Machine Learning Techniques and Analytics for Cloud Security

Scrivener Publishing
100 Cummings Center, Suite 541J
Beverly, MA 01915-6106

Advances in Learning Analytics for Intelligent Cloud-IoT Systems

Series Editor: Dr. Souvik Pal and Dr. Dac-Nhuong Le

The role of adaptation, learning analytics, computational Intelligence, and data analytics in the field of cloud-IoT systems is becoming increasingly essential and intertwined. The capability of an intelligent system depends on various self-decision-making algorithms in IoT devices. IoT-based smart systems generate a large amount of data (big data) that cannot be processed by traditional data processing algorithms and applications. Hence, this book series involves different computational methods incorporated within the system with the help of analytics reasoning and sense-making in big data, which is centered in the cloud and IoT-enabled environments. The series publishes volumes that are empirical studies, theoretical and numerical analysis, and novel research findings.

Submission to the series:
Please send proposals to Dr. Souvik Pal, Department of Computer Science and Engineering, Global Institute of Management and Technology, Krishna Nagar, West Bengal, India.
E-mail: souvikpal22@gmail.com

Publishers at Scrivener
Martin Scrivener (martin@scrivenerpublishing.com)
Phillip Carmical (pcarmical@scrivenerpublishing.com)

Machine Learning Techniques and Analytics for Cloud Security

Edited by

Rajdeep Chakraborty
Anupam Ghosh
and
Jyotsna Kumar Mandal

Scrivener
Publishing

WILEY

Wiley Global Headquarters
111 River Street, Hoboken, NJ 07030, USA

For details of our global editorial offices, customer services, and more information about Wiley products visit us at www.wiley.com.

Limit of Liability/Disclaimer of Warranty
While the publisher and authors have used their best efforts in preparing this work, they make no representations or warranties with respect to the accuracy or completeness of the contents of this work and specifically disclaim all warranties, including without limitation any implied warranties of merchant-ability or fitness for a particular purpose. No warranty may be created or extended by sales representatives, written sales materials, or promotional statements for this work. The fact that an organization, website, or product is referred to in this work as a citation and/or potential source of further information does not mean that the publisher and authors endorse the information or services the organization, website, or product may provide or recommendations it may make. This work is sold with the understanding that the publisher is not engaged in rendering professional services. The advice and strategies contained herein may not be suitable for your situation. You should consult with a specialist where appropriate. Neither the publisher nor authors shall be liable for any loss of profit or any other commercial damages, including but not limited to special, incidental, consequential, or other damages. Further, readers should be aware that websites listed in this work may have changed or disappeared between when this work was written and when it is read.

Library of Congress Cataloging-in-Publication Data

ISBN 978-1-119-76225-6

Cover images: Pixabay.Com
Cover design by Russell Richardson

Set in size of 11pt and Minion Pro by Manila Typesetting Company, Makati, Philippines

10 9 8 7 6 5 4 3 2 1

Contents

Preface

Our objective in writing this book was to provide the reader with an in-depth knowledge of how to integrate machine learning (ML) approaches to meet various analytical issues in cloud security deemed necessary due to the advancement of IoT networks. Although one of the ways to achieve cloud security is by using ML, the technique has long-standing challenges that require methodological and theoretical approaches. Therefore, because the conventional cryptographic approach is less frequently applied in resource-constrained devices, the ML approach may be effectively used in providing security in the constantly growing cloud environment. Machine learning algorithms can also be used to meet various cloud security issues for effective intrusion detection and zero-knowledge authentication systems. Moreover, these algorithms can also be used in applications and for much more, including measuring passive attacks and designing protocols and privacy systems. This book contains case studies/projects for implementing some security features based on ML algorithms and analytics. It will provide learning paradigms for the field of artificial intelligence and the deep learning community, with related datasets to help delve deeper into ML for cloud security.

This book is organized into five parts. As the entire book is based on ML techniques, the three chapters contained in "Part I: Conceptual Aspects of Cloud and Applications of Machine Learning," describe cloud environments and ML methods and techniques. The seven chapters in "Part II: Cloud Security Systems Using Machine Learning Techniques," describe ML algorithms and techniques which are hard coded and implemented for providing various security aspects of cloud environments. The four chapters of "Part III: Cloud Security Analysis Using Machine Learning Techniques," present some of the recent studies and surveys of ML techniques and analytics for providing cloud security. The next three chapters in "Part IV: Case Studies Focused on Cloud Security," are unique to this book as they contain three case studies of three cloud products from a security perspective. These three products are mainly in the domains of public cloud, private cloud and hybrid cloud. Finally, the two chapters in "Part V: Policy Aspects," pertain to policy aspects related to the cloud environment and cloud security using ML techniques and analytics. Each of the chapters mentioned above are individually highlighted chapter by chapter below.

Part I: Conceptual Aspects of Cloud and Applications of Machine Learning

- Chapter 1 begins with an introduction to various parameters of cloud such as scalability, cost, speed, reliability, performance and security. Next, hybrid cloud is discussed in detail along with cloud architecture and how it functions. A brief comparison of various cloud providers is given next. After the use of cloud in education, finance, etc., is described, the chapter concludes with a discussion of security aspects of a cloud environment.

- Chapter 2 discusses how to recognize differentially expressed glycan structure of H1N1 virus using unsupervised learning framework. This chapter gives the reader a better understanding of machine learning (ML) and analytics. Next, the detailed workings of an ML methodology are presented along with a flowchart. The result part of this chapter contains the analytics for the ML technique.
- Chapter 3 presents a hybrid model of logistic regression supported by PC-LR to select cancer mediating genes. This is another good chapter to help better understand ML techniques and analytics. It provides the details of an ML learning methodology and algorithms with results and analysis using datasets.

Part II: Cloud Security Systems Using Machine Learning Techniques

- Chapter 4 shows the implementation of a voice-controlled real-time smart informative interface design with Google assistance technology that is more cost-effective than the existing products on the market. This system can be used for various cloud-based applications such as home automation. It uses microcontrollers and sensors in smart home design which can be connected through cloud database. Security concerns are also discussed in this chapter.
- Chapter 5 discusses a neoteric model of a cryptosystem for cloud security by using symmetric key and artificial neural network with Mealy machine. A cryptosystem is used to provide data or information confidentiality and a state-based cryptosystem is implemented using Mealy machine. This chapter gives a detailed algorithm with results generated using Lenovo G80 with processor Intel® Pentium® CPU B950@210GHz and RAM 2GB and programming language Turbo C, DebC++ and disc drive SA 9500326AS ATA and Windows 7 Ultimate (32 Bits) OS.
- Chapter 6 describes the implementation of an effective intrusion detection system using ML techniques through various datasets. The chapter begins with a description of an intrusion detection system and how it is beneficial for cloud environment. Next, various intrusion attacks on cloud environment are described along with a comparative study. Finally, a proposed methodology of IDS in cloud environment is given along with implementation results.
- Chapter 7 beautifully describes text-based sentiment analysis for cloud security that extracts the mood of users in a cloud environment, which is an evolving topic in ML. A proposed model for text-based sentiment analysis is presented along with an experimental setup with implementation results. Since text-based sentiment analysis potentially identifies malicious users in a cloud environment, the chapter concludes with applications of this method and implementation for cloud security.
- Chapter 8 discusses zero-knowledge proof (ZKP) for cloud, which is a method for identifying legitimate users without revealing their identity. The ZKP consist of three parts: the first is ticket generator, the second is user,

and the third is verifier. For example, to see a movie in a theater we purchase ticket. So, the theater counter is the ticket generator; and while purchasing a ticket here we generally don't reveal our identifying information such as name, address or social security number. We are allowed to enter the theater when this ticket is verified at the gate, so, this is the verifier algorithm. This chapter also discusses ZKP for cloud security.

- Chapter 9 discusses an effective spam detection system for cloud security using supervised ML techniques. Spam, which is an unwanted message that contains malicious links, viral attachments, unwelcome images and misinformation, is a major security concern for any digital system and requires an effective spam detection system. Therefore, this chapter begins by discussing the requirements for such a system. Then, it gradually moves towards a supervised ML-technique-based spam detection system, mainly using a support vector machine (SVM) and convolutional neural network (CNN). Implementation results are also given with application in cloud environment.

- Chapter 10 describes an intelligent system for securing network from intrusion detection and phishing attacks using ML approaches, with a focus on phishing attacks on the cloud environment. It begins by describing different fishing attacks on cloud environment and then proposes a method for detecting these attacks using ML. Next, analysis of different parameters for ML models, predictive outcome analysis in phishing URLs dataset, analysis of performance metrics and statistical analysis of results are presented.

Part III: Cloud Security Analysis Using Machine Learning Techniques

- Chapter 11 discusses cloud security using honeypot network and blockchain. It begins with an overview of cloud computing and then describes cloud computing deployment models and security concerns in cloud computing. Then the honeypot network and its system design are discussed, followed by the use of blockchain-based honeypot network. A good comparative analysis is given at the end of the chapter.

- Chapter 12 includes a survey on ML-based security in cloud database. The chapter starts with a discussion of the various ML techniques used to provide security in a cloud database. Then a study is presented which mainly consists of three parts: first, supervised learning methods, such as support vector machine (SVM), artificial neural network, etc., are given; second, unsupervised learning methods, such as K-means clustering, fuzzy C-means clustering, etc., are given; third, hybrid learning techniques, such as hybrid intrusion detection approach (HIDCC) in cloud computing, clustering-based hybrid model in deep learning framework, etc., are given. Comparative analyses are also given at the end.

- Chapter 13 provides a survey on ML-based adversarial attacks on cloud environment. The chapter starts with the concepts of adversarial learning followed by the taxonomy of adversarial attacks. Various algorithms found in the literature for ML-based adversarial attacks on cloud environment are also presented. Then, various studies on adversarial attacks on cloud-based platforms and their comparative studies are discussed.

- Chapter 14 provides a detailed study of the protocols used for cloud security. The chapter starts by discussing the system and adversarial models, and then the protocols for data protection in secure cloud computing are given followed by a discussion of the protocols for data protection in secure cloud storage. Finally, various protocols for secure cloud systems are discussed. The authors also attempt to give a futuristic view of the protocols that may be implemented for cloud security.

Part IV: Case Studies Focused on Cloud Security

- Chapter 15 is a detailed presentation of the Google cloud platform (GCP) and its security features. It begins by discussing GCP's current market holdings and then describes the work distribution in GCP. Next, the chapter gradually moves towards a basic overview of security features in GCP and describes the GCP architecture along with its key security and application features. Then, an interesting part is presented that describes various computations used in GCP, followed by a discussion of the storage, network, data and ML policies used in GCP.
- Chapter 16 presents a case study of Microsoft Azure cloud and its security features. The beginning of the chapter covers Azure's current market holdings and the Forrester Wave and Gartner Magic Quadrant reports. Then, the security infrastructure of Azure is given, which covers its security features and tools, Azure network security, data encryption used in Azure, asset and inventory management, and the Azure marketplace. Next, details of Azure cloud security architecture are presented along with its working and design principles, followed by the components and services of Azure architecture. The chapter ends with a discussion of its various features and why Azure is gaining popularity.
- Chapter 17 presents a case study on Nutanix hybrid cloud from a security perspective. Nutanix is a fast-growing hybrid cloud in the current scenario. The chapter begins with the growth of Nutanix and then presents introductory concepts about it. Next, Nutanix hybrid cloud architecture is discussed in relation to computation, storage and networking. Then, reinforcing AHV and controller VM are described, followed by disaster management and recovery used in Nutanix hybrid cloud. A detailed study on security and policy management in Nutanix hybrid cloud is then presented. The chapter concludes with a discussion of network security and log management in Nutanix hybrid cloud.

Part V: Policy Aspects

- Chapter 18 describes a data science approach based on user interactions to generate access control policies for large collections of documents in cloud environment. After a general introduction to network science theory, various approaches for spreading policies using network science are discussed. Then, evaluations and matrices to evaluate policies for cloud security are described. This chapter concludes with a presentation of all the simulation results.

- Chapter 19 discusses the policies of iSchools with artificial intelligence, machine learning, and robotics through analysis of programs, curriculum and potentialities towards intelligent societal systems on cloud platform. iSchools are a kind of consortium that develops with the collection of information and technology-related schools and academic units. In the last decade there has been a significant growth in the development of such academic bodies. This chapter provides a policy framework for iSchools, the methodology involved and a list of available iSchools. The chapter concludes with some policy suggestions and future work related to iSchools.

The Editors
October 2021

Part I

CONCEPTUAL ASPECTS ON CLOUD AND APPLICATIONS OF MACHINE LEARNING

Hybrid Cloud: A New Paradigm in Cloud Computing

Moumita Deb* and Abantika Choudhury†

RCC Institute of Information Technology, Kolkata, West Bengal, India

Abstract

Hybrid cloud computing is basically a combination of cloud computing with on-premise resources to provide work portability, load distribution, and security. Hybrid cloud may include one public and one private cloud, or it may contain two or more private clouds or may have two or more public clouds depending on the requirement. Public clouds are generally provided by third party vendors like Amazon, Google, and Microsoft. These clouds traditionally ran off premise and provide services through internet. Whereas private clouds also offer computing services to selected user either over the internet or within a private internal network and conventionally ran on-premise. But this scenario is changing nowadays. Earlier distinction between private and public clouds can be done on the location and ownership information, but currently, public clouds are running in on-premise data centers of customer and private clouds are constructed on off premise rented, vendor-owned data centers as well. So, the architecture is becoming complex. Hybrid cloud reduces the potential exposure of sensitive or crucial data from the public while keeping non-sensitive data into the cloud. Thus, secure access to data while enjoying attractive services of the public cloud is the key factor in hybrid cloud. Here, we have done a survey on hybrid cloud as it is one of the most promising areas in cloud computing, discuss all insight details. Security issues and measures in hybrid cloud are also discussed along with the use of artificial intelligence. We do not intend to propose any new findings rather we will figure out some of future research directions.

Keywords: PaaS, SaaS, IaaS, SLA, agility, encryption, middleware, AI

1.1 Introduction

Cloud computing is catering computing services such as storage, networking, servers, analytics, intelligence, and software though the internet on demand basis. We typically have to pay for only for the services we use. IT is a growing industry and catering its service requirement is challenging. On-premise resources are not sufficient always, so leveraging attractive facilities provided by cloud service providers is often required. Typical services

---

**Corresponding author*: moudeb@gmail.com

†*Corresponding author*: abantika_choudhury@rediffmail.com

Rajdeep Chakraborty, Anupam Ghosh and Jyotsna Kumar Mandal (eds.) Machine Learning Techniques and Analytics for Cloud Security, (3–24) © 2022 Scrivener Publishing LLC

provided by cloud computing are Platform as a service (PaaS), Software as a service (SaaS), and Infrastructure as a service (IaaS). But all the clouds are not same and no one particular cloud can satisfy all the customer. As a result, various types of services are emerging to cater the need of any organization. The following are the facilities cater by cloud computing.

- **Scalability:** IT services are not restricted to offline resources anymore, online cloud services can do a wonder. Any business can be extended based on the market need through the use of cloud computing services. A client needs almost nothing but a computer with internet connection, rest of the services can be borrowed from cloud vendors. Business can grow according to the requirement. Scalability is the key factor in adoption of any new paradigm. An organization meant for 100 people can be easily scaled up to 1,000 (ideally any number) people with the help of the cloud computing services.
- **Cost:** Since cloud provides services pay as you use basis, cost of setting up a business has reduced manifolds. Capital expense in buying server, software, and experts for managing infrastructure is not mandatory anymore; vendors can provide all these services. Cost saving is one of the most lucrative features of cloud computing. Any startup company can afford the cost of the setup price required for the orchestration of public cloud; thus, they can engage their selves exclusively for the development of their business.
- **Speed:** Cloud computing helps to speed up the overall functioning of any organization. Several lucrative easy-to-use options are just one click away, so designers and programmers can freely think about their innovations, and as a result, the speed and performance can be enhanced. Moreover, since most of the background hazards are handled by the cloud service providers as a result implementation of any advanced thinking can be made possible quickly and effortlessly.
- **Reliability:** Reliability is a key factor where huge data need to handle all the time. Periodic data backup and use of disaster recovery methods helps to increase the data reliability in cloud computing. Also, since space is not a constraint anymore, clients can keep mirrored data. A reliable system often leads to a secure system. Any organizations need to handle huge user centric sensitive data as well as business related data. Maintaining the reliability in the data need several rules and regulations to be enforced.
- **Performance:** Improved operation, better customer support, and flexible workplace aid companies to perform better than conventional on-premise system. Amazon helps Car company Toyota to build cloud-based data centers. The company is going to use the behavioral data of the user of the car, and based on that, they will send service and insurance related data [1]. User can also use Facebook or Twitter in their car dashboard. This is only an example; there is lot more. Adaptation of advanced technology excels the performance of existing system as cloud plays a crucial role here.

- **Security:** Cloud service providers use many security mechanisms like encryption, authentication of user, authorization, and use of some Artificial Intelligence (AI)–based method to secure their app, data, and infrastructure from possible threats.

A combination of secure open source technologies along with integrated network may be used for secure hybrid cloud deployment like it does in HCDM [16]. But, before deployment, the customer need to determine what type of cloud computing architecture is best suitable. There are three different ways to organize cloud: private, public, and hybrid. Here, we will discuss about hybrid cloud, its benefits, and security aspects.

Thus, motivation of this review is to provide a broad details of hybrid cloud computing, why it is gaining popularity, how business is going to be affected through the use of cloud adaption in near future, what security aspects need to dealt by vendors, and how AI can help in this regard. The following sections deal with all this topics.

1.2   Hybrid Cloud

If we go by the definition of National Institute of Standards and Technology [3], hybrid cloud is a "composition of two or more different types of cloud infrastructure that are bind together with the help of proprietary and standardized technology for the purpose of data and application portability. So, Simple amalgamation of cloud and on-premise data should not misinterpret as hybrid cloud. It should also provide the following facilities [2]:

- Workload distribution by portability.
- Networking between system and devices, by the use of LAN, WAN, or VPN.
- Use of a comprehensive unified automation tool.
- A complex powerful middleware for abstracting the background details.
- Incorporating availability and scalability of resources.
- Integrating disaster management and recovery strategies.

Thus, it enables the customer to extend their business by leveraging the attractive services provided by public cloud as well as securing the delicate data through the use of private cloud. When the demand of a business fluctuates that may be sudden peak in the business come or sudden fall down, in those scenarios, hybrid cloud is the best possible option as it has that flexibility [8]. Organizations can seamlessly use public cloud amenities without directly giving access to their data centers which are part of their on-premise servers. So, business critical data and applications can be kept safe behind, while computing power of the public cloud can be used for doing complex tasks. Organizations will only have to pay for the services it is using without considering the capital expenditure involve in purchasing, programming and maintaining new resources which can be used for a short span of time and may remain idle for long. Private cloud on the other hand is more like public cloud, but generally installed on clients datacenter and mainly focus on self-servicing, scalable structure. Single tone service nature, service-level agreement (SLA), and similar association make the relationship between client and cloud stronger and less demanding [33, 34].

1.2.1   Architecture

There may be any combination of cloud services when to deploy a hybrid cloud. It may the client has its own on-premise private cloud as IaaS and leverage public cloud as SaaS. Private cloud may be on premise or sometimes off premise on a dedicated server [10]. There is no fixed fits for all architecture. Private clouds can be made individually, whereas public cloud can be hired from vendors like Amazon, Microsoft, Alibaba, Google, and IBM. Next, a middleware is required to combine public and private cloud mostly provided by the cloud vendors as a part of their package. Figure 1.1 gives general diagram of a hybrid cloud.

In case of hybrid cloud architecture, the following is a list of properties that must to be kept in mind [4]:

    a. Multiple devices need to be connected via LAN, WAN, or VPN with a common middleware that provides an API for user services. Rather than using a vast network of API, a single operating system must be used throughout the network and APIs can be built on top of that.

    b. Resources are made available to all the connected devices via virtualization and it can be scaled up to any limit.

    c. The middleware does all the coordination between devices and resources are made available on demand basis with proper authentication.

1.2.2   Why Hybrid Cloud is Required?

Hybrid cloud means different service to different people [5]. Need of an organization depends on diverse aspects of IT. As the perspective of application designer, business developer, and infrastructure support personnel is different from one another, their expectation from the system also varies.

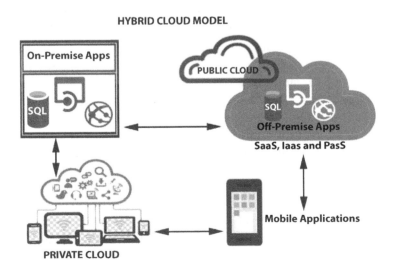

Figure 1.1 General architecture of hybrid cloud.

- ***Application programmer always requires support for edge technologies.*** Availability of high-end resources and cutting edge technology support is the primary concern of a developer. Off premise support for such is essential. Flexibility in deployment of changing technology services, speedy availability of the new resources required by the solution, peak support for on-premise system, and seamless and continuous integration of system services are key issues need to be dealt in hybrid cloud. Disaster management is also an integral part of it.
- ***On the contrary, infrastructure support personnel always look for a steady build in support for smooth execution of overall activities of the organization.*** Off premise support for virtualized computing resources is often necessary in IT. In this scenario, the role of infrastructure support team is very crucial. Visibility of all the resources wherever it is, monitoring them in federated way following SLA, management of deployed setup for auditing and security management, accessibility of all resources, and control provisioning are key consideration in case of hybrid cloud.
- ***Business developer, on the other hand, focuses on consumer marketing in cost-effective manner*** [6]. The need of IT business has manifolds. Support for newly growing technology like mobile or web-based application requires agile and easy to extend network, and at the same time, consistent system and stable process management services cannot be replaced. So, business developers have to look into all these aspects, and at the same time, they have to focus on the cost. The maintenance and management cost should not exceed the overall financial budget. Looking at the SLAs and software license exposure, they need to design financial plans that can fulfill the whole organization's prerequisites.

No matter how well we plan the future, it still remains uncertain and hybrid cloud provides the facility to use cloud services as and when it is required. It is also quite unlikely that workload of an organization remains same throughout the whole year. Suppose an organization is working on big data analytics, it can take help of public cloud computing resources for high complex computations but that too is not needed for long run, may be require for few months. Here, public cloud resources can be borrowed for few months only. In the same way, startup companies can start with some trivial private resources and take cloud services for rest of the processing. Then, based on the performance, they can plan to expand the business with the help of public cloud. All these are possible only in case of hybrid cloud as it has ***agility***, ***scalability***, ***data reliability***, ***speedy recovery***, and ***improved connectivity*** and ***security***.

1.2.3   Business and Hybrid Cloud

According to Hybrid Cloud Market report, in 2018, hybrid cloud market was USD 44.6 billion and expected to grow to USD 97.6 billion by the end of 2023 with Compound Annual Growth Rate (CAGR) of 17.0% [9]. IaaS is expected to hold a large market in the forecast period as it facilitates to migrate workload from on premise to off premise in high peak hours. Hybrid web hosting also hold a big market as it provides management of all

Hybrid Cloud Market - Growth Rate by Region (2020 - 2025)

Regional Growth Rates
High
Mid
Low
Source: Mordor Intelligence

Figure 1.2 Market trend of hybrid cloud [14].

hosting services in just single point of contact. North America was the most promising hybrid cloud market place in 2018 and Asia Pacific areas shows the highest CAGR. So, hybrid cloud is a promising area in business. Major sectors using hybrid cloud computing are healthcare, retail, government, or public sectors, banking, entertainment media, insurance, finance, communication media, etc. [14]. According to a report published by Mordor Intelligence, North America, Middle East, Africa, Europe, and Asia Pacific are top growing regions worldwide. Figure 1.2 shows the hybrid cloud market. Green portions represent highly growing market. Hybrid cloud management software solution is the main reason of this popularity. Starting from deployment to quota management, customization of service library, costing, performance management, and governance, everything is taken care of, like the software management tool. Mostly, the services provided by public providers are restricted to some architecture or technology and vendor specific. But the management tool provided by hybrid providers helps to amalgamate different services provided by various vendors. Amazon and Microsoft, the giants in this field, are working hard in the up gradation of their management software by including advanced infrastructure templates, libraries, API, and apps. In India, IBM is also approaching toward hybrid cloud and AI [15]. IBM invested $1 billion into a cloud ecosystem project in the month of August. They are expected to invest more in the coming time. In India, 17% of organizations are planning to spend investment from 42% to 49% on hybrid cloud by 2023 according to a study by IBM IBV. Since India is heading toward a digital transformation and self-reliant camping, so the opportunity of new technology adaptation also increasing.

1.2.4   Things to Remember When Deploying Hybrid Cloud

Having an understanding what hybrid cloud is and how it facilitates the activities of any organization, now, we need to understand some factors that have to be considered before the deployment of hybrid cloud.

- *Selection of best suitable platform for cloud:* As discussed, the need of every organization is not same. Before deployment of the hybrid cloud, organizations need to have a plan for the services; it will borrow from the public cloud. If it is going to use only SaaS, then it is not a problem but it is going to use IaaS or PaaS and then it is very important to take the correct decision from the commencement of the service as building a hybrid structure that would not be able to handle additional workload generates severe problem.

- **Whether to use unified OS or not:** In true hybrid cloud, a unified OS is installed in the middleware that basically governs the overall functionalities. But in some cases, on-premise system may be operated by its own OS then just with the help of internet they can connect to public cloud. The performance of this architecture will be vast different from unified OS. OpenStack, VMWare cloud, Nutanix, and Kubernetes are some example of cloud OS framework. These frameworks are sufficient building the middleware and it provides OS and all supporting application for the smooth execution of all activities in hybrid cloud.

- **How to manage different activity:** Huge amount of data need to be handled in case of hybrid cloud. A hybrid system should look into smooth accessibility of data, and at the same time, security of data needs to be guaranteed. Anyone cannot host any data onto the public cloud. Proper personnel with adequate experience need to be engaged for the management of dedicated applications.

- **How security of data will be guaranteed:** Since data is moving in between public and private cloud, it needs to be secured. Through security mechanisms of public cloud, it has developed much from its early date but still it is not 100% secure. There are always threats of data breach. Migration of sensitive need special care as sight alteration in business sensitive data might cause severe problem in the business.

- **How to integrate public cloud with existing on-premise system:** Amalgamation of public cloud onto an existing on-premise system often needs several alterations in the working of the existing on-premise system. Overall performance of the system should always improve with the addition of the public cloud, and it should not degrade.

- **How to manage common backup and disaster recovery:** Data need to be backed up to ensure reliability and availability. Backing up of all the data both in private and public cloud need to be done. At the same time, the system should be able to handle catastrophic failure or disaster. How to maintain a common routine for all the operational data to accommodate those situations is key to the success of hybrid cloud deployment.

Building a hybrid cloud is a complex procedure but successful implementation will provide scalability, flexibility, security, and cost saving. More and more organizations approaching toward hybrid cloud for the current benefit and future growth.

1.3   Comparison Among Different Hybrid Cloud Providers

The major famous leading cloud computing vendors are Google Cloud, AWS, and Microsoft Azure. They have their some advantages and disadvantages. These three leading cloud providers have important role in the PaaS and IaaS markets. Synergy Research Group reported that the growth of Amazon is very significantly high in overall growth of market. It possesses a share of 33% of cloud market throughout the world. In second position, there is Microsoft. Microsoft is very fast growing and in the last four quarters, and its share has been increased by 3% and it reaches at 18%. Nowadays, cloud computing is become much matured. It is becoming hybrid cloud, and it also becomes more enhanced as market share. New trends have come to improve cloud computing system in 2020 than that of 2017, 2018, and 2019 [17].

Hybrid cloud [17] provides strategy for enterprises that involve operational part of varieties of job in varieties infrastructure, whether on private cloud and public cloud with a proprietary different layers at the top level. Multi-cloud concept is similar kind of but not to involve any private cloud. Hybrid cloud is the most popular strategy among enterprises; 58% of respondents stated that it is their choice able approach while 10% for a single public cloud provider and 17% for multiple public clouds.

- **Microsoft Azure Stack:** Microsoft is a popular vendor that provides hybrid cloud. Because it has huge on-premises legacy. The services of MS Azure are developed on Windows Server. The .Net framework and the Visual Studio provide better features of on apps for their smoother services [17].
- **AWS Outposts:** Amazon's Amazon Web Services (AWS) is a one of the best product. It is one of the most popular in market and its share is next to the Microsoft leading competitor. This company has variety of services and largest data center that continues to provide facilities to billions of customers. AWS is very well-known public cloud that offers many services to connect for installations to the cloud. It also serves everything like disaster recovery and burst capacity [17].
- Google Cloud Anthos: The Google Cloud Platform is another one popular in hybrid cloud. It is a competitor of Microsoft AWS and IBM. Google primarily made pure cloud system, but later, they changed policy and started to work with on-premise systems for disaster recovery, elastic infrastructure, Big Data, and DevOps. It also provides a huge number of cloud-based services. The services are based on AI efforts based on AI processor and TensorFlow. No one can buy TensorFlow system but can run AI and machine learning apps on Google Cloud [17, 18].
- Oracle Cloud at Customer: This is another one popular hybrid cloud service provider. It provides mostly on-demand service, in its own cloud system. Unlike Azure, AWS, and GCP, this provider does not allow its software to execute in virtual instances for any operation. But it runs on metal servers; Oracle also offers this kind of service. Oracle cloud is also very easy to run its apps on-premise on the cloud [18].
- IBM: IBM merged all of its cloud services, called IBM Cloud. It possesses more than 170 types of services for public cloud and on-premise. These services are not only limited to bare metal hosting and virtualized mode, containers, and server less computing, DevOps, AI/ML, HPC, and blockchain.

It also offers to do lift and shift on-premise apps, executing on IBM platforms [18].

- Cisco Cloud Center: Cisco is popular for private cloud that also offers hybrid solutions via its partner. Cisco Cloud Center is more secured to manage and deploy the applications in different data centers in both private and public cloud environments. Cisco's partner networks are Google, CDW, Accenture, and AT&T. Google is the biggest partner among them. It offers the hybrid connectivity and their solutions [18].
- VMware vCloud Suite: VMware provides vendor for virtualized services. It is relatively new than that of other service providers. VMware has the vSphere hypervisor. Customers can run in some known public clouds or their own data centers or cloud provider partners. These cloud providers are able to run vSphere on-premise that creates a stable hybrid cloud infrastructure [19].

1.3.1   Cloud Storage and Backup Benefits

Protection of the confidential data is very difficult. Automatic backup of cloud storage is flexible. It also provides data security.

Microsoft Azure is very effective in SaaS. Whereas, Google Cloud is strong in AI [18]. Table 1.1 gives a comparison among them.

1.3.2   Pros and Cons of Different Service Providers

All the cloud service providers have their own pros and cons. Their make themselves a suitable choice for different purposes. Here, the advantages and disadvantages are described for all the providers. Table 1.2 provides a comparative study on this.

Table 1.1 Comparison between AWS Outpost, Microsoft Azure Stack, and Google Cloud Anthos.

AWS Outpost	Microsoft Azure Stack	Google Cloud Anthos
Amazon has a huge tool set and that too is rapidly growing. No service providers can match with it. But the pricing is bit puzzling. Though providing service for hybrid or public cloud is not amazon's primary focus thus incorporation of cloud services with on-premise data is not in top priority [20]. They primarily focus on public cloud.	The customer can run in their own data center. Azure tries to incorporate with that. It provides the facility of hybrid cloud [19]. A customer can replicate his environment in Azure Stack. This is very useful in case of backup disaster and for cutting cost.	Google has come to the cloud market later. So, it does not have that much level of focus to incorporate the customers. But the strength is its technical efficiency. Some of its efficient tools are applicable in data analytics, machine learning, and deep learning.

Table 1.2 Pros and cons between AWS Outpost, Microsoft Azure Stack, and Google Cloud Anthos.

Vendor	Strength	Weakness
AWS Outpost	1. Dominant market position 2. Extensive, mature offerings 3. Effective use in large organizations	1. Managing cost 2. Very difficult for using 3. Options are overwhelming
Microsoft Azure Stack	1. Second largest service provider 2. Coupling with Microsoft software 3. Set of features is vast 4. Provides Hybrid cloud 5. Open source supported	1. Poor documentation 2. Management tooling is incomplete
Google Cloud Anthos	1. Designed to serve for cloud-native enterprises 2. Provides portability and allows open source 3. Huge discounts and suitable contracts 4. Expertise in DevOps	1. Enters late in IaaS market 2. Less services and features 3. Not focused for enterprise

1.3.2.1 AWS Outpost

The strongest strength of Amazon is its effectiveness in public cloud. They provide services through the world for its public cloud infrastructure. This cloud provider is very popular because of its varieties operational scope. AWS provides different kind of services. It also has a large network for worldwide data centers. The "Gartner" reported that this provider is the most mature and enterprise-ready. It also has capabilities to govern a large amount of resources and customers. But the weakness is its cost. Customers face difficulty to understand its cost structure. It is also difficult to manage the costs while running a large volume of workloads.

1.3.2.2 Microsoft Azure Stack

Microsoft provides on-premises software—SQL Server, Windows Server, SharePoint, Office, .Net, Dynamics Active Directory, etc. The reason of its success is most of the enterprises uses Windows and its related software. As Azure is tightly coupled with its other software applications, the enterprises, that use many Microsoft software, they find Azure as a suitable platform. This is how it builds good relationship with their existing customers. They also provide a remarkable discount on variety of services to their existing customer. But, Gartner also reported some faults in their some of the platforms [21].

1.3.2.3 Google Cloud Anthos

AWS and Azure offer the Kubernetes standard which is developed by Google. GCP is expert in machine learning and Big Data analytics. It provides huge offers on that. It also provides offers in load balancing and considerable scale. Google is also efficient knowledge about different data centers and quick response time. Google stands in third in the field of market share [21]. But, it is rapidly increasing its offers. As per Gartner, clients choose GCP as a secondary provider than that of primary provider.

1.3.3   Review on Storage of the Providers

1.3.3.1   AWS Outpost Storage

- **SSS to EFS:** The storage services of AWS include its Elastic Block Storage (EBS), Simple Storage Service (S3), and Elastic File System (EFS) for persistent block storage, object storage, and file storage, respectively. It also provides some new innovative products for storage that includes the Snowball and Storage Gateway. Snowball is a physical hardware device, whereas Storage Gateway creates a hybrid storage environment.
- **Database and archiving:** Aurora is a compatible database of SQL by Amazon. It consists of different services like DynamoDB NoSQL database, Relational Database Service (RDS), Redshift data warehouse, ElastiCache in-memory data store, Neptune graph database, and Database Migration Service. Amazon also offers long term storage known as Glacier. It is having very low charges [20].
- **Storage services:** The storage services of Microsoft Azure include Queue Storage, Blob Storage, File and Disk Storage for large-volume workloads, and REST-based object storage of unstructured data respectively. Data Lake Store is another storage that is used for big data applications.
- **Extensive database:** This extensive database provides three SQL-based options. They are Database for MySQL, SQL Database, and Database for PostgreSQL. Data Warehouse service is also provided as well. The services are Table Storage for NoSQL and Cosmos DB. Its in-memory service is Redis Cache and the hybrid storage service is Server Stretch Database. Those are designed for the organizations that use Microsoft SQL Servers [22]. Unlike AWS, Microsoft offers an actual Site Recovery service, Archive Storage, and Backup service.

1.3.3.2   Google Cloud Anthos Storage

- **Unified storage and more:** GCP has enormous level of storage services. The unified object storage service is cloud storage. It also provides persistent disk storage. It also offers a Transfer Appliance which is a similar kind of AWS Snowball and online transfer services.
- **SQL and NoSQL:** GCP possesses the SQL-based Cloud and also provides a relational database known as Cloud Spanner. Cloud Spanner is designed for critical and complex workloads. It also provides NoSQL. They are Cloud Datastore and Cloud Bigtable. No backup services and archive services are provided.

Table 1.3 Comparison between VMware Microsoft Amazon AWS.

Category	VMware	Microsoft	Amazon AWS
Delivery mode	Very simple	Easy to follow	Very easy
Ability to apply the technology	Cost-effective virtualization solution, manage to virtualize the X86 computer architecture	Estimated cost was around $4.99 per month [19]	Very affordable, $32 to $255 per month [19]
Integration with other applications	It is an Edge PC Virtualization, Workstation 12.5 Pro, Fusion 8.5 - Windows on Mac®, Workstation 12 Player- streamlined PC Virtualization for Business	Computes engine for networking, virtual machines, SQL databases, storage, containers, security, API integration, etc.	Web application, website and database storefront.
Security	Secure virtual box is possible to create, manages files, using SSL, SSH, etc.	Reliable	Tight
Operating system and mobile compatibility	Many operating systems like Windows, Linux and Mac, etc.	Windows 8 and Windows 10	Both Linux and Windows. Able to compute, storage, database, networking, and content delivery.
Upgrades	On demand Products available at less price.	Able to run updates.	
Service-level agreements		Azure Cloud provides Container services speedily and in simple way.	Easy
Training/support			Auditing, monitoring/ logging, storage creating
Scalability and vendor reliability			Vendor is dependable and revenue growth is stable for Elastic Cloud Compute (EC2) and database usage [19]

1.3.4   Pricing

Pricing is one of the challenging scenarios among these three hybrid cloud providers. Table 1.3 lists all the pricing related issues involved here.

- **AWS Outpost:** The pricing of Amazon is very inscrutable. Though it offers a cost calculator, many variables involved here make it very difficult for proper estimation [23].
- **Azure Stack:** Microsoft Azure is also complicated software. The licensing options and their uses are applicable in specified case discounts. The pricing structure is also difficult to understand of this provider.
- **Google Cloud Anthos:** The pricing of Google is different. It offers are customer-friendly. So, it provides the least price than that of the other providers. It also provides huge discounts and flexible contracts to fulfill the purpose of customers.

1.4   Hybrid Cloud in Education

Apart from business sectors, educational institutions can also take help of the hybrid cloud for extending their on-premise legacy system [31]. They can build some application on to the public cloud to student data management, resource management, employee data management, etc., at ease releasing their IT team to do some other jobs. An example can be some database of the student can be kept on-premise server while front end web applications for the students can run onto the public cloud. Based on specific performance or regularity needs, they can also move workloads dynamically between public and private cloud may be for the specific period of time. Student and staff and institutional data are very sensitive; they can be kept secure behind with their own firewall and antivirus. Whereas with the help of the public cloud, several attractive features can be provided, like job getting opportunity trend, research work prospect, and study and lecture material of renowned professors, virtual labs, etc., without installing any additional hardware or software solution system. Thus, by using "Build the base rent the spike" deployment model, they can save the money. But security policies have to be strict. Applications and infrastructures should be guided by different security policies. Edge systems like email server, web server, and routers should be kept protected as they can communicate with inside and outside the organization.

1.5   Significance of Hybrid Cloud Post-Pandemic

Adaptation of cloud-based services has grown tremendously after pandemic. Due to COVID-19, every sector faces losses. Rapid shifting of business into online mode is the current requirement. Organizations that have legacy infrastructure on premise cannot shift to public cloud in a day and security also is a matter of consideration. As a result, hybrid cloud is the most preferred solution.

- In COVID-19 pandemic situation, the world is compelled to move for remote work. So, the video conferencing is tremendously increasing and all the related data moves to the cloud. Enterprises are considering the cloud as a digital transformation engine and as well. As the work is done remotely, the jobs are majorly done in cloud infrastructure. Collaboration with Microsoft Teams or Google Meet becomes very strong with the companies in broader cloud ecosystem [17].
- Hybrid cloud has an aspiration to achieve target for companies. Companies are well aware about their vendors and they want to transfer their applications to clouds. The multi-cloud conception is yielded among different vendors. The vendor plug with many clouds like VMware or Red Hat [17, 18].
- Customers are getting tackier to the cloud service providers as more and more corporate data are stored on the cloud. It is known that cloud computing vendors are trying enterprises to use their platforms to accumulate data from everywhere.
- IoT, AI, edge computing, and data analytics will make difference among the top cloud service providers. The market share grab has largely gone to AWS, which was early, adds services at a rapid clip, and is the go-to cloud service provider. AWS' ability to upsell to AI, IoT, and analytics will be critical. Microsoft Azure Stack is also looking to differentiate via AI and machine learning [18].
- If we look at the records provided by IDC, in the year 2020, public cloud expenses have made a mark, for the first time, it has left behind old-style IT structure. An increase of 34.4% has been recorded in cloud including private and public. Whereas traditional IT infra fall out by 8%.
- Public hybrid cloud providers have the gap of capability between hyper scale cloud providers. Competition for enterprise workloads yields secondary markets throughout the world. The cloud service providers like Microsoft Azure Stack, AWS Outpost, and Google Cloud Anthos have become financially strong.

1.6   Security in Hybrid Cloud

A properly designed, managed, and integrated hybrid cloud is considered to be as secure as on-premise infrastructure. But reality is bit different. Gartner and WSJ [7] have recently reported that 95% data breaches occur in cloud computing due to human error. Here, in hybrid cloud, also human error plays a crucial role. Misconfiguration, misunderstanding of system use, and accidental data sharing all results threat to security. Security is essential in all application areas. Suppose in healthcare organizations patients' data should be kept hidden. Pathological reports of any patient are not expected to be accessed by any unauthenticated person. Similarly in financial industry, trust is the most important factors. Details of all customers' sensitive data have been kept like their income related info; their identification info their tax related document everything has been kept there. Customer should feel protected about their data. It happens in all sectors. With the help of public server and data centers, the business world is forwarding toward a new server free era but security measures have to be adjusted so that it can reap up ultimate technological and financial benefits. Since hybrid cloud is a *"one size fits for all"* solution for business development, it is advisable to look into the security issues more closely as threats to sensitive data might cause problem. Here is a list of issues specific to hybrid cloud security [11]:

- *Authority:* In hybrid environment, multiple functioning components scattered through private and public cloud. Multiple services can also be taken from multiple public clouds. So, customers of hybrid cloud should decide the governance rule for components, functions, and data beforehand both for private and public cloud.
- *Portability:* Supporting infrastructure must be there so that applications and data may move between public and private cloud. Data portability causes additional risk in hybrid cloud. Private data can be made secure by applying encryption techniques but when portability is allowed then who will be responsible for the protection of data in transit need to be addressed.
- *Presence of multiple interface:* Multiple cloud may be present in a network and each of them most likely is to have their own set of security and privacy policy compounds. This acts as a back door for data breaching in case of hybrid cloud.
- *Lack of separation wall:* Cloud customers have seamless access to private and public resources. As a result of that, sometimes, intruders take an indirect entry to penetrate the delicate data.
- *Security issues handling:* Reporting and subsequent measures for security issues need to be shared to the customer as well as service providers so that they will be extra cautious from the next access. Sometimes, customers face unacceptable delay due to security issues, so in the SLA, it should be mentioned when and how they will be notified.
- *Application and data protection:* Protections offered by the cloud providers are getting stronger day by day but still they are not enough. Advanced security information and event management (SIEM) solution need to be implemented.
- *Vendor lock-in:* Sometimes, due to lack of scalability or security issues, cloud needs to be shifted from one vendor to other vendor. If the cost of switching is so high that the customer is forced to stick to the origin, it is known as vendor lock-in. Avoiding vendor lock-in needs to be included in the business policy.
- *Guard against shadow IT practice:* Sometimes, within the organization, some person or departments are using sensitive data without the knowledge of the security group. This is called shadow IT practice, and often severe risks are associated with it.

Although hybrid cloud is considered more secure than public cloud as it provides greater control over the data but still data leakage, corruption, improper or unauthorized access, and data deletion can only be handled by secure channel, access control, data validation, and encryption. By doing the vulnerability management also security can be enhanced [32]. Risk assessment is often done to reduce vulnerability.

1.6.1   Role of Human Error in Cloud Security

As discussed, 95% of error in cloud security happens because of human error. Most of the time errors are not intentional but lack of seriousness, lack of overall knowledge of the system, poorly configured servers, misconfiguration, absence of proper authorization, etc., are players behind error generation. As a result, human expertise is not always believed to make safeguards against security threats. New kind of services and technologies are evolving every day for providing better services. There are automated security tools which can scan cloud configuration regularly and can enforce security policies which will not let intruders to get access.

1.6.2   Handling Security Challenges

When any organization is planning to deploy hybrid cloud, some box of tricks needs to apply to reduce the security threats. Though cloud vendors generally provide security measures but still they see the task as shared responsibility, also in case of multi-tenant cloud security algorithms are not same for all vendors. So, planning and standardization of all activities can handle security challenges to a great extent. Some best ever practices are as follows:

- *Encrypt all data:* Best possible means to secure data is to do the encryption. Encrypt all data irrespective of their location. In hybrid cloud, data often move between two or more clouds and in transit data is vulnerable. Encrypted data is less likely to be compromised. Selective encryption can be more vulnerable as it is easy to identify which is encrypted and which is not. Target selection becomes easier in this case and data becomes more susceptible to threats.
- *Strengthen authentication and authorization process:* Access to data should only be provided to authenticated user. Unnecessary and unauthorized access has to be prevented. In hybrid cloud, different applications run on different cloud, so access rights of different customer will not be same.
- *Customer awareness:* One of the most important part in security as it can reduce human error to some extent. Customers should follow common guidelines for accessing data and services. They should be aware of the security threats and will take measures accordingly. They should use strong passwords and prevent access to sensitive data by any unauthenticated application.
- *Application of standardized process:* Uniform standards have to be maintained; it should not be like any one can use anything. Network configuration, password structure, firewall setup, auditing and monitoring, and database maintenance everything need to be regulated. Regular updation of OS and applications is essential.

- **Strong disaster recovery plan:** Though event of system or application failure in hybrid cloud is much less than other cloud, but still it can happen. Disaster recovery plans should take action in those scenarios. Regular backup and configuration of failover system should be a part of disaster recovery plan.
- **Employ right security personnel:** Infra and network administrators have the most vital role to play in hybrid cloud computing. Employment of correct personnel with adequate knowledge and experience can apprehend potential threats beforehand and therefore can accommodate the system accordingly.
- **Endpoint security:** Hybrid cloud has more endpoints than on-premise system. Each open endpoint is also entrance for potential attackers. Strict security measures should be application for all inbound data.
- **Multi-faced approach:** It basically deals with both internal and external vulnerabilities. Protecting our network from external threats is not enough here, we need to concentrate on the internal threats also as the frequency of internal threats is higher than external and also it has bigger effect onto the organization.
- **Pervasive encryption:** It is a consumable approach for in flight and in rest data encryption. Huge amount of data can be encrypted easily and in cost-effective way. IBM Z15 is a platform which provides pervasive encryption in digital enterprise [26].

1.7   Use of AI in Hybrid Cloud

Organizations now completes for the customer satisfactions and operational efficiency. AI and machine learning are the light bearer in this regard [12, 13]. A term in this regard often circulated, i.e., "AI in the cloud". Most of the cloud-based services provider designs their management tool where some AI-based technologies are incorporated. This helps the customer a range of facilities starting from image recognition to big data analysis [24]. The biggest advantage of this adaptation is that you do not need expertise for deployment, or configuration or management of the architecture models and prototypes are already there for the developers. Banking sectors, automobile industries, e-commerce trades, etc., all the approaching toward hybrid cloud and AI. For example in case of banking sector, they can keep their customer details in private datacenters and can leverage public cloud services for operational need. AI will help to analyze customer specific data, which can help the organization to provide loans or offers customized according to the present need of the customer. Also with help of the AI, 24x7 service can be provided, without actual intervention of customer care executives. AI can also help in incident analysis. If sometimes the system became irresponsive, AI can judge the situation and can suggest recovery measures. Disaster recovery plans can also be toughen with the help of AI. Based on the previous observations, AI can generate the pattern of the system might causes disaster, and therefore, preventive actions can be taken in advance. Automobile industries also approaching toward adaptation of AI and hybrid cloud to provide best ever services and hazard free maintenance. In case of e-commerce business, AI has most lucrative role to play. Analyzing the buying pattern of the customer not only helps business to expand, it also can serve the customer need in best possible way.

But is this adaptation sustainable is a million dollar question. Some experts commented that use of AI is a fashion. But the easy-to-use nature and strong data mining methods makes is worthy. Now, what about data privacy? Is the use of AI has any role to play in data privacy? The answer is yes. In this case, AI has a major role to play. It can analyze the attacker's behavior and attacking pattern and accordingly can guide the network admin to take corrective steps and measures.

Mainly, AI requires large amount of data for their data mining operations and these data may come from several sources some internal and some external. When AI is used in public cloud, we might hesitate to use the data which is highly secure. But the quest for data of an AI engine is huge, as a result potential threats may arise. In July 2019, an incident was happen between AWS and financial giant Capital One. A person was arrested for hacking the data from the server of Capital One containing customer financial information. That person was a former employee of AWS. Capital One uses AWS for sorting the data and also on top of cloud; they built their app for analyzing the data. FBI then called and they investigated that there was some issue in the firewall of Capital One, buy using which the intruder has gain access to the data. AWS quickly responded that there was no issue from their end and Capital One rectifies the misconfiguration in the firewall. But the data breach has already happened. So, cloud security still in immature state as old approaches for securing internal data does not go the cloud. Here comes the hybrid cloud. Data security can be ensured efficiently and adaptation of AI-based technologies is also possible as internal data are kept hidden in private data centers, public cloud has no access to it.

Nutanix [27] provides a solution which is a turnkey for infra, aps, ops, and disaster recovery. A ready-made platform which helps to make a secure private cloud, streamline manual boring data operations, provides less complex management of database by using a single policy for all data, manages data in a better way by storing all data in a single storage, secures all data by providing visualization of policy and traffic works in different segments, detects and quarantines infected portion of the network, automates IT operations with the help of AI and ML, and does periodic backup of all data. This type of solution is highly acceptable in the industry. Special use of AI makes Nutanix very attractive for building secure hybrid cloud.

The amalgamation of AI into cloud has bring an evolution as AI was still complex, expensive, and high-end technology which was out of the reach of the general masses [25]. But now services of AI can be utilized by general masses without actually knowing the background technology. Several mobile apps and IoT work in this regard in an effective way. Human like interfaces, self-service, and customer-oriented application are made possible through the use of hybrid cloud and AI.

Use of AI made hybrid cloud more intelligence by playing a key part in cost analysis, real-time decision-making, policy optimization, and workload distribution leaving the IT experts to work on complex things rather than doing trivial tasks. AI-as-a-service is heading toward next level. Cloud giants AWS, Microsoft, IBM, and Google all are doing investments on this to make their service better as this is a competitive world. Whoever will provide better service in less cost will be more popular.

Quantifi [28] is one such solution. They are using AI/ML to perform risk analysis, data analytics, portfolio management, and trading predictions. Some major banking sectors, asset management companies, pension funds, and financial institutions are their customer. By the use of AI, big data, Lamda architecture, and in-memory computing, Quantifi is one of the front benchers in risk assessment. Cross platform which supports Windows, Linux, MacOS, and Adaptation of ELT layer provides various external data sources to communicate bi-directionally at ease; rich API helps to provide tools and functionalities to clients so that they can extend their business without knowing much of the technical details; real-time business analysis and predictions are just one click away. Quantifi uses Microsoft Azure for its cross platform application development.

IBM Watson [29, 30] is another pioneer in this regard. It a tool where can give their instructions using natural language. This AI-powered search engine can answer complex business queries on demand. The natural language understanding capability makes it more interesting as otherwise for getting high-end business insight may be lines of code has to be written. Watson is also used with other AI-based tools for providing a platform which provides better customer services. This allows client to run all Watson products, IBM's own AI products on IBM cloud or any cloud from other vendors. It can club private cloud services also.

Lots of other tools are also available which use AI and hybrid cloud for better customer services.

1.8   Future Research Direction

The adaptation of hybrid cloud still is in nurture state. It is not exhaust in nature. High possibility of amalgamation of different technologies makes it useful and difficult to handle also in some cases. Here is a list of future research directions:

- Standardization is a vital part of cloud architecture. No uniform standard is there for setting up the hybrid cloud architecture. Research can be done in this direction.
- Orchestration of hybrid cloud often requires huge power consumption and high-end networking. Use of green energy sources can be kept as an option.
- Security is always a concert. Intrusion detection and encryption techniques should be able to handle advanced threats. The pattern of attacks is changing every day so to cope up with that security measures also need to be updated also. Thus, it a subject of research all the time.
- Use of AI and data analytics can do wonders. Many researches are already going on in this direction but still scopes are there.
- Reliability still is a major issue in hybrid cloud computing, some portion of the network may remain unavailable for some period of time. How failover plans can be made stronger so that it can handle these issues in transparent way is a matter of consideration.
- SLA is a portion where more research should be done. Miscommunication, misinterpretation, and lack of information often cause problem. In multi-cloud system, it is more prominent.

1.9   Conclusion

Hybrid cloud offer several benefits but complex large and distributed nature makes it hard to handle. It keeps business sensitive data in private data centers for their protection and use public cloud for additional services. But still, management and monitoring of all in bound data is not always possible. As a result, security issues always happen. IT security is always challenging, and in case of hybrid platform it seems more complicated. Use of AI can do miracles in cloud computing. Adaptation of AI and hybrid cloud is new trend in the industry. So, by taking reasonable thoughts and with judiciously designed automation system in middleware hybrid cloud can offer exciting features in cost-effective way. Leading organizations are moving forward the adaptation of hybrid cloud and AI as it can provide scalable, cost-effective, flexible, user friendly, and secure solution.

References

1. Toyota Coud based Service, https://www.gadgetsnow.com/tech-news/amazon-to-help-toyota-build-cloud-based-data-services/articleshow/77609555.cms. Accessed on 9th Oct, 2020.
2. Hybrid Cloud, https://www.redhat.com/en/topics/cloud-computing/what-is-hybrid-cloud, Accessed on 31/07/2020.
3. National Institute of standard Technology, https://nvlpubs.nist.gov/nistpubs/Legacy/SP/nistspecialpublication800-145.pdf, Accessed on October, 2020.
4. Hybrid Cloud: https://phoenixnap.com/blog/what-is-hybrid-cloud, Accessed on October, 2020.
5. 'Practical guide to hybrid cloud'- Cloud standard and customer council, February, OMG standard Development Organization, 2016, https://www.omg.org/cloud/deliverables/CSCC-Practical-Guide-to-Hybrid-Cloud-Computing.pdf.
6. Lakshmi Devasena, C., Impact study of cloud computing on business development. *Oper. Res. Appl.: An Int. J. (ORAJ)*, 1, 1, pp. 1–7 August 2014.
7. Human Error in Cloud: https://www.wsj.com/articles/human-error-often-the-culprit-in-cloud-data-breaches-11566898203, Accessed on 31/07/2020.
8. Hybrid cloud: https://azure.microsoft.com/en-in/overview/what-is-hybrid-cloud-computing/, Accessed on 9th Oct, 2020.
9. Cloud Market: https://www.marketsandmarkets.com/Market-Reports/hybrid-cloud-market-1150.html, Accessed on 10th Oct, 2020.
10. Hybrid Cloud Architecture: https://www.vxchnge.com/blog/building-hybrid-cloud-architecture, Accessed on 10th October, 2020.
11. *Solution brief: What Is hybrid cloud. A crash course on combining private and public cloud Infrastructure*, Intel, https://cdw-prod.adobecqms.net/content/dam/cdw/on-domain-cdw/brands/intel/intel-hybrid-cloud-brief.pdf, 2016.
12. AI in Hybrid Cloud, https://www.ibm.com/blogs/client-voices/digital-transformation-ai-hybrid-cloud/, Accessed on October, 2020.
13. AI galvanizing with cloud, https://cio.economictimes.indiatimes.com/news/cloudcomputing/galvanizing-the-new-age-of-it-with-ai-and-hybrid-cloud/74722393, Accessed on 10th October, 2020.
14. Market Hybrid Cloud, https://www.mordorintelligence.com/industry-reports/hybrid-cloud-market, Accessed on 10th October, 2020.

15. Hybrid Cloud Opportunity, https://www.thehindu.com/business/Industry/india-is-key-to-ibms-pursuit-of-a1-trillion-hybrid-cloud-opportunity/article33201906.ece. Accessed on 12th October, 2020.

16. Aryotejo, G., Kristiyanto, D.Y., Mufadhol, Hybrid cloud: bridging of private and public cloud computing. *IOP Conf. Series: J. Physics: Conf. Ser.*, 1025, 012091, 2018.

17. Hybrid Cloud Providers, https://www.loomsystems.com/blog/hybrid-cloud-providers, Accessed on 10th November, 2020.

18. Top 5 Cloud Providers, https://www.cloudmanagementinsider.com/top-five-cloud-computing-news-june-2020, Accessed on 20th November, 2020.

19. SaaS-Cloud-Providers, https://www.zdnet.com/article/the-top-cloud-providers-of-2020-aws-microsoft-azure-google-cloud-hybrid-saas. Accessed on 20th November, 2020.

20. Kumar, S., Kumar, S., Bajwa, M.S., Sharma, H., A Comparative Study of Various Cloud Service Platforms. *J. Adv. Database Manage. Syst.*, 6, 1, pp. 7–12, 2020.

21. Islam, N. and Rehman, A., A comparative study of major service providers for cloud computing, in the Proceedings of 1st International Conference on Information and Communication Technology Trends, at Karachi Pakistan, 2014.

22. Kimmy, A Comparative Study Of Clouds In Cloud Computing. *Int. J. Comput. Sci. Eng. Technol. (IJCSET)*, 4, pp. 843–849 2013.

23. Sharma, A. and Garg, S., Comparative Study of Cloud Computing Solutions. *IJCST*, 6, 4, pp. 231–233, Oct - Dec 2015.

24. Data Protection in Cloud, https://www.nutanix.com/theforecastbynutanix/technology/protecting-data-when-running-ai-in-the-cloud, Accessed on 10th December, 2020.

25. AI and Hybrid Cloud, https://www.hcltech.com/blogs/growing-bond-between-ai-hybrid-cloud, Accessed on 5th December, 2020.

26. Pervasive Encryption, https://www.ibm.com/support/z-content-solutions/pervasive-encryption/, Accessed on 6th December, 2020.

27. Nutanix, https://www.nutanix.com/, Accessed on 10th December, 2020.

28. Quantifi, https://www.quantifisolutions.com/overview, Accessed on 10th December, 2020.

29. IBM Watson, https://www.ibm.com/in-en/watson, Accessed on 7th December, 2020.

30. Watson Blog, https://www.ibm.com/blogs/watson/2019/09/gartner-names-ibm-a-leader-in-2019- magic-quadrant-for-insight-engines/, Accessed on 7th December, 613, pp. 480–489, 2020.

31. Hybrid cloud in Education, https://www.intel.fr/content/dam/www/public/us/en/documents/education/hybrid-cloud-in-education.pdf, Accessed on 10th December, 2020.

32. Dhinakaran, K., Kirtana, R., Gayathri, K., Devisri, R., Enhance hybrid cloud security using Vulnerability Management. *Adv. Intell. Syst. Comput.*, 613, pp. 480–489, December 2018.

33. Vaishnnave, M.P., Suganya Devi, K., Srinivasan, P., A Survey on Cloud Computing and Hybrid Cloud. *Int. J. Appl. Eng. Res.*, 2019.

34. Cearley, W. and Hilgendorf, K., Cloud Computing Innovation Key Initiative Overview, Gartner Research Database, Volume 15 pp. 45–52, 2014.

Recognition of Differentially Expressed Glycan Structure of H1N1 Virus Using Unsupervised Learning Framework

Shillpi Mishrra

Department of Computer Science and Engineering, Techno India University, Kolkata, India

Abstract

Influenza A (H1N1) virus created a pandemic situation around the world from 1918 to 1919. More than 10,000 cases have been reported to the World Health Organization (WHO). It affects species and sometimes in humans. Binding of hemagglutinin and some types of glycan receptors is the major ingredients for virus infections. In this work, we take both H1N1 infected human and non-infected human glycan datasets and identify differentially expressed glycans. In this work, we narrate a computational frame work using the cluster algorithm, namely, k-means, hierarchical, and fuzzy c-means. The entire methodology has been demonstrated on glycan datasets and recognizes the set of glycans that are significantly expressed from normal state to infected state. The result of the methodology has been validated using t-test and F-score.

Keywords: Glycan receptors, differentially expressed glycan, clustering, k-means, fuzzy, F-score, glycan cloud

2.1 Introduction

Influenza A is a widespread infectious disease caused by the influenza virus that can easily spread from one person to another by coughing, sneezing, etc. This virus infects hosts like humans, sea-mammals, and swine. The first reported pandemic from 1918 to 1919 and the other two pandemics occurred in the 20th century [1–3]. Every year, 250,000 to 500,000 deaths occurred worldwide for this virus. In the past few years, there are lots of disasters that occurred, for example, pandemic named "Spanish Flu" caused the global death of 60 to 100 million people in the 1918. In 2009, scientists recognized a particular strain of influenza A virus which is known as H1N1 [4, 5]. H1N1 is normally found in swine. For this reason, it is also called "Swine Flu" or "Pig Flu" or "Swine influenza viruses (SIVs)". It is a human respiratory infection caused by the H1N1 influenza that is basically started in pigs and contains RNA virus with a segmented genome. It is also called orthomyxovirus because it contains haemagglutinin and neuraminidase glycoproteins. Transmission of swine flu to humans is

Email: shllpimishrra91@gmail.com

Rajdeep Chakraborty, Anupam Ghosh and Jyotsna Kumar Mandal (eds.) Machine Learning Techniques and Analytics for Cloud Security, (25–40) © 2022 Scrivener Publishing LLC

rare. But, swine flu can be transmitted to humans via contact with infected swine or environments contaminated. Once a human gets infected, humans can then spread this virus to other humans, and in the same way, swine flu is spread (i.e., cough or sneezing). It is a mystery that when and where pandemic reassortments will happen. Lots of reports suggest that this type of reassortments is very frequent between human viruses [6]. Influenza has been found very frequently with co-infections and reassortment of swine and human. Cell surface oligosaccharide receptors of the swine windpipe present a NeuAcalpha2, 6 Gal linkages, and preferred by human viruses. Some glycans with sialic acid α2,6-linked (SA2,6Gal) are detected more immense in the upper airways than the lower airways in the human body [7–10]. According to the "central dogma" biological concept, double-stranded DNA is simulated into RNA and this RNA carries some instructions for making proteins that mean DNA to RNA to protein. Glycosylation and phosphorylation are the post-translational modifications techniques that are required to estimate for the accurate regulation that is required by the living system. Every cell is wrapper up with a coat (solid) of glycans to create interface of molecular between the cells and environment of cells. Glycosylation is basically enzymatic techniques where this technique is the key factors to establish the connection of carbohydrates to proteins through nitrogen and oxygen links. Whole process happens with the Endoplasmic Reticulum (cell) that arranged with different types of glycol-sialyltransferases and glycosidases [9–16]. The immune system is an important component to keep up a hygenic and well balanced system that is very organized by a sequence of stimulatory and restrictive ways. If whole system is broken down, then autoimmunity can occur for loss of immune tolerance and it can also effect in unusual costimulatory signals. The proper growth and function of the immune system confide pair on the glycan-structures (expression) and glycan-binding proteins, and the association between them. Innate immune is responsible to identify the molecular "patterns" that basically find on microbes. Microbes are responsible to bind by pattern recognition receptors that is one kind of protein to identify molecules in pathogen, C-type (calcium-dependent), lectins (types are Dectin-1 and DC-SIGN), and mannose-binding lectin. The glycans that are found on sensors of innate immune system can be classified by two effects they are "direct" and "indirect" effects [11–15] and these are playing important role in influencing microbe-host interactions and T and B cell identification. Glycan-binding proteins known as GBP are very important within the immune systems that are basically the lectins and the sialic acid-binding immunoglobulin (Siglecs). Within the lectin family, lots of pattern recognition receptors are present like as DC-SIGN and Dectin-1 and the selectins that are L-selectin, E-selectin, and P-selectin. For leukocyte function, lectins are very complex to communicate with the glycans of cell surface that are basically sialyl-LewisX and 6′-sulfo-sialyl-LewisX. To bind the glycoprotein as counter receptors, L-lectins are expressed by leukocytes on endothelial cells for directing naive T cells. In contrast, on endothelial cells, E-lectins and P-lectins are both expressed as a impact of inflammation. The selectins and their glycan ligands interactions facilitate adherence of leukocytes along the endothelium and allowing the cells to migrate into tissues in response to chemokines that are bound to glycol-saminoglycans [12–18]. This way, communication of glycans and selectins are responsible for leukocyte function by arranging restricted to the ideal anatomic field. Another group of glycan-binding molecules are siglecs. But siglecs' function is perfectly separate from lectins (c-type) and galectins. Siglecs are also receptors of cell surface for recognizing sialic acids and high-ranking vertebrates. It has also cytoplasmic tails that holds more than immune-receptor inhibitory motif sequences (tyrosine-based). Glycans holds different types of effects (indirect) on lymphocyte function [12–19]. To reduce the N-glycans' complexity on T-cell receptors, these effects are resulted to raised T-cell receptors clustering and signaling at antigen density (lower). In the T-cell receptors signaling process, galectin is not directly engaged and Mgat5 enzyme plays an important role to contribute of N-glycan complexity that increase autoimmune disorders of H1N1 disease and had raised sensibility to empirical autoimmune encephalitis. Similarly, decease of N-glycan complexity on glycoproteins of the cell surface is changed the signaling via lectins and cytokine receptors [17–22].

In 2015, a framework has been proposed of the genetics of the new strain and recognized its nearest relatives in swine using a cluster analysis approach like as the PCA and k-means clustering algorithm and suitable with a reassortment of Eurasian and North American swine viruses [5, 20]. Glycoproteins are the key elements of human pathogenic viruses and perform important roles in infection and immunity. The influenza A virus contains two surface glycoproteins which consist of hemagglutinin (HA) and neuraminidase (NA) that dominate the virion exterior and form antibodies. One major of the components of the outermost layer of viruses is glycans. The communication between the viral pathogens with pathogens' hosts is affected by the glycans' pattern and glycan-binding receptors. Due to the mass branching of carbohydrates, they are the complex bio-molecules, and in this process, various glycoproteins are used to recognize with human pathogens (virus). Infectious glycans can be either virus-encoded or can be host-derived that usually obtained by humoral immune responses (high) within the human body. HA and NA both are responsible for creating a connection with envelope glycoproteins of the influenza virus. When HA communicates with terminal sialyl residues of oligosaccharides that ensure the binding of the virion to the cell surface. To eliminate sialyl residues from oligosaccharides contained in cell and virus components, NA is also needed. It is a receptor-destroying enzyme that prevents aggregation of virus particles [7, 25].

In this paper, our goal is to identify differentially expressed glycan. The clustering algorithms have been applied to H1N1 infected human datasets and non-infected human dataset. After that, we compare infected with the non-infected dataset and identify differentially expressed glycan.

2.2   Proposed Methodology

Input: Let, the dataset **D** consists of "n" number of glycan with "m" number of parameter values like RFU (relative fluorescence units), STDEV (standard deviation), and SEM (squared error mean). Each glycan is a vector and is represented by $g_1, g_2, g_3, ..., g_j, ..., g_n$. The dataset **D** has two states normal (represented by $\mathbf{D_N}$) and diseased or H1N1 infected state (represented by $\mathbf{D_I}$).

Output: Differentially expressed glycan identification **G'**

Step-1: Apply clustering algorithm "C" on normal (represented by $\mathbf{D_N}$) and diseased or H1N1 infected state (represented by $\mathbf{D_I}$).

Step-2: Result for normal state = $\mathbf{C_N} = \left(C_1^N, C_2^N, C_3^N, ..., C_j^N, ..., C_k^N \right)$; similarly, result for infected state = $\mathbf{C_I} = \left(C_1^I, C_2^I, ,, ..., C_k^I \right)$; Here, clusters number is k.

Step-3: Find out the identical clusters or matched clusters between normal states to infected states.

Step-4: Perform cluster comparison and identify the differentially expressed glycan set **G** that has been changed quite significantly.

$$G = \left(C_1^N \cap C_2^I \right) \cup \left(C_1^N \cap C_3^I \right) \cup \ldots \left(C_1^N \cap C_k^I \right) \cup \ldots \left(C_{k-1}^N \cap C_k^I \right)$$

Step-5: For multiple glycan datasets D_1, D_2,..., D_t, the resultant glycan set will be represented as $G' = G_1 \cap G_2 \ldots \cap G_t$; here, G_1 is the differentially expressed glycan set obtained in Step 4 for dataset D1.

The entire methodology has been depicted in Figure 2.1. In this paper, three clustering algorithms are used:

The first algorithm has been applied that is the k-means clustering and was proposed by scientist J.B. Macqueen. The actual idea behind this algorithm is to identify k centroids one for each cluster or group.

(1) At first, choose some points to represent initial cluster focal points.
(2) Secondly, assign each object to a cluster that has closed centroids.
(3) Thirdly, when all objects are assigned, then recalculate the position of the k centroids, and lastly, this process will be continued until the centroids no longer move and this basically produces separation of the objects into clusters from which the metric is to be minimized can be calculated [23].

The hierarchical clustering is the second algorithm. It groups similar objects into groups (cluster). In this algorithm, it basically treats every observation as an individual cluster. After that, it iterates the following steps continuously:

(1) At first, consider the two clusters or groups that are closest together.
(2) Then, combine the two most similar clusters. Until all the clusters are combined together, this process continues [24].

The fuzzy c-means clustering is the last and third algorithm. This algorithm's concept is very like to the k-means clustering. The algorithm is as follows:

(1) At first, identify clusters number.
(2) Then, randomly assign coefficients to each data point for being in the clusters.
(3) Until the algorithm has converged, repeats (1) and (2) step:
    (i) Compute centroid of each cluster or group.
    (ii) For every data point, compute the coefficient of being in the cluster.

2.3 Result

Result section consists of description of datasets, analysis of results, and validation of results.

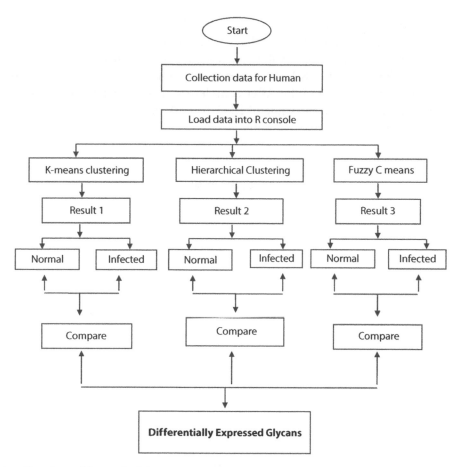

Figure 2.1 Flowchart of the methodology.

2.3.1   Description of Datasets

Influenza sequences (glycan dataset) are taken from the National Centre for Biotechnology Information. At first, to perform searching operation, Basic Local Alignment Search Tool (BLAST) has been applied on H1N1 infected human datasets of Influenza A/447/08 at Oklahoma, Influenza A/1138/08 at Oklahoma, and Influenza A/447/08 at Oklahoma and on non-infected normal human of Influenza A/California/04/2009-4C. The dataset of H1N1 contains glycan data in Oklahoma City and the dataset of normal human contains glycan data in California City. The dataset consists of 442 different glycans and list of linkers are sp0, sp8, sp9, sp12, etc. Individual columns of the dataset represent the glycan numbers, glycan structure, the RFU, the STDEV value, and the SEM.

2.3.2   Analysis of Result

In this paper, unsupervised machine learning method like as k-means, hierarchical, and fuzzy c-means algorithm are shown to prove excellent classification performance and have been successfully applied in data analysis of H1N1 infected and non-infected datasets. At first, k-means clustering algorithm are applied on H1N1 infected dataset Influenza

A/447/08 at Oklahoma, Influenza A/1138/08 at Oklahoma, and Influenza A/447/08 at Oklahoma and on non-infected dataset Influenza A/California/04/2009-4C that are shown in Figures 2.2 to 2.5. Same process will be repeated for hierarchical clustering algorithms that are shown in Figures 2.6 to 2.8. Fuzzy c-means has applied on above-mentioned datasets that are shown in Figures 2.9 to 2.11. After completing cluster analysis, we have collected those glycan structures where the value of RFU, STDEV, and SEM has been significantly changed from normal state to infected state.

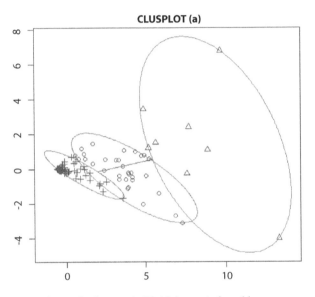

Figure 2.2 K-means cluster analysis of Influenza A (H1N1) non-infected human.

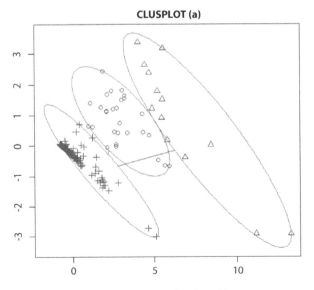

Figure 2.3 K-means cluster analysis of Influenza A (H1N1) infected human.

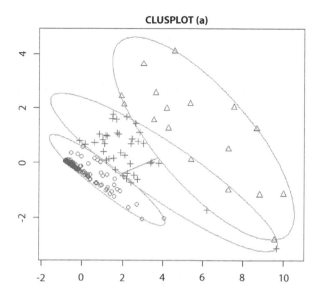

Figure 2.4 K-means cluster analysis of Influenza A (H1N1) infected human.

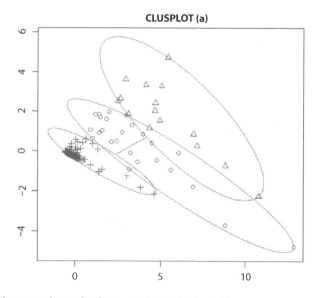

Figure 2.5 K-means cluster analysis of Influenza A (H1N1) infected human.

2.3.3   Validation of Results

2.3.3.1   T-Test (Statistical Validation)

The t-test statistical validation has been applied for comparing the means of two samples (infected and normal), even if they have different number of glycans. The following steps are used to solve t-test validation:

a) List H1N1 infected datasets for sample 1.

b) List normal dataset for sample 2.
c) Record the number replicates (in the data set, n = 3) for sample (The number of replicates for sample1, i.e., n1 is 3, the number of replicates for sample2, i.e., n2 is 3).
d) Compute the mean of both n1 and n2 (x_1', x_2'). [mean = total/n]
e) Compute the standard deviation (σ) for each sample ($\sigma1$, $\sigma2$). Where, $\sigma^2 = \Sigma d^2/(n-1)$
f) Compute the variance that is the difference between the two means $\left(\sigma_b^2\right)$. Where $\sigma_b^2 = \sigma_1^2/n1 + \sigma_2^2/n2$
g) Compute σ_b (square root of σ_b^2).
h) Compute the p value as follows:

$$p = (x1' - x2') / \sigma_b$$

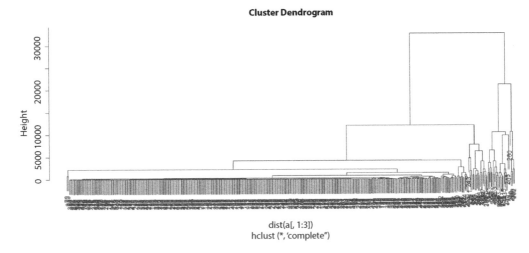

Figure 2.6 Hierarchical cluster analysis of Influenza A (H1N1) infected human.

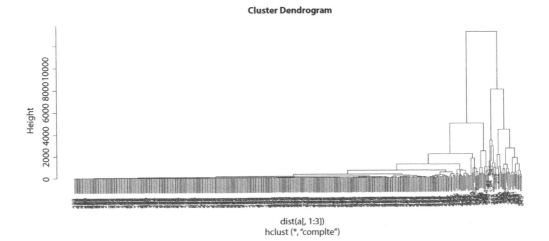

Figure 2.7 Hierarchical cluster analysis of Influenza A (H1N1) infected human.

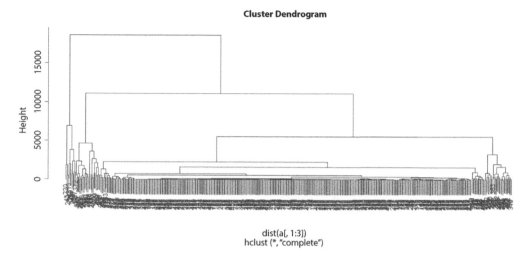

Figure 2.8 Hierarchical cluster analysis of Influenza A (H1N1) infected human.

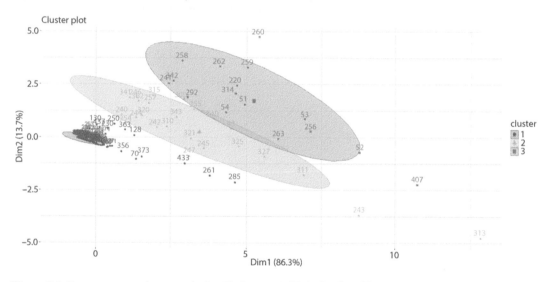

Figure 2.9 Fuzzy c-means cluster analysis of Influenza A (H1N1) infected human.

2.3.3.2   Statistical Validation

In this article, on both datasets, k-means algorithm has been applied where k value is 3. Secondly, on the same datasets, hierarchical algorithm has been applied. At last, on the same datasets, fuzzy c-means algorithm has been applied where cluster number is 3. Total numbers of glycans are 442 that are present in all datasets. On host cell surfaces, these 442 glycans are displayed and act as sensory receptors that basically identify the glycoproteins of the viral surface. Consider an example where these 442 glycan structures concluded by sialic acid a2, 3- or a2, 6-linked that is called N-acetyl neuraminic acid which acts as receptors for H1N1. The upper respiratory surface of human mainly displays sialylated glycan receptors that are executed with a2 to 6-linked sialic acid. Moreover, various types of glycan receptors are responsible to identify the hemagglutinin glycoprotein (HA) on the outermost

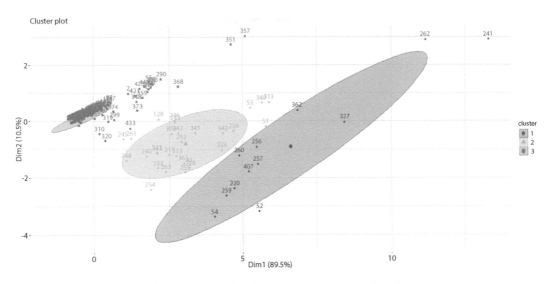

Figure 2.10 Fuzzy c-means clustering algorithm of Influenza A (H1N1) infected human.

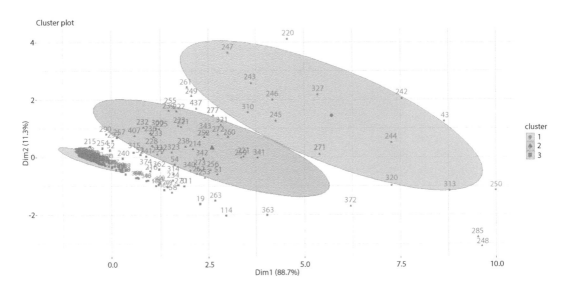

Figure 2.11 Fuzzy c-means clustering algorithm of Influenza A (H1N1) infected human.

part of influenza A viruses. This way, human can be infected and H1N1 viruses transmit via respiratory droplets in humans. Nineteen differentially expressed glycans are found out of 442 after applying three clustering algorithms. After that, t-test statistical validations are applied on the infected and non-infected (normal) datasets. In Table 2.1, nineteen differentially expressed glycans are found after t-test validation.

After that, type-I and type-II errors are used for finding the accuracy and predicting the output between the actual and predicted values. Table 2.2 is represented as rows and columns where rows are experiment and columns are represented as gold set. The meaning of true positive (TP) is that the set of glycans are identified by our experiment as same as the result mentioned in the gold set. True negative (TN) means that the set of glycans are identified by

Table 2.1 Significant glycan list.

Sr. no.	Structure
1	Neu5Aca2-3(6-O-Su)Galb1-4(Fuca1-3)GlcNAcb-Sp8
2	Neu5Aca2-6Galb1-4GlcNAcb1-3Galb1-4(Fuca1-3)GlcNAcb1-3Galb1-4(Fuca1-3)GlcNAcb-Sp0
3	Galb1-4GlcNAcb1-2Mana1-3(Neu5Aca2-6Galb1-4GlcNAcb1-2Mana1-6)Manb1-4GlcNAcb1-4GlcNAcb-Sp12
4	GlcAb1-3GlcNAcb-Sp8
5	Mana1-2Mana1-2Mana1-3(Mana1-2Mana1-6(Mana1-2Mana1-3)Mana1-6)Mana-Sp9
6	GlcNAcb1-2Mana1-3(Galb1-4GlcNAcb1-2Mana1-6)Manb1-4GlcNAcb1-4GlcNAc-Sp12
7	Galb1-4GlcNacb1-2(Galb1-4GlcNacb1-4)Mana1-3(Galb1-4GlcNacb1-2(Galb1-4GlcNacb1-6)Mana1-6)Manb1-4GlcNacb1-4GlcNacb-Sp21
8	Galb1-3Galb1-4GlcNAcb-Sp8
9	Galb1-3(Neu5Aca2-6)GalNAca-Sp14
10	Neu5Aca2-6Galb1-4Glcb-Sp0
11	Neu5Aca2-3Galb1-4GlcNAcb1-2Mana1-3(Neu5Aca2-3Galb1-4GlcNAcb1-2Mana1-6)Manb1-4GlcNAcb1-4GlcNAcb-Sp12
12	Neu5Aca2-6Galb1-4GlcNAcb1-2Mana1-3(Neu5Aca2-3Galb1-4GlcNAcb1-2Mana1-6)Manb1-4GlcNAcb1-4GlcNAcb-Sp12
13	Neu5Aca2-6GlcNAcb1-4GlcNAcb1-4GlcNAc-Sp21
14	Neu5Aca2-3Galb1-4GlcNAcb-Sp8
15	Neu5Aca2-6Galb1-4GlcNAcb-Sp0
16	Neu5Gca2-3Galb1-4(Fuca1-3)GlcNAcb-Sp0
17	Neu5Aca2-3Galb1-4GlcNAcb1-3Galb1-3GlcNAcb-Sp0
18	Neu5Aca2-6Galb1-4GlcNAcb1-3Galb1-6GlcNAcb-Sp8
19	Neu5Aca2-3Galb1-3GalNAcb1-4(Neu5Aca2-8Neu5Aca2-3)Galb1-4Glcb-Sp0

Table 2.2 The tabular format has been created from the above diagram.

		Gold Set	
		Positive (+)	**Negative (−)**
Our experiment	Positive (+)	T_Pos	F_Pos
	Negative (−)	F_Neg	T_Neg

our experiment not same as the result mentioned in the gold set. False negative (FN) means that the set of glycans are identified by our experiment which is missing in our experiment. False positive (FP) means that the set of glycans are identified by our experiment that positive but missing in the gold set. Type-I and Type-II errors are described in Figure 2.12.

The performance of the method has been validated using various statistical measurements & metrices. For details, please refer to Table 2.3. The visual representation of the method's performance has also been depicted in Figure 2.13.

In our experiment, the value of t-pos = 14, F_pos = 5, F_Neg = 5, and T_neg = 418. Performance of our method using various metrices.

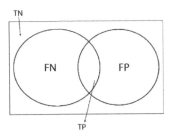

Figure 2.12 Concepts of type-I and type-II error in terms set.

Table 2.3 Performance of the method using various metrices.

Parameter	Value
Sensitivity	0.736
True negative rate	0.976
Precision	0.736
Negative-predictive value	0.163
Miss rate	0.263
Fall out	0.011
False discovery rate	0.357
False omission rate	0.011
Threat score	0.583
Prevalence threshold	0.149
Accuracy	0.977
Balance accuracy	0.856
Matthews correlation coefficient	0.725
Fowlkes-Mallows index	0.736
Informedness or bookmarker informedness	0.712
Markedness	−0.101
F-score	0.736

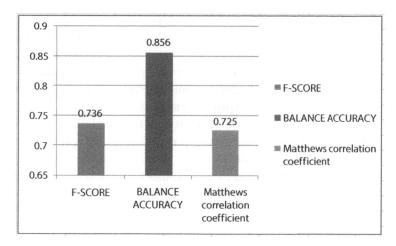

Figure 2.13 Performance measurements of the F-score, balance accuracy, and Matthews correlation coefficient.

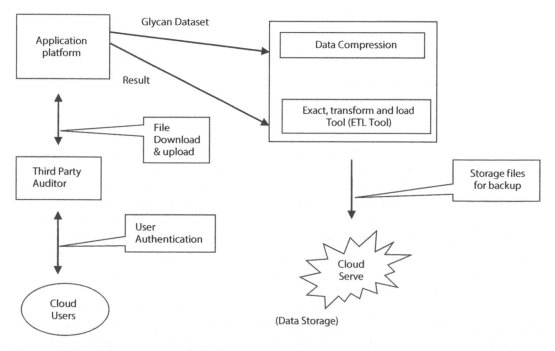

Figure 2.14 Block diagram of glycan cloud.

2.3.4   Glycan Cloud

There are two types of data sets stored in the cloud, namely, glycan dataset and result data. In Figure 2.14, dataset can be stored either. Dataset can be stored either in the form of files or in form of blocks in the cloud. Accessing the cloud is based on internet or intranet. To store the glycan dataset in the cloud storage system, one can move to any location that supports internet access. To save and recover the information, it is not essential to carry physical storage device or use the same computing systems. In this cloud system, security is also a major issue. When data will be stored securely in the cloud, security measures will be followed by authentication, encryption, tokens, and data replication. Authentication is the key security features where authorized user can access this glycan dataset stored in the cloud storage. Dataset of glycan and generated data should be encrypted first and store in the cloud. Only authorized user should know about the decryption key to access the dataset and final resulting framework. Tokens are generated by the third party auditor to check all data set and certify that whether the resultant information is corrupted or not. Hence, the data compression is used to speed up file transfer and decrease the cost of storage hardware, whereas the Exact, Transpose, and Load tool (ETL tool) is used to avoid redundancy, save space, and filter data for data replication. Moreover, data replication is used to back up multiple copies of data at different locations.

2.4   Conclusions and Future Work

In this paper, the deep study of epidemic models and methodologies has been investigated, and hence, we proposed a new model that has not been used in the earlier studies. This model will include unsupervised algorithms in which the system will be trained in order to capture and react to influenza-like activities so that the preventive measures can be taken to get rid of the epidemic as early as possible and we have established a proposed method for identifying of differentially expressed glycans. We will extend this work in future to find bonding between glycoproteins structure and moreover how the structure of glycan will change from host to host and estimate the mathematical parameters for the molecular insight of epidemiological characteristics in pandemic H1N1 influenza virus and also find the relationship between biosecurity and glycan. Biosecurity basically defines lots of attempts that secure biological dynamism, abnormality, and future of biology. In this article, we have to take some biosecurity concerns to control arising infectious diseases and pandemic flu and also organize some biosecurity events for the swine flu pandemic. The novel H1N1 virus has been recognized within swine in various countries like as Asia and Europe. Swine producers should be responsible to save themselves, farm workers, and swines from the further develop of H1N1. They should take biosecurity precautions that are respecting to the virus. The National Pork Board is requesting farm producers and veterinarians to maintain the precautions. At first, maintain biosecurity cultures to prevent the H1N1 to take entry their swineherd and also pay attention thoroughly for swines' health, and take some necessary precautions to reduce its spread. Farm producers need to follow up all rules to prevent spread of the H1N1 virus between human to human.

Several of the herds have been infected with the H1N1 virus that infected farm workers likely passed the virus to pigs. If producers restrict the crowd of people in their swine farm, also spread and implement bio-security rules for farm workers like as do not allow people who suffer flu-like symptoms, this way they can prevent H1N1. It is also essential that when workers will enter the pig farm, they require valveless respirators mask, gloves, and other personal protective equipment to prevent it. Before entering the pig farm, all people must clean up hands and arms with hot water and soap and produces should arrange the clothing and shoe (farm-specific) for entering within the pig farm. Cheer up farm workers to maintain all rules of biosecurity. Symptoms of the H1N1 influenza virus are basically fever, cough, body aches, and sometimes vomiting. They should provide farm workers with personal protective equipment and training. Vaccination is very important to stop human infections from stain of seasonal human influenza. Still, vaccination will decrease the amount of spreading H1N1 and virus shed if infected during outbreaks of human influenza and will give a boundary for human influenza virus infection of swines.

References

1. Jones, S., Nelson, S., Pillai, M.R., Evolutionary, genetic, structural characterization and its functional implications for the Influenza A (H1N1) infection outbreak in india from 2009 to 2017. *Sci. Rep.*, 9, 14690, 2019.

2. Rabadan, R., Levine, A.J., Knitz, M., Non-random reassortment in humaninfluenza A viruses. *Influenza Other Respir. Viruses*, 2, 1, 9–22, PubMed.gov, 2008, 2002.

3. Solovyov, A., Palacios, G., Briese, T., Lipkin, I.W., Rabadan, R., cluster analysis of the origins of the new Influenza A (H1N1) virus, *Eurosurveillance*, 2009;14(21):19224.

4. Eichelberger, M.C. and H.W., Influenza neuraminidase as a vaccine antigen. *Curr. Top. Microbiol. Immunol.*, 386, 275–299, 2015.

5. York, A.I., Stevens, J., Alymova, V.I., Influenza virus N-linked glycosylation and innate immunity. *Biosci. Rep.*, 39, BSR20171505, https://doi.org/10.1042/BSR20171505, 2018.

6. Wanzeck, K., Boyd, L.K., McCullers, A.J., Glycan Shielding of the Influenza Virus Hemagglutinin Contributes to Immunopathology in Mice. American journal of respiratory and critical care medicine, 183, 767–773, October 8, 2010, 2011.

7. Rahul, R., Kannan, T., V.S., Ram, S., Glycan–protein interactions in viral pathogenesis. *Curr. Opin. Struct. Biol.*, 40, 153–162, 2016.

8. Mena, I., Origins of the 2009 H1N1 Influenza pandemic in swine in Mexico. *eLife*, 5, e16777, 2016.

9. Rajoura, O.P., Roy, R., Agarwal, P., Kannan, A.T., A Study of the Swine Flu (H1N1) Epidemic Among Health Care Providers of a Medical College Hospital of Delhi. *Indian J. Community Med.*, 36, 3, 187–190, 2011.

10. Choudhury, A., Emergence of pandemic 2009 influenza A H1N1, India. *Indian J. Med. Res.*, 135, 534, 2012.

11. Iwasaki., A. and Pillai., P., Innate immunity to influenza virus infection. *Nat. Rev. Immunol.*, 14, 5, 315–328, 2014.

12. Biondo, C., Lentini, G., Beninati, C., Teti, G., The dual role of innate immunity during influenza. *Biomed. J.*, https://doi.org/10.1016/j.bj.2018.12.009.

13. Dandagi, G. and Byahatti, S., An insight into the swine-influenza A (H1N1) virus infection in humans. Lung India: Official Organ of Indian Chest Society, 28, 1, 34–38, 2011 Jan-Mar.

14. Ann, Y., McCullers, J.A., Alymova, I., Parson, L.M., Cipollo, J.F., Glycosylation analysis of engineered H3N2 influenza A virus hemagglutinins with sequentially added historically relevant glycosylation sites. *J. Proteome Res.*, 14, 3957–3969, 2015.

15. Wang, T., Maamary, J., Tan, G., Bournazos, S., Davis, C., Krammer, F., Schlesinger, S., Palese, P., Ahmed, R., Ravetch, J., Anti-HA glycoforms drive B cell affinity selection and determine influenza vaccine efficacy. *Cell*, 162, 160–169, 2015.

16. Mkhikian, H., Mortales, C., Zhou, R.W., Khachikyan, K., Wu, G., Haslam, S., Kavarian, P., Dell, A., Demetriou, M., Golgi self-correction generates bioequivalent glycans to preserve cellular homeostasis. *Elife*, 5, e14814, 2016.

17. Le, N., Bowden, T., Struwe, W., Crispin, M., Immune recruitment or suppression by glycan engineering of endogenous and therapeutic antibodies. *Biochim. Biophys. Acta*, 1860, 1655–1668, 2016.

18. Cedeno-Laurent, F., Opperman, M., Barthel, S., Metabolic inhibition of galectin-1-binding carbohydrates accentuates antitumor immunity. *J. Invest. Dermatol.*, 132, 410–420, 2012.

19. Maverakis, E., Kim, K., Shimoda, M., Gershwin, E., Patel, F., Wilken, R., Raychaudhuri, S., Ruhaak, L.R., Lebrilla, Glycans In The Immune system and The Altered Glycan Theory of Autoimmunity: A Critical Review. *J. Autoimmun.*, 57, 1–13, 2015 February 1st.

20. Pereira, M., Alves, I., Vicente, M., Campar, A., Silva, C.M., Padrao, A., Dias, M.A., Pinho, S.S., Glycans as key checkpoints of T cell Activity and Function. Frontiers in immunology, https://doi.org/10.3389/fimmu.2018.02754, 2018.

21. Baum, G.L. and Cobb, A.B., The direct and indirect effects of glycans on immune function. *Glycobiology*, 27, 7, 619–624, July 2017.

22. Reily, C., Stewart, J.T., Novak, J., Glycosylation in health and disease. 15, 6, 346–366, 2019.

23. Youguo, L. and Haiyan, W., A Clustering Method Based On K-means Algorithm, Elsevier. *Phys. Proc.*, 25, 1104–1109, 2012.

24. Murtagh, Fionn and Contreras, Pedro, Algorithms for hierarchical clustering: an overview, II, Wiley Interdisciplinary Reviews: Data Mining and Knowledge Discovery, 7, 6, e1219, 2017.

25. Taubenberger, J.K. and Morens, M.D., The Pathology of Influenza Virus Infections. *J. Clin. Micriobiol.*, 2008.

Selection of Certain Cancer Mediating Genes Using a Hybrid Model Logistic Regression Supported by Principal Component Analysis (PC-LR)

Subir Hazra*, Alia Nikhat Khurshid and Akriti

Meghnad Saha Institute of Technology, Kolkata, India

Abstract

In recent times, gene selection whose mutation is associated with some cancers is a promising research area. An important tool to progress in this research work is analyzing microarray gene expression data. Literature survey shows that different algorithms based on Machine Learning have been found effective in cancer classification and gene selection. The selected genes play a significant role as a clinical decision-making support system. It becomes helpful in diagnosing cancer by identifying genes whose expression level changes significantly. As microarray gene expression data is huge in number, so developing gene selection algorithm through Machine Learning approach incurs high computational complexity. Too many features can cause of over fitting and gives poor performance for the algorithm. In the present article, we developed a hybrid approach where we reduced number of features using Principal Component Analysis (PCA) and then applied Logistic Regression model for prediction of genes. After fitting Logistic Regression on test data, it is compared with an accuracy score. By checking the accuracy score, finally, the set of candidate genes is selected whose expression levels are manifested disproportionately. The generated sets of genes are identified for having correlation with certain cancers. The proposed method is demonstrated with two datasets, *viz.*, colon and lung cancer. The result has been finally validated biologically using NCBI database. The efficacy and robustness of the method have also been evaluated.

Keywords: Gene expression, PCA, Logistic Regression, dimensionality reduction, accuracy score, classification, F-score

3.1 Introduction

All cancer is the result of gene mutations. Mutations may be caused by several factors. Normal cells turn into cancerous cells largely due to mutations in their genes. Often, it is observed that a cell becomes cancer cell, when several mutations are involved. The mutations can influence various genes that control the division and growth of cells. Identifying

---

*Corresponding author: hazrasubir@gmail.com

Rajdeep Chakraborty, Anupam Ghosh and Jyotsna Kumar Mandal (eds.) Machine Learning Techniques and Analytics for Cloud Security, (41–60) © 2022 Scrivener Publishing LLC

the genes having correlation with certain cancer is a challenging task. Gene expression data obtained by high-performance–based technology, *viz.*, DNA sequencing and DNA microarray, both have been proven to have high impact in cancer research [1]. Gene selection can help in many ways like cancer treatment, proper diagnosis, and drug discovery [2]. With the invention and advancement of DNA microarray technology, monitoring the levels of expression of thousands of genes is possible but the key task is to derive information from the vast amount of biological data and realizing the underlying patterns [3]. Over the past few decades, a lot of tools based on various computational techniques have been developed in the domain of cancer classification for making advancement in medical science which essentially improves the competence of biologists and physicians for detecting cancer mediating biomarkers [4].

Cancer classification with the help of analyzing microarray gene expression data is a conventional method nowadays. The biological relevance of genes substantially influences the accuracy of cancer classification. Thus, selection of genes plays a pivotal role and might be observed as main factor for classification of cancer on the basis of microarray data. The process of gene selection relates to the task of selecting a few significant genes that better characterizes the variations [5]. It is always effective to put focus some important genes which are obviously smaller in number and might differ in their expression levels from non-cancerous state to cancerous one. Thus, from the whole genome, only a few number of genes which are dominant should be identified by using effective gene selection method [6]. But extracting information from the vast amount of biological data and understanding the patterns is the most appealing task. This correlation is more pronounced when these genes are located on the same biological path. In this situation, the procedures traditionally used for feature selection often overlook the relationships between genes and select only a few the set of genes which are mostly linked. The irrelevant genes not only contribute to lower output of the classification but also bring additional difficulties in locating genes which are descriptive in nature [7].

Analyze microarray data and selection of informative genes is always a demanding task. Due to presence of diversity and complexity in different types of cancer, the task is more challenging. With the emergence in the field of biotechnology a bulk amount of data is being generated by utilizing high-density oli-gonucleotide chips and cDNA arrays [8, 9]. Researchers now can measure thousands of gene expression data simultaneously. But there is lack of suitable algorithm to extract knowledge and mine the information from this type of biological data source which is very much significant. So, the increased demand always persists to explore and design suitable algorithm/s. While analyzing microarray data, one of the most significant applications is to classify the tissue samples that belong to normal and cancerous state. Nevertheless, during such application, it has always been observed that a large number of genes are identified which are irrelevant. So, this genes has got no impact on clinical application, and as a result, the efficiency of the method gets compromised [10, 11]. On the other side of the coin, working and interpreting with the huge number of genes incurs lack of feasibility. Thus, it is obvious to select accurate number of relevant genes by analyzing microarray data and has become really a promising one. Selecting these important genes is very much important from different angles of medical science which includes drug discovery, targeted therapy, prognosis, and sometimes early detection [12, 13].

Gene expression data generated through high-throughput technology comes in the form of matrix where each rows represents gene expression level but columns are the samples. As gene expression is considered as the features which is a very large but the experimental data, i.e., the samples are very few in numbers so it becomes really a complex task to work with. This is a real problem to start with the work with such huge dimensionality. Many algorithms based on different Artificial Intelligence (AI) techniques have been experimented over the years to find solution. Different algorithm based on Machine Learning (ML) approach, a branch of AI has been used over the years as an effective analytical tool this type data [14]. In ML technique model, data used in past is utilized in order to predict future result. Different learning methods based on statistical and probabilistic model and optimization techniques can be implemented for analyzing data. Learning methods like Logistic Regression (LR), artificial neural networks (ANN), K-nearest neighbor (KNN), decision trees (DT) and Naïve Bayes are widely used in different context [15, 16]. Two categories of learning in ML techniques are mainly used, i.e., supervised and unsupervised learning. The learning model implemented through learning from known classes (labeled training data) is termed as supervised learning. On the other hand, unsupervised learning methods learn from unknown class data often termed as unlabeled training data [17]. Algorithms designed by ML approach have been used for different purpose like classification of groups and kcy feature training and recognition. The real power of ML algorithms is it could recognize patterns from datasets which are large, noisy, and difficult to discern. This property is very much useful to process complex genomic data, specifically in the field of cancer related studies [18, 19].

While building a prediction model, LR is reckoned as a popular method where the outcome is binary and has been expanded to provide classification of disease with microarray data. Here, it is necessary to incorporate a feature (gene) selection technique and should be induced to penalize the logistic model. The fundamental reason is that, here, the number of genes is very large compare to number of samples. So, selection of proper model in this procedure needs new statistical methods. This is important because while predicting error assessment, the step for selecting features if ignored, could have impact of severely downward biased. The widely used methods which are mostly generic like cross-validation and non-parametric bootstrap may be not so effective owing to the huge vulnerability in predicting the error estimation process. The classification of diseases like cancer using microarray data has been considered the subject of extensive research in order to provide more precise diagnostic methods than the conventional pathological approach alone can provide. The expression of genes can also be used to predict survival time, disease prognosis and treatment response. The overall impact is very much significant as all the factors are having major clinical consequences. To design a logistic prediction model using microarray data, however, has got a fundamental difference from the standard logistic model owing to the observed number of genes, which often becomes thousands in number while the number of arrays (samples) observed is generally very lesser which is often less than one hundred. A common wise used approach is to combine a step in gene selection with a penalized inference of probability, called selection of features, which selects a subset of genes for inclusion in the LR model.

LR is a tool borrowed from the domain of statistics by ML. This method is used for classification problems which are binary in nature (problems having two values in the class). LR is widely used in the biological sciences where the dependent variable is categorical, i.e., it is a widely used method to build predictive models where the outcome is binary and is extended for utilizing as disease classification using microarray data [20]. In the present article, we have developed an algorithms using LR model to select feature (gene) whose mutation is having correlation with certain cancers. While designing proper gene selection algorithm using a ML model, it is a challenging task to reduce the computational complexity as because the dataset is of huge volume. The total number of genes (features) is very large in number. In the LR model, having too many features can cause of over fitting and performance of the algorithm is compromised [21]. There are many standard techniques which are widely used to reduce the dimensionality such as Kernel PCA, Linear Discriminant Analysis (LDA), and Principal Component Analysis (PCA). It is observed that, when the number of samples per class is smaller, PCA performs better, while LDA operates better for large datasets of multiple classes. While minimizing the dimensionality class repairability is considered as an essential factor. As our aim is to develop a binary classifier model, where we have overcome this by developing a hybrid approach where the number of features has been reduced using PCA. Although there are many techniques to do this, with PCA, loss of data is minimum in the context of the dataset it is appropriate to get better outcome. After that, the output of PCA is applied LR model for prediction of genes. A threshold value has been calculated and set for this binary classification which is applied on some test data to select which genes are selected as candidate genes or cancer mediating genes. The statistical and biological validation of obtained resultant set of genes has been accomplished at end.

3.2   Related Methods

Linear regression and LR both are statistical methods widely used by ML algorithms. Linear regression is effective for regression or for prediction of values continuous in nature, whereas LR is effective in both regression and classification problems. However, it is widely used mainly in the domain of classification algorithm. Models of regression seek to project values on the basis of independent characteristics. The key distinction which makes them different is when the dependent variables are assumed to be binary; LR is useful. However, when dependent variables are continuous, linear regression seems to be more effective.

In mathematics, linear models are well defined. For the purpose of predictive analysis, this model is commonly used nowadays. It uses a straight line to primarily address the relationship between a predictor and a dependent variable used as target. Basically, there exists two categories of linear regression, one is known as simple linear regression and the other one is known as multiple regressions. In linear regression, there could be independent variables which are either of type discrete or continuous, but it will have the dependent variables of type continuous in nature. If we assume that we have two variables, X as an independent variable and Y as a dependent variable, then a perfectly suited straight line is fit in linear regression model which is determined by applying a mean square method for finding the association between the independent variable X and the dependent variable Y. The relationship between them is always found to be linear. The key point is that in linear regression, the number of independent variable is one, but in case of multiple regressions, it can be one or more.

Although LR is commonly utilized for classification but it can effectively be applied in the field of regression also. The respondent variable being binary in nature can appear to any of the classes. The dependent variables aid in the process of predicting categorical variables. When there exists two classes and it is required to check where a new data point should belong, then a computing algorithm can determine the probability which ranges 0 to 1. LR model calculates the score of weighted summation of input and is given to the sigmoid function which activates a curve. The generated curve is popularly known as sigmoid curve (Figure 3.1). The sigmoid function also known as logistic function generates a curve appears as a shapes like "S" and acquires any value which gets converted in the span of 0 and 1. The traditional method followed here is that when the output generated by sigmoid function is greater than 0.5, then it classifies it as 1, and if the resultant value is lower than 0.5, then it classifies it to 0. In case the generated graph proceeds toward negative direction, then predicted value of y will be considered as 0 and vice versa.

Building predictions by applying LR is quiet a simple task and is similar to numbers that are being plugged into the equation of LR for calculating the result. During the operating phase, both LR and linear regression proceeds in the same way for making assumptions of relationship and distribution lying within the dataset. Ultimately, when any ML projects are developed using prediction-based model then accuracy of prediction is always given preference over the result interpretation. Hence, any model if works good enough and be persistent in nature, then breaking few assumptions can be considered as relevant. As we have to work with gene expression, data belong to both normal and cancerous state and at the end want to identify the candidate genes whose expression level changes beyond a threshold level. This group of collected genes will be determined as genes correlated to cancer. So, the rest of the genes will automatically be excluded from the list of candidate genes. So, the whole task becomes a binary classification where LR fit well and has been used in the present work.

While learning the pattern with given data, then data with larger dimension makes the process complex. In ML, there are two main reasons why a greater number of features do

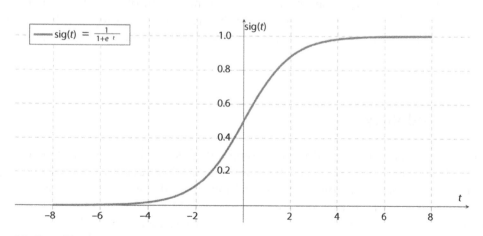

Figure 3.1 Sigmoid curve.

not always work in favor. Firstly, we may fall victim to the "curse of dimensionality" that results in exponentially decreasing sample density, i.e., sparser feature space. Secondly, the more features we have, the more storage space and computation time we require. So, it can be concluded that excess amount of information is bad because the factors like quality and computational time complexity make the model inappropriate to fit. If the data is having huge dimension, then we should find a process for reduction of the same. But the process should be accomplished in such a manner where we can maintain the information which is significant as found in the original data. In this article, we are proposing an algorithm which serves that particular task. This is a very prominent algorithm and has been used extensively in different domain of work. It is named as Principal Component Analysis (PCA). PCA is primarily used to detect the highest variance dimensions of data and reshape it to lower dimensions. This is done in such a manner that the required information will be present, and when used by ML algorithms, it will have little impact on the perfection.

PCA transforms the data of higher dimension to lower dimension by incorporating a new coordinate system. In that newly introduced system, one axis is tagged as principal component which can express the largest amount of variance the data is having. In other way, it can simply be stated that the method PCA extracts the most significant variables from a large set of variables found in any available dataset and is marked as principal components. It retains most of the critical information from the actual dataset having higher dimension. The space defined in the new dimension designates the actual data in the form of principal component. It is important to understand how PCA is used to speed up the running time of the algorithm, without sacrificing much of the model performance and sometimes even improving it. As the most challenging part is which features are to be considered, the common tendency is to feed all the features in the model going to be developed. But doing so, the problem of over fitting in developed model will be introduced which is unlikely. So, to eliminate this problem two major things are considered, i.e., feature elimination and feature extraction. Feature elimination, i.e., somewhat arbitrarily dropping features, is problematic, given that, we will not obtain any information from the eliminated variables at all. Feature extraction, however, seems to circumvent this problem by creating new independent variables from the combination of existing variables. PCA is one such algorithm for feature extraction. In the process, it also drops the least important variables (i.e., performs feature elimination) but retains the combinations of the most important variables.

3.3   Methodology

The aim of the proposed methodology presented in this article is to select a set of genes whose mutations have been observed in certain cancers. For accurate analysis and proper identification, the dataset belong to both carcinogenic and normal state has been examined. The main focus is to pick out some genes whose variations is observed in experiment and can be considered the most significant. These genes might be termed as the genes having association with cancer as because their expression level has been observed as crucially changed from their initial state. Finding these genes can have contribution in different ways to biologists, medical practitioners, pathologists, and many more. As we know that all genes do not mutate in all cancers, so our target is to segregate the genes which are mutated notably from their original state. The method first used PCA to reduce number of features (genes) which overcomes the curse of dimensionality and then LR is used for binary classification and identifies the set of genes which are expressed differentially [22, 23].

3.3.1   Description

The implementation of our work started with gene expression data which is mathematically viewed as a set $\mathbf{G} = \{\mathbf{g_1}, \mathbf{g_2}, \mathbf{g_3}, ..., \mathbf{g_a}\}$. Each member $\mathbf{gi}$ of $\mathbf{G}$ can be further expressed as $\mathbf{g_i} = \{\mathbf{g_{i1}}, \mathbf{g_{i2}}, \mathbf{g_{i3}}, ..., \mathbf{g_{ib}}\}$. Thus, the entire mathematical expression G can be considered as vector of vectors. In this context, g_i can be thought as a vector/gene comprising of feature. More specifically, the entire dataset is represented in a matrix format of dimension a × b where a is number of genes and b is number of samples and a >> b. So, the number of samples is very less in compare to number of genes, considered as features. Two separate sets of data belong to two different states: normal and carcinogenic are taken here for generating the result from the proposed method. The whole dataset is represented mathematically as a set G = $\{G^N, G^C\}$ where the dataset G^N represents normal or non-cancerous state and G^C belongs to cancerous state. Two such datasets, *viz.*, lung and colon pertaining to non-cancerous and cancerous states, are studied to get experimental result, i.e., the set of genes whose mutations have been observed.

In the present work, PCA is applied for the purpose of subgrouping the variables that preserves as much information present in the complete data as possible and also to speed up ML algorithm. The gene expression data G is presented here as a mathematical notation depicted as $\mathbf{G} = \{g_1, g_2, g_3, ..., g_a\}$. The dataset used here belongs to two states, i.e., normal and cancerous states and treated here for determining the genes associated with cancer. The proposed algorithm works by reducing the size of features using PCA and then applying LR model on both datasets.

Here, we have applied LR as because the dependent variable (target) is categorical in nature. A threshold value has been considered here which helps to predict the class belongingness of a data. On the basis of the set threshold value, the predicted probability is realized for classification. After calculating the predicted value if found ≥ threshold limit, then gene is said to be cancerous in nature, otherwise non-cancerous. Considering x as independent variable and y as dependent variable in our LR model, the hypothesis function $h_\Theta(x)$ ranges between 0 and 1. As it works as a binary classifier, the result of prediction with the classification becomes y = 0 or y = 1. The hypothesis function $h_\Theta(x)$ actually can have values <0 or > 1. The mathematical expression in logistic classification used in the method is defined as $0 \le h_\Theta(x) \le 1$.

As in our Logistic Regression model, we want $0 \le h_\Theta(x) \le 1$, so our hypothesis function might be expressed as

$$h_\Theta(x) = g(\Theta^T x) \tag{3.1}$$

Replacing $\Theta^T x$ by t, the equation becomes

$$g(t) = \frac{1}{1+e^{-t}} \tag{3.2}$$

The above equation is known as sigmoid function

$$h_\Theta(x) = \text{sig}(t) \tag{3.3}$$

If "t" proceeds toward infinity, then the predicted variable Y will become 1. On the other hand, if "t" moves to infinity toward negative direction, then prediction of Y will be 0. Mathematically this can be written as

$$h_\theta(x) = P(y = 1 \,|x; \theta) \tag{3.4}$$

Computing the probability that y = 1 when x is given and it is parameterized by θ

$$p(y = 1|x; \theta) + p(y = 0|x; \theta) = 1 \tag{3.5}$$

$$p(y = 0|x; \theta) = 1 - p(y = 1|x; \theta) \tag{3.6}$$

While implementing the proposed method, we are selecting a bunch of r genes at random. This dataset of r × n (r denotes number of genes and n denotes number of samples) is partitioned into two sets, i.e., train and test. A certain percentage, say, p%, of the data is chosen as training set and rest is used as test set.

Features need to be scaled down before applying PCA. Standard scalar is used here for standardizing the features of the available dataset. Here, it is taken a onto unit scale (mean value is taken as 0 and variance is taken as 1). Now, PCA is applied with α as the number of parameters signified as components. It means that scikit-learn choose the minimum number of principal such that α% of the variance is retained.

After applying PCA, selected genes are fitted into the LR model. Test data and predicted data values are compared, and accuracy score is calculated. To obtain the gene with good accuracy score, the iterative LR and PCA was fitted at each iteration step and every time r random genes were selected. After the completion of the iterative process, the final list was sorted in descending order of the calculated accuracy score and top genes were selected.

From then "a" number of genes ${}^a C_r$ different combinations can be made by selecting r genes at random. Our algorithm works on M such combinations.

3.3.2   Flowchart

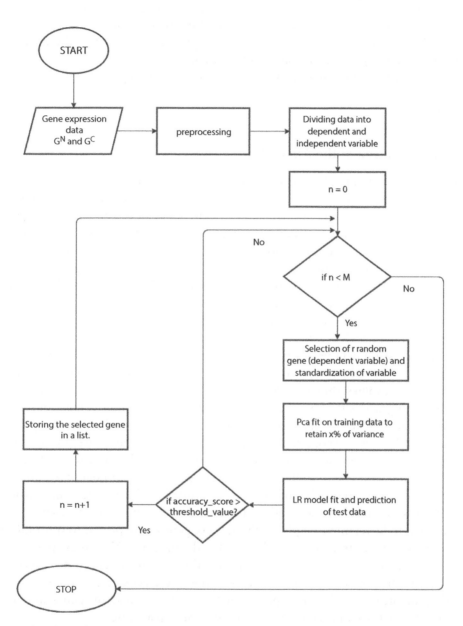

Figure 3.2 Flowchart of PC-LR algorithm.

3.3.3   Algorithm

Step 1: Read dataset $G = \{G^N, G^C\}$ and make $G = (G^N)^T \cup (G^C)^T$.
Step 2: Partition dataset into training and test dataset with a ratio.
Step 3: Standardize the dataset's value onto unit scale.
Step 4: Repeat steps 5 to 9 till all genes are selected and processed.

Step 5: Selecting r genes at random and mark them.
Step 6: Applying PCA on selected genes to retain α% of the variance.
Step 7: Training the selected gene on Logistic Regression model.
Step 8: Predicting accuracy score by comparing the test data and predicted data
Step 9: If accuracy_score>threshold_value, then
          store these genes in a new list as resultant set of gene.
   [end if]
Step 9: Stop

3.3.4   Interpretation of the Algorithm

The pictorial representation of the algorithm gives clear idea of the working model (Figure 3.2). The proposed algorithm works with gene expression dataset that belongs to both normal and cancerous state which is available in the form of a matrix where rows are genes and columns are the samples. The matrix is transposed so that samples were made as rows and all the genes were made as columns. So, this transposed matrix is given as the input. The whole dataset is partitioned into two categories: one is used for training purpose and the other one is for testing purpose. The model gets trained with the help of training data, and then, test data is used to measure the correctness of the model. The division of the data is done with the ratio 0.2 that means for training, 80% of the data is applied for training the model where as 20% data is applied for testing the same model.

The gene expression data values in the dataset vary in size. The numerical columns of the dataset need to be reduced to a common scale without any distortion of the differences lying in the range of values; therefore, standardization is needed to be used. Standardization is a form of scaling where the values are considered as centered on the basis of mean with a standard deviation taken as another component. Now, to start the iterative process for working a set of "r" genes were selected at random, and these genes were passed to train the model. Once these genes are selected, these are marked so that they will not be selected again in the iterative process. As in the dataset, it is observed that number of features (genes) is very large in compare to number of samples. In order to reduce curse of dimensionality, PCA was applied on the above selected "r" genes and a certain percentage, say, α%, of the variance is tried to be retained. Applying PCA, these genes were passed to train LR model. After training the model, test data is used to predict the outcome. Now, these predicted outcomes were checked against the actual outcomes of the test data and accuracy is calculated. If its accuracy level founds to be more than 85%, then these genes are extracted and stored in a list of candidate genes. The entire process gets repeated until all the genes were marked as selected in the dataset and accuracy was found to be considerate.

3.3.5   Illustration

The accessible dataset persists in two states, i.e., G^N and G^C, where G^N denotes dataset of non-cancerous and G^C denotes dataset of cancerous state. The designed algorithm is examined on both lung and colon dataset. Both G^N and G^C are combined and grouped together as one dataset G. Then, the dataset was transposed, i.e., rows became columns and columns became rows. A target variable Y was chosen and dataset was divided into dependent (Y) and independent (X) data.

In an M iterative process, a group of five genes is selected at random from the independent (X) data. Now, these five selected gene become X, i.e., dependent data, and Y, i.e., independent data, which is the same as earlier. This X × Y matrix is then divided into training and test data in 80:20 ratios.

After dividing into training and test data, the feature of the dataset is scaled down onto unit scale. Then, PCA is fitted onto training and test data of X to retain 95% of the variance. Then, LR was fitted on the training data of X and Y and predicted value is calculated using test data of X. At last, accuracy score was calculated by comparing the test data of Y and the predicted values. If the accuracy was found to be more than 85%, then those genes are considered as cancer mediating genes and stored in a new list as result set.

3.4   Result

The output of the proposed algorithm is a set of genes which are identified as their expression level changes significantly and can be referred as genes having correlation with cancer. The algorithm actually is experimented with some authentic dataset accessible from NCBI database. Two datasets, *viz.*, lung and colon, have been utilized for examination purpose. Data of both normal and carcinogenic states are given as the input of the algorithm to generate the target output. The algorithm follows a hybrid approach where PCA has been incorporated for minimization of dimensionality of the dataset. Then, prepared logistic model is applied as a binary classifier to detect the collection of genes which might have possible relation with cancer. Our developed PC-LR model is applied on both lung and colon data.

3.4.1   Description of the Dataset

In our algorithm, two datasets, *viz.*, lung and colon, are considered for testing and getting the output. With the help of microarray experiments, human gene expression is measured for lung and the data is obtained for tumor and normal sample. Total of 96 samples are collected of which 86 samples belong to tumor and 10 as normal state. In a more descriptive manner, it can be stated that among 86 samples of lung adenocarcinoma, 67 belong to stage I and 19 is of stage III. Ten lung samples are identified as neoplastic sample. The colon data consists of 7,464 genes with 18 samples that belong to carcinogenic state and 18 with normal state. More detailed information can be accessed from the site https://www.ncbi.nlm.nih.gov

3.4.2   Result Analysis

While executing the algorithm taking r = 5, i.e., a group of five genes is selected at random at a time. So, for lung dataset, it consisting of 5 cols (genes/features) and 96 rows (samples), which is divided into test and training dataset. For colon, it is 5 and 36, divided in same manner. Here, test data consist of 20% of the dataset and rest 80% belongs to training dataset. This dataset is scaled down by applying standard scalar and features of dataset is brought down onto unit scale. Then, PCA is applied on the selected 5 × 96 matrix. While applying PCA, the variance α is taken as 0.95 as number of components, parameter on both lung and colon datasets.

After reducing the dimensionality of the dataset, LR is applied using "sag" method for faster convergence. Predictive value is calculated based on the training dataset and then accuracy is calculated by comparing this predicted value and test data. When the accuracy was found to be more than 85%, those genes were selected as cancer mediating gene and stored in a new list.

For lung dataset, 886 genes were selected. When these genes were matched with the genes in the NCBI database, 102 were found to be true positive (TP). For colon dataset, 207 genes were selected out of which 85 were found to be TP when matched with NCBI database.

3.4.3   Result Set Validation

The generated result set genes for lung and colon dataset having correlation with cancers have been validated biologically using NCBI database. NCBI provides a gene database (http://www.ncbi.nlm.nih.gov/Database) where the disease mediating gene list corresponding to a specific disease can be obtained. The list is arranged in terms of relevance of the genes. We have got different sets of genes for lung cancer and colon cancer. The algorithm has selected 886 genes for lung and 207 for colon cancer as mutated genes. For lung expression data, we have compared this set of genes with 1,067 genes from NCBI. Here, we have identified 102 common in both the sets. We call these genes TP genes (Figure 3.4). Thus, 784 (886 − 102) genes are not in the list of genes obtained from NCBI. We denote these genes as false positive (FP) and 965 (1,067 − 102) genes are identified as false negative (FN). Likewise, for colon data, 1,223 genes are in the NCBI database. In this case, our algorithm has identified 207 genes. So, when compared with NCBI database, 85 genes got matched and marked as TP and 1,138 (1,223 − 85) genes are identified as FN and 122 (207 − 85) genes are FP (Figure 3.3).

It is very important while developing an efficient algorithm using ML model with a skewed dataset. For example, if the dataset is about cancer detection, then the task becomes more significant. Accuracy alone cannot decide for a skewed dataset whether the algorithm is working efficiently or not. What happens is that if we see in the dataset that in 99% of the time, then there is no cancer. In a binary classification problem, we can easily predict 0 all the time (predicting 1 if cancer and 0 if no cancer) to get a 99% accuracy. If we implement that model, then we will have a 99% accurate model based on ML algorithm but we will never detect cancer. If someone has cancer, then s/he will never get detected and will not get treatment. In our problem, we want to detect cancer mediating genes whose expression

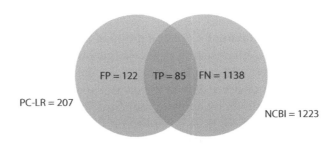

Figure 3.3 FN, TP, and FP values for colon.

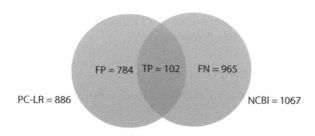

Figure 3.4 FN, TP, and FP values for lung.

level changes significantly from normal state to cancerous state. So, here also, only accuracy is not going to work. There are different evaluation matrices that can help with these types of datasets. Those evaluation metrics are called precision-recall evaluation metrics. The F-score is a way of combining the precision and recall of the model, and it is defined as the harmonic mean of the model's precision and recall. The F-score is commonly used effectively for many kinds of ML models. Moreover, for a binary classification problem, it is very much significant to analyze the accuracy vs. F-score to evaluate the efficiency of the model. Accuracy is defined as simply the number of correctly categorized examples divided by the total number of examples. Accuracy can be useful but does not take into account the subtleties of class imbalances, or differing costs of FN and FP. On the other hand, F-score is an effective measure when there are either differing costs of FP or FN or where there is a large class imbalance. As our proposed method works with gene expression data where number of genes is very large in number but the number of genes whose mutation is correlated to cancer will be very less, so in this case, the accuracy would be misleading, since a classifier that classifies set of genes not related to cancer would automatically get 90% accuracy but would be useless for the proposed work and hence will have little contribution in real-world application specially in the field of medical science. As a result, F-score has been given importance to evaluate the efficacy of the proposed model by proper application precision and recall.

Precision is the fraction of TP examples among the examples that the model classified as positive. In other words, it is the number of true positives divided by the number of FP plus true positives. Recall, also known as sensitivity, is the fraction of examples classified as positive, among the total number of positive examples. In other words, this is the number of true positives divided by the number of true positives plus FN. In our model, the resultant set of genes has been validated using NCBI database for both colon and lung. From the diagram, the intersection part for colon dataset (Figure 3.3), and for lung dataset (Figure 3.4), the number of TP genes is identified. At the same time, FP and FN values are also identified from the figures in the same way.

Further, we have calculated the precision, recall, and F-score values to check how good our model is. Precision tells us how precise/accurate our model is out of those predicted as positive and how many of them are actual positive. The formula that is used to calculate for precision [Equation (3.7)] and recall [Equation (3.8)] is clearly mentioned.

$$\text{Precision} = \frac{\text{True positive}}{\text{True positive} + \text{False positive}} = \frac{\text{True positive}}{\text{Total predicted} + \text{positive}} \quad (3.7)$$

Recall calculates the actual number of positives recorded by our model, i.e., what proportions of actual positives was identified correctly.

$$\text{Recall} = \frac{\text{True positive}}{\text{True Positive} + \text{False Negative}} = \frac{\text{True positive}}{\text{Total Actual} + \text{Positive}} \quad (3.8)$$

Unfortunately, a trade-off was seen between both precision and recall. With higher the value of Recall, then lower will be the precision value and vice versa. As a result, we are getting different impression of the outcome in the result set found for two different datasets (Figures 3.5 and 3.6). In order to overcome this trade-off, F1-score has been calculated, to find an optimum point where both the precision and recall values are high.

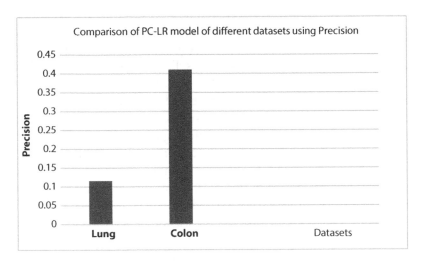

Figure 3.5 F-score for lung and colon using precision.

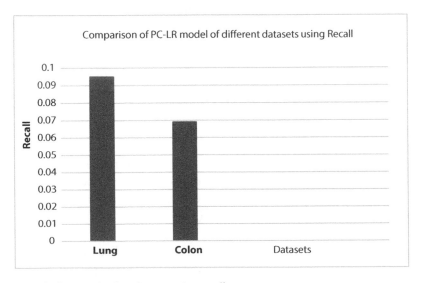

Figure 3.6 F-score for lung and colon dataset using recall.

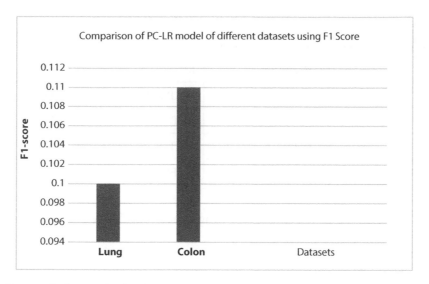

Figure 3.7 F1 score for lung and colon dataset.

Further, we have computed F1 score values using the formula [Equation (3.9)] for two datasets considered here and it is observed that our PC-LR method generates optimal result for colon dataset compared to lung dataset (Figure 3.7).

$$\text{F1 Score} = \frac{2 * \text{Recall} * \text{Precision}}{\text{Recall} + \text{Precision}} \tag{3.9}$$

It should be noted that the generalized formula for F-score is actually known as F_β-score. The F-score when used in a regulated manner helps us to weight recall and precision more accurately for our working model. The equation in that becomes little different.

$$F_\beta = (1 + \beta^2) * \frac{precision * recall}{(\beta^2 * precision) + recall} \tag{3.10}$$

Here in the equation of F_β-score [Equation (3.10)], the factors are indicating about in what extent recall is having more importance over precision. For instance, setting the value of β to 2 indicates that recall is being given importance two times higher than precision. The standard practice is to set the value of β to 1, while using in F-score [Equation (3.10)] which causes our equation to be as Equation (3.9) and by observing the comparative study by giving different weigh on precession and recall, it can be concluded that F1 score can measure the performance of the working model more accurately.

The proposed method has identified 102 genes for lung cancer and 85 genes for colon cancer as cancer mediating genes. The result is generated by validating with NCBI database where some already identified genes are available. Some of the gene symbols are given in the tables below generated by our developed methodology. Table 3.1 contains

Table 3.1 Resultant genes (gene symbols) identified by PC-LR method.

Significant true positive genes for lung cancer			
KRAS	CHRNA3	MIF	GSTP1
TP53	SOX9	MAP2K1	VDR
IGFIR	TNF	RET	SYK
IFGBP3	CDH2	MET	PGR
STAT3	CDH1	TGFB1	IL10

some the significant TP gene symbols for lung cancer and Table 3.2 contains the same for colon cancer.

3.5 Application in Cloud Domain

Cloud computing is a terminology widely used in the field of information technology. It illustrates the basic idea about how an end user can avail different types of resources related to IT like software services and hardware resources. There is no standard accepted definition about cloud is available. But still, it could be defined as a set of virtualized computers which are interconnected and provisions are made dynamically to make them available as computing resources depending on service level agreement. Several categories of services are available in cloud computing domain.

- Infrastructural service: Here, different computational resources like processors and storage are provided to the end users in raw format. In this model, users are allowed to install different supplications as well as the operating system in the infrastructure provided to them. This can be thought as users are getting some space for computational purpose on a rental basis. So, the cloud domain can be effectively utilized as research tool for genomic study.
- Platform service: While developing and launching new software applications this type of service becomes very important as it needs proper platform for the purpose of implementation.

Table 3.2 Resultant genes (gene symbols) identified by PC-LR method.

Significant true positive genes for colon cancer			
MSH2	IGF1	PKM	IL33
TP53	CCND1	MIF	ITGA5
VEGFA	VDR	TERT	CSK
PTGS2	IGF1R	TAC1	SDC2
AKT1	HIF1A	CDKN1A	EGFR

- Software services: This type of service is required by users for different applications like Dropbox if storage is an issue or Google Docs in case the requirement is an application which is as good as word processor.

In the present article, our focus is to avail infrastructural service in the field of cloud computing or more specifically storage as a service. Our study is based on processing of biological data and generates resultant bio markers. As we have developed a model where gene expression data of both normal and cancerous state is analyzed and identified, the cancer mediating genes can be beneficial in the field of medical science and can help biologists in different perspective.

The biggest challenge for research community in the field of genomic science is to develop infrastructure with a huge number of computers and some efficient software tools for analyzing the genomic datasets more exhaustively in the field biomedical research and to some extent in clinical practice. People who are doing research in this domain are getting toward cloud domain. To find a solution of different biomedical problems, it is very much important to analyze data effectively. Thus, integrating data from genomics, systems biology, and biomedical data mining always becomes promising one [24]. In our proposed model, we have worked on a dataset as a file (.csv format), and after processing by the developed methodology, we have produced a resultant dataset which is again sorted in a text file. So, our concerns how all these data can be made available in cloud environment so that it can be accessed by other user of the research community for further progress. But there are some parameters of concern [25].

In the domain of cloud computing maintaining the secrecy of the data is a major concern that needs special attention with utmost priority. As we are here only concerned about the confidentiality of the data at the same time in a simplified manner without going insight the architectural detail. This also attracts the other benefits and advantages of cloud computing like lowering cost and greater efficiency. Besides, these other points of concern are data security and confidentiality. In cloud service, there are many commercial offering but these are heterogeneous in nature and deals with different needs which depends on the customers. The primary contestants in this field are Microsoft Azure, Google AppEngine, Amazone Web Service (AWS), IBM cloud, and many more. Amazon Simple Storage Service also known as Amazon S3 provides an object-based storage service that offers scalability considered as industry-leading, security, performance, and, of course, the availability of data. As our requirement is to store the files and get the security over the dataset so Amazon Web Service can be a good choice as because, AWS provides a Simple Storage Service (S3) for storing of data. It provides object storage to all the software developers and group of people related to IT which is highly secured, scalable, and durable as well. It offers a web interface which is easy to use and provides facility to store and retrieve data from anywhere on the web without considering the amount of data being consumed. It is a place where we can store our files on the AWS cloud Dropbox by simplifying the user interface of S3. The Dropbox here acts as a layer built on top of S3. Data is spread across multiple devices and facilities. Although S3 can be used for many purposes but in the present context, it can be used as storing files in Buckets/Folders in a secured way.

It is to be noted that as security is a major issue so storing the data in Amazon S3 and keeping it secure from the other users is a major parameter to be considered. It has to be implemented by applying encryption features and with different access management tools.

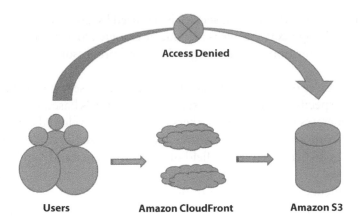

Figure 3.8 Storing and accessing the data values in Amazon S3.

The only available object-based storage service is S3 that can block public access to all the objects stored in the bucket. It can also perform the account level restriction with S3 Block Public Access mechanism. In order to ensure that different objects will never have public access, presently or in the future, S3 Block Public Access provides various controls across in different level like the entire AWS Account or at the individual bucket stage. Objects and buckets are given public access either by access control lists (ACLs), or policies framed for the bucket, or sometimes by using both. For ensuring blocking of public access to all the S3 buckets and objects, it is required that at account level we should switch on block all public access. These settings are utilized will all the account for all the buckets used in present or in future. Although restricting the public access is suggested by AWS by turning on the block option but while doing so it must be ensured that all applications can run properly without having public access. We can configure the settings as per the requirement at individual level below to fit our unique storage use cases for some degree of public access for the objects and buckets. Public access permission of S3 can be redefined by Block Public Access defined by S3. By doing so, it becomes easier for the administrator for setting up a centralized control system which can prevent any changes in the configuration of the security mechanism, no matter in which way the insertion of an object or bucket is formed. While writing an object to an S3 bucket or AWS Account having S3 Public Access Block, and if some form of public permission is designated by any object through ACL or by means of any Policy, then blocking of those public permissions will still remain. Figure 3.8 gives the idea about how to store/access the data in AWS S3.

3.6   Conclusion

The proposed method PC-LR uses a hybrid approach which is chosen as a ML technique to generate the target output. As our task is to select the driver genes which are related to certain cancers, so it is better to design an algorithm which can act as a binary classifier and identify the relevant genes. It is to be noted that LR always works well for this model. But the gene expression data is of huge volume and so to get rid of the curse of dimensionality is mandatory before start working with LR. This is done using PCA. Our implemented approach has established a group of genes very precisely that are expressed differentially and are correlated to some cancers. The experimentation is executed over two datasets, *viz.*, colon and lung, and has determined a gene set. The creativity and robustness of the system is clearly defined. It is to be noted that mutations of genes might have correlations among themselves and it may or may not vary with different stages of cancer. So, identifying these is also a challenging task. Those genes can effectively be examined by research scientists and biologists for the purpose of laboratory testing by focusing on less number of genes instead of whole genome.

Our work is having scope of extension in future for identifying more genes which might be correlated to mutations. Further identifying interactions among those genes can be very much helpful in prognosis, cancer prevention and treatment. Analyzing interactions of Gene-Gene will be beneficial for finding out more TP genes having key role for mediating cancer. The extension of our study using other omics data might help researchers and biologists to concentrate on cancer study in a targeted way.

References

1. Soh, K.P., Szczurek, E., Sakoparnig, T., Beerenwinkel, N., Predicting cancer type from tumour DNA signatures. *Genome Med.*, 9, 104, 2017.
2. Hao, X., Luo, H., Krawczyk, M., Wei, W., Wang, W., Wang, J. *et al.*, DNA methylation markers for diagnosis and prognosis of common cancers. *Proc. Natl. Acad. Sci. U.S.A.*, 114, 28, 7414–19, 2017.
3. Yang, Z., Jin, M., Zhang, Z., Lu, J., Hao, K., Classification based on feature extraction for hepatocellular carcinoma diagnosis using high-throughput dna methylation sequencing data. *Proc. Comput. Sci.*, 107, 412–417, 2017.
4. Rachman, A.A. and Rustam, Z., Cancer classification using Fuzzy C-Means with feature selection. *12th International Conference on Mathematics, Statistics, and Their Applications (ICMSA)*, pp. 31–34, 2016.
5. Ghosh, A. and De, R.K., Fuzzy Correlated Association Mining: Selecting altered associations among the genes, and some possible marker genes mediating certain cancers. *Appl. Soft Comput.*, 38, 587–605, 2015.
6. Mao, Z.-Y., Cai, W.-S., Shao, X.-G., Selecting significant genes by randomization test for cancer classification using gene expression data. *J. Biomed. Inform.*, 46, 4, 549–601, 2013.
7. Cao, J., Zhang, L., Wang, B., Li, F., Yang, J., A fast gene selection method for multi-cancer classification using multiple support vector data description. *J. Biomed. Inform.*, 53, 381–389, 2015.
8. Dashtban, M. and Balafar, Gene selection for microarray cancer classification using a new evolutionary method employing artificial intelligence concepts. *Genomics*, 109, 2, 91–107, 2017.
9. Mirza, B., Wang, W., Wang, J., Choi, H., Chung, N.C., Ping, P., Machine Learning and Integrative Analysis of Biomedical Big Data. *Genes*, 10, 2, 87, 2019.
10. Hoadley, K.A. *et al.*, Multiplatform analysis of 12 cancer types reveals molecular classification within and across tissues of origin. *Cell*, 158, 929–944, 2014.
11. Yang, A. *et al.*, Bayesian variable selection with sparse and correlation priors for high-dimensional data analysis. *Comput. Stat.*, 32, 1–17, 2016.
12. Danaee, P., Ghaeini, R., Hendrix, D.A., A deep learning approach for cancer detection and relevant gene identification. *Pac. Symp. Biocomput.*, 22, 219–229, 2017.

13. Kourou, K., Exarchos, T.P., Exarchos, K.P., Karamouzis, M.V., Fotiadis, D.I., Machine learning applications in cancer prognosis and prediction. *Comput. Struct. Biotechnol. J.*, 13, 8–17, 2014.
14. Tabl, A.A., Alkhateeb, A., ElMaraghy, W., Rueda, L., Ngom, A., A machine learning approach for identifying gene biomarkers guiding the treatment of breast Cancer. *Front. Genet.*, 10, 256, 2019.
15. Huang, S., Cai, N., Pacheco, P.P., Narrandes, S., Wang, Y., Xu, W., Applications of Support Vector Machine (SVM) Learning in Cancer Genomics. *Cancer Genomics Proteomics*, 15, 1, 41–51, 2018.
16. Rajaguru, H., Analysis of Decision Tree and K-Nearest Neighbor Algorithm in the Classification of Breast Cancer. *Asian Pac. J. Cancer Prev.*, 20, 12, 3777–378, 2019.
17. Neha, K. and Verma, K., Volume 10, May-June 2019.A survey on various machine learning approaches used for breast cancer detection. *IJARCS*, 10, 3, 76–79, 2019.
18. Libbrecht, M.W. and Noble, W.S., Machine learning applications in genetics and genomics. *Nat. Rev. Genet.*, 16, 321–332, 2015.
19. Gao, F., Wang, W., Tan, M. *et al.*, DeepCC: a novel deep learning-based framework for cancer molecular subtype classification. *Oncogenesis*, 8, 9, 44, 2019.
20. Sultana, J., Predicting Breast Cancer using Logistic Regression and Multi-Class Classifiers. *Int. J. Eng. Technol.(UAE)*, 7, 4.20, 22–26, 2018.
21. Alkuhlani, A., Nassef, M., Farag, I., Multistage feature selection approach for high-dimensional cancer data. *Soft Comput.*, 21, 6895–6906, 2017.
22. Kavitha, R.K., Ram, A.V., Anandu, S., Karthik, S., Kailas, S., Arjun, N.M., PCA-based gene selection for cancer classification. *2018 IEEE International Conference on Computational Intelligence and Computing Research (ICCIC)*, Madurai, India, pp. 1–4, 2018.
23. Wu, W. and Faisal, S., A data-driven principal component analysis-support vector machine approach for breast cancer diagnosis: Comparison and application. *Trans. Inst. Meas. Control*, 42, 7, 1301–1312, 2020.
24. Deshmukh, P., Design of Cloud Security in the EHR for Indian Healthcare Services. *J. King Saud Univ. – Comp. Info. Sci.*, 29, 3, 281–287, 2017.
25. Langmead, B. and Nellore, A., Cloud computing for genomic data analysis and collaboration. *Nat. Rev. Genet.*, 19, 4, 208–219, 2018.

Part II

CLOUD SECURITY SYSTEMS USING MACHINE LEARNING TECHNIQUES

Cost-Effective Voice-Controlled Real-Time Smart Informative Interface Design With Google Assistance Technology

Soumen Santra[1], Partha Mukherjee[2] and Arpan Deyasi[3]*

[1]Department of Computer Application, Techno International Newtown, Kolkata, India
[2]Infiflex Technologies Pvt Ltd, Kolkata, India
[3]Department of Electronics and Communication Engineering, RCC Institute of Information Technology, Kolkata, India

Abstract

In 21st century, passive intelligence makes a new surrounding around humans through various natural and intelligent interfaces which are interconnected with different computing devices. It creates a user-authenticated and also authorized smart milieu for endowing efficient support to individual communications and convenience. This technology integrates reasoning, processing, sensing, and capabilities of network formation along with other diverse relevance and applications, supports, and services, providing easy access to web contents (audio, video, text, and other file formats). The present work as proposed here is directed and sharply focused toward architectural design and improvement of a mirror boundary with smart informative system embedded within it for the smart terrain environment of home.

Here, we propose a smart real-time interface in such a way that even though it provides us with the mirror like effect, it also smart enough to view us multiple information like news, clock, calendar events, and fitness tracking on the background. The information is relayed with the help of a LCD screen behind the glass. The proposed automation system is associated where voice instructions (Google Assistance) in alliance with sensors are utilized for controlled authoritarian measures.

The proposed system/architecture has high reliability for the senior citizen and also for handicapped or especially able people moving with wheelchair and is dependent on others. It is also applicable on the areas where you need your appliance to work without reaching the switch board and for saving energy. By virtue of its real-time nature due to application of machine intelligence, it may be the system can be implemented in households with very less cost.

Keywords: Informative interface, passive intelligence, real-time smart system, voice-controlled mechanism, Google Assistant technology, cloud console

Corresponding author: deyasi_arpan@yahoo.co.in

Rajdeep Chakraborty, Anupam Ghosh and Jyotsna Kumar Mandal (eds.) *Machine Learning Techniques and Analytics for Cloud Security*, (63–80) © 2022 Scrivener Publishing LLC

4.1   Introduction

The rapid evolution of smart industry [1] in the first part of 21st century is in synchronous with growth of semiconductor industry, and as per the latest available data, it is close to a 50 billion industry. This exponential advancement becomes realizable due to the growth of information and communication technology which ensures the transform of computer-aided industry to embedded system-based industry [2, 3], where decision-making becomes totally data-driven, augmented with emotional intelligence, and sentiment analysis. The role of Internet of Things (IoT) here is to make sustainable connection between corporeal industrial environments [4, 5] with cyberspace of calculating systems. The proper augmentation generates a new system, termed as Cyber-Physical System (CPS), which makes a large paradigm shift in the industrial progress. The rapid multidisciplinary industrial wings as obtained after inclusion of IoT, in terms of living, manufacturing, food industry, travel, and utilities, improve the efficacy of production by enhancing work flow [6, 7], whereas machine effort reduces the physical manpower requirement, and therefore, quality of output is enhanced. The major challenges that the emerging industry face can effectively subdued through [i] proper decentralization of systems, [ii] assortment of systems and associated devices, [iii] data complexity and heterogeneity, and [iv] complexity of existing network. Major security issues are nullified through incorporation of these features [8, 9]. In particular, IoT-enabled system contains the following assets:

- Across various IoT-based devices, the ability to exchange information between the systems/devices applied in households/industrial sectors plays the key role in making it suitable for all classes of candidates. This unique property can be achieved through network-composite layer which enables to provide uniform access to all systems. This is made on the top of an overlay P2P (peer-to-peer) network.
- IoT data can be traceable, i.e., its temporal and spatial information can be detected and verified/authenticated/validated when saved inside the memory device. This memory device is always associated to the timestamp which efficiently makes the data tracing at real-time. Also historical information can easily be retrieved.
- Another combined features associated closely with IoT data are reliability and flexibility. It is the data which is considered as asset. Novel cryptographic mechanisms are incorporated in order to ensure the data integrity. This can be achieved through inclusion of hash functions, asymmetric encryption algorithms, and digital signature.
- Interactions in automatic mode are another important property which ensures the capability of the system under consideration for mutual interaction with similar kind of systems, and the major advantage is that any trusted third party intervention is not at all required.

In today's developing world, living in a house has become an important part of our day-to-day life. A substantial amount of resources as well as expenditure that we would carry might not always be pleasurable as there are various problems such as accidents caused in house with the lonely child or old-aged person. These accidents happened due to various human errors. Also, the problem that haunts all the people is the possibility of theft of the household appliances by unauthorized people. To overcome these challenges, there is a pressing need to develop automated smart home system [10] or smart homes. This can be reached using the IoT-based platforms and services.

Many applications have been developed using IoT methodologies. The platform for developing such technologies is Raspberry Pi, Arduino, or other microcontrollers [11, 12] which are responsible for controlling various operations. These systems can be controlled and monitored from a registered device which is present with the user and install with the household devices.

4.2 Home Automation System

In today's life, we are very much comfortable to use wireless system, i.e., Wi-Fi. It is very much general for home network or public network system. Our traditional home system totally based on wired system. Every home appliances system such as light, fan, television, and refrigeration through connected wired system. A home automation system means controlling all home appliances through a Wi-Fi system which varying as per environment. Most of the traditional home electricity system based on wired and depends on inner building construction. To avoid this building and wiring cost, we can move toward an automated system based on Wi-Fi system to access the appliances from anywhere of the home as well as from the outside of the home also. An automated home electricity system defines as an automated one which not only accesses the electric devices for turn on and off even this system but also notifies about the status and internal condition of the system.

In India, most of the accident of electric appliances happened due to internal fault of wired system. In wired system, we have to maintain lots of control points. In most of the cases, the short falls happen from these control points. To avoid this type of accident, home automation system is one of the ways especially for those people who are aged and staying alone.

Home automation is a building automation for home. Home automation system will command or observe the home aspects such as various electrical appliances including lighting arrangements and entertainment systems. These automation devices are the essential parts of IoT. Centrally located server can control these automated systems, with proper internet connectivity and simultaneously the mobile-based applications also. Before getting into the details of home automation, let us take a closer look on IoT.

Automation means controlling several objects or tasks with minimum human labor. Home automation system using IoT refers to the way of operating our home appliances such as lights, fans, air conditioners, televisions, security, fire alarm, and many more appliances using our mobile phones, computers, or other gadgets through a connection to the internet. Several components are used to make such a model. Few of them are sensors, protocols, IoT clouds, and databases. We are making a primary list for significant components for the automation system.

4.2.1 Sensors

There are many sensors which can be used in our home automation system. A few of them are as follows:

Temperature sensors: They directly sense temperature and adjust our home temperature for us. They are also used in several appliances where they can automatically switch it off when it reaches a certain temperature.

Lux sensors: They measure the intensity of the lights and adjust it accordingly. For example, if we are watching any horror movie, then it senses and it dims the light to give us a theatre like movie experience. We can control it manually from our connected devices as well.

Sound detection sensor: They are very helpful in monitoring babies and switching the lights on or off for them. It can also automatically recognize the voices of the householders and open the gates for them.

There are also sensors which can open the blinds and windows during sunrise and shut them at sunset. Sensors can switch on our coffee machine and switch to our favourite news channel in the morning.

The commonly used programming languages in the development of automated homes are Python, C, JavaScript, Shell, etc.

Development of ancient homes to automated homes using IoT is making our lives much easier and comfortable. It is also converting our house to a smart home. It appears to be a very useful advancement in technology and is expected to grow in the near future. Though it is expensive, but it is also helping us in saving energies in different forms.

4.2.2 Protocols

The protocols considered for making any gateways, sensory systems, or servers are most important while dealing with any arbitrary home automation product. These protocols are used by all types of devices. At the end part of 20th century, these problems are solved by mostly using Bluetooth. Also, Wi-Fi and GSM networks are used but are not appropriate due to cellular internet connectivity. However, looking at the commonly preferred home automation protocols as follows:

- Bluetooth low energy or Bluetooth smart: data encryption and decryption algorithms are embedded with different protocols used for wireless communications, and essentially security and mesh size become the crucial factors.
- From security perspective, Z-wave is specialized for all types of home automation system.
- Royalty is ensured with free protocol.

4.2.3 Technologies

Home automation is prevailing in a variety of domain; some of them includes the following:

- Thermostat and air monitoring: Internet connectivity is essential to satisfy this requirement, and user-friendly device with that facility is incorporated for controlling purpose.

- Lighting: Central computing systems or devices are incorporated through any smart network in order to provide efficient communication between different lighting inputs and outputs.
- Home automation for elderly and disabled: It primarily concentrates on completing the required things/instructions which makes life easier for elderly and people with disabilities, so that they can make their livelihood comfortable.
- Voice control: Amazon Alexa or Google home are very accepted devices for controlling as well as providing proper execution of instructions which are very much common and popular.

4.2.4   Advantages

- Error probability reduced when IoT is implemented, as it senses the data perfectly, and corresponding actions are performed.
- Ease of access for all age f people, provided put at convenient location.
- Reduces human effort, so brigs home comfort for all classes of people.
- Smarter processing and services which increases its popularity.
- Alert system is quick in any case of an emergency.

4.2.5   Disadvantages

- Security concerns, as data may be trapped by hackers.
- Most of the times range is restricted, because every router has its own periphery of operation.
- High dependency on sensor which makes the system vulnerable if sensor fails.
- System compatibility is major concern, as microcontrollers with different architecture require different types of memory.
- Cost of implementation t the initial level is not in the reach of all classes of people (financially).

4.3   Literature Review

Very recently, literatures are available on home automation system where Wi-Fi–based microcontrollers are embedded [13] along with authentication facility. Energy management perspectives are also considered [14] for multiple users. A voice recognition characteristic [15] is also invoked to operate primary electrical appliances, and this particular facility is precisely helpful for blind people. Facial recognition is also proposed [16], but it contains some practical limitations, which is generally ignored. Earlier people tried to include different facial gestures like sad and angry for the same purpose [17], but complexity of the algorithm and time-variant of the expressions makes it little successful. OpenHAB framework is also considered for secure wireless network design [18] and is in experimental stage. For complex data transmission condition, various sensor nodes are considered [19] where encryption algorithm is incorporated for security purpose. Thermal comfort is prioritized

[20] by a few groups of workers, whereas others prioritized the mobile app development [21]. Temperature sensor plays an important part for automatic truing of air-conditioner system [22] under closed door arrangement. GPS facility is also added for tracking the person [23]. However, the present system also deals with the cost of the total system, and therefore proposed novel architecture for the purpose of improvement of the quality of operation along with multiple feature facility.

4.4   Role of Sensors and Microcontrollers in Smart Home Design

A smart home was designed using components such as an Arduino module, ultrasonic sensor, GPS receiver, sound sensor, IR sensor, GSM shield, LCD, LED, and buzzer. There were three sections: input section, processing unit, and output section. The ultrasonic sensors were installed to detect any signal such as movement, sound, or gesture that come in the way. The range of operation was to be increased when detecting signal which was achieved by the RF module. For determining the exact location of the household appliances, a GPS-enabled Wi-Fi receiver was used in order to track the target device's (household appliances) condition and signal. To sense the sound honking in the surrounding, a sound sensor was used. To sense the motion moving in the surrounding, a motion sensor was used. The Arduino module, which is the main platform, has four loops, namely, loop 1, loop 2, loop 3, and loop 4. Loop 1 activated when the target device was powered ON and the also true key was present. It also contained loop 2 which ran when the mode or context switches was enabled. Loop 3 initiated when the conditions of Loop 1 were negated. Loop 4 started when the target device was turned on even though the true key was absent.

There are several sensors present in the system, each having specific task as follows:

[i]   Level sensor: It checks the oxygen–carbon dioxide level in the room.
[ii] Humidity sensor: It checks the humidity level of the room.
[iii] Light sensor: It measures intensity, technically called luminance.
[iv] Door lock sensor: It checks whether the door is locked or not.
[v]   Temperature sensor: It checks the temperature of the room.
[vi] Motion sensor: It calculates the speed or RPM of fan which is moving in the room.
[vii] Ultrasonic sensor: It calculates the distance of any object from the target device.

In this module, we will be making a home automation system controlled using IoT embedded with advanced level microcontroller (Raspberry Pi) and cloud architecture (Particle Cloud) or Blynk application using IFTTT or Mosquito agent. Here, we will be creating a raspberry pi application to control home AC, fan, light (staircase or bedroom or corridor or front door, etc.), television, mirror, and appliances using Particle Mobile app and online particle IDE. It requires the following components:

[i]   Raspberry Pi 3 with Raspbian installed in it
[ii] Relay Module
[iii] 220v bulbs

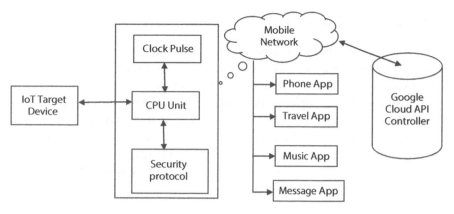

Figure 4.1 IoT-based smart home automation system.

[iv]   Jumper wires
[v]   Motor

First, we will make an account on the Particle.io. Then, particle agent will be installed with the Raspberry Pi of the embedded system so that interface can be made with particle cloud. This is background software which is able to interact with the Raspberry pi through GPIO pin. Here, we can add new devices as well as create mesh networks, integrated with IFTTT, Microsoft Azure, and web IDE. A block diagram is presented below.

In Figure 4.1, household appliances (fan, light, TV, AC, etc.) represent as target devices which connect with IoT devices or smart sensors which embedded with code. When this IoT device connects with mobile network, it can directly attach with Google API through Google Cloud Console. Using this mobile network, every application of smart phone which acts as tune device can connect with IoT device and can use every module or technique of Google Cloud Console.

Voice-operated room switching control system is the smarter version of the remote-controlled switching system. As titled, these systems are controlled over voice commands over the internet, thus providing you with no bound for the control. Home is a place where people incline to at the day end. After a long tiring day when people return exhausted, they may find it tough to move around the corner of the room where the switch board for the room appliance control is situated at the convenient locations, closer to the sitting or bed arrangement. It is also difficult for a person to locate the switch board of the staircase, or the room main entrance in the dark. So, if a small technology helps them to switch their room light and fan or other electrical appliances of low wattage or read out the news to them, with a single voice command through their smart phone or table or the control dock settled in their room, it will enhance the comfort experience to next level.

Earlier days, millionaires used to keep housekeepers and other sorts of human assistance for easing up their day. But, for the common man in the society, they were not eligible to taste the crunch of that facility. Even today, when technology is so close by, only established and wealthy people in this contemporary civilization are benefited with these new technologies of elegant house, as these devices are still too expensive. Since everyone in this society are not so wealthy enough to afford smart home kit, thus the need for these in expensive smart kits keeps growing.

4.5 Motivation of the Project

This project proposes one very low-priced economical system, where Google Assistant technology (provided by Google to all their OS, and if necessary, it can be downloaded to other smart phone makers too like IOS by Apple) is utilized: the IFTTT server and application, The Blynk application, and Google Cloud Console. In the hardware part, The NodeMCU 8266 micro-controller acts as the major communicator as it receives and sends data to our apps and server, along with a relay board of 4/8 channel, whose regulatory voltage is 5 V and has the capability for handling 10-A current through it. We use our natural language to give command to our Google Assistance and receive data on our Blynk app. We have hereby segregated the total manuscript into two parts: at first, the device, and second, the control unit.

4.6 Smart Informative and Command Accepting Interface

Passive Intelligence (PI) is a very important aspect in today's world and makes a paradigm shift in view of industry initiatives for realizing smart environments. Everyday's smart devices like smart bag, smart watch, and smart wallet provide that required heterogeneous intelligent interfaces along with other natural devices, and these together makes a complex computing scenario, which, thereafter, generates the vision of PI. The environment becomes respondent to each individual, and therefore, anyone can interact with the surrounding with 1:1 basis. Therefore, user-empowered smart environment can be generated using PI, which provides the required support to human for various interactions.

In this connection, it should be mentioned that the environment, interfaced with PI, may be the home (comfortable) or a distributed one. For the said purpose, different smart technologies are considered as per the demand. All these technologies are integrated with the environment, for the purpose of sensing and data processing. Networking is also an important phase of this integration in order to provide remote service and also of digital materials. The actual question comes to the embedding of all these smart devices, and here lies the real challenge of PI.

PI can be obtained at the home comfort when proper key technological fruits are perfectly blended with virus smart interfaces (programmable). For the purpose, several smart

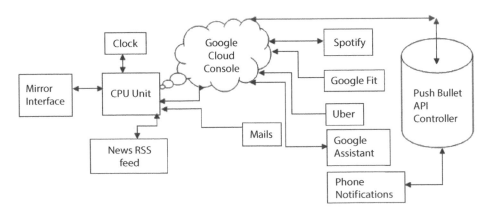

Figure 4.2 Command accepting interface.

devices and appliances are invoked, and anyone can be considered as an interface with the real world. In this particular work, authors have tried and successfully implemented a mirror interface with proper incorporation of smart informative system, precisely to get smart home environment. This is depicted in Figure 4.2, embedded with Google Cloud Console. The console has an interface with API controller.

The major objective of making a PI at the home is originated from the safety and security concern, associated with efficiency of the system along with convenience. Precisely, elderly people and people with physical disabilities required better attention, when other family members are absent. PI greatly influences not only home automation systems, but also socialization, communication, entertainment, refreshment, proper rest, and various physical activities like sports, working, online learning through MOOCs or in general YouTube videos.

Another aspect that will engage their footstep with these PI modules will be digital marketing. Henceforth, proper architecture should be considered for convenient and user-friendly PI design where both the technological advancement should be clubbed with home comfort and convenient for the residents.

4.7 Data Flow Diagram

The workflow for the proposed work can be explained using the dataflow diagram described in Figure 4.3. A bidirectional network is established between mosquito server and IoT controller where data is continuously flowing and periodic update is taking place. The mosquito server is fed through IFTTT, whereas all the applets (including triggering applet) are given similar instructions by the same. Google Cloud Console is the heart of this total workflow,

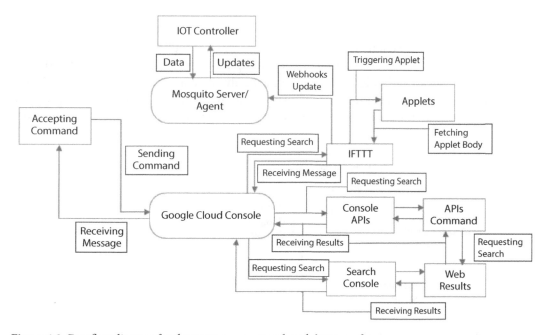

Figure 4.3 Dataflow diagram for the message, command, and data transfer.

which always dynamically interacts with command interface. It also makes a bidirectional communication with IFTTT, console APIs, and search console. Console APIs receives and also sends commands to command APIs. Web results are retrieved from the search console. The transfer of data and different messages are schematically represented in the diagram given below (Figure 4.2).

4.8   Components of Informative Interface

The most important interface is the mirror. The mirror considered here is architecture for doing multiple functions in same time slot, i.e., the concept of multiplexing is applied. The interface is made in such a way that even though it provides us with the mirror like effect, it also smart enough to view us multiple information like news, clock, calendar events, and fitness tracking on the background. Information is relayed with the help of a LCD screen behind the glass. The key factor is the smoothness of the surface, as rough surfaces scatter light instead of reflecting it. Since the propositions of installing multiple smart informatics are embedded inside the system as per user's choice.

One of the major interfaces is clock, which is real time and updates itself using time server of Google NTP (Network Time Protocol). NTP provides accurate and synchronized time across the Internet.

On the top left position of the mirror, we have the email sync option. This uses SMTP protocol to receive mails from your mailing servers to the screen. Our mirror has only the option of incoming mailing view notification feature for obvious reasons.

Uber is the largest cab industry business globally recognized. Uber has multiple integrations with Google and other smart device manufacturers. Uber has free API distribution developer platform that provides us with the API keys for free. So, we have used that API interface along with our cloud server to be more specified, Google Cloud Console. To obtain the data against our Uber account that are sync to the Uber Technologies Servers from our mobile phones, we have used a buffer mosquito server in between UBER and our Google Cloud Console. Schematic block diagram is given in Figure 4.4.

Now, we consider a music streaming device in digital form, called Spotify that provides access of digital audio and video files from a normally huge database along with podcasts and videos. The major acceptance and corresponding overwhelming response to Spotify is due to the fact that all the contents under this umbrella are free with a simple authentication

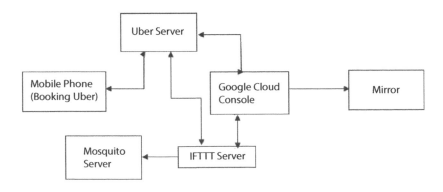

Figure 4.4 Block diagram that exhibits the linkage between Uber server and IFTTT server.

Figure 4.5 Block diagram for Spotify server connection.

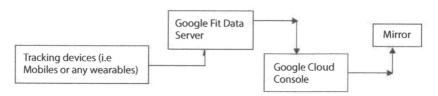

Figure 4.6 Block diagram for fitness tracking using Google Fit.

through email or Facebook account. This module shows user the current playback on Spotify app from any devices like iPad, iPhone, any Android Phones, and computers using the same Spotify account. Block diagram is given in Figure 4.5.

Fitness-freak persons are increasing in day by day in the modern lifestyle and therefore can be considered an essential part while making the present proposal. The embedded fitness tracker does the same. Google Fit is a free-to-use application developed by Google for multiple devices like mobile phones based on Android and IOS. It also has extended its support to multiple wearable operating system and devices like iWatch, MI watch, Fitbit, and other smart watches. Data of one's daily activity are stored through these devices and are synced to the cloud via internet. Here, the user can sync his/her account of Google Fit to the mirror by replicating the data from Google Fit server to our Cloud Console and then viewing the data on owns Mirror. Block diagram is given in Figure 4.6.

News updates are fetched within the mirror directly from Times of India world news with 1 hour interval. The present proposal deals with one extremely essential feature which is given at free of cost; that is weather predictions with utmost accuracy. This is helpful for making daily routine for people with whatever professions. Phone notifications are fetched into the mirror and stayed tuned.

4.9   Results

The total result section in this manuscript is subdivided into three parts: circuit design, LDR data display, and API data from the informative interface. In the circuit design section, we have discussed about PIR sensor and its connections, LDR, control unit design, and Rasberry Pi configuration. In the display section, we have shown the variation of data in LDR, and API data using Google Cloud Console is exhibited in the last phase of this section.

4.9.1   Circuit Design

We have started with the setting up of Raspberry Pi 3 Model B+, which operates at 1.4GHz. This is supported by Bluetooth 4.2.1, along with wireless ac Wi-Fi. The process begins with connecting the microphone and speaker to the Raspberry Pi and then by inserting the SD card into it. Thereafter, USB keyboard, mouse, and HDMI monitor are added sequentially.

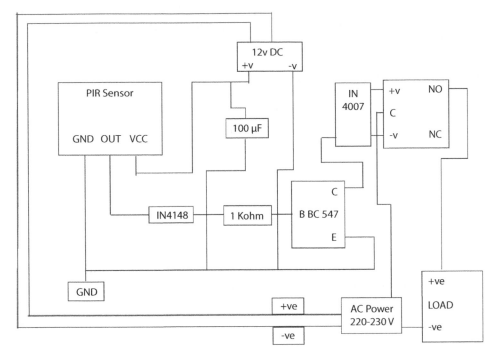

Figure 4.7 Implementation of PIR sensor in our system.

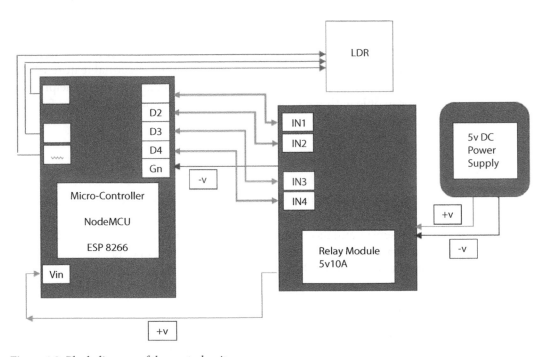

Figure 4.8 Block diagram of the control unit.

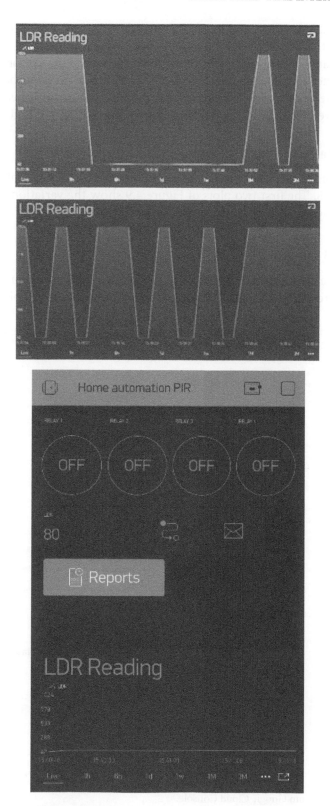

Figure 4.9 Live streaming results of the LDR sensor.

At last, Ethernet cable is connected to Wi-Fi network. After successful configuration, date and time will be set.

The next important hardware part is the Pyroelectric Infrared (PIR) Sensor Module, required for human body detection. Its implementation into the interface circuit is shown in Figure 4.7.

In the next phase, control unit is designed. Microcontroller is connected with relay module and LDR, where proper power supply is required. Block diagram is given in Figure 4.8.

4.9.2 LDR Data

After finalizing the circuit, LDR gives data as output which is a series of pulses. Plots are shown in Figure 4.8. The first two plots of Figure 4.9 show the variation of pulses in LDR where the third diagram shows the reading across the device.

4.9.3 API Data

At first, we analyze the results obtained from Google Cloud Console and provided them sequentially (Figures 4.10, 4.11, 4.12, and 4.13) below. Figure 4.10 exhibits the operational

Figure 4.10 API keys operational workbook.

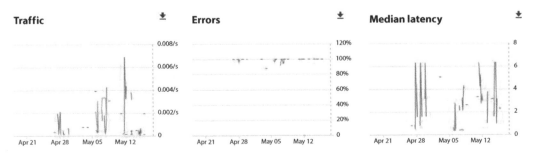

Figure 4.11 API graphs from Google Cloud Console.

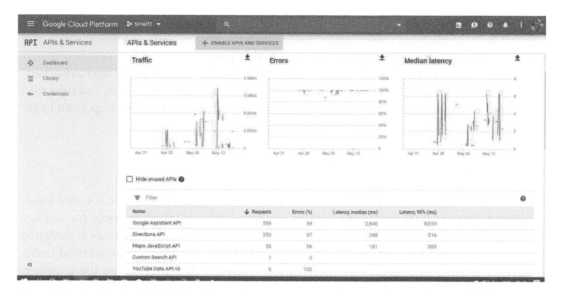

Figure 4.12 API data call counter log.

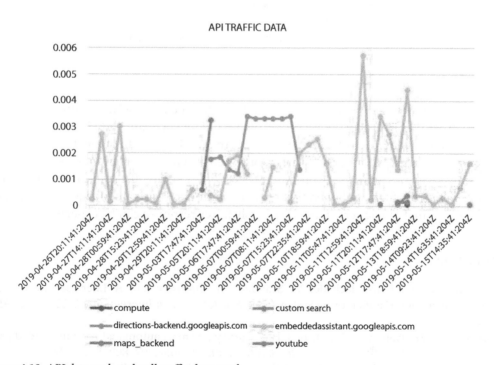

Figure 4.13 API data push and pull traffic data graph.

workbook with API keys, whereas in Figure 4.11, corresponding graphs are provided in different days, as obtained from cloud console. Traffic variations, corresponding error, and median latency for the same days are provided in that plot.

For different APIs, call log is extremely important in order to note down the busy schedule. Therefore, important APIs like Google Assistance, JavaScript, Directions, YouTube, and custom search are noted. This is shown in Figure 4.12. In this case, it is also important to get view about the variations of traffic, as shown in Figure 4.13.

4.10 Conclusion

The smart real-time prototype developed as explained in this manuscript is really interesting and efficient in terms of the ease of response and accuracy, precisely for old age people, and also for people who needs special care. Total informative interface is designed using Google Cloud Console so that the operation can be possible for the android users. In absence of any help, people can operate basic electrical appliances using the interface, which is precisely voice-controlled. Moreover, it can search the web for your query and read out the results or inform you about the weather when you ask for it. It also smartly helps you to reduce the energy consumption by switching off the device when not needed. At extreme urgent condition, people can take help of cab service, which can save time and life. Interface with personal mosquito server can also be possible through IFTTT server, and that makes the system more robust. The most important part is that it can be integrated with the existing electrical circuit of one's home, and therefore, it makes huge cost saving.

4.11 Future Scope

The present prototype can be augmented in near future to generate a large complex yet compact system with smart incorporation of artificial intelligence and therefore can be made scalable for embedding with future controllers. This adds with the benefit of less power requirement and ideal for modern home automation system. Several new and essential features can be easily ties up with the proposed system architecture like coffee machine operation, speed control of fan, and operation of air-conditioner. If private Mosquitto server can replace the original public server, then obviously faster response can be expected.

References

1. Alcácer, V. and Cruz-Machado, V., Scanning the Industry 4.0: A Literature Review on Technologies for Manufacturing Systems. *Eng. Sci. Technol., an International J.*, 22, 3, 899–919, 2019.
2. Al-wswasi, M., Ivanov, A., Makatsoris, H., A survey on smart automated computer-aided process planning (ACAPP) techniques. *Int. J. Adv. Manuf. Technol.*, 97, 809–832, 2018.
3. Tan, Y., Yang, W., Yoshida, K., Takakuwa, S., Application of IoT-Aided Simulation to Manufacturing Systems in Cyber-Physical System, Machines, 7(2), 1-13, 2019.
4. Boyes, H., Hallaq, B., Cunningham, J., Watson, T., The industrial internet of things (IIoT): An analysis framework. *Comput. Ind.*, 101, 1–12, 2018.
5. Saqlain, M., Piao, M., Shim, Y., Lee, J. Y., Framework of an IoT-based Industrial Data Management for Smart Manufacturing, Journal of Sensor and Actuator Networks, 8(25), 1-21, 2019.

6. Xu, H., Yu, W., Griffith, D., Golmie, N., A Survey on Industrial Internet of Things: A Cyber-Physical Systems Perspective. *IEEE Access*, 6, 78238–8259, 2018.

7. Kavitha, B.C. and Vallikannu, R., IoT Based Intelligent Industry Monitoring System. *6th International Conference on Signal Processing and Integrated Networks*, Noida, India, 7-8 March 2019.

8. Maple, C., Security and privacy in the internet of things. *J. Cyber Policy*, 2, 2, 155–184, 2017.

9. Sfar, A.R., Natalizio, E., Challal, Y., Chtourou, Z., A roadmap for security challenges in the Internet of Things. *Digital Commun. Networks*, 4, 2, 118–137, 2018.

10. Ranjan, R., Sharma, A., Tanwar, S., Voice-Controlled IoT Devices Framework for Smart Home, in: *Proceedings of First International Conference on Computing, Communications, and Cyber-Security (IC4S 2019)*. Lecture Notes in Networks and Systems, vol. 121 Springer, Singapore, pp. 57–67, 2020.

11. Wu, Z., Qiu, K., Zhang, J., A Smart Microcontroller Architecture for the Internet of Things. *Sensors (Basel)*, 20, 7, 1821, 2020.

12. Mendoza, J.F., Ordóñez, H., Ordóñez, A., Jurado, J.L., Architecture for embedded software in microcontrollers for Internet of Things (IoT) in fog water collection. *Proc. Comput. Sci.*, 109, 1092–1097, 2017.

13. Singh, H.K., Verma, S., Pal, S., Pandey, K., A step towards Home Automation using IOT. *12th International Conference on Contemporary Computing*, Noida, India, 8-10 Aug. 2019.

14. Singh, U. and Ansari, M.A., Smart Home Automation System using Internet of Things. *2nd International Conference on Power Energy, Environment and Intelligent Control*, Greater Noida, India, 18-19 Oct. 2019.

15. Elsokah, M.M., Saleh, H.H., Ze, A.R., Next Generation Home Automation System Based on Voice Recognition. *6th International Conference on Engineering & MIS*, vol. 72, pp. 1–7, 2020.

16. Haria, H. and Mohammad, B.N.S., Home Automation System Using IoT and Machine Learning Techniques. *3rd International Conference on Advances in Science & Technology*, 2020.

17. Soumya, P.C., Design and Implementation of Home Automation System Using Facial Expressions, in: *Proceedings of the 3rd International Conference on Frontiers of Intelligent Computing: Theory and Applications*, Advances in Intelligent Systems and Computing, vol. 327, Springer, Cham, 2015.

18. Sowah, R. A., Boahene, D. E., Owoh, D. C., Addo, R., Mills, G. A., Owusu-Banahene, W., Buah, G., Sarkodie-Mensah, B., Design of a Secure Wireless Home Automation System with an Open Home Automation Bus (OpenHAB 2) Framework, Journal of Sensors: Integration of Sensors in Control and Automation Systems, 2020, 8868602, 2020.

19. Pirbhulal, S., Zhang, H., Alahi, M.E.E., Ghayvat, H., Mukhopadhyay, S.C., Zhang, Y.T., Wu, W., A Novel Secure IoT-Based Smart Home Automation System using a Wireless Sensor Network. *Sensors*, 17, 1, 69, 2017.

20. Al-Kuwari, M., Ramadan, A., Ismael, Y., Al-Sughair, L., Gastli, A., Benammar, M., Smart-home automation using IoT-based sensing and monitoring platform. *IEEE 12th International Conference on Compatibility, Power Electronics and Power Engineering*, Doha, Qatar, 10-12 April 2018.

21. Jabbar, W.A., Alsibai, M.H., Amran, N.S.S., Mahayadin, S.K., Design and Implementation of IoT-Based Automation System for Smart Home. *International Symposium on Networks, Computers and Communications*, Rome, Italy, 19-21 June 2018.

22. Veeranjaneyulu, N., Srivalli, G., Bodapati, J.D., Home Automation and Security System Using IOT. *Rev. d'Intelligence Artif.*, 33, 1, 21–24, 2019.

23. Amudha, S., Sankar, S.S.R., Rajkumar, M.N., Jain, A., Enhancement of smart home automation system using secure geofence concept in IoT. *AIP Conference Proceedings*, vol. 2112, p. 020036, 2019.

Symmetric Key and Artificial Neural Network With Mealy Machine: A Neoteric Model of Cryptosystem for Cloud Security

Anirban Bhowmik[1*], Sunil Karforma[2] and Joydeep Dey[1]

[1]*State Aided College Teacher, Dept. of Comp. Science, M.U.C. Women's College, Purba Bardhaman, WB, India*
[2]*HoD, Dept. of Computer Science, The University of Burdwan, Purba Bardhaman, WB, India*

Abstract

Cloud computing is defined as the distribution of computing which include hardware and software program to the patron through the Internet. In the technology of ICT, cloud computing has encouraged via many industries which includes technology, enterprise, management, logistics, and numerous other enterprises. But some new kind of risks and vulnerabilities exist in cloud environment. Users of cloud services are under constant threat. Hence, security-related risks are the main drawback of cloud computing. The aim of this paper is to enhance the cloud security by designing a secure cryptosystem. At first, we have emphasized on secure key generation algorithm based on coupled artificial neural network (ANN) with Mealy machine and then weight vector-based authentication mechanism. We have used coupled multilayer feedforward neural network and Mealy machine for security issues of cloud computing. Machine learning is done "n" times between two ANNs, and after several steps, we have generated session key for encryption. A novel key wrapping protocol has also introduced using one way function. For encryption and decryption, we have used XOR and CLS (Circular Left Shift) operation and for authentication purpose weight vectors of ANN with hash function is used. Different types of experimental results and analysis prove the efficiency and robustness of our technique in the field of artificial intelligence.

Keywords: Cloud computing, Mealy machine, machine learning, ANN, symmetric key, key wrapping, authentication

5.1 Introduction

In today's time, cloud computing is a quick flourishing area in computational studies and Industry 4.0. It is an Internet-based computing that offers services using IT assets on call for of the users. It employs parallel processing, distributed processing, grid computing, and allotted database to enhance processing. Cloud computing means distribution of

Corresponding author: animca2008@gmail.com

Rajdeep Chakraborty, Anupam Ghosh and Jyotsna Kumar Mandal (eds.) Machine Learning Techniques and Analytics for Cloud Security, (81–102) © 2022 Scrivener Publishing LLC

computing to the consumers through the Internet. Many organizations like technology, business, management, and logistics are influenced by cloud computing. According to the company's need, cloud computing has three specific provider fashions which includes platform as a provider (PaaS), software as a carrier (SaaS), and infrastructure as a carrier (IaaS) [6]. It has four deployment models that are public cloud, hybrid cloud, and private cloud and community cloud. The main drawback in cloud computing is security attacks because it stores data from the different geographical locations. There are different types of attacks and their security issues exist in cloud computing environment. All these security problems are of categories which can be safety issues confronted through cloud carriers and safety issues confronted by way of their customers. Both have exceptional set of equipment like encryption, robust password and authentication virtual signature and so on to guard towards safety breach. At present, machine learning, deep learning, etc., are latest trends in computer science. The amalgamation of machine learning and deep learning with cloud computing is an interesting area in the field of research and commercial implementation. The concept of neural network in machine learning is an attracted field for developer and invertors.

Machine learning and artificial neural network (ANN): The idea of ANNs is based definitely on the perception that operating of human mind by using making the proper connections may be imitated the usage of silicon and wires as residing neurons and dendrites. The human brain consists of 86 billion nerve cells known as neurons. They are related through the use of Axons to other thousand cells [1].

ANNs are composed of more than one node, which imitate organic neurons of human brain. The neurons are linked with the aid of links and they have interaction with every distinct. The nodes can take input information and perform easy operations on the records. The give up end result of these operations is exceeded to other neurons. The output at each node is referred to as its activation or node cost. Each link is associated with weight. ANNs are capable of mastering, which takes region through changing weight values. Figure 5.1 illustrates a simple ANN structure.

Types of ANNs: There are two forms of ANN topologies: feedforward and feedback.

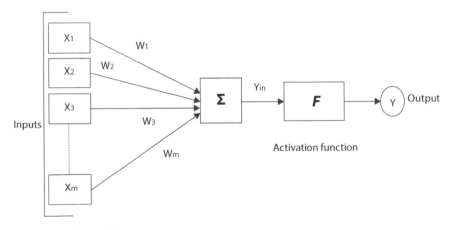

Figure 5.1 Diagram of ANN [5].

Feedforward ANN: In this ANN, the information float is unidirectional. A unit sends records or data to different unit from which it does not get preserve of any statistics. There are no feedback loops. They are used for pattern generation or pattern reorganization or class. They have steady inputs and outputs [14].

Feedback ANN: Here, comments loops are allowed. They are utilized in content material addressable memories.

Working of ANNs: It receives n-inputs and every accelerated with weights. Now, activation function is applied to the sum of expanded results and output cease result is received [15].

If the community generates a "high-quality or preferred" output, then there is no need to adjust the weights. However, if the network generates a "negative or undesired" output or a blunder, then the machine alters the weights in an effort to improve subsequent effects.

Machine Learning in ANNs:
ANNs are able to getting to know and that they need to learn. There are numerous getting to know techniques as follows.

1. Supervised Learning: It involves a teacher this is pupil than the ANN itself. For instance, the trainer feeds a few example information approximately which the teacher already knows the answers. For example, pattern spotting. The ANN comes up with guesses at the same time as recognizing. Then, the teacher gives the ANN with the answers. The network then compares it guesses with the instructor's "accurate" answers and makes adjustments in step with mistakes.
2. Unsupervised Learning: It is required while there is no instance facts set with identified answers. In this situation, clustering, i.e., Dividing a set of things into organizations regular with some unknown pattern is finished based totally on the prevailing statistics units present [19].
3. Reinforcement Learning: This strategy built on remark. The ANN makes a selection with the aid of way of looking at its surroundings. If the statement is negative, then the community adjusts its weights so that it will make a notable required choice the subsequent time [2, 3].

Mealy Machine: Finite automata might also have outputs similar to each transition and this is called transducer. There are sorts of finite nation machines that generate output: i. Mealy Machine and ii. Moore Machine [26].

Mealy Machine:
A Mealy Machine is an FSM whose output depends on the present state as well as the present input.

It can be described by a 6 tuple $(Q, \Sigma, O, \delta, X, q0)$ where

- *Q is a finite set of internal states, and Σ is a finite set of input alphabet.*
- *O is a finite set of the output alphabet, and $q0$ is the initial state* (q0 $\in$ Q).

- **δ** *is the transition function where* δ: $Q \times \Sigma \rightarrow Q$.
- **X** *is the output transition function where* X: $Q \times \Sigma \rightarrow O$.

The state Table 5.1 of a Mealy machine is shown below.

Table 5.1 Mealy machine.

| Present state | Next state | | | |
| | input = 0 | | input = 1 | |
	State	Output	State	Output
→ A	B	x_1	C	x_1
B	B	x_2	D	x_3
C	D	x_3	C	x_1
D	D	x_3	D	x_2

The state diagram of the above Mealy machine is shown if Figure 5.2.

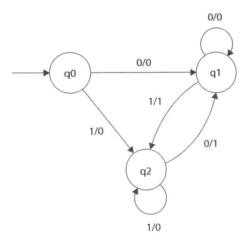

Figure 5.2 State diagram of Mealy machine [26].

Cryptography: Cryptography is the have a look at of mathematical techniques associated with elements of records security which includes confidentiality, statistics integrity, entity authentication, and information starting place authentication. The cryptographic dreams are 1. privacy, 2. data integrity, 3. authentication, and 4. non-repudiation. These desires are measured by way of stage of safety, capability, strategies of operation, overall performance, and ease of implementation [4, 5].

An encryption scheme is said to be breakable if a third party, without earlier understanding of the important thing pair (*e, d*), can systematically recover plaintext from corresponding cipher text inside some suitable time frame. A finite set referred to as the alphabet of definition. For instance, *A* = 0, 1, the binary alphabet, is a frequently used alphabet of definition. A set called the message area. The message region consists of strings of symbols from an alphabet of definition. A set referred to as the cipher textual content place which incorporates strings of symbols from an alphabet of definition, which may also additionally range from the alphabet of definition shape message space. Each element $e \in$ *key vicinity* (K) uniquely determines a bijection from message place to cipher textual content area, denoted through E_e. E_e is known as an encryption function or an encryption transformation. Now, each $d \in K$, D_d denotes a bijection from cipher text area to message space, D_d is referred to as a decryption function or decryption transformation.

The encryption scheme is stated to be symmetric key if for every associated encryption/decryption key pair (e, d), its miles computationally smooth to decide d information best e, and to determine e from d. Since $e = d$ in most realistic symmetric key encryption schemes, the time period symmetric key becomes appropriate. There are classes of symmetric key encryption schemes which might be generally outstanding: block ciphers and move ciphers. An identification or entity authentication approach assures one birthday party of each the identity of a second birthday celebration involved, and that the second became lively at the time the proof turn out to be created or received. Consider an encryption scheme which includes the sets of encryption and decryption modifications. The encryption technique is stated to be a public-key encryption scheme if for every related encryption/decryption pair (e, d), one key e (the general public key) is made publicly to be had, while the alternative d (the non-public key) is stored mystery. For the scheme to be cozy, it must be computationally infeasible to compute d from e.

In this paper, we have emphasized on symmetric key, session key, multi-layer neural community, and mealy machine.

5.2   Literature Review

Moghaddam F. *et al.* [8] proposed a hybrid encryption model wherein category indexing attributes and time-based procedures are focused mainly. The idea of hybrid ring and attribute-based statistics classifications are used. This technique securely protect the illegal access of data. The end result and evaluation show that the hybrid ring model is efficient and reliable for facts safety applications.

Dhamija Ankit *et al.* [9] proposed cloud structure in which the technique of cryptography and steganography are mixed for at ease facts transmission. In this paper, a two-way facts safety has proposed. First, the records that are received are transformed into cipher textual content through the usage of encryption algorithm and then this cipher text code layout is again transformed into a difficult picture through the usage of steganography. Steganography also hides the existence of the message and this ensures that the minimum chances of statistics.

Neetha Xavier, V. Chandrasekar [10] described a holistic view cloud computing via authentication and encryption. An authentication method is proposed for cloud companies.

Li *et al.* (2017) [11] provided a message that outsourcing is an excellent option for machine learning. Machine learning processes large amount of data; also, it requires complex and powerful computer system. A huge amount of storage is required for designing such advanced and complex computing system. Hence, cloud computing provides all the necessary resource and also offers large storage.

Kaur K., Zandu V [12] addressed different types of security risks related to cloud computing. They proposed a frame work to address these security issues at the authentication and storage level in cloud computing. A data classification approach based on confidentiality of data in machine learning is described in this paper.

Dhivya R and Dharshana R [13] have particularly emphasized on numerous security attacks like denial-of-service (DOS) attack, malware injection assault, side-channel assault, man-in-the-middle attack, authentication attack inside the cloud, and the machine learning algorithms used for detecting the attacks.

Awodele O. *et al.* [16] indentified the key security and privacy problems of cloud and its solutions. They have also addressed cloud deployment fashions consist of public, private, network, and hybrid clouds.

Sundharakumar KB *et al.* [17] defined a singular cloud-based totally fitness care system where the Wireless Body Area Networks aggregate the records to the non-public server that encompasses STORM. It is a real-time computation gadget with Fuzzy inference gadget.

Yunchuan Sun *et al.* [18] have studied exceptional security techniques and challenges from both the nook of software program and hardware for shielding facts within the cloud the intention of this have a look at is to decorate the facts protection and privacy protection for the trustworthy cloud environment.

5.3 The Problem

The literature review section provides some advanced techniques and solutions for cloud security but till security-related problems are exists in cloud system. Data security and network security are two main issues in cloud system. Different types of privacy and security-related issues have long-term significance for cloud computing which are governance, compliance, malicious insiders, and account or service hijacking, hypervisor vulnerabilities, insecure APIs, etc. [9]. Cloud computing loses its popularity till now for these problems. The above literatures have tried to overcome these problems using different types of concepts and computational tools like fuzzy concepts, data classification, and hybrid ring but not fully successful. These literatures cannot provide a specific direction or model in security issues.

5.4 Objectives and Contributions

In this paper, our objectives is to develop a secure cryptosystem for cloud data security because the security issue is one of the parameter among different parameters of cloud computing that control the usage of cloud in different platforms. So, we should focus on security issues of cloud computing. Any cryptosystem has three basic modules: key generation and key transmission, encryption-decryption algorithm, and authentication [7]. Although above literatures provide different types of cryptosystem for security issues but all the modules are not under one umbrella.

Novelty of Proposed System: Here, we have proposed a cryptosystem which includes all the three basic modules using the concept of coupled ANN, transducer, and digital logic.

The machine learning–based algorithm is more secured and efficient because of its ability to recognize data as per the priority and sensitivity. Our new concept about cloud security is given below.

If we want to transmit data or information through wireless channel, then sender sends some input data to the receiver via public channel; this input data is transformed to another data via transducer. The significance of use of transducer is the data transformation and this transformation is hidden from outside by using specific Mealy machine structure. The output of transducer is treated as input of ANN. In this way, we have secured the input of ANN, i.e, first level security.

A specific learning method is used for weight vector updating in both side. The weight vectors of layer2 are used as session key, and weight vectors of layer1are used for key transmission purpose and also authentication purpose. The weight vectors of layer1 are same for both sides. The output of last layer (output layer) is compared between sender and receiver and for different output, a specific learning method is used in both side for weight vector updating. This process is continued for "n" times. After "n" times, we have assumed that both the machines are coupled and ready for session key generation. Thus, in our article, we have used coupled ANN to generate encryption key as well as key transmission protocol and authentication.

5.5   Methodology

Here, our concept of cryptosystem is divided into four modules. The details of each module are given below. After proper integration of each module, we can get a secured cryptosystem for cloud computing.

MODULE-1

Concept: Here, we have designed a Mealy machine (design may change, not fixed) for data transformation and output of the machine is input vector to ANN. The structure of Mealy machine is same for both sender and receiver.

Input: Any numbers in binary format which are same for both sender and receiver.

Output: Transformed numbers which are used as input to ANN.

Algorithm:

Step1: Let M= (Q, q_0, Σ, O, σ,λ) where Q is *finite set of internal* states, q_0 is the *initial state*, Σ is the finite set of input *alphabet*, O is the *output alphabet*, σ is the *transition function* which maps $Q \, x \, \Sigma \rightarrow Q$, and λ is the *output function* which maps $Q \, x \, \Sigma \rightarrow O$.

Step2: Transition function for *input* 0, $q_0 \rightarrow q_1$ *Output* 0 $q_1 \rightarrow q_1$ *output* 0 $q_2 \rightarrow q_1$ *output* 1

Step3: Transition function for *input* 1, $q_0 \rightarrow q_2$ *Output* 0 $q_1 \rightarrow q_2$ *output* 1 $q_2 \rightarrow q_2$ *output* 0

Step4: Strings of {0, 1} as output.

Step5: End.

The output of module-1 is transferred to module-2 as input.

MODULE-2

Concept: Here, we have developed a coupled multi-layer feedforward ANN for receiver and sender. Using this coupled ANN, session key is generated for encryption-decryption.

A $4 - 4 - 4 - 1$ ANN structure is used in this work. Let there be r processing units in each hidden layer ($r < N$). The expression for the network input to the hidden layer units and the output units are obtained as $HL1\_in = X \times W$, $HL2_{in} = HL1_{out} \times V$ and $HL3\_in = HL2\_out \times U$ where $X = [x_1, x_2,...,x_N]$, X is the input vector. $HL1\_in = [hl1\_in_1, hl1\_in_2,...,hl1\_in_r]$ is the input vector to the hidden layer1. $HL1\_out = [hl1\_out_1, hl1\_out_2,...,hl1\_out_r]$ output vector from the hidden layer1. $HL2\_in = [hl2\_in_1, hl2\_in_2,...,hl2\_in_r]$ is the input vector to the hidden layer 2. $HL2\_out = [hl2\_out_1, hl2\_out_2,...,hl2\_out_r]$ is the output vector from the hidden layer2. $OL\_in = [ol\_in_1, ol\_in_2,...,ol\_in_r]$ is the input vector to the output layer (OL). The layer1 weight vectors (W) are same for both ends and it is generated from symmetric key via a functional unit (combination of non-linear function and modulo operation) but layer2 weight vectors (V) and output layer weight vectors (U) are not same. At each iteration on *ANN* the outputs for the both sides are compared. According to the result of comparison, the appropriate rules are applied for updating weight vectors. This iteration is continued up to "*n*" times. Now, we have saved k_1th, k_2th ($1 < k_1$ and $k_2 < n$) vector of layer1 for key transmission purposes. The values of "*n*", k_1, and k_2 are generated from symmetric key and these are same for both ends.

Activation function: Two activation functions are used in our proposed technique. Activation function2 (activFunc2) is used in layer1 and layer2, and activation function1 (activFunc1) is used in output layer. They are actually threshold function. Its design is given below:

Activation function1 (activFunc1):   *Activation function2 (activFunc2):*

$$F(x) = \begin{cases} 1 & if \ x > 0 \\ 0 & if \ x = 0 \\ -1 & if \ x < 0 \end{cases}$$

$$F(x) = \begin{cases} b - (x\%(b-a)) & if \ x > b \\ a + (x\%(b-a)) & if \ x < 0 \\ x & if \ a \le x \le b \end{cases}$$

The values of *a* and *b* are the range within which functional values lies. These values need not negotiated between two parties, it is fixed for ANN structure.

W_{11}	W_{12}	...	W_{1m}		V_{11}	V_{12}	...	V_{1m}		u_1
W_{21}	W_{22}	...	W_{2m}		V_{21}	V_{22}	...	V_{2m}		u_2
...	...	...	...		...	...	...	...		...
W_{N1}	W_{N2}	...	W_{Nm}		V_{r1}	V_{r2}	...	V_{rm}		u_r

W matrix   V matrix   U matrix

Input: output of module-1.
Output: session key
Algorithm:
Step1: set k as integer, input [ ] [ ] as integer array.
     {/* Calculation for input values of hidden layer 1 */}

Step2: set $[x_1, x_2, ..., x_N] \leftarrow$ get_values ( ).   //same for both sender and receiver.
Step3: *for i* = 1 *to N*   //'N' numbers of vector.
    $k \leftarrow x_i$.
Step4: *for j* = 1 *to m*   // "m" dimension vector.
Step5: *input*[*i*][*j*] $\leftarrow$ (*w*[*i*][*j*] * *k*).
    End for
    End for
Step6: *for i* = 1 *to m*
Step7: *for j* = 1 *to N*
Step8: $hl1\_in_1 \leftarrow$ cal_sum (*input*[*j*][*i*]), $hl1\_in_2 \leftarrow$ cal_sum (input[j][i]),..., $hl1\_in_r \leftarrow$ cal_sum (*input*[*j*][*i*]).
    End for
    End for
Step9: $hl1\_out_1 \leftarrow$ activFunc2 ($hl1\_in_1$), $hl1\_out_2 \leftarrow$ activFunc2 ($hl1\_in_2$)... $hl1\_out_r \leftarrow$ activFunc2 (
    $hl1\_in_r$)
                {/* *Calculation for hidden layer 2* */}
Step10: *for i* = 1 *to r*
    $p \leftarrow hl1\_out_i$.
Step11: *for j* = 1 *to m*
Step12: *input*[*i*][*j*] $\leftarrow$ (*v*[*i*][*j*] * *p*).
    End for
    End for
Step13: *for i* = 1 *to m*
Step14: *for j* = 1 *to r*
Step15: $hl2\_in_1 \leftarrow$ cal_sum (*input*[*j*][*i*]), $hl2\_in_2 \leftarrow$ cal_sum (*input*[*j*][*i*])... $hl2\_in_r \leftarrow$ cal_sum (*input*[*j*][*i*]).
    End for
    End for
Step16: $hl2\_out_1 \leftarrow$ activFunc2 ($hl2\_in_1$), $hl2\_out_2 \leftarrow$ activFunc2 ($hl2\_in_2$)... $hl2\_out_r \leftarrow$ activFunc2 (
    $hl2\_in_r$).
  {/* *Calculation for output layer* */}
Step17: *for i* = 1 *to r*
    $p \leftarrow hl1\_out_i$.
Step18: $ol\_in_i \leftarrow$ (*u*[*i*] * *p*).
    End for
Step19: *for i* = 1 *to r*
Step20: $OL\_in \leftarrow$ cal_sum (ol_in_i).
    End for
Step21: $OL\_out \leftarrow$ activFunc1 (ol_in).
Step22: End
Following is the pseudo code of activation function.

activFunc1 (integer x): x is a parameter.   *activFunc2 (integer x)*: x is a parameter

Step1: set f_val as integer.
Step2: if $(x > 0)$
    $f\_val \leftarrow 1$.
Step3: else if $(x = 0)$
$f\_val \leftarrow 0$.
Step4: else $f\_val \leftarrow (-1)$
Step5: Return (f_val)
Step6: End

Step1: set f_val as integer.
Step2: if $(x > b)$
    $f\_val \leftarrow b - (x \% (b - a))$.
Step3: else if $(x < a)$
$f\_val \leftarrow a + ((x \% (b - a)))$.
Step4: else if $(a \leq x \leq b)$ $f\_val \leftarrow x$
Step5: Return (f_val)
Step6: End

Same algorithm is used and processed in both ends in parallel. Now, we have compared the output i.e, OL_out "n" times between sender and receiver. Here, we have used two rules for weight vector updating. If the value of output layer of ANN is same, then we have used rule-1, and otherwise, we have used rule-2. The unsupervised learning concept is used in the design of rule-1 and rule-2.

Rule-1: $w_{ij}(new) = w_{ij}(old) + floor(\mu X [x_i - w_{ij}(old)])$ where $\mu = 0.4$.
Rule-2: $w_{ij}(new) = w_{ij}(old) + ceiling(\mu X [x_i - w_{ij}(old)])$ where $\mu = 0.5$.

Thus, after comparing and iterating the above process "n" times, the required session key is generated from weight vectors of layer2 of sender's ANN. We have saved k_1th and k_2th weight vectors of layer1 for key transmission purposes.

Limitations: i. the values of W and Input are not same for ANN. The row wise values of W must be different.

ii. Weight vector (U) may contain negative weight vectors.

MODULE-3

Concept: In this module, we have checked authentication specially user authentication mutually. In module 2, we have saved k_1th, k_2th vector of layer1of sender's and receiver's ANN. Now, XOR operation is done between k_1 and k_2th vectors and MD5 hash algorithm is used on XOR operation.

Input: k_1th and k_2th weight vectors.
Output: Authentication check.
Algorithm:

Step1: set $R_a [ ]$, $P_a [ ]$ as character.
Step2: $R_a[] = k_1 XOR k_2$.
Step3: $P_a[] = MD5 (R_a[])$.
Step4: End

This $P_a [ ]$ is exchanged between sender and receiver sides. Each side checks it is calculated $P_a [ ]$ and received $P_a [ ]$, if it is same, then authentication proved and encryption key can be transmitted.

MODULE-4

Concept: In this module, we have discussed on key wrapping protocol that transmit session key between sender and receiver. In this protocol, modulo operation is used between k_1th, k_2th weight vectors of layer1of sender's ANN. These k_1th, k_2th weight vectors of layer1of sender's ANN have already saved, and in the receiver end, k_1th, k_2th weight vectors of layer1of ANN have also saved at the same time. An output weight vector is generated after modulo operation between k_1th, k_2th weight vectors, and XOR operation is done between output weight vector and session key. The output weight vectors are generated in both sides, so we have only shared the output of XOR via secure channel.

Input: k_1th and k_2th weight vectors, session key.
Algorithm: (Key Wrapping Algorithm)

Step1: set P_k [ ], R_k [ ] as character array.
Step2: P_k [ ] ← K_1 MOD K_2.
Step3: R_k [ ] ← P_k [] xor Session key.
Step4: End

R_k [ ] is transmitted to the receiver end through secure channel. Using unwrapping protocol, the session key is redeemed. This session key is used to generate plain text.

MODULE-5

Concept: This module mainly focuses on cipher text generation. XOR and CLS (circular left shift) operation is done between plain text and session key for generating cipher text. In recipient end, the plain text is generated using decryption process.

Input: Session key, Plain text
Output: Cipher text.
Algorithm (Encryption):

Step1: set pt [ ], ct [ ], tmp [ ], session key [ ], s_key [ ] as character.
Step2: tmp [ ] ← pt [] xor session key.
Step3: s_key [ ] ← get_CLS (session key, 1st element (k_1th vector)) // Circular left shift operation on session key.
Step4: ct [ ] ←tmp [] xor s_key[].   // ct [ ] is cipher text.
Step5: End.

This ct [ ] is transmitted to recipient end where decryption algorithm (reverse of encryption algorithm) is used for plain text generation.

Details ANN structure and a complete flowchart are given below for clear understanding the proposed technique.

The input values and the weight vectors of first layer (W) are same for both ends Figure 5.3 represents the ANN structure of sender & receiver. Figure 5.4 represents the flow chart of proposed technique.

5.6   Results and Discussions

A good cryptosystem should be designed in such a way that it must robust against different types of cryptanalytic, statistical, and brute-force attacks. In this section, we have discussed different types of security analysis of our proposed scheme [11].

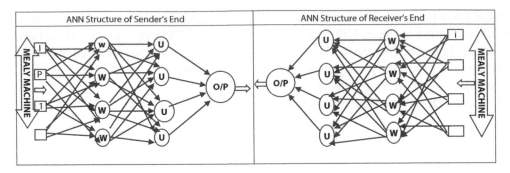

Figure 5.3 ANN structure [27].

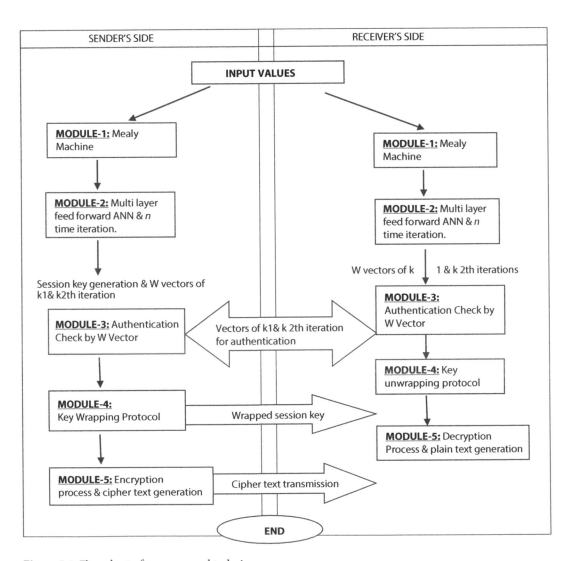

Figure 5.4 Flow chart of our proposed technique.

Table 5.2 Specifications of H/w and S/w used in the experiment.

Computer	*Lenovo G80*
Processor	Intel® Pentium® CPU B950@210GHz
RAM	2GB
Compiler	Turbo C, DebC + +
Disc Drive	SA 9500326AS·ATA
Operating System	Windows 7 Ultimate (32 Bits)

The Table 5.2 shows specifications of H/w and S/w.

5.6.1   Statistical Analysis

Nowadays, different sorts of statistical assaults and statistical evaluation are utilized by intruders or hackers to analyze the cipher text for decryption. Therefore, a great cipher text ought to be robust towards any statistical attacks. To prove the robustness of our proposed scheme, we have accomplished the histogram evaluation, avalanche impact evaluation, and randomness test [20].

(a) Histogram Analysis: A textual content-histogram describes [21] how distinctive characters in a text are disbursed with the aid of graphing the variety of characters at every stage. Here, histogram analysis is finished on the numerous encrypted as well as its authentic textual content documents which have extensively unique content. We have proven the encrypted documents of the authentic documents (simple textual content) using the secret keys *ApMn1808AB81* (in decimal) in Figure 5.5.

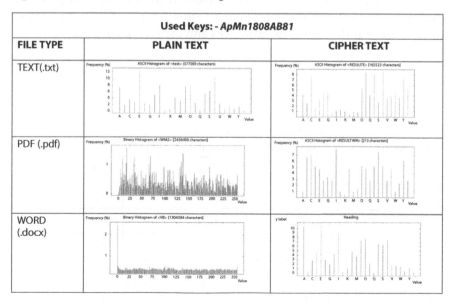

Figure 5.5 Histogram analysis [27].

Observations: It is plain from Figure 5.5 that the histograms of the encrypted documents are quite uniform and significantly changed from the respective histograms of the unique files (plain text) and consequently does no longer provide any clue to hire any statistical attack on the proposed encryption process.

5.6.2   Randomness Test of Key

Randomness approach all factors of the series that are generated independently of every other and the value of the following element within the series cannot be predicted, no matter how many elements have already been produced. Random and pseudorandom numbers that are generated for cryptographic programs have to be unpredictable (ahead and backward). The outputs of a PRNG are deterministic capabilities of the seed; i.e., all authentic randomness is depended on seed generation. An RNG uses a nondeterministic source, i.e., the entropy supply. Here, we have used RNG for generating weight vectors of ANN, and after some learning process, the weight values of a particular layer of ANN are used for session key generation. To prove the randomness of our session key, we have used serial test [3, 10]. The following statics is used for serial test [13].

$$X = \frac{4}{(n-1)}\left(n_{00}^2 + n_{01}^2 + n_{10}^2 + n_{11}^2\right) - \frac{2}{n}\left(n_0^2 + n_1^2\right) + 1$$

which approximately follows a χ^2 distribution with two degrees of freedom if $n \geq 21$. Table 5.3 is given below.

Observation: For a significance level of $\alpha = 0.05$, the threshold values of X for serial test are 1.11, 1.2, 1.26, 2.12, 11.01, and 19.04, respectively. Thus, the sequence generated by the above algorithm passes serial test. Table 5.3 and Figure 5.6 prove that our proposed technique is secure against different statistical attacks and differential attacks.

Table 5.3 Serial test.

Key size (byte)	Result of proposed tech.	Result of only PRNG() [3]	Result of only RNG() [10]
16	1.11	1.08	1.08
24	1.2	1	1.02
36	1.26	1.25	1.20
48	2.12	2.14	2.13
56	11.01	8.99	10
64	19.04	17.02	18.04

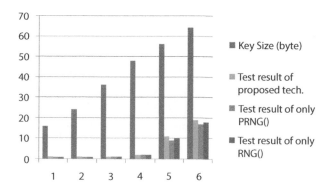

Figure 5.6 Graph of Table 5.3.

5.6.3 Key Sensitivity Analysis

An ideal encryption technique should be sensitive with recognize to the name of the secret key, i.e., a single bit trade within the mystery key have to produce a very unique cipher text. For checking out the sensitivity of the proposed encryption technique, we have completed the encryption scheme within the documents (.txt) with moderate adjustments using the secret key. The avalanche effect is shown below only for changed session key and with fixed session key. Table 5.4 and Figure 5.7 show the total scenario [15, 22].

Observation: We have got shown the effects of a few attempts to decrypt an encrypted file with barely one of kind secret keys than the only used for the encryption of the unique report. Table 5.4 shows the added characters, deleted characters, and changed characters

Table 5.4 Avalanche effect: change in session key.

Key	Ascii difference	Total number of added characters	Total number of deleted characters	Total number of changed characters
cryptann@12345	0	3,526	3,540	2,541
cyyptann@12345	8	3,717	3,714	2,363
cryptBnn@12345	9	3,862	3,836	2,272
cryptann@12346	108	3,929	3,878	2,219
cryptann#12345	30	3,614	3,612	2,456
crystann@12345	81	4,263	4,247	1,893
cryptann@1234z	8	3,794	3,776	2,315
cryptann@12445	120	3,867	3,843	2,247
cryptann@02345	6	4,108	4,082	2,044
Aryptann@12345	69	4,094	4,089	2,031

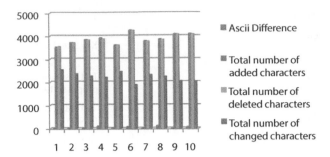

Figure 5.7 Graph of Table 5.4.

with slight change (one byte or two bytes) in session key, and the above graph (Figure 5.7) also shows the increasing and decreasing performance among added characters, deleted characters, and changed characters for one byte change in key. It is obvious that the decryption with a slightly extraordinary key fails absolutely and hence the proposed encryption system is highly key touchy.

5.6.4   Security Analysis

Key Space Analysis: The required belongings of a terrific encryption algorithm are the massive key area by way of which algorithm can face up to distinct types of attacks. The total range of various keys in encryption procedure shows the dimensions of key area. The brute-pressure assault is impractical in such crypto structures where key area is huge. Now, we do not forget a general case in which the dimensions of secret keys k bits, i.e., k the length of key in bits. Now, the key space is 2^k, and if the important thing space is large, then attack is not possible. There is a proportional relation among key space and key size [17, 23].

Brute-Force Attack: The massive key space makes the brute force assault [24] infeasible. In this attack, attacker attempts to translate the cipher textual content into undeniable textual content using every possible key. On common, half of all viable keys are enough for attaining success. Algorithms are recognized to all in maximum networking machine however brute-force assault will not possible if the algorithm uses massive key space.

If an eavesdropper listen this coupled feedforward ANN structure and accessing every public parameter (input values), then it can act as genuine participant. But it is very difficult for eavesdropper to get access of the symmetric key, and since the weight vectors of each layer is not publicly accessible, then the attacker link weight may not be same at the of time learning process in each iteration [27].

5.6.5   Dataset Used on ANN

The values of input vectors and W weight vectors are same for both sides and V weight vectors and U weight vectors are different in Table 5.5. These weight vectors are updated using rule-1 and rule-2 in both sides according to the values of output layer of ANN.

Table 5.5 Input vector and initial weight vectors.

Input vector	W vector				V vector				Input vector
3	2	1	3	2	1	2	3	2	8
6	1	2	1	4	2	2	1	4	2
10	3	4	0	1	2	1	2	3	5
5	1	3	2	2	1	2	4	1	3

Table 5.6 Updated weight vectors.

	W Vector				V Vector			
Iteration-1	2	2	4	2	2	4	2	4
	3	3	2	5	5	6	5	4
	6	7	4	5	2	2	3	6
	3	4	3	2	1	1	5	4
Iteration-2	2	5	4	1	4	8	2	5
	5	7	3	6	6	4	6	1
	4	4	9	1	2	9	4	6
	2	5	3	4	3	4	7	1
Iteration-3	5	6	8	2	5	8	1	6
	3	1	2	6	2	3	4	9
	4	7	4	2	1	6	7	5
	3	6	5	2	4	10	6	11
Iteration-4	2	5	4	1	4	7	6	2
	2	7	6	5	1	2	10	5
	3	2	11	4	4	11	6	5
	6	4	1	2	6	3	12	2
Iteration-5	2	4	1	3	1	5	4	2
	5	7	6	10	8	9	7	1
	2	3	4	6	3	6	4	9
	7	1	6	2	11	4	6	12

Observation: Table 5.6 shows the updated weight vectors of layer1 and layer2 in each iteration. Let $n = 5$, i.e., according to our proposed rule, 5 iterations are done on both sides. Weight vector updating is done according to the result of the output layer of ANN.

The unsupervised learning concept is used in weight vectors updating. The values of V vectors at iteration-5 are the required session key in sender end and this key is transmitted to the receiver end by amalgamating the values of W vectors of iteration-k_1 and iteration $-k_2$. It is seen that there is no correlation between input vectors and session key. This session key is used for encryption decryption purposes.

5.6.6   Comparisons

In comparisons with tree parity machine (TPM), our proposed scheme shows good result with respect to time and complexity. Many research papers has used coupled TPM for machine synchronization and encryption key generation but we have used the concept of coupled feedforward ANN instead of TPM which improves the quality of protocol for synchronization and key generation (Table 5.7).

Table 5.8 shows comparative study among different existing techniques and our proposed technique. This study also proves the efficiency of our protocol (Table 5.8).

Table 5.7 Comparison between coupled TPM and coupled feedforward ANN.

Scheme using coupled TPM [25]	Scheme using coupled feedforward ANN
Each time weight vectors are exchanged.	Weight vectors are exchanged one time in the whole process.
Input vectors are changed frequently depending on output.	Input vectors are not changed for whole process.
More time consuming for machine synchronization.	Less time consuming for machine synchronization.
Less structural complexity.	More structural complexity.

Table 5.8 Comparison table.

Schemes→ Security properties↓	Ref [7]	Ref [15]	Ref [21]	Ref [22]	Ref [23]	Ref [27]	Proposed technique
Confidentiality	Yes	No	No	No	Yes	Yes	Yes
Integrity	No	No	No	No	Yes	Yes	Yes
Authenticity (user authentication)	Yes	No	No	Yes	No	Yes	Yes
Defend against man-in-the-middle attack	No	No	No	No	No	No	Yes

(Continued)

Table 5.8 Comparison table. (*Continued*)

Schemes→ Security properties↓	*Ref* [7]	*Ref* [15]	*Ref* [21]	*Ref* [22]	*Ref* [23]	*Ref* [27]	**Proposed technique**
Defend against replay attack	No	No	No	No	No	No	Yes
Vulnerability	No	No	No	*Yes*	Yes	Yes	Yes

Defend against
  impersonation
  attack
	No	*Yes*	No	Yes	Yes	No	Yes

Cryptanalysis (linear and differential)	No	No	No	Yes	Yes	Yes	Yes
Session key establishment	No	No	No	No	Yes	Yes	Yes

Secure against
  information-
  leakage attack
	Yes	No	No	Yes	Yes	Yes	Yes

5.7   Conclusions

The data security and privacy issues are main barrier toward the rapid growth of cloud computing. A number of techniques have been proposed for data protection and these techniques also attain highest level of data security in the cloud. However, there are still many gaps in this field and need more researches to make these techniques more effective. Our proposed technique shows a novelty in neural cryptography and also provides a new direction in key generation and authentication using coupled feedforward ANN. Here, ANN generates outputs using few iterations of unsupervised learning process. So, this technique is faster and effective than other TPM-based techniques. Different types of analysis prove its robustness in security issues and it also improves various limitations of previous techniques in neural cryptography. It is not only applicable in cloud security but also in big data security or any other information security system.

References

1. Michalski, R., Carbonell, J., Mitchell, T., *Machine learning: An artificial intelligence approach*, Springer Science & Business Media, London, 2013.
2. Haykin, S., *Neural networks: A comprehensive foundation*, 2nd ed., Prentice Hall, New Jersey, 2009.
3. Goswami, B. and Singh, S.N., Enhancing Security in Cloud computing using Public Key Cryptography with Matrices. *Int. J. Eng. Res. Appl. (IJERA)* ISSN: 2248-9622, 2, 4, 339–344, July-August 2012.

4. Hassan, W., Chou, T., Tamer, O., Pickard, J., Appiah-Kubi, P., Pagliari, L., Cloud computing survey on services, enhancements and challenges in the era of machine learning and data science. *Int. J. Inf. Commun. Technol.*, 9, 117–139, 2020.

5. Bhalekar, P.D. and Shaikh, M.Z., MACHINE LEARNING: SURVEY, TYPES AND CHALLENGES. *Int. Res. J. Eng. Technol. (IRJET)*, 6, 3, 8131–8136, 2019.

6. Ahmad, I., Cloud Computing - Threats and Challenges. *J. Comput. Manage. Stud.*, 5, 9, 120–135, 2017.

7. Kiran, and Sharma, S., Enhance Data Security in Cloud Computing using Machine Learning and Hybrid Cryptography Techniques. *Int. J. Adv. Res. Comput. Sci. (IJARCS)*, 8, 9, 393–397, November – December 2017.

8. Moghaddam, F.F., Vala, M., Ahmadi, M., Khodadadi, T., Madadipouya, K., A reliable data protection model based on Encryption Concepts in cloud environments. *2015 IEEE 6th Control and System Graduate Research Colloquium (ICSGRC)*, pp. 11–16, 2015.

9. Dhamija, A. and Dhaka, V., A novel cryptographic and steganographic approach for secure cloud data migration. *2015 International Conference Green Computing and Internet of Things (ICGCIoT)*, pp. 346–351, 2015.

10. Xavier, N. and Chandrasekar, V., Security of PHR in Cloud Computing by Using Several Attribute Based Encryption Techniques. *Int. J. Commun. Comput. Technol.*, 1, 114–118, 2013.

11. Yang, C., Huang, Q., Li, Z., Liu, K., Hu, F., Big Data and cloud computing: innovation opportunities and Challenges. *Int. J. Digital Earth*, 10, 1, 13–53, 2017, DOI: 10.1080/17538947.2016.1239771.

12. Kaur, K. and Zandu, V., A Secure Data Classification Model in Cloud Computing Using Machine Learning Approach. *Int. J. Grid Distrib. Comput.*, 9, 13–22, 2016, 10.14257/ijgdc.2016.9.8.02.

13. Dhivya, R., Dharshana, R., Divya, V., Security Attacks Detection in Cloud using Machine Learning Algorithms. *Int. Res. J. Eng. Technol. (IRJET)*, 6, 2, 223–230, February 2019.

14. Gander, M., Felderer, M., Katt, B., Tolbaru, A., Breu, R., Moschitti, A., Anomaly Detection in the Cloud: Detecting Security Incidents via Machine Learning. Commun. *Comput. Inf. Sci.*, 379, 103-116, 2013.

15. Siva Kumar, R.S., Wicker, A., Swann, M., Practical Machine Learning for Cloud Intrusion Detection. *ACM*, 2017.

16. Omotunde, A., Oludele, A., Kuyoro, S., Chigozirim, A., Survey of Cloud Computing Issues at Implementation Level. *J. Emerg. Trends Comput. Inf. Sci.*, 4, 1, 90–96 2013.

17. Sundharakumar, K.B., Dhivya, S., Mohanavalli, S., Vinob Chander, R., Cloud Based Fuzzy Healthcare System. *Proc. Comput. Sci.*, 50, 2015.

18. Sun, Y., Zhang, J., Xiong, Y., Zhu, G., Data Security and Privacy in Cloud Computing. *Int. J. Distrib. Sens. Netw.*, 9, 3, 157, July 2014.

19. Sharma, R., Gourisaria, M.K., Patra, S.S., Cloud Computing—Security, Issues, and Solutions, in: *Communication Software and Networks. Lecture Notes in Networks and Systems*, vol. 134, S.C. Satapathy, V. Bhateja, M. Ramakrishna Murty, N. Gia Nhu, J. Kotti (Eds.), Springer, Singapore, 2021, https://doi.org/10.1007/978-981-15-5397-4_70.

20. Harfoushi, O. and Obiedat, R., Security in Cloud Computing Using Hash Algorithm: A Neural Cloud Data Security Model. *Mod. Appl. Sci.*, 12, 143, 2018, 10.5539/mas.v12n6p143.

21. Ghosh, P., Hasan, M.H., Atik, S.T., Jabiullah, M.I., A Variable Length Key Based Cryptographic Approach on Cloud Data. 2019 *International Conference on Information Technology (ICIT)*, pp. 285–290, 2019.

22. Hassan, W., Chou, T.-S., Tamer, O., Pickard, J., Appiah-Kubi, P., Pagliari, L., Cloud Computing survey on services, enhancements and challenges in the era of machine learning and data science. *Int. J. Inf. Commun. Technol. (IJ-ICT)*, 9, 117–139, 2020, 10.11591/ijict.v9i2.

23. Al-Khateeb, B., Mahmood, M., Alwash, W.M., Review of Neural Networks Contribution in Network Security. *J. Adv. Res. Dyn. Control Syst.*, 4(11), pp. 1-22, 2019.
24. Hitaswi, N. and K. Chandrasekaran, A bio-inspired model to provide data security in cloud storage. *2016 International Conference on Information Technology (InCITe) - The Next Generation IT Summit on the Theme - Internet of Things: Connect your Worlds,* 203–208, 2016.
25. Almorsy, M., Grundy, J., Ibrahim, A.S., Collaboration- Based Cloud Computing Security Management Framework. *IEEE Conference of cloud computing,* Washington (DC), pp. 364–371, 2011.
26. Srimani, P. and Nasir, S., *A Textbook on Automata Theory,* Foundation Books, Cambridge University Press India Private Ltd., 2007.
27. Ganesan, P., Priyanka, B.R., Sheikh, M., Murthy, D.H.R., Patra, G.K., A secure key exchange protocol using link weights and dynamic tree parity machine (TPM). *ACCENTS Trans. Inf. Secur.*, 2, 8, 2017, http://dx.doi.org/10.19101/TIS.2017.2800.

6

An Efficient Intrusion Detection System on Various Datasets Using Machine Learning Techniques

Debraj Chatterjee

Department of CSE, Techno International New Town, Kolkata, India

Abstract

The sudden surge in the relentless usage of networks in the last few years has compelled the creation of Intrusion Detection Systems (IDSs), which are distinctively used to identify various irregularities and outbreaks persisting in these networks. To eradicate the existing problems of IDSs, various machine learning and data mining techniques are being employed to ease the detection process. This work aims to traverse through the various IDSs and some state-of-the-art machine learning classifiers that can be deployed to enhance the performance of the IDSs. The author also proposes a machine learning classifier–based model of an effective IDS that can detect a network good or bad with the help of different machine learning techniques. The Logistic Regression, Naïve Bayes, Stochastic Gradient Descent, K-Nearest Neighbours, Decision Tree, Random Forest, and Support Vector Machine classifiers have been implemented to calculate the accuracy of the models. Popular yet standard datasets KDD 1999, NSL KDD, and DARPA have been used for the implementation. The model gives a permissible accuracy of over 80% when tested for each of the attacks.

Keywords: Network, attacks, intrusion, detection, feature selection, machine learning, accuracy

6.1 Introduction

With the vast increase of networks and its associated ancillaries, maintaining the security of these networks is a big issue. It is implied that an attack of any manner in the network can lead to a loss, however small it might be. In an organization, it is always anticipated that there will never arise a situation in which the security is breached through any means. Maintaining security should be one of the top priorities of any organization that plan to run fruitfully in the long run. Compared to the amount of security trespassing mechanisms that has been rising from attackers, the market has been substantial enough to deploy a good number of tools which can detect attacks in the networks from intruders. Generally, various methods like firewalls, spam filters, and anti-malware programs are arranged to save the terminals from intruders. Keeping the security line of control intact is one of the

Email: debuchat08@gmail.com

Rajdeep Chakraborty, Anupam Ghosh and Jyotsna Kumar Mandal (eds.) Machine Learning Techniques and Analytics for Cloud Security, (103–128) © 2022 Scrivener Publishing LLC

major concerns of organizations worldwide, irrespective of its size. Other than the popularity of the mentioned attack prevention systems, the network fraternity has seen the rise of a superior tool named Intrusion Detection System (IDS) [1] in recent times. Just like the traffic police who maintain the traffic of the road and reports of any unwanted incident to its immediate superior, the same happens in case of IDS. IDS may be termed as a program utilized to identify the overall scenario of the passage through the particular network and which subsequently awakes the user when an illegal admission takes place. By implementing such attack identification systems, the attacks generating within the network and those that have by some means skipped through the firewall can be alerted to the administrator. As no network security is infallible and neither is any firewall, intruders are on the constant search for devising mechanisms to intrude into the network and dodge the precautions made at entry points. The main aim of arranging IDSs in a system is that through it, the company is made aware of the presence of wary activities in the network. Hence, the concerned person can take proper action to prevent further entry of the attack. Referring to the current situation of the world, there has been a revolution in digitization. Each transaction in all types of business is bound to go online and hence any minor unwanted malicious behavior in the network should be monitored. Shielding is becoming a necessity with the incessant rise of online banking and e-commerce business. Monitoring must be done in both the network level and within the host machine also.

According to study the use of traditional methods responds to selective attacks. Though sometimes, passive threats also arise and for which a generalized system can be prepared that will detect and treat all attacks equally. Hence, the idea of machine learning technique is applied for intrusion detection. Though many machine learning techniques like SVM and feedforward networks are having some loopholes like time factor or size of data access, but ultimately by reducing redundancy or false negative alarms, the accuracy becomes higher. This work hence implements various hyper-parametric state-of-the-art machine learning classifiers and find out the accuracy after executing them with three different datasets.

The rest of the manuscript is arranged as follows: Section 6.2 contains the motivation and justification of the work done. Section 6.3 contains brief descriptions about the terms that are related to IDSs. Section 6.4 mentions some of the intrusion attacks on cloud environment. Section 6.5 contains the literature survey of the work done. Section 6.6 describes the proposed methodology along with its implementation details followed by Section 6.7 containing the comparative results executed on the datasets. Finally, Section 6.8 contains the conclusion and future scope.

6.2 Motivation and Justification of the Proposed Work

With the growth of new technologies and ecommerce, it was observed that threats and suspicious attacks increased a lot. The intruders or hackers with the hacking tools are invading any system profusely. The attackers by using a camouflage enter through the backdoor of the network to gain access of the system. This results in a huge data loss as well as security breach which can inadvertently lead to a breakdown of the organization. The primary goal to stop this unauthorized access is tightening the security. This is the main reason why the author decided to work in this field to devise methods to efficiently handle intrusions in computer networks through latest technologies.

IDS and IPS came into being to encounter the attacks made to the vulnerabilities in the infrastructure securities. As traditional mechanism to secure networks is not capable of effectively identifying security breaches, the author prioritizes the proposal of IDS to investigate and identify the security of the system. As it is inherent that IDS deal with a lot of data, machine learning techniques are utilized to deal with the huge. Clustering techniques like KNN [2], Naïve Bayes [3], and SVM [4] are widely used for the construction of IDS. But the exact machine learning algorithm that is to be used in a particular problem is entirely dependent on the nature of the data set that is used. Hence, the usage of the machine learning classifiers has been stressed in this work. It is anticipated that this can solve the persisting problem of unavailability of proper benchmarked dataset in the field of intrusion detection or detection of attacks in networks.

6.3   Terminology Related to IDS

Theoretically, IDS is the technique which is able to detect the occurrence of invasive activities. It includes all the methods which are utilized to search for unauthorized access within a network and its components. Hence, a brief description of the terms associated with IDS is presented in the section below.

6.3.1   Network

Network is an amalgamation of threads or wires connecting different machines such as computers [5]. It can be hailed as a connection through twisted pair cables, telephone lines, radio waves, satellites, or optical fibre cables. It basically is a man-made system having certain patterns or topologies. Some examples of topologies are ring, bus, mesh, tree, and star. The end-to-end connection established in networks helps in transmitting or receiving information to and from various devices within the networks. Reportedly, the first network was designed by the United States Department of Defence and it was named as the Advanced Research Projects Agency Network (ARPANET) [6]. Currently, there are several network technologies like LAN, MAN, WAN, IAN, SAN, WLAN, GAN, PAN, and CAN [7].

6.3.2   Network Traffic

Network traffic and its consequent analysis are very important to strengthen the network by identifying and averting obstruction and searching suspicious data packets by detecting inconsistencies. It is responsible for displaying the amount of data transferring in the network within a specified time. Generally, the data present in the network is encapsulated in form of packets. In order to measure the efficiency of a network through controlling and simulation, network traffic plays an important role [8]. Quality of service greatly depends on the existing network traffic. Network traffic can be classified into busy traffic where the consumption of bandwidth is high, interactive traffic where prioritization of bandwidth on application is necessary, and non-real time traffic where utilization of bandwidth is during working hours. Regular traffic analysis has taken a toll in recent times as they result in providing proper network security.

6.3.3 Intrusion

Anomaly and abnormality in network traffic can be termed as intrusion which directly threatens the entire security system of an organization. The network intrusion is basically the access of a system by an unauthorized user. This access without having any prior defence breaches the security of the system which results in loss of information [9]. Some of the well-known attacks are Asymmetric routing, Buffer overflow, Common gateway interface attack, Protocol specific attack, Traffic flooding, Trojans, and Worms [10–14]. Through these attacks, they invade into the file repositories or overload the system server and thus break the smooth flow of data packets.

6.3.4 Intrusion Detection System

An IDS can be said to be a tool or software or a technology to monitor intrusion in network traffic [15]. Various malicious or unwanted activities occur in a system for which the systems are thoroughly scanned. It detects the threat that occurs in the communication path of the network. It analyzes both inbound and outbound network traffic by checking the threats. If there are any types of abnormalities regarding breaching of network, then it eventually gives an alert. This malicious threat or violation is reported either to an administrator or stored centrally using a security information and event management (SIEM) system. A SIEM system checks the threats from the stored collection and segregates the result from false alarms. Figure 6.1 represents the functionalities IDS in a nutshell.

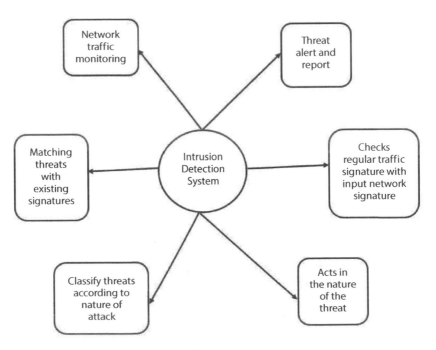

Figure 6.1 Intrusion detection system in a nutshell.

There are several tools available for IDS [16]. Some of them are as follows:

Snort: It was developed by Cisco. It is an open-source tool which can be easily installed in windows operating system. It is the leading network-based IDS software which also acts as an intrusion prevention system (IPS). There are three modes of Snort. They are Sniffer mode, Packet logger, and Intrusion detection.

OSSEC: It is known as open-source host IDS. It is entirely free to use in both windows operating system and Linux operating system. The prime focus of it is the log files installation location. It checks all the log files for error detection before concluding. It monitors the attempt to enter the root location in Linux. The main features of OSSEC are Log file analyzer, Free policies and Alerting system.

Suricata: It is an alternative to snort. The main advantage is that it collects data at the application layer. It works in the application layer but also monitors the lower-level protocol activity such as ICMP, TCP, and UDP. It also inspects instantaneous traffic for several network applications that includes FTP and HTTP. It also focuses on the DNS calls and the requests made by HTTP.

Zeek: It was previously known as BRO. Though it is a free network IDS, it also monitors the network traffic. There are two phases of Zeek: traffic logging and analysis. A major advantage of Zeek is that the packet analysis operates on the application layer. This provides a clear understanding of packets to analyze network protocol activity. The main features of Zeek are signature detection and anomaly analysis. It can be used in Unix, Linux, and Mac operating system.

Sagan: It is a host-based IDS tool for log analysis. It can be available freely and an alternative for OSSEC. Sagan is independent of dedicated hardware. It can analyze both network traffic data and host logs. It also helps to monitor the geographical location of the suspicious IP addresses.

Security Onion: Its idea is to monitor the network for suspicious activities and check the security of the network for any unexpected occurrences.

AIDE: The Advanced Intrusion Detection Environment is a host IDS. It is used in operating systems like Unix, Linux, and Mac. It monitors and rolls back any unauthorized changes done in the system.

OpenWIPS-NG: It is a wireless network IPS that runs on Linux. It is a free software. After gathering information through wireless channel by the server, the intrusion pattern is detected and monitored by the analysis engine in the server program.

Samhain: It is a simple host-based IDS. It can be carried out in more than one host. It uses a centralized data gathering by monitoring on the events identified by the agents present on each host. The agents in the individual system monitors the port and log files. Samhain uses a technology, known as steganography, to prevent its processes from the attack or manipulation of log files by unauthorized users. It is used in operating systems like Linux, Unix, and Mac OS.

Fail2Ban: It is a simple and free host-based IDS. It focuses mainly on identifying problematic events recorded in logs. Excessive login failure is an example of this. If any suspicious actions are reported, then the system blocks the IP address.

6.3.4.1   Various Types of IDS

IDS can be classified into five categories depending on the types of nature of incident they monitor and the type of attack they handle:

1. Network Intrusion Detection System (NIDS) [17]:
   It is placed within the network to analyze traffic from all devices on the network. It inspects the traffic on the entire network and matches the traffic that is forwarded on the subnets to the set of known attacks. Once an attack is detected or abnormalities are observed, the alert is transferred to the administrator. It is installed on the subnet where firewalls are present to look at if somebody is trying to crack the firewall.
2. Host Intrusion Detection System (HIDS) [18, 19]:
   It operates on individual hosts or devices on the network. It examines both the arriving and departing packets from the device only. If any irregularities or abnormalities come, then it will notify the administrator. It takes a view of the existing files in the system and goes for a comparison with the previous ones. If any change in the file system were done, then the administrator receives an alert.
3. Protocol-based Intrusion Detection System (PIDS) [20]:
   It consists of a system that controls and check the protocol between a device and a server. Its aim is to secure the web server by frequent monitoring of the HTTPS protocol.
4. Application Protocol-based Intrusion Detection System (APIDS) [21]:
   This system resides within a group of servers. The intrusion in this case is identified by thorough checking and monitoring the communication over the specific protocols.
5. Hybrid Intrusion Detection System [22]:
   This system is an amalgamation of many approaches of the IDS where host is merged with network information to create a thorough view of the network system. It is more effective than other IDSs.

Table 6.1 illustrates a comparative table of NIDS and HIDS based on various criteria.

6.3.4.2   Working Methodology of IDS

An IDS detects planned and prospective attacks based on two methodologies.

Signature-Based Detection
In this method [23, 24], it compares signatures with monitored actions to detect probable events. If by default any of the event matches, then immediately it issues an alert.

Table 6.1 Comparative table of NIDS and HIDS.

Type of IDS	Consists of	Area to be monitored	Advantages and Disadvantages
NIDS	A network sensor along with a Network Interface Card incorporated on the boundary of a network to be able to track the entire network.	Monitors the entire network or the segment in whose boundary the NIDS has been placed.	• Flexible and portable compared to other IDSs and is generally self-regulating by nature. • Easier to implement and incorporate in networks. • Auto-updation of attacks is not possible in many cases.
HIDS	Sensors which are installed in particular machines which is to be monitored.	Keeps track for trespassing in the workplace where it has been placed.	• Versatile in many cases as they are able to function in encrypted situations also. • Unable to monitor multiple workstations at a single time. • Can be rendered inoperative by intruders easily

The advantage of this detection is that it gives more accuracy and generates an alarm easily understandable by user. The probable events or alerts can be a malware, server attack, or network attack. Attackers frequently change information regarding place of attack or possible occurrences of the attack to access the signature-based IDS which results in loss of signature from the database. If the database is large, then processing speed increases to analyze the workflow.

Anomaly-Based Detection

This method [25, 26] compares characteristics of regular activity with monitored events to detect the substantial deviations. It looks for unknown attacks that signature-based IDS were unable to check. It frequently observes and compares the network traffic with the statistical model. If any fault or breaching occurs, then the admin receives and alert. Anomaly-based IDS network behavior are always predictable and can easily be guessed which one is a good traffic and which one is bad traffic. One disadvantage of anomaly-based IDS is that it looks at the nature of traffic and not the payload. If a network is operating on a basic pattern, then the IDS faces problems of guessing which traffic to flag. Generally, most IDSs nowadays work on the hybrid models combining both signature-based and anomaly-based detection systems. While signature-based IDSs match the attack faced to a database of identified intrusion techniques, anomaly-based IDSs work on the principle of searching for doubtful behavior in the network to identify threats. Table 6.2 illustrates a comparative table of the above mentioned intrusion detection mechanisms.

6.3.4.3 Characteristics of IDS

• It analyzes and monitors different activities of system. Before any real damage occurs to a system, it catches the unauthenticated user.

Table 6.2 Comparative table of signature-based and anomaly-based IDS.

Type of IDS	Characteristics	Advantages	Disadvantages
Signature-Based IDS	It attempts to track intrusion by matching patterns on trials of attacks made to the system. Based on the assumption of various attempts made on the system, the intrusion is detected.	• Simple and efficient in nature • Less time is required.	• A matching pattern needs to exist in order to identify the attack. • Updation of new attacks requires unnecessary time wastage caused after the attack. • Excess traffic in the network may lead to problem as the method requires one-to-one packet inspection.
Anomaly-Based IDS	It prioritizes abnormal intrusions focussing mainly on the software aspects. It is specifically used to track the veracity of the data during the attack.	• There is no necessity for upgradation of attacks in the database. • Extensive usage of the system leads to more efficiency in identifying threats. • Little or no maintenance is required.	• While the system is creating its profile based on the attacks, the system can be susceptible for intrusion. • Attacks poised as normal traffic may lead to no alarm generation in the system.

- If any notification regarding security arises, then it generates an alarm to inform security admin. The key objectives for an IDS implementation are to decrease risk, detect error, enhance network, give a view to threat levels, and alter user behavior.
- It also detects breaches and faults in system configuration. It needs human or system interaction to work as it does not act on its own.
- If any alteration in the data files occurs, then the IDS detects it and spontaneously reports to the admin. Deciding where to set the probes is not easy. It can be placed outside the firewall tocollect data on attacks from the Internet, but normally they are placed near servers, or interfaces between safe regions.
- An IDS helps to explore odd traffic on the network. It is mainly used in an investigated mode but can also be used in a defensive mode (through interrupting system calls for the host-based result or avoiding the network product). It reviews the reliability of the data files and the system.

6.3.4.4   Advantages of IDS

There are numerous advantages of IDS. IDSs when placed tactically over a network, deploying appropriate hardware sensors or if deployed in a single system can efficiently supervise trespassing activities within a network. Not only that attacks are identified, but also patterns of security infringements are also detected leading to a low-risk network system. The following points may be considered as advantages of IDS:

1. It allows admin to organize and analyze the logs and events done in the system.
2. Provides a user-friendly system for non-expert users.
3. It can detect any change occurring in the data file.
4. It reacts very first by blocking the intruders breaching into the system by giving an alert to the admin.
5. It easily recognizes the intruder and the data files altered by the intruder time to time.
6. The HIDS monitors and analyze encrypted data and by which it informs whether an intrusion will occur or not.
7. As host IDS never uses extra hardware facility, hence it is easy to use.
8. Wireless IDS manages the wireless protocol activity.

6.3.4.5   Disadvantages of IDS

The major disadvantage of IDS is that it secures the entire network when it fails to identify the source of the intrusion. It also needs the permission to access the entire network to perform monitoring for intrusion. In many cases, IDS requires immense amount of storage space. Apart from these, the following maybe considered as the disadvantages of IDS:

1. Sometimes, single information does not give a clear view of the intruder.
2. One main disadvantage is that whether the message was sent securely or not is unclear.
3. High chances of false alarm can be observed due to fixed user profile.
4. If the operating system fails, then the host intrusion detection also fails.
5. The host IDS fails to monitor denial-of-service (DoS) attack.
6. The network IDS cannot analyze or detect encrypted traffic.
7. The network IDS has a restricted view on the host system.

6.3.5   Intrusion Prevention System (IPS)

The IPS helps in monitoring malicious activities, identify them, gather information about those activities, and take actions to block them. Here, IDS also operate on the network traffic for monitoring the activities. Hence, IPS [27] is an extended version of the IDS.

The IPS is divided into four categories as follows.

6.3.5.1   Network-Based Intrusion Prevention System (NIPS)

It examines the entire network for unwanted traffic by investigating the protocol activity. It is the system used for monitoring a network as well as protecting the reliability, privacy, and accessibility of a network. It protects the network from various risks, such as DoS and unauthorized access or usage of the network.

6.3.5.2   Wireless Intrusion Prevention System (WIPS)

It investigates a wireless network for unwanted traffic by checking the wireless networking protocols. This system observes network connections for the trait of a malicious attack, links a series of actions to identify an unwanted attack, and takes specified actions to prevent the malicious attack.

6.3.5.3   Network Behavior Analysis (NBA)

It monitors the network traffic to recognize risks that breaks the normal flow of traffic. An example of such risk is distributed DoS (DDoS) attacks and violations of policy. It is a system for network monitoring that certifies the security of a private network. This analysis improves network safety by acutely monitoring traffic for suspicious activity. Traditional ways of securing a network against malicious data involves signature detection, data packet testing, and periodic checking of infected sites.

6.3.5.4   Host-Based Intrusion Prevention System (HIPS)

It checks the activities that are occurring inside a host. If any threats are scanned, then it immediately takes actions within that host. The HIPS is a software package built inside the system. It runs on a single host having a problem. This method is used to protect systems containing essential data against known as well as unknown malicious threats and attacks. This system frequently verifies the traits of a particular host and the several actions that appear inside the host for irregular activities. There are some detection methods for IPS. Some of them are as follows:

Signature-Based Detection
It is a method where a unique key is created on a recognized risk so that the risk can be detected further. A distinct form of a code pattern can be used for scanning code or it may be simply a characteristic of a recognized infected file. If that specific form is detected again, then the file is recognized as infected one. It manages packets in the network with the help of signatures. It compares the packets with existing patterns.

Statistical Anomaly-Based Detection
This method analyzes network traffic and compares it with a pre-existing one baseline. The work of this baseline is to identify which is suitable for the network and with respect to that which protocol is to be used. If the baseline is not configured properly, then it might give a false alert.

Stateful Protocol Analysis Detection
This method identifies deviation of protocols by comparing monitored events with existing ones showing no threat or risks. The crucial features of it are that it detects sudden change in pattern of commands and checks for regular protocol analysis.

6.3.6   Comparison of IPS With IDS/Relation Between IDS and IPS

The difference between IPS with IDSs is as follows:

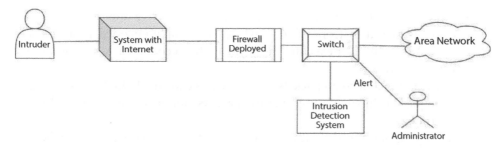

Figure 6.2 (a) Basic architecture of intrusion detection system (IDS).

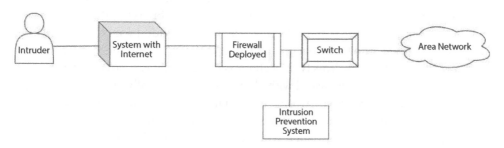

Figure 6.2 (b) Basic architecture of intrusion prevention system (IPS).

1. IDSs are monitoring and detection tool, whereas IPSs are a control system that can actively prevent or block intrusions that are detected.
2. IDS cannot take actions on their own, whereas IPS can take actions by sending an alarm, dropping the identified malicious packets, re-establishing a connection, or preventing traffic from the infected IP address.
3. IDS requires the intervention of another system or human to check the results, whereas IPS helps in checking cyclic redundancy check (CRC) errors, reduces TCP issues, and removes unnecessary transport layer and network layer options.
4. Both IDS and IPS interpret network packets and relate the contents to a known threat database.

Figures 6.2a and b depict the difference in the basic architecture of IDS and IPs.

6.3.7 Different Methods of Evasion in Networks

An IDS can be evaded in many ways. Without informing the host, an attacker can easily manipulate the host. Some of the evading methods are described as follows:

1. Encoding and encryption: The IDS should be aware of all the encrypted packets. But the IDSs were unable to read the attacks of some protocols like HTTPs unless it has a copy of the private key that was previously used by the server. The server uses this private key for encrypting the communication. If the signatures were unable to match with the traffic, then attackers invade the system.

2. Polymorphism: The attacker forms a series of innovative attack patterns. A decoder is placed in front of the payload and finally encoded in a typical pattern. When the user executes the payload, the decoder starts its work thus affecting the IDS.

3. Fragmentation and small packets: The attackers can attack the IDS by changing the packets in such a way that the packets can be splitted into multiple small fragments.

4. Overlapping of fragments: It is an evasion process of overlapping the TCP/IP packets sequence number. There is a sequence of the TCP packets where the first packet and the second packets are containing some bytes which are different. If the IDS were unable to match this TCP stream, then it can be easily manipulated by inserting malicious data, thus breaking the signature.

5. Protocol ambiguities: If the IDS was unable to provide proper TCP and IP protocols, then ambiguity occurs, and attackers can invade the system easily.

6. Low bandwidth attack: This type of attack is basically a password cracker where the hacker matches a password with all the users individually. If by any how the user makes a password type wrong, then it takes the fault and matches it.

7. CPU exhaustion: This is DoS attack. Here, captured packets are stored in a buffer if the CPU is overloaded with previous packets. With prolonged wait of the new packets, they eventually lead to packet drop. The attacker matches the pattern of the incoming and outgoing packets thus making the CPU time maximum and overloads it.

8. Memory exhaustion: Here, the signatures of certain malicious packets are monitored and then compared. The IDS monitors TCP blocks (TCB) that contain information of the protocol in chunks inside the memory. Many times, when transferring of data in the memory packets are dropped which leads to memory exhaustion and attacker at this point overloads the memory by repetitive connections of TCP or fragmenting larger packets into smaller ones. This is an example of DoS attack.

9. Operator fatigue: Here, the attacker generates huge alert signatures. Thus, threat increases in the IDS. But it will not hamper the IDS where the application protocol context is present.

6.4   Intrusion Attacks on Cloud Environment

Cloud computing refers to the mechanism that allows easy, demand-based entry to a network which contains a shared pool of organized computing sources that can be readily prepared and utilized with minimum amount of manpower involvement or service supplier dealings [28]. Due to the virtualization idea, cloud security works on standard internet protocols. This gives a loophole as well as a weakness in the cloud environment and thus unauthenticated users breach the system. The use of firewall is a traditional method which protects the system from the access of the unauthenticated users by allowing or blocking IP addresses. But it becomes hard to detect the insider attacks or threats as they are too complicated. Thus, the idea of IDS comes into limelight for cloud security. Some of the IDS for cloud security are as follows:

1. Host Intrusion Detection System

   This IDS monitors and inspects the accumulated data like system calls, network activities, and type of host file system from a particular host. It also monitors the changes done in the host file system or unusual behavior of the system. If it observes any change, then it confirms and report to the admin that an attack or a threat is present in the host [29]. For the cloud security, it monitors keenly on the log files, access control, and the login phase of the user.

2. Network Intrusion Detection System

   This IDS aims to identify unwanted activities like DoS attacks, scanning of ports and accessing system in an unauthenticated way. The data absorbed first from the network and scanned thoroughly. Through rigorous checking, it is matched with some known threats in real time analysis. It utilizes both signature-based and anomaly-based intrusion detection procedure. But if a network is already encrypted, then NIDS cannot work on that network. It mainly highlights IP monitoring for detecting intrusion on individual packets. One disadvantage of network intrusion in cloud is that it has inadequate access within the host system. It is the sole responsibility of the cloud provider or owner to install the network intrusion detection system inside.

3. Distributed Intrusion Detection System

   It is a combination of all IDS which works on large networks. There can be a master server which controls or monitors all the other machines or systems or there can be a connection between individual ones. They gather and filter the information received from the systems and produce it to a uniform method which is then transferred to the key analyzer. Both anomaly- and signature-based procedures are used for analyzing the information. The advantage of using a distributed intrusion detection system is that it can be applied in both host system and acting server processing the information in a cloud.

4. Hypervisor-Based IDS

   A hypervisor can also be said to be a virtual machine (VM) monitor. It is software for creating VMs. A hypervisor shares its resources like memory and thus forms a relation between one host with multiple guest VMs. This system specifically designed for hypervisors which monitors and identifies network communications between the VMs. This technique is one of the best for detecting intrusion or breach in cloud environment.

   Usually, intrusion detection is performed at the network layer in case of general environments. Unprocessed data is collected, and prototype matched for the relevant type of signature-based or anomaly-based attacks. But this is not possible for cloud environments. The limitation of clouds resists the users from collecting raw data for further matching [30]. Hence, the nature of intrusion detection always depends on the type of cloud service that is being used.

   a) Software as a Service (SaaS): Unfortunately, the service providers of SaaS extensively perform detection of intrusion.

   b) Platform as a Service (PaaS): It works almost same as SaaS, where the provider is responsible for most of the detection for trespassing within the cloud, but certain mechanisms can be deployed wherefrom monitoring of the network can be done.

c) Infrastructure as a Service (IaaS): This is the only method through which consumers get a maximum opportunity of deploying intrusion detection within networks. The monitoring is generally done in the VM, host system, virtual network as well as in the traditional network.

6.5   Comparative Studies

Researchers are constantly on the move to devise latest mechanisms to propose efficient IDSs. Table 6.3 presents a tabular view of few of the latest research made in this field.

Table 6.3   Some of the works pertaining to IDS in recent years.

Ref. no.	Aim of the work	Methodologies used	Dataset	Outcome, future scope, and limitations
[31]	For calculating and improving the classification accuracy by reducing false positive rate, an ensemble method for intrusion detection system is used.	A unique idea of the Bagging method along with REP Tree is used for implementing intrusion detection system.	The updated version of KDD99 dataset, that is, NSL-KDD dataset has been used.	It can be said that the Bagging machine learning method detects highest classification accuracy on the NSL-KDD dataset. But in this method only one data set was taken for the test.
[32]	To identify the number of clusters by lessening the false negative rate.	With K-means algorithm and unsupervised machine learning technique, the Intrusion Detection was carried out. Here, the proposed model follows a signature-based approach along with the K-means clustering.	Due to the dearth of latest datasets, the NSL-KDD dataset was used.	When the correct number of clusters is identified, then the efficiency rate of the system increases, whereas fluctuations in the cluster number leads to a loss in efficiency. But if the number of clusters is described previously, then it can run properly; otherwise, it will be very complex.

(Continued)

Table 6.3 Some of the works pertaining to IDS in recent years. (*Continued*)

Ref. no.	Aim of the work	Methodologies used	Dataset	Outcome, future scope, and limitations
[33]	The main aim is to reduce the attack before it occurs and identify the threats properly. The idea is to find the anomalies present in the system and to reduce the training time by preparing a high-speed algorithm.	In this work, an idea of outlier detection technique is used where the dataset is evaluated by a factor called the NOF. Large datasets are utilized for this process of intrusion detection.	Self-extracted datasets from Big data–enabled systems were collected and compared to the popular KDD dataset to show the efficiency of the proposed model.	Due to some issues like excess training time, low accuracy checking and attack classification, high speed model comes into. The proposed model for IDS is giving a higher performance speed and detecting all the anomaly data present in the network system. This idea is better than the remaining approaches of machine learning.
[34]	To find the best possible set of characteristics with the help of methods like discretized differential evolution (DDE) and C4.5 ML.	Decision Trees and Differential Evolution methods have been used in the proposed model.	The standardized NSL-KDD Cup'99 dataset was used.	The proposed method was able to efficiently identify sixteen features to be able to categorize the associations. The model yielded an accuracy of 88.73% while detecting novel attacks. As a limitation to the work, the generalization of the features was required to be eradicated in future work. Also, live networks could be explored to retrieve connections.

(*Continued*)

Table 6.3 Some of the works pertaining to IDS in recent years. (*Continued*)

Ref. no.	Aim of the work	Methodologies used	Dataset	Outcome, future scope, and limitations
[35]	A network intrusion detection is proposed with constructive approach to existing extreme learning (C-ELM) machines in which concealed neurons are added in such a augmented way that the hidden neurons may not be recreated from scratch every time that it is being tested.	Three-layer structure is used comprising of inlet, concealed and outlet layers. Random weights were taken as input along with the bias.	The NID dataset has been used but comparisons have also been made with the mostly used KDD Cup'99 dataset.	It was anticipated that the adaptive method used in adding the neurons would save time and cost of composing an efficient C-ELM. The only drawback of the method is that much amount of time is consumed to find the exact number of hidden neurons through trial-and-error method.
[36]	Machine Learning–based techniques have been applied to detect interference and to afford more security-based solutions to cloud-based environments.	Logistic Regression and propagation methods have been deployed to find out the occurrence of attacks in the network.	Malware and non-malware samples from Packet storm were examined with the proposed method.	Attacks are efficiently detected in real time with the help of machine learning mechanisms through the use of anomaly-based recognition schemes. The work could further be implemented with deep learning techniques to identify an attack.

(*Continued*)

Table 6.3 Some of the works pertaining to IDS in recent years. (*Continued*)

Ref. no.	Aim of the work	Methodologies used	Dataset	Outcome, future scope, and limitations
[37]	An effective IDS has been proposed based on machine learning	An assortment of classifiers and feature selection methods were used to detect attacks in the dataset.	NSL-KDD, the adapted version of the KDD99 dataset, was reduced and used for the purpose.	Significant accuracy was achieved implementing the mix of the classifiers and selection techniques. A requirement of a system which can efficiently detect an attack in the entire dataset can be treated as a future scope of this work.
[38]	To create a Machine Learning–supported IDS to survey the problem of invasion identification in industrial IOT devices.	A testbed had been developed impersonating an actual industrial plant. Attacks have been performed deliberately to gather real data for the purpose.	The dataset was gathered through Argus and Wireshark network instruments.	This work was the first to initiate machine learning oriented IDS in SCADA systems for backdoor attacks. A hybrid model implementing various types of algorithms is referred to as a future scope in this work.

(*Continued*)

Table 6.3 Some of the works pertaining to IDS in recent years. (*Continued*)

Ref. no.	Aim of the work	Methodologies used	Dataset	Outcome, future scope, and limitations
[39]	To authenticate and create a model for intrusion detection in wireless sensor networks using Automated Validation of Internet Security Protocols and Applications (AVISPA) tool and a high-level protocol specification language (HLPSL) language.	Supervised machine learning algorithm is used considering back-ends like OFMC, CL-AtSe, SATMC, and TA4SP as a protocol analyzer.	Raw data is taken as input and fed to the system, maybe in the form of a packet.	The system is proposed to offer a threat analysis in the case of wireless sensor networks with the help of security verification tool.
[40]	Decision Tree and rule-based algorithms are used to devise a new intrusion detection method to help efficiently identify attacks within the system.	REP Tree, JRip algorithm, and Forest PA classifiers which are widely recognized are used in the work.	CICIDS2017 dataset has been considered and compared to other existing datasets in this field.	Both regular and irregular attacks can be identified with a low false alarm rate and high detection rate. The method resulted in high accuracy with the dataset.

6.6   Proposed Methodology

It has been observed that the huge rise of data generated from existing networks and its peripherals compels the usage of machine learning mechanisms on IDSs for proficient identification of attacks within the system. The machine learning–based model with an assortment of classifiers which has been used in this paper has been illustrated in Figure 6.3.

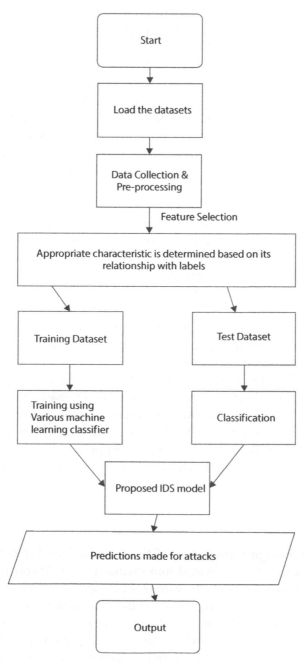

Figure 6.3 The flowchart of the proposed IDS used in this work.

Three standard datasets have been used in this work to establish the result variation in the proposed model, namely, the DARPA 2000, KDD Cup'99, and the improvised NSL-KDD [41]. While KDD99 is the characteristic removed version of DARPA dataset, NSL-KDD is eliminated of redundancy abolishing the chance of the classifiers being biased while producing the results. As these are very commonly used datasets, much description about the same is not included here. The attacks in the datasets are generalized and categorized into four classes of DoS attack, Probe attack, User-to-Root attack (U2R), and Remote-to-Local attack (R2L) [42]. The DoS attack is a threat where the target machine is over flooded with trash information and thus making the expected users to be on a hold by crashing the system or shutting down the network.

The probe is a threat or an attack where the hacker tries to detect an open port. It is created in such a way that the target identifies it and informs it with a familiar identification. The hacker then tries to find out the details of the detector and invade in the system. A U2R attack first gains access over the remote system as a normal user through TELNET. Gradually with a combination of patterns, it tries to access the system as a super-user. A R2L attack is like the U2R attack but is more limited to its work. Here, the intruder sends a packet to the target with the intention of making the host vulnerable to attack by disclosing all the target systems information.

The data in all the cases has initially been pre-processed for transforming of the unqualified data into its numerical counterpart and ultimately helping enhance the performance of the classifiers. The diminution of the data has been performed by Principal Component Analysis to convert the dataset into a compact form. This particular method has been chosen as though PCA reduces the number of variables in a data set, it performs the trick by retaining the maximum amount of data possible. PCA standardizes the continuous values of the data set so that there is equal contribution of all the variables to the analysis. Then, the co-variance matrix is computed to get the idea of how the input variables are varying from the mean in comparison to its peers. The eigen vectors and eigen values are calculated next to find out the principal components of the dataset. By this method, the principal components are found out by representing them in terms of linear components of the input variables. This method is followed by the decision-making phase of abandoning the components which are of comparatively lower significance, leading to the creation of feature vectors. The final step comprises of redistribution of the values from the initial axes to the principal component ones. This method is obtained by performing the multiplication of the transpose of the dataset along with the transpose of the obtained feature vector.

6.7   Result

The datasets are fed through various state-of-the-art classifiers. Etymologically, classification is the method where data is divided into various classes. Through classification, it is easier to depict the classes in which the variables belong. This work presents the comparative result of various state-of-the-art classifiers used in machine learning. The process of classification involves the classifier to be initialized, train it, forecast the target and finally evaluate the model. The hyper-parametric classifiers [43] like Logistic Regression, Naïve Bayes, Stochastic Gradient Descent, K-Nearest Neighbors, Decision Tree, Random Forest, and Support Vector Machine have been implemented in this work. It is to keep in mind that the linear models provide the same output each time the data is fed to the model. In some case of classifiers, random weights are considered, which initially may not be optimum, but on continuous training performed on the model, the results improve. This work intends to present a thorough performance evaluation of different classifiers on the datasets. Out of the classifiers executed in this experiment, Logistic Regression is an algorithm based on machine learning. It is based on a logistic function and is very effective in categorizing as it very well understands the pressure of multiple autonomous variables on a particular output variable. Naïve Bayes algorithm works based on the Bayes theorem assuming that there is no dependency between any pair of characteristics. This is treated as one of the most efficient classifier providing excellent results in innumerable real-time cases. They require a small amount of data and produces result in less amount of time. The stochastic gradient descent classifier is very straightforward and is very well suited for linear models. For neighbor-related classification, the k-Nearest Neighbor classifier computes result for storing instances of the trained data. Decision Tree classifiers are easy to implement and are able to deal with both numbers and classified data. It provides a succession of rules which is eventually used to classify the data. Random Forest Classifier uses the technique of averaging to fit decision trees on multiple data samples. This is an effectual classifier that is responsible for controlling over-fitting and gives more precise results than decision trees. Finally, Support Vector Machine works by embodying trained data in the form of points in space and is divided into different classes which are highly separated from one another. The new samples of data are ultimately mapped to that particular space and the forecast is done depending on the class in which they lie. Tables 6.4a, b, and c illustrate the accuracies obtained on the three different datasets using the above-mentioned classifiers.

Further to exploit the utility of the data, cross-validation has been introduced further in this experiment. Generally, when a machine learning model is created the data is divided

Table 6.4 (a) The accuracies yielded through various state-of-the-art classifiers implemented in DARPA dataset.

Classifiers	Attacks			
	DOS (%)	Probe (%)	U2R (%)	R2L (%)
Logistic Regression	**87**	85	85	83
Naïve Bayes	86	84	86	84
Stochastic Gradient Descent	85	83	84	84
k-Nearest Neighbor	80	79	81	81
Decision Tree	82	81	82	83
Random Forest Classifier	85	82	84	81
Support Vector Machine	86	86	83	83

Table 6.4 (b) The accuracies yielded through various state-of-the-art classifiers implemented in KDD Cup'99 dataset.

Classifiers	Attacks			
	DOS (%)	Probe (%)	U2R (%)	R2L (%)
Logistic Regression	94	94	92	92
Naïve Bayes	94	93	91	93
Stochastic Gradient Descent	92	92	91	92
k-nearest neighbor	89	91	88	91
Decision Tree	92	90	91	92
Random Forest Classifier	93	93	92	91
Support Vector Machine	93	91	92	91

Table 6.4 (c) The accuracies yielded through various state-of-the-art classifiers implemented in NSL-KDD dataset.

Classifiers	Attacks			
	DOS (%)	Probe (%)	U2R (%)	R2L (%)
Logistic Regression	95	92	92	93
Naïve Bayes	93	93	91	92
Stochastic Gradient Descent	92	89	91	90
k-Nearest Neighbor	91	92	92	90
Decision Tree	92	91	90	91
Random Forest Classifier	93	90	88	92
Support Vector Machine	93	93	92	91

into train and test sets. While the set for training is utilized to train the model, the set is used to authenticate the data to be tested. Traditionally, the data is divided into 80% and 20%, and it may vary with 70% and 30%, 90% and 10% also. The difference in the cross-validation method is that multiple divisions are made of the dataset. The number of splits varies from 2, 5, 10, 30, and 50 or any random number of splits. The number of splits is termed as K. The splits or divisions are also called as folds, and hence, a dataset with 10 splits is called as a 10-fold cross-validation. There are various ways in which the folds are

Table 6.5 The accuracies yielded through various state-of-the-art classifiers implemented in NSL-KDD dataset.

	Cross-validation folds				
	2	5	10	30	50
DoS Attack	0.995	0.996	0.9974	0.9968	0.9971
Probe Attack	0.9908	0.992	0.9907	0.9916	0.9909
U-to-R Attack	0.995	0.996	0.9965	0.997	0.9964
R-to-L Attack	0.981	0.988	0.984	0.983	0.9853

created. The simple k-folds method comprises of dividing the dataset into K parts, and the models are trained with up to $(K - 1)$th parts and tested with Kth part. Another method is the leave one out method, in which a model is built using all data in the dataset and the same is done for each data in the dataset. The final testing is done on the chosen dataset. It is to be made sure that the dividing of data into folds is done in such a manner that the whole dataset is properly present within those folds. Though most of the times this is done in a haphazard manner, but in cases where there is large amount of data associated, a proper distribution should be imposed on the dataset. This method is known as stratified cross-validation. Table 6.5 represents the accuracies in decimal places yielded after applying stratified cross-validation on the NSL-KDD dataset. The number of folds has been taken randomly as 2, 5, 10, 30, and 50.

6.8   Conclusion and Future Scope

The comparative tables provide a clear view of the fact that the NSL-KDD dataset performs better that the other two existing datasets. The reason for this might be the elimination of redundancy in the NSL-KDD dataset compared to its earlier KDD Cup'99 datasets. As every work comes with limitations, this also is not an exception. The number of attacks could be further explored in the experiment. As is evident from the table, the logistic regression classifiers show the best performance, but it carries with itself overhead, which is a disadvantage. The most important point of this model is that it is extremely simple and easier to understand.

One of the future works in this field is to prepare a generalized dataset with minimum error and duplicity. More robust mechanisms using deep learning approaches should be applied to efficiently find out attacks in real time. The main challenge in this field lies in collecting and utilizing data in real time and then check for attacks accurately. This work also could be further extended by employing mechanisms to prevent the IDS itself being infected with various attacks. Big data and deep learning can also be deployed to further extend this work.

References

1. Liao, H.J., Lin, C.H.R., Lin, Y.C., Tung, K.Y., Intrusion detection system: A comprehensive review. *J. Netw. Comput. Appl.*, 36, 1, 16–24, 2013.

2. Sameera, N. and Shashi, M., Protocol specific intrusion detection using KNN classifier. *Int. J. Res. Appl. Sci. Eng. Technol. (IJRASET)* 1927–1935, 6, V, 2018.

3. Kannan, A., Maguire Jr., G.Q., Sharma, A., School, Genetic algorithm-based feature selection algorithm for effective intrusion detection in cloud networks, in: *IEEE 12th International Conference on Data Mining Workshops*, pp. 416–423, 2012.

4. Thaseen, I.S. and Kumar, C.A., Intrusion detection model using fusion of chi-square feature selection and multi class SVM. *J. King Saud Univ.-Comp. Info. Sci.*, 1;29, 4, 462–72, 2017.

5. https://en.wikipedia.org/wiki/Internet, Anonymous, Retrieved on 2nd July, 2021.

6. McQuillan, J., Richer, I., Rosen, E., The new routing algorithm for the ARPANET. *IEEE Trans. Commun.*, 28, 5, 711–719, 1980.

7. McQuillan, J., Falk, G., Richer, I., A Review of the Development and Performance of the ARPANET Routing Algorithm. *IEEE Trans. Commun.*, 26, 12, 1802–1811, 1978.

8. Ramamurthy, B., *Design of optical WDM networks: LAN, MAN and WAN architectures*, vol. 603, Springer Science & Business Media, US, 2012.

9. Gábor, S. and Csabai, I., The analogies of highway and computer network traffic. *Physica A: Stat. Mech. Appl.*, 307, 3–4, 516–526, 2002.

10. Starsman, R.S., Asymmetric routing, in: *MILCOM 97 MILCOM 97 Proceedings*, 1997, November, vol. 2, IEEE, pp. 1021–1025.

11. Deckard, J., *Buffer overflow attacks: detect, exploit, prevent*, Elsevier, Amsterdam, Netherlands, 2005.

12. Kruegel, C. and Vigna, G., Anomaly detection of web-based attacks, in: *Proceedings of the 10th ACM conference on Computer and communications security*, 2003, October, pp. 251–261.

13. Salmani, H., Tehranipoor, M., Plusquellic, J., A novel technique for improving hardware trojan detection and reducing trojan activation time. *IEEE Trans. Very Large Scale Integr. (VLSI) Syst.*, 20, 1, 112–125, 2011.

14. Erbschloe, M., *Trojans, worms, and spyware: a computer security professional's guide to malicious code*, Elsevier, Amsterdam, Boston, 2004.

15. Escamilla, T., *Intrusion detection: network security beyond the firewall*, vol. 8, John Wiley, Hoboken, New Jersey, 1998.

16. Alsakran, F., Bendiab, G., Shiaeles, S., Kolokotronis, N., Intrusion detection systems for smart home IoT devices: experimental comparison study, in: *International Symposium on Security in Computing and Communication*, Springer, Singapore, pp. 87–98, 2019, December.

17. Mukherjee, B., Heberlein, L.T., Levitt, K.N., Network intrusion detection. *IEEE Network*, 8, 3, 26–41, 1994.

18. Liu, M., Xue, Z., Xu, X., Zhong, C., Chen, J., Host-based intrusion detection system with system calls: Review and future trends. *ACM Comput. Surv. (CSUR)*, 51, 5, 1–36, 2018.

19. Chawla, A., Lee, B., Fallon, S., Jacob, P., Host based intrusion detection system with combined CNN/RNN model, in: *Joint European Conference on Machine Learning and Knowledge Discovery in Databases*, Springer, Cham, pp. 149–158, 2018, September.

20. Wu, M.F., Protocol-based classification for intrusion detection, in: *WSEAS International Conference. Proceedings. Mathematics and Computers in Science and Engineering (No. 7)*, World Scientific and Engineering Academy and Society, 2008, March.

21. Pei, L., Schütte, J., Simon, C., Intrusion detection system. Carlos Simon, 2007.

22. Aydın, M.A., Zaim, A.H., Ceylan, K.G., A hybrid intrusion detection system design for computer network security. *Comput. Electr. Eng.*, 35, 3, 517–526, 2009.

23. Kumar, V. and Sangwan, O.P., Signature based intrusion detection system using SNORT. *Int. J. Comput. Appl. Inf. Technol.*, 1, 3, 35–41, 2012.

24. Hubballi, N. and Suryanarayanan, V., False alarm minimization techniques in signature-based intrusion detection systems: A survey. *Comput. Commun.*, 49, 1–17, 2014.

25. Jose, S., Malathi, D., Reddy, B., Jayaseeli, D., A survey on anomalybased host intrusion detection system. *J. Phys.: Conf. Ser.*, 1000, 1, 012049, IOP Publishing, 2018, April.

26. Jyothsna, V. V. R. P. V., Prasad, V.R., Prasad, K.M., A review of anomalybased intrusion detection systems. *Int. J. Comput. Appl.*, 28, 7, 26–35, 2011.

27. Zhang, X., Li, C., Zheng, W., Intrusion prevention system design, in: *The Fourth International Conference on Computer and Information Technology*, CIT'04, 2004, September, IEEE, pp. 386–390, 2004.

28. Shelke, M.P.K., Sontakke, M.S., Gawande, A.D., Intrusion detection system for cloud computing. *Int. J. Sci. Technol. Res.*, 1, 4, 67–71, 2012.

29. Deshpande, P., Sharma, S.C., Peddoju, S.K., Junaid, S., HIDS: A host based intrusion detection system for cloud computing environment. *Int. J. Syst. Assur. Eng. Manage.*, 9, 3, 567–576, 2018.

30. Patel, A., Taghavi, M., Bakhtiyari, K., JúNior, J.C., An intrusion detection and prevention system in cloud computing: A systematic review. *J. Netw. Comput. Appl.*, 36, 1, 25–41, 2013.

31. Gaikwad, D.P. and Thool, R.C., Intrusion detection system using bagging ensemble method of machine learning, in: *2015 International Conference on Computing Communication Control and Automation*, IEEE, pp. 291–295, 2015, February.

32. Duque, S. and bin Omar, M.N., Using data mining algorithms for developing a model for intrusion detection system (IDS). *Proc. Comput. Sci.*, 61, 46–51, 2015.

33. Jabez, J. and Muthukumar, B., Intrusion detection system (IDS): anomaly detection using outlier detection approach. *Proc. Comput. Sci.*, 48, 338–346, 2015.

34. Popoola, E. and Adewumi, A.O., Efficient Feature Selection Technique for Network Intrusion Detection System Using Discrete Differential Evolution and Decision. *IJ Netw. Secur.*, 19, 5, 660–669, 2017.

35. Lee, C.H., Su, Y.Y., Lin, Y.C., Lee, S.J., Machine learning based network intrusion detection, in: *2017 2nd IEEE International Conference on Computational Intelligence and Applications (ICCIA)*, IEEE, pp. 79–83, 2017, September.

36. Krishnan, N. and Salim, A., Machine Learning Based Intrusion Detection for Virtualized Infrastructures. *2018 International CET Conference on Control, Communication, and Computing (IC4)*, Thiruvananthapuram, pp. 366–371, 2018.

37. Biswas, S.K., Intrusion detection using machine learning: A comparison study. *Int. J. Pure Appl. Math.*, 118, 19, 101–114, 2018.

38. Zolanvari, M., Teixeira, M.A., Gupta, L., Khan, K.M., Jain, R., Machine Learning-Based Network Vulnerability Analysis of Industrial Internet of Things. *IEEE Internet Things J.*, 6, 4, 6822–6834, Aug. 2019.

39. Chandre, P.R., Mahalle, P.N., Shinde, G.R., Machine Learning Based Novel Approach for Intrusion Detection and Prevention System: A Tool Based Verification. *2018 IEEE Global Conference on Wireless Computing and Networking (GCWCN)*, 2018.

40. Chandre, P.R., Mahalle, P.N., Shinde, G.R., Machine Learning Based Novel Approach for Intrusion Detection and Prevention System: A Tool Based Verification. *2018 IEEE Global Conference on Wireless Computing and Networking (GCWCN)*, 2018.

41. Srivastava, D., Classification of various Dataset for Intrusion Detection System, International Journal of Emerging Technology and Advanced Engerineering, ISSN 2250-2459, ISO 9001:2008 Certified Journal, 8, 1, 40–48, January 2018.

42. Kaushik, S.S. and Deshmukh, P.R., Detection of attacks in an intrusion detection system. *Int. J. Comput. Sci. Inf. Technol. (IJCSIT)*, 2, 3, 982–986, 2011.
43. Chakraborty, K., Bhatia, S., Bhattacharyya, S., Platos, J., Bag, R., Hassanien, A.E., Sentiment Analysis of COVID-19 tweets by Deep Learning Classifiers—A study to show how popularity is affecting accuracy in social media. *Appl. Soft Comput.*, 106754, 2020.

7

You Are Known by Your Mood: A Text-Based Sentiment Analysis for Cloud Security

Abhijit Roy[1] and Parthajit Roy[2*]

[1]Dr. Bhupendra Nath Dutta Smriti Mahavidyalaya, Burdwan, West Bengal, India
[2]Department of Computer Science, The University of Burdwan, Burdwan,
Purba Bardhaman, West Bengal, India

Abstract

Context is an important aspect for security decisions. Contexts like spatial and temporal are used for analysis of patterns but the context which is often ignored in the realm of cloud security is the human sentiment or mood. In a complex cloud-based distributed environment, end-users are often lucrative targets and pose a high risk of getting contaminated with intruders. Behaviors or moods are highly individual traits and thus carries a potential as identification tools. So, the idea of context sensitive behavior analysis and providing security based upon that can be a major achievement for fair usage of the cloud platform.

In the present paper, we propose a novel web-text–based sentiment analysis for understanding the mood, and based upon that, some access-control/secrecy protocol in cloud architecture. For the present study, we have considered stock market persons and their behaviors. This is because stock market buyers and sellers always remain under pressure and suffer from anxiety for their invested money, profits and losses. In the present study, we have analyzed web-texts for stockists using state-of-the art machine learning tools like Support Vector Machine, Artificial Neural Network, and Naïve Bayes Classifier and have tried to identify their usage patterns and have used them for security monitoring. We have also proposed some cryptographic remedies to the problems for cloud-based platforms using homomorphic computations.

Keywords: Sentiment analysis, mood detection, machine learning, homomorphic computations, cloud computing, financial stock market, web-text analysis, natural language processing

7.1   Introduction

Context is an important aspect for security decisions. The common applications of contexts are time of the day (temporal context), geographical locations (spatial contexts), user ID, user defined security questions (execution context) [1, 2], etc. The context which is of immense potential but often ignored in the realm of cloud security is the human sentiment or mood. In the internet domain, users generate a lot of textual data that can be meaningfully

[*]Corresponding author: roy.parthajit@gmail.com

Rajdeep Chakraborty, Anupam Ghosh and Jyotsna Kumar Mandal (eds.) *Machine Learning Techniques and Analytics for Cloud Security*, (129–148) © 2022 Scrivener Publishing LLC

classified in different human sentiments and moods using natural language processing algorithms [3]. When these texts are analyzed in certain contexts, the security aspects get a different dimension. Certain words or sentences, which are absolutely acceptable in some context, may be suspicious in some other context. As a second example, a person's pattern of operations or pattern of word selection for expression may easily be understood and can be a point of threat to him. So, the analysis of the context-sensitive behavior of users may be a potential domain of research work. The importance becomes exponential, if the underlying platform is cloud and the concern is cloud security. The identification of suspicious groups and informing the same to the vulnerable groups though context-sensitive behavior analysis may be a major achievement for fair usage. The application of such type of mood analysis ranges from product reviews, stock market investment discussions, special purpose social media groups, business news discussion forums, etc.

In the present paper, we propose a novel web-text–based sentiment analysis for understanding the behavior of the user. Then, we have proposed some methods as an access-control protocol in cloud architecture [4]. In a complex cloud-based environment, the operations are very complex. End-users are not (in most of the cases) experts in internet security. So, with their naïve knowledge, end-users are often lucrative targets and pose a high risk of getting contaminated with intruders. This is because behavioral, sentimental, or mood-based aspects are highly individual specific traits. This fact carries a great potential as an identification tool [5]. An intruder or the competitor of the person may follow her web-texts and can impersonate as the original person and can do the cloud related activities. The present study handles this in the following way.

The objectives of the present study is as follows. The first objective is to analyze whether the web-texts reveal any pattern/mood or not. If there is a clear pattern and the mood can easily be detected from his web-texts, then the second objective is how to protect cloud related important activity as secret. Also, if there is a strong pattern, then to provide a second layer of access control to her in the cloud domain. For detection of the mood, we have considered machine learning tools, and for the security, we have considered homomorphic computation–based [6] cryptographic model.

In the present research, we have Twitter texts around the discussions about stock market investments. Stock markets are a bit more interesting because buyers and sellers always remain under pressure and always suffer from anxiety for their invested money, profit and loss. So, their mood transitions are momentary and sharp and do not sustain for a long time. Further, if they get an outcome (success or failure), then they generally switch to their next level of planning (which is their trading strategy and that is different for different persons depending upon their experiences, expertise and information asymmetry), and so, their behavior on the trading and texts generated in the discussion forum becomes remarkably different. In the present paper, we have tried to address two security aspects. Firstly, whether the real person is doing the transactions, or the account has been controlled by some anonymous intruder, based on their present and past text patterns. Secondly, whether they are changing their patterns for a certain period and to inform them about the fact. The second situation is important because they may be influenced by someone unconsciously. Finally, we propose how to formalize the access control so that the intruder cannot win.

The rest of the chapter is structured in the following way. A state-of-the-art review in the domain of machine learning, sentiment analysis, and security aspects have been presented in Section 7.2. The backgrounds which are needed to understand the proposal is presented in Section 7.3. The proposed work has been explored in Section 7.4. We have discussed the data that we have taken and the performance measurement tools in Section 7.5. The results of the sentiment analysis has been discussed in Section 7.6, and the possible remedies to the threats in the cloud architecture have been proposed in Section 7.7. The conclusion as well as the future research directions are given in Section 7.8.

7.2 Literature Review

Access control rules form the basis of information security. In an automated environment, an access control protocol decides who can have access to particular resources and this is considered to be a critical issue in security aspect [7]. Temporal context for information security considers a newer piece of Information to be more relevant [8]. The temporal context when combined with spatial footprints makes the access control mechanism much more robust. It is now well accepted fact that there are three basic features for secured access control mechanisms, these are consistency, completeness, and accuracy [9] which are satisfied by the combination of different contexts. Considering these key features, extracting access control rules from natural language processing (NLP) has been gaining prominence.

Empirical approach of NLP has got momentum with large datasets of annotated texts and application of probabilistic methods for analysis [3]. These form the foundation of modern NLP where the empiric is based on certain formalization like tokenization of text, lemmatization, and parts-of-speech tagging. Tokenization is a simple task of separation or identification of words. After this, parts-of-speech is identified for each word. Lemmatization is about finding the original word that reduces the noise in language processing.

Apart from software-based security protocols, the NLP is also proposed for implementation of privacy policies of organizations [5]. In this paradigm, privacy policies of organizations are empirically investigated with the help of machine algorithm and later mapped with compliance tools to find out if the proposed policy is working as intended. The mapping mechanism is very similar to the access control protocol of the information security systems. Using NLP, Xiao *et al.* [10] studied the consistency and correctness of this access control protocol studying software documents which are usually written in natural languages. In a similar work, natural language descriptions of mobile applications are analyzed using NLP for risk assessment [11].

In the present paper, we use NLP for user pattern identification by studying the mood or sentiment patterns of user created texts. So, we resort to more of sentiment analysis of texts which will be used for user identification as an added layer of security. As a use-case, we have taken twitter texts for mapping "positive" and "negative" sentiments of the users. So, for the present study, apart from access control policy and information security related literature, we have extensively drawn social media analytics to classify moods or sentiments of users. In an interesting study by Antweiler and Frank [12], the Yahoo stock message board is analyzed to understand investors' sentiment about stock market investment. Analyzing 1.5 million small talk messages using Bayes classifier and Support Vector Machine (SVM), the study predicts the intention of investors to buy, hold or sell a particular stock. This user specific information is dynamic and highly valuable for user authentication purpose. In another study, a social networking application for investors called "StockTwits" is studied to identify disagreements between different investors for a given stock [13]. Sourav and

Dey [14] studied a large Twitter data from UK-based users to identify the mood dimensions of users and how these are related to stock market movements. The study finds that the predictability of Artificial Neural Network (ANN)–based model is higher in compared to decision tree, discriminant analysis, or SVM. In different context, Twitter sentiments are analyzed for retail brands [15]. Giannini and Irvine [16] studied the Twitter dataset to identify the divergence of opinion and the impact of such divergence. So, the users of social media release a substantial amount of personalized, sentiment or mood-based identifiers that may be immensely helpful for authentication purposes. The volume of personalized information is the strength as well as weakness of NLP using social media texts. Personalized information contains a lot of noise that reduces the predictability of the models used. In probabilistic models like Naïve Bayes Classifier, a text sentiment is classified using a pre-identified special purpose lexicon. So, in a primarily English language text, a mix of meaningful word from a different language becomes a noise if the lexicon is in English language. This indicates toward the unrealistic assumption of independent predictor [17] of Naïve Bayes Classifier. On the other hand, SVM underperforms when the target classes are overlapping though it does not suffer the problem of data dimensionality [18]. In the next section, we discuss these classification tools in detail.

While sentiment is one dimension of our work, security is another dimension also. We may view the research work from two aspects. One is sentiment vs. security and the other is problem vs. solution. So, if sentiment and the pattern is the problem, then breaking that pattern and providing security is the solution. Security is an important context in the cloud domain. There are handful of symmetric key ciphers that successfully solves the problem of encryption. 3DES and AES are a few to name [19]. There are mathematical tools that successfully solves the problem of digital signature [20–22] and the problem of integrity using hash [23, 24]. But the cryptographic community now believes that the most challenging part of security protocol design is the operational security. The problem becomes even more challenging when it is the question of cloud-based computing. We will first discuss a brief introduction of the cloud architecture and thereafter we will identity the potential areas where the security may be compromised and then we shall go further in the context of our work.

According to NIST [4], cloud has three main types of service models. These are Software as a Service (SaaS), Platform as a Service (PaaS), and Infrastructure as a Service (IaaS). In all of the cases, a third party offers the service (Software, Platform, or Infrastructure) [25, 26]. So, in front of the user or customer, there are several parties. Parties who provide software, parties who provide platform or the parties who provide infrastructure. The main problem here is that the presence of third party for storage of the data and computations. Here comes the two major issues in cloud computing. The first one is whether the data and the storage provider can see your data, and whether the entire operational procedure is secure or not. The effect of cloud architecture in service performance has been addressed by Zhang [27]. We shall discuss these two problems in detail.

The cloud is a great opportunity for storing the user data. While this can be a fantastic solution for location transparent storage, there is also threat. This threat is related to privacy. The fundamental question is whether the provider of the cloud can be trusted or not and how not to reveal the information to the provider. There has been several attempts in this line. The first one is obviously the use of traditional encryption. While this is good, we cannot do computations on encrypted data. The most popular attempt is based on homomorphic computations [6, 28]. In this model, data is transferred from one domain into another domain in such a way that the computation is possible in that domain without knowing the actual data. Further, the reversibility of the data is also possible after computation. There are several interesting application of homomorphic computations. Purchase history analysis using homomorphic comoutation has been done by Yasuda [29]. Statistical learning–based homomorphic computations have been proposed by Jiang *et al.* [30].

7.3 Essential Prerequisites

Up to this, we have learned about the objective of the present work. This is simply analyzing the patterns and providing the security based on that. Now, we shall discuss the backgrounds that are needed to understand the model. As security (on cloud domain) is the main goal of our work, we shall first present security related or specially cryptography related backgrounds and thereafter we shall present the machine learning tools.

7.3.1 Security Aspects

The cryptography related tool that we shall use for security is homomorphism. Let us now discuss the homomorphic computations that is needed for the solutions to the problem of pattern revealing. Homomorphic computation means computations will be performed in some transformed domain, i.e., instead of multiplying a number a with b directly, we shall first transfer both a and a into their corresponding homomorphic images as follows:

$$\mathcal{H}_a = H(a)$$

$$\mathcal{H}_b = H(b)$$

where $H(\cdot)$ is the homomorphic transformation function and that $\mathcal{H}_a$ and $\mathcal{H}_b$ are the homomorphic images of a and b, respectively. Then, we shall perform some suitable operation on $\mathcal{H}_a$ and $\mathcal{H}_b$ as follows:

$$\mathcal{H}_{ab} = \mathcal{H}_a \circ \mathcal{H}_b$$

thereafter, we shall perform the reverse computation on $\mathcal{H}_{ab}$ and we shall get back the resultant multiplication of a and b as follows:

$$H^{-1}(\mathcal{H}_{ab}) = a \times b$$

The main advantage is, if we cannot guess a from $\mathcal{H}_a$ or b from $\mathcal{H}_b$, i.e., if the homomorphism acts like a one-way function, then we can successfully put the homomorphic image to the cloud and still do computations on the cloud. This will help us a lot in the security. Mainly, the cloud information need not be decrypted for computations and thus will significantly reduce the threat of information revealing. To work with this, we really do not need a true one-way function. We need a one-way trapdoor function. So, that whenever needed, the owner can do the reverse computations using the trapdoor information. In our proposal, we have given RSA-based model as a proposal. In real cloud, we need many other homomorphic models for computations but in all the cases the working principle will be same. RSA-based homomorphism has been used by Chaum [31] for signature purposes. We will now present the model.

In RSA-based homomorphic model, we select two large primes p and q. These are large primes of more than 1,000 bits. Then, we compute Euler's Totient function $\phi(n) = (p - 1)(q - 1)$. Then, we compute the homomorphic forward transformation exponent h. h should be such that $gcd(h, \phi(n)) = 1$, i.e., they are co-prime to each other[1]. After this, we compute the inverse of h as d. In our proposal, both h and d will be kept secret by the owner. Now, transferring an integer into homomorhic domain can he done using Equation (7.1) and the reverse computation is done by Equation (7.2). Clearly, we cannot learn about a from $\mathcal{H}_a$ because this is RSA encryption and its security is based upon primer factorization which is extremely hard.

$$\mathcal{H}_a = a^h (mod\, n) \tag{7.1}$$

$$a = \mathcal{H}_a^d (mod\, n) \tag{7.2}$$

Let us now try to multiply two numbers in homomorphic domain. We want to multiply a and b. What we will do, is we will first transfer both a and b to their respective homomorphic images. Equations (7.3) and (7.4) show these operations.

$$\mathcal{H}_a = a^h (mod\, n) \tag{7.3}$$

$$\mathcal{H}_b = b^h (mod\, n) \tag{7.4}$$

After this, we multiply the $\mathcal{H}_a$ and $\mathcal{H}_b$ in homomorphic domain using the operation "multiplication modulo n" and and get

$$\mathcal{H}_a \times \mathcal{H}_b = \mathcal{H}_a \times \mathcal{H}_b (mod\, n)$$
$$= \mathcal{H}_{ab} (mod\, n) \tag{7.5}$$
$$= \mathcal{H}_{ab}$$

then we try to reverse the result obtained in Equation (7.5). The process is shown in Equation (7.6).

$$(\mathcal{H}_{ab})^d = (\mathcal{H}_a \times \mathcal{H}_b)^d (mod\, n)$$
$$= (a^h \times b^h)^d (mod\, n)\ follow\ Equations\,(7.3)\ and\ (7.4).$$
$$= (a^h \times b^h)^d (mod\, n) \tag{7.6}$$
$$= (a \times b)^{hd} (mod\, n)\ but\ h \times d(mod\, n) = 1.\ So,$$
$$= a \times b$$

---

[1] This constrain is essential because it ensures the existence of the inverse computation key!

It can be noted that we have multiplied the numbers a and b in the homomorphic domain without knowing the actual numbers. In this method, we are going to use in our proposed solution.

7.3.2   Machine Learning Tools

Access control policies based on texts depend on the ability of the machine to classify texts based on contexts. The contexts may vary depending on the use-case. For example, if we consider texts of product reviews, then it may be features of products that are preferred or not, associated product ratings or related attributes should be analyzed. In case of banking transactions, the most common size of transactions may form the context for the access control policies. In the context of social media like Twitter, the sentiment or mood of the texts may form the basis for a good classifier. If the social media platforms are focused, like political or business news related groups, then texts may be analyzed in the context of politics or business to identify the orientation of the user to be used as access control protocol. So, the key aspect in the context specific text analysis for security protocol is to classify the text-based sentiments of users and thus to understand the behavioral patterns of such users in relation to certain contexts and to use such patterns as the authentication of identity of users. Now, we discuss the classification tools that we use in this study.

7.3.2.1   Naïve Bayes Classifier

This is supervised model of classification where we use training data to define prior probabilities and use those probabilities to measure posterior probabilities of documents falling into certain category. In text classification context, we normally use lexicon. A context specific lexicon, for example, lexicons for movie reviews, or for stock market, small discussions, etc., lead to more accurate classification outcome. Now, let us assume there are D documents to be classified into C categories based on a lexicon of T words with polarity tags. So, we have d_i documents where $i = 1, 2,...,D$, lexicon with t_j words, where $j = 1,2,...,T$, to be classified into c_k classes, where $k = 1, 2,...,C$. Suppose we are analyzing texts related to stock market–related discussions and we wish to classify the mood of the texts as bullish ($c1$) or neutral ($c2$) or bearish ($c3$). This means we have three classes of text documents, that is bullish, neutral, and bearish, and so, $C = 3$. Now, we train Bayes classifier with pre-classified documents. The total numbers of documents are D. So, if we are working on Twitter texts, then total number of twits pre-classified for training is D. Now, we take a word t_j, and we find the probability of that word to be present in training documents classified as c_k. Thus, we calculate the prior probability of each word from the lexicon to be present in the document class c_k. We denote this probability as $p(t \mid c)$. For example, in bullish documents, if the word "grab" appears to be 15% of all the words in the specific document class, then $p(t \mid c) = 0.15$ becomes the prior probability of the word "grab". Technically, we compute $p(t \mid c)$ as follows:

$$p(t|c) = \frac{n(t|c)+1}{n(c)+T} \tag{7.7}$$

Here, $n(t \mid c)$ is the frequency of word t in the document class c and $n(c)$ is the total word count in the document class c. Note that, if any term in the lexicon does not appear in the document class altogether, then it carries a non-zero probability of $1 / (n(c) + T)$ for such term. So, the multinomial probability of a document di to appear in class c_k is measured in the following way:

$$p(d \mid c) = \frac{n(d)!}{n(t_1 \mid d)! \, . n(t_2 \mid d)! \cdots n(t_T \mid d)!} \times p(t_1 \mid c) . p(t_2 \mid c) \cdots p(t_T \mid c) \qquad (7.8)$$

This $p(d \mid c)$ is the prior probability of the training data. Here, $n(d)$ denotes the total number of words in a document d_i and $p(tj \mid d)$ is the frequency of word t_j in the document d_i. Now, we calculate posterior probability on the testing dataset, using this prior probability in Bayes classifier. The procedure is as follows:

$$p(c \mid d) = \frac{p(d \mid c) . p(c)}{\sum_k p(d \mid c_k) . p(c_k)}, \forall k = 1, 2, \cdots, C \qquad (7.9)$$

Here, we assign a class to document d for which the posterior probability for the class c_k is maximum. When text data is informal and ambiguous Bayes classifier is expected to give better results given a good lexicon with prior probabilities for each words.

7.3.2.2   Artificial Neural Network

ANN has been a highly popular tool in machine learning. ANN is a computational system which is inspired by structure and processing methods of biological brains for learning about patterns. This is a non-parametric approach to make sense out of fuzzy and unclear information. It uses a large number of weighted connections between elements with distributed representations. In our proposal, we have used ADAM Optimizer [32] and Gradient Descent–based Neural Network Model [33]. We have chosen these two models because they are very stable optimizer. Further, ADAM Optimizer learns and adjusts learning rates internally.

7.4   Proposed Model

In this section, we shall discuss the proposed model of sentiment analysis and the remedies to the possible threats to behavioral pattern due to that. Figure 7.1 gives an outline of the proposed model and its working principle. Here, we have taken twit data for sentiment analysis. If we want to understand the behavioral pattern of a person, then we need some of his past twits in the related domain. In our case, this is stock market–related twits. As we have stated earlier, this research work identified three models of machine learning, namely, Naïve Bayes Classifier, Neural Network (NN), and SVM. All these are training-based classifier. That means we need training and testing samples. The proposed model is a word-based sentiment analysis model. Meaning some predefined set of words tagged with positive or negative sentiment will be used for analysis purposes. In our proposed model, we have

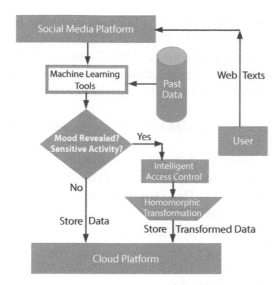

Figure 7.1 A block diagram of the proposed mood-based sentiment analysis and the solution to the related threat in the cloud domain.

taken two sets of words: a standard "bag of words" [34, 35] and a dynamically generated "bag of words". The dynamically generated set is generated from the testing sample every time we need to understand the pattern. So, the analyzer is supposed to maintain a database of labeled data for stock related data also. The advantage here is that the model will consider some text styles that are unique to every person and which do not follow grammar or dictionary. As an example, "zzzactly", "comin!!!" (coming), and "#WOW!" are specific to a person. So, not only we have considered the standard set of words but also we have used a set of domain specific words. To make the system more informative, we have excluded the sentiment neutral punctuation marks like dot and comma and included the sentiment specific punctuation marks like exclamatory sign and hash tag.

Once the "bag of words" have been identified, we pre-process the twit data. Here, we match the each and every twit to four different sets. Namely,

1. positive standard "bag of words"
2. negative standard "bag of words"
3. positive dynamic "bag of words"
4. negative dynamic "bag of words"

and we count the number of matches. Thus, we generate a four-dimensional vector (n_1, n_2, n_3, n_4) for every twit where n_1 is the number of words matches with positive standard "bag of words", n_2 is the number of words matches with negative standard "bag of words", and so on. The idea is if the twit is having a "positive" sentiment, then values of n_1 and n_3 will be larger than n_2 and n_4. The dual statement it true for negative sentiment twit also, i.e., if n_2 and n_4 contains larger number than n_1 and n_3, then the sentiment is "negative".

We have used three types of machine learning models, namely, Naïve Bayes Classifier, NN, and SVM. In NN, we have further considered two variants, namely, ADAM Optimizer [32] and Gradient Descent–based Neural Network. In both cases, we have run the NN with 10 neurons and 5 neurons. The number of hidden layers, however, has been fixed to 2 for all the cases. We call them ADAM10, ADAM5, GD10, and GD5, respectively, in our paper. So, all together, we have six different models: Bayes, GD5, GD10, ADAM5, ADAM10, and SVM. We first train each model with 80% data and thereafter test the performance of the model for the rest 20% of the data. The proposed model in algorithmic form is given in Algorithm 7.1.

Algorithm 7.1 The algorithm for ADAM Optimizer–based neural network model.

1. **procedure** Sentiment-Analysis (*TrainingDataset, TestingDataset*)
2.   *stdWordSet* ← Std-Bag-of-Word (*WordList*)
3.   *dynamicWordSet* ← Dynamic-Bag-of-Word (*WordList*)
4.   *Algorithm* ← *ADAM*
5.   Set-Num-Neuron (*ADAM*, 10)
6.   Set-Hidden-Layer (*ADAM*, 2)
7.   Train-Neural-Net(*ADAM*),*TrainingData,stdWordSet,dynamicWordSet*)
8.   **for** *twit*$_i$ ∈ *TestingSet* **do**
9.   *result* ← Neural-Network (*ADAM*10, *twit*$_i$)
10.   **if** *result* = *Positive* **then**
11.   Add-twit (*PositiveSet, twit*$_i$)
12.   else
13.   Add-twit (*NegativeSet, twit*$_i$)
14.   **end if**
15.   **end for**
16.   *Generate Accuracy Percentage*
17. end procedure

After this, we have run all the models ans have generated the results. We compare the performances of the different algorithms in different indexes also. The experimental setups, i.e., dataset and indexes, have been given in Section 7.5, whereas, the results and the analysis of the proposed sentiment-based analysis is given in Section 7.6.

7.5   Experimental Setup

To test the strength of our proposed model, we have carefully chosen the dataset. We have taken standard twitter dataset for finance market [36, 37]. This dataset has 5,000 twit dataset. They are preprocessed manually and has been labeled with *positive* and *negative* tags. Also, we have taken a standard "bag-of-words" [34, 35]. Further, we have generated a dynamic "bag-of-words" for our training purposes. We have developed in-house program (partly in C language and partly in python) for the entire process. The data cleaning and processing part as well as feature vector extraction part has been done using C program. The machine learning–based mood analysis part has been done in Python.

We have used eight indexes for comparison purposes. These are Czekanowski-Dice index, Jaccard index, Folkes-Mallow index, Kulczynski index, and Rogers-Tanimoto index for measuring the performances. Further, to know the false negative and false positive, we have used two other indexes, namely, precision index and recall index. Finally, to check if the result is like randomly opted results or is truly gathering the sentiment, then we have used rand index. A good literature review of all such indexes is given in [38]. All these index values vary from 0 to 1. The more the value, the better the performance.

7.6   Results and Discussions

Let us now consider the results of the proposed model. As we have said, we have taken a set of 5,000 twits and have used 80% of the same for training and 20% for testing, i.e., we have taken 4,000 twits for training and 1,000 data for testing. As the dataset is a standard benchmark dataset and the labels are given by the domain experts, we did not validate the dataset; instead, we have assumed that it is validated. The results of sentiment analysis is presented in this section.

The performance of the proposed models have been shown in the form of confusion matrix in Figures 7.2a–c and 7.3a–c. These matrices show the percentage of true positive, true negative, false positive, and false negative detection out of 1,000 testing samples. For example, consider Figure 7.2a. This is the confusion matrix for Naïve Bayes Classifier. Here, 64.1% is positive and identified by the model as positive. In addition, 3% however are actually positive but the model has been misclassified them. On the other hand, 5.8% negative sentiment has been predicted successfully, whereas 27.1% are misclassified. So, the accuracy is (64.1 + 5.8) = 69.9%. On the other hand, in Figure 7.3c, the performance of SVM model has been given. Using the same logic, we can say that the accuracy percentage for this model is (66.6+21.3) = 87.9%. The colors also play an informative role. The smaller the number in the cell, the whiter the color. The larger the number in the cell, the deeper blue is the color. So, from that, also, we can identify the accuracy levels.

Now, let us come to the comparative study of the proposed models. Confusion matrices are good as an indicator, but we need some well established indexes for measuring the performances. We have measured the performances in various indexes. Figures 7.4 and 7.5 show the performances of the models in Czekanowski-Dice and Jaccard index, respectively. Figure 7.4 shows that only Naïve Bayes Classifier is having a bit poor performance. The rest of the models are above 0.8 range. In Jaccard Index, the same trend is observed. The performances are significant.

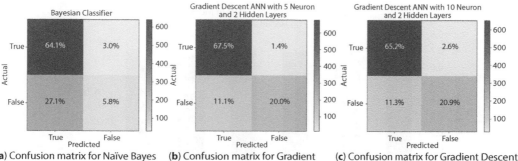

(a) Confusion matrix for Naïve Bayes Model. In this model a Bayes classifier has been used for classification.

(b) Confusion matrix for Gradient Descent Neutral Network with 5 neuron and 2 hidden layers.

(c) Confusion matrix for Gradient Descent Neural Network with 10 neuron and 2 hidden layers.

Figure 7.2 Confusion matrices for Bayes, Gradient Descent with five neuron, and Gradient Descent Descent model with 10 neurons, respectively. The colors indicate the percentage values. The deeper blue color indicates higher percentages, whereas whitish colors indicate lower percentage.

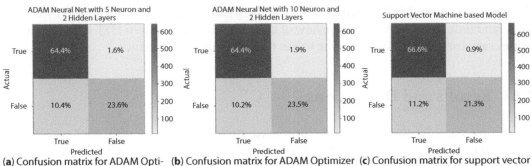

(a) Confusion matrix for ADAM Optimizer Neural Network with 5 neuron and 2 hidden layers.

(b) Confusion matrix for ADAM Optimizer Neural Network with 10 neuron and 2 hidden layers.

(c) Confusion matrix for support vector machine model. The SVM shows best performance.

Figure 7.3 Confusion matrices for ADAM Optimizer with 5 neuron, ADAM Optimizer with 10 neurons and Support Vector Machine model, respectively. The colors indicate the percentage values. The deeper blue color indicates higher percentages whereas whitish colors indicate lower percentage.

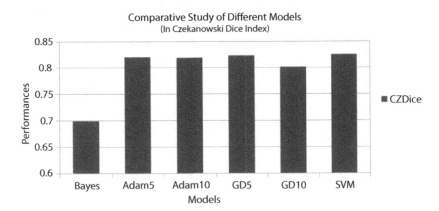

Figure 7.4 Performance of the proposed Naïve Bayes, Adam5, Adam10, GD5, GD10, and SVM models in Czekanowski-Dice index. Higher value means better performance. The best performance is 1.00.

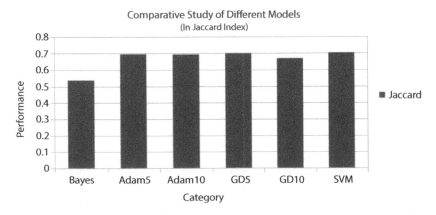

Figure 7.5 Performance of the proposed Naïve Bayes, ADAM5, ADAM10, GD5, GD10 and SVM models in Jaccard index. Higher value means better performance. The best performance is 1.00.

In Table 7.1, the performances of the proposed models have been shown on Folkes-Mallows, Kulczynski, and Rogers-Tanimoto index. Overall, the performances are good. Rogers-Tanimoto index considers true-negative counts where as Kulczynski index considers precision and recall with equal weight-age. The reason we have used so many indexes is because several index gives several aspects of the results. Some considers true positive, some gives more weight to true positive than to true-negative, etc. We wanted to see the results from all such aspects to come to an unbiased decision.

The measurement precision and recall has been given in Figure 7.6. Precision is measuring the true classification out of total points and Recall is the measurement of true classification out of total true points. In our proposed models, except, Naïve Bayes Classifier, in all cases, the precision is near 0.8 and recall is near 0.9, respectively. This shows that the results are really very impressive.

The Final index is Rand index. The performances of the proposed models have been shown for Rand index in Figure 7.7. If Rand index value is around 0.5, then it is believed that the result is no better than randomly selected decisions. But in our case, all the results (Except Naïve Bayes Classifier) are well beyond random. So, this Rand index essentially proves that the proposed models truly learns and understands, and then, it predicts the results like an intelligent system.

Table 7.1 Performance in different indexes.

Model	Folkes-Mallows	Kulczynski	Rogers-Tanimoto
Bayes	0.7131606	0.7280641	0.4072424
ADAM5	0.8213698	0.8229153	0.6509668
ADAM10	0.8199028	0.8212817	0.6488985
GD5	0.8248989	0.8272122	0.6407309
GD10	0.802489	0.8041447	0.6134268
SVM	0.8272011	0.8296567	0.6488985

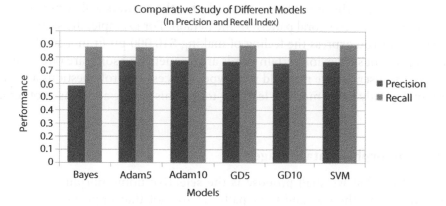

Figure 7.6 Performance of the proposed Naïve Bayes, ADAM5, ADAM10, GD5, GD10, and SVM models in precision and recall index. Higher value means better performance. The best performance is 1.00.

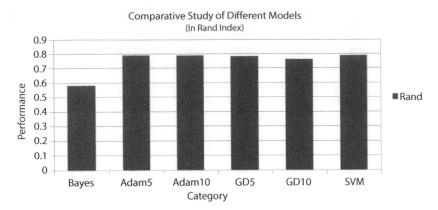

Figure 7.7 Performance of the proposed Naïve Bayes, ADAM5, ADAM10, GD5, GD10, and SVM models in Rand index. Higher value means better performance. The best performance is 1.00.

7.7   Application in Cloud Security

Now, we have understood that there are strong patterns in the behavior of the persons in the stock market. But the responsibility of every positive research work is not only to identify the problem but also to suggest the remedies. What to do then? We cannot control the emotions of the persons because that is inherent. So, we will propose some different paths of solutions. We will once again note that we are working on a cloud platform. Considering that, we shall suggest three solutions. These solutions may be used alternatively or may be used as a combination. The solutions are as follows:

1. Ask an intelligent security question.
2. Homomorphic Data Storage
3. Data Diffusion.

7.7.1   Ask an Intelligent Security Question

In this proposal, cloud platform will ask an intelligent security question based on the past twits or past web-texts. The questions will be such that the answers will be personalized and that is based upon the behavioral pattern of the person. For example, the security question may be "How will you express the feeling of making $10,000 profit in a single sentence?" Now, based upon one's behavior, certain words are frequent and some are rare. These words vary from user to user. So, we may add such type of access control questions and can analyze them intelligently using machine learning tools. This can be added as another layer of security.

7.7.2   Homomorphic Data Storage

The next solution that we shall propose is the selective homomorphic data storage. It can be noted that all the text and their patterns are not that important for all aspects. For example, whenever we are concentrating on stock market and the persons related to that, then the main concern of the competitors is which stock a peron is dealing with.

For example, let Alice be a stock trader and Eve be a competitor of Alice. Eve and Alice have information asymmetry, i.e., Alice is better informed about the stock market. Now, Eve's main concern will be how many units Alice is selling or buying and for which company. If Alice stores only these information secret, then her purchase habit can be kept secret. As we are dealing with cloud, we have to store our data in the cloud. eve is not concerned with all the cloud data. Eve is concerned only about the numbers, i.e., how many units Alice is purchasing. So, instead of keeping all the things secret, we shall keep only those numbers secret.

We will do that using homomorphism. Encryption scheme is not suitable for such type of cases because we cannot compute (add or multiply etc.) on encrypted data. But in the homomorphic domain, we can. Let us suppose, initially, Alice decided to purchase 1423 units of share and later changed her mind and has made the number triple. How she is going to update her cloud data. In the homomorphic domain, we do not need to decrypt the data. We can directly update the data in the homomorphic domain. This reduces a significant amount risk of information leakage.

To understand this, we have selected an Integer Ring–based homomorphic domain. The domain on which RSA model relies. Let p and q be two 50 bit numbers. (We have taken small integer for better understanding purposes.) Let p and q be two primes.

$$p = 945717688523953 \ and$$

$$q = 655049301394981$$

The public component n can be computed as

$$n = p * q = 619491711184491652737732479893$$

Let us suppose we have selected forward homomorphic transformation key

$$h = 59. \quad as \quad gcd(h, \phi(p^*q)) = 1.$$

Using extended Euclidean algorithm, the inverse of h for $\phi(p^*q)$ has been computed. The computed value is

$$d = 346495363882850368051432279859$$

Now, suppose Alice wants to buy 1423 units of share and wants to store this information in the cloud. So,

$$m = 1423$$

She is going to store the homomorphic image of the number 1423, i.e., she is going to store me (*mod n*), i.e., homomorphic image,

$$\mathcal{H}_m = 1423^{59}(mod \ n) = 600534975958695264032041441627$$

Note that from the homomorphic image $\mathcal{H}_m$ in the cloud, Eve will not get any idea about Alice's purchase. Now, come to the second step. Let us suppose Alice has changed her mind and has finally purchase three times the initial decision, i.e., 4269 units of share. To do this, she is not going to decrypt the $\mathcal{H}_m$. What she is going to do is she is going to take forward homomorphic image if 3, i.e., she is going to compute $3^h(mod\ n)$, i.e.,

$$\mathcal{H}_3 = 3^{59}(mod\ n) = 141303860917387345047648 11067$$

and she is going to multiply this number with previous number, i.e.,

$$6005349759586952640320414416 27 * 141303860917387345047648 11067\ (mod\ n)$$

So, her updated information is

$$\mathcal{H}_{m_{new}} = 13120529227781355485276045 1329$$

The beauty of this model is that whenever she decrypts, she gets back 4269, i.e.,

$$\mathcal{H}_{m_{new}}^{-1} = 4269 = 3 \times 1423 = 3 \times \mathcal{H}_m^{-1}\ [follow\ Equation\ (7.6)]$$

In this way, we can reduce the understanding of purchase habit even if we store the data in the cloud and perform update operation on the cloud data. This is an example of multiplication, and we can do addition also.

7.7.3   Information Diffusion

The final solution is information diffusion. Suppose Eve has somehow managed to own a very powerful cryptanalytic method by which she can mount an attack to the previously proposed homomorphic model if she provides very hard work. Now, here comes the idea of information diffusion. Instead of putting only essential numbers into homomorphic domains, we are proposing to put many other unnecessary parts into homomorphic domains. We know that text and numbers all will be transferred to numbers in the homomorphic domain when texts are treated as ASCII numbers. So, Eve's task will just become much much more harder by many factors. Eve will eventually use cryptanalytic methods on the numbers which will end up with unnecessary text. This will waste her time and effort and the information will remain secret for longer time.

7.8   Conclusion and Future Scope

In this research work, we have shown that the Twitter-based sentiment analysis for stock traders is definitely possible. Several methods of machine learning have been applied. Several performance measurement tools have been used ti judge the results. In all of the cases, the only outcome is that the mood or patterns are revealed. We have also shown that in cloud domain, pattern of a person's behavior is a potential threat.

So, in our present research work, we have also suggested some of the remedies to reduce the threats.

Though this research work shows potential, there are scopes of improvements also. The first improvement can be made in understanding the patterns themselves. As of now, we have only positive and negative classifications, i.e., two valued classifications, multi-class classification will greatly help us understanding subpatterns within the patterns also. The introduction of more sophisticated lexicons may be another research dimensions. The second improvement is toward the solutions. Here, instead of RSA-based homomorphic models, some more recent models can be incorporated. Further breaking of pattern may also be a very good future research direction.

References

1. Enck, W. and Xie, T., Tutorial: Text analytics for security, in: *Proceedings of the 2014 ACM SIGSAC Conference on Computer and Communications Security*, pp. 1540–1541, 2014.
2. Slankas, J., Xiao, X., Williams, L., Xie, T., Relation extraction for inferring access control rules from natural language artifacts, in: *Proceedings of the 30th Annual Computer Security Applications Conference*, pp. 366–375, 2014.
3. Jurafsky, D. and Martin, J.H., *Part-of-speech tagging. speech and language processing: An introduction to natural language processing, speech recognition, and computational linguistics*, Prentice Hall, London, 2009.
4. Mell, P. and Grance, T., *The nist definition of cloud computing*. NIST Special Publication 800-145, National Institute of Standards and Technology, U.S. Department of Commerce, USA, September, 2011.
5. Brodie, C.A., Karat, C.-M., Karat, J., An empirical study of natural language parsing of privacy policy rules using the sparcle policy workbench, in: *Proceedings of the second symposium on Usable privacy and security*, pp. 8–19, 2006.
6. Yi, X., Paulet, R., Bertino, E., *Homomorphic Encryption and Applications*, 1st edition, Springer, Cham, 2014.
7. Samarati, P. and de Vimercati, S.C., Access control: Policies, models, and mechanisms, in: *International School on Foundations of Security Analysis and Design*, pp. 137–196, Springer, Berlin, Heidelberg, 2000.
8. Russell-Rose, T. and Tate, T., Chapter 3 - context, in: *Designing the Search Experience*, T. Russell-Rose and T. Tate (Eds.), pp. 47–69, Morgan Kaufmann, Springer, Berlin, Heidelberg, 2013.
9. Zowghi, D. and Gervasi, V., On the interplay between consistency, completeness, and correctness in requirements evolution. *Inf. Software Technol.*, 45, 14, 993–1009, 2003.
10. Xiao, X., Paradkar, A., Thummalapenta, S., Xie, T., Automated extraction of security policies from natural-language software documents, in: *Proceedings of the ACM SIGSOFT 20th International Symposium on the Foundations of Software Engineering*, pp. 1–11, 2012.
11. Pandita, R., Xiao, X., Yang, W., Enck, W., Xie, T., {WHYPER}: Towards automating risk assessment of mobile applications, in: *22nd {USENIX} Security Symposium ({USENIX} Security 13)*, pp. 527–542, 2013.
12. Antweiler, W. and Frank, M.Z., Is all that talk just noise? the information content of internet stock message boards. *J. Finance*, 59, 3, 1259–1294, 2004.
13. Cookson, J.A. and Niessner, M., Why don't we agree? evidence from a social network of investors. *J. Finance*, 75, 1, 173–228, 2020.

14. Saurabh, S. and Dey, K., Unraveling the relationship between social moods and the stock market: Evidence from the united kingdom. *J. Behav. Exp. Finance*, 26, 100300, 2020.

15. Souza, T.T.P., Kolchyna, O., Treleaven, P.C., Aste, T., Twitter sentiment analysis applied to finance: A case study in the retail industry, Handbook of Sentiment Analysis in Finance. *arXiv preprint arXiv:1507.00784*, 2015.

16. Irvine, P.J. and Giannini, R.C., The impact of divergence of opinions about earnings within a social network, SSRN Electronic Journal. *Available at SSRN 2024559*, 2012.

17. Rish, I. *et al.*, An empirical study of the naive bayes classifier, in: *IJCAI 2001 workshop on empirical methods in artificial intelligence*, vol. 3, pp. 41–46, 2001.

18. Srivastava Durgesh, K. and Lekha, B., Data classification using support vector machine. *J. Theor. Appl. Inf. Technol.*, 12, 1, 1–7, 2010.

19. Schneier, B., *Applied Cryptography: Protocols, Algorithms, and Source Code in C*, 2nd edition, Juhn Wiley, New Jersey, USA, 1995.

20. Rivest, R.L., Shamir, A., Adleman, L., A method for obtaining digital signatures and public-key cryptosystems. *Commun. ACM*, 21, 2, 120–126, February 1978.

21. Elgamal, T., A public key cryptosystem and a signature scheme based on discrete logarithms. *IEEE Trans. Inf. Theory*, 31, 4, 469–472, September 2006.

22. Johnson, D., Menezes, A., Vanstone, S., The elliptic curve digital signature algorithm (ecdsa). *Int. J. Inf. Secur.*, 1, 1, 36–63, August 2001.

23. Al-Kuwari, S., Davenport, J.H., Bradford, R.J., *Cryptographic hash functions: Recent design trends and security notions*. Cryptology ePrint Archive, Report 2011/565, IACR, USA, 2011, urlhttps://eprint.iacr.org/2011/565.

24. Dobraunig, C., Eichlseder, M., Mendel, F., Analysis of sha-512/224 and sha-512/256, in: *Advances in Cryptology – ASIACRYPT 2015*, T. Iwata and J.H. Cheon (Eds.), pp. 612–630, Springer Berlin Heidelberg, Berlin, Heidelberg, 2015.

25. Albini, A. and Rajnai, Z., General architecture of cloud. *Proc. Manuf.*, 22, 485–490, 2018. *11th International Conference Interdisciplinarity in Engineering, INTER-ENG*, Tirgu Mures, Romania, 5-6 October 2017, 2017.

26. Odun-Ayo, I., Ananya, M., Agono, F., Goddy-Worlu, R., Cloud computing architecture: A critical analysis, in: *2018 18th International Conference on Computational Science and Applications (ICCSA)*, pp. 1–7, 2018.

27. Zhang, R., The impacts of cloud computing architecture on cloud service performance. *J. Comput. Inf. Syst.*, 60, 2, 166–174, 2020.

28. Gentry, C. and Halevi, S., Implementing gentry's fully-homomorphic encryption scheme, in: *Advances in Cryptology – EUROCRYPT 2011*, K.G. Paterson (Ed.), pp. 129–148, Springer Berlin Heidelberg, Berlin, Heidelberg, 2011.

29. Yasuda, M., Shimoyama, T., Kogure, J., Secret computation of purchase history data using somewhat homomorphic encryption. *Pac. J. Math. Ind.*, 6, 1, 5, Oct 2014.

30. Jiang, L., Xu, C., Wang, X., Lin, C., Statistical learning based fully homomorphic encryption on encrypted data. *Soft Comput.*, 21, pp. 7473–7483, Aug 2016.

31. Chaum, D., *Blind Signatures for Untraceable Payments*, pp. 199–203, Springer US, Boston, MA, 1983.

32. Kingma, D.P. and Ba, J., Adam: A method for stochastic optimization, arXiv preprint, arXiv:1412.6980, 2017.

33. Haykin, S., *Neural Networks and Learning Machines*, Prentice Hall, 3rd edition, 2008.

34. Liu, B., Hu, M., Cheng, J., Opinion observer: analyzing and comparing opinions on the web, in: *Proceedings of the 14th international conference on World Wide Web*, pp. 342–351, 2005.

35. Hu, M. and Liu, B., Mining and summarizing customer reviews, in: *Proceedings of the tenth ACM SIGKDD international conference on Knowledge discovery and data mining*, pp. 168–177, 2004.

36. Oliveira, N., Cortez, P., Areal, N., On the predictability of stock market behavior using stocktwits sentiment and posting volume, in: *Progress in Artificial Intelligence - 16th Portuguese Conference on Artificial Intelligence, EPIA 2013*, Angra do Heroísmo, Azores, Portugal, September 9-12, 2013. *Proceedings*, volume 8154 of *Lecture Notes in Computer Science*, L. Correia, L.P. Reis, J. Cascalho (Eds.), pp. 355–365, Springer, Berlin, Heidelberg, 2013.

37. Cortez, P., Oliveira, N., Ferreira, J.P., Measuring user influence in financial microblogs: Experiments using stocktwits data, in: *Proceedings of the 6th International Conference on Web Intelligence, Mining and Semantics, WIMS 2016*, Nîmes, France, June 13-15, 2016, R. Akerkar, M. Plantié, S. Ranwez, S. Harispe, A. Laurent, P. Bellot, J. Montmain, F. Trousset, (Eds.), pp. 23:1–23:10, ACM, Paris, France. 2016.

38. Desgraupes, B., *Clustering indices*, vol. 1, p. 34, University of Paris Ouest-Lab Modal, Paris, France, 2013.

The State-of-the-Art in Zero-Knowledge Authentication Proof for Cloud

Priyanka Ghosh

Faculty of Computer Science & Engineering, Brainware University, Kolkata, India

Abstract

The security of information has now become the utmost priority for the users as breach of information may cause significant losses to individuals and organizations. To ensure the security and privacy of information, Zero-Knowledge Authentication technique will play a vital role. The Zero-Knowledge Proof (ZKP) operates on the concept that the system will have zero knowledge about the content of the data transactions. With the technical advancement, the computing needs has taken a new shape. Data accessibility from any point and at any given time has become a primary need for any technology which can only be served through cloud computing. The cloud computing has become a sustainable, scalable, and reliable platform for computing for millions of technologies. Cloud computing is not impeccable; it poses a significant threat of data leakage. In this paper, a survey of ZKP algorithms and comparative study will be done while focusing on the concept of cloud security.

Keywords: Zero-knowledge proof, authentication, IoT, security, cloud security, cryptographic, key, cloud architecture

8.1 Introduction

With the advancement of technology, the mobility has increased by many folds and the need to access the same data from different devices and locations has become primary requirement. This multiple access of data from multiple locations and devices could have possible by cloud technology. In cloud technology, all the computing and storages are done on centrally located servers or data centers instead of local devices. As the interaction between human and technology is becoming more prevalent, a user wants to access data from smart phones, computers, and in other platforms for overwhelming number of applications like mails, documents, social media, shopping, food delivery, cab service, news, and a lot more. The cloud servers support a user to access his personal data anytime, anywhere, and for any platform he uses.

Email: aecpriynaka@gmail.com

Rajdeep Chakraborty, Anupam Ghosh and Jyotsna Kumar Mandal (eds.) Machine Learning Techniques and Analytics for Cloud Security, (149–170) © 2022 Scrivener Publishing LLC

The cloud technology has also helped several small and medium IT enterprises to reduce the cost of keeping and maintaining local servers. Small and medium companies are storing their data into the cloud servers; they are also becoming free of location restrictions. Through cloud technology every employee of company can access the data at the same time from almost anywhere in the world. This brings ease of doing business and readiness of data.

The cloud technology has completely changed the way people use to perceive internet. Earlier, the cloud term was meant to demonstrate a network of servers and machines. With the increasing ease of shifting more of the computing processes to cloud, the cloud technology has become new style of computing. Thus, the cloud technology is now widely recognized by the word cloud computing. Cloud computing mainly works upon technology called virtualization. The virtualization mimics the existence of a physical computer in the form of purely simulated and digital only computers, called virtual machines. Several virtual machines can be implemented in a single computer. These virtual machines can behave as per the requirement of the user. If required, the virtual machines can be sandboxed from one another, so that they do not have any interaction and access of data of other virtual machines while existing in the same physical machine. This way, optimum utilization of hardware can be done, where a number of virtual machines can be implemented in a single physical machine. Via cloud technology, servers will also be able to act as multiple servers, and thus, data centers will also be able to serve multiple organizations simultaneously.

Cloud also supports users to access the service from any device they use through browsers or apps. With the increasing number of users, the concern of maintenance, readiness, and availability of cloud servers are also increasing. The cloud vendors take back up of the servers in multiple machines, in multiple locations to avoid any chance of data loss. The degrees of readiness of these servers are also way better than the local servers as they are continuously monitored and kept under controlled conditions. Though the technology seems very costly, but as the numbers of users are significantly high, the technology cost gets evenly distributed among all and the individual cost becomes reasonable.

With the huge amount of data and services provided by cloud technology, the security concerns also rise simultaneously. The data in the cloud storage may be of different kind and highly important to individuals, corporations, and governments. Leakage or theft of data from data centers can cause unimaginable complex problems possibly to the whole world. So, cloud security is an equally important process which is provided using combination of different methods to safeguard the data. To maintain the cloud security, Firewall plays a vital role. Firewall helps to protect the organization and the users from several fatal threats. It also helps in controlling data transfers and threats imposed by different applications in cloud.

Access controls is used to distribute the access rights among the users. By this process, a set of access rules can be applied for different group of users or individuals. For example, in an organization, only accounts staff can access the financial data and it is restricted for any other user. This will help to protect confidential business insights from ignorant or malicious insiders, who can pose a threat to the organization. Cloud service providers make sure to implement access control quite efficiently to handle the flow of data.

Information security systems use Virtual Private Networks (VPNs) and Encryption techniques to provide security. VPN like micronetworks within a network ensures security and access of data for a particular set of users. For example, an employee can access all his assigned data of his organization without any physical barrier. The employee will be able to work from any device as if he is seating in the office. The VPN also helps in controlling the data flow.

Data masking is a technique that provides and extra layer of privacy. It helps in keeping data parameters hidden from unwanted users. Like an organization can publish opinions, feedbacks, and other information without disclosing the name or identity of the person.

Disaster restoration is vital to security since it encourages user recuperate information that are lost or stolen. While not a security segment fundamentally, the cloud administrations supplier may have to consent to information stockpiling guidelines. A few nations necessitate that information should be put away inside their nation. On the off chance that a nation has this necessity, one needs to check that a cloud supplier has server farms in the same nation.

Cloud Security Provided Following Field:

Data center security: Data center security (Figure 8.1) is of highest priority for any cloud provider. The data center holds sensitive and critically important information of clients which can be leaked or theft via different avenues. There are two different aspects of data center security like physical security and network security. A proper location planning for data center establishment is required to prevent any physical break-ins and breaches. Recently, renowned cloud providers are considering sea beds as the safest place for data center establishment. The network security of the data centers is equally vital. Several firewalls and anti-malware systems have been in place to prevent any threat or breaches. This security system also includes the user education and awareness, lack of which can impose critical threat to the data centers.

Access control: In this era, the data has become the most valuable asset for any company, safeguarding which is of the utmost priority. Access control system (Figure 8.1) is used to store, observe, and control the flow of data for different users. Company can make different policies to restrict or allow user to access the data as per the company policy. The data access control can be implemented for specific device, time, IP address, browsers, and other technical conditions. This provides a complete control to company to safeguard their business data and control the flow of information at different levels.

Threat prevention: With the increasing number of cloud service users, the vulnerability is also increasing. As the cloud provider does not have the control over choosing the users, the risk of data leakage and breaches is increasing day by day. To prevent the risk caused by the behavior of users, training and awareness programs need to be setup. The employees need to develop the sense of obligation for the data security. Routine network security checks, frequent change of passwords, access allowed, and SOP in case of breach need to be readily available with the employees to reduce the risk of data breaches.

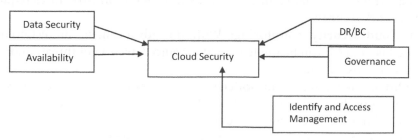

Figure 8.1 Requirement of cloud security.

Threat mitigation: Though the threats and attacks remain same for the cloud data centers and traditional data centers, there is an advantage of using cloud services, (Figure 8.1) i.e., threat mitigation. The liability of threat mitigation is shared between the cloud service provider and the user. Though the core architecture of the cloud is still exposed to different threats, the mitigation strategies bring a sense of responsibility and reliability to the system.

Redundancy: With the increasing security threats and technical complexities, the availability of data centers is always being challenged. To hedge the risk of corruption and system failures, data are being stored in duplicates to back up in any such situations. This strategy is called redundancy. The cloud service providers are cognizant of such situations and provide four level of redundancy to handle any unwanted scenarios.

Hardware-level redundancy: The hardware redundancy is a solution toward the hardware failures. In this modern age where most of the business are contingent of software and computing services, hardware tolerance is something which is a concern for every business.

Process redundancy: A business runs upon a number of processes which may be physical or can be implemented using software. At this age of digitization, most of the business has migrated their processes to software. To function smoothly, a business needs all these processes to be up and working continuously or to be ready whenever asked. To gain this reliability and stability, a business might think of complete redundant solution but that will quickly add up to the cost. As a solution, a business will need to priorities the processes as per their criticality and can design redundant solution for the required vital processes.

Network redundancy: Availability of network is the primary requirement for any organization to function. While procuring network services, redundancy is one of the features which most sought for by the consumers. The network redundancy service provides multiple routes of connectivity and reduces the risk of network failures. An organization should understand the criticality of this service while choosing the network service provider.

Geographic Redundancy: Geographic redundancy is the technique to safeguard the data and data centers from any natural disasters or physical threats. The data centers are strategically placed and at a sufficient space that no one natural disaster or any unwanted threat can affect both the data centers at once.

Cloud-based security system has below mentioned benefits:

Protection to business from threats: Most of the data centers have not event implemented proper encryption techniques to protect their database. To ensure the business information, the underneath referenced measures can be taken to accomplish a more significant level of security.

Conduct a cloud security assessment regularly: Choose reliable cloud service providers to prevent data leaks. A regular security assessment of cloud infrastructures required to re ensure the network security.

Implement cloud security monitoring: With the advancement of technology, now, Artificial Intelligence (AI) can be implemented for auto detection of threats and also helps in minimizing the cost of monitoring.

Establish solid access management policies: Data access control is a healthy strategy to control and monitor the flow of information. Restriction of data access for different level of employees will improve the security. A closer look and routine check-up are required to restructure the flow of information within and outside of the organization.

Create a disaster recovery plan: Redundancy strategy is always helpful to quickly recover from the disasters. A regular back up of data and SOP in case of data breach is helpful as recovery plan.

Encrypt data: A business always need to use standard encryption techniques before uploading any data over cloud.

Consider edge computing for IoT: Data need to be decentralized to increase the data protection. It is always recommended to store the data at the edge of the network rather than put everything one place that is cloud.

Raise employee awareness: Regular employee training and awareness sessions are needed to be conducted to develop the sense of obligation among the employees. Every employee should understand the criticality of data security and standard procedures to be maintained while handling business data.

Preventing data loss: Though the cloud technology has been in the picture for a long time but still there are huge security loopholes mainly caused by ignorance. The online threats and attacks are becoming more sophisticated and eminent. Here are some steps that can be followed to prevent data loss.

1. **Perform a cloud risk assessment:** Company should focus and be curious about to understand how the data is being stored and how the cloud architecture is operating.
2. **Evaluation of deficits between suggested security and implemented security:** The business should be aware of the PCI and HIPAA guidelines and need to assess regularly to the gaps between implemented and suggested security guideline.
3. **Prevention plan for shadow IT:** With the overwhelming number of applications and services, the threat of shadow IT has become prevalent. The employees while using unauthorized applications may end up with leaking important data to third parties which can create severe security problems for the organization.
4. **Choose a cloud framework to deploy:** The business will need to choose reliable service providers who can offer all the security features planned and assessed by the organization.
5. **Determine and implement cloud best practices:** Every business should come up with well though and curated business policies to implement the best practices to prevent network security threats.
6. The shadow IT and unauthorized application users have proved to be a major threat for the organizations these days.

8.2   Attacks and Countermeasures

This section explains the different types of attacks and the counter measures can be taken. Some prominent threats and attacks have been taken into consideration for better understanding of the scenario.

8.2.1   Malware and Ransomware Breaches

Malware is a type of attack which most of the organizations face today. The malwares are generally received through e-mails, which employees could not recognize and download them in system. The malwares are sophisticated enough to be under disguise and perceived as attractive. After being downloaded, it can seize or steal data from the organizations. Ransomwares are a type of malware which demands monetary settlement in exchange of seized data. In recent times, a number of renowned organizations faced this issue and ended up paying a significantly huge amount to recover what was seized. Most of the could service providers implement prevention strategies like spam channels, firewalls, and other methods to identify the malwares and keep them away from the user's mailbox.

8.2.2   Prevention of Distributing Denial of Service

DDOs or Distributing Denial of Service is a kind of attack which tries blocked websites to be available to its users, which can cause severe reputational damage and business loss to the organizations. In DDOs attack, a website gets overloaded with zombie requests and makes your slow and unstable for loading. These attacks may get continued from few hours to weeks, causing severe business losses. The government organizations, telecom, IT, and e-commerce websites are mostly in targets of such kind of attacks causing harassment and losses for a number of people. The attacker creates a zombie network and starts sending overwhelming number of requests to the website which is much higher than the webservers handling capacity causing the website functions slow or completely crashed. Cyber security systems can be implemented to filter out the junk requests and safeguard the cloud service providers from DDOs attacks.

8.2.3   Threat Detection

Security is distributed computing can ensure better security and threat detection capabilities. The cloud servers filter out the threats before sending it to the clients which enhances the entry point level of security for the organizations.

Cloud technology has clear advantages over individual servers. As the cloud server supports higher number of users, the requirement of threat detection technique is more critical. Cloud service providers look for most sophisticated technologies like Machine Learning (ML) for threat detection. Through cloud any small and medium enterprises can afford the higher level of security for their data.

8.3   Zero-Knowledge Proof

The traditional authenticating process, where a user produces its password to the verifier, can be vulnerable if the password gets leaked over the network. To handle this threat, a new user authentication technique was conceptualized where the user does not have to disclose any secret information over the network the authentication can take place without compromising on security standards. The Zero-Knowledge Proof (ZKP) process was first introduced in 1985 by Goldwasser *et al.* [1], where the authentication can happen without sharing any secret key or password.

With the new technology new threats are also emerging. As the cloud provider handles a huge amount of data, most of the time they spread the data in different servers to lower the risk of hardware failures and data loss due to same. This, in turn, increases the risk of data leakage due to the untrustworthy servers. In most of the time, cloud server stores data in redundancy protect to prevent data loss that also adds up to risk of data theft. The data center becomes the primary targets for most of the cyber criminals as well.

ZKP is an interactive authentication system (P, V), where the Prover (P) and Verifier (V) prove their legitimacy through exchanging Language (L) Statements {0,1}.

The membership instance can be considered as x ϵ L. x is the common input shared by both prover and verifier, connected through a common communication channel. The P and V exchange a sequence of numbers to prove the authenticity. This sequence is represented as proof transcript, which has a predefined set of exchange sequences a1, b1, a2, b2, ..., an, bn. Here, the one party (prover) tries to proof the other party (verifier) that they hold the secret information without actually sharing it. The implementation of ZKP is still far to go, though a lot has been done as Mathematical Models and toward its applications. More about Zero-Knowledge Protocols can be found in [3].

Peggy, the prover: Peggy holds a secret key S, which she will prove to Victor without actually sharing it.
Victor, the verifier: Victor is verifier who requests a set of information from Peggy to verify the authenticity and confirms that Peggy holds the secret key S. By this process, Victor will have zero knowledge about the S key.
Eave, the eavesdropper: Eave is untrusted third party who listens to the complete conversation. A complete zero conversation will make sure that Eave will not be able to crack the S key out of the conversation.

An efficient ZKP system will satisfy two conditions:

1. **Completeness:** Peggy in priority will try to convince Victor that she knows S.
2. **Soundness:** Peggy will have very little chance to fake Victor if she does not know S.

Zero-knowledge protocols make sure that the verifier will have zero knowledge about the secret.

The concept PDP was conceptualized by Ateniese *et al.* in [4]. In this scheme, the user divides the data D into blocks and tag them with cryptographic tag s *bi* as $Ti,b = (H(Wi) gbi)d)modN$, where N is an RSA modulus, g is a public parameter, d is the secret key of the user, and $H(Wi)$ is chosen randomly. In this scheme, the data blocks need not be recovered for verification. Though the scheme is effective, but the computational complexity with the random numbers and verification of the user by secret key creates hurdle for actualization. In [2], Ateniese *et al.* introduced a newer version which allows open verification system where any user can reach cloud server for verification. This system has loopholes in dynamic scenarios where it loses the homomorphism and the verification standard falls, as it [5] depends upon the index of data blocks for proofing and verification.

Xu *et al.* [6] have proposed a unique concept of server data possession. In this system, the user uses polynomials for tagging and uses coefficient of polynomials for tagging the data blocks. This improves the standard the proof generation procedure as it uses the evaluations of polynomials. L. Krzywiecki and M. Kutylowski [7] have also focused on Lagrangian Interpolation for designing the similar scheme. Simari, Gerardo I in 2002 [8] explained in research about identity-based encryption system to implement access control in cloud-based computing systems.

8.4   Machine Learning for Cloud Computing

ML technology is serving the humanity in a best possible way by reading patterns, behaviors, predictions, and calculated moves backed up by data. ML itself requires expert support of data, computing, and storages to function efficiently. Cloud, on the hand, is capable of providing most versatile computing and storage services. When ML is implemented with cloud, the leverage can be amplified by many folds. This model is called "Intelligent Cloud". By using cloud technology, ML complexities can be simplified, and processes can be accelerated.

8.4.1   Types of Learning Algorithms

8.4.1.1   *Supervised Learning*

This is one of most important branch of ML. Every model comprises of learning agent and supervisor. The supervisor possesses a concealed a desired copy of output. The learning agent produces an actual output based on calculations. The performance of the learning agent is evaluated based on difference between the desired output and the actual output. The learning agent will learn from the environment and the error. The learning agent rectifies its further output focusing on to produce closest of desired output.

8.4.1.2   *Supervised Learning Approach*

To train a machine to produce a desired output, supervised learning model can be implemented to train the machine. This includes a labeled data set as input and the desired output. The output can be defined by human experts or measurements. The labeled data set can be in a table format indicating different features of the input to design a structure of understanding indicating toward the output. The input features cannot be very detailed due to the challenge of complexity but has to be detailed enough to train the machine. These set of labeled input and the defined output are considered as trends, based on which the future output will be generated. The accuracy of the learning function depends upon the input features used. For example, to create a model of recognizing handwriting, the input data set should have enough parameters that can be a single letter, a word, or a sentence. The input data set can include numeric data and categorical data. Some supervised learning algorithm requires user intervention to define the control parameters. There are two types of supervised learning: classification and regression. After optimizing the input data set, a test run is done on test data set before running on the actual training dataset.

The evaluation and correction of learning function is done repetitively to achieve the desired level of functionality.

8.4.1.3   Unsupervised Learning

Unsupervised learning, as the name implies, the model is not supervised for training but rather model is left to learn itself from the unnoticed parameters and invisible information to the human eye. Unsupervised learning uses ML algorithms that draw calculations on unlabeled data. It uses more sophisticated algorithms for analysis as the very little of zero knowledge is available about the data set and the desired outcome to be expected. The unsupervised learning is used for cluster or group analysis for what they performed, estimation of density, and reduction of dimensionality [14]. As the input data is unlabeled, a few tests and few models exist for unsupervised learning. The controlling parameters for unsupervised learning are also minimal as the machine itself generates the outcome.

8.4.2   Application on Machine Learning for Cloud Computing

- In the age of Industry 4.0, ML has become one of the most prominent technologies which are helping humanity in diverse areas. Data has become the language of the 21st century. To implement ML efficiently, it requires continuous support of data and computing, which has become possible due to the existence of cloud technology.
- As the cloud technology is cost efficient, it has become affordable for the small and medium enterprises to implement ML technology without spending much on the servers.
- Cloud being one of the emerging technologies is able to support the user with various services, which reduces the higher order of technical capabilities.

8.4.2.1   Image Recognition

Image recognition is one of the most effective uses of ML. The image recognition technique can be deployed for a variety of purpose like authentication, identification, analysis, attendance, human emotions, and in other several purposes. The technique identifies pixels as black and white or as red, green, and blue for identifying an image. It creates different categories for every set of attributes. The recognition is also called classification as it classifies almost everything as per the attributes. The attributes depend upon the objects it is identifying. This can be used for recognizing any living or non-living objects like human face, buildings, cars, or even handwriting and letters.

8.4.2.2   Speech Recognition

Speech recognition broadly use for recognition and translation of human language to text. The inputs can be taken from the human speech, recorded files, or other sources. The emerging tech corporations have implemented speech recognition technologies in a number of devices to get operated using voice commands. Siri, Alexa, and Google Assistant or Translate are one of the most common applications of this category.

8.4.2.3   Medical Diagnosis

ML has a wide application in the field of medical sciences. ML can be used to monitor health conditions and to create an alarm for the medical supervisors in case of emergency health situations of a patient. It monitors a number of parameters to detect and trigger output. The information gathered in different cases can be used to predict disease progression and knowledge creation through research.

8.4.2.4   Learning Associations

ML algorithms can be used in defining associations between products which have been perceived as unassociated so far. For example, this includes study of human purchasing behavior and micro and macro market conditions to define associations.

8.4.2.5   Classification

Classification is a process of segregating each object under study in different classes as per the features. The features help to analyze any object and classify them. To make the analysis effective, a number of relevant features or measurements are defined. For example, stock broker company can analyze a number of parameters of a company before suggesting their clients to invest. The features in this case may be quarterly profits, dividends, NPA, assets, and liabilities of the company and its trend of performances.

8.4.2.6   Prediction

ML is used in a wide variety of fields for predictions. The predictions done by the ML are scientific, based on data and based on past records and trends that make it a reliable application. A lot of sectors like trade, banking, health science, meteorology, and psychology have a great level of dependency on ML predictions.

8.4.2.7   Extraction

Extraction is one of the most common uses of ML. This process helps to analyze a huge chunk of unstructured data and creates a structured database and insights which can be used in a lot of fields. In extractions, a huge number of documents are taken as inputs and the output will be a structured dataset. E-commerce, financial corporations, media houses, and a lot other fields have a major dependency over this feature.

8.4.2.8   Regression

It can be likewise actualized that the AI in the relapse too. In relapse, the rule of AI can be utilized to upgrade the boundaries. It can likewise be utilized to diminish the estimation blunder and compute the nearest conceivable result. Likewise, the streamlining capacity of AI can be utilized. One can likewise decide to modify the contributions to request to get the nearest conceivable result.

8.4.2.9 Financial Services

AI has a ton of potential in the monetary and banking area. It is the main thrust behind the prevalence of the monetary administrations. AI can help the banks and monetary establishments to settle on more astute choices. AI can assist the monetary administrations with recognizing a record conclusion before it happens. It can likewise follow the spending example of the clients. AI can likewise play out the market examination. Shrewd machines can be prepared to follow spending designs. The calculations can distinguish the trends effectively and can respond continuously.

8.5 Zero-Knowledge Proof: Details

In straightforward secret key conventions, an inquirer A gives his secret phrase to a verifier B. In the event that specific safeguards are not taken, a snoop can get the secret word that was moved, and from that point on, he can imitate A to his advantage. Different conventions attempt to enhance this, as on account of challenge reaction frameworks [8]. The ZKP is an interactive system where the one party tries to prove that it holds a secret key, without actually revealing it. As per [9], the two parties can be denoted as P (prover) and V (verifier). The prover (P) tries to prove that it holds the secret key and the verifier (V) validates the statement of the prover through some mathematical transactions. Typical utilization of zero-information evidence is in verification frameworks where a substance demonstrates his character to the prover without revealing his mystery [10].

8.5.1 Comparative Study

Diffie-Hellman (D-H) key exchange algorithm is known as one of the earliest practical instances of Zero-Knowledge Protocol where two sides share one non-private communication channel to interact and the authentication process takes place without sharing any secret information. No side will require any prior information to authenticate and the transaction lefts no traces of the secret information. Each side uses a common shared key which is a symmetric key cipher to encrypt the communications.

Quite possibly the most entrancing employments of zero-information evidence inside cryptographic conventions is to uphold legit conduct while looking after protection. Generally, the thought is to authorize a client to demonstrate, utilizing a zero-information verification, that its conduct is right as indicated by the convention. Due to adequacy, it is realized that the client should truly act really to have the option to give a legitimate confirmation. Due to zero information, it is evident that the client does not bargain the protection of its privileged insights during the time spent giving the confirmation [11, 12].

8.5.1.1 Fiat-Shamir ZKP Protocol

In Fiat-Shamir ZKP protocol, it satisfies the condition of zero knowledge, where the two parties (prover and verifier) complete the authentication process without any prior knowledge and sharing the secret information. The prover focuses on proving that it holds the secret information and does not need to reveal it for authentication process [13]. In Fiat-Shamir protocol, a trusted third party chooses to large random numbers, p and q and calculates n (n = p * q). The third party reveals the value of n as public key while keeping the value of p and q secret. Figure 8.2 illustrates the transactions take place in the process. The prover P and verifier B follows the below mentioned steps to complete the process [21].

1. The prover Alice (P) chooses a random number r and calculates $\{x = r^2 \bmod n\}$, where n is the shared public key.
2. Alice shares the value of x with the verifier Bob (b) as witness.
3. Bob chooses a number between 0 and 1 and sends it as challenge (C) to Alice.
4. With the help of value of C, Alice calculates Y $\{Y = r^2 \bmod n\}$.
5. Alice shares the Y with Bob as response to the challenge.
6. Bob the verifier calculates $Y^2 \bmod n$ and $xv^c \bmod n$.
7. Bob compares both the values, if they are same, then Alice is authentic; otherwise, Bob considers this as a failure of authentication.
8. The process gets iterated for one to six times with different values of C as 0 or 1. The prover needs get through every time to prove its authenticity.

There is another similar protocol as Feige-Fiat-Shamir protocol, which follows a series of private keys and public key and array of challenges for the authentication process.

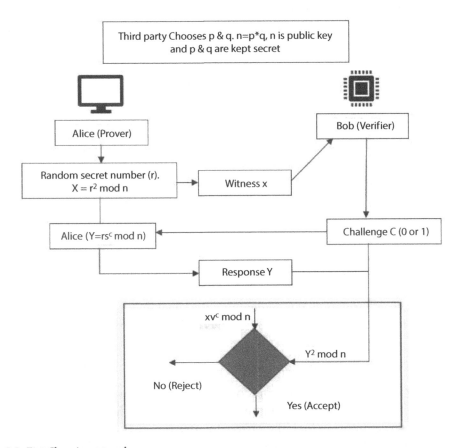

Figure 8.2 Fiat-Shamir protocol.

8.5.2 Diffie-Hellman Key Exchange Algorithm

D-H key exchange program was conceptualized in 1976 by Whitfield Diffie and Martin Hellman, which was the first practical ZKP protocol. Here, the prover and the verifier establish communication over a public communication channel and performs a set of mathematical transactions to authenticate the prover without revealing the secret. This algorithm uses multiplicative group of integers modulo $p(Zp^*, x)$, where P is a prime number, and 1 to $p - 1$ is used for different mathematical operations. The two parties choose random value of p and g. g is a primitive root in the group. The value of p and g are made public and follows the procedure as shown in Figure 8.3 [14, 20, 21].

1. Alice chooses a random value for x between 0 and p and calculates $R_1 = g^x \bmod p$.
2. Bob the verifier picks up another random value for y and calculates $R_2 = g^y \bmod p$.
3. Bob and Alice exchange R_1 and R_2.
4. Bob and Alice decode and calculate K_{Alice}, K_{bob}, respectively.

The D-H key exchange algorithm is prone to "man-in-the-middle" and "discrete algorithm" attacks [6]. These operations of these two attacks are described as below.

8.5.2.1 *Discrete Logarithm Attack [6]*

Any untrusted third party can overhear the value of R1 and R2 by placing itself in the middle. It can then recalculate the value of x and y by performing ($R_1 = g^x \bmod p$ and $R_2 = g^y \bmod p$). These values will reveal the value of $K = g^{xy} \bmod p$.

As preventive measure, the below mentioned changes can be done:

1. The value of P has to be large enough.

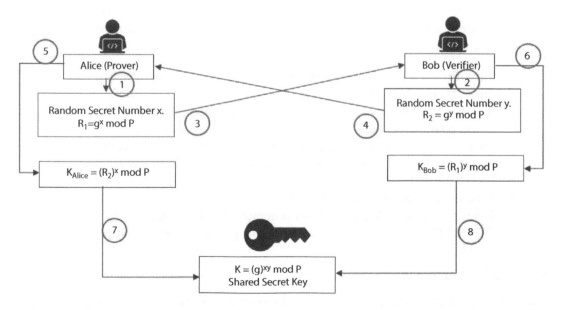

Figure 8.3 Diffie-Hellman key exchange algorithm.

2. g should be able to be beyond the group limit.
3. The values of x and y chosen by prover and verifier has to be for single use and extremely large.

As these measures will increase the mathematical complexity by multiple times, thus practical implementation will not be possible [22, 23].

8.5.2.2 Man-in-the-Middle Attack

The untrusted third party can replicate the prover and the verifier by placing itself in the middle. It will receive R_1 from Alice and R_2 from Bob.

1. The prover selects random value of x, and calculates $R_1 = g^x \bmod p$, then transmits the R_1 to Bob.
2. Eve, untrusted third party, selects random number z and calculates $R_2 = g^z \bmod p$ then transmits R_2 to both Alice and Bob.
3. Bob chooses random number y and calculates $R_3 = g^y \bmod p$ and then transmits R_3 to Alice.
4. R_3 is blocked and captured by Eve, which then never reaches Alice.
5. Alice and Eve both calculate $K_1 = g^{xz} \bmod p$, which will then work as a shared key between them.
6. Eve and Bob both calculates $K_2 = g^{zy} \bmod p$, which will then work as a shared key between them. The man-in-the-middle attack can be prevented by implementing a two-way validating technique where both prover and verifier prove to each other that they are authentic [14].

8.5.3 ZKP Version 1

In this protocol [17], a trusted third party chooses two random numbers p and g and makes them public, where p is a large prime number and g is primitive root of order $p - 1$. Figure 8.4 illustrates the working principle of the model.

1. Alice, the prover, chooses a random number x and calculates $R_1 = g^x \bmod p$ and sends the R_1 to the Bob (the verifier).
2. Bob, the prover, chooses another random number Y and calculates $R_1 = g^y \bmod p$ and sends the R_2 to Alice.
3. Then, Alice calculates the value of secret key K_1 using the R_2 received from the verifier $K_1 = (R_2)^x \bmod p$. Alice encrypts the K_1 and R_2 and generates $C_1 = E(K_1, R_2)$.
4. Alice sends C_1 to Bob for verification.
5. Bob generates $K = (R_1)^y \bmod p$ and generates $C_2 = E(K_1, R_2)$.
6. If C_1 and C_2 are same, then it proves that the prover, Alice, is authentic.

8.5.4 ZKP Version 2

The proposed ZKP1 model is vulnerable to the man-in-the-middle attack as an interceptor can place itself in the middle and can replicate the opposite parties and retrieve the

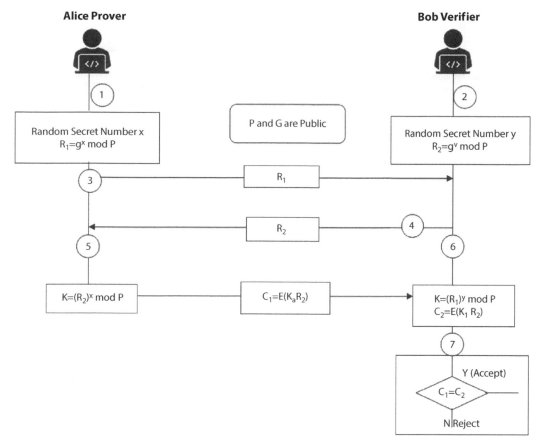

Figure 8.4 ZKP version 1 [17].

secret key K. To avoid the situation, the proposed ZKP model 2 [17] added one extra layer of authentication to verify the authenticity of the verifier. Same as the previous model, a trusted third party selects two random numbers p and g and makes them as public key. Figure 8.5 illustrates the working principal of the model.

1. Alice selects a random number x and calculates $R_1 = g^x \bmod p$ and sends the R_1 to Bob, the verifier.
2. Bob chooses a random number y and calculates $R_2 = g^y \bmod p$.
3. Bob calculates the secret key $K = (R_1)^y \bmod p$ and encrypts it with R_2. Encrypted $C_1 = E(K_1 R_2)$.
4. Bob sends the R_2 and C_1 to Alice.
5. Alice then generates secret Key $K_2 = (R_2)^x \bmod p$.
6. Alice calculates R_2 by decrypting the C_1 and checks whether $R_2 = R_2$. If the values are same, then the verifier is authentic; otherwise, it stops the process.
7. If the prover finds the verifier is authentic, then it sends $K_1 R_1$ and R_2 by encrypting as C_2.
8. Bob receives the C_2 and decrypts it. Bob will be able to calculate R_1.

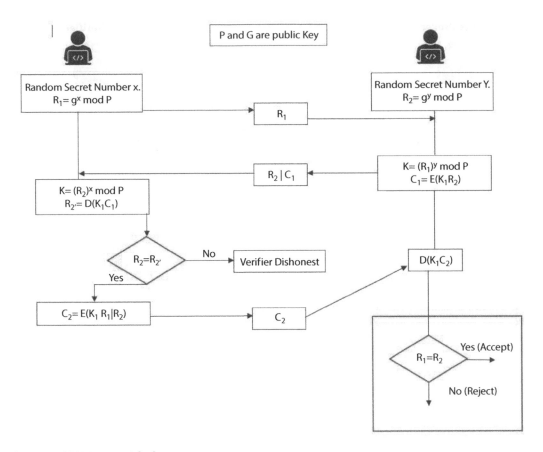

Figure 8.5 ZKP Version 2 [17].

9. If the verifier finds that the R_1 is equal to R_2, then it satisfies the conditions and the authentication process gets completed; otherwise, the transaction is rejected.

8.5.5   Analysis

According to the meaning of ZKP, the proposed conventions are intelligent framework, where a mix prover and verifier (P, V) is executed for confirmation and for demonstrating a language participation proclamation over {G}, where G is a gathering $<z_p^*,x>$. R_1, R_2, C_1, and C_2 are participation occurrences of G gathering and verification record. Prover (P) and verifier (V) ascertain and trade a predefined set of number arrangements while blending them with new contributions from each new exchange. After the cooperation is finished, the yield of the conventions is thought about, and choices are made for acknowledgement or rejection. These depicted conventions ready to meet the ZKP properties and are sufficiently productive to oppose regular assaults with its functionalities. See Table 8.1.

1. Completeness: The prover and the verifier register the mystery key K by following the predefined convention, which is equivalent to (k = gxy mod P). On the off chance that both the prover and the verifier are an endless supply of the association, they will wind up with producing a similar mystery key

Table 8.1 Comparative study.

Techniques	Interaction technique	Third party involvement	Possible threats	Encryption technique	Operating technique	Limitations
Fiat-Shamir ZKP Protocol	Exchange challenge and witness	Yes	Discrete logarithm attack and man-in-the-middle attack	No	Utilizations measured number juggling and equal check measure	Repetitive and infeasible
Diffie-Hellman Key Exchange Algorithm	Exchange keys	No	Discrete logarithm attack and man-in-the-middle attack	No	Utilizations a multiplicative gathering of whole numbers module	Infeasible due to technical complexity
ZKP Proposed Model 1	Exchange Keys in encrypted format	No	Man-in-the-middle attack	Yes	Utilizations a multiplicative gathering of whole numbers module	Vulnerable to man-in-the-middle attack
ZKP Proposed Model 2	Exchange Keys in encrypted format	No	None	Yes	Uses multiplicative group of integers module	None

K and the confirmation will be acknowledged. Else, they will produce distinctive mystery key which will prompt dismissal of the verification. In this way, the convention is fit to produce unmistakable choices upon finish and accordingly fulfils the culmination property.

2. If the prover neglects to process the right mystery key K, the scrambled answer $[C_2 = E(K_{Alice}, R_2)]$ will be unique in relation to the worth registered by the verifier $[C_2 = E(K_{Bob}, R_2)]$. As the cycle fuses irregular choice of numbers, speculating the C_1 and C_2 is practically incomprehensible, which guarantees just two prospects; either equivalent $(C_2 = C_2')$ or extraordinary $(C_1 \neq C_2')$. So the convention is sound and does not founded on probabilities.

3. Zero knowledge: In this convention, the prover and the verifier are not needed to share or uncover any data which can force danger of assaults or pantomime. Both the gatherings will be left distinctly with their own mystery number and the determined mystery key which gets changed after every exchange. The mystery numbers like x, y, and K were not uncovered to the next gathering during the cycle and each gathering is left with zero information about the other.

4. The proposed convention form - 2 is protected from man-in-the-center assault, as the assailant would not have the option to figure or ascertain two mystery keys; $\left(K_1 = R_1^z \bmod p\right)$ and $\left(K_2 = R_2^z \bmod p\right)$ to be imparted to Alice and Bob.

5. The proposed convention can be secured against discrete logarithm assault, by applying the suggestion.

8.5.6 Cloud Security Architecture

Cloud computing is the modern technique of computing in which the data and computing services can be made readily available to any user at any geographical location. The user does not have to be involved in the active management of the servers.

Cloud technology is capable of providing great scalability, device independency, location independency, and agility to any user in very low cost. By cloud technology, a user is free from managing the risk of data security and readiness.

A large portion of the current mists are based on top of present-day server farms. It redesigns its Infrastructure as a Service (IaaS), Platform as a Service (PaaS), and Software as a Service (SaaS) and offers them to the end user. The end user pays only for its usage and thus reduces the burden of cost. Figure 8.6 shows a various leveled see for distributed computing.

Information centers: The information centers are the locations where the data servers are established to support cloud services. These centers are strategically placed where resources can be made available in optimum cost. While looking at the geographical locations of the information centers, it is important to choose locations which are less prone to natural disasters.

Foundation as a service: It exists in the data centers to support consumers with computing capabilities and storage and other facilities to function as per their requirements. This helps the consumers their preferred scheme to further cut down the cost [24].

Software as a service
Platform as a service
Infrastructure as a service
Data center

Figure 8.6 Cloud architecture.

Stage as a service: This is also known as PaaS and provides platform services to the consumer, where the consumer doe not need to download or install any application in their local system and can work collaboratively in any project irrespective of their geographical locations [25].

Programming as a service: This is also known as SaaS and is service generally provided to the end user as per requirements. This enables users to access a software without local maintenance and monitoring. There are a number of large-scale software and Enterprise Resource Management software are preferably deployed by this layer to serve a large number of employees without the physical barrier. The layer supports to integrate these software packages with other software to increase their productivity and utility.

8.5.7 Existing Cloud Computing Architectures

Examination on distributed computing has pulled in both the scholarly community and industry to concoct inventive and viable distributed computing models. A great deal has been done here and a few distributed computing structures have been proposed.

A number of modern day cloud architectures do not interact with other clouds which makes the resources limited and utility goes down due to the rigidity in the structures.

8.5.8 Issues With Current Clouds

Migration from cloud provider: Though cloud services helps to reduce a significant amount of time and money for different services but when an organization wishes to move its applications to another, it becomes more expensive and time consuming to migrate [15].

Rigidity of computing components: The computing needs of a user may changeover the time and the user may wish to include or discard feature to a system. In physical machines, a user can build its own computer or can buy a system as per the current requirements, but in case of cloud computing, the user will need to choose the components only from offerings of its cloud provider [16].

Lack of multi-tenancy supports: To achieve the low cost goals the cloud services are often shared with multiple clients [18]: While sharing the cloud services with other clients, the three major issues are often faced:

1. Resource sharing: The cost of management, maintenance, and equipment needs to be reduced for each client.

2. Security confinement: To ensure the security protocols are maintained between the clients.
3. Localization: To ensure to meet the individual need of each client in terms of data access, user interface, and usability.

Lack of flexibility for user interface: The user interface defines the usability of system to a user. As every customer has a different perseverance toward systems, the user interface needs will be unique each time. Due the cloud rigid framework, this need cannot be made most of the time [19].

8.6   Conclusion

With the modernization of workplace, mobility has increased immensely and the traditional way of computing has become a bottleneck for many functionalities and services. The cloud technology offers applications, computing, and storage services irrespective of the physical machines and geographical locations. This flexibility has helped millions of people to enter the globalization process of their business. It is evident from the current style of living that technology has flooded in every aspects of human life. Staring from social media, banking, online marketplace, medical facilities, food delivery, and other several services entirely depend upon the cloud services. Any user can access their data from any location by using any device of their choice. This has reshaped the world of work entirely and moving faster than ever before. Cloud services can be hold responsible for bringing the paradigm shift in the way the companies customize their promotions and sales. Consumerism has reached at its zenith and will continue to go up for at least several decades. Not only through its own services but also cloud has served a platform to other wonderful technologies like AI and ML which has brought a drastic change in the way human use to think. AI and ML, which are considered as the technology of the future, are heavily dependent on the cloud services. The cloud has made us able to store immense volume of data and to analyze them to generate business intelligence, national security, and medical attention and has opened several avenues in the field of research and academia. The cloud technology has several distinct advantages over the traditional computing style.

The cloud technology is cost effective as it does not impose a heavy burden of procuring hardware to offer any service. This encourages small and medium business to go online and flourish. The data centers maintain 99.9% availability which ensures maximum uptime and minimizes the risk of losing business. The features like redundancy adds extra layer of prevention from data loss, which makes cloud services more versatile and reliable. A business can customize the services, to solve its purpose and make changes to the service requirements without being worried about adding extra hardware or cost. As per the business needs, services can be prioritized and hedged to ensure the functionality. As the data centers can achieve higher degree of security and safeguarding data, it reassures the clients about the data security. Now, business can rely upon the cloud services without being worried about the external threats. Cloud computing handles critically important data for businesses and other important clients but still the cloud architecture is exposed to several internet threats. To overcome through critical security threats, Zero-Knowledge Proof techniques can be implemented. This section illustrates Zero-Knowledge Proof in details and the existing protocols like fait Shamir Protocol and D-H Protocol. This paper also explains about different Cloud Computing Architectures, applications of cloud computing. A survey of zero-knowledge existing algorithm has also been explained in this paper.

This survey paper has a future scope to explore further work on existing algorithms of Zero-Knowledge Proof with cloud computing and modification of the existing algorithm to achieve higher degree of security.

References

1. Goldwasser, S., Micali, S., Rckoff, C., The Knowledge Complexity of Interactive Proof Systems. *SIAM J. Comput.*, 18, 186–208, 1989, July.

2. Goldreich, M. and Wigderson, Proofs that Yield Nothing But their Validity or All Languages in NP have Zero-Knowledge Proof. *JACM*, 38, 1, 691–729, 1991.

3. Goldreich, O. and Oren, Y., Definitions and Properties of Zero-Knowledge Proof Systems. *J. Cryptol.*, 7, 1, 1–32, 1994.

4. Ateniese, G., Burns, R., Curtmola, R., Herring, J., Kissner, L., Peterson, Z., Song, D., Provable data possession at untrusted stores, in: *Proceedings of the 14th ACM conference on Computer and communications security, CCS '07*, ACM, New York, NY, USA, pp. 598–609, 2007.

5. Ateniese, G., Burns, R., Curtmola, R., Herring, J., Khan, O., Kissner, L., Peterson, Z., Song, D., Remote data checking using provable datapossession. *ACM Trans. Inf. Syst. Secur.*, 14, 1, 12:1–12:34, June 2011.

6. Xu, J. and Chang, E.-C., Towards efficient proofs of retrievability, in: *Proceedings of the 7th ACM Symposium on Information, Computer and Communications Security, ASIACCS '12*, ACM, New York, NY, USA, pp. 79–80, 2012.

7. Krzywiecki, L. and Kutylowski, M., Proof of possession for cloud storage via lagrangian interpolation techniques, in: *Proceedings of the 6th international conference on Network and System Security, NSS'12*, Springer-Verlag, Berlin, Heidelberg, pp. 305–319, 2012.

8. Simari, G.I., *A Primer on Zero Knowledge Protocols*, Technical report, UniversidadNacional del Sur, Buenos aires, argentina, 2002.

9. Velten, M., *Zero-Knowledge The Magic of Cryptography*, Saarland University, Carbondale, August, 2006.

10. Mohr, A., *A Survey of Zero-Knowledge Proofs with Applications to Cryptography*, Southern, Illinois University, Carbondale, 2007.

11. Krantz, S.G., Zero Knowledge Proofs. *AIM Preprint Series*, vol. 10–46, July 25, 2007.

12. Ueli, M., Unifying Zero-Knowledge Proofs of Knowledge. *Africacrypt 2009, LNCS*, vol. 5580, pp. 272–286, 2009.

13. Kizza, J.M., Feige-Fiat-Shamir ZKP Scheme Revisited. *Int. J. Comput. ICT Res.*, 4, 1, pp. 9–19, 2010, June.

14. Hinton, G. and Sejnowski, T., *Unsupervised Learning: Foundations of Neural Computation*, MIT Press, 1999.

15. Huang, Y. *et al.*, A Framework for Building a Low Cost, Scalable and Secured Platform for Web-Delivered Business Services. *IBM J. Res. Dev.*, 53, 6, 4:1–4:14, 2010.

16. Golden, B., Computer World. [Online]http://www.computerworld.com/s/article/9126620/The_case_against_cloud_computing_part_one, 2009, January.

17. Ibrahem, M.K., Modification of Diffie-Hellman key exchange algorithm for Zero knowledge proof. *2012 International Conference on Future Communication Networks*, 2012.

18. Gao, B., Guo, C., Wang, Z., An, W., Sun, W., Develop and Deploy Multi-Tenant Web-delivered Solutions using IBM middleware: Part 3: Resource sharing, isolation and customization in the single instance multi-tenant application. [Online]. http://www.ibm.com/developerworks/

webservices/library/wsmultitenant/index.html, Proceedings of the 2007 IEEE International Conference on ECommerce Technology and the IEEE International Conference on Enterprise Computing, E-Commerce, and EServices, 551–558. IEEE. 2009, March.

19. Tsai, W.-T., Huang, Q., Elston, J., Chen, Y., Service-Oriented User Interface Modeling and Composition, in: *International Conference on e-Business Engineering*, Xi'an, pp. 21–28, 2008.

20. Hellman, M.E., An Overview of Public Key Cryptography. *IEEE Commun. Mag.*, 40, 42–49, May 2002.

21. Bhattacharya, P., Debbabi, M., Otrok, H., Improving the Diffie-Heliman Secure Key Exchange. *International Conference on Wireless Networks, Communications and Mobile Computing*, 2005.

22. Stallings, W., *Cryptography and Network Security*, 5th Ed, Prentice Hall, Upper Saddle River, NJ, USA, 2010.

23. Back, A., The Diffe-Hellman Key Exchange, 2009, December 2, 2009, *Intl. J. Innov. Res. Electron. Commun. (IJIREC)*, 1, 4, 26–36, July 2014. http://129.81.170.14/~erowland/courses/2009-2/projects/Back.pdf.

24. Wikipedia, Cloud Computing. [Online]. http://en.wikipedia.org/wiki/Cloud_computing.

25. Vecchiola, C., Chu, X., Buyya, R., Aneka: A Software Platform for.NET-based Cloud Computing, in: *High Speed and Large Scale Scientific Computing*, pp. 267–295, 2010.

A Robust Approach for Effective Spam Detection Using Supervised Learning Techniques

Amartya Chakraborty[1*], Suvendu Chattaraj[2], Sangita Karmakar[2] and Shillpi Mishrra[2†]

[1]Department of Computer Science and Engineering, University of Engineering and Management, Kolkata, India
[2]Department of Computer Science and Engineering, Techno India University, Kolkata, India

Abstract

In this age of popular instant messaging applications, Short Message Service or SMS has lost relevance and has turned into the forte of service providers, business houses, and different organizations that use this service to target common users for marketing and spamming. A recent trend in spam messaging is the use of content in regional language typed in English, which makes the detection and filtering of such messages more challenging. In this work, an extended version of a standard SMS corpus containing spam and non-spam messages that is extended by the inclusion of labeled text messages in regional languages like Hindi or Bengali typed in English has been used, as gathered from local mobile users. Monte Carlo approach is utilized for learning and classification in a supervised approach, using a set of features and machine learning algorithms commonly used by researchers. The results illustrate how different algorithms perform in addressing the given challenge effectively.

Keywords: Spam detection, supervised learning, regional spam, Monte Carlo approach, deep learning, convolutional neural networks, SMS spam, TF-IDF vectorization

9.1 Introduction

Man is a social animal, and the very essence of this socializing nature lies in their ability to effectively communicate. From the cave drawings in early ages to the blazingly fast instant messaging applications prevalent in these times, the need for effective and timely communication has always been a priority in human life.

The basic components of a typical communication are as shown in Figure 9.1 where a communication medium is used by sender(s) to communicate with the receiver(s). This medium of communication has taken several forms over the many decades of human civilization. For instance, cave walls, letters (pages), and text messages are all different forms of communication medium that man has used.

---

*Corresponding author: amartya3@gmail.com
†Corresponding authors: shllpimishrra91@gmail.com

Rajdeep Chakraborty, Anupam Ghosh and Jyotsna Kumar Mandal (eds.) Machine Learning Techniques and Analytics for Cloud Security, (171–192) © 2022 Scrivener Publishing LLC

Figure 9.1 Components of a communication.

With the onset of mobile technology in human lives, the concept of hand-written letters was replaced by a new form of communication, referred to as the Short Message Service or SMS. The first instance of sending a mobile device–based text message was recorded in the year 1992 [1], and it has come a long way since then. This service gained popularity at a very rapid rate, and became an integral part of technology enriched human life in the last two decades. Using the SMS, each mobile device user can compose a textual message of length up to 160 characters including alphabets, numeric values, and special symbols [2]. This constitutes the "short message" that can be sent to a recipient (another mobile device user). This mode of communication has utility especially in cases where short pieces of information need to be urgently conveyed or where attending calls is not plausible.

However, the last decade has witnessed the meteoric rise in the use of internet-based messaging services which are faster and cheaper than SMS in most cases. Also, such services are made more attractive with no message length limit, inclusion of stickers, GIFs, and other application specific enhancements to make them the primary choice of mobile-based communication. This has pushed the erstwhile default communication medium to a secondary position, and nowadays it is seldom used in day-to-day communication by general mobile users. Instead, this service has become a handy tool for different service and/or product-based companies, who use it to implement their strategy of direct marketing.

The SMS-based marketing strategy adapted by different companies provides a unique opportunity to identify and incite their potential clients by providing them attractive incentives and offers on chosen products or services. A recent survey revealed that 96% of the participants from India admitted they receive unwanted spam message every day, of which 42% receive almost 7 such SMS per day [3]. Despite the regulatory and preventive norms put in place by the Telecom Regulatory Authority of India (TRAI) on the broadcast of unwanted messages, only about 6% of Indian mobile users find the Do Not Disturb (DND) service useful [4].

A general understanding of spam as unwanted or unsolicited messages is essential in order to effectively prevent or detect and filter such messages at the user end. Oblivious mobile users are highly prone to signing up for such irritating SMS automatically when they are availing a service or purchasing a product of their choice. Online marketing, banking, telecom service, etc., constitute a bulk of the unwanted or spam messages that Indian users usually receive. Yet more harmful is the set of fraudulent spam messages that target innocent users and aim to lure them and extract crucial information regarding their personal details, banking passwords, etc., as shown in Figure 9.2.

On the other hand, the desired electronic texts that a mobile user expects to receive are called ham messages. Such SMS could be bank account related updates or travel ticket-based information, etc. So, it is essential to accurately distinguish between these two types of SMS. Typically, the SMS-based communication including spam filtering may be illustrated as represented as shown in Figure 9.3.

Congrats 9593XXXX14 !
You are selected for Free Test
Drive. Verify details now.

http://z2az.com/GFkPC

Figure 9.2 An example of malicious spam message.

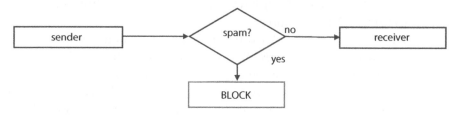

Figure 9.3 Flowchart of spam filtered communication system.

Over the years, there has been extensive research on different spam detection and filtering techniques, though not all of them have resulted in efficient and productive end user applications. The current work deals with the determination of robustness of the commonly used classification algorithms consisting of conventional machine learning classifier models as well as contemporary Deep Neural Network architecture–based models. This is undertaken by utilizing the Monte Carlo approach by performing the training and classification tasks on different combinations of both spam and ham data for up to 100 times. As a result, the definitive performance statistics for each classification model can be realized and the best performing model may be chosen as the ideal one. The state of the art of research on spam identification has been discussed in the following Literature Review.

9.2   Literature Review

In this section, the authors have discussed some recent state of the art research works in the field of spam detection on SMS messages, going up to the last 5 years. The discussed works have proposed and implemented novel features, effective processing techniques and different advanced machine learning algorithms toward developing an efficient SMS spam recognition system.

Back in 2015, Agarwal *et al.* [5] utilized the comprehensive data corpus consolidated by [6] and extended it by adding a set of spam and ham SMS collected from Indian mobile users. They demonstrated how different learning algorithms like Support Vector Machine (SVM) and Multinomial Naïve Bayes (MNB) performed on the Term Frequency–Inverse

Document Frequency (TF-IDF)–based features extracted from the corpora. Starting at around this time, a plethora of research works have used the same corpus and similar set of features and learning algorithms for designing spam detection systems. In the following set of similar works, it is observed that a set of learning and classification algorithms are used for a performance comparison study. Also, there is a paradigm shift toward neural network-based learning algorithms in more recent times.

In such a work in 2017, Suleiman *et al.* [7] demonstrated a comparative study of the performance of MNB, Random Forest, and Deep Learning algorithm–based models by using the H2O framework and a self-determined set of novel features on the same SMS corpus.

Using word embedding features, Jain *et al.* [8] showed in 2018 how Convolutional Neural Network (CNN) can be utilized to achieve a better performance than a number of other baseline machine learning models in determining the spam messages from the corpus of [6]. In the same year, Popovac *et al.* [9] illustrated how CNN algorithm performs on the same SMS corpus using TD-IDF features.

In 2019, Gupta *et al.* [10] proposed a voting ensemble technique on different learning algorithms, namely, MNB, Gaussian Naïve Bayes (GNB), Bernoulli Naïve Bayes (BNB), and Decision Tree (DT) for spam identification using the same corpus.

The trend of classifier performance comparison continues till recent times in 2020, where the work by Hlouli *et al.* [11], illustrated how Multi-Layer Perceptron (MLP), SVM, k-Nearest Neighbors (kNN), and Random Forest algorithms perform on the same SMS corpus for detecting spam and ham using Bag of Words and TF-IDF–based features. In a similar contemporary work, GuangJun *et al.* [12] highlighted the performance of kNN, DT, and Logistic Regression (LR) models on SMS spam corpus, though the feature extraction techniques were not discussed.

A recent but different type of work by Roy *et al.* [13] shows how the same SMS corpus by Hidalgo *et al.* [6] is classified using Long Short Term Memory (LSTM) and CNN-based machine learning models with a high accuracy. The authors also noted that dependence on manual feature selection and extraction results often influences the efficacy of the spam detection system and consequently utilized the inherent features determined by the LSTM and CNN algorithms.

Another interesting observation stems from the inclusion of SMS content in languages other than English for spam and ham identification, as undertaken by Ghourabi *et al.* [14] in their recent work. The authors used TF-IDF and word embedding–based features for the conventional machine learning models (such as SVM, kNN, DT, and MNB) and proposed CNN-LSTM hybrid model, respectively. This is the only recent research work that intends to identify the spam content in non-English language from a multi-lingual corpus.

9.3   Motivation

It is observed that in spite of the comparative study of classification performance undertaken by the aforementioned state-of-the-art works, none of them have attempted to determine and establish the robustness of the classification techniques in spam identification. Also, the abundance of spam messages in regional language (typed in English) is largely ignored in such works.

Taking cue from the aforementioned observations, the authors have made the following contributions in the current work:

1. We introduce the novel context of identifying spam and ham SMS in regional languages that are typed in English, along with the general English corpus of spam and ham by extending it.
2. We employ a Monte Carlo approach to repeatedly perform classification using different machine learning algorithms on different combinations of spam and ham text from the extended corpus (with k-fold cross-validation for a large value of k = 100) in order to determine the efficiency of baseline learning algorithms in comparison to the CNN-based model.

9.4   System Overview

The current work follows a series of steps as illustrated in Figure 9.4. The corresponding discussions are provided in the following sections.

The SMS corpus with added Indian context, described in Section 9.5, is initially processed in a series of operations as discussed in Section 9.6. The processed text corpus is then vectorized and the TF-IDF vector is determined for the corpora as its feature. This procedure is illustrated in the Section 9.7. The different supervised learning techniques that have been trained and evaluated in this work are discussed in Section 9.8. The experimental setup and evaluation techniques have been discussed in Sections 9.9 and 9.10, respectively. The experimental results and analysis have been provided in Section 9.11. The adaptation of proposed framework in cloud architecture is discussed in brief in Section 9.12. Finally, the concluding remarks have been offered in Section 9.13.

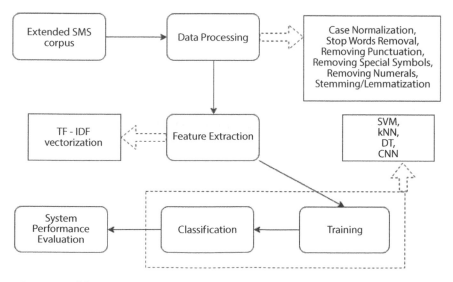

Figure 9.4 Overview of the system.

9.5   Data Description

The authors have utilized the comprehensive and popular SMS dataset made available by [6], which has been the choice of many state-of-the-art works in this domain even in recent years. This spam and ham text corpus is compiled using free sources on the World Wide Web and corresponds to SMS messages from places like the United Kingdom (UK) and Singapore. The corpus originally consists of 5,574 texts written in English and each such message is appropriately labeled as a spam message or a ham message. The authors have further extended this data set during a period of 2 years by introducing the context of Indian spam messages. The speciality of the collected corpus is that it consists of spam SMS that the Indian companies and service providers use for marketing purposes. These messages are mostly regional language-based texts that are in typed in English (shown in Figure 9.5), while some of them are written in English (shown in Figure 9.6). This set of SMSs has been collected from the students and faculties of Techno India University, West Bengal. The final corpus prepared and used in this work consists of more than 7,000 text messages. The data corpus has two columns corresponding to the message text and the label, respectively. This corpus is processed as described in the next section.

9.6   Data Processing

As evident from the illustrated spam SMS screenshots, each text contains different types of symbols, numeric values, as well as English and regional language–based words typed in English. In order to be able to extract meaningful features for the classifiers to learn, these pieces of text need to be thoroughly cleaned or normalized. Unlike usual sensory data cleaning, in such cases, the elimination of outliers and value standardization is not appropriate. The process of text normalization or cleaning ensures that all possible "noise" is

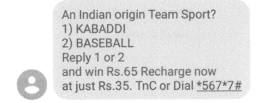

Figure 9.5 A sample spam message in regional language typed in English.

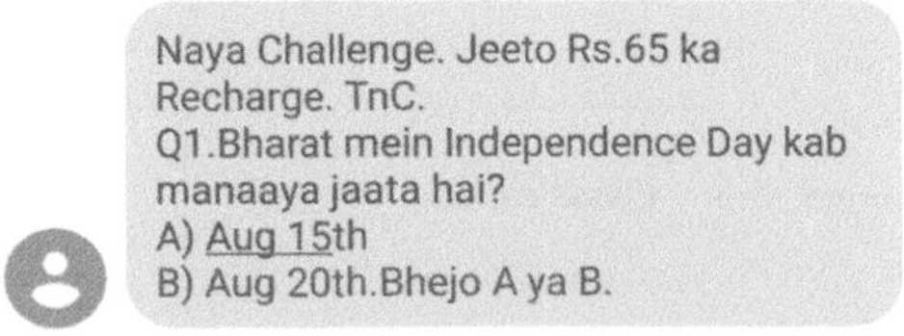

Figure 9.6 A sample spam message in regional language typed in English.

eliminated from the data, semantic identification and grouping is feasible, and the inherent features of the text data may be accurately represented in a simpler manner as features for the learning algorithms.

The data corpus used in this work is available in the form of a text file, which has been read and converted to a data-frame in using python-based library called pandas. The two columns of this data-frame correspond to the label and the text, and for each row in this data-frame, a set of operations is performed which are described below:

i. Case normalization: Each text message may contain different words that are capitalized, or some of whose alphabets are capitalized. For the current purpose of spam identification, there is no requirement of maintaining this distinction among words of the same meaning. For instance, different SMS texts may contain the same word "boy" written as "BOY", "Boy", "BoY", etc. In such case, it is prudent to normalize the case of each occurrence of this word such that all have the same common form "boy". In this manner, every word in every text is normalized to lower case. This is the first step that has been used to process each text in our SMS corpus.

ii. Stop-word removal: Every piece of text commonly contains a number of "stop-words", a term coined by Hans Peter Luhn which signifies their essential lack of importance in text processing. Such words are generally removed during text processing as they only contribute to computational complexity and hardly contribute to the task of learning spam or ham feature, while their contribution to syntactical understanding of sentence structure is undeniable. Some common stop-words are "a", "an", "the", "I", "to", "because", "for", "in", etc. As a second step of data processing, we have completely eliminated the stop words from the text output of the previous step.

iii. Removing punctuations and special symbols: The usual messages contain a good number of punctuation marks and special symbols such as ";", "/", "?", "!", "@", "%", and "&". These symbols, though essential for sentence structuring, do not actually contribute much to the determination of spam or ham related characteristics. Hence, as a third step of text normalization, all such punctuation marks and special symbols are removed from each piece of text from the previous step.

iv. Removing numerals: Numbers are also widely present in SMS text messages, both spam and ham. They, too, do not contribute to the training of classification algorithms and subsequent identification of spam or ham messages. Thus, we have removed all numerals present in each text message in the extended corpus used in this work.

v. Stemming or Lemmatization: In English, there is a scope of extracting the "root form" or "word of origin" for words in a particular piece of text. These "root forms" are derived using the "inflected" state of the word that is in use in the SMS text. For instance, the words "running", "ran", "runs", etc., all have the same "word of origin" that is "run". This operation has been performed for each SMS text in our corpus in order to generate an intermediate form of processed text. However, it is to be noted that this step is not much instrumental on SMS texts in the current work, as most of them are usually types in colloquial English, and in our case, they also consist of regional words typed in English.

After the aforementioned processing techniques have been carried out on each text in our extended corpus, it is the further used for feature extraction as discussed in the next section

9.7   Feature Extraction

The processed SMS data is to be finally used by the mathematical model–based supervised learning algorithms. These algorithms fail to deal with textual content in the data and are more comfortable with numeric values. This method of converting a text to vector rich, directly classifiable form is called vectorization. In essence, each piece of text is converted to a matrix of numbers, and every row of this matrix corresponds to a particular label which in our case is restricted to ham and spam.

Though there is a plethora of such vectorizers that may be used for transforming texts to classifiable form, not all of them are effective in every case. For the currently undertaken work, the authors have chosen to use a common vectorization technique called TF-IDF [15]. Its efficiency has been noted in state-of-the-art research works studied in the Literature Review.

In this vectorization technique, each document is transformed into a document vector, where each element is the statistic derived between every term in the vocabulary and the document itself. This method of textual feature extraction makes use of the importance of each term to the document as a whole. The TF-IDF vector for a particular document j and the number of constituent terms i is calculated after the process of determining the TF and IDF is carried out, as discussed below:

- Term Frequency (TF): The individual words in a piece of text document can be individually extracted as "tokens" or "terms' in a process of "tokenization". In this work, a word level tokenizer is utilized as the texts also contain colloquial English and regional words typed in English. The number of times that each such term occurs in the document as a whole is determined as its "Term Frequency". Mathematically, TF can be defined as in Equation (9.1):

$$TF = \frac{Number\ of\ times\ a\ token\ appears\ in\ the\ corpus}{Total\ number\ of\ tokens\ in\ the\ corpus} \tag{9.1}$$

- Inverse Document Frequency (IDF): The measure of the importance of any term or token in a particular document can be analyzed using a simple logic. In natural language processing, this importance is said to be decreasing with the increasing frequency of the term in a particular corpus. This same logic can be mathematically expressed as in Equation (9.2):

$$Importance\ of\ token\ i \propto \frac{1}{frequency\ of\ token\ i\ in\ the\ document} \tag{9.2}$$

It follows that the IDF can be determined as in Equation (9.3):

$$IDF = log_{10} \frac{Total\ number\ of\ documents}{Number\ of\ documents\ in\ which\ token\ i\ appears} \tag{9.3}$$

- Calculation of TF-IDF: Finally, the consolidated TF-IDF value needs to be determined. It signifies the weightage of the TF of every token i in the document j corresponding to the IDF value of the token i. This ensures that the least common words in the document possess more weightage and vice versa. The mathematical expression of TF-IDF score for every word in the document is expressed as in Equation (9.4):

$$TF - IDF = TF\ x\ IDF \tag{9.4}$$

The vectorized data corpus is further used during experimentation by the different mathematical learning algorithms for system performance evaluation, as discussed in the succeeding sections.

9.8 Learning Techniques Used

The duly processed and vectorized, feature-rich, labeled text corpus is used for training the following classification algorithms in a supervised approach. The notion of supervised classification is that an algorithm will attempt to learn from a given set of labeled inputs and then use that knowledge to further determine the class of a new set of observed data. In the current work, the problem of determining spam and ham SMS has been addressed in this manner.

9.8.1 Support Vector Machine

The SVM algorithm [16] trains a model using labeled data to find an optimal plane of separation that can be used to classify the new test data. In our case of a binary problem, the objective is to identify a hyperplane which has maximum distance from data points of both the classes during training. This hyperplane ensures the presence of a maximum number of possible points of a class on one side, given two separate classes of data. Mathematically, the hyperplane can be represented by Equation (9.5) where the value of $||w||$ is to be minimized:

$$w^T x + b = 0 \tag{9.5}$$

where, w is the weight vector, x is input vector, and b is the bias.

Specific data points that lie closest to the hyperplane act as support vectors and help in determining the performance of the classifier. These support vectors are determined by Lagrangian multiplier method. In the current work, the SVM algorithm with a linear kernel has been employed, as the text corpus is feature-rich and the data is linearly separable.

9.8.2   k-Nearest Neighbors

The kNN classification technique [17] attempts to learn the nearness or proximity between a set of points, in order to determine their individual class as class label. This class label is chosen by a simple voting mechanism where the class with maximum number of votes in the defined neighborhood is chosen as the class of the element vector. Certain standard distance metrics are popularly used for determining this proximity, for example, the Manhattan distance, which is calculated as in Equation (9.6):

$$f = \sum_{i=1}^{k} |x_i - y_i| \tag{9.6}$$

In the processed and labeled corpus, the kNN algorithm is used to learn and find the nearest class label for every vectorized text during experimentation.

9.8.3   Decision Tree

The DT classifier is based on a cascading tree structure, where the whole corpus is broken down into smaller subsets, with increasing depth. The *leaf nodes* correspond to the class labels, and all internal decision nodes represent the tests on attributes. Beginning with the entire data at the root node, the decision rules are applied at each node, to predict the outcome and generate the next node.

The current work uses Classification and Regression Tree (CART)–based [18] DT algorithm with Gini index as cost function, which is given by the formula in Equation (9.7):

$$Gini = 1 - \sum_{i=1}^{n} (p_i)^2 \tag{9.7}$$

9.8.4   Convolutional Neural Network

Mostly used with two-dimensional vectors such as images, the Convolutional Neural Network [19] learning mechanism can also be utilized in training a classifier to recognize spam and ham text messages in a corpus. Inherently, every neural network has a set of layers which can be configured as required, and the layers are capable of extracting features from the input data and map them to the respective classes/labels.

In any neural network, generally, the layers are fully connected with corresponding activation functions, whereas in CNNs, there are convolutional layers, pooling layers, etc., along with fully connected layers in the end. The convolutional layers repeatedly use filters on the input data to generate feature-based maps for the specific training data. In all the experiments performed in this work, the CNN classifier utilizes the concept of early stopping, where incremental weight updation and testing is performed until there is no loss minimization for a limit of 10 epochs. This helps to eliminate over-fitting and subsequent poor performance of the classifier.

The architecture of CNN-based models can be customized as per requirement of the given problem statement, and the CNN architecture used in this work is as described below.

The first two sections consist of convolutional layers, each of which uses the given kernel values to convolve the input (or previous layer's output stream). Also, in each layer, the output is mapped by Rectified Linear Unit (ReLu) activation function [20], given by Equation (9.8):

$$relu(x) = \max{(0, x)} \tag{9.8}$$

This activation function re-enforces non-linearity in the feature set after the convolution operations.

- *First Layer*: A 1D convolutional layer that takes the vectorized spam and ham texts as input streams of data. A total of 32 feature detectors or filters have been used here, each with a kernel size of 3. This allows the layer to learn 32 different basic features from the input data.
- *Second Layer*: The neuron matrix from the first layer is fed in to this CNN layer, and 64 new filters are used for training, with 3 kernels in use.
- *Third Layer*: After two convolutional layers, a max-pooling layer [21] is used, which helps to eliminate the dependence on the feature position in the vector. This is obtained by down-sampling the data from the last layer while retaining the effective features. The down-sampling is done with a sliding window of height 2 across the data, such that it is replaced by the maximum value. In the process, 50% of the data in the neuron matrix is discarded.
- *Fourth Layer*: The next layer is dropout [22], which makes our CNN model ignore certain neurons randomly during training by assigning them zero weight. This ensures that there is a proper learning of the model, less sensitivity to minute variations in data or specific neuron weights, thus preventing over-fitting. With the use of dropout, the classifier is also able to perform better when tested with new data. The authors have experimentally determined a dropout rate of 0.4, meaning 40% of data values are given a zero-weight value.
- *Fifth Layer*: The flatten layer is used next to convert the previous output to a 1D vector such that it can be directly fed to the succeeding fully connected network.
- *Sixth Layer*: The final section consists of two fully connected (dense) layers with an intermediate normalization layer. The first dense layer takes the flattened feature vector as input and applies the ReLu activation function on this input, with 100 neurons as output. The result is normalized by scaling it to a mean of zero and unit standard deviation in the intermediate layer. As the addressed challenge is a two-class problem, the final dense layer takes the normalized feature vector and applies the Sigmoid activation function to predict the probability as output (between 0 and 1). These probabilistic

values along with the true labels are then used by the cost function for model performance evaluation.

The architecture of the CNN classifier designed for this spam classification problem is illustrated in Figure 9.7

9.9   Experimental Setup

The labeled and vectorized spam and ham SMS texts are used in the experiment where the previously discussed classifiers are trained on the data and then their classification performance is recorded. In each case, a k-fold cross-validation technique is used to split the complete feature vector into training and testing sets randomly. This ensures that there is no bias in the trained models, no dependence on the particular splits of data, and no persisting holdout problem.

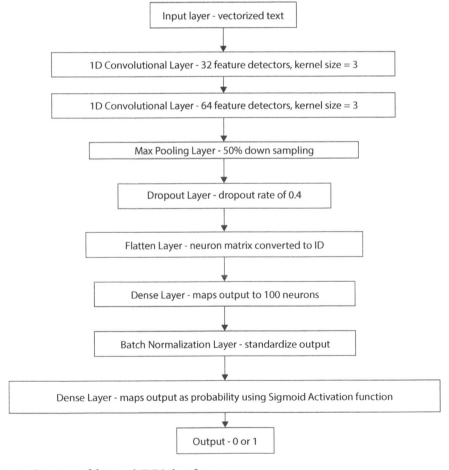

Figure 9.7 Architecture of designed CNN classifier.

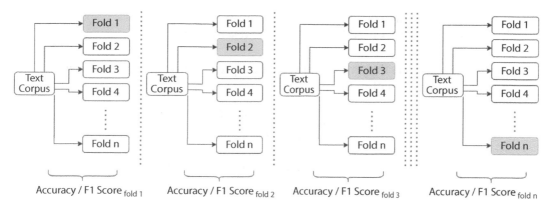

Figure 9.8 Illustrative example of the k-fold cross-validation technique.

The k-fold cross-validation technique may be better realized with the help of a simple example, as shown in Figure 9.8. Assuming the determined number of folds is k, the complete text corpus will be broken into k equal parts. From this point onward, an iterative process will follow. In the first iteration, all but the first fold of data will be utilized for training the model, while the first fold will serve the purpose of testing model performance. Similarly, in the second iteration, all but the second fold of data will be used for model training and the second fold itself will be utilized for model evaluation via testing. This iterative process continues for all the k-folds of data, and the model performance is expressed as the mean of model performance in all k cases.

In this work, the classification and evaluation are designed in a Monte Carlo [23] approach where the concept of repeated random sampling is used for training and testing the classifiers. As already stated, the k-fold cross-validation is a standard technique that is very popularly used with the supervised learning techniques. However, a low standard value of 5 or 10 folds is employed in the majority of research works. This minimum number of folds of training and evaluation, while computationally easy, is not appropriate to provide a proper idea regarding the robustness of the classification model in use, i.e., they cannot be judged properly.

In order to address this issue, the authors have performed the experiments using the set of previously discussed classifiers, and by training and testing them for a high number of randomly sampled sets of spam and ham data. For this purpose, a substantially high value of k is used in k-fold cross-validation, which has been set at a maximum of 100. Each classifier is thus trained and tested on random splits using the cross-validation technique where the value of k is kept between 10 and 100, with intervals of 10 folds. Also, the evaluation of classifier performance has been done with the help of a set of standard evaluation metrics, as discussed in the next section.

9.10   Evaluation Metrics

To serve the purpose of determining classifier performance, a set of standard metrics need to be utilized such that the results may be considered as valid. It enables a comparison of the system performance with that of the state-of-the-art in SMS message-based spam recognition. The set of such metrics used in this work, are discussed below:

- Accuracy denotes the proper and accurate representation of each event detection, given by Equation (9.9):

$$Accuracy = \frac{TP + TN}{TP + TN + FP + FN} \tag{9.9}$$

- Precision denotes the correctly classified events out of all detected events, given by Equation (9.10):

$$Precision = \frac{TP}{TP + FP} \tag{9.10}$$

It is defined as ratio of all true positives to all events flagged as positives by the classifier.
- Recall denotes the ratio of correctly detected events of all true events, using Equation (9.11):

$$Recall = \frac{TP}{TP + FN} \tag{9.11}$$

It is defined as ratio of all true positives to all events flagged as positives by the classifier.
- F1 score: this is a measure of the harmonic mean of the precision and recall determined in the previous steps, calculated using Equation (9.12):

$$F1\ score = 2x \frac{Precision\ x\ Recall}{Precision + Recall} \tag{9.12}$$

In each of the above metrics, the terms TP, TN, FP, and FN have been repeatedly used. These can be interpreted as discussed here:

- True Positive (TP) denotes the case where the model has correctly assigned the data to a particular class, i.e., the model has correctly determined a spam message as spam.
- True Negative (TN) means the model has correctly determined that the data does not belong to the class, i.e., the model has correctly determined a text as not spam.
- False Positive (FP) means the model has wrongly assigned the data to a class, i.e., the model has wrongly determined a spam message as a ham message.
- False Negative (FN) means the model has incorrectly determined that the data does not belong to the class, i.e., the model has incorrectly determined a spam message as not belonging to the class of spam messages.

The results of the experiments are expressed in terms of these metrics and illustrated in the next section.

9.11   Experimental Results

The classifiers that have been previously discussed, namely, CNN, SVM, kNN and DT, are used for the system experiments. Each classifier is trained on k − 1 out of k randomly generated folds of data and evaluated on the remaining data by testing. Also, as discussed, the k-fold cross-validation–based evaluation is repeated for values of the fold k, where $10 \leq k \leq 100$, k = k + 10. The motive of this methodology is to gain clarity about the robustness of the classifier performance based on repeated random sampling using Monte Carlo approach.

The processed and vectorized corpus of spam and ham SMS is learned and classified by each classifier.

The mean of mean accuracies for all the determined folds of evaluation up to 100 is illustrated in Table 9.1. The classification accuracies for each of the 10 steps of experiments are also visualized in the accuracy plot in Figure 9.9.

Similarly, in Table 9.2, the mean of mean F1 scores achieved by the four different classification models has been illustrated. The same has been graphically demonstrated in Figure 9.10. From the figures and the tables listed above, it is obvious that CNN has the best performance in accurately classifying the extended spam and ham message corpus used in this work. This is true in both the cases of accuracy and F1 scores. The maximum system performance is indeed achieved by the deployed CNN classifier, with an accuracy as high as 99.85% and a mean accuracy of 99.48%. Similarly, a maximum F1 score of 99.83% is

Table 9.1 Mean of mean accuracies of different classifiers in k-fold cross-validation.

Classifier	k = 10	k = 20	k = 30	k = 40	k = 50	k = 60	k = 70	k = 80	k = 90	k = 100	Mean	Std. Dev.
SVM	98.08	98.31	98.34	98.59	98.54	98.35	98.42	98.56	98.48	98.51	98.42	0.15
kNN	94.71	94.87	94.62	94.84	94.72	94.91	94.78	94.77	94.48	94.88	94.76	0.13
DT	96.11	97.12	97.24	97.11	97.29	97.17	97.03	97.11	97.25	97.25	97.17	0.08
CNN	99.35	99.27	99.39	99.38	99.83	99.41	99.28	99.77	99.71	99.64	99.50	0.2

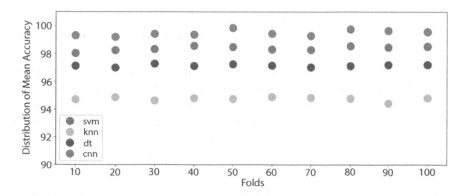

Figure 9.9 Mean of mean accuracies of the different classification models.

Table 9.2 Mean of mean F1 scores of different classifiers in k-fold cross-validation.

Classifier	k = 10	k = 20	k = 30	k = 40	k = 50	k = 60	k = 70	k = 80	k = 90	k = 100	Mean	Std. Dev.
SVM	98.04	98.25	98.34	98.57	98.49	98.31	98.28	98.55	98.46	98.52	98.38	0.16
kNN	94.73	94.88	94.65	94.82	94.77	94.91	94.86	94.79	94.45	94.83	94.77	0.13
DT	96.94	97.01	97.29	97.13	97.26	97.16	97.04	97.13	97.21	97.22	97.16	0.08
CNN	99.31	99.20	99.42	99.37	99.85	99.44	99.28	99.75	99.65	99.57	99.48	0.2

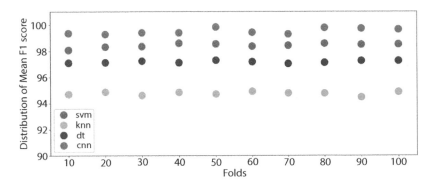

Figure 9.10 Mean of mean F1 scores of the different classification models.

exhibited by this classification model with a mean score of this observed performance is indeed remarkable and can be attributed to the convolution-based learning, deep and connected networks, and inherent error minimization capacity of the CNN model.

In contrast, the conventional machine learning algorithms fail to perform as good as the CNN model. However, it is observed that SVM performs the best among all the machine learning algorithms both in terms of accuracy and F1 scores, with mean of mean values of 98.38% and 98.42%, respectively. Thus, we can state that SVM performs robustly among all the baseline machine learning algorithms that have been tested in this work.

Analysis of the DT-based classification results show that it closely follows SVM in terms of F1 score and accuracy measures. This classifier model fairs well with mean accuracy and F1 scores above 97%. Consequently, the worse performance is noted on the part of the kNN algorithm–based classifier which performs with a high accuracy and F1 score of about 94% in all cases but is comparatively poorer in spam detection from the extended SMS corpus used in this work.

A statistical analysis of classifier performance in the overall experiment in terms of the mean and standard deviation of the mean accuracy and F1 score values are illustrated in Figures 9.11 and 9.12. It is evident from these figures that the CNN learning model has the best mean performance and the maximum standard deviation among all classifiers used, though the standard deviations in all cases in only fractional. The standard deviation for SVM is lower, followed by that of kNN. Notably, the standard deviation for DT is the lowest with a good classification performance. Very similar statistical values are also noted in the case of F1 score of the classifiers. The standard deviation is the same in case of mean F1 scores for all classifiers except SVM where the value is fractionally reduced.

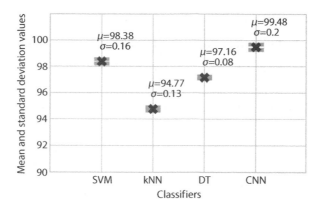

Figure 9.11 Statistical distribution of classifier performance in terms of mean accuracies.

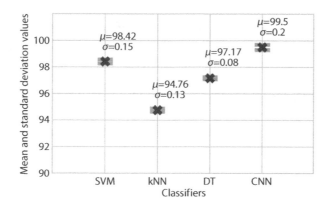

Figure 9.12 Statistical distribution of classifier performance in terms of mean F1 score.

Remarkably, the illustrations in Figures 9.9 and 9.10 show the efficiency and capability of the developed spam detection framework. The graphical representations are very much alike, which highlights that the adopted technique of k-fold cross-validation for high value of k (=100) has helped in eliminating the inconsistency in system performance graphs for all the classifiers, in terms of both accuracy and F1 score. Indeed, the statistical analysis in Figures 9.11 and 9.12 is evidence of the success of our implemented Monte Carlo–based testing mechanism that has resulted in a stable performance for all the classifiers, with a very irrelevant and small standard deviation in each case.

Thus, on the basis of classification performance in terms of accuracy and F1 score, we determine that the developed system is indeed robust to the underlying patterns and features of spam and ham messages of both the types—those that are originally in English and typed in English, and the ones that are originally in regional languages but typed in English.

9.11.1   Observations in Comparison With State-of-the-Art

A few observations can be highlighted based on results of the experiments in relation with the state-of-the-art research works conducted in the domain of SMS spam classification, as follows:

Table 9.3 Performance comparison with contemporary works.

Article	Performance achieved	Dataset used	Additional data (If any)
Ghourabi et al. [14]	Accuracy: 98.37%	Almeida et al. [6]	Arabic spam and ham messages
Roy et al. [13]	Accuracy: 99.44%		None
Popovac et al. [9]	Accuracy: 98.40 %		None
Jain et al. [8]	Accuracy: 98.65%		None
Barushka et al. [24]	Accuracy: 98.51%		None
Our work	**Accuracy: 99.85%**		**Regional messages typed in English**

- The superior performance of the CNN classifier is established in our experiments, and it can be deduced that CNN is the best candidate for building a robust spam identification system. This corroborates with the recent works [8, 9, 13, 14] that have been studied in our Literature Review. Table 9.3 highlights the efficient performance and provides a comparison of our proposed system with these works.
- Among the conventional learning techniques, SVM shows the best and most robust performance in comparison to the other models based on algorithms of kNN and DT. This is in keeping with the observations of state-of-the-art works by Agarwal et al. [5], Jain et al. [8], El Hlouli et al. [11], and Ghourabi et al. [14]. In each of these works, it is noted that the SVM classifier model achieves the highest accuracy of classification among all other learning algorithms.
- The poor performance of DT classifier model is also substantiated by state-of-the-art research works [10, 12, 14]. Thus, it is deduced that the DT classifier is not suitable for deploying a robust spam detection system. It needs to be mentioned that this is not because of poor performance of DT, but the superior learning and classification capability of such data as exhibited by CNN and other baseline machine learning algorithms.

9.12   Application in Cloud Architecture

The proposed system determines that the CNN-based trained classifier performs more robustly than the conventionally used machine learning algorithms, even when trained with the set of spam messages including regional texts typed in English. When adapted in the cloud, the overall system may be represented as in Figure 9.13. This architecture is loosely based on the recent patent by Skudlard et al. [25].

As seen in the figure, the mobile or portable devices DEVICE 1 and DEVICE 2 (which may be smartphones or tablets capable of sending and receiving SMS messages) are

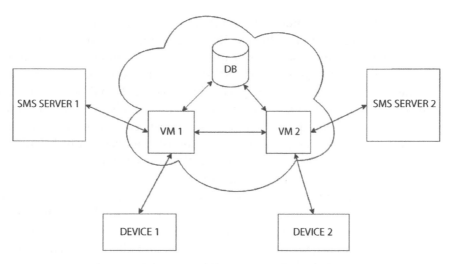

Figure 9.13 Illustration of the proposed CNN-based model in cloud architecture.

in communication with the virtual machines VIRTUAL MACHINE 1 and VIRTUAL MACHINE 2, respectively. Each of these VMs may be sharing the same hardware or may be based on separate pieces of hardware with the capacity for intercommunication using all standard protocols. Also, each VM maintains the trained CNN-based classifier with the data from the shared database DB.

All SMS messages from SMS SERVER 1 and SMS SERVER 2 to the user devices (DEVICE 1 and DEVICE 2) are intercepted by VIRTUAL MACHINE 1 and VIRTUAL MACHINE 2, respectively. The text is processed and classified using the trained models in the VM before transmission to the user devices. If a particular piece of SMS text is flagged as spam by the respective VIRTUAL MACHINE, then the flagged message is forwarded to the user for confirmation. Once the user confirms that the SMS is indeed spam, the shared database DB is updated accordingly. On the other hand, if in case the text is not classified as spam, then it is directly forwarded to the user. Given that the system is not ideal, i.e., it may not be 100% accurate, there may arise a case where a particular message that the user feels is spam, it is not flagged accurately. In any such case, the user has the option to report the text as spam and the bi-directional feedback system ensures that the database DB is updated accordingly. This, in turn, results in an updated classifier in the VMs, which learns the new user preference and works more efficiently thereafter.

9.13   Conclusion

Effective spam detection and filtering is a very well visited field of research, and there is a wide variety of feasible solutions that have been proposed. It is obvious from a review of relevant, recent state-of-the-art literature that the most distinct progress is in the use of newer, advanced algorithms that are capable of learning more about the inherent patterns of different spam and ham messages in a text corpus. Such algorithms are mostly based on Neural Networks and variants of Deep Neural Networks, such as CNN and LSTM. In the current work, a spam detection system that takes as input a comprehensive and well tested

SMS corpus, which has been extended by including the context of regional messages typed in English, has been designed and evaluated. The system employs a Monte Carlo approach to determine which of the supervised classification algorithms among CNN and other conventional machine learning algorithms like SVM, kNN, and DT and is the most robust in detecting the spam messages accurately. For this purpose, k-fold cross-validation has been utilized with a high value of k = 100, at intervals of 10 folds. It has been determined experimentally that the proposed approach results in consistent performance in case of all the classifiers and that CNN emerges as the most robust classification technique with an accuracy and F1 score about 99.5%. Also, among the conventional learning algorithms, SVM is the most robust with standard evaluation metric values of above 98%. Thus, the given novel text corpus has been effectively classified by the designed system and CNN can be utilized as a robust learning and classification technique. A cloud-based framework for implementing the proposed classifier is also discussed. In future, this work can be used as a reference for building robust, real-time spam detection and filtering systems that need to work on SMS corpora that is challenging and contains novel contexts.

References

1. Hppy bthdy txt!, BBC, BBC News World Edition, UK, 3 December 2002, [Online]. Available: http://news.bbc.co.uk/2/hi/uk_news/2538083.stm. [Accessed October 2020].
2. Short Message Service (SMS) Message Format, Sustainability of Digital Formats, United States of America, September 2002, [Online]. Available: https://www.loc.gov/preservation/digital/formats/fdd/fdd000431.shtml. [Accessed, October 2020].
3. India's Spam SMS Problem: Are These Smart SMS Blocking Apps the Solution?, Dazeinfo, India, August 2020, [Online]. Available: https://dazeinfo.com/2020/08/24/indias-spam-sms-problem-are-these-smart-sms-blocking-apps-the-solution/. [Accessed October 2020].
4. The SMS inbox on Indian smartphones is now just a spam bin, Quartz India, India, March 2019, [Online]. Available: https://qz.com/india/1573148/telecom-realty-firms-banks-send-most-sms-spam-in-india/. [Accessed October 2020].
5. Agarwal, S., Kaur, S., Garhwal, S., SMS spam detection for Indian messages, in: *1st International Conference on Next Generation Computing Technologies (NGCT) 2015*, UCI Machine Learning Repository, United States of America, IEEE, pp. 634–638, 2015.
6. Almeida, T.A. and Gómez, J.M., SMS Spam Collection v. 1, UCI Machine Learning Repository, United States of America, 2012. [Online]. Available: http://www.dt.fee.unicamp.br/~tiago/smsspamcollection/, [Accessed October 2020].
7. Suleiman, D. and Al-Naymat, G., SMS spam detection using H2O framework. *Proc. Comput. Sci.*, 113, 154–161, 2017.
8. Jain, G., Sharma, M., Agarwal, B., Spam detection on social media using semantic convolutional neural network. *Int. J. Knowl. Discovery Bioinf. (IJKDB)*, IGI Global, 8, 12–26, 2018.
9. Popovac, M., Karanovic, M., Sladojevic, S., Arsenovic, M., Anderla, A., Convolutional neural network based SMS spam detection, in: *2018 26th Telecommunications Forum (TELFOR)*, Serbia, 2018.
10. Gupta, V., Mehta, A., Goel, A., Dixit, U., Pandey, A.C., Spam detection using ensemble learning, in: *Harmony Search and Nature Inspired Optimization Algorithms*, pp. 661–668, 2019.
11. El Hlouli, F.Z., Riffi, J., Mahraz, M.A., El Yahyaouy, A., Tairi, H., *Detection of SMS Spam Using Machine-Learning Algorithms, Embedded Systems and Artificial Intelligence: Proceedings of ESAI 2019, Fez, Morocco*, 1076, 429, Springer Nature, Singapore, 2020.

12. GuangJun, L., Nazir, S., Khan, H.U., Haq, A.U., Spam Detection Approach for Secure Mobile Message Communication Using Machine Learning Algorithms. *Secur. Commun. Netw.*, Hindawi, 2020, 1–6, 2020.

13. Roy, P.K., Singh, J.P., Banerjee, S., Deep learning to filter SMS spam. *Future Gener. Comput. Syst.*, 102, 524–533, 2020.

14. Ghourabi, A., Mahmood, M.A., Alzubi, Q.M., A Hybrid CNN-LSTM Model for SMS Spam Detection in Arabic and English Messages. *Future Internet*, 12, 156, 2020.

15. Sammut, C. and Webb, G.I., TF-IDF, in: *Encyclopedia of Machine Learning*, pp. 986–987, Springer, US, 2010.

16. Gunn, S.R. and others, *Support vector machines for classification and regression*, ISIS technical report, vol. 14, pp. 5–16, University of Southampton, UK, 1998.

17. Altman, N.S., An introduction to kernel and nearest-neighbor nonparametric regression. *Am. Stat.*, 46, 175–185, 1992.

18. Loh, W.-Y., Classification and regression trees, in: *Wiley Interdisciplinary Reviews: Data Mining and Knowledge Discovery*, pp. 14–23, 2011.

19. Goodfellow, I., Bengio, Y., Courville, A., *Deep learning*, vol. 1, MIT press, Cambridge, 2016.

20. Krizhevsky, A., Sutskever, I., Hinton, G.E., Imagenet classification with deep convolutional neural networks. *Advances in neural information processing systems*, pp. 1097–1105, 2012.

21. Yamaguchi, K., Sakamoto, K., Akabane, T., Fujimoto, Y., A neural network for speaker-independent isolated word recognition, in: *First International Conference on Spoken Language Processing*, 1990.

22. G.E. Hinton, A. Krizhevsky, I. Sutskever, N. Srivastva, System and method for addressing over-fitting in a neural network. USA Patent US Patent 9, 406, 017, 2016.

23. Kalos, M.H. and Whitlock, P.A., *Monte carlo methods*, John Wiley & Sons, New York, USA, 2009.

24. Barushka, A. and Hajek, P., Spam filtering using integrated distribution-based balancing approach and regularized deep neural networks. *Appl. Intell.*, 48, 1–19, Springer, 2018.

25. A.E. Skudlark, L.K. Tran, Y. Jin, Cloud-Based Spam Detection. USA Patent US Patent App. 16/901,056, 2020.

An Intelligent System for Securing Network From Intrusion Detection and Prevention of Phishing Attack Using Machine Learning Approaches

Sumit Banik*, Sagar Banik and Anupam Mukherjee

Siliguri Institute of Technology, Siliguri, West Bengal, India

Abstract

Phishing attacks are one of the most popular attacks in compromising user's data and performing malicious activities. It was discovered during the mid-1990s, and to this present day, it is one of the severe cybercrime methods to hijack user's data. This is a serious issue as people still fall for the trap of logging into a phished website and giving out all the details which result in loss of bank balance, getting their files breached, and also the hacker trying to impersonate the person at a maximum level. Many algorithms are proposed to counter this attack. Various machine learning approaches are used to employ and check the detection of phishing websites. The problem is that there is no existing analysis at a detailed level about the URLs, the type of domains, origin, and other important aspects. To date, there is no exact way of saying whether a website is genuine or phishing related but the study of the website pattern and its structure will play an important role in dealing with the detection. In this study, we propose the estimation of the phishing websites and put in a detailed analysis comparing pre-existing malicious URLs which will help to filter the websites effectively and create a comparison of all the attributes in them. The advantages, drawbacks, and the comparison with the pre-existing research on this field have been discussed.

Keywords: Phishing, fake websites, detecting fraud, cyber-attack, vectorization, supervised learning, Logistic Regression, Naïve Bayes

10.1 Introduction

Phishing is an attempt to trick someone and make them enter their sensitive details which might be their bank account passwords and social media accounts which would allow the hacker to gather the above-mentioned data in no time. The term has been derived from the concept of fishing where the fisherman catches fishes using the "bait", the same goes in the case of phishing [1]. During the mid-1990s, America Online (AOL) warned its users that there are a group of hackers who tries to trick the customers and obtain their credentials and steal their account at last. The scenario during those days was like this that a

---

*Corresponding author: sumitbanik02@gmail.com

Rajdeep Chakraborty, Anupam Ghosh and Jyotsna Kumar Mandal (eds.) *Machine Learning Techniques and Analytics for Cloud Security*, (193–212) © 2022 Scrivener Publishing LLC

random member in the chat room would receive a message from another account claiming it to be a bank's executive and in turn, granting the user's credentials which, in turn, makes their account vulnerable to data stealing and above all stealing money from their accounts [2]. Phishing is a crime that employs technical deception and social engineering. Technical Deception means that the hacker will try to install malicious applications on the victim's side and will wait for it to get executed which, in turn, will give full access to the hacker stealing the credentials and getting added privilege in controlling the device. Social Engineering [37] mimics the actual service of what is provided by the official organization such as banks and social media. The hacker designs the phishing website with similar looks so that the victim can be trapped, when the user logs into this phished website the credentials are either emailed to the hacker or the data is stored in the database of the private server [3]. There can be several reasons why the user might fall into this trap. Consider there is an online sale taking place in any e-commerce website; what the hacker will do is create a phished website of the e-commerce sale page and prompt the user to authenticate via any social media accounts by saying that we will be getting a 50% off on the selected product. Now, the user might fall into this trap and will eventually submit the social media details thus getting compromised.

Despite being an old-school approach to hacking users' accounts, phishing attacks are still growing in numbers accounting for millions of data loss and monetary setbacks. According to the report published by APWG [4], there were around 146,994 phished websites detected during the second quarter of 2020. In comparison to the first quarter, there is a decline of around 11% as, during the Q1 of 2020, the total phished websites detected were 165,772.

In Figure 10.1, we can see that the maximum number of phishing URLs was detected in March which is approximately equal to 60,000. At this month, the whole world was under lockdown, and due to which, there was a rise in the number of phishing websites and malicious activities happening worldwide. In the same report, there is also an analysis of the affected sector due to phishing attacks. Notably, the attacks targeting the social media sector increased in the second quarter by about 20% as compared to the first quarter of 2020. According to Kaspersky, the rise of social engineering will increase as the other

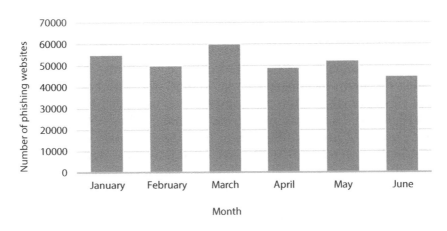

Figure 10.1 Phishing websites in Q1 and Q2, 2020.

methods of hacking are now restricted to ideal scenarios only due to advanced cybersecurity measures [5].

10.1.1   Types of Phishing

Though the underlying technique of phishing is to basically trick a user and give the credentials deliberately, it can be further classified into five different categories.

10.1.1.1   Spear Phishing

It deals with compromising a specific organization or dedicated group of people for which the hacker gets to manipulate the users or to gain unethical access over something else [6]. For this, detailed research about the organization or specific group of people is carried out; the reason to do this is to make further communications with the victims to sound authentic. Spear phishing is the initial step for getting access to an organization for carrying out further attacks.

Nowadays, this method has turned into a business for which many big players are using it as a political and diplomatic tool [7]. In July and August 2018, Microsoft shut down various malicious websites that were mimicking the political organizations [8]. The group named APT28 was responsible for creating the fake websites which were linked to previous US Elections of 2016. The six domains which were mimicked were created for fooling people that one of the websites belongs to International Republican Institute, the Hudson Institute, and the rest were vague attempts to make people realize that it belongs to US Senate. Later in that year, Twitter had banned around 10,000 accounts which were discouraging people not to vote during the elections [9]. Another case where a Junior Scientist's email was compromised and the medical research data was sent to another company based on Indore [10].

10.1.1.2   Whaling

It refers to spear-phishing attacks that are specifically dedicated to senior executives in an organization. Like normal spear attacks, hackers try to mimic the higher authorities of an organization and try to make a communication with its subordinates of the same organization or its partners. Most of the time, the employees fail to contact the actual authority of whether they sent out the email or not thus losing data or the company's monetary deposits.

In 2015, The Scoular Co. faced a loss of 17.5 million USD because an employee forwarded the amount in multiple investments to banks in China [11] as the company was having a business deal scheduled with another organization based out there for which the mail was thought to be genuine.

10.1.1.3   Catphishing and Catfishing

It is a method where the hacker gets to know someone for which information of sensitive credentials are gained, and malicious activities are carried out pretending to be the person who is a victim. Catfishing deals with impersonating a fake account pretending to be an actor, sportsman, or any other celebrity and trapping various people to donate to a fake organization, sending unsolicited pictures, etc.

In 2015, a 31-year-old person impersonated the NBA star [12] online and tried to blackmail the actual person.

10.1.1.4   Clone Phishing

In this method, the hacker copies an authentic message from a trusted organization, and in turn, what it does is replaces the actual website link with the phished website address and in some cases also attach malicious software in email attachments. Nowadays, this method is used with the concept of spear-phishing attacks for which there is a huge loss in various companies and the general person who, in turn, gets trapped in it for claiming a fake offer.

10.1.1.5   Voice Phishing

Also known as Vishing [38], it is a type of phone fraud where the hacker tries to impersonate that the call is from an authentic organization that is distributing financial rewards on basis of a certain occasion. Initially, the fraudsters use to buy SIM cards in bulk, and whenever the limit had been reached, the card was discarded. At this moment, due to technological advances, they prefer VoIP numbers so that it becomes more difficult to trace back to the actual source of the call.

In August 2020, police arrested five fraudsters [13] who were trying to mimic themselves as a part of customer care and steal the credit card information of normal people.

10.1.2   Techniques of Phishing

10.1.2.1   Link Manipulation

In this technique, the hacker tries to create a similar website that has the same user interface and a misleading URL having the same set of characters that is present in the original website but in a different order for which sometimes it is hard to figure out the difference between the phished domain and the original one. At last, the victim gets trapped and gives out the credentials. Another type of link manipulation that is very popular nowadays is the IDN Homograph Attack [14]. In this method, the underlying process is that there are many set of languages, which has similar resemblance with the English characters and for which the hacker uses it as an advantage and make the phishing website's domain very similar to the original website.

10.1.2.2   Filter Evasion

In this method, the hacker tries to insert a phished website into any type of multimedia [15] as in the present-day emails have smart filtering to recognize a phishing email for which the hacker takes the help of any multimedia objects and embed the phished website link into it.

10.1.2.3   Website Forgery

In this process, the hacker tries to run scripts at the client end using JavaScript which not only redirects to the phishing website but with the help of the script the hacker tries to mimic the URL which will be displayed in the address bar and to which the victims give out the data [16]. This method is normally employed on banking websites and trading websites. Several scams have been done in the past using this method, and currently, Cryptocurrency trading websites are the big targets due to two reasons. Firstly, crypto transactions cannot be reversed and are very hard to trace back, and secondly, the price boom keeps on rising the value of any crypto assets. In 2019, a security researcher cracked out one of the phishing websites of one of the popular crypto exchanges, Binance [17]. The researcher found out that the script which was deployed in the forged website was to collect the users' credentials and to fool them to give the two-factor authentication codes.

10.1.2.4   Covert Redirect

It is one of the methods where it depends on the authentication token of another website. Consider an example, where a user clicks on the phishing link posted on Facebook and on the new tab it asks for the allowance to continue using the application, what happens is that the hacker gets the user tokens and can now harvest any personal data such as email, birthdate and so on. Though it is not a bigger threat, getting access to emails and phone numbers can make the hacker easy to target via the above channels which will act as step 0 to initiate the phishing attack on the victim. In serious cases, if the hacker gets an upscaled privilege, another set of sensitive information might be leaked.

In the present scenario, phishing attacks have now been shifted into the cloud environment [26] too where the attacker mimics as a cloud service provider agent and tricks the customer to feed in the details of their cloud access credentials. Moreover, the dominance of cloud computing taking up for hosting the websites increases the chances of hosting phishing websites overcloud. According to a recent report, the online prime day sale of Amazon has led to a rise in phishing attempts [27].

In the later part of this study, we have arranged the topics as follows: Section 10.2 talks about the previous studies conducted in this domain of detection of fake and phishing websites; Section 10.3 gives a detailed understanding of the dataset and the methodology which could make the research study possible and the list of algorithms used; Section 10.4 gives us the analysis of the model performance and concerning other performance metrics the comparison is made; Section 10.5 concludes the paper.

10.2   Literature Review

Subasi *et al.* [18] proposed a study in which the labeling of the website is done by various classification algorithms such as Artificial Neural Network (ANN), Support Vector Machine (SVM), k-Nearest Neighbor (k-NN), Random Forest (RF), and Rotation of Forest (RoF). The dataset used in this study was taken from the UCI machine learning repository and for furthering assessing the different model efficiencies Waikato Environment for Knowledge Analysis (WEKA) machine learning tool was used. The parameters that were employed to study the performance were the accuracy, ROC curve score, and F-measure, and on conducting the study, it was concluded that the RF algorithm performed very well as compared to the other mentioned algorithms which gave an accuracy of around 97.36% and also has a faster runtime.

Ankit *et al.* [23] conducted a study of detecting phishing websites based on hyperlinks information. In this study, the specific features of the hyperlink (HL) are divided into 12 categories and further used those features to train the machine learning models. Initially, the website structure is studied and the hyperlinks which are embedded in it were extracted. After the extraction of all the hyperlinks included in the website, each of them is further divided into specific attributes such as no HL, total HL, internal and external HL, internal and external error, internal and external redirection, login link, null HL, Cascading Style Sheet HL, and internal and external favicon HL. This study does not depend on any other third-party service providers which make it easy to implement on the client-side. Several models are used for this study and the most superior algorithm was the Logistic Regression which gave an accuracy of around 98.42% and precision of 98.8%.

Ammara *et al.* [24] presented a framework that detects phishing websites using the stacking model. Initially, the phishing dataset's top attributes analysis is done using various algorithms of feature selection. On getting the strongest and weakest attributes, the latter is stored in N1 and the former is stored in N2; then, the features were normalized; then, using the Principal Component Analysis (PCA), the data is then fed to various Machine Learning classifiers followed by the stacking of the highest performance algorithms which were the bagging classifier, neural net, and the RF. These three algorithms outperformed all the other algorithms and the stacking algorithm was used on these. It also compared with the other studies and concluded that the process of stacking 97.4% accuracy was achieved.

Ishant *et al.* [25] study could detect zero-hour phishing and newer types of phishing attacks that used various machine learning models to predict the same as it stated that present-day internet crimes need to tackle. Their dataset consisted of 30 attributes for detection purpose which were named as having an IP address, long URL length, shortened URL, having at the rating symbol, double slash redirects, iframe tags, prefix/suffix, anchor tags, right-click disable, meta links and script links, domain age, records, and other prominent features. It also proposed that the hacker might add the word HTTPS in the URL itself to trick users into believing it for a legitimate website. Majorly, three algorithms were considered to detect the output in which the RF Classification algorithm performed well to give an accuracy of around 96.71% upon which after implementing PCA, the score turned out to be 98.40%.

Opara *et al.* [35] designed a deep learning framework named WebPhish that extracts the HTML characteristics from the input URL for which the classification has to be made and it concatenates at the end of the domain name, then feeding it into the neural network that will further give the desired output. On the test dataset which they have used in their study, the accuracy score was around 94.1%.

Hakim *et al.* [36] used a hybrid machine learning approach where they used 56 domain features like count of special characters, suspicious Top Level Domain, and other features like that followed by 24 content features and seven external features of the websites such as domain age which are obtained from a service provider like WHOIS [39]. Upon selecting appropriate features, several machine learning classification algorithms are used for predicting the label of a given input website, and the accuracy of the approach came to be 96.61%.

The model comparison as compared to the literature survey works is shown in Table 10.1.

Table 10.1 Model comparison.

Ref.	Source of dataset	Features	Model implemented	Accuracy score
[18]	UCI Machine Learning Repository	30	Random Forest, Rotation Forest	97.36%
[23]	Phishtank, Alexa	13	SMO, Random Forest, Logistic Regression	98.42%
[24]	Kaggle	32	KNN, SVM, Random Forest,	96.9%
[25]	UCI Machine Learning Repository	30	Decision Tree, Random Forest, GBM	98.40%
[35]	Phishtank, Alexa.com	2	Neural Network	94.1%
[36]	OpenPhish, Alexa	87	Random Forest, Hybrid Model	96.61%

10.3   Materials and Methods

10.3.1   Dataset and Attributes

The dataset used in this research has been collected from the Phishtank [19] having 53,000 phishing URLs records, 2,462 phishing URLs collected from Openphish [20], 1,713 collected from MalwareDomainList [21], and 100,000 collected from Alexa [22]. The dataset provides information about the URL and whether it is a phishing URL or not. The attributes are shown in Table 10.2. The dataset consists of two attributes: the first one is the domain and the other output label is the outcome.

As the output of this model will give whether the URL is phishing or not, i.e. Good=1 or Bad=0. So, this problem is treated as a Binary Classification.

10.3.2   Proposed Methodology

The work consists of detecting whether a website is phishing or not for which the data collection is done and then the lexical analysis is done on each URL as shown in the Figure 10.2, which is stored in another data frame consisting of the individual features as shown in Table 10.3.

Accordingly, after that the machine learning model performance is compared and then the appropriate model is selected and is further implemented. This is shown in Figure 10.3.

Table 10.2 Dataset attributes and its description of phishing URLs.

Attributes	Description
URL	Collection Phishing and Legitimate URLs
Outcome	Whether phishing URL or not (Good=1/Bad=0)

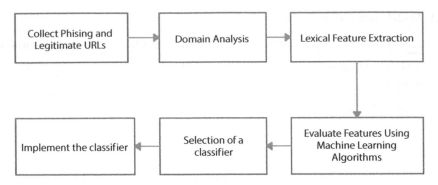

Figure 10.2 Feature extraction.

Table 10.3 Dataset attributes and its description of URLs.

Attributes	Description
RegistrationDate	Registration date of domain
ExpiredDate	Expired date of domain
UpdatedDate	Update date of domain
CountDot	Dot count of URL
UrlLength	Length of URL
CountDigit	Count of digit in URL
CountSpecial	Count of Special character in URL
CountHyphen	Count of hyphen in URL
DoubleSlash	Count of double slash in URL
SingleSlash	Count of single slash in URL
AtSign	Count of at sign in URL
WebTarfiic	Count of web traffic of domain
Label	Phishing (0) or Legitimate (1)

In Figure 10.3, the complete method is depicted. Firstly, the URL dataset is loaded, and all the missing and inappropriate data are removed. Secondly, only relevant features are used for further study as compared to other features that will be beneficial for the study, the attributes consisted of URLs features and the label as described in Table 10.3. The URL attribute consists of string values that are then tokenized and convert into vectors so that word-based analysis can be conducted.

It is also kept in mind that phishing websites might also have a few sets of characters to trick the user into believing it to be the legitimate website for which after tokenization, text stemming is performed. The dataset is then divided into two sets: one being the training set consisting of 80% of the dataset and the other is the testing set which comprises 20% of the

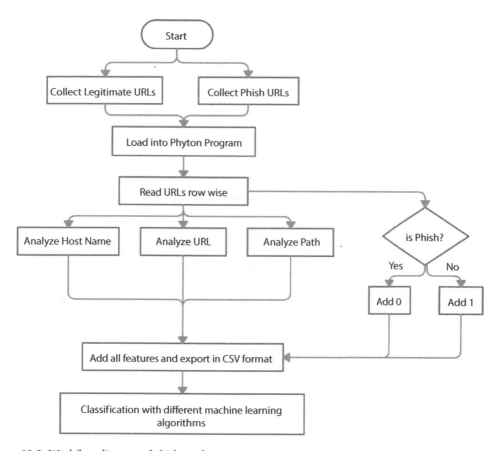

Figure 10.3 Workflow diagram of phishing detection.

dataset. On the training set, several sets of algorithms are used to estimate the model performances: (a) Logistic Regression, (b) Naïve Bayes, (c) SVM, and (d) Voting Classification, upon then, the metric comparison is done for choosing the appropriate algorithm for URL classification.

The collection of data is done using the APIs provided by Alexa which gives us an output of legitimate websites, and for the malicious/phishing website, Phishtank's API is used to collect the corresponding labeled data, when both of the categorized data are collected, it is merged onto a single dataset for further analysis. The step-by-step approach is discussed in Algorithm 10.1.

Algorithm 10.1 Data collection.
Input: API endpoint for Alexa, Phishtank
Output: List of legitimate and phishing websites
Steps

    1. if request (Alexa's API).status_code is 200, then
         1.1 write the legitimate URLs in data.csv

2. else
   2.1 echo "Error in connection"
3. if request (Phishtank's API).status_code is 200, then
   3.1 write the phishing URLs in data.csv
4. else
   4.1 echo "Error in connection"

10.3.2.1   Logistic Regression

This method of regression is a famous method after Linear Regression [29]. Though both are regression algorithms, the underlying difference is that the Logistic Regression is used for classification tasks while the other is used for predicting or forecasting data provided to the model [28]. This algorithm also uses a linear equation to predict the value, but the output range lies between negative and positive infinity. To have a classification output, we will be having binary data for which 1 means Yes and 0 means No which sums it up to have the range 0 to 1. For squeezing the output data to be in this range, the sigmoid function is used as shown in Equation (10.1). The working of logistic regression is shown in Figure 10.4

$$s(m) = \frac{1}{1 + e^{-m}} \tag{10.1}$$

- s(m): Probabilistic Estimate (output)
- m: Input to the function
- e: Base of natural log

10.3.2.2   Naïve Bayes

As the name suggests, this algorithm acts as a base to compare with the other sets of algorithms while estimating the model performance because it assumes that the data

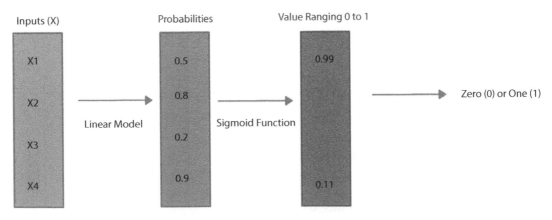

Figure 10.4 Working of logistic regression.

in the dataset are not correlated in any manner [30]. It uses the Bayes Theorem [31] to calculate the probability of the input which we provide as shown in Equation (10.2). The underlying concept is that it makes a probability based on any prior knowledge provided to it.

$$P(X|Y) = \frac{P(Y|X)P(X)}{P(Y)} \tag{10.2}$$

- P(X|Y): Conditional probability that event X occurs, given that Y has occurred.
- P(X) and P(Y): The probability of X and Y independent of each other.
- P(Y|X): Conditional probability that event Y occurs, given that X has occurred.

This means that to train our model we will need the output value P(X|Y) but the parameters might exceed the count in large numbers, and due to this reason, the algorithm assumes no correlation.

10.3.2.3 Support Vector Machine

SVM [32] employs the classification for both the types of data like non-linear and linear data. This algorithm is preferred as it may produce significant accuracy with lesser power of computation. Though it is helpful in regression and classification tasks it is mainly used for later purposes. Its objective to find a hyperplane [33] that will create a fine boundary within two classes of data, if the input features count is two the boundary becomes a straight line and if the features count is three then it becomes a 2D plane. To find the optimal hyperplane to be fitted two more of them are used as a boundary which will bifurcate the two classes, our objective is to minify the distance between the dedicated hyperplane with the optimal hyperplane.

Parameter tuning is done to various models which gives us an improved performance in comparison to the base model.

10.3.2.4 Voting Classification

In this method [34], we aggregate all the classification algorithms for which we have two options to choose, one of which is *hard voting* and the other is *soft voting*. In the first type of voting, we simply choose the classifier which has the highest accuracy among others, and the latter being the one that will assign weights to different classification algorithms and then create an average classification out of it. This is represented in Figure 10.5.

In Figure 10.6, the complete process is shown where the dataset collection is followed by cleaning the dataset with appropriate extraction of features and then correspondingly separating it into two groups named as train and test dataset followed by the training using different algorithms for which the different performance metrics are compared to decide which model to go with.

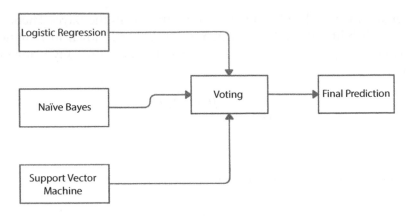

Figure 10.5 Working of voting classification.

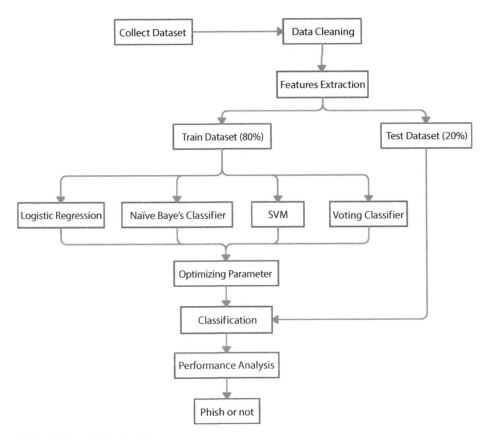

Figure 10.6 Phishing URL classification process.

10.4   Result Analysis

10.4.1   Analysis of Different Parameters for ML Models

To fine-tune the model for comparison and final classification, some parameters need to be altered accordingly which boosts the overall performance of a model. For this study, a few parameters also needed to be changed in a manner so that the near about optimal result can be achieved and help classify the URL accordingly.

In Table 10.4, the parameter values are compared for the different machine learning algorithms which are used to conduct the study of predicting the URLs which belong to the phishing category or not. The parameter tuning is done to fine-tune the model and improve its performance which is later compared using the accuracy score and other metrics.

10.4.2   Predictive Outcome Analysis in Phishing URLs Dataset

In machine learning, the performance of individual model which is tested is measured by the following factors:

Recall: It is one of the metrics which is defined as the count of true positives divided by the total count of false negatives and true positives [40].

Accuracy: It is one of the metrics which is used to compare the correct predictions with all the data points of the classifier [41].

Precision: It is one of the metrics which is defined as the count of true positives divided by the total count of false positives and true positives [42].

F1 Score: It is one of the metrics which is explained as the weighted average of precision and recall [43].

Table 10.4 Comparison of the parameter values for different models.

Algorithms	Parameters
Logistic Regression	dual = False, fit_intercept = True, random_state = 42, multi_class = ovr, warm_start = False, n_jobs = None, verbose = 0
Naïve Bayes	var_smoothing = 1e-09, priors = None
SVM	gamma = 'scale', shrinking = True, probability = False, tol = 0.001, class_weight = None, verbose = False, break_ties = False, random_state = 42
Voting Classifier	voting = 'soft', weights = None, n_jobs = None, flatten_transform = True, verbose = False

Table 10.5 Comparison of the various models for its metrics.

Algorithm/Metrics	Accuracy	Precision	Recall	F1 score
Logistic Regression	99.02%	98.62%	98.89%	98.75%
Naïve Bayes	97.49%	96.81%	97.56%	97.18%
SVM	89.70%	90.12%	89.65%	89.88%
Voting Classifier	99.52%	98.51%	98.98%	98.74%

Table 10.5 shows the performance of various models compared to each other which gives us an idea that Voting Classifier is superior to other machine learning which is used for this study.

10.4.3 Analysis of Performance Metrics

The first and the most common metric for comparison is the accuracy score which is mathematically depicted in Equation (10.3):

$$Accuracy = \frac{True\ Positive + True\ Negative}{Total\ Number\ of\ data\ points} \tag{10.3}$$

The accuracy score is the highest for the Voting Classification model as compared to the other algorithms which are shown in Figure 10.7.

Next, we have the *precision* metric for comparison which is mathematically depicted in Equation (10.4):

$$Precision = \frac{TruePositives}{TruePositives + False\ Positives} \tag{10.4}$$

The precision is the highest for the Logistic Regression model as compared to the other algorithms which are shown in Figure 10.8.

Next, we have the recall metric for comparison which is mathematically depicted in Equation (10.5):

$$Recall = \frac{True\ Positives}{True\ Positives + False\ Negatives} \tag{10.5}$$

The recall is the highest for the Voting Classification model as compared to the other algorithms which are shown in Figure 10.9.

Lastly, we have the recall metric for comparison which is mathematically depicted in Equation (10.6).

$$F1\ Score = \frac{2 \times (Precision \times Recall)}{Precision + Recall} \tag{10.6}$$

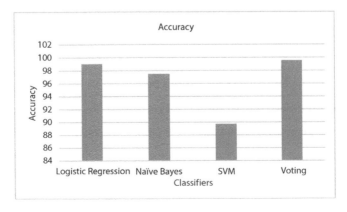

Figure 10.7 Comparison of accuracy scores.

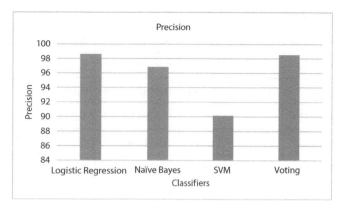

Figure 10.8 Comparison of precision scores.

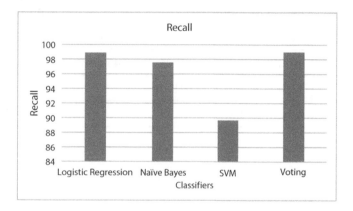

Figure 10.9 Comparison of recall scores.

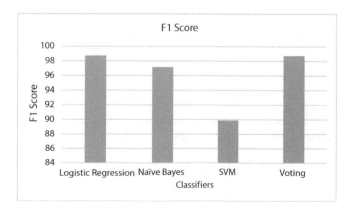

Figure 10.10 Comparison of F1 scores.

Table 10.6 Summary.

Groups	Count	Sum	Average	Variance
0.9749	3	2.9155	0.971833333	1.40633E-05
0.897	3	2.6965	0.898833333	5.52E-06
0.9952	3	2.9623	0.987433333	5.52E-06
0.9862	3	2.8544	0.951466667	0.001967303
0.9889	3	2.8619	0.953966667	0.002527223
0.9875	3	2.858	0.952666667	0.002237053

Table 10.7 ANOVA.

Source of variation	SS	df	MS	F	P-value	F crit
Rows	0.0134223	2	0.00671116	657.3124388	9.20E-06	6.944272
Columns	9.38E-06	2	4.69E-06	0.459353575	0.66133	6.944272
Error	4.084E-05	4	1.021E-05			
Total	0.0134725	8				

Table 10.8 Summary.

Groups	Count	Sum	Average	Variance
0.9902	3	2.8671	0.9557	0.002687
0.9862	3	2.8544	0.951467	0.001967
0.9889	3	2.8619	0.953967	0.002527
0.9875	3	2.858	0.952667	0.002237

Table 10.9 ANOVA.

Source of variation	SS	df	MS	F	P-value	F crit
Between Groups	2.96E-05	3	9.88E-06	0.004194	0.999593	4.066181
Within Groups	0.018838	8	0.002355			
Total	0.018867	11				

Table 10.10 Descriptive statistics.

Accuracy		Precision	
Mean	0.964325	Mean	0.96015
Median	0.98255	Median	0.9766
Standard Deviation	0.045706555	Standard Deviation	0.040163873
Standard Error	0.022853277	Standard Error	0.020081936
Mode	NA	Mode	NA
Sample Variance	0.002089089	Sample Variance	0.001613137
Kurtosis	3.237676171	Kurtosis	3.060722267
Skewness	−1.795901295	Skewness	−1.761036034
Range	0.0982	Range	0.085
Minimum	0.897	Minimum	0.9012
Maximum	0.9952	Maximum	0.9862
Sum	3.8573	Sum	3.8406
Count	4	Count	4
Confidence Level (95.0%)	0.072729328	Confidence Level (95.0%)	0.063909684
Recall		F1 Score	
Mean	0.9627	Mean	0.961375
Median	0.98225	Median	0.9796
Standard Deviation	0.044608295	Standard Deviation	0.042364008
Standard Error	0.022304148	Standard Error	0.021182004
Mode	NA	Mode	NA
Sample Variance	0.0019899	Sample Variance	0.001794709
Kurtosis	3.541712156	Kurtosis	3.33600785
Skewness	−1.878222658	Skewness	−1.827587171
Range	0.0933	Range	0.0887
Minimum	0.8965	Minimum	0.8988
Maximum	0.9898	Maximum	0.9875
Sum	3.8508	Sum	3.8455
Count	4	Count	4
Confidence Level (95.0%)	0.070981752	Confidence Level (95.0%)	0.06741059

The F1 score is the highest for the Logistic Regression model as compared to the other algorithms which are shown in Figure 10.10.

10.4.4   Statistical Analysis of Results

In this section, the relationship between the models is done using the ANOVA test. In Section 10.4.4.1, the two-factor test is discussed and in Section 10.4.4.2, the single factor test is discussed.

10.4.4.1   ANOVA: Two-Factor Without Replication

The summary of the ANOVA two-factor test is summarized in Table 10.6, and the details about the p-value and F-score are in Table 10.7 where SS denotes sum-of-squares, df means the degree of freedom, MS means mean squares, and the p-value is the probability value.

10.4.4.2   ANOVA: Single Factor

The summary of the ANOVA single factor test is summarized in Table 10.8, and the details about the p-value and F-score are in Table 10.9.

In Table 10.10, the statistical values are listed displaying the metrics like mean, median, and standard deviation.

10.5   Conclusion

Phishing is a technique to trick people into giving out credentials, bank details, and other sensitive information on another website that exactly looks like the legitimate one, thus getting access to the user's data and, in turn, doing financial scams and another type of crime depending on the hacker's motive. To stop internet crime, phishing attacks need to be controlled and mitigated at a very low level. In this study, using various machine learning approaches, we came with an approach that detects whether a website URL is a phishing domain or not.

Several website URLs are compared using various machine learning algorithms. To protect the end-users from entering these phishing websites, we tried to analyze the severity by tokenizing the URLs and also generate similar tokens related to it by stemming the text. In this study, we propose the estimation of the phishing websites and also put in a detailed analysis comparing pre-existing malicious URLs which will help to filter the websites effectively. ML algorithms such as Logistic Regression, Naive Bayes, and SVM were used and it came to the notice that the first algorithm performs better than the other mentioned algorithms. The accuracy score was found to be 0.9976.

Future studies into phishing detection should utilize this study for detailed analysis about how to proceed in labeling a website URL is in the phishing category or not. In future work, the study will be expanded to detect phishing URLs on mobile environments as mobile devices contribute to be more than 60% of the internet traffic which means the hackers can also target mobile devices. Thus, detection and preventing mobile-based phishing is a challenge for further research and development on this type of internet crime.

References

1. Chiew, K.L. *et al.*, A Survey of Phishing Attacks: Their Types, Vectors, and Technical Approaches. *Expert Syst. Appl.*, 106, Elsevier BV, 1–20, Sept. 2018.

2. AOL Users Warned of Hackers, CNET, 27 June 1997, www.cnet.com/news/aol-users-warned-of-hackers/. Accessed 4 Oct. 2020.

3. Volkman, E., The Definition of Phishing, Phishlabs.Com, 2014, info.phishlabs.com/blog/the-definition-of-phishing. Accessed 4 Oct. 2020.

4. APWG, Phishing Activity Trends Reports, Apwg.Org, 2020, apwg.org/trendsreports/. Accessed 4 Oct. 2020.

5. Comparitech, Phishing Statistics and Facts for 2019–2020, Comparitech.Com, 2019, www.comparitech.com/blog/vpn-privacy/phishing-statistics-facts/. Accessed 4 Oct. 2020.

6. Bullee, J.-W., Montoya, L., Junger, M. and Hartel, P., Spear phishing in organisations explained. *Inf. Comput. Sec.*, 25, 5, 593–613, 2017. https://doi.org/10.1108/ICS-03-2017-0009

7. Steer, J., Defending against spear-phishing. *Comput. Fraud Secur.*, 2017, 8, 18–20, 2017.

8. Cimpanu, C., Microsoft Disrupts APT28 Hacking Campaign Aimed at US Midterm Elections, BleepingComputer, 21 Aug. 2018, www.bleepingcomputer.com/news/security/microsoft-dis rupts-apt28-hacking-campaign-aimed-at-us-midterm-elections/. Accessed 4 Oct. 2020.

9. Bing, C., Exclusive: Twitter Deletes over 10,000 Accounts That Sought to Discourage U.S. Voting. Reuters, Thomson Reuters, 2 Nov. 2018, http://www.reuters.com/article/us-usa-election-twitter-exclusive-idUSKCN1N72FA, Accessed, 4 Oct. 2020.

10. Mayur Joshi, C.A., Case of Spear Phishing in India, Indiaforensic, 21 Nov. 2012, indiaforensic.com/case-of-spear-phishing-in-india/. Accessed 4 Oct. 2020.

11. Korolov, M., Omaha's Scoular Co. Loses $17 Million after Spearphishing Attack, CSO Online, 13 Feb. 2015, www.csoonline.com/article/2884339/omahas-scoular-co-loses-17-million-after-spearphishing-attack.html. Accessed 4 Oct. 2020.

12. Ingold, J., Woman Who Catfished Chris 'Birdman' Andersen Online Sentenced to Jail, The Denver Post, 28 Oct. 2015, www.denverpost.com/2015/10/28/woman-who-catfished-chris-birdman-andersen-online-sentenced-to-jail/. Accessed 4 Oct. 2020.

13. Aryan, A., Jamtara Is Back, This Time in a New e-SIM Phishing Racket, The Indian Express, 26 Aug. 2020, indianexpress.com/article/india/jamtara-e-sim-phishing-fraud-racket-6569962/. Accessed 4 Oct. 2020.

14. Hannay, P. and Baatard, G., The 2011 IDN Homograph Attack Mitigation Survey. in: *Proceedings of International Conference on Security and Management (SAM'12).* pp. 653–657, Las Vegas, NV, 2012.

15. Ke, L., Li, B., Vorobeychik, Y., Behavioral Experiments in Email Filter Evasion. *AAAI*, 2016.

16. Waziri, I., Website forgery: Understanding phishing attacks and nontechnical Counter-measures. *2015 IEEE 2nd International Conference on Cyber Security and Cloud Computing*, IEEE, 2015.

17. Biggs, J., *Security Researcher Tears Up a Binance Scam Site to Find the Hackers - CoinDesk*, CoinDesk, 3 June 2019, www.coindesk.com/security-researcher-tears-up-a-binance-scam-site-to-find-the-hackers. Accessed 10 Oct. 2020.

18. Subasi, A. *et al.*, Intelligent Phishing Website Detection Using Random Forest Classifier. *2017 International Conference on Electrical and Computing Technologies and Applications (ICECTA)*, IEEE, 2017.

19. PhishTank, Join the Fight against Phishing, Phishtank.Com, 2020, www.phishtank.com/. Accessed 10 Oct. 2020.

20. OpenPhish, Phishing Intelligence, Openphish.Com, 2020, openphish.com/. Accessed 10 Oct. 2020.

21. MDL, Malwaredomainlist.Com, 2020, www.malwaredomainlist.com/. Accessed 10 Oct. 2020.

22. Alexa.Com., Alexa.Com, 2016, www.alexa.com/. Accessed 10 Oct. 2020.

23. Jain, A.K. and Gupta, B.B., A Machine Learning Based Approach for Phishing Detection Using Hyperlinks Information. *J. Ambient Intell. Hum. Comput.*, 10, 5, 2015–2028, Springer Science and Business Media LLC, Apr. 2018.

24. Zamir, A. *et al.*, Phishing Web Site Detection Using Diverse Machine Learning Algorithms. *Electron. Libr.*, 38, 1, Emerald, 65–80, Jan. 2020.

25. Tyagi, I. *et al.*, A Novel Machine Learning Approach to Detect Phishing Websites. *2018 5th International Conference on Signal Processing and Integrated Networks (SPIN)*, IEEE, 2018.

26. Whitney, L., *How phishing attacks have exploited Amazon Web Services accounts*, 2020, August 25, Retrieved December 5, 2020, from TechRepublic website: https://www.techrepublic.com/article/how-phishing-attacks-have-exploited-amazon-web-services-accounts/.

27. Amazon Prime Day leads to spike in phishing attempts, 2020, October 12. Retrieved December 5, 2020, from Securitymagazine.com website: https://www.securitymagazine.com/articles/93593-amazon-prime-day-leads-to-spike-in-phishing-attempts.

28. Kleinbaum, D.G. *et al.*, *Logistic regression*, Springer-Verlag, New York, 2002.

29. Montgomery, D. *et al.*, Introduction to Linear Regression Analysis. vol. 821, 5th Edition. John Wiley & Sons, 2012.

30. Murphy, K.P., Naïve bayes classifiers, vol. 18, p. 60, University of British Columbia, Vancouver, Canada, 2006.

31. Efron, B., Bayes' theorem in the 21st century. *Science*, 340, 6137, 1177–1178, 2013.

32. Wu, Q. and Zhou, D.-X., Analysis of support vector machine classification, *J. Comput. Anal. Appl.*, 8, 2, 99–119, 2006.

33. Ding, S., Hua, X., Yu, J., An overview on nonparallel hyperplane support vector machine algorithms. *Neural Comput. Appl.*, 25, 5, 975–982, 2014.

34. Zhang, Y. et al., A Weighted Voting Classifier Based on Differential Evolution. *Abstr. Appl. Anal.*, 2014, 1–6, 2014. doi:10.1155/2014/376950

35. Opara, C. *et al.*, Look Before You Leap: Detecting Phishing Web Pages by Exploiting Raw URL And HTML Characteristics. ArXiv:2011.04412 [Cs], abs/2011.04412, Nov. 2020. arXiv.org, http://arxiv.org/abs/2011.04412..

36. Hakim, Z.M. *et al.*, The Phishing Email Suspicion Test (PEST) a Lab-Based Task for Evaluating the Cognitive Mechanisms of Phishing Detection. *Behav. Res. Methods.*, 53, 3, 1342–1352, 2020. doi:10.3758/s13428-020-01495-0

37. Hadnagy, C., *Social engineering: The art of human hacking*, John Wiley & Sons, 2010.

38. Choi, K., Lee, J.-l., Chun, Y.-t., Voice phishing fraud and its modus operandi. *Secur. J.*, 30, 2, 454–466, 2017.

39. WHOIS Search, Domain Name, Website, and IP Tools - Who.Is, Who.Is, 2020, who.is/.

40. Goutte, C. and Gaussier, E., A probabilistic interpretation of precision, recall and F-score, with implication for evaluation. *European conference on information retrieval*, Springer, Berlin, Heidelberg, 2005.

41. Sokolova, M., Japkowicz, N., Szpakowicz, S., Beyond accuracy, F-score and ROC: a family of discriminant measures for performance evaluation. *Australasian joint conference on artificial intelligence*, Springer, Berlin, Heidelberg, 2006.

42. Sklearn.Metrics.Precision_score — Scikit-Learn 0.23.2 Documentation, Scikit-Learn.org, 2020, scikit-learn.org/stable/modules/generated/sklearn.metrics.precision_score.html.

43. Sklearn.Metrics.F1_score — Scikit-Learn 0.23.2 Documentation, Scikit-Learn.org, 2020, scikit-learn.org/stable/modules/generated/sklearn.metrics.f1_score.html?highlight=f1%20score#sklearn.metrics.f1_score.

Part III

CLOUD SECURITY ANALYSIS USING MACHINE LEARNING TECHNIQUES

11

Cloud Security Using Honeypot Network and Blockchain: A Review

Smarta Sangui* and Swarup Kr Ghosh

Department of Computer Science, Sister Nivedita University, Kolkata, India

Abstract

Cloud technology has revolutionized the domain of computing in recent years. The cloud has succeeded to attract many businesses to use cloud resources or host most of their data in the cloud with their reduced prices, accelerated application deployment, and dynamic resources. With the COVID-19 pandemic disrupting the usual offline mode of sales, many businesses are going online and using cloud services. Recent statistics have shown that over 80% of industry workloads will be in the cloud by the end of 2020 and over 90% of industries already use a cloud service, with many more to come very soon. Despite having numerous benefits, security has always been a concern for cloud services. With the improvement of technology, related threats are also getting more complicated and advanced. Cloud services are facing attacks more than ever and this will keep increasing in the coming years. The swift development and popularity of cloud computing make cloud security an important necessity. In this paper, we have discussed security challenges and reviewed cloud security using blockchain technology and honeypot networks. This article is focused on the recent advancement in the implementation of honeypots to detect new attacks while minimizing resource overhead and blockchain to enhance cloud security using it is decentralized and distributed nature.

Keywords: Cloud computing, cloud security, honeypot, blockchain, privacy, intrusion detection, distributed storage

11.1 Introduction

Cloud services are accepted widely in this era, and they are often used to handle crucial and confidential data which can be accessed remotely from anywhere via the internet that makes security a very significant concern [1]. Cloud computing is invariably transforming the way we store, utilize, and share data, applications, systems, and workloads. With these changes, it has also induced new security threats and challenges. Cloud Security Alliance's (CSA) survey reveals that over 70% of the world's businesses now use cloud technology in some way or other [8]. As day by day, more and more data make its way to the cloud, and resources deployed in the cloud become targets of cybercriminals.

---

*Corresponding author: smartasangui@gmail.com

Rajdeep Chakraborty, Anupam Ghosh and Jyotsna Kumar Mandal (eds.) *Machine Learning Techniques and Analytics for Cloud Security*, (215–238) © 2022 Scrivener Publishing LLC

In this paper, we have reviewed recent progress in honeypot networks and blockchain technology addressing cloud security concerns. A honeypot is primarily a bait (or fake sensitive data) that are deliberately made very tempting and accessible. The intention is to trick and lure attackers who attempt to get unauthorized access to the network [2, 3]. A deliberately compromised computer system permits attackers to abuse the vulnerabilities so that you can analyze them to improve your security loopholes [35]. The honeypot is monitored by security teams. It helps us to know the activities of the attacker like how the attacker got into the system, from where (e.g., from where the data is accessed and IP addresses of where the stolen data is travelling to), what is being erased or added (e.g., if the intruder tries to become an admin), keystrokes of the attacker, and the malware used. The overall purpose is to find alerts worth investigating, alternative to thwart ransomware, identify insider threats, and monitor decrypted data.

The main reason that clients lack trust in the cloud as a third party is due to security loopholes. So to address this, blockchain can be used which has made its mark as a trusted third-party (TTP) with its implementation in cryptocurrency (e.g., Bitcoin) [4]. Blockchain's decentralized and distributed storage system takes the client's information and divides it up into little lumps. They provide an additional layer of security as information is distributed throughout the system. Blockchain technology gives us the edge via its hashing capability, encryption, and exchange records. Each part of the data is stored in a decentralized area.

11.2   Cloud Computing Overview

Cloud computing helps us use computing services like storage, database, servers, and processing power over the internet rather than using local solutions. Clients would typically pay only for cloud services they use, which helps them to run their infrastructure more efficiently, lower the operating expenses, and scale as their business requirements change. The cloud computing architecture is shown in Figure 11.1.

11.2.1   Types of Cloud Computing Services

Primarily, there are three different types of service models in cloud computing. These services are Software as a Service (SaaS), Infrastructure as a Service (IaaS), and Platform as a Service (PaaS). Each service model has its own distribution of responsibility for the resources as shown in Figure 11.2.

11.2.1.1   *Software as a Service*

This cloud service provides third-party applications to users via the web. On utilizing this service, clients would not have to install and run the application on their personal computers or in their own data centres, it is hosted on a remote server, it runs on the web directly, and it is managed from a central location. This excludes the cost of hardware procurement, provisioning and maintenance and also software licensing, support, and installation. Another advantage of SaaS is the capability to scale the use of applications based on the need.

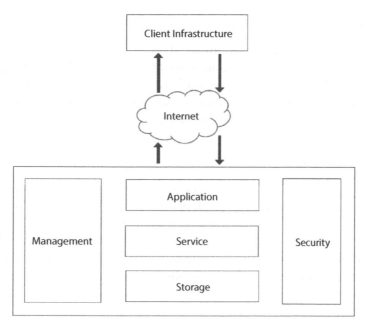

Figure 11.1 Cloud computing architecture.

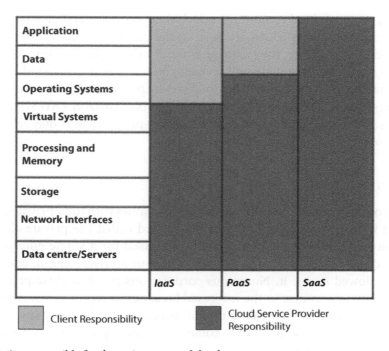

Figure 11.2 Entity responsible for the maintenance of cloud system resources.

11.2.1.2   Infrastructure as a Service

IaaS is the most adaptable cloud service model. It enables consumers to outsource their IT infrastructures like servers, processing, networking, virtual machines, storage, and other resources through virtualization technology. Clients can dynamically scale the system configuration to meet their changing requirements and are charged only for the services used using the IaaS platform layer as given in Figure 11.1.

11.2.1.3   Platform as a Service

PaaS gives us a cloud platform for the end users to develop, manage, and run applications without installing any tool. It enables developers to basically rent everything they require to develop an application/software and count on the service provider for tools, operating systems, and infrastructure. It also integrates the database and web services. PaaS helps us to create applications more swiftly than would be possible if developers had to worry about things like creating, configuring, and provisioning their platforms and backend infrastructure. The principal benefit of PaaS is its ability to be efficiently converted to hybrid.

11.2.2   Deployment Models of Cloud Computing

Cloud computing usually has four deployment models. These are public cloud, private cloud, community cloud, and hybrid cloud.

11.2.2.1   Public Cloud

Public cloud is a type of cloud computing model where the data generated or processed are stored on third-party servers which are open to the general public. The service provider owns the server infrastructure, they manage it and distribute pool resources, so that client companies do not have to purchase and manage their hardware. This kind of cloud computing is an example of a cloud where the cloud service providers deliver services to numerous consumers. Cloud service provider companies like Amazon (AWS) and Microsoft (Azure) offer services which are free of cost or on a pay-per-use. Users may scale computing resources up and down as needed.

11.2.2.2   Private Cloud

A third-party organization is often not trusted by companies with their private information, so a different kind of cloud computing model is used called the private cloud. It has a similar infrastructure as the public cloud, but it is used for a single enterprise. Only a few authorized persons have access to the data kept in a private cloud, and the general public is not allowed to use it. Numerous corporations prefer a close private cloud to get better security in response to the increased breaches in recent years. A private cloud provides broad possibilities for scaling the infrastructure to the company's needs [2]. A private model is particularly fitting for companies which give priority to security and with changing requirements.

11.2.2.3 Community Cloud

A community cloud is quite similar to the private ones; the difference is only the client set. Here, only one organization may own a cloud server but the infrastructure and resources of the cloud are shared by several other organizations if the organizations have comparable security, privacy, storage, and computing power. A community cloud is an appropriate solution for joint business ventures, research organizations, etc., as it will enhance their effectiveness. A centralized cloud helps in development, management, and implementation. The clients share all the incurred expenses.

11.2.2.4 Hybrid Cloud

As the name suggests a hybrid cloud consists of an architecture which combines two or more cloud models like private, public or community. Sensitive and critical processes are done in a private cloud to prevent data breaches while the less risky jobs are done in the public cloud. The hybrid cloud model protects important digital assets and manages tasks strategically and does so in a cost and resource-effective manner. This method benefits in data and application portability.

11.2.3 Security Concerns in Cloud Computing

Cloud computing services and platforms addressed in this chapter face the very security threats that most internet-connected systems are facing. But due to the shared or collaborative character of cloud computing, various threats, and vulnerabilities [36] have increased. The CSA has provided a reference in their list of the top 11 cloud computing threats which they call The Egregious Eleven [8].

11.2.3.1 Data Breaches

In case of a data breach in a system, any secured, classified, or sensitive data might be published, viewed, stolen, or used by an unapproved entity. A breach can occur due to various reasons, and it may be the primary intention of a targeted attack or simply application vulnerabilities [37], bad security practices, or the consequence of human error. It usually involves any sort of information which is not for public releases, such as personally identifiable information (PII), personal health information, business secrets, intellectual property, and financial information.

11.2.3.2 Insufficient Change Control and Misconfiguration

When the computing assets are set up inaccurately, frequently making them exposed to attackers, we call this misconfiguration. For example, security controls disabled, unsecured storage containers, etc. Misconfiguration of cloud services is a major reason for data breaches and it would open possibilities for alteration or deletion of resources and interruption of services. A common cause of misconfiguration in a cloud environment is the lack of efficient change control.

11.2.3.3   Lack of Strategy and Security Architecture

Businesses are trying to get themselves online, and in order to do so, there is a migration of their entire database being shifted to the cloud, in such event, one of the main hindrances during this transition is to implement a proper security and a strategy in order to prevent it from breaches and attacks. Business data may get compromised via various threats when companies do a migration to the cloud porting their present security controls and IT stack to a cloud. Another relevant factor is the absence of perception of the model of shared security responsibility. Risk and cost can be reduced by leveraging the cloud-native tools to enhance visibility in cloud ecosystems. The chance of security trade-off will reduce significantly by such precautions.

11.2.3.4   Insufficient Identity, Credential, Access, and Key Management

Credential, identity, and access management systems have protocols and tools which enable corporations to secure access, manage, and monitor important resources. Examples may include physical resources, such as server rooms and buildings, computer systems, and electronic files and data.

11.2.3.5   Account Hijacking

In the situation of account hijacking, a malicious attacker gains access to and may misuse accounts that are private. In a cloud-based ecosystem, the accounts are at more risk of being hijacked due to the integration of accounts to unknown sources which may be a phishing attack, exploitation of the cloud-based system, or compromised account [39]. These threats are potentially strong and unique which may cause a substantial disorder of the cloud environment, like dysfunction of operations and loss of data and assets. The delivery model of the cloud services, as well as its governance and organization, are responsible for these risks: applications and data in the cloud services, which reside in an account.

11.2.3.6   Insider Threat

The capability of an individual with authorized access to an organization's assets to use their access, either maliciously or unintentionally, to behave in a manner that could adversely affect the organization is defined as insider threat by Carnegie Mellon Computer Emergency Response Team (CERT). Insiders can be other business partners, former or present employees, contractors, etc. Unlike the external threat players, insiders do not have to deal with the security defense. Insiders leverage the company's circle of trust where they get straight access to computer systems, sensitive data, and other parts of the network [7]. Employee negligence was the primary reason for 62% of the insider incidents reported, while 23% were associated with criminal insiders and 13% to the theft of credentials, according to [6]. Few usual situations are employees being a victim of phishing attacks and misconfigured cloud servers.

11.2.3.7   Insecure Interfaces and APIs

Clients interact and manage with cloud services via APIs and software user interfaces (UIs) which the Cloud Service Providers (CSP) gives access. The security of these APIs is responsible for the availability and security of the general cloud services. Authentication, activity monitoring, access control and encryption, and interfaces should be devised to defend against unintended or intended attempts to breach the security system. Exposed, hacked, or broken APIs have resulted in many big breaches. The security requirements and protocols about creating and using these interfaces on the internet should be followed meticulously. The most vulnerable segments of a system are the APIs and UIs and are prone to repeated attacks. Thus, security and safety by design and sufficient controls for protection are necessary.

11.2.3.8 Weak Control Plane

There are many challenges for developing an adequate data protection and storage program while migrating to the cloud from the data centre. The user now needs to make new processes for data duplication, storage, and migration. With the security and integrity that would complete the data plane (it grants runtime and stability), a control plane is an ideal solution to these obstacles. A weak control plane jeopardizes the data infrastructure's logic, verification, and security. These deficiencies may result in data unavailability, leakage or corruption [5].

The other concerns are metastructure and applistructure failures, limited cloud usage visibility, and abuse and nefarious use of cloud services.

11.3 Honeypot System

The concept and methodology for honeypots [14] were first introduced by Lance Spitzner in 1999. Honeypots have become a very popular tool for network security and threat monitoring systems ever since. Honeypots help us to capture and analyze intruder behavior. They are not for directly aiding cloud protection like encryptions and firewalls. Thus, the infrastructure resources get wasted when no attacks are received. They lure the attackers and keep them busy with fake data while keeping the main system out of attackers' reach.

Over time, various kinds of open-source honeypots were developed. Figure 11.3 shows a typical honeypot system. A few prominent honeypots are heralding [28], conpot, dionaea [29], kippo [30], honeyd [31, 32], and sebek [33]. Honeypots are usually categorized into two types: high interaction and low interaction. High-interaction honeypots [34] tend to be costly and possess a greater probability of getting hijacked by an intruder [25]. On the other hand, the low-interaction honeypots are economical and are less likely to be hijacked by an attacker [25]. Nevertheless, the low-interaction honeypots emulate operating systems and other services, and they also have a higher possibility of getting attacked by an identity probing or fingerprinting attack, which would compromise the honeypot. Wang *et al.* (2008) [26] proposed an advanced peer-to-peer botnet which can help us to test a honeypot's security and prepare accordingly for future attacks.

11.3.1 VM (Virtual Machine) as Honeypot in the Cloud

Lavrov *et al.* [11] introduced COR-Honeypot which solves critical challenges by presenting a personalized honeypot which is similar to the victim system and it is created only if an attack is detected so that it can be used for security while operating everything efficiently. Thus, COR-Honeypot has proved to be effective, simulating whatever service required

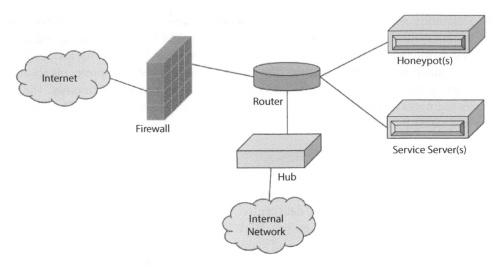

Figure 11.3 Honeypot system diagram.

including restrictive implementations, and can be implemented in real-world cloud systems for protection.

The victim system and the intruder are distinguished via their IP addresses whenever an attack is detected by the honeypot. Then, the malicious data/traffic is restrained in a buffer, and then, it is isolated from the network. While the COR-Honeypot method is applied to the victim system, the cloning of the system is done using the COR-Cloning technique. Then, the sensitive data is replaced with fake data so that, when an intrusion happens, it makes the intruder believe that the attack was successful. Then, the honeypot is isolated from the existing network and buffered and the active traffic is redirected to a new honeypot. Lastly, the system captures the attacker activity that can be used later on for analysis and improving the loopholes revealed. The implementation is done by using KVM as Hypervisor, JITRSwitch as a software network switch, libvirt for the virtualization control API, and Snort [12] for IDS.

The COR-Honeypot is compared with conventional honeypots on Gestalt similarity. The client was a simulated intruder, and the server signifies the victim, COR-Honeypot, and the usual honeypot for each case, respectively. To make the server respond to a trigger, a request query is sent to the service repeatedly for three times. As observed after 12 hours, this system consumed 65% lesser CPU time than Wordpot and 72% lesser than Honeyd.

The present honeypot systems just managed to obtain 6% to 47% of response similarity. Whereas the COR-honeypot attains 100% similarity for POP3 services, FTP, and Telnet. Usually, the error in response similarity is less than 2%. The case of MySQL was the only exception where the honeypot gave 8% error because of the use of ephemeral keys in the service. These results showed that the COR-Honeypot was able to produce the victim system behavior much better than conventional Honeypot solutions.

11.3.2   Attack Sensing and Analyzing Framework

Fraunholz *et al.* [13] proposed an advanced method at interpreting data acquired by their honeypot framework. The framework facilitates the accumulation and processing of data from various honeypots. Statistical methods are applied to the collected data, familiar credentials (usernames and passwords) used by malicious users are recognized. No matches were found in an IP comparison with anonymization services, inferring that all attacks either used unknown anonymization services or originated on bots. Attacks targeted on IoT-devices were identified. Apart from that, a metric of comparison between dictionaries was established. This metric was applied to the acquired data to find relationships among IPs adopted by malicious users. The results showed that, though none of the dictionaries was entirely disjoint, some were a perfect match. Along with other information, it revealed that a large number of malicious users work quite inefficiently [given in Equation (11.1)].

$$Inefficiency = \frac{Login\ attempts - Unique\ Credentials}{Login\ attempts} \tag{11.1}$$

The framework is formed of several modules as sensor, backend, analyzer, and frontend. Information such as username, password, timestamp, MAC, IP, protocol, and OS are collected from unauthorized login attempts by the sensor. Then, the data sent to the backend (comprises a set of relational databases) after encryption. The received data is improved and enhanced with geoinformation and information regarding anonymization services (like the TOR network) from the central database. The analyzer produces simple statistics like passwords, usernames, password lengths and combinations, and attack efficiency. Finally, the frontend helps to observe the statistics and raw data in a comprehensible form.

During the 111 days after deployment, they received more than 300,000 login attempts from more than 2,000 unique IP addresses and that too from about a hundred different countries. There was an average of 136 attempts per IP. An IP with 90,000+ login attempts was discerned, while maximum IPs attempted to log in only once. The IPs from where the login attempts took place were compared to known free proxy servers, TOR exit nodes, and OpenVPN servers. It was observed that virtually no IP (<0.1%) from the dataset matched one of the above-named services. So, it can be concluded that maximum attacks originated directly from unfamiliar proxies, the malicious user's system, or compromised hosts.

11.3.3   A Fuzzy Technique Against Fingerprinting Attacks

Naik *et al.* [18] proposed a fuzzy method to predict and identify fingerprinting attacks. It showed an evaluation of the fingerprinting attack against a honeypot known as KFSensor which is of low-interaction type. Based on the experimental assessment, a mechanism for detection of fingerprinting attacks in low-interaction type honeypots, which incorporates the fundamental ideas of modern fingerprinting attack tools, is proposed. Ultimately, a fuzzy technique is proposed for this. It is a generic fuzzy technique which we can deploy into any type of low-interaction honeypot to help us identify any fingerprinting attack while it is happening.

A total of 50 fingerprinting attacks were conducted and 10 repetitions of each fingerprinting attack. Out of the 50 attacks, 47 attacks were successfully predicted by this fuzzy technique categorizing 31 attacks as high probability and 16 attacks as a medium probability. Just three attacks were predicted as low probability attacks. Therefore, it can extend the life of the honeypot by preventing the attacks. Though this fuzzy technique gives hope, it might not be useful in cases wherever any new fingerprinting probes are utilized that were not taken into consideration in this detection technique. Hence, it is crucial to continue modifying this technique and also introduce some recent attack methods. Moreover, it would be profitable to modify this technique as an adaptive method based on Dynamic FRI and adaptive FRI framework so that it can be more useful for varying attack patterns.

11.3.4   Detecting and Classifying Malicious Access

Saikawa *et al.* [21] deployed the Dionaea honeypot which is a low-interaction honeypot on the Sakura cloud to obtain data regarding attacks and malware binaries; results are analyzed, it was also analyzed with data gathered by other researchers, and the latest trends in attacking patterns and techniques are studied. As Dionaea has the highest amount of available services, it was used as a core of the honeypot. Dionaea is coupled with python as the scripting language and using libemu for shellcodes detection. It emulates services such as SIP, SMB, TFTP, MySQL, HTTP, MSSQL, FTP, and others. These services emulated an exposed and vulnerable server operating on Windows. The main protocol Dionaea uses is the SMB protocol and uses the traditional port 445.

Dionaea was set up in a cloud environment (as shown in Figure 11.3) as a virtual private server (VPS) deployment. After the setting up of Dionaea is completed, they set the DionaeaFR. To prevent honeypot detection, an approach of study [22] was used where the honeypot is activated every morning and stopped it every evening. The present practice in web server connections has moved to HTTPS protocol from HTTP. The key result from this is a notable decrease in port 80 attacks. Presently, the most prevalent malware is WannaCry [23]. It is a combination of self-propagating worms and ransomware. It uses the vulnerability of the SMB protocol which uses the SMB protocol's vulnerability. The SMB service (port 445) faced the highest number of attacks and their aim was to download malware in the servers. Database attacks like on Microsoft SQL and MySQL are well known on the Internet. Dionaea is an efficient honeypot to monitor and identify intruder access. It is important to administer Dionaea discreetly to defend it from attacks because the honeypot itself has a vulnerability.

11.3.5   A Bayesian Defense Model for Deceptive Attack

This paper by Guan *et al.* [24] proposes deception detection technologies and the game theory in network security. They examined the deficiencies and benefits of the Bayesian model and proposed a game model which is based on the historical returns and gave a complete mathematical explanation of the results of the relative model. They took the benefits of the two different models and designed a Bayesian improved model, and they further advanced the enhanced model to compensate for the flaws of the Bayesian model so that the system can get the most advantage.

Based on different possible scenarios, few income parameters in the game matrix (attack defense) were considered. The identity of the malicious intruder is determined randomly by the roulette bets. Every signal is correlated with two separate and distinct intruders with a different identity. Different strategies were analyzed via Bayesian rules. There are a set of two optimal strategies (Pb is the probability of user identity as a malicious user, and Pt is the threshold probability). The victim's Nash equilibrium is dependent on the exact value of p with the comparison of Pt.

They consider X (Regular Behavior) = {(X|N), (X|M)} and Y (Suspicious Behavior) = {(Y|N), (Y|M)}, where M represents malicious users and N represents normal users. (α, β) is used to denote belief of a defender in a rival.

$$\alpha = Pb(M|X), 1 - \alpha = Pb(N|X); \tag{11.2}$$

$$\beta = Pb(M|Y), 1 - \beta = Pb(N|Y); \tag{11.3}$$

α [given by Equation (11.2)] and β [given by Equation (11.3)] are the probabilities of a malicious user receiving signal X and Y, respectively.

According to Bayesian rules, α and β can be represented using the Equations (11.4) and (11.5).

$$\alpha = \frac{P(X|M)P(M)}{P(X|M)\,P(M) + P(X|N)\,P(N)} \tag{11.4}$$

$$\beta = \frac{P(S|M)\,P(M)}{P(S|M)\,P(M) + P(S|N)\,P(N)} \tag{11.5}$$

H represents that the honeypot system is deployed and U represents the access to usual systems. There are two strategies: X and Y, and we consider the expectation in both strategies. The threshold probability (Pφ) as shown in Equation (11.6) can be considered only when the two are equal, i.e., E(X) = E(Y),

$$P\varphi = \frac{b_a + c_h}{b_c + b_a + c_h + c_a + 2e} \tag{11.6}$$

where b_a is profit after defender serves the normal user, b_c is the profit after the defender successfully captures an attack, c_h is the cost of the defender arranging an extra honeypot system, and c_a is the loss after the defender was successfully attacked.

When p ≥ Pφ, strategy H is the best choice, else strategy U is better. We get inequalities given in Equations (11.7) regardless of the attacker's identity:

$$\beta b_c > 0 > -\beta c_a - (1 - \beta)c_t \tag{11.7}$$

For avoiding the probability calculation of negative income, relative income is taken. With the help of this income, the confidence degree can be computed. We can set p equals to Pφ in the Relative Historical Income (RHI) model, and the actual situation determines the value of a. Trust coefficient of the normal user in the improved model is represented by *a*, the value of the coefficient changes the equilibrium between security cost and system security. A lower value of the trust coefficient requires more cost for security. If they concentrate more on the cost, they would have to modify the following actual situation. The system is rarely attacked when the value of p is extremely low like p = 0.01. In actual circumstances, the RHI model is better and more active. If p is high, then the performance of the RHI model would be extremely close to the revised model, though this is highly unlikely in real situations. It was found that the Bayesian model and the RHI model have an efficiency dividing line. When the value of p is less than 0.5 (excluding when p tends to zero RHI infinitely), the Bayesian model is more beneficial, else the RHI model would be more helpful. This model is based on the RHI model and the Bayesian model. It was updated and enhanced in overall performance, and even without the knowledge about the value of p, the system can reach the best defense state.

11.3.6   Strategic Game Model for DDoS Attacks in Smart Grid

Wang *et al.* [27] addressed DDoS attacks in smart grids by introducing honeypots into the AMI network. Furthermore, they have also taken the anti-honeypot issue into account. They investigated the crucial interactivity amidst the intruder and the user. As per the observation, using the recommended system, there was an improvement in the rate of detection and consumption of energy. Therefore, a game strategy honeypot implemented in an AMI network can protect the data and ensure network security. However, traditional AMI(s) used single way communication, and modern AMI(s) allows both ways: communication among the meters and utility companies. AMI comprises data aggregators, smart meters, meter data management system (MDMS), central system (known as AMI headend), and enabling communication technologies and the communication networks.

The payoff of the real services for Ω_1 (system provides service) is given as $J_{Z1}(\Omega_1)$ given by Equation (11.8) where Z1 is real communication, U_1 is real users, U_2 is attackers, V_1 is visitor access, λ is real user payoff, and ϕ is attack damage factor.

$$J_{z1}(\Omega_1) = P(U_1 \mid V_1) * (-\phi * \lambda) + P(U_2 \mid V_1) * (\lambda)$$
$$= (\theta - \phi + \theta\phi) * \lambda \tag{11.8}$$

Likewise, the payoff of the actual services for $\Omega 2$ (the system does not provide service) was computed by Equation (11.9).

$$J_{z1}(\Omega_2) = P(U_1 \mid V_1) * 0 + P(U_2 \mid V_1) * (\lambda)$$
$$= -\theta\lambda \tag{11.9}$$

In the AMI networks, different simulations were conducted to get a proper honeypot system for DDoS attacks. The selected one consists of smart meters, honeypots, routers, anti-honeypots, and servers. The performance was compared with Cluster Head (CH) model [42] and All Monitor (AM) model [43]. The proposed model was better with energy consumption rates. The average detection rate is around 50% that indicates an unstable detection performance. The results imply that by raising honeypots in an AMI network, the anti-honeypots can be reduced to keep balance with the servers. In this way, the general servers were prevented from intruders significantly.

Table 11.1 lists the few recent studies done on the advancements in honeypot the cloud to protect the main network and analyze the attack patterns and methodology of attackers. To apprehend the attack traffic, Wang *et al.* in [44] discussed distributed and hybrid architecture for honeypots. Hastings *et al.* [45] recorded and analyzed data on attacks on a low-interaction honeypot in the smart grid for six months. A new hybrid detection method is

Table 11.1 List of recent studies on the improvement of honeypots in the cloud.

Reference number	Problem addressed	Techniques used
[11]	Efficient use of resources, less prone error and faster	Hypervisor (KVM), virtualization control API (libvirt), IDS (Snort), software-network switch (JITRSwitch)
[13]	Highly-scalable WAN network attack sensing and Analyzing framework	Encryption, relational databases, anonymization services (TOR)
[18]	Identifying and inhibiting fingerprinting attacks on low-interaction honeypots	KFSensor as low-interaction honeypot, fuzzy techniques, fingerprinting detection
[21]	Detection and classification of malicious Access	Consortium blockchain, encryption, and conditional proxy re-encryption
[24]	Improved defense model for deceptive attack	Game theory, Bayesian models
[27]	Preventing DDoS attacks and preventing anti-honeypots attacks	Game strategy, Bayesian model, OPNET

Shadow honeypot [46]; it checks for unusual diagnosis and uses a feedback tool to enhance the hybrid detection algorithm. The analysis of the security of critical systems is done using Game Theory. Reiher and Mirkovic [47] showed an analysis of DDoS attacks and defense techniques. Chai *et al.* [48] suggested a continuous setting in the game model, and then, the Nash equilibrium is calculated to resolve the attack detection issues.

11.4 Blockchain

We can define blockchain as a set of blocks that are connected via cryptography, and they keep growing as new blocks are added. Every block comprises a cryptographic hash of the former block, transaction data and a timestamp. A blockchain is immutable. Transactions between various parties are recorded efficiently. Blockchain's distributed storage splits up the client's data into small lumps or blocks as in Figure 11.4. Now, an additional layer of protection is added so it gets dispersed all through the system. This is made possible using the hashing ability, public or private key encryptions, and exchange records of the blockchain [49]. Every bit of data is put away in a decentralized section as shown in Figure 11.4. Blockchain gave rise to popular cryptocurrencies like Bitcoin [50] and Ethereum.

The three most prominent types of blockchain are public, private, and consortium blockchain. In a public blockchain, anyone can read and access the information and developers do not bother the users. All the information is public by default. It is primarily applied to Ethereum, Bitcoin, Hyperledger, and other fields. In the case of a private blockchain, the write permission is only available to an individual or organization, and the read and other permissions are restricted. A private blockchain provides superior security in terms of data

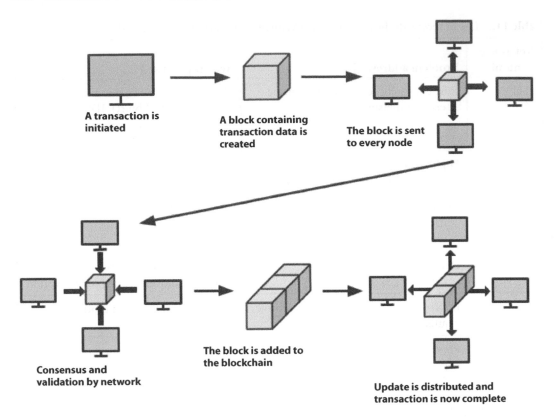

Figure 11.4 Blockchain architecture.

privacy and faster transaction speeds in comparison to public blockchains. A consortium blockchain gives us what we may call "partial decentralization", the users can trade and consult, but they would not be able to verify the transaction or publish smart contracts without the permission of the consortium. In this section, a few recent papers related to blockchain technology in management, storage, and movement of the data in the cloud are reviewed.

11.4.1   Blockchain-Based Encrypted Cloud Storage

Gochhayat *et al.* [9] proposed a novel encrypted cloud architecture called Yugula, which gives file integrity and confidentiality by adopting blockchain and revised convergent encryption. Mainly, two approaches were employed for data security and confidentiality: one uses symmetric encryption and the other uses double hashing. The Yugala cloud service is highly scalable as it was created over the Mystiko blockchain. As Mystiko blockchain principally targets big data, IoT requirements can be supported and managed with Yugala as well.

For the implementation, the authors consolidated Mystiko Blockchain's [15] platform. The primary reason to use Mystiko Blockchain was due to its high scalability features and transaction throughput. The encrypted files are stored in the cloud. The encryption of the files only allows the users to verify it is existence, not the cloud. The files in blockchain are distributed in multiple servers and the information is irrelevant that is why the cloud storage cannot remove the file on its own, therefore giving reliability and system integrity.

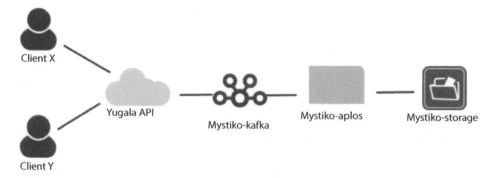

Figure 11.5 Yugala architecture.

In Mystiko blockchain, every peer has a Cassandra node; they form a ring-like cluster architecture as they are connected with one other. When a transaction gets completed, the state update in a peer gets shared and duplicated using sharding with the algorithm of Cassandra's Paxos. Figure 11.5 depicts the architecture of Yugala. Mystiko offers the Aplos smart contract platform as a substitute for the smart contract on current blockchains. Consistent transaction throughput is maintained by every peer in the blockchain. When the number of Blockchain peers was increased, the transaction throughput linearly increased.

11.4.2   Cloud-Assisted EHR Sharing via Consortium Blockchain

Wang *et al.* [17] introduced a blockchain-based EHR sharing system with conditional proxy re-encryption and conjunctive keyword searchable encryption to achieve privacy and security of the data being shared between various medical organizations. A legitimate block is formed of a header, data admin signature, block body, and timestamp. The block header consists of five elements: preceding block's hash, block size, block ID, Merkle root [52], and a random number. Data transaction consists of the transaction type, keyword ciphertext, transaction ID, doctor's signature, and patient's account. A consensus mechanism called proof of authorization is proposed to ensure high-efficiency, safety, and authenticity of the blockchain network and create the regulation for the consortium blockchain. The protocol is composed of three layers: a data-sharing layer, data storage layer, and data generation layer.

The doctors encrypt the EHR with their private key and patient's public key along with a set of keywords. So that decryption of the ciphertext becomes impossible without the keywords and doctor's public key and the patient's private key. Thus, only the appointed doctor can decipher the ciphertext, which improves data confidentiality. The EHR consortium blockchain system distinguishes various nodes and their validity. The doctor can assert the ciphertext sent by the cloud by examining whether he/she can decrypt the ciphertext. It will not disclose any information regarding the patient while searching for the keyword. Given k (security parameter), the Data Provider (DP) generates a prime number q and selects a bilinear pairing ê: $C1 \times C1 \rightarrow C2$, where C1 is an additive cyclic set and C2 is a multiplicative cyclic set with an equal prime order q. The DP takes three distinct one-way collision-proof hash functions given in Equations (11.10), (11.11), and (11.12).

$$H1: \{0,1\}^{*} \to C1 \tag{11.10}$$

$$H2: \{0,1\}^{*} \times C1 \times C1 \to C1 \tag{11.11}$$

$$H3: \{0,1\}^{*} \to Zq^{*} \tag{11.12}$$

The proposed scheme was implemented on the popular Ethereum platform to check its performance. The consensus mechanism, network model and data structure are created for consortium blockchain to ensure the efficient performance of the model. Further, encryption with keyword-searchable mechanism was used to assure data security including search capabilities and proxy re-encryption (conditional) was employed to achieve privacy protection while sharing data.

11.4.3 Blockchain-Secured Cloud Storage

Zou *et al.* [16] proposed a cloud-based file system with enhanced security by using a blockchain named ChainFS to fight against forking attacks. It has cloud storage for data files and it sends crucial operations to the blockchain for file operation logging and key distribution. The user's important files are managed by the client's device and a FUSE client helps to store those securely. The SUNDR [10] protocol was considered on the data plane that manages a pair of server elements: the block which stores the content of the files and a consistency server. The directory of the public keys and the SUNDR server both were hosted on insecure platforms like the public cloud. The blockchain was mainly used to detect or prevent forking attacks and the blockchain ledger can act as a witness system.

The performance result with small files analyzing the typical case that operates an S3FS without blockchain showed that with 10 KB files the ChainFS had up to 35% overhead of performance. As the files become bigger, the overhead gets reduced. The performance is not balanced when the files are very small. Files of size ranging from 1 MB to 1 GB were generated. The execution time was measured. The result showed the overhead rises as the files become bigger and reach a peak of 28% (1 GB file). In the big file perspective, transferring data over the Internet was the bottleneck.

11.4.4 Blockchain and Edge Computing–Based Security Architecture

Zhang *et al.* [19] introduced a novel security architecture for Vehicular Ad hoc Network (VANET) based on Edge Computing (EC) and blockchain systems. It has a three-level structure consisting of perception level, edge level, and cloud service level. The blockchain solves the security challenges in the transmission of data in the perception level. The edge computing segment gives edge cloud services and computing resources for the perception layer.

In [53], the public key infrastructure (PKI) with the transport along with the roadside unit (RSU) develops a blockchain network to enhance security. To prevent delay and poor network performance when lots of consensus job of blockchain is performed in the Roadside Unit (RSU), the computationally intensive work is offloaded to EC, and then, the outcome is delivered to the RSU when completed. The VANET produces a lot of data all of which we cannot store in blockchain as it will use more resources. So, only the very important part of the data is stored in the blockchain, the rest is stored in the cloud (with encryptions and other securities).

11.4.5   Data Provenance Architecture in Cloud Ecosystem Using Blockchain

In this paper, Liang *et al.* [54] introduced the architecture of a data provenance system (ProvChain) meant for auditing in the cloud. It uses blockchain which helps in increasing availability and preserving privacy. The blockchain helps by creating an unchangeable timestamp and generating tokens for validation. ProvChain was developed using own-Cloud [55] (an open-sourced app) to obtain data for provenance. Ongoing works show that this architecture can fulfill the requirements of validation and proof in various cases. The evaluation showed that ownCloud coupled with this architecture brought a lower system overhead.

The critical components of ProvChain are Cloud User, Cloud Service Provider (CSP), Provenance Database, Provenance Auditor (PA), and Blockchain Network. Files in the cloud are used as data units. Provenance data is generated when a file operation is detected which is uploaded in the blockchain network by the service provider. Each block consists of a block header and a transactions list. ProvChain's implementation is based on a three-layered structure, comprising the storage, the blockchain network, and the database for provenance. In addition, 6.49% of overhead is found in the proposed architecture than the original one based on response time, but considering the robust security, it is acceptable.

Table 11.2 lists a few recent studies done on advancements on implementation of blockchains in the cloud to solve various security issues and improve trust and credibility of data. Zyskind *et al.* [56] (2015) proposed an approach of decentralized data privacy

Table 11.2 List of recent studies application of blockchain for security in the cloud.

Reference number	Problem addressed	Techniques and technology used
[16]	Prevention of forking attacks	Ethereum, S3FS, FUSE clients and Amazon S3 cloud storage
[19]	A better security architecture of VANET	Blockchain and MEC
[9]	Secured cloud storage	Mystiko Blockchain, double hash, symmetric encryption
[17]	Security and privacy preservation in EHR sharing via cloud	Consortium blockchain, encryption and conditional proxy re-encryption
[20]	Secured and faster Dependency Attestation Framework	Ethereum, IPFS, TPM, cloud database
[54]	Data provenance with enhanced privacy and availability	ownCloud, blockchain database

which will ensure that the users have control over their data. The system consists of the blockchain system, users, and the providers. Data sharing models based on blockchain is an approach getting popular to preserve the privacy of the electronic medical records in the cloud [17, 57].

In Shafagh *et al.* [58], a blockchain network is used by the authors to manage and securely store the access permissions. The corresponding access permissions and the control of the data comprise the blockchain transactions. But in applications of IoT systems, the scalability and the latency issues are yet to be fixed. Ensuring data provenance in the cloud ecosystems requires techniques that are similar to auditing and logging systems. Many of these methods control system resources like PASS [59], S2Logger [60], and SPROVE [61]. In [62], a blockchain architecture for data provenance and tracking data accountability is proposed by Neisse *et al.* Similar to [63], smart contracts are used by this approach in blockchains to inculcate the data access protocols. The system consists of data processors, data subjects, and data controllers.

Table 11.3 Honeypots for cloud security analysis.

Reference number	Advantages	Disadvantages
[26]	Can be used to address the shortcomings of honeypots, test a honeypot system.	Attackers can use this to get past inefficient honeypots or render them useless.
[29]	Gives limited access to attackers, economic, low chances of being hijacked.	Easy to predict, not engaging, static.
[30]	More realistic, attackers get more access, and provide more analytics data.	Harder to predict, needs more resources and energy, and is more vulnerable.
[11]	Economical, auto-detects attacks, uses less computation power, less error-prone.	May not withstand/detect modern attacks.
[13]	Good analytics tool, analysis from multiple honeypots can be done.	Not a direct security measure, just an analytics tool.
[18]	Protection against fingerprinting attacks can be modified to an adaptive (D-FRI) framework.	Designed for low-interaction honeypots only, medium prediction results.
[21]	Detection and classification of attacks in details.	Easy to predict, not engaging, static.
[24]	Improved model.	More resources needed.
[27]	Protection against DDoS attack, better attack detection.	Multiple nodes, large data exchange, multiple interfaces.

11.6   Comparative Analysis

Here, we present a brief outline of the benefits and drawbacks of the studies and methods reviewed in this literature.

Table 11.3 lists some advantages and disadvantages of recent studies on using honeypot systems for cloud security, while Table 11.4 lists the same on using blockchain for cloud security. Although several innovative and effective techniques were introduced in the past few years, the review demonstrates that there are still some loopholes in the proposed systems which can be addressed in future to safeguard against new and unconventional attacks.

11.7   Conclusion

We have conducted a study to review the advancement in cloud security with a focus on honeypot networks and cloud security. We studied more than 15 techniques which aided in strengthening cloud security in recent years. The papers we reviewed used several techniques to increase security and prevent attacks. In light of the variation and frequency of attacks in recent times, we recommend using honeypot and blockchain technology in the cloud along with proper cryptographic encryption to ensure maximum security in cloud environments. The improvements of honeypot networks are discussed in Table 11.1. Honeypots will provide us with intel on attacks which can be analyzed, lure attackers, and

Table 11.4 Blockchain for cloud security analysis.

Reference number	Advantages	Disadvantages
[9]	Better data confidentiality using double hash and using symmetric encryption.	Slower when files are large.
[17]	Highly efficient, authentic and safe	The amount of the keyword set should not be too large, gas consumption increases with the increase of the length of the data package.
[16]	Prevents forking attacks, highly secure	30%–35% performance overhead
[19]	Secured and less prone to failure	Might be slow, yet to test in the real world
[20]	High accuracy, fast, and safe	Network routing channel attack and memory overflow attack might affect it
[54]	Better privacy and availability	6.6% overhead in response time
[58]	Secure storage and management	Latency and scalability
[63]	Secure and economical	Mining speed affects execution duration

keep them occupied with fake information though we should take precautions so that the attacker cannot use the honeypot as leverage. To ensure this, monitoring of honeypot is essential. We can use multiple honeypots according to our requirement and resources. Blockchain will help to implement the idea of distributed storage so even if the network gets compromised the attacker would not get the whole information rather some chunks of it which may not be of any value at all. But blockchain might bring overall system resources overhead when dealing with big data. Table 11.2 lists the problems addressed using blockchain in the cloud.

As the COVID- 19 pandemic changed, the usual ways of the world many businesses are migrating online thus using cloud services. We will use this study to further dive deep into various security concerns that will arise in the future. Since honeypots and blockchain are developing technologies, we are expecting to see further development in recent years which will make cloud computing more secure.

References

1. Dillon, T., Wu, C., Chang, E., Cloud Computing: Issues and Challenges. *2010 24th IEEE International Conference on Advanced Information Networking and Applications*, Perth, WA, pp. 27–33, 2010.
2. Sotomayor, B., Montero, R.S., Llorente, I.M., Foster, I., Virtual Infrastructure Management in Private and Hybrid Clouds. *IEEE Internet Comput.*, 13, 5, 14–22, Sept.-Oct. 2009.
3. Spitzner, L., Honeypots: catching the insider threat. *19th Annual Computer Security Applications Conference, 2003. Proceedings*, Las Vegas, NV, USA, pp. 170–179, 2003.
4. Zhu, L., Wu, Y., Gai, K., Choo, K.K.R., Controllable and trustworthy blockchain-based cloud data management. *Future Gener. Comput. Syst.*, 91, 527–535, 2019.
5. Lacoste, M. *et al.*, User-Centric Security and Dependability in the Clouds-of-Clouds. *IEEE Cloud Comput.*, 3, 5, 64–75, Sept.-Oct. 2016.
6. https://www.observeit.com/wp-content/uploads/2020/04/2020-Global-Cost-of-Insider-Threats-Ponemon-Report_UTD.pdf
7. Kandias, M., Virvilis, N., Gritzalis, D., The Insider Threat in Cloud Computing. *Critical Information Infrastructure Security*. Lecture Notes in Computer Science, vol. 6983, pp. 93–103, Springer-Verlag, Berlin Heidelberg, 2013.
8. https://cloudsecurityalliance.org/press-releases/2019/08/09/csa-releases-new-research-top-to-cloud-computing-egregious-eleven/.
9. Gochhayat, S.P., Bandara, E., Shetty, S., Foytik, P., Yugala: Blockchain Based Encrypted Cloud Storage for IoT Data. *2019 IEEE International Conference on Blockchain (Blockchain)*, Atlanta, GA, USA, pp. 483–489, 2019.
10. Li, J., Krohn, M.N., Mazieres, D., Shasha, D.E., Secure Untrusted Data Repository (SUNDR), in: *OSDI*, vol. 4, pp. 9–9, 2004.
11. Lavrov, D., Blanchet, V., Pang, S., He, M., Sarrafzadeh, A., COR-Honeypot: Copy-On-Risk, Virtual Machine as Honeypot in the Cloud. *2016 IEEE 9th International Conference on Cloud Computing (CLOUD)*, San Francisco, CA, pp. 908–912, 2016.
12. https://snort.org.
13. Fraunholz, D., Zimmermann, M., Anton, S.D., Schneider, J., Dieter Schotten, H., Distributed and highly-scalable WAN network attack sensing and sophisticated analysing framework based on Honeypot technology. *2017 7th International Conference on Cloud Computing, Data Science & Engineering - Confluence*, Noida, pp. 416–421, 2017.

14. Spitzner, L., *Honeypots: Tracking hackers. 2. print*, Addidon-Wesley, Boston, 2003.

15. Bandara, E., Ng, W.K., DE Zoysa, K., Fernando, N., Tharaka, S., Maurakirinathan, P., Jayasuriya, N., Mystikoblockchain meets big data, in: *2018 IEEE International Conference on Big Data (Big Data)*, IEEE, pp. 3024–3032, 2018.

16. Tang, Y. *et al.*, ChainFS: Blockchain-Secured Cloud Storage. *2018 IEEE 11th International Conference on Cloud Computing (CLOUD)*, San Francisco, CA, pp. 987–990, 2018.

17. Wang, Y., Zhang, A., Zhang, P., Wang, H., Cloud-Assisted EHR Sharing With Security and Privacy Preservation via Consortium Blockchain. *IEEE Access*, 7, 136704–136719, 2019.

18. Naik, N., Jenkins, P., Cooke, R., Yang, L., Honeypots That Bite Back: A Fuzzy Technique for Identifying and Inhibiting Fingerprinting Attacks on Low Interaction Honeypots. *2018 IEEE International Conference on Fuzzy Systems (FUZZ-IEEE)*, Rio de Janeiro, pp. 1–8, 2018.

19. Zhang, X., Li, R., Cui, B., A security architecture of VANET based on blockchain and mobile edge computing. *2018 1st IEEE International Conference on Hot Information-Centric Networking (HotICN)*, Shenzhen, pp. 258–259, 2018.

20. Zhao, Z., Shen, Q., Luo, W., Ruan, A., CloudCoT: A Blockchain-Based Cloud Service Dependency Attestation Framework, in: *Information and Communications Security*. ICICS 2019. Lecture Notes in Computer Science, vol. 11999, J. Zhou, X. Luo, Q. Shen, Z. Xu (Eds.), Springer, Cham, 2020.

21. Saikawa, K. and Klyuev, V., Detection and Classification of Malicious Access using a Dionaea Honeypot. *2019 10th IEEE International Conference on Intelligent Data Acquisition and Advanced Computing Systems: Technology and Applications (IDAACS)*, Metz, France, pp. 844–848, 2019.

22. Tsikerdekis, M., Zeadally, S., Schlesener, A., Sklavos, N., Approaches for Preventing Honeypot Detection and Compromise. *2018 Global Information Infrastructure and Networking Symposium (GIIS)*, Greece, pp. 1–6, 2018.

23. CERT-MU Whitepaper, THE WANNACRY RANSOMWARE, 7, 1, Port Louis, May 2017.

24. Guan, R., Li, L., Wang, T., Qin, Y., Xiong, W., Liu, Q., A Bayesian Improved Defense Model for Deceptive Attack in Honeypot-Enabled Networks. *2019 IEEE 21st International Conference on High Performance Computing and Communications; IEEE 17th International Conference on Smart City; IEEE 5th International Conference on Data Science and Systems (HPCC/SmartCity/DSS)*, Zhangjiajie, China, pp. 208–214, 2019.

25. Spitzner, L., Honeypots: Tracking Hackers. vol. 1, Addison-Wesley Reading, United States, 2003.

26. Wang, P., Sparks, S., Zou, C.C., An Advanced Hybrid Peer-to-Peer Botnet. *IEEE Trans. Dependable Secure Comput.*, 7, 2, 113–127, April-June 2010.

27. Wang, K., Du, M., Maharjan, S., Sun, Y., Strategic Honeypot Game Model for Distributed Denial of Service Attacks in the Smart Grid. *IEEE Trans. Smart Grid*, 8, 5, 2474–2482, Sept. 2017.

28. https://www.honeynet.org/2016/03/23/heralding-the-credentials-catching-honeypot/

29. https://github.com/DinoTools/dionaea

30. https://github.com/desaster/kippo

31. Provos, N., Honeyd: A Virtual Honeypot Daemon, 1, 5, Michigan, 2003.

32. Provos, N. and Holz, T., Virtual Honeypots : From Botnets Tracking to Instrusion Detection, Addision Wesley Professional, United States, 2007.

33. http://www.cs.jhu.edu/~rubin/courses/sp04/sebek.pdf

34. T. H. Project, Know Your Enemy, 2nd ed., Addison-Wesley, United States, 2004.

35. Grimes, R.A., Honeypots, in: *Hacking the Hacker: Learn from the Experts Who Take Down Hackers*, John Wiley & Sons, Inc., Indianapolis, Indiana, 2017.

36. Grobauer, B., Walloschek, T., Stocker, E., Understanding Cloud Computing Vulnerabilities. *IEEE Secur. Privacy*, 9, 2, 50–57, March-April 2011.
37. Xiao, Z. and Xiao, Y., Security and Privacy in Cloud Computing. *IEEE Commun. Surv. Tutorials*, 15, 2, 843–859, Second Quarter 2013.
38. Wang, K., Du, M., Sun, Y., Vinel, A., Zhang, Y., Attack detection and distributed forensics in machine-to-machine networks. *IEEE Network*, 30, 6, 49–55, 2016.
39. Tirumala, S.S., Sathu, H., Naidu, V., Analysis and Prevention of Account Hijacking Based INCIDENTS in Cloud Environment. *2015 International Conference on Information Technology (ICIT)*, Bhubaneswar, 2015.
40. Koo, J., Kim, Y., Lee, S., Security Requirements for Cloud-based C4I Security Architecture. *2019 International Conference on Platform Technology and Service (PlatCon)*, Jeju, Korea (South), 2019.
41. Wang, K., Du, M., Maharjan, S., Sun, Y., Strategic Honeypot Game Model for Distributed Denial of Service Attacks in the Smart Grid. *IEEE Trans. Smart Grid*, 8, 5, 2474–2482, Sept. 2017.
42. Wang, K., Du, M., Yang, D., Zhu, C., Shen, J., Zhang, Y., Game theory based active defense for intrusion detection in cyber-physical embedded systems. *ACM Trans. Embedded Comput. Syst.*, 16, 1, Article 18, pp. 21, 2016.
43. Moosavi, H. and Bui, F., A game-theoretic framework for robust optimal intrusion detection in wireless sensor networks. *IEEE Trans. Inf. Forensics Secur.*, 9, 9, 1367–1379, 2014.
44. Wang, K., Du, M., Sun, Y., Vinel, A., Zhang, Y., Attack detection and distributed forensics in machine-to-machine networks. *IEEE Network*, 30, 6, 49–55, 2016.
45. Hastings, J. and Laverty, D.M., Tracking smart grid hackers. *49th International Universities Power Engineering Conference (UPEC)*, pp. 1–5, 2011.
46. Anagnostakis, K.G., Sidiroglou, S., Akritidis, P., Polychronakis, M., Keromytis, A.D., Markatos, E.P., Shadow honeypots. *Int. J. Comput. Netw. Secur.*, 2, 9, 1–15, 2010.
47. Mirkovic, J. and Reiher, P., A taxonomy of DDoS attack and DDoS defense mechanisms, in: *Proc. ACM SIGCOM*, pp. 39–53, 2004.
48. Chai, B., Chen, J., Yang, Z., Zhang, Y., Demand response management with multiple utility companies: a two-level game approach. *IEEE Trans. Smart Grid*, 5, 2, 722–731, 2011.
49. Zyskind, G., Nathan, O., Pentland, A., Decentralizing Privacy: Using Blockchain to Protect Personal Data. *2015 IEEE Security and Privacy Workshops*, San Jose, CA, 2015.
50. https://bitcoin.org/bitcoin.pdf
51. https://ethereum.org/en/whitepaper/
52. Patel, D., Bothra, J., Patel, V., Blockchain exhumed. *2017 ISEA Asia Security and Privacy (ISEASP)*, Surat, pp. 1–12, 2017.
53. Lasla, N., Younis, M., Znaidi, W. et al., Efficient Distributed Admission and Revocation using Blockchain for Cooperative ITS[C]//New Technologies, Mobility and Security (NTMS). *2018 9th IFIP International Conference on*, IEEE, 2018.
54. Liang, X., Shetty, S., Tosh, D., Kamhoua, C., Kwiat, K., Njilla, L., ProvChain: A Blockchain-Based Data Provenance Architecture in Cloud Environment with Enhanced Privacy and Availability. *2017 17th IEEE/ACM International Symposium on Cluster, Cloud and Grid Computing (CCGRID)*, Madrid, 2017.
55. https://owncloud.org/.
56. Zyskind, G., Nathan, O., Pentland, A., Decentralizing Privacy: Using Blockchain to Protect Personal Data, in: *2015 IEEE Security and Privacy Workshop*, San Jose, CA, 2015.
57. Xia, Q., Sifah, E.B., Smahi, A., Amofa, S., Zhang, X., BBDS: Blockchain-Based Data Sharing for Electronic Medical Records in Cloud Environments. *MPDI, Information*, MPDI, 8, 44, 2017.

58. Shafagh, H., Burkhalter, L., Hithnawi, A., Duquennoy, S., Towards Blockchain-based Auditable Storage and Sharing of IoT Data, in: *2017 ACM Cloud Computing Security Workshop (CCSW)*, Dallas, Texas, USA, 2017.

59. Muniswamy-Reddy, K.K., Holland, D.A., Braun, U., Seltzer, M., II, Provenance-aware storage systems, in: *USENIX Annual Technical Conference*, General Track, 2006.

60. Suen, C.H., Ko, R.K., Tan, Y.S., Jagadpramana, P., Lee, B.S., S2logger: End-to-end data tracking mechanism for cloud data provenance, in: *12th IEEE International Conference on Trust, Security and Privacy in Computing and Communications*, 2013.

61. Hasan, R., Sion, R., Winslett, M., Sprov 2.0: A highly configurable platform-independent library for secure provenance, in: *ACM Conference on Computer and Communications Security (CCS)*, Chicago, IL, USA, 2009.

62. Neisse, R., Steri, G., Nai-Fovino, I., A Blockchain-based Approach for Data Accountability and Provenance Tracking, in: *12th International Conference on Availability, Reliability and Security*, Reggio Calabria, Italy, 2017.

63. Ramachandran, A. and Kantarcioglu, M., Using Blockchain and smart contracts for secure data provenance management, arXiv, abs/1709.10000, 2017.

12

Machine Learning–Based Security in Cloud Database—A Survey

Utsav Vora*, Jayleena Mahato, Hrishav Dasgupta, Anand Kumar and Swarup Kr Ghosh

Sister Nivedita University, Kolkata, India

Abstract

Cloud computing has grown as an innovative technology providing physical as well as logical resources over the internet and changing the way of collecting and sharing data files. This growth is a reflection of the rapid transition and intense interest of academic and industrial organizations in this technology. Despite having several advantages, cloud security has always been a concern for cloud services. With the evolution of technology worldwide, the threats are also getting more complicated and advanced such as data breaching, insecure interfaces, shared technology vulnerabilities, and distributed attacks. A safe environment for cloud services is highly essential. For this, Intrusion Detection Systems based on various Machine Learning (ML) algorithms, Supervised, Unsupervised, or Hybrid, have been developed. In this review, we focus on understanding the current status of ML algorithms and emphasize those Intrusion Detection Systems which are evaluated using either of the two worldwide recognized datasets, NSL-KDD dataset, and UNSW-NB15 dataset. Related research papers are examined with respective experimental setups and other important factors. We stress our research on addressing security threats, issues related to cloud security, and the advantages and disadvantages that are faced on implementation of ML for detection of attacks in the cloud. We also aim to deliver effective solutions and put forth some open challenges as well for future research and development on cloud security.

Keywords: Cloud computing, cloud security, machine learning, NSL-KDD, UNSW-NB15, intrusion detection systems

12.1 Introduction

The term "Cloud" was coined from the computer network diagrams which used it to conceal the complexity of infrastructure involved [1, 49]. Cloud consists of several servers that store customer data and for this it is also called a Data Center [2]. It can be limited to one organization, called as Enterprise Cloud, or convenient to numerous firms, called as Public Cloud. This technology leads us to "cloud computing" which is a popular phrase and can be explained as a centralized pool of assets and outsourcing mechanism that provides various services to users whenever needed [3].

Corresponding author: utsavvora0809@gmail.com

Rajdeep Chakraborty, Anupam Ghosh and Jyotsna Kumar Mandal (eds.) Machine Learning Techniques and Analytics for Cloud Security, (239–270) © 2022 Scrivener Publishing LLC

The primitive concept of time-sharing systems was mostly popularized by Remote Job Entry (RJE). This concept was common among big companies like IBM and DEC. By the 1970s, full time-sharing solutions were available on Multics, Cambridge CTSS, and early UNIX ports. Telecom companies in the early 1990s offered committed Point-to-Point data services. They started Virtual Private Network (VPN) Services with well-matched services at lower costs. The Telecom companies saw an effective increase in the usage of network bandwidth and for balancing the usage of servers, switching of network traffic was used. They started utilizing cloud symbols to distinguish between what the supplier was in charge of and what the user was responsible for. Cloud metaphor usage is credited to David Hoffman, the General Magic Communications Employee. Cloud computing was uplifted by Amazon with its Elastic Compute Cloud (E2C), Google with its Google App Engine in 2008, and NASA with its OpenNebula, which became the first open-source development software for private and hybrid clouds.

Many sectors such as Healthcare [4, 45, 46], Transport, Social Networking, Communication System [48], and Education are shifting their applications and data from local computers to remote cloud environments and experiencing the benefits [5]. Cloud computing has become a social phenomenon used by most people every day. Regardless of its advantages in various fields, security has always been a major area of concern. While safeguarding the security could increase the popularity of this technology extensively, compromising with the same could lead to the abandonment of the technology [6].

Cloud security [50] can be defined as a set of several strategies and technologies utilized to secure virtualized IP, servers, data, and other applications available under the cloud environment. The need for cloud security is generally because of the threats such as unauthorized data access, risk related to data theft, and many more faced by both cloud providers and customers. Threats faced by the cloud providers are usually based on the softwares, platforms, and infrastructures provided on the cloud, whereas issues faced by the customers are mainly regarding the applications used to store data on the cloud. The distributive nature of the cloud encourages information sharing but also enhances security problems related to user's information. A number of organizations still hesitate in using this technology just because of a fear of compromising with the security of sensitive business information. Though full security is difficult to achieve, it requires immense attention [7]. However, the responsibility of being secure has to be shared by both the cloud providers and the customers. On one end, the providers must confirm that the information-sharing infrastructure is safe and their client's data is secured, whereas, on the other end, customers must make sure that they protect their information using strong password authentication measures.

With the increasing need for security, the Intrusion Detection Systems came up with a strong defense mechanism, which the traditional Firewall failed to provide. An Intrusion Detection System finds out the intrusions and raises alarms and warnings for the administrator [36]. These systems are of two types. First is Misuse or Signature-based mechanism in which predefined rules or signatures of known attacks are used for detection of attacks. However, this mechanism fails to identify any unknown attack or deviation from known attacks. To overcome this, Anomaly-based mechanism was introduced which understands the general behavior of the system first and, after that, detects the actions which deviate from normal behavior. Those deviated actions were considered to be anomalies. Well, the conventional security systems have secured cloud systems for a long time and are still doing

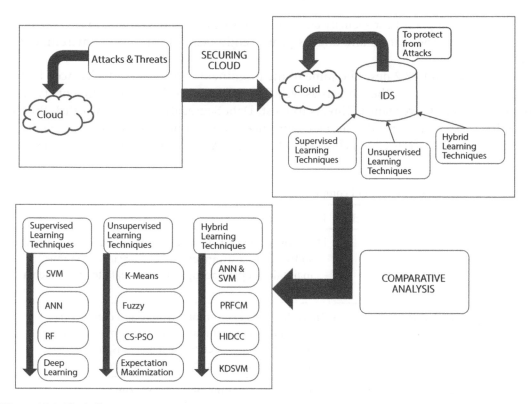

Figure 12.1 Block diagram.

it but in reality, due to several evolving threats and issues, those conventional systems are now becoming incapable [37].

To upgrade the security system, several Machine Learning (ML)–based methodologies have been developed as well as analyzed by many researchers in the past few decades. This review literature emphasizes on ML approaches for cloud security as well as analyzes those intrusion detection systems whose performance was evaluated using the NSL-KDD and the UNSW-NB15 datasets. The workflow of the article is shown in Figure 12.1. The rest of the literature is divided into some divisions. Section 12.2 provides knowledge about the security threats and attacks faced in cloud environments. Then, Section 12.3 gives a brief background of the datasets, NSL-KDD, and UNSW-NB15. In Section 12.4, we present ML algorithms proposed by several researchers and developers that include different Supervised, Unsupervised, and Hybrid approaches. With the descriptions, we have also added suggested future works as well. In Section 12.5, we come up with advantages and disadvantages of the reviewed articles. Finally, in Section 12.6, we conclude and discuss future research scopes.

12.2   Security Threats and Attacks

With the rise in advantages and usage of cloud technology, the threats and attacks have also evolved and their advancement has pushed all the researchers and developers to work and develop a robust security environment for cloud and its users. In this segment, an overview of the threats and attacks prominently faced in the cloud environment is delivered.

Tables 12.1 and 12.2 describe some of the prominent threats and attacks faced by the cloud users. There are other threats as well that still exist in cloud environments [9–12], such as, Loss of Governance, Threats to trust, Data Segregation, Unknown Risk Profile, Isolation Failure, and Insufficient Due Diligence. Concerning attacks, there are plenty of them such as Backdoor Channel Attack, Dictionary Attack, and Prefix Hijacking [8, 52].

Table 12.1 Threats faced in cloud computing.

Sr. no.	Name of threat/attack	Description
1.	Data Loss [51]	Data Loss occurs due to deletion, modification and other software or hardware errors. The organization must maintain proper backups of all the data to avoid such a threat.
2.	Data Breach	This refers to collection of sensitive and confidential information in an unauthorized manner. It arises due to improper security mechanisms, unreliable authentication, or authorization failure.
3.	Shared Technology Vulnerabilities	In general, these vulnerabilities are seen in multi-user environments where different services are shared between various users. The intruders may get control over the virtual machines or even the host itself by exploiting vulnerabilities in any part of the shared framework and cause significant damage.
4.	Malicious Insiders [42, 43]	They are those trusted people in organizations who can access confidential data. They may perform some unprivileged activities to infiltrate organizational confidential assets but showing it to be a legal activity.
5.	Insecure Interfaces and APIs	This refers to those protocols and standards, in which customers connect with cloud services. The APIs should have high standard credentials, better access mechanisms, and active monitoring mechanisms to avoid attacks. Cloud developers must implement strong APIs.
6.	Identity Theft	This takes place when the attacker acts as someone else to collect user's information and access the confidential assets.
7.	Abusive Use of Cloud Services	This occurs when customers use Cloud services for unethical and illegal actions. Poor Infrastructure, high-resource provisioning, and weak registration procedures lead to misuse. Cloud Service Providers such as Amazon, Facebook, and Google had been used to launch Trojans and Botnets.

Table 12.2 Attacks faced in cloud computing.

Sr. no.	Name of threat/attack	Description
1.	Denial-of-Service Attacks [40]	These attacks overload the system and disables the accessibility of services assigned to various users by incorporating SYN flooding, UDP flooding, ICMP flooding, etc. DDoS attacks are even more dangerous among the advanced types of DoS attacks. This is because in DDoS attacks the incoming traffic comes from multiple sources.
2.	Wrapping Attacks	On a user's request for a virtual machine, a SOAP message gets generated. In wrapping attacks, this message gets translated by the attacker, which then gets passed on to the server and in this way, the attackers intrude the services. These attacks are also considered as a good example for Man-in-the-Middle Attack.
3.	Cross Site Scripting Attacks	Here, the attacker redirects a user to the attacker's website for accessing sensitive data.
4.	Structured Query Language Injection Attacks	Here, the attacker manipulates standard SQL code, to get access to the website and gain knowledge about the database and functionality of the website.
5.	Man-in-the Middle Attacks	Here, false information is injected, by the attacker, in an ongoing conversation to access sensitive information being shared.
6.	Cookie Poisoning Attacks	In these attacks, the content of the user's cookies is modified by the attacker for accessing unauthorized applications and performing illegal activities.
7.	Sniffer Attacks	This type of attack is performed using programs that grant permission to a host for capturing flowing packets in the Ethernet network. The attackers insert malicious code into the host's Network Interface Card (NIC) in order to launch this attack.
8.	Malware Attacks [41, 44]	Here, the attacker installs a malicious software in the user's device without taking permission. Through that software, the attacker accesses the user's personal information. Different types of malware are viruses, spyware, ransomware, and trojan horses.
9.	Crypto Jacking	Crypto jacking emerged intensively last year because of the popularity cryptocurrency was getting. The attackers use the resources of a particular user for processing cryptocurrency transactions, simply inserting a crypto mining script in the servers.

Although security attacks are not only found in the cloud but all these attacks lead to the fact that a robust detection system is highly essential. The technology has a composite and dynamic nature and for this reason, it requires more than the traditional security.

12.3   Dataset Description

Intrusion detection systems are of great importance for securing the cloud environment. A number of researchers and developers have proposed several security systems using different ML algorithms. To understand and inspect the performance of the proposed methodologies for the detection of intrusions, a comprehensive dataset is required. In this literature, we analyze those intrusion detection systems whose performance and efficiency were evaluated using the following two datasets.

12.3.1   NSL-KDD Dataset

For many years, the KDDCup99 dataset has served as a benchmark dataset for performance evaluation, but it suffers from some disadvantages. The NSL-KDD dataset suggested by Travallaee et al. [13] was better than KDDCup99. This dataset overcomes most of the disadvantages of KDDCup99 dataset, as stated below:

- In order to avoid biased behavior toward frequent records and improve the performance for detection, all the redundant and duplicate records were removed from the dataset.
- The dataset holds a reasonable number of train and test records that helped the experiments to run easily without randomly selecting some portion from the records.

The dataset has 125,973 train data instances and 22,544 test data instances. Each record is composed of 41 features, among which 3 are non-numeric attributes and rest are numeric ones. With respect to attacks, there are about 24 different types in the train set and additional 14 in the test set. However, it has certain problems as discussed in McHugh [14]. The major disadvantage is its failure in representation of the modern low footprint attack scenarios. Looking at the nature of the security domain a real-world security dataset is quite difficult to obtain, but this dataset has been widely used since proposed, despite having some issues, for anomaly detection research [15].

12.3.2   UNSW-NB15 Dataset

The NSL-KDD and KDDCup 99 have been widely used for evaluating purposes but these evaluations do not support the real output due to several reasons. According to Moustafa et al. [16], the existing benchmark datasets are unable to represent the modern developing network traffic and attacks comprehensively. Countering this challenge, they proposed the UNSW-NB15 dataset for understanding the efficiency of various detection systems. The dataset contains 2.5 million records and 49 features. It is attack data can be categorized into Fuzzers, Analysis, Backdoors, DoS, Exploits, Generic, Reconnaissance, Shellcode, and Worms. In comparison with the dataset, the existing benchmark datasets had less attacks and information on outdated packets.

12.4   Machine Learning for Cloud Security

ML has grown as the most important technology of the present world and will remain to be in the future as well. It concentrates on understanding various patterns and structures that are related to the data available and then makes decisions based on them which are sometimes not even possible to make by humans. With its various methods, ML has put a significant impact on various fields like Data Science, Virtual Platforms, and Medical sector. Since the past few decades, ML has also attracted several researchers and developers for using it in developing secure cloud environments. The following subdivisions briefly discuss different Supervised, Unsupervised, and Hybrid techniques under ML used for securing cloud environments.

12.4.1   Supervised Learning Techniques

Supervised learning techniques are those ML techniques that require a labeled dataset. The train and test data deployed here must be allocated to a correct label: normal or attack data instances [17]. The detection systems based on Supervised techniques [18] are generally signature-based detection systems. Although having significant labels in a dataset is a challenging task as the dataset can have noise that leads to high false alarm rates. Following are some Supervised techniques introduced for developing intrusion detection systems in past few years.

12.4.1.1   Support Vector Machine

This is a strong learning method used to build several practical projects, for example, recognizing patterns, classifying text and images, handwriting recognition, bioinformatics analysis, and many more. It supports both multi-class and binary classifications [19].

Pervez *et al.* [19] applied this classifier on the NSL-KDD dataset. Their motive was to increase the strength of intrusion classification using reduced feature sets from the training data. For this, they proposed a feature selection algorithm that initially built the classifier with all the features from the train set then permanently removed features one by one, after comparing the accuracies of the initial set and the set without that particular feature. In this way, a proper set of input features was selected. After feature selection, SVM classifier was implemented on the dataset with selected features, 10-fold cross-validated train set, and test set, respectively. Results showed that the highest classification accuracy achieved was 99% with 41 and 36 features, respectively. They suggested the use of other learning classifiers along with SVM to get even better detection rates for minority class instances.

Jing *et al.* [20] proposed a non-linear scaling approach with SVM classifier for classification. To evaluate this approach, the UNSW-NB15 dataset was utilized. They used 257,673 instances of the dataset, among which 175,341 instances were for training and 82,332 instances were for testing. This scaling method was independent of the data values, unlike the minmax normalization and that came up as an advantage because the data of UNSW had several dissimilarities among each other.

$$\underset{\sim}{h}x' = log_{10}(x) \tag{12.1}$$

Equation (12.1) shows the log function used for scaling. In this model, Kernel functions helped in mapping low and high dimensional space. Among different kernel functions, RBF kernel got the best overall performance in terms of time and accuracy.

$$K(x_m, x_n) = exp(\gamma||x_m - x_n||^2) \tag{12.2}$$

The expression in Equation (12.2) is used in RBF Kernel. After scaling and preprocessing, the model was implemented. For binary classification, the approach got 97.10% of accuracy for the train set and 85.99% of accuracy for the test set. For multi-class classification, the approach got 83.59% accuracy for the train set, and 75.77% accuracy for the test set. The detection rate for generic instances was the best but not that good for normal instances. With respect to false positive rate, worms, generic, and backdoor got better results. However, these fluctuant values were because of imbalanced distribution of classes in the dataset. The weighted average detection rate was 50.9% and false positive rate was 3.0%. The authors also compared this method with different detection classifiers and found that the approach got effective results for anomaly detection.

Wang *et al.* [21] proposed another effective approach using Stacked Contractive Autoencoder (SCAE) method with SVM classifier. They considered two datasets KDDCup99 and NSL-KDD datasets for performance evaluation. At first, the SCAE model was designed which included several hidden layers for encoding and decoding.

$$\text{Encoding: } x^a = p(w^a x^{a-1} + b^a) \tag{12.3}$$

$$\text{Decoding: } z^{a-1} = q(w'^a z^a + b'^a)a = 1,...,h \tag{12.4}$$

The encoding and decoding processes were expressed using Equations (12.3) and (12.4) where p and q represented functions for activation, w and w' were the weight matrices, b and b' determined the bias values, and h was the count of hidden layers. The mapping of h-th order features was allowed layer-wise for reconstruction of z^0 by considering, $x^h = z^h$. The a-th encoder was represented by $\theta^a = \{w^a, b^a\}$ and decoder was represented by $\theta'^a = \{w'^a, b'^a\}$.

$$J_M = \sum_{a=1}^{h}\sum_{j=1}^{d}\left(L(x^{(j,a-1)}, q_\theta a(p_\theta a(x^{(j,a-1)}))) + \lambda^a\left\|J_p(x^{(j,a-1)})\right\|_F^2\right) \tag{12.5}$$

The maximization function of SCAE was expressed using Equation (12.5) where λ was the coefficient for penalty and $\left\|J_p(x)\right\|_F^2$ was the square of Jacobian matrix's Frobenius norm. But the objective function had some practical problems. First, it failed for deep networks having several layers. To overcome that, the greedy layer-wise strategy was followed that divided the learning process into basic CAEs and then stacked them into deep neural networks after training separately. Second was higher values of penalty term than the reconstruction error. To tackle that, smaller values for λ were used.

$$J^a = \frac{1}{d} \sum_{j=1}^{d} (x^{(j,a-1)} - z^{(j,a-1)})^2 + \lambda^a \sum_{j=1}^{d}$$
$$\left(\frac{1}{l_n} \sum_{k=1}^{l_n} \left(x_k^{(j,a)} \left(1 - x_k^{(j,a)}\right) \right)^2 \times \frac{1}{l_a l_{a-1}} \sum_{i=1}^{l_{a-1}} \left\| w_{ik}^a \right\|^2 \right) \tag{12.6}$$

The function for each CAE network was represented by Equation (12.6) where l_a, l_{a-1} represented dimensions of a–1th and ath layer features. λ^a was the penalty coefficient of the ath CAE network whose value was set less but order of magnitude was the same as that of reconstruction error. Now, training was done. At first, the unsupervised greedy layer-wise approach trained a number of basic CAEs. Then, each basic CAE was unrolled and a deep CAE network (SCAE) was constructed. Finally, fine-tuning was performed using multiclass cross-entropy loss function. In this way, an optimal model was deduced. For evaluating with NSL-KDD dataset, the SCAE structure had three layers having 28, 16, and 8 features, respectively. In this way, essential features were generated and further used for classification. However, SCAE was weaker to do classification and for this SVM classifier was used. The SDN technology was used to develop the detection system. For implementation with NSL-KDD dataset, five models were created and the highest accuracy reached was 87.33%. Again, with KDDCup99, 98.11% accuracy was gained for binary classification and 97.87% accuracy was gained for multi-class classification. The authors concluded that the combination of SVM and deep learning methods was much more effective than the shallow SVM alone.

12.4.1.2 Artificial Neural Network

It is an approach in which several interlinked nodes, also called neurons, are used for processing the data. Ingre *et al.* [22] applied this method for classification purposes using NSL-KDD dataset. Before proceeding, data preprocessing, feature selection, and normalization were performed to get better results. For data preprocessing, all the non-numeric attributes were converted into numeric inputs. Then, among the 41 features of NSL-KDD, 29 features were selected using Information Gain attribute evaluation, Gain ratio attribute evaluation, and Correlation attribute evaluation algorithms. Finally, the dataset was normalized using the Z-score algorithm.

$$x(i) = \frac{x(i) - \mu(X)}{\sigma(X)} \tag{12.7}$$

The Z-score algorithm was denoted by Equation (12.7), where X determines the attribute, $x(i)$ was the ith value of X, μ, and σ were mean and standard deviation, respectively. For the training process, tansig transfer function, Levenberg Marquardt (LM), and BFGS quasi-newton backpropagation algorithms were used to change the values for weight and bias. Since the dataset had unequal distribution of patterns among different classes, R2L and U2R had low patterns. For equality and better training speed, 18,718 patterns were chosen. Most of them were chosen from normal, DoS, and probe classes. On implementation, results showed that for the train set, binary classification got the best accuracy of 99.3% with LM, whereas five-class classification got the best accuracy of 98.9% with BFGS. While for the test set, binary classification (with feature reduction) got 81.2% and five-class classification (without feature reduction) got 79.9% accuracy. In comparison with other reputed techniques, the approach got better binary classification accuracy. Although the detection rate and accuracy were much better, the false positive rate was considerably higher which may affect the utilization of the proposed method in future.

Aboueata *et al.* [23] explored the applicability of ANN and SVM classifier for detection of intruders. The performances of both algorithms were assessed using the UNSW-NB15 dataset. The train set of UNSW was utilized for training the algorithms using different parameters. The validation set incorporated 80% of the test set of UNSW and was utilized in optimizing the algorithm parameters. The remaining data was deployed for performance assessment of trained models. However, training of both the algorithms could be time consuming, especially for a large dataset. For this, at first feature categorization was applied and five different sets of training parameters were created, basic, content, time, general, and connection. Then, feature selection methods, $ChiX^2$ and Principal Component Analysis (PCA), were applied for generating relevant features. After feature selection, parameter tuning was also performed. The parameters for SVM were kernel function and penalty-C coefficient (pC) and that for ANN were activation and optimization functions, count of layers and neurons. On implementation of SVM, the general category with sigmoid kernel function and pC as 20, got the best outcome having an accuracy of 92%, precision rate of 92%, and recall of 92%. In the case of ANN, model generation required three phases. First phase was initialization of weights (W) and bias (b) values. A random matrix W_r with dimension $J \times K$, where J and K represented neurons of present and previous layers, respectively, was used for initialization of weights of the layers [Equation (12.8)].

$$W[L] = W_r \times \sqrt{\frac{2}{J}} \tag{12.8}$$

Second phase was forward propagation. Here, the values for input X were modified using weight and bias values via Equation (12.9).

$$Y = W^{(l)}X + b^{(l)} \tag{12.9}$$

Then, a simple ReLU activation function [Equation (12.10)] was applied for output generation of each hidden layer and sigmoidal function [Equation (12.11)] was utilized for the output layer.

$$relu(Y) = M(0, Y) \tag{12.10}$$

$$sigmoid(Y) = \frac{1}{1 + e^{-Y}} \tag{12.11}$$

$$C.E = -\frac{1}{m}\sum\nolimits_{r=0}^{m}(T^{(r)}logt^{(r)}) \times ((1-T^{(r)})(1-logt^{(r)})) \qquad (12.12)$$

Finally, a cross-entropy loss function was used for calculation of model evaluation cost. It was represented using Equation (12.12), where $t^{(r)}$ denoted training sample r's prediction and T was the true label of training sample r. The third phase was backward propagation. The weights and biases values were updated on account of the prediction errors calculated earlier. To tackle over-fitting, regularization was used and on parameter tuning, it was found that Adam optimization, ReLU activation function, 5 layers, and 25 neurons outperformed. Finally, on implementation of ANN, results showed the general category got best results again with accuracy of 91%, precision rate of 93%, and recall of 92%. Comparatively, the authors concluded that the ANN model performed slightly better than SVM. However, both algorithms effectively maximized the accuracy of classification.

12.4.1.3 Deep Learning

With the continual progress of ML, its subset Deep Learning has also developed expeditiously [47]. The approach is designed to learn better feature representations from a number of unlabeled data and then apply those learned features to the classification. It can effectively detect intrusions and classify them using its high dimensionality and complex features.

Zhang *et al.* [24] proposed an approach which learnt features of the data and also adjusted itself according to previous undefined attacks. For evaluation, the NSL-KDD dataset was utilized. The authors used the encoder of Autoencoder, a popular technology, and an unsupervised approach of neural networks for learning and extracting features. Then, for classification, soft-max regression was employed. After preprocessing, the dataset consisted of 122 features including 3 protocol types, 70 services, and 11 flags. Then, the dataset was normalized to the range of [0, 1] with max-min operation. Now, the processed data was deployed as input to the encoder. For activation, ReLU function [Equation (12.10)] was used.

$$k_{W,b} = f(Wx + b) \qquad (12.13)$$

The nodes in hidden and output layers were calculated using Equation (12.13) where k determines a nonlinear function with parameter weight (W) and bias (b). The cost function [Equation (12.14)] minimized the reconstruction error in learning process and learnt an output X^- similar to X.

$$C = \frac{1}{2m}\sum\nolimits_{j=1}^{m}\left|x_j - x_j^-\right|^2 \qquad (12.14)$$

Although this neural network benefitted compression coding and feature learning in an unsupervised form, it also constructs a simple model for faster prediction of abnormal traffic. With encoder compression feature technique, the input of 122 features was reduced to only 5. After which the SoftMax layer classified the data and finally the output layer received the results. Though the accuracy evaluated the practicability of the model, due to the unbalanced sample data, precision, recall, and f1 score were also added which eventually represented the generalization ability of the model. For multi-class classification, the model got an accuracy of 79.74%. This was not that poor but the individual rates for R2L and U2R attacks were low which influenced the overall accuracy. The authors suggested modifying and adding other classifiers to refine the detection accuracy rate and considering the problem of real-time detections as future works.

Zhiqiang *et al.* [25] proposed another deep learning approach based on Feed Forward network, Back propagation, and Stochastic gradient. For evaluation, the UNSW dataset was utilized. The deep learning classifier was trained using the entire dataset. The performance parameters were computed using three experiments. The first experiment looked for a suitable activation function. Then, in the next experiment, that activation function was deployed for identification of key attributes using the Gedeon method. Finally, the last one was understanding the unseen data, developed using the dataset, in accordance with the findings from the previous two experiments. The proposed model had 10 hidden layers with hundred neurons. On implementation, 99.5% accuracy was achieved. For future works, the authors recommended self-taught learning systems for reducing dimension and lower the false alarm rates.

Yin *et al.* [26] proposed yet another interesting deep learning classifier based on recurrent networks and for performance evaluation, NSL-KDD dataset was used. The recurrent networks introduced directional loops that memorized previous information and applied them to current output. These loops differed them from traditional Feed Forward networks.

$$x_k = \frac{x_k - m}{M - m} \tag{12.15}$$

After converting all the non-numeric values into numeric ones, the dataset was normalized using a logarithmic scaling method as represented by Equation (12.15), where m denotes minimum value and M indicates maximum value for each feature (x_k). The training of the model was performed in two stages. First, forward propagation computed the output values, and then back propagation passed the collected residuals to update the weights. On implementation, this approach got 99.81% accuracy with the train set and 68.55% accuracy with the test set for binary classification, on the other hand, for multi-class classification, the model got 99.53% accuracy with the train set and 64.67% accuracy with the test set. When compared with orthodox classifiers the proposed model obtained much higher accuracy and relatively less false alarm rate, especially for multiclass classification. Although the model effectively improved accuracy for intrusion detection and recognition ability, the training time was high, and for that, the authors advised the use of GPU acceleration. They also recommended for avoiding exploding and vanishing gradients and use of the Bidirectional RNNs algorithm for intrusion detection.

12.4.1.4   *Random Forest*

An ensemble classifier, used to obtain better predictive performance, Random forest method consists of several decision trees. In terms of classification error, the classifier is better than other traditional classification algorithms [44].

Choudhury *et al.* [27] compared various classification techniques and learning algorithms using WEKA tools. Among different classifiers present, nine befitting classifiers, BayesNet, Logistic, IBK, J48, PART, JRip, Random tree, Random forest, and REPTree were selected. The NSL-KDD dataset was utilized for evaluation purposes. Results showed that IBK and Random forest had the highest true positive rate (88.68%), whereas REPTree had the lowest true positive rate (79.78%). In case of true negative rate, BayesNet got the highest rate (96.18%) and Logistic got the lowest rate (82.2%). For accuracy, Random forest got the best figures, 91.52%. The authors concluded that Logistic was the worst classifier and Random forest was optimal. Finally, the authors suggested utilizing these algorithms for constructing an efficient intrusion detection system for security purposes in various organizations.

Salman *et al.* [28] investigated both identification and classification of anomalies using Random forest and Linear regression approaches. They utilized the UNSW dataset for performance evaluation. Among the attacks of dataset, Fuzzer attack was excluded due to its scarcity in multi-cloud environments. For feature selection, the best-fit feature selection technique was deployed which showed that the optimal performance could be reached using Linear regression with 18 features, and using Random forest with only 11 features. After feature selection, the models were constructed and implemented on the dataset. Results of evaluation showed that the detection error rate was 1% for Random forest, whereas 4.5% for Linear regression. Indeed, Random forest had the best figures for detection of anomalies. The authors also introduced the Step-wise attack categorization method for classification of data into different attack categories. Both classic and proposed categorization methods were compared and results showed that the accuracy for classic categorization was 80% and that of proposed one was 93.35%. However, for DoS, analysis, and backdoor attacks, the accuracy was less because of feature similarities and unbalanced data. At the end, the authors commented that although the higher detection rate may not lead to higher classification rate.

With respect to Supervised ML techniques (Table 12.3), we found the Deep Learning approach with the best detection rates.

12.4.2 Unsupervised Learning Techniques

Unsupervised Learning Techniques are those ML techniques that do not require a labeled dataset [17]. The detection systems based on these techniques are generally not signature based but more anomaly based or behavior based. Although it overcomes the drawback of supervised techniques to some extent, the percentage of false positive rates remains high. The following are some Unsupervised techniques introduced for developing intrusion detection systems in past few years.

Table 12.3 Supervised learning techniques with the highest accuracy.

Sr. no.	Method name	Dataset used	Highest accuracy reached
1	Support Vector Machine [19–21]	NSL-KDD	99
2	Artificial Neural Network [22, 23]	NSL-KDD	81.2
3	Deep Learning [24–26]	NSL-KDD	99.81
4	Random Forest [27, 28]	UNSW-NB 15	99

12.4.2.1   K-Means Clustering

This clustering approach is among the most popular unsupervised techniques. It has the ability to handle high volumes of data [31]. It classifies a given dataset using a couple of clusters based on some predefined conditions.

Verma *et al.* [29] proposed an intrusion detection model using classification algorithms and clustering. They compared the XGBoost and AdaBoost algorithms with and without clustering and computed their performance using the NSL-KDD dataset. The AdaBoost algorithm, introduced in 1996, transforms weak classifiers into strong ones.

$$c(x) = sign\left(\sum_{j=1}^{M} \theta_j\, w_j(x) \right) \tag{12.16}$$

Equation (12.16) represented the classification equation for AdaBoost, where w_j stands for jth weak classifier, θ_j for corresponding weighs, and M indicates the total number of weak classifiers. On the other hand, XGBoost accepts multiple forms of input data and is also optimized for sparse input.

$$\frac{\partial L(y, w^{(j-1)}(x) + w_j(x))}{\partial w_j(x)} = 0 \tag{12.17}$$

The algorithm determines the steps directly by solving Equation (12.17), where L indicates the loss function. Before proceeding for evaluation, the dataset was preprocessed. This preprocessing included removal of redundant records, factorization and one hot encoding, and feature scaling and finding of optimal number of clusters. Thereafter, algorithms were trained using the train set and assessed using the test set. In the first approach, XGBoost with its default parameters (100 estimators, maximum depth = 3, regularization alpha = 0, and lambda = 1) and AdaBoost with decision tree classifier as base estimator and 50 other estimators were assessed. Then, the CFS subset selection algorithm was used to choose a subset of the dataset and re-evaluate the algorithms, but accuracy had no improvement. In the second approach, classifiers were trained for different clusters of data points. Then, prediction was made for data points, from the test set, about the cluster in which they were located and the corresponding classifier was selected to classify the data points. The Grid search helped in tuning the parameters of classifiers. Finally, the results were compared. On the train set, the XGBoost and AdaBoost algorithms got the accuracy of 99.70% and 90.39%, respectively, without k-means clustering, whereas the accuracy of 99.86% and 99.84%, respectively, was achieved with k-means clustering. On the test set, the XGBoost and AdaBoost algorithms got the accuracy of 80.24% and 80.73%, respectively, without k-means clustering, whereas the accuracy of 84.25% and 82.01%, respectively, was achieved with k-means clustering. The authors suggested improvement of the same model using hybrid approach, incorporating different classifiers as future works.

12.4.2.2 Fuzzy C-Means Clustering

This clustering method is also considered as a mining algorithm. In this approach, all records are divided into different clusters based on some membership grade measured as degrees within the range 0 and 1 [30].

Bhattacharjee *et al.* [30] compared two algorithms, Fuzzy C-Means and K-Means clustering using the NSL-KDD dataset. The K-Means clustering, implemented over 20% dataset and 42 features, got the accuracy of 99.90% in the fourth iteration of the first cluster and other three clusters had comparatively much less accuracy. Thereafter, the same algorithm was again evaluated, but now with 28 features and an accuracy of 44.72% was achieved without biasing a particular cluster. After this observation, the Fuzzy C-Means clustering was assessed.

$$J_F = \sum_{p=1}^{P} \sum_{q=1}^{Q} v_{pq}^m \cdot d(x_p, y_q)^2 \tag{12.18}$$

The objective function for this clustering is given by Equation (12.18), where P represented connections, Q represented clusters, v_{pq} determines the degree of membership ($0 \le v_{pq} \le 1$) of a connection x_p to qth cluster center, and y_q determines the center of qth cluster.

$$v_{pq} = \frac{1}{\sum_{L=1}^{Q} \left[\dfrac{d(x_p, y_q)}{d(x_p, y_q)} \right]^{\frac{2}{(m-1)}}} \tag{12.19}$$

$$y_q = \frac{\sum_{p=1}^{P} v_{pq}^m x_p}{\sum_{p=1}^{P} v_{pq}^m} \tag{12.20}$$

The objective function was iterated over using different values of v_{pq}, computed using Equation (12.19) and y_q, computed using Equation (12.20), to generate the cluster center matrix and fuzzy partition matrix. The iteration was continued until $||v^{l+1} - v^l|| < \xi$ was satisfied where $0 \le \xi \le 1$. Now, on implementing this clustering with the same amount of dataset and 42 features, accuracy of 45.93% was achieved. Again, the same algorithm was assessed with 28 features and accuracy of 45.95% was achieved. Hence, Fuzzy C-Means clustering got a comparatively higher accuracy for attack detection than K-Means clustering. The authors recommended using hybrid variants of Fuzzy C-Means clustering in intrusion detection systems for attack detection.

12.4.2.3 Expectation-Maximization Clustering

Expectation-Maximization clustering algorithm is a clustering technique where the parameter values are randomly initialized. The Expectation step allocates values to the hidden variables and the Maximization step computes the parameters based on fully observed data [31]. Sangve *et al.* [31] proposed a new approach using the multi-start metaheuristics method and enhanced clustering algorithms for intrusion detection. They compared K-Means clustering with Expectation-Maximization clustering utilizing the NSL-KDD dataset.

$$T_N = \frac{T - u_T}{\sigma_T}, \sigma_T \neq 0 \tag{12.21}$$

$$T_N = T - u_T, \sigma_T = 0 \tag{12.22}$$

In the first stage, preprocessing was performed and then normalization of train set was done using the Equations (12.21) and (12.22), where T represented attributes of the train set, and u and σ were mean and standard deviation, respectively. The test set was also normalized using the same Equations (12.21) and (12.22) but the only difference here was the use of test set attributes. In the second stage, clustering algorithms reduced the training dataset into clusters for decreasing processing and time complexity. After the division into clusters, detector generation was done using metaheuristic algorithms. A number of initial start points were selected from the clustered dataset using multi-start strategy and distributed over clusters for generating a hyper-sphere shape. Then, detector radius $D_r = \{r \in D_r \mid 0 < r \leq hru\}$ was calculated where hru was the upper bound of the radius of the hyper-sphere.

$$F(D_i) = N_{abnrml}(d_i) - N_{nrml}(d_i) \tag{12.23}$$

Equation (12.23) represented the objective function for controlling detector generation process, where $N_{abnrml}(d_i)$ determines those samples, covered by detector d_i, which were abnormal and $N_{nrml}(d_i)$ determines those samples, covered by detector d_i which were normal. For the optimization purpose of detector radius, the Genetic Algorithm was deployed that focused on non-overlapping of hyper-sphere detectors. It generated various random patterns and compared them with self-defined patterns; if any of them got matched with the self-defined pattern, then they were not considered as detector patterns.

$$F(r_i) = N_{abnrml}(r_i) - N_{nrml}(r_i) \tag{12.24}$$

The fitness function, given by Equation (12.24), was used to optimize the detector radius, where $N_{abnrml}(r_i)$ represented the hyper-sphere radius for those samples that were abnormal and $N_{nrml}(r_i)$ represented the hyper-sphere radius for those samples that were normal. Finally, on evaluation, the Expectation-Maximization clustering got 98.28% detection accuracy and false positive rate of 0.0041, whereas K-Means got 95.18% detection accuracy and around 0.0052 false positive rate. Comparatively, detector generation time was also less in Expectation-Maximization with respect to that in K-Means. Hence, the Expectation-Maximization clustering performed better than K-Means clustering algorithm.

12.4.2.4   *Cuckoo Search With Particle Swarm Optimization (PSO)*

Ghosh *et al.* [32] proposed an efficient approach using Cuckoo search with PSO. They used the NSL-KDD dataset for evaluation purposes. Initially, feature selection was done on the preprocessed and normalized dataset. For this, N data points were selected from the dataset and then the objective function and fitness values were computed for all the data points. Along with the individual best values (pbest), best values produced by the group (gbest) were also checked using particle swarm optimization technique which represented a good example of exploitation concept.

$$x_{pq}^{k+1} = x_{pq}^k + s_{pq} \times \alpha \times L(\lambda) \tag{12.25}$$

$$L(\lambda) = \left(\frac{\Gamma(1+\lambda) \times sin\left(\frac{\pi \times \lambda}{2} \right)}{\Gamma\left(\frac{1+\lambda}{2} \right) \times \lambda \times s^{\frac{\lambda-1}{2}}} \right)^{\frac{1}{\lambda}} \tag{12.26}$$

$$s_{pq} = x_{pq}^k - x_{fq}^k \tag{12.27}$$

Setting the limit for iterations ($1 \le \lambda \le 3$), nest positions were searched using cuckoo search given by Equation (12.25), and levy flight technique [$L(\lambda)$] given by Equation (12.26). Here, size, given by Equation (12.27), was the step size associated with problems of interest. If size was large, then a far location was obtained, and if size was small, then a close location was obtained. The cuckoo search used with levy flight technique represented a good example of exploration concept. After this, the objective function and fitness values were again calculated for all data points.

$$prob_p = \left(\frac{0.45 \times fit_p}{pbest_p} \right) + \left(\frac{0.45 \times fit_p}{gbest_p} \right) + 0.1 \tag{12.28}$$

Now, for each egg, a probability to be found by the host bird was computed using Equation (12.28), where fit_p was the value for fitness. For checking, whether the egg was recognized, σ was generated. If $prob_p$ value for an egg was lower than the value of σ, then that particular egg was considered to be recognized by the host bird.

$$V_{pq}^{k+1} = V_{pq}^k + c_1 r_1 (x_{pbest\,pq} - x_{pq}) + c_2 r_2 (x_{gbest\,pq} - x_{pq}) \tag{12.29}$$

$$new_i = x_{pq}^k + V_{pq}^{k+1} \tag{12.30}$$

For each new egg, a new nest position was explored using Equations (12.29) and (12.30). These new nest positions (new_i) were added to the set of data points. Then, objective and fitness functions were again calculated. Now, the fitness values were sorted in descending order and among them, the first N number of points was selected for the next generation. After some iterations, the feature subset with best fitness values was considered to be the most relevant set of features. The proposed algorithm effectively solved the trade compromisation between exploitation and exploration. Feature Selection from a high-dimensional dataset benefitted in reducing training time, memory storage and even boosted the proficiency of the system. Now, the accuracy of three classifiers, Logistic, AdaBoost, and Random forest, was compared. Results showed that Logistic got accuracy of 75.5%, AdaBoost got accuracy

Table 12.4 Unsupervised learning techniques with the highest accuracy.

Sr. no.	Method name	Dataset used	Highest accuracy reached
1	K-Means Clustering [29]	NSL-KDD	99.86
2	Fuzzy C-Means Clustering [30]	NSL-KDD	45.95 (over 28 features)
3	Expectation-Maximization Clustering [31]	NSL-KDD	98.28
4	CS-PSO [32]	NSL-KDD	75.5

of 75.2%, and Random forest got accuracy of 75.3%. Hence, the two nature-inspired approaches together formed an effective system for attack detection in cloud environments.

In the case of Unsupervised ML techniques (Table 12.4), we found the K-Means Clustering Algorithm with the best detection rates.

12.4.3   Hybrid Learning Techniques

Hybrid Learning Techniques are the combination of multiple ML methods. They hold the advantages of Supervised and Unsupervised learning [17]. However, these techniques also have less detection and high false alarm rates. The following are the Hybrid approaches introduced for developing intrusion detection systems.

12.4.3.1   HIDCC: Hybrid Intrusion Detection Approach in Cloud Computing

Hatef *et al.* [33] proposed HIDCC which comprehensively and accurately detected intrusions. They performed their approach in four phases and evaluated the approach using the NSL-KDD dataset. In the first phase, the Snort tool was applied to prevent the known attacks. This phase compared the data packets with predefined signatures and patterns, kept the attack log, and generated warnings for every known attack. The second phase trapped those attacks that were not detected in the first phase. Here, at first, the Information Gain mechanism was used for selecting that feature which had the highest Information Gain value. For a feature, Information Gain meant the entropy reduction value generated by separating data on the basis of that feature.

$$IG = E(d) - E_{exp} \tag{12.31}$$

$$E(d) = -\sum_{m=1}^{r} (P)_m \times log^2_{((P)m)} \tag{12.32}$$

$$E_{exp}(d) = \sum_{s=1}^{k} \left(\frac{|d_s|}{|d|} \right) \times E(d_s) \tag{12.33}$$

The Information Gain was computed using Equation (12.31). The entropy and expected entropy were calculated using Equations (12.32) and (12.33), where r determined classification classes, P was the packet weighted frequency, k represented different values for a feature, d was the train set, and d_s was the subset of d. After selecting the feature with best value, C4.5 algorithm was applied to classify the packets.

$$E_f(d) = -\sum_{s=1}^{k}\left(\frac{|d_s|}{|d|}\right) \times log_2\left(\frac{|d_s|}{|d|}\right) \tag{12.34}$$

$$IG_r(F) = \frac{IG(F)}{E_f(F)} \tag{12.35}$$

The algorithm computed the Information Gain ratio, given by Equation (12.35) where Split Entropy was computed using Equation (12.34), for all features then selected that feature which had the highest Information Gain ratio. Now, using the selected feature, the train set was divided into subsets. In this way, the algorithm constructed a decision tree from the train set and classified the packets that remained undetected in the first phase. For the known packets, a simple warning was generated but the unknown ones were passed to the next phases. However, in case of higher unknown instances, the decision tree may get higher branches which may lead to overfitting problem, ultimately reducing the accuracy for the algorithm. In the third phase, the patterns of unknown one was updated in the known attacks database, so that in future, the Snort immediately detects it and prevents it from entering. This indeed increased the speed of detection and even reduced the number of iterations for the second phase. Finally, the fourth phase updated the derived attack database with derived attack patterns generated from that unknown attack. The approach was implemented and compared with seven other methods. The approach got the highest efficiency (up to 25%), least false positive rate, precision rate over 99% which was an acceptable one, highest accuracy rate (up to 15%), and 0.01 to 0.14 higher values of F-Score than other methods. It proved to be one of the robust solutions for the security of cloud systems.

12.4.3.2 Clustering-Based Hybrid Model in Deep Learning Framework

Tao *et al.* [34] presented an approach applying K-Means clustering, deep networks, and SVM classifier. To assess the method, six datasets were randomly generated from KDDCup'99 and NSL-KDD datasets. Initially, the training sets were divided into a number of subsets. After division, the center points were calculated for each subset and then the deep networks were trained using them. This aided in getting information about different characteristics of the subsets or precisely clusters. Now, the k-means algorithm divided the testing sets using the center points calculated earlier. The subsets generated were used with the trained deep networks for attack type detection. Every deep network had the SVM classifier as the top layer. The approach efficiently improved detection rates and accuracy. When compared with four other methods (SVM, BPNN, DBN-SVM, and BAYES), the proposed one got the best results for attack detection and classification. The algorithm also efficiently classified U2R and R2L types of attacks, whose instances were quite low. Despite having good efficiency, the SVM parameters optimized by heuristic algorithms and deep network parameters such as weight and threshold turned out to be the drawbacks of the approach.

12.4.3.3   K-Nearest Neighbor–Based Fuzzy C-Means Mechanism

Ghosh *et al.* [35] introduced an intrusion detection method using Penalty Reward-Based Fuzzy C-Means clustering (PRFCM) and modified K-Nearest Neighbor (KNN) algorithm. They utilized NSL-KDD dataset to assess the approach. Initially, non-numeric data of the dataset was converted into numeric data. Then, the dataset was normalized using min-max normalization. The Fuzzy C-Means clustering has a disadvantage of being responsive to noise, due to which it stucks at local optimal values. In the training phase, PRFCM was implemented to overcome the limitation of simple Fuzzy C-Means clustering. It efficiently handled noise by tuning the coefficient values of penalty and reward parameters.

$$J = J_F + J_{pe} - J_{Re} \tag{12.36}$$

$$J_{Pe} = \sum_{k=1}^{K} \sum_{p=1}^{P} \sum_{q=1}^{Q} W \cdot v_{pq}^{m} \cdot v_{kq} \cdot \ln \alpha_q \tag{12.37}$$

$$J_{Re} = \sum_{k=1}^{K} \sum_{p=1}^{P} \sum_{q=1}^{Q} W \cdot v_{pq}^{m} \cdot (1 - v_{kq}) \cdot \ln(1 - \alpha_q) \tag{12.38}$$

The objective function for PRFCM was given by Equation (12.36), where J_F was the objective function for Fuzzy C-Means clustering, given by Equation (12.18), J_{Pe} and J_{Re} were the objective function with penalty and reward parameters added, respectively, given by Equations (12.37) and (12.38). J was optimized by iterating the function over different values of membership and cluster center. The membership values were updated using Equation (12.39), where L was the collection of labels for different classes into which a connection could be classified and the center of every cluster was updated using Equation (12.20).

$$v_{pq} = \frac{\left[d(x_p, y_q)^2 + W \sum_{k=1}^{K} v_{kq} \cdot \ln a_q - w \sum_{k=1}^{K} (1 - v_{kq}) \cdot \ln(1 - \alpha_q) \right]^{\frac{-1}{(m-1)}}}{\sum_{L=1}^{Q} \left[d(x_p, y_L)^2 + w \sum_{k=1}^{K} v_{kL} \cdot \ln \alpha_L - W \sum_{k=1}^{K} (1 - v_{kL}) \cdot \ln(1 - \alpha_L) \right]^{\frac{-1}{(m-1)}}} \tag{12.39}$$

For penalizing (J_{Pe}) or rewarding (J_{Re}) a connection, KNN connections were used where K was calculated experimentally. The accuracy of the algorithm increased with rising values of K but after a certain limit accuracy started to decline. The algorithm was again tested on different values for the bias constant W (between 0 and 1) but the result was similar to that of K values. This showed clearly that if only K neighbors were considered then the result may become biased resulting in less accuracy and for this reason, only a part of impact was taken into account. The variable α_q in Equation (12.37) and (12.38) was the fraction of membership values of qth cluster by that of other clusters. This was repeated until the objective function reduced or reached a convergence. After PRFCM clustering, every connection of the cluster was assigned with a final membership value which signifies only its decision.

$$S(x_p) = \frac{1}{K} \sum_{k=1}^{K} C(x_p, x_k) \tag{12.40}$$

A strength term, given by Equation (12.40), was also introduced to every connection in the train set that determined trustworthiness. In the strength term, $C(x_p, x_k)$ signifies a function which returns 1 when both x_p, x_k belong to the same class otherwise returns 0. Finally, the training phase ended with generation of a collection of rules R using the strength and membership values assigned. In the testing phase, an updated version of KNN algorithm was implemented that generated the collection of best rules R' from R, considering the closest rules to that of the incoming connection and then assigned the weights in R', on the basis of distance, from the incoming connection. For more distance, the incoming connection had low influence, but for less distance, that connection had high influence.

$$w_p = \frac{d(x_{far}, i_c) - d(x_p, i_c)}{d(x_{far}, i_c) - d(x_{ne}, i_c)} \tag{12.41}$$

The weight for a connection was calculated using Equation (12.41), where x_{far} determines the farthest rule from incoming connection (i_c), x_{ne} determines the nearest rule, and $d(x_p, i_c)$ determines the Euclidean distance measure between x_p connection and i_c. Along with the weight, strength of each connection was also incorporated to generate the effective weight.

$$\delta_{pq} = \frac{v_{pq}}{\sum_{L=1}^{Q} v_{pL}} \tag{12.42}$$

After effective weight, a confidence value (δ_{pq}), given by Equation (12.42), was also generated, proportional to membership value, for each connection. Finally, the best rule set R', effective weights and confidence values were used as evidence in Dempster-Shafer rule for attack and normal hypothesis. In this rule, Basic Probability Assignment (BPA), for all the evidence in R', was calculated to provide mass to each element in the power set, and after that, three basic evidential functions, Belief, Plausibility, and Uncertainty, were also obtained [35].

$$\rho(L_p) = m(L_p) + \frac{m(L')}{Q} \tag{12.43}$$

Finally, the pignistic probability function, given by Equation (12.43), was computed, where $m(L')$ determines the mass assigned to the frame. Each incoming connection was allocated to a class based on best values of pignistic function. Thereby, the incoming connections were classified into normal or attack classes in the testing phase successfully. The proposed approach was assessed in two parts. At first, it was analyzed using fixed values of K and W. Then, the accuracy was computed. The proposed clustering method got 88.33% accuracy, whereas on implementing the Fuzzy C-Means clustering, 82.65% accuracy was achieved. Therefore, the authors stated that the novel approach generated an efficient and reliable intrusion detection system.

12.4.3.4 K-Means Clustering Using Support Vector Machine

Aljamal *et al.* [36] proposed a method that used combined K-Means Clustering and SVM classifiers. They considered the UNSW-NB15 dataset for performance evaluation.

$$\forall D_k^| = \frac{D_k}{10^M} \tag{12.44}$$

At first, preprocessing was performed then Decimal scale normalization technique, given by Equation (12.44), was used to normalize the dataset. Thereafter, for removing the non-contributing features, PCA was used.

$$C_m = \frac{1}{M-1} \sum_{k=0}^{N-1} (D^k)(D^k)^T \tag{12.45}$$

For reducing the dataset from N-dimensions to K-dimensions, Covariance matrix (C_m) was computed using Equation (12.45), where D^k determined the matrix from the original dataset and $(D^k)^T$ its transpose. Then, the Singular value decomposition function was applied on the matrix which resulted in three more matrices, U, S, and V. Finally, from matrix U, the first K features were taken. In this work, KNIME platform was used for data preprocessing. About 36 features were selected after applying PCA. On evaluation of the output features using Random forest classifier and predictor, first 25 features were selected. The approach had two parts. The first one included K-Means clustering which labeled the data values as normal or attack class. Before implementation, the authors adjusted the most critical parameters: α (to select small clusters), β (to select large clusters), and γ (to select sparsest clusters). Reviewing some previous works and analysis, five models were created using K-Means with 10, 16, 32, 45, and 64 numbers of clusters, respectively. After evaluation, the model with 64 clusters got the highest accuracy. The second part of the system used the model with 64 clusters to train the SVM classifier for detection of intrusions. The classifier got the accuracy of 86.7%. This could have been better if there was no variance among the data instances of the online dataset. The performance of the system was 77% accurate, which was pretty low compared to other intrusion detection systems. But using the test data, the SVM model achieved an accuracy of 0.847 which was sustainable for a hybrid model. The major disadvantage was high false alarm rates that may affect the entire system.

12.4.3.5 K-Nearest Neighbor–Based Artificial Neural Network Mechanism

Ghosh *et al.* [37] proposed a reliable and secure intrusion detection system by collaborating the Network Intrusion Detection System (NIDS) and Host Intrusion Detection System (HIDS). They utilized the NSL-KDD dataset for evaluation purposes. Using the Information Gain method on the dataset, 25 features were selected. The multi-threaded

NIDS monitored the user requests and also processed the client's end requests. The NIDS model was divided into three parts. The first part was Capture and Query, where capturing and receiving of inbound and outbound data packets was performed, the order of the packets was also maintained and packets were placed into a shared queue. Then, the second part was Analysis, where multiple threads were constantly checked for any intrusion. In this part, at first, all the packets were classified into normal or abnormal categories using the KNN algorithm. After that, all the abnormal packets were again subdivided into specific attack types by Neural network algorithm. On implementation, the hybrid model of KNN and NN classifiers got a better accuracy rate in classification (76.54%) than individual KNN (72.49%) and NN (73.03%). Finally, the third part was the Reporting module where the Cloud administrator was notified about any intrusion. However, another intrusion could be faced in the hypervisor server. Those intrusions were tackled using HIDS which monitored the hypervisor. Hence, merging of both NIDS and HIDS together made the system more secure and reliable. For any data loss or breakdown, the concept of restore point was also used. Thereby, a secure model was generated for attack detection in the cloud systems.

12.4.3.6   Artificial Neural Network Fused With Support Vector Machine

Omrani *et al.* [38] presented a hybrid approach combining ANN and SVM classifiers. These classifiers are very expensive ML algorithms if used individually and hence they came up with this hybrid approach. They considered NSL-KDD dataset for performance evaluation. At first, for proper balancing of attack types some DoS and probe attacks were removed. The dataset was divided into three sets, train, test, and validation. Finally, 1,000 instances were selected for validation and test sets randomly. After preprocessing, two types of features were extracted, low and high. The classification results of ANN, SVM, and the combined one along with variation and replacement of flag, service, and protocol features were collected, and it was found that the combination of classifiers outperformed. The authors suggested modeling the attack analysis problem of network connection as a multi-class classification issue and recommended regression for estimating the attacks.

12.4.3.7   Particle Swarm Optimization–Based Probabilistic Neural Network

Rabbani *et al.* [39] proposed another interesting hybrid approach based on PSO and neural networks. They utilized the UNSW-NB15 dataset for evaluation purposes. The proposed system was divided into two parts. First one was Data preprocessing which involved feature reduction using PCA and normalization using the min-max method. Second part was the Recognition module where a model was created based on users' activities, for predicting whether the user was normal or malicious. The model was trained using the hybrid approach proposed. The equal numeric values of feature vectors were provided as input to the approach.

$$F_{p,q}(X) = \frac{1}{(2\pi\sigma)^{\frac{\pi}{2}}} exp\left(-\frac{\| X - X_{p,q} \|^2}{2\sigma^2} \right) \tag{12.46}$$

Table 12.5 Hybrid Learning Techniques with the highest accuracy.

Sr. no.	Method name	Dataset used	Highest accuracy reached
1	HIDCC [33]	NSL-KDD	99.38
2	Deep Neural Network, K-Means, SVM [34]	NSL-KDD	92.1
3	PRFCM [35]	NSL-KDD	88.33
4	K-Means Using SVM [36]	UNSW-NB 15	77
5	KNN, ANN [37]	NSL-KDD	76.54 (over 25 features)
6	ANN, SVM [38]	NSL-KDD	79.71
7	PSO-PNN [39]	UNSW-NB15	98

The output for each neuron, in the pattern layer of the approach, was computed using Gaussian kernel, given by Equation (12.46), where $X_{p,q}$ represented the center of kernel and σ was the spread parameter which was optimized using PSO technique.

$$G_p(X) = \sum_{q=L}^{M_p} w_{pq} F_{pq}(X), p \in (1, \ldots, P) \qquad (12.47)$$

After the pattern layer, the summation layer, with the help of previously obtained densities, computed the approximate class probability as given by Equation (12.47).

$$S(X) = argmax_{1 \le p \le P}(G_p) \qquad (12.48)$$

Lastly, the output was predicted after processing all the neurons using Equation (12.48). On implementation, the proposed approach had an overall accuracy of 98% in classification between normal and malicious attacks, whereas 96.2% in classification of attack type. Hence, the authors successfully designed the hybrid ML system which effectively detected attacks.

With respect to Hybrid ML techniques (Table 12.5), we found the HIDCC approach with the best detection rates.

12.5   Comparative Analysis

Here, the various advantages and disadvantages of all the works reviewed in this literature are discussed.

Table 12.6 discusses some advantages and disadvantages about Supervised Learning Techniques, whereas Table 12.7 discusses Unsupervised Learning Techniques and Table 12.8 discusses Hybrid Learning Techniques. Although a number of innovative and effective techniques were introduced in past few years, the analysis demonstrates that there are still some loopholes in the proposed systems which may harm the cloud environment and open it to both conventional and unconventional attacks and threats.

Table 12.6 Supervised learning analysis.

Article/ Paper	Dataset used	Advantages	Disadvantages
Pervez et al. [19]	NSL-KDD	Better classification accuracy was achieved.	i) False Positive Rate was much higher, about 7%–15% ii) Despite performing feature selection, the highest accuracy was achieved using all 41 training features.
Jing et al. [20]	UNSW-NB15	Overcome the disadvantage of MinMax normalization, using a non-linear scaling method.	In multiclass classification, i) Analysis, Backdoor, DoS, and Worms had low detection rates. ii) Exploits and Fuzzers had high false positive rates.
Wang et al. [21]	KDDCup99 and NSL-KDD	i) Greedy-layer wise strategy was applied to overcome the complexity of deep networks. ii) Smaller values of penalty-coefficient were used to maintain its value below reconstruction error. iii) The combined approach was superior to standalone SVM.	i) On doing multi-class classification task, buffer_ overflow, nmap, and pod had low detection rate. ii) SVM was unable to detect modern attacks in the test set effectively hence more optimized classifiers are required. iii) Controller's bottlenecks could be reduced to increase the detection rate.
Ingre et al. [22]	NSL-KDD	Better accuracy was achieved for binary classification (99.3%).	For five-class classification, the detection rate for R2L and U2R was low.
Aboueata et al. [23]	UNSW-NB15	i) Feature selection algorithms, $ChiX^2$ and Principal Component Analysis (PCA), effectively reduced the feature dimensionality. ii) The proposed model reduced the training time and complexity.	Moreover, general category got the highest accuracy, but in terms of SVM, all other categories of training parameter got much lower accuracies.
Zhang et al. [24]	NSL-KDD	i) The proposed neural network benefitted in compression coding and feature learning.	The detection rate for R2L and U2R was low which affected the overall accuracy.

(Continued)

Table 12.6 Supervised learning analysis. (*Continued*)

Article/ Paper	Dataset used	Advantages	Disadvantages
		ii) Encoder Compression Technique, effectively reduced the features.	
Zhiqiang *et al.* [25]	UNSW-NB15	False alarm rate was much better.	Data preprocessing and Normalization was not performed.
Yin *et al.* [26]	NSL-KDD	The RNNs introduced directional loops that memorized previous information and applied them to current output. These loops differed them from traditional Feed Forward Neural Networks.	i) The training time was high. ii) Exploding and Vanishing gradients were not avoided.
Choudhury *et al.* [27]	NSL-KDD	Effectively compared several classifiers and algorithms.	Weka tool, used for comparison purpose, failed to handle bigger datasets.
Salman *et al.* [28]	UNSW-NB15	i) For optimization, the Fuzzer attack was excluded. ii) To overcome the misclassification error of single-type categorization model, a new Step-wise categorization technique was introduced.	Attack categorization for DoS, Analysis, and Backdoor was low.

12.6 Conclusion

With the rise in advancement of cloud technology, complexities in its services and various threats and attacks have also been increasing day by day. Various researchers have developed several algorithms and systems to secure the cloud environment. In this article, we have reviewed several research papers related to cloud security and highlighted the current status of ML and intrusion detection systems. We considered two datasets, NSL-KDD and UNSW-NB15, for their high effectiveness and popularity in intrusion detection systems. ML is classified into Supervised, Unsupervised, and Hybrid learnings, and keeping in mind about these three types, we categorized our review.

Table 12.7 Unsupervised learning analysis.

Article/ Paper	Dataset used	Advantages	Disadvantages
Verma *et al.* [29]	NSL-KDD	Clustering applied with boosting algorithms achieved better accuracy.	False positive rate was high
Bhattacharjee *et al.* [30]	NSL-KDD	Fuzzy C-Means Clustering was proved to be better than K-Means clustering algorithm.	Features could be reduced for getting better classification and accuracy.
Sangve *et al.* [31]	NSL-KDD	i) In comparison with K-Means, the Expectation-Maximization was better. ii) Genetic Algorithm effectively helped in optimization.	Expectation-Maximization converged to local optima only.
Ghosh *et al.* [32]	NSL-KDD	i) Good examples for exploitation and exploration concepts were provided. ii) Feature Selection was effectively performed.	False positive rates were still higher.

Among Supervised techniques, we got an accuracy of 99% in almost all the approaches. On the other hand, among both Unsupervised and Hybrid techniques, we got an accuracy of around 75%–99%. Despite these high accuracies, ML techniques are still suffering from high false alarm rates which may harm the entire cloud system and hence requires more attention. With respect to datasets, the most used dataset by the researchers is NSL-KDD, the modified version of KDDCup 99. However, the dataset still suffers from some drawbacks, and for this, we suggest the use of UNSW-NB 15 Dataset which overcomes most of the drawbacks of the NSL-KDD Dataset.

For future, we focus on proposing a hybrid detection model taking the best methods among Supervised and Unsupervised techniques to overcome the limitations and increase the overall performance of the intrusion detection systems which can lead to a robust solution for security in the cloud environment.

Table 12.8 Hybrid learning analysis.

Article/ Paper	Dataset used	Advantages	Disadvantages
Hatef *et al.* [33]	NSL-KDD	i) For clustering, a low-cost learning vector quantization algorithm was used. ii) Better results were achieved	Overfitting may occur.
Tao *et al.* [34]	NSL-KDD	The algorithm efficiently classified sparse cases of U2R and R2L. It also improved detection accuracy in real security systems.	The SVM parameters were optimized using heuristic algorithms and DNN parameters of weights and threshold.
Ghosh *et al.* [35]	NSL-KDD	i) The proposed approach overcomes the drawback of Fuzzy C-Means Clustering. ii) The introduced strength value favored in overcoming the drawback of lower accuracy rates of KNN algorithm	The false alarm rate of proposed method was slightly higher than Fuzzy C-Means Clustering.
Aljamal *et al.* [36]	UNSW-NB15	Clustering accuracy was better	High false alarm rates.
Ghosh *et al.* [37]	NSL-KDD	Merging of both NIDS and HIDS together made the system more secure and reliable.	HIDS are sometimes harder to manage and configure. They can be disabled by certain denial-of-service attacks.
Omrani *et al.* [38]	NSL-KDD	Fusion of ANN and SVM effectively reduced the cost than using them individually.	The classifiers failed to detect each network attack.
Rabbani *et al.* [39]	UNSW-NB15	The proposed approach extracted meaningful information and behavioral patterns of a user effectively from the network traffic and used them for detection of malicious behaviors in cloud environments.	i) Backdoor attacks had low classification accuracy. ii) The false positive rate was a little higher.

References

1. Birje, M., Challagidad, P., Goudar, R.H., Tapale, M., Cloud computing review: Concepts, technology, challenges and security. *Int. J. Cloud Comput.*, 6, 32, 2017.
2. Fernandes, D.A.B., Soares, L.F.B., Gomes, J.V., Security issues in cloud environments: a survey. *Int. J. Inf. Secur.*, 13, 113–170, 2014.
3. Doshi, R. and Kute, V., A Review Paper on Security Concerns in Cloud Computing and Proposed Security Models. *2020 International Conference on Emerging Trends in Information Technology and Engineering (ic-ETITE)*, Vellore, India, pp. 1–4, 2020.
4. Marwan, M., Kartit, A., Ouahmane, H., Security Enhancement in Healthcare Cloud using Machine Learning. *Procedia Computer Science*, 127, pp. 388–397, 2018.
5. Shyam, G.K. and Doddi, S., Achieving Cloud Security Solutions through Machine and Non-Machine Learning Techniques: A Survey. *J. Eng. Sci. Technol. Rev.*, 12, 3, 51–63, 2019.
6. Alrehaili, A., Mir, A., Junaid, M., A Retrospect of Prominent Cloud Security Algorithms. *Int. J. Innov. Technol. Exploring Eng. (IJITEE)*, 9, 2278–3075, 2020.
7. Subramanian, E.K. and Tamilselvan, L., A focus on future cloud: machine learning-based cloud security. *SOCA*, 13, 237–249, 2019.
8. Naseer, A., Zhiqui, H., Ali, A., Cloud Computing Security Threats and Attacks with Their Mitigation Techniques. *2017 International Conference on Cyber-Enabled Distributed Computing and Knowledge Discovery (CyberC)*, pp. 244–251, 2017.
9. Maniah, Abdurachman, E., Gaol, F.L., Soewito, B., Survey on Threats and Risks in the Cloud Computing Environment. *Procedia Computer Science*, 161, pp. 1325–1332, 2019.
10. Singh, S., Jeong, Y., Park, J.H., A survey on cloud computing security: Issues, threats, and solutions. *Journal of Network and Computer Applications*, 75, pp. 200–222, 2016.
11. Efozia, N. F., Ariwa, E. , Asogwa, D. C., Awonusi, O., Anigbogu, S. O., A review of threats and vulnerabilities to cloud computing existence. *2017 Seventh International Conference on Innovative Computing Technology (INTECH)*, pp. 197-204, 2017.
12. Tabrizchi, H., Kuchaki Rafsanjani, M. A survey on security challenges in cloud computing: issues, threats, and solutions. *J Supercomput*, 76, 9493–9532, 2020.
13. Tavallaee, M., Bagheri, E., Lu, W., Ghorbani, A.A., A detailed analysis of the KDD CUP 99 data set. *2009 IEEE Symposium on Computational Intelligence for Security and Defense Applications*, Ottawa, pp. 1–6, 2009.
14. McHugh, J., Testing Intrusion Detection Systems: A Critique of the 1998 and 1999 DARPA Intrusion Detection System Evaluations as Performed by Lincoln Laboratory. *ACM Trans. Inf. Syst. Secur.*, 3, 262–294, 2000.
15. Thomas, R. and Pavithram, D., A Survey of Intrusion Detection Models based on NSL-KDD Data Set. *The Fifth HCT Information Technology Trends (ITT 2018)*, Dubai, UAE, 2018.
16. Moustafa, N. and Slay, J., UNSW-NB15: a comprehensive data set for network intrusion detection systems (UNSW-NB15 network data set). *2015 Military Communications and Information Systems Conference (MilCIS)*, Canberra, ACT, pp. 1–6, 2015.
17. Eltanbouly, S., Bashendy, M., AlNaimi, N., Chkirbene, Z., Erbad, A., Machine Learning Techniques for Network Anomaly Detection: A Survey. *2020 IEEE International Conference on Informatics, IoT, and Enabling Technologies (ICIoT)*, pp. 156–162, 2020.
18. Bhamare, D., Salman, T., Samaka, M., Erfad, A., Jain, R., Feasibility of Supervised Machine Learning for Cloud Security. *2016 International Conference on Information Science and Security (ICISS)*, 2016.
19. Pervez, M.S. and Farid, D.M., Feature selection and intrusion classification in NSL-KDD cup 99 dataset employing SVMs. *The 8th International Conference on Software, Knowledge, Information Management and Applications (SKIMA 2014)*, pp. 1–6, 2014.

20. Jing, D. and Chen, H., SVM Based Network Intrusion Detection for the UNSW-NB15 Dataset. *2019 IEEE 13th International Conference on ASIC (ASICON)*, pp. 1–4, 2019.

21. Wang, W., Du, X., Shan, D., Qin, R., Wang, N., Cloud Intrusion Detection Method Based on Stacked Contractive Auto-Encoder and Support Vector Machine. *IEEE Trans. Cloud Comput.*, 1, 1–1, 2020.

22. Ingre, B. and Yadav, A., Performance analysis of NSL-KDD dataset using ANN. *2015 International Conference on Signal Processing and Communication Engineering Systems*, Guntur, pp. 92–96, 2015.

23. Aboueata, N., Alrasbi, S., Erbad, A., Kassler, A., Bhamare, D., Supervised Machine Learning Techniques for Efficient Network Intrusion Detection. *2019 28th International Conference on Computer Communication and Networks (ICCCN)*, Valencia, Spain, pp. 1–8, 2019.

24. Zhang, C., Ruan, F., Yin, L., Chen, X., Zhai, L., Liu, F., A Deep Learning Approach for Network Intrusion Detection Based on NSL-KDD Dataset. *2019 IEEE 13th International Conference on Anti-counterfeiting, Security, and Identification (ASID)*, pp. 41–45, 2019.

25. Zhiqiang, L., Mohi-Ud-Din, G., Bing, L., Jianchao, L., Ye, Z., Zhijun, L., Modeling Network Intrusion Detection System Using Feed-Forward Neural Network Using UNSW-NB15 Dataset. *2019 IEEE 7th International Conference on Smart Energy Grid Engineering (SEGE)*, pp. 299–303, 2019.

26. Yin, C., Zhu, Y., Fei, J., He, X., A Deep Learning Approach for Intrusion Detection Using Recurrent Neural Networks. *IEEE Access*, 5, 21954–21961, 2017.

27. Choudhury, S. and Bhowal, A., Comparative analysis of machine learning algorithms along with classifiers for network intrusion detection. *2015 International Conference on Smart Technologies and Management for Computing, Communication, Controls, Energy and Materials (ICSTM)*, pp. 89–95, 2015.

28. Salman, T., Bhamare, D., Erbad, A., Jain, R., Samaka, M., Machine Learning for Anomaly Detection and Categorization in Multi-Cloud Environments. *2017 IEEE 4th International Conference on Cyber Security and Cloud Computing (CSCloud)*, pp. 97–103, 2017.

29. Verma, P., Anwar, S., Khan, S., Mane, S.B., Network Intrusion Detection Using Clustering and Gradient Boosting. *2018 9th International Conference on Computing, Communication and Networking Technologies (ICCCNT)*, pp. 1–7, 2018.

30. Bhattacharjee, P.S., Fujail, A. K. Md, Begum, S.A., A Comparison of Intrusion Detection by K-Means and Fuzzy C-Means Clustering Algorithm Over the NSL-KDD Dataset. *2017 IEEE International Conference on Computational Intelligence and Computing Research (ICCIC)*, pp. 1–6, 2017.

31. Sangve, S.M. and Kulkarni, U.V., Anomaly Based Improved Network Intrusion Detection System Using Clustering Techniques. *Int. J. Adv. Res. Comput. Sci.*, 8, 808–815, 2017.

32. Ghosh, P., Karmakar, A., Sharma, J., Phadikar, S., CS-PSO based Intrusion Detection System in Cloud Environment, in: *Emerging Technologies in Data Mining and Information Security. Advances in Intelligent Systems and Computing*, vol. 755, Abraham, A., Dutta, P., Mandal, J., Bhattacharya, A., Dutta, S. (Eds.), 2019.

33. Hatef, M., Shaker, V., Reza Jabbarpour, M., Jung, J., Zarrabi, H., HIDCC: a hybrid intrusion detection approach in cloud computing. *Concurr. Comp.: Pract. Exp.*, 30, 3, e4171, 2018.

34. Ma, T., Yu, Y., Wang, F., Zhang, Q., Chen, X., A Hybrid Methodologies for Intrusion Detection Based Deep Neural Network with Support Vector Machine and Clustering Technique, in: *Frontier Computing*. FC 2016. Lecture Notes in Electrical Engineering, vol. 422, Yen, N. and Hung, J. (Eds.), 2018.

35. Ghosh, P., Shakti, S., Phadikar, S., A Cloud Intrusion Detection System Using Novel PRFCM Clustering and KNN Based Dempster-Shafer Rule. *Int. J. Cloud Appl. Comput. (IJCAC)*, 6, 4, 18–35, 2016.

36. Aljamal, I., Tekeoğlu, A., Bekiroglu, K., Sengupta, S., Hybrid Intrusion Detection System Using Machine Learning Techniques in Cloud Computing Environments. *2019 IEEE 17th International Conference on Software Engineering Research, Management and Applications (SERA)*, pp. 84–89, 2019.

37. Ghosh, P., Mandal, A., Kumar, R., An Efficient Cloud Network Intrusion Detection System. *Adv. Intell. Syst. Comput.*, 339, 91–99, 2015.

38. Omrani, T., Dallali, A., Rhaimi, B.C., Fattahi, J., Fusion of ANN and SVM classifiers for network attack detection. *Proc. 18th Int. Conf. Sci. Techn. Autom. Control Comput. Eng. (STA)*, pp. 374–377, 2017.

39. Rabbani, M., Wang, Y.L., Khoshkangini, R., Jelodar, H., Zhao, R., Hu, P., A hybrid machine learning approach for malicious behaviour detection and recognition in cloud computing. *Journal of Network and Computer Applications*, 151, 102507, 2020.

40. He, Z., Zhang, T., Lee, R.B., Machine Learning Based DDoS Attack Detection From Source Slide in Cloud. *2017 IEEE 4th International Conference on Cyber Security and Cloud Computing*, New York, NY, pp. 114–120, 2017.

41. Kumar, S. and Singh, C.B.B., A zero-day resistant malware detection method for securing Cloud using SVM and Sandboxing Techniques. *2018 Second International Conference on Inventive Communication and Computational Technologies (ICICCT)*.

42. Nathezhtha, T. and Vaidehi, V., Cloud Insider Attack Detection Using Machine Learning. *2018 International Conference on Recent Trends in Advance Computing (ICRTAC)*, Chennai, India, pp. 60–65, 2018.

43. Feng, W., Yan, W., Wu, S., Liu, N., Wavelet Transform and Unsupervised Machine Learning to Detect Insider Threat on Cloud File-Sharing. *2017 IEEE International Conference on Intelligence and Security Informatics (ISI)*, Beijing, pp. 155–157, 2017.

44. Watson, M.R., Shirazi, N., Marnerides, A.K., Mauthe, A., Hutchison, D., Malware Detection in Cloud Computing Infrastructures. *IEEE Trans. Dependable Secure Comput.*, 13, 2, 192–205, 2016.

45. Farnaaz, N. and Jabbar, M.A., Random Forest Modeling for Network Intrusion Detection System. *Proc. Comput. Sci.*, 89, 213–217, 2016.

46. Zhang, Y., Xu, C., Li, H., Yang, K., Zhou, J., Lin, X., HealthDep: An Efficient and Secure Deduplication Scheme for Cloud-Assisted eHealth Systems. *IEEE Trans. Ind. Inf.*, 14, 9, 4101–4112, 2018.

47. Shone, N., Ngoc, T.N., Phai, V.D., Shi, Q., A Deep Learning Approach to Network Intrusion Detection. *IEEE Trans. Emerging Top. Comput. Intell.*, 2, 1, 41–50, 2018.

48. Qureshi, K.N., Bashir, F., Iqbal, S., Cloud Computing Model for Vehicular Ad hoc Networks. *2018 IEEE 7th International Conference on Cloud Networking (CloudNet)*, Tokyo, 2018.

49. Kaur, A., Singh, V.P., Gill, S., The Future of Cloud Computing: Opportunities, Challenges and Research Trends. *2018 2nd International Conference on I-SMAC (IoT in Social, Mobile, Analytics and Cloud) (I-SMAC)I-SMAC (IoT in Social, Mobile, Analytics and Cloud) (I-SMAC), 2018 2nd International Conference on*, India, pp. 213–219, 2018.

50. Bharadwaj, D.R., Bhattacharya, A., Chakkaravarthy, M., Cloud Threat Defense – A Threat Protection and Security Compliance Solution. *2018 IEEE International Conference on Cloud Computing in Emerging Markets (CCEM)*, Bangalore, India, pp. 95–99, 2018.

51. Markandey, A., Dhamdhere, P., Gajmal, Y., Data Access Security in Cloud Computing: A Review. *2018 International Conference on Computing, Power and Communication Technologies (GUCON)*, Greater Noida, Uttar Pradesh, India, pp. 633–636, 2018.

52. Sun, X., Critical Security Issues in Cloud Computing: A Survey. *2018 IEEE 4th International Conference on Big Data Security on Cloud (BigDataSecurity), IEEE International Conference on High Performance and Smart Computing, (HPSC) and IEEE International Conference on Intelligent Data and Security (IDS)*, Omaha, NE, pp. 216–221, 2018.

13

Machine Learning Adversarial Attacks: A Survey Beyond

Chandni Magoo* and Puneet Garg

J.C. Bose University of Science and Technology, Faridabad, India

Abstract

Machine Learning (ML) has fascinated researchers and developers to an extent that it has been now considered as an astute to most of them. To this continuation, ML integrated with Natural Language Processing (NLP) has yielded extraordinary results in many fields. ML began to splutter in early 2000 and has now been to its zenith. It has radically proved to be sure-fire to the human level performance in many tasks. Many huge companies like Google and Amazon are providing Cloud-based ML as a service (MLaaS) which can be efficiently used by an end user to perform numerous tasks in fields like NLP and Recommender systems. However, these services and their applications like sentiment analysis and text entailment are prone to adversarial attacks which force them to misclassify. This issue has been considered in depth in this chapter with analysis based on comparative study of some of the popular text-based attacks. The chapter also focuses on attacks, namely, in domains like Image, Cloud-based services, and Recommender-based systems.

Keywords: Machine Learning, NLP, adversarial attacks, recommender systems, Cloud-based services

13.1 Introduction

Machine Learning (ML) has created a niche in research field like Natural Language Processing (NLP) [1, 2], medical diagnostic [4], human interaction systems [3], and many more. Though they have carved their place in every field but are unable to save themselves from adversarial attacks. These research claims that numerous Deep Neural Network (DNN) and ML techniques are victim of severe adversary attacks leading to degradation of the performance. Many classification algorithms are forced by the adversary attackers to produce false negative results thus aiming to manipulate classification. Papernot, N. *et al.* [5] generated few small perturbations on the images for the classification problem and deceived DNNs with high probability. These misclassified samples are known as adversarial examples. In the layman's terms, it can be said that a small imperceptible change in data can be a threat to security and integrity of many ML algorithms [6, 7]. The scope of research in adversarial

---

Corresponding author: chandnimagoo@yahoo.com

Rajdeep Chakraborty, Anupam Ghosh and Jyotsna Kumar Mandal (eds.) Machine Learning Techniques and Analytics for Cloud Security, (271–292) © 2022 Scrivener Publishing LLC

attacks has significantly increased from image classification [8, 9] to NLP [10] and Cloud-based services provided by Google, Microsoft, Amazon, and other popular cloud companies. But these companies do not pay much attention to these attacks

This chapter is organized as follows: The mathematics behind adversarial learning inter-twined with ML is discussed in Section 13.2. Section 13.3 gives the brief introduction to various types of attacks in ML followed by Section 13.4 which starts by highlighting the excellent related work previously done by the researchers and analyzing some of the well-known text-based attacks, followed by adversarial attacks on cloud-based services in Section 13.5, and finally conclusion in Section 13.6.

13.2   Adversarial Learning

We have been living in this illusion till date that ML has been an outstanding performer in many human-related tasks by its surprising learning and efficacy. But this delusion broke when some of its techniques started acting differently on some of the instances. This is con-sidered as an attack and a name given to this attack is "adversarial attack" [5, 6, 10]. The idea behind this attack is to introduce an imperceptible change in the data to fool the system (say classifier) to produce wrong results. The change is slight that it is unnoticeable to humans also but in case of playing with images and not for text.

13.2.1   Concept

Let us consider x as input label and y as output class label, thus defining the traditional clas-sifier mathematically as

$$f(x) = y \tag{13.1}$$

Now, by adding small noise (δ) to the input function results in the equation as

$$f(x+\delta) \neq y \tag{13.2}$$

The classifier during its training aims to reduce the loss between the target and the pre-dicted class label which can be mathematically formulated as below where h is the hypoth-esis and $X = \{x_1, x_2,..., x_n\}$ and $Y = \{y_1, y_2,..., y_n\}$ and l is the loss function.

$$\underset{h}{\mathrm{argmin}} \sum_{x_i \in X} l(h(x_i)(y_i)) \tag{13.3}$$

Whereas during the testing phase, the error is calculated as the accumulation of the loss between the target and the predicted output label. The mathematical formulation is given as below where A represents input test data, i.e., $A = \{x_1, x_2,..., x_n\}$ and output labels as $O' = \{y_1, y_2,..., y_n\}$.

$$\sum_{x_i \in A} l(H(x_i)(y_i)) \tag{13.4}$$

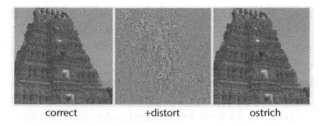

Figure 13.1 Blind spots in neural networks (source: Szegedy *et al.* [11]).

Though the discussion about the concept of adversarial attacks started in early 2000, it catches pace in recent years when ML was at its boom and security became the crucial aspect. Many researchers came up with many hypothetical reasons of the occurrence of these adversaries. Szegedy, C. *et al.* [11] made a breakthrough by discovering that even robust ML techniques like neural network suffered from adversarial attacks. The research found that even a small change in an image tends to misclassification as shown in Figure 13.1. It was further added that the main reason for the occurrence of these adversaries is the non-linearity nature in neural network by taking into consideration two main counter-intuitive properties of DNN. The first property showed that the entire activation functions provide important semantic information rather than some individual units. The randomness of the features proved better than the single feature. Further to this, their research was able to identify those parts of the inputs which are hidden and lead to the generation of adversary effect. Also, an observation was made that the adversarial examples are not the result of overfitting and are rather universal. To this contrary, Goodfellow *et al.* [12] came with the well-proved theory that the sufficient reason for the occurrence of adversaries is the strict linearity nature of neural network. Regularizing the model by using ways like dropout and pretraining do not effectively contribute to the reduced vulnerability to adversarial attacks. They came out with a technique named fast gradient sign method (FGSM) for generating adversarial examples. This method is explained in detail in the subsequent Section 13.3.

13.3   Taxonomy of Adversarial Attacks

Different researchers and reviewers have created their own way to classify different types of attacks. In this section, a related taxonomy is described which is mapped with different adversarial techniques in Section 13.5.

13.3.1   Attacks Based on Knowledge

As per the generalized form, the attacks can be categorized, namely, x.

13.3.1.1   *Black Box Attack (Transferable Attack)*

This attack basically deals with the transferability notion that adversaries generated to attack surrogate model S can achieve good results for the targeted model T [13]. Simple steps to perform black box attack are as follows:

1. The target model T is trained in a closed environment which is unknown to the adversary.
2. Model A which is a surrogate form of model T is developed to generate adversarial instances.
3. By using the transferable methods, the adversaries can be injected to attack model T.
4. The attack can be used for both known and unknown dataset of model T.

In the case of the awareness of the dataset to the adversary, the model A can be easily trained to that dataset to mimic model T. However, when the training set is not known, then the attacker's goal is to find the error between its behavior on the training inputs to that of the target model's behavior on the same input on which it is trained. Both the model prediction is analyzed. This is called membership inference [14].

13.3.1.2 White Box Attack

This results when the attacker has complete knowledge or access to the target model. The access is to parameters, input, output, and its architecture. It is considered more harmful than black box attack. Many novel techniques have been proposed [15, 16].

The adversarial instances can be created by analyzing the inputs near to the decision boundaries and learning them to modify till they cross the boundary and perform misclassification. In Figure 13.2, only a minor change in some of the inputs can change the class and perform misclassification. The arrow in "red" indicates the shifting of the inputs after perturbation. The adversarial instances are created by identifying the inputs near the boundary of the decision line and modifying them till the misclassification occurs. In Figure 13.3, the probabilities indicate that the image is of panda, whereas Figure 13.4 indicates the drastic change in the probabilities. As it can be seen after making small changes in the image pixels, the value of panda is decreased and cat is increased. This indicates that making small changes in the input image is to an extent not perceived by the human but misclassified by the classifier. The concept of generating adversarial examples [13, 14, 16] is explained in detail in Section 13.4.

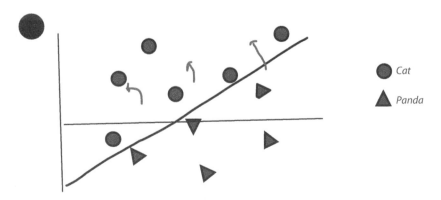

Figure 13.2 Representing a decision boundary with two classes separated by it.

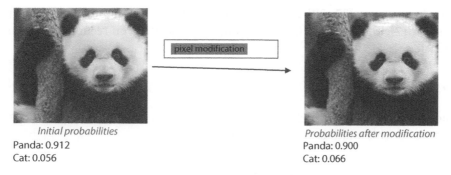

Figure 13.3 Panda image with initial probabilities and final probabilities.

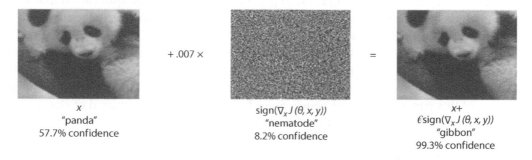

Figure 13.4 Example of adversarial effect on panda image (source: Goodfellow *et al.* [12]).

13.3.2 Attacks Based on Goals

The adversarial attacks can also be classified based on whether the adversarial class should be a target specified class or any other class unknown to the classifier.

13.3.2.1 Target Attacks

This attack aims to give incorrect class label for adversarial instances. The input is slightly changed and will be classified as a target label unknown to the classifier.

13.3.2.2 Non-Target Attacks

This attack misclassifies to any label unknown to the classifier. It is easy to generate a non-target attack rather.

13.3.3 Attacks Based on Strategies

The following is the categorization of attacks based on strategies applied on various ML techniques.

13.3.3.1 Poisoning Attacks

The attacker can pollute the data by injecting the designed instances during the training phase to compromise the entire learning phase. This type of attack is commonly used for recommender systems [37, 38] and supervised learning techniques like support vector machines [16, 17]. The detailed discussion of this type of attack on recommender systems is discussed later.

13.3.3.2   Evasion Attacks

This attack is incorporated by manipulating adversary test samples but do not change the training process. This attack is active at test time.

13.3.4   Textual-Based Attacks (NLP)

NLP models human language understanding. NLP has a widespread application like sentiment analysis [41], recommendation systems [38, 39], question answering systems [43], spam detection [44], paraphrasing [23], and text summarization [42]. DNNs are the main source of executing NLP. So, it is hard to ignore the fact that NLP is another victim of adversarial attacks other than images. Text-based adversarial attacks are more challenging as compared to image as a small change in the text can impact the semantics of the input. The focus of this paper will be on English. Since English language composed of characters, words, and sentences, it is obvious that the attack can be made at any level from characters to sentences and the result would be intimidating. Huq *et al.* [18] have mentioned different types of NLP attacks at character, word, and sentence level. The research in this field has started taking big leaps.

13.3.4.1   Character Level Attacks

Ebhramini *et al.* [19] performed editing at character level to create adversarial instances. Though character level has a low impact on human understanding, but they are highly vulnerable to adversaries. The character level attacks involve operations like flipping, insertion, and deletion. A detailed overview of these operations has been discussed in Section 13.4.

13.3.4.2   Word-Level Attacks

The words are replaced by their synonyms, antonyms, or deleting the word completely or replacing the word with an entire new word unknown to the model [20–22].

13.3.4.3   Sentence-Level Attacks

The entire sentence can be replaced by a new sentence in this type of attack. Many paraphrasing attacks can be included in this category [23].

13.4   Review of Adversarial Attack Methods

This section reviews various adversarial attacks applied on text and images.

13.4.1   L-BFGS

Box constrained L-BFGS [11] can be able to find adversarial instances. It deals with the minimization problem. The variable r should be minimum so that it can be shown that even a small amount of noise can have adverse effect.

$$\text{Minimize } r \tag{13.5}$$

$$\text{Such that } f(x + r) = l \text{ and } (x + r) \in D \tag{13.6}$$

where $(x + r)$ is the perturbed image and r is the amount of perturbation. D is the domain representing perturbed samples. It is computationally expensive but gives good results.

13.4.2   Feedforward Derivation Attack (Jacobian Attack)

It showed how slight input perturbations generated using the feed forward derivative can bring large variations in the output. Papernot *et al.* [24] used the feedforward derivative approach followed by saliency maps to generate adversarial instances with a small change in the actual input. Jacobian matrix was used to define the derivative during learning by the neural network. The forward derivative can be calculated using gradient function as function f is given by

$$\nabla f(x) = \left[\frac{\partial f_j(x)}{\partial x_i} \right] \text{ for } j=1,2,....N \text{ and } i=1,2,.....M \tag{13.7}$$

The forward propagation of the gradient helped to find the input components leading to change in the network outputs. Moreover, the idea of choosing saliency maps is to restrict to limited and efficient number of input features for perturbation. They are used to solve target specific problems. It further uses the forward derivative calculated to find those inputs which can lead to misclassification. The saliency value can be calculated by using following equation:

$$S(x,t)[i] = \begin{cases} 0 \text{ if } \dfrac{\partial f_t(x)}{\partial x_i} < 0 \text{ or } \displaystyle\sum_{j \neq t} \dfrac{\partial f_j(x)}{\partial x_i} > 0 \\[4mm] \left(\dfrac{\partial f_t(x)}{\partial x_i} \right) \left| \displaystyle\sum_{j \neq t} \dfrac{\partial f_j(x)}{\partial x_i} \right| \text{ otherwise} \end{cases} \tag{13.8}$$

where $\dfrac{\partial f_j(x)}{\partial x_i}$ can be easily calculated using Equation (13.1). High saliency values correspond to the input features desired for misclassification. This is a complex method with high computational cost. The same method was applied on RNN's and LSTM model [25].

13.4.3   Fast Gradient Sign Method

Goodfellow *et al.* [12] explained that simple linear model can have adversarial instances and how softmax function is vulnerable to attacks. The linearity of the cost function is calculated by finding its gradient. Mathematically, it can be defined as

$$\eta = \epsilon \ (\ sign(\nabla_x J(\Theta, x, y))) \tag{13.9}$$

$$x^* = x + \epsilon \ (sign(\nabla_x J(\Theta, x, y))) \tag{13.10}$$

where ∇_x as its gradient w.r.t. to x(input), y(true label), Θ (parameter), and J(cost function).

As in Figure 13.4, a small change in the original image brings no visual change in the final image but leads to misclassification. Hence, it can be deduced that adversarial instances can be generated through simple linearity of any model. Models which can be easily optimized can also be easily perturbed. Even the ensemble-based models are vulnerable to adversarial attacks.

13.4.4   Methods of Different Text-Based Adversarial Attacks

Word-level attack [20] is based on sememes word substitution method as shown in Figure 13.5 and particle swarm optimization search algorithm.

This method outperformed on many factors like good quality adversarial instances, attack success rate, and high transferability, which makes the victim model highly robust. Only the words which carry meaning are substituted with sememes words. Li *et al.* [26] introduced TextBugger that proves to be effective in generating adversarial instances and providing adversarial training to defend these attacks. Both white and black box models are considered for adversaries. The method used for white box explained in easy way below. Five proposed bugs generated to create adversarial examples are shown in Table 13.1. White box setting has been explained in detail as: In steps 2 to 3, the most important words are selected by calculating the importance score of each word. The importance score is calculated by finding the partial derivative of the confidence value C based on the predicted class y w.r.t. x(input). The confidence value C is calculated by computing the Jacobian matrix for input text $x = (x_1, x_2, x_{3...} x_m)$

$$J(f(x)) = \frac{\partial f(x)}{\partial x} = \left[\frac{\partial f_j(x)}{\partial x_i} \right] where \tag{13.11}$$

Original Sentence

The film's biggest is its complete and utter **lack** of tension.

(Prediction = Negative)

Attacked sentence

The film's biggest is its complete and utter dearth of tension.

(Prediction = Positive)

Figure 13.5 Example of adversarial effect on word (source: Zang *et al.* [20]).

Table 13.1 Types and examples of five bugs generated methods [26].

Bug	Purpose	Original word	Perturbed word
Insert	It is generated by applying space between two characters.	Good	G ood
Swap	Randomly two adjacent characters are swapped except first and last character.	Worse	Wrose
Delete	To remove any character of a word except first and last.	Good	God
Sub-C	Substitute characters with similar non-characters like numerals/alphanumeric.	Good	Go0d
Sub-W	Replace the selected word with top(k) nearest neighbors in vector space.	Good	Poor

$$i = 1, 2 \ldots N, \quad \text{and } j = 1, 2, \ldots m \text{ and } J(f(x)) \text{ is Jacobian function matrix}$$

Steps 3 to 4 determine the selection of the bug at the character level and word level. For word-level perturbation, pretrained Glove model is used to select top five semantically similar neighbors to the original word. In character-level and word-level perturbation, several types of bugs are generated as mentioned in Table 13.1 like Insert, Swap, and Sub-W. From several generated bugs, the most optimal bug is generated which reduces the confidence value. The most favored bug replaces the word or character to new text x'. If the classifier changes the original output, thereby maintaining the semantic similarity, then that text is considered as an adversarial example. For black box attack, since the gradient is not known, the method to choose the important sentences following important words among each sentence is implemented. After selecting the preferred sentence, the important words are selected and modified by controlling the semantic similarity. For selecting the important words, the authors use the method of removing j^{th} word from the text and the score is calculated by evaluating the prediction, before and after removing that word. The score of each word reflects its importance in the text.

$$C_{wj} = F_y(w_1, w_2, \cdots, w_m) - F_y(w_1, w_2, \cdots, w_{j-1}, w_{j+1}, \ldots w_m) \tag{13.12}$$

where C_{wj} is the function score to determine the relevance of each word. The bug generation method is same as white box attack method.

Algorithm 13.1 TEXTBUGGER under white box setting [26].

Input: Sentence X worth its true label Y, classifier f(.) and threshold e.
Output: Adversarial Sentence x_{adv}
Step 1: X' ← X
Step 2: for each word X_i in X

$$Cx_i = \frac{\partial f_y(x)}{\partial x_i}$$

Step 3: W_{ord}= desc-sort($X_1, X_2, X_{3...} X_m$) by Cx_i
Step4: for each w_k in W_{ord}
Bug= *select_bug (X_i, X', Y, f(.))

        X'← substitute w_k
        if S'(X, X') ≤ ε then
          return
        else if f_i(X') ≠ y then
          solution found
          return X'

    *For select_bug function please refer [26]

Textfooler [27] is also considered as an adversarial attack generator specifically for pretrained models like BERT. Some instances of original and adversarial sentences from Textfooler are shown in Table 13.2. The bugs proposed in [26] resulted in some unnatural and irrelevant words in the sentences can be considered as incorrect or irrelevant words to humans. Huq *et al.* [18] was the first to challenge the robust BERT model by its attack. The attack is based on black box model where the attacker is unaware of the architecture, training data, and victim model's parameters. The experimental results on adversarial examples are better as compared to [26] by considering only the word replacement feature using cosine similarity method. Based on black box attack method, the framework of TextFooler is applied to various state-of-the art deep learning models in five text classification tasks and two text entailment tasks. The method is able to reduce the accuracy of the deep learning models, namely, BERT, wordLSTM, and wordCNN to below 10% by only less than 20% perturbed words. The TextFooler algorithm generates adversarial examples of text as shown in Algorithm 13.2. Steps 2 to 3 correspond to selecting the most significant words that influence the final predictions and maintaining the semantic similarity. The importance score is thus calculated as the change over after and before deletion of the word w_i as shown in step 2 of the algorithm 11.2. Steps 5 to 8 correspond to replacing the word by the most similar option. The replacement criteria are as follows: (1) semantically similar to the original word, (2) context-based, (3) pushing target model toward wrong prediction.

Algorithm 13.2 Textfooler [27].

Input: Sentence S ={ $x_1, x_2, x_{3...} x_m$ }, true label = y, target model M, sentence similarity function sim(.), similarity threshold ε. Word embeddings (emb), vocabulary (voc)
Output: adversarial sentence S_{adv}
Step 1: S_{adv} ← S
Step 2: for each word x_i in S do
    If(M(S) = M($S_{\backslash x_i}$) = y)
        Ix_i = M_y(S) − M_y($S_{\backslash x_i}$),
    Else if(M(S) = y && M_y($S_{\backslash x_i}$) = y' && y≠y'
        Ix_i = (M_y(S) − M_y($S_{\backslash x_i}$)) +($M_{y'}$($S_{\backslash x_i}$) − $M_{y'}$(S))
Step 3: Create set W with words in order of high importance and so on.
Step 4: Filter out stop words like "the", "then" which are placeholders.

Step 5: for each word x_j in W do
      candidate ← cos_sim(emb_{xj} = emb_{word}) for all words in vocab
      candidate ← posfilter(candidate)
Step 6: for each c_k in candidate do
      Create S' containing c_k replaced for x_j
   if Similarity between S' and S_{adv} is less then threshold then
      fcandidate ← ck
      y_k ← M(S')
      p_k ← My_k(S')
Step 7: if there exists ck s.t. y_k ≠ y then
      fcandidate ← ck
Step 8: From the fcandidate set, if there exist a candidate which changes the output of target model,
      word with maximum similar semantics is chosen from fcandidate set
      else
      choose the word with least confidence score of label y for word x_i and repeat step 2.

TextTricker [28] is a white box model for text classification and is directed for both target and non-target attacks. The gradient-based method is implemented for efficiency and loss-based method is performed for high success rate. The performance was much better than some previous techniques [21, 22].

Algorithm 13.3 The TextTricker [28].

Input: S = ($t1,t2....tm$) and the target label y; Classifier f; Pre-trained word embeddings *Epre*; Stop words *Tstop*; Maximum allowed valid perturbation N; Maximum nearest neighbor M
Output: The adversarial example *Sadv*.
Step1: for each t in S do
      Compute S_t as $||\nabla_t loss(f, S, y)||_2$
Step 2: tscore ← sort t with score in decreasing order
Step 3: Let Sadv= S and count=0
Step 4: for each t in tscore
      if t ε *Tstop* then continue
   if count==N then break
   Tcandidate ← k nearest neighbors of t but with same POS stored in *Epre* and add special tokens "pad" and "unk"
   t, $loss'$ ← *calculate loss using target loss based/gradient-based loss methods
   if $loss'$< $loss(f, Sadv, y)$ then
      Sadv ← t'
      Count++
      if $f(Sadv)$ == y then
      Return Sadv
Return none
*for target loss based the word which minimizes the loss is chosen.
*for gradient-based loss, the word embedding of t word should minimize the loss
*for detailed algorithm on both loss methods please refer [28].

Table 13.2 Instances of original and adversarial sentences [27].

Reviews of movie [Negative (NEG) ↔ Positive (POS)]	
Original (Label: Negative)	The cast in impossibly **contrived situations** is **totally** estranged from reality.
ttack (Label: Positive)	The cast in impossibly **engineered circumstances** is **fully** estranged from reality.

Gao *et al.* [29] proposed a technique named DeepWordBug, based on black box model to misclassify text by generating small text perturbations. The technique is specifically designed for non-targeted attacks. The method is a two-step process:

> Step 1: Calculating score for each token and ranking it to choose the most important one for prediction. Four scoring functions are 1 Score, Temporal Head Score (THS), Temporal Tail Score (TTS), and Combined Score (CS). Best k tokens to perturb are selected based on these scores.
>
> Step 2: Transforming the token using different operations like deletion, insertion, swap, and substitution, as shown in Table 13.3.

Ebrahimi *et al.* [19] proposed an efficient white box model for generating adversarial examples at character level. It is a character level attacker and can be used at word level also. Flips can be used to perform different character level operations like deletion, insertion other than substitution (flipping) as shown in Table 13.4. The flipping takes place simply by using a single pass to estimate the best flip. The technique chose the character flipping, which results in maximum loss. Mathematical representation of the loss calculation is given as

$$\max \nabla_x J(x,y)^T = \vec{v}_{ijb} = \max_{ijb} \frac{\partial y}{\partial x_{ij}}^{(b)} - \frac{\partial y}{\partial xij}^{(a)} \tag{13.13}$$

TextAttack [30] is an open source library and used as an attack model to test the robustness of the NLP model. It is used for attacks on NLP applications like Text Entailment and Text classification.

$$S = (x_1, x_2, x_3 ... x_m) \qquad //x_i \text{ can be a word or character} \tag{13.14}$$

$$S_{adv} = (x_1, x_3 ... x_m) \text{ or} \qquad //\text{Deletion} \tag{13.15}$$

$$S_{adv} = (x_1, x_{21}, x_3 ... x_m) \text{ or} \qquad //\text{Replacement of } x_2 \text{ with } x_{21} \tag{13.16}$$

Table 13.3 Different transformer functions with results [29].

Original word	Insert	Swap	Delete	Substitute
Place	Placer	Place	Plae	plade

Table 13.4 Nearest neighbor words based on cosine similarity when hotflip is applied on CNN-STM [19].

Deletion	Substitution	Insertion
actor → actr	Local → loral	Past → pas!t
Act	Moral	Pasture
Acting	Floral	Task
Acts	Coral	Pastor

$$S_{adv} = (x_1, x_2, x_{21}, x_{3...} \ x_m) \qquad //\text{insertion} \qquad (13.17)$$

The tool designed takes into considerations all important aspects required for generating an adversarial attack technique. It includes important search methods like greedy with word importance ranking and beam search. The tool also supports various transformation operations like word swap and composite transformation. It is integrated directly with Transformers by Hugging Face's and various NLP libraries. It provides pretrained data models like BERT, wordCNN, and wordLSTM on popular datasets like Rotten Tomatoes Movie review, quora question paraphrase, and many more. The idea behind TextAtaack is to train various attacks for different language models on popular datasets. The command-line API is used to allow users to specify attack recipe and test it on different models and datasets. We implemented TextAttack framework to compare some of the effective text-based adversarial methods like TextFooler, Deepwordbug, and hotflip. We explain the step-by-step command line arguments to implement TextAttack for comparing various attacks supported by them.

Strategy behind TextAttack:

1. The framework is designed to compare various NLP attacks on standard models and datasets.
2. Time efficacy by simply using the command-line API for different attacks and thus forbidding users from implementing previous work which is a tedious and error-prone task.

Run an attack (Command)

$$\textit{textattack attack --model lstm-mr --recipe textfooler --num-examples 300} \tag{13.18}$$

View any dataset details (Command)

$$\textit{textattack peek-dataset --dataset-from-huggingface mr} \tag{13.19}$$

We have compared TextFooler, DeepwordBug, and TextBugger attacks using TextAttack framework to show the effectiveness of each attack. Researchers can easily replicate the recipe name (attack name) and model name in Command in Equation (13.19) to compare various attacks for further scope.

The analysis in Table 13.5 shows that TextFooler has the highest attack success rate among other popular attack methods and achieves a significant success rate of 90% on BERT model and 94% on Roberta-base model, both of which are widely used language models.

13.4.5   Adversarial Attacks Methods Based on Language Models

Fursov *et al.* [31] proposed a strong and efficient adversarial model DILMA (Differentiable Language Model Attack) which make use of pre-trained language models to make robust adversarial attack model. It uses MLM (masked to masked) model used in BERT [32]. The method includes many hyperparameters like learning rate (α) and coefficient (β) in loss function, which are missing in [12]. Due to pretrained language models, it can perform efficiently on variety of datasets.

Garg *et al.* [33] generated grammatically correct and semantically similar adversarial instances. The technique is based on BERT and named as BAE (BERT-based Adversarial examples) where the masked token is replaced by another word which is similar or related to the words in the left and right position. This is possible due to the context consideration feature of BERT which automatically replaces the word with the word based on the context.

Li *et al.* [34] proposed BERT-attack model which generates adversarial examples to attack BERT model using its own pretrained model. It is based on white box attacking model. It got a green signal by taking into considerations major qualities required to generate adversarial attacks. Many existing models like [19] fail to keep one of the factors of preserving grammaticality and semantic nature of output with input. Since BERT is highly trained language model which makes it more challenging to get attacked but besides that it is based on masked language model technique making it to generate semantic consistent perturbed words for attack. The model initially finds the most vulnerable words and then substituting semantically correct and similar word against it to create adversarial instances. Attacking language models is challenging because of its robustness and is an emerging topic of research. The method got better results than [18].

13.4.6   Adversarial Attacks on Recommender Systems

One of the most popular applications of NLP is recommender systems. Hardly any application of NLP is left which is not affected by adversarial attacks. Recommender systems are widely used today and so are prone to adversarial attacks. The designing of adversarial attacks in recommendation systems are far more challenging and difficult then in image classification domain or any other NLP domain. Many of such systems are based on collaborative filtering where similar users rate items in similar fashion. Thus, the dependency among each other helps in making the system robust.

13.4.6.1   *Random Attack*

This type of attack creates a fake profile and selects randomly the items to rate and their ratings. There can be a nuke attack where the rating of an item can be reduced or can be push attack where the predicted rating of an item can be increased. Lam *et al.* [39] used this

Table 13.5 Comparison of various attacks using TextAttack framework.

Dataset	Rotten tomatoes movie review								
Samples taken	300								
Text attack	TextFooler			DeepwordBug			TextBugger		
Model Trained	LSTM	Roberta-Base	Bert-base-uncased	LSTM	Roberta-Base	Bert-base-uncased	LSTM	Roberta-Base	Bert-base-uncased
Original Accuracy	78%	85%	81.67%	78%	85.65%	81.67%	78%	85.65%	81.67%
Accuracy under attack	0.67%	5%	8.0%	13.67%	19.65%	22.0%	16.67%	28.33%	30.67%
Attack Success Rate	99.15%	94%	90.01%	82.48 %	77%	73.06 %	78.63%	66.93%	62.45%
No. of successful attacks	232	242	221	193	198	179	184	172	153
No. of failed attacks	2	15	24	41	59	66	50	85	92
No. of skipped attacks	66	43	55	66	43	55	66	43	55

Table 13.6 Sample output from various text attacks during execution.

Text attack	Movie review (Negative (NEG) ↔ Positive (POS))
TextFooler [27]	Bears could be even *worse* than I imagined a movie could ever be (negative -98%)
	Bears could be even *greatest* than I imagined a movie could ever be (positive -53%)
DeepwordBug [29]	More *trifle* than triumph (negative - 73%)
	More *Btrifle* than triumph (positive - 63%)
TextBugger [26]	Overburdened with complicated plotting and banal dialogue (negative - 97% →failed)

attack by creating fake users profiles and the ratings is the result of distribution of the user ratings of the dataset. The process is called shilling.

13.4.6.2   Average Attack

Like random attack but the ratings are created by the mean of each item. The shill should be aware of the average ratings of each item. Lam *et al.* [39] showed that this attack is more effective then random attack.

13.4.6.3   Bandwagon Attack

In this type of attack, only limited popular items are given high ratings [40]. This type of attack is based on zip's law that some limited numbers of items are more likely to get in users' profile.

13.4.6.4   Reverse Bandwagon Attack

This is just opposite of bandwagon attack [40]. In this technique, some of most non-popular items are given low ratings.

Christakopoulou *et al.* [35] provide an insight to how fake user profiles can hamper the efficiency of any recommender system. This paper addresses the issues with collaborative recommender systems in which similar users tend to rate items in a similar way. This interdependency makes the attacks cascading by affecting the single user and influencing many others. An oblivious recommender is considered which is unaware of the adversarial attack and is based on white box attack model. The model is formed on the Min-Max game theory where there are two players, one is rec called recommender system and other is adv, i.e., adversary. Both the players have the loss function which needs to be minimized as

$$\theta_R^{t+1} = \underset{\theta_R}{\operatorname{argmin}} f_R(\theta_R, Z^t)$$

(13.20)

$$Z^{t+1} = argmin_{\theta_Z} f_A(\theta_R^t, Z^t) \qquad (13.21)$$

The relying on GAN [36] leads to solving of the Min-Max problem.

Mobasher *et al.* [40] proposed different ways to detect fake user profile which is commonly called injection attack. The attributes are designed for reverse bandwagon attack because of its effectiveness. Mean time interval (MTI) which is used to fetch the rating time interval between two ratings so that the generic and the fake profile can be distinguished. Weighted User Rating Distribution (WURD) emphasizes on the probability if low ratings of items. User similarity Distribution Center (USDC) is also used to distinguish fake user to generic user.

13.5   Adversarial Attacks on Cloud-Based Platforms

In the recent years, ML and DNN techniques have become a lifeline for many companies like Amazon, Google, and Microsoft for their cloud-based services. To meet the requirements of users of not having ample amount of resources to complete their tasks efficiently and effectively, cloud-based services have proved to be flexible and cost-effective solution. ML cloud-based service (MLaaS) is getting recognition as unfailing solution to many real-time applications. These applications typically utilize ML and DNNs techniques to perform some tasks like classification and detection. The key is in the fact that user need not to bother about the actual computation. Amazon's Amazon ML, Microsoft's Azure ML, IBM's Watson, and Google Cloud ML are some of the leading providers of MLaaS services. But it is quite possible for an adversary to steal models from cloud-based platforms, by continuously querying the public prediction API with malicious inputs. Tramer *et al.* [45] demonstrated various model extraction attacks which hamper the confidentiality in ML models. Since the model and the trained data is black box, the adversary's goal is to extract near-equivalent model by extracting exact parameters like decision tree paths. Dmitrenko *et al.* [46] also proposed a model extraction attack that plays around hyperparameters selected for attacker model. The mimicked model is an improvement to many existing attacks [45, 47]. Besides the model, the data used for training the models can also be leaked through query process. Shokri *et al.* [14] proposed an attack method based on membership inference which determines whether the training set has data records. Long *et al.* [47] also discuss about various membership attacks existing in overfitting and generalized models. Most of these methods are not worth for real world scenarios as they mainly target small-scale ML models like support vector machines, decision trees, and massive prediction queries query.

Yu *et al.* [48] proposed a FeatureFool attack model thereby decreasing the queries as compared to the previous attack models. The transfer framework for the FeatureFool attack is shown in Figure 13.6.

In FeatureFool framework, the unlabeled dataset is generated for a specific domain and the victim model is queried with the dataset generated. The labeled dataset is trained by the new substitute model which consists of copied layers and layers from the new substitute model.

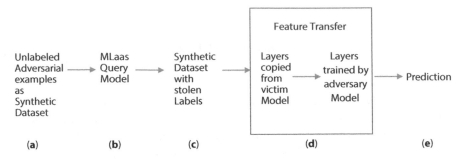

Figure 13.6 Overview of FeatureFool framework [48]. (a) generate unlabeled dataset. (b) query victim model. (c) labeled adversarial examples with the output of the victim model. (d) training substitute model with synthetic dataset. (e) use model for prediction.

The predictions are generated which matches the performance of the victim model. The proposed method was able to reduce the queries to ~3K from ~ 112K [45] and 100M [47].

The paper of Goodman *et al.* [49, 50] focuses on the Cloud Vision API of some popular cloud-based companies and reviews the attacks against the ML applications and describes effective defenses and mitigation.

13.6   Conclusion

Despite of highly effective and efficient ML techniques, the applications based on these techniques are vulnerable to many adversarial attacks which can lead to dangerous consequences. The chapter is basically the in-depth review of various types of adversarial attacking techniques popular among various ML techniques in various domains like Images, NLP, language models, recommendation systems, and various cloud-based services. The unique part of this paper is the thorough review of various attacks on popular language models and recommendation systems and analysis of some of the popular text-based attacks has been done. Upon in depth review, it has been observed that the wings of adversarial attacks are slowly spawning over cloud-based services and more often real-time applications.

References

1. Otter, D.W., Medina, J.R., Kalita, J.K., A survey of the usages of deep learning for natural language processing. *IEEE Trans. Neural Networks Learn. Syst.*, 32, 604–624, 2020.
2. Zhang, L., Wang, S., Liu, B., Deep learning for sentiment analysis: A survey. *Wiley Interdiscip. Rev.: Data Min. Knowl. Discovery*, 8, 4, e1253, 2018.
3. Wu, W. and Yan, R., Deep chit-chat: Deep learning for chatbots, in: *Proceedings of the 42nd International ACM SIGIR Conference on Research and Development in Information Retrieval*, 2019, July, pp. 1413–1414.
4. Esteva, A., Robicquet, A., Ramsundar, B., Kuleshov, V., DePristo, M., Chou, K., Dean, J., A guide to deep learning in healthcare. *Nat. Med.*, 25, 1, 24–29, 2019.
5. Papernot, N. *et al.*, Practical Black-Box Attacks Against Machine Learning, in: *Proceedings of the 2017 ACM on Asia Conference on Computer and Communications Security. ASIA CCS '17*, ACM, pp. 506–519, 2017.

6. Kurakin, A., Goodfellow, I., Bengio, S., Adversarial examples in the physical world. *International Conference on Learning Representations. arXiv preprint arXiv:abs/1607.02533*, 2016.

7. Kurakin, A., Goodfellow, I., Bengio, S., Adversarial machine learning at scale. *International Conference on Learning Representations. arXiv preprint arXiv:abs/1611.01236*, 2016.

8. Fischer, V., Kumar, M.C., Metzen, J.H., Brox, T., Adversarial examples for semantic image segmentation. *International Conference on Learning Representations. arvix*, abs/1703.01101, 2017.

9. Krizhevsky, A., Sutskever, I., Hinton, G.E., Imagenet classification with deep convolutional neural networks, in: *Advances in neural information processing systems*, pp. 1097–1105, 2012.

10. Liang, B. *et al.*, Deep text classification can be fooled. *Proceedings of the 27th International Joint Conference on Artificial Intelligence*. AAAI Press, *arXiv preprint arXiv:1704.08006*, 4208–4215, 2017, 9780999241127.

11. Szegedy, C., Zaremba, W., Sutskever, I., Bruna, J., Erhan, D., Goodfellow, I., Fergus, R., Intriguing properties of neural networks. 2nd International Conference on Learning Representations, {ICLR} 2014, *CoRR, arXiv preprint arXiv:1312.6199*, abs/1312.6199, 2013.

12. Goodfellow, I.J., Shlens, J., Szegedy, C., Explaining and harnessing adversarial examples. *CoRR, arXiv preprint arXiv:1412.6572*, abs/1412.6572, 2014.

13. Liu, Y., Chen, X., Liu, C., Song, D., Delving into transferable adversarial examples and black-box attacks. *Arvix, arXiv preprint arXiv:1611.02770*, abs/1611.02770, 2016.

14. Shokri, R., Stronati, M., Song, C., Shmatikov, V., Membership inference attacks against machine learning models, in: *2017 IEEE Symposium on Security and Privacy (SP)*, IEEE, pp. 3–18, May, 2017.

15. Nazemi, A. and Fieguth, P., Potential adversarial samples for white-box attacks. *Arvix, arXiv preprint arXiv:1912.06409*, abs/1912.06409, 2019.

16. Biggio, B., Nelson, B., Laskov, P., Support vector machines under adversarial label noise, in: *Asian conference on machine learning*, pp. 97–112, November, 2011.

17. Biggio, B., Nelson, B., Laskov, P., Poisoning attacks against support vector machines. *Proceedings of the 29th International Conference on International Conference on Machine Learning, June 2012*, Omnipress, *arXiv preprint arXiv:1206.6389*, 1467–1474, 2012.

18. Huq, A. and Pervin, M., Adversarial Attacks and Defense on Textual Data: A Review. *Arvix, arXiv preprint arXiv:2005.14108*, abs/2005.14108, 2020.

19. Ebrahimi, J., Rao, A., Lowd, D., Dou, D., Hotflip: White-box adversarial examples for text classification. Association for Computational Linguistics. *Proceedings of the 56th Annual Meeting of the Association for Computational Linguistics, arXiv preprint arXiv:1712.06751*, 31–36, 2017.

20. Zang, Y., Qi, F., Yang, C., Liu, Z., Zhang, M., Liu, Q., Sun, M., Word-level Textual Adversarial Attacking as Combinatorial Optimization, in: *Proceedings of the 58th Annual Meeting of the Association for Computational Linguistics*, pp. 6066–6080, July, 2020.

21. Papernot, N., McDaniel, P., Swami, A., Harang, R., Crafting adversarial input sequences for recurrent neural networks, in: *MILCOM 2016-2016 IEEE Military Communications Conference*, IEEE, pp. 49–54, November, 2016

22. Alzantot, M., Sharma, Y., Elgohary, A., Ho, B.J., Srivastava, M., Chang, K.W., Generating natural language adversarial examples. Association for Computational Linguistics. *Proceedings of the 2018 Conference on Empirical Methods in Natural Language Processing, arXiv preprint arXiv:1804.07998*, 2890–2896, 2018.

23. Iyyer, M., Wieting, J., Gimpel, K., Zettlemoyer, L., Adversarial example generation with syntactically controlled paraphrase networks. Association for Computational Linguistics. *Proceedings of the 2018 Conference of the North American Chapter of the Association for Computational Linguistics: Human Language Technologies, arXiv preprint arXiv:1804.06059*, 1, 1875–1885, 2018.

24. Papernot, N., McDaniel, P., Jha, S., Fredrikson, M., Celik, Z.B., Swami, A., The limitations of deep learning in adversarial settings, in: *2016 IEEE European symposium on security and privacy (EuroS&P)*, IEEE, pp. 372–387, March, 2016.

25. Hochreiter, S. and Schmidhuber, J., Long short-term memory. *Neural Comput.*, 9, 8, 1735–1780, 1997.

26. Li, J., Ji, S., Du, T., Li, B., Wang, T., Textbugger: Generating adversarial text against real-world applications. *CoRR, arXiv preprint arXiv:1812.05271*, abs/1812.05271, 2018.

27. Jin, D., Jin, Z., Zhou, J.T., Szolovits, P., Is bert robust? natural language attack on text classification and entailment. *Proceedings of the AAAI Conference on Artificial Intelligence, arXiv preprint arXiv:1907.11932*, 34, 8018–8025, 2019.

28. Xu, J. and Du, Q., TextTricker: Loss-based and gradient-based adversarial attacks on text classification models. *Eng. Appl. Artif. Intell.*, 92, 103641, 2020.

29. Gao, J., Lanchantin, J., Soffa, M.L., Qi, Y., Black-box generation of adversarial text sequences to evade deep learning classifiers, in: *2018 IEEE Security and Privacy Workshops (SPW)*, IEEE, pp. 50–56, 2018, May

30. Morris, J.X., Lifland, E., Yoo, J.Y., Qi, Y., TextAttack: A framework for adversarial attacks in natural language processing. Proceedings of the 2020 EMNLP, *Arvix, arXiv preprint arXiv:2005.05909*, abs/2005.05909, 119–126, 2020.

31. Fursov, I., Zaytsev, A., Kluchnikov, N., Kravchenko, A., Burnaev, E., Differentiable Language Model Adversarial Attacks on Categorical Sequence Classifiers. *Arvix, arXiv preprint arXiv:2006.11078*, abs/2006.11078, 2020.

32. Devlin, J., Chang, M.W., Lee, K., Toutanova, K., Bert: Pre-training of deep bidirectional transformers for language understanding. Proceedings of NAACL-HLT 2019, *arXiv preprint arXiv:1810.04805*, 4171–4186, 2018.

33. Garg, S. and Ramakrishnan, G., BAE: BERT-based Adversarial Examples for Text Classification. *Proceedings of the 2020 Conference on Empirical Methods in Natural Language Processing (EMNLP)*, Association for Computational Linguistics, *arXiv preprint arXiv:2004.01970*, 6174–6181, 2020.

34. Li, L., Ma, R., Guo, Q., Xue, X., Qiu, X., Bert-attack: Adversarial attack against bert using bert. *Proceedings of the 2020 Conference on Empirical Methods in Natural Language Processing*, Association for Computational Linguistics, *arXiv preprint arXiv:2004.09984*, 6193–6202, 2020.

35. Christakopoulou, K. and Banerjee, A., Adversarial attacks on an oblivious recommender, in: *Proceedings of the 13th ACM Conference on Recommender Systems*, 2019, September, pp. 322–330.

36. Goodfellow, I., Pouget-Abadie, J., Mirza, M., Xu, B., Warde-Farley, D., Ozair, S., Bengio, Y., Generative adversarial nets, in: *Advances in neural information processing systems*, pp. 2672–2680, 2014.

37. Li, B., Wang, Y., Singh, A., Vorobeychik, Y., Data poisoning attacks on factorization-based collaborative filtering, in: *Advances in neural information processing systems*, pp. 1885–1893, 2016.

38. Fang, M., Yang, G., Gong, N.Z., Liu, J., Poisoning attacks to graph-based recommender systems, in: *Proceedings of the 34th Annual Computer Security Applications Conference*, 2018, December, pp. 381–392.

39. Lam, S.K. and Riedl, J., Shilling recommender systems for fun and profit, in: *Proceedings of the 13th international conference on World Wide Web*, 2004, May, pp. 393–402.

40. Mobasher, B., Burke, R., Bhaumik, R., Sandvig, J.J., Attacks and remedies in collaborative recommendation. *IEEE Intell. Syst.*, 22, 3, 56–63, 2007.

41. Goel, P., Goel, V., Gupta, A.K., Multilingual Data Analysis to Classify Sentiment Analysis for Tweets Using NLP and Classification Algorithm, in: *Advances in Data and Information Sciences*, pp. 271–280, Springer, Singapore, 2020.

42. Verma, P. and Verma, A., Accountability of NLP Tools in Text Summarization for Indian Languages. *J. Sci. Res.*, *64*, 1, 258–263, 2020.

43. Azevedo, P., Leite, B., Cardoso, H.L., Silva, D.C., Reis, L.P., Exploring NLP and Information Extraction to Jointly Address Question Generation and Answering, in: *IFIP International Conference on Artificial Intelligence Applications and Innovations*, 2020, June, Springer, Cham, pp. 396–407.

44. Saidani, N., Adi, K., Allili, M.S., A Semantic-Based Classification Approach for an Enhanced Spam Detection. *Comput. Secur.*, *94*, 101716, 2020.

45. Tramer, F., Zhang, F., Juels, A., Reiter, M.K., Ristenpart, T., Stealing ` machine learning models via prediction apis, in: *25th USENIX Security Symposium (USENIX Security 16)*, pp. 601–618, 2016.

46. Dmitrenko, A. *et al.*, *Dnn model extraction attacks using prediction interfaces*, Aalto University. School of Science, 2018.

47. Long, Y., Bindschaedler, V., Wang, L., Bu, D., Wang, X., Tang, H., Gunter, C.A., Chen, K., Understanding membership inferences on well generalized learning models, *ArXiv*, arXiv preprint arXiv:1802.04889, *ArXiv*, abs/1802.04889, 2018.

48. Yu, H. *et al.*, Cloudleak: Large-scale deep learning models stealing through adversarial examples. *Proceedings of Network and Distributed Systems Security Symposium (NDSS)*, 2020.

49. Goodman, D., Transferability of adversarial examples to attack cloud-based image classifier service. *arXiv*, abs/2001.03460, 2020.

50. Goodman, D. and Xin, H., Attacking and defending machine learning applications of public cloud. *Arvix*, *ArXiv preprint arXiv:2008.02076*, abs/2008.02076, 2020.

14

Protocols for Cloud Security

Weijing You[1]* and Bo Chen[2]

[1]School of Computer Science and Technology, University of Chinese Academy of Sciences (UCAS), Beijing, China
[2]Department of Computer Science, Michigan Technological University, Houghton, MI, United States

Abstract

Nowadays, cloud service providers (CSPs), like Amazon, allow users to outsource the entire IT infrastructures to significantly reduce their cost for running businesses. This, however, brings severe security concerns due to the out-of-control nature of the cloud services. To ensure cloud security, various protocols have been designed in the literature. In this chapter, we review protocols for securing cloud data in two categories: the secure cloud computing and the secure cloud storage. For the secure computing, we review a few protocols which can support trusted computation in the untrusted cloud environment, including the homomorphic encryption, the searchable encryption, the ciphertext-policy attribute-based encryption, and the secure multiparty computation. For the secure cloud storage, we review protocols ensuring confidentiality, integrity, and reliability of the cloud data, which are defined as proofs of encryption (PoEs), proofs of storage (PoSs), and proofs of reliability, respectively. In addition, we briefly review protocols for securing cloud systems. Lastly, we discuss some potential future directions for cloud security.

Keywords: Cloud security, homomorphic encryption, searchable encryption, secure multi-party computation, ciphertext-policy attribute-based encryption, proofs of encryption, proofs of storage, proofs of reliability

14.1 Introduction

The cloud computing services have been widely used nowadays. The public cloud service providers (CSPs), e.g., Amazon, Microsoft Azure, iCloud, and Google Drive, provide software-, platform-, or infrastructure-as-a-service online. The cloud customers (individuals, companies, and organizations) host applications or store data in the public clouds by purchasing customized cloud computing and cloud storage services conveniently and economically. According to IDC [1], nearly half of data will be stored in the clouds by 2025.

The cloud computing has brought immense conveniences and benefits to the society. This, however, raises significant security concerns which unseen before. In the cloud

---

*Corresponding author: youweijing16@mails.ucas.ac.cn

Rajdeep Chakraborty, Anupam Ghosh and Jyotsna Kumar Mandal (eds.) Machine Learning Techniques and Analytics for Cloud Security, (293–312) © 2022 Scrivener Publishing LLC

outsourcing, all the resources including the system and the data have been hosted by the CSPs. This implies that the cloud users have effectively lost their control over their critical resources. Compared to hosting everything locally, severe security concerns arise. First, when operating resources locally, the users are clear that each operation (or execution) has been run correctly; on the contrary, when operating remotely, how can the users ensure that each operation will be run exactly as they wish? Second, when performing computation locally, the data are located inside the bound of the organization (e.g., behind the firewall); but in cloud computing, when performing computation in a remote site, how can the users ensure that the sensitive data being processed will not be leaked? Third, when storing the resources locally, the users are sure that the resources are well maintained and protected according to a certain policy or a regulation; however, when storing resources in the remote clouds, how can the users be convinced that all the valuable resources are stored, maintained, and protected in a desired manner? This chapter thus aims to discuss the security concerns and the known protocols for cloud, including security protocols for both cloud data and cloud systems. Considering data is more significant for machine learning, we mainly center around cloud data security from two dimensions, namely, the cloud computing and cloud storage.

For cloud computing in the untrusted public clouds, the most significant issue is how to perform computation securely without leaking the sensitive or even mission critical data. This issue is especially important for strictly regulated industries such as health care and digital economy. Therefore, the sensitive data which will be processed in the clouds should be encrypted. But performing computation over the encrypted data would be challenging since encryption may have removed the effective information from the data. The homomorphic encryption [2] can support computation over the encrypted data, so that the final results can be obtained by the cloud users through performing decryption directly. This can enable various operations, e.g., predictive analytics and model training, on the encrypted data. In addition, the searchable encryption (SE) [3] allows the cloud users to conduct searching over the encrypted cloud data, without leaking the underlying sensitive data to the clouds. To facilitate data sharing in cloud, the cloud users adopt attribute-based encryption (ABE), especially the ciphertext-policy ABE (CP-ABE) [4] to allow a group of users to effectively decrypt specific ciphertext when the attributes of their decryption keys match attribute set of the encrypted data. Another line of promising protocols, the multi-party computation (MPC) [5], allows cloud users to collaboratively compute a function based on individual inputs while keeping those inputs private to each other. This essentially enables a secure cloud collaboration on computing in a privacy-preserved manner.

For cloud-based storage outsourcing, a significant obstacle which prevents data owners from outsourcing their sensitive data is that they are not able to obtain a guarantee that the outsourced data will be correctly stored and maintained by the CSPs over time. This guarantee should cover the typical CIA, namely, confidentiality, integrity, and availability. A set of security protocols have been designed to achieve these guarantees, including proofs of encryption (PoEs), secure message-locked encryption (MLE), proofs of storage (PoSs), proofs of ownership (PoWs), and proofs of reliability. PoEs [6–8] are protocols by which the data owner can effectively verify whether the cloud server has encrypted the outsourced data following special encryption algorithms, and hence, confidentiality of the outsourced data can be ensured. MLE [9–11] protocols allow the users to encrypt their outsourced data without hindering the deduplication. PoSs [12–14] ensure that the outsourced data will not be modified over time, which is usually achieved by conducting a periodical integrity checking on the outsourced data. PoWs [15, 16] are protocols by which the cloud server can efficiently verify whether a cloud user really owns a claimed file. Proofs of reliability include proofs of replications, co-residency checking, and geolocation of cloud data. Checking co-residency ensures the cloud data are stored redundantly in multiple cloud servers, and any data corruption will be detected and repaired in a timely manner. This renders the outsourced data recoverable and available at any point over time. Geolocation of cloud data is a protocol [17] respecting to recently proposed laws and regulations pertained to the cloud storage and use of data, in which cloud customers can determine where to distribute their outsourced data to avoid legal issues.

For securing cloud systems, the user and corresponding VMs placed in the cloud should be properly managed, which can be accomplished by applying access control and protocols for securely initiating VMs remotely.

Chapter Organization. The rest of the chapter is organized as follows: We review the typical systems and adversarial model in Section 14.2. We then describe protocols for security of cloud data, including secure cloud computing and secure cloud storage, in Section 14.3 and Section 14.4, respectively. Protocols for ensuring security of cloud systems are presented in Section 14.5. Finally, we discuss future research for cloud security in Section 14.6 and conclude in Section 14.7.

14.2   System and Adversarial Model

14.2.1   System Model

A typical cloud computing system contains two parties: the cloud server (i.e., the CSPs) and the cloud users (i.e., the customers which use the cloud services). The cloud server provides various services, including cloud computing and cloud storage, to the cloud users. The cloud users purchase customized services from the CSPs according to their requirements and outsource their computations and/or data to the cloud server. Especially, a cloud user who uploads data to the cloud server will be further considered as a "data owner" of the data. The cloud server and the cloud users connect with each other via the Internet, and the communication channel is always protected by SSL/TLS.

14.2.2   Adversarial Model

Each party in clouds, i.e., the cloud server and the cloud user, may misbehave as elaborated in the following:

The cloud server. The cloud server is usually not trustworthy in practice. In general, its adversarial behaviors can be classified as follows:

- *Cheap-and-lazy* [6–8]. This type of attacker is motivated by economic intentions. Specifically, "cheap" here means the cloud server may be incapable to implement adequate security measures, and "lazy" indicates that the cloud server may discard security requirements from cloud users to reduce cost of running cloud services. The cheap-and-lazy cloud server will misbehave when they could gain more economical advantages than behaving honestly;

- *Honest-but-curious* [16, 18]. This type of cloud server is the most common attacker in the literature. It takes economic gains and reputation into account. The cloud server will "honestly" respond to and execute operations required by cloud users but is "curious" about the outsourced data. The honest-but-curious cloud server attempts to obtain user data by all means as long as its misbehavior will not be discovered by the cloud users;
- *Malicious*. A malicious cloud server is the strongest attacker among the three types. When the cloud server is compromised by internal (e.g., the careless manager) or external attackers (e.g., the hackers), it will behave arbitrarily regardless of economic gains and reputation. The malicious cloud server aims at disturbing the cloud services.

The cloud user. The cloud users may not be honest either. In general, we can assume that a special type of cloud users, i.e., the data owners, are fully trusted, since they pay for resources in cloud computing and own the data outsourced to the cloud storage, and they do not have the motivation to cheat. However, the other cloud users, e.g., the subscribers in a content delivery network, may misbehave and, their adversarial behaviors can be classified as follows:

- *Semi-honest* (or a *passive attacker*). The semi-honest cloud user is assumed to gather information out of the protocol but does not deviate from the protocol execution;
- *Malicious* (or an *active attacker*). The malicious cloud user may arbitrarily deviate from the protocol specification for cheating.

14.3 Protocols for Data Protection in Secure Cloud Computing

One of the most significant products for commercial clouds is the cloud computing, which provides various computational platforms and resources. Typically, in the machine learning area, the cloud users outsource large volume of data and heavy computations to the cloud server for accelerating processing with rather low cost. As the public cloud providers may not be trusted, the most critical security concern for the cloud users is losing data when using public cloud services. Therefore, to protect confidentiality of their sensitive data in cloud computing, the outsourced data should be encrypted before uploading, and after the data are processed, the results should be encrypted as well. To support processing of encrypted outsourced data, various special encryption algorithms have been designed, and special form of encryption algorithms are used to support operations on encrypted cloud data, including 1) the homomorphic encryption, which supports operation on encrypted data; 2) the SE, which enables efficient searching on encrypted data; 3) the CP-ABE, in which the data is encrypted based on an access tree and only the key generated from an attributes set matching this access tree can be used to decrypt the ciphertext; and 4) MPC, which supports operations on encrypted data shares. These special encryption algorithms will be introduced in detail in the following.

14.3.1   Homomorphic Encryption

Homomorphic encryption is such an encryption with a special feature that allows users to calculate the encrypted data directly, and the result after calculation is still in an encrypted form. When the encrypted result is decrypted, the output is the same as if performing the same calculation on the unencrypted data. Therefore, the homomorphic encryption can be used to preserve data confidentiality in cloud computing. Specifically, the user can encrypt their data and outsource the encrypted data to the cloud server for processing without revealing the original data and internal state. The general workflow of secure cloud computing with homomorphic encryption enabled is shown in Figure 14.1.

- The cloud user encrypts outsourced data (f) to ciphertexts (C) by using the homomorphic encryption[1] with its own secret (k). C will be sent to the cloud server.
- The cloud server processes C, e.g., adds, multiplies, classifies, performs data training, to obtain the results in an encrypted manner (M). M will be sent to the cloud user.
- The cloud user decrypts M with k to obtain the final computation result he/she intends (m). By using the homomorphic encryption, m will be the same to the result which is generated through applying the same procession on f directly.

The homomorphic encryption can be categorized as *fully homomorphic* (FHE), *leveled fully*, *somewhat homomorphic*, and *partially homomorphic* encryption. The well-known encryption cryptosystems, e.g., the unpadded RSA, the ElGamal, and the Goldwasser-Micali encryptions, are typical partially homomorphic cryptosystems which support evaluation of limited types of circuits, e.g., addition or multiplication, which are far from applicable. FHE cryptosystems, which allow evaluations on arbitrary circuits of unbounded depth, such that have great practical implications in the context of cloud computing. However, FHE suffers from performance problem. The Gentry-Halevi implementation of Gentry's original cryptosystem shown that it will consume about 30 minutes for per basic bit operation [19], which is unacceptable in practice.

The latest generation FHE, e.g., the CKKS scheme [20] is focused as a solution for secure outsourced machine learning, in which the privacy of input data and output model should be protected at cost of modest additional overhead. The fundamental idea is trading accuracy for efficiency. Unlike previous generations of FHE, the latest generation FHE generates *approximately* the same answer rather than *exactly* the same answer from the encrypted data with what is computed from the unencrypted data. In this manner, the accuracy of results after approximating logistic regression based on the encrypted data is good enough for application, while the performance can be significantly improved.

---

[1] Note that the term *homomorphic encryption* here is used for referring to all encryption algorithms which have homomorphic property.

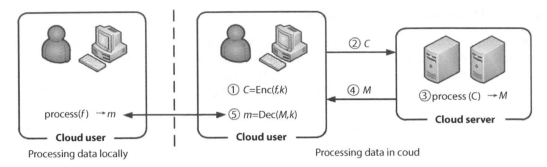

Figure 14.1 Homomorphic encryption in clouds.

14.3.2   Searchable Encryption

The SE [3] allows users to search over the encrypted data. In secure cloud computing, the cloud users can efficiently locate their encrypted data remotely without disclosing the underlying data to the untrusted cloud server by using SE. In general, SE schemes can be classified into two categories: the symmetric key–based SE (SKBSE) and the public key–based SE. The SKBSE is much more efficient and thus is more widely adopted in practice.

At a high level, data owners, i.e., the users who possess the data, extract distinct keywords from the original file (or file collections) and map each encrypted file blocks to each encrypted keyword. The authenticated or authorized user uses a special searching token derived from a secure trapdoor generation algorithm to perform searching over the encrypted data. The typical SE system works as shown in Figure 14.2.

- The cloud user, i.e., the data owner, extracts specific keywords from the file (f), and then encrypts f and derives searching tags (*tag*) for keywords using its own secret (*sk*). The encrypted file (C) and *tag* will be sent to and stored by the cloud server;
- The cloud user, i.e., data owner or its authorized user, generates secure searching token (*query*) and sends it to the cloud server, which will not leak the underlying f when performing searching;
- Based on *query* and C, the cloud server locates and replies specific encrypted file blocks (C_i) to the cloud user;
- The cloud user decrypts C_i using *sk* to obtain the underlying original file blocks (f_i).

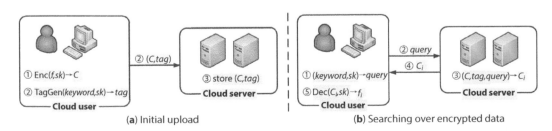

(a) Initial upload   **(b)** Searching over encrypted data

Figure 14.2 Searchable encryption in clouds.

14.3.3   Attribute-Based Encryption

Data sharing has been increasingly common in cloud computing. A straightforward solution for the data owner to share its data is to encrypt data using each subscriber's private key and to propagate the encrypted data to specific subscriber, which is far from efficient and is not applicable in cloud computing. An alternative solution is the ABE. As a sub-field of public key encryption, in ABE, the secret key of a user and corresponding ciphertext are associated to pre-defined attributes, such that when the set of attributes of key matches the attributes of ciphertext, this key can be used to decrypt this ciphertext. In this manner, the data can be efficiently shared to multiple users in one time with access control in place. Roughly speaking, ABE can be categorized into the CP-ABE [4] and the key-policy ABE (KP-ABE) [21]. Since the access strategies associated to private keys are controlled by the data owner in the CP-ABE, the CP-ABE is more adopted for sharing data in cloud computing.

The main idea of the CP-ABE is that the data owner uses the access tree, in which the access rules are organized in a tree structure, to encrypt data, and generates users' secret keys based on a set of attributes. By using the special secret key, the user could obtain specific data shared by the data owner. The CP-ABE works as follows (as shown in Figure 14.3).

- The data owner chooses and publishes system parameters, including a public key (PK) and a master key (MK);
- The data owner picks a polynomial for each node in a pre-defined attribute tree (T), which are contracted in a top-down manner.
- Start from the tree root that the data owner recursively evaluates each polynomial by taking parent of current node (C_y) as input (for the tree root, the input is "0"). The outsourced data is thus encrypted by the output of polynomial of the root of T. The encrypted data ($\tilde{C}$), T, the value of all polynomials of C_y will be uploaded to the cloud server as ciphertext;

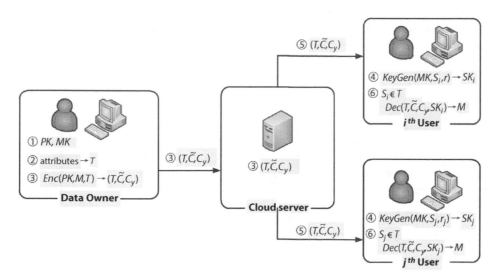

Figure 14.3 Ciphertext-policy attribute-based encryption in clouds.

- The user generates private key (*SK*) based on *MK*, a sub-tree of $T(S)$, which is a subset of attributes that are organized in a top-down manner, and a randomly picked value *r*;
- The user recursively takes ciphertext and *SK* as input to decrypt $\tilde{C}$. If *S* satisfies *T*, the user can successfully obtain the specific data. Otherwise, the decryption will fail.

In addition, the ability to decrypt the outsourced data can be delegated by re-randomizing the secret key, i.e., choosing another *r*, such that the delegated key is equivalent to the one generated by the data owner directly.

14.3.4 Secure Multi-Party Computation

The secure MPC [5] enables multiple parties to jointly evaluate their own inputs with preserving privacy of these inputs. Different from traditional cryptographic solutions, e.g., the homomorphic encryption, which focus on against the adversary outside the computing community, i.e., the untrusted cloud server and cloud users who do not participant in the computing, the secure MPC protects participants' privacy from each other. By using secure MPC in cloud computing, the cloud users and the cloud server, or cloud servers owned by different cloud users, can collaborate to perform computations without losing privacy.

The two-party computation (2PC) is a special case of MPC but there are major differences between the two groups of protocols. Besides different system settings, the techniques applied on 2PC may not work in the multi-party case. Two parties who take part in a 2PC protocol are called the "sender" and the "receiver", respectively. The two main building blocks in the typical 2PC protocol are the garbled circuit (GC) [5] and the oblivious transfer (OT) [22]. The main ingredient in a GC is a double-keyed symmetric encryption scheme, in which each party can securely obtain their own output from the randomized truth table corresponding to each gate in the circuit by taking their own inputs as keys. The truth table is initially encrypted and garbled by the sender. The one out of two OT protocol allows the sender who possesses two values, to send one query by the receiver without knowing what value is transferred, and the receiver could only learn the value it requests. The sender and receiver interact as shown in Figure 14.4.

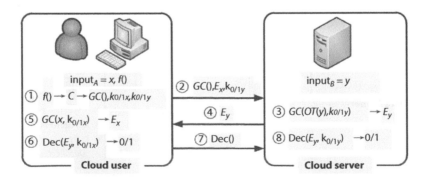

Figure 14.4 Two-party encryption.

- The sender first equally transfers the evaluation function ($f()$) to a circuit (C), which will be further processed to be a garbled circuit ($GC()$). Then the sender will select its own encoding keys out of two distinct keys ($k_{\{0/1\}x}$), and remains two keys for the receiver ($k_{\{0/1\}y}$);
- The sender encodes its inputs (x) through GC. The resulting E_x will be sent to the receiver with GC and $k_{\{0/1\}y}$;
- The receiver evaluates the circuit through OT and learns the encodings (E_y) corresponding to sender's and its own outputs;
- The receiver sends back E_y corresponding to sender's output;
- The sender computes his part of output (0/1) based on E_y and $k_{\{0/1\}x}$;
- The sender helps the receiver to map E_y to the final output (0/1).

Most MPC protocols, different from 2PC ones, require private channels unconditionally, and each party acts as a participant in a secret sharing process. Shamir secret sharing and additive secret sharing are the two most widely adopted secret sharing mechanisms in MPC.

14.4   Protocols for Data Protection in Secure Cloud Storage

The cloud storage is an instant and easy-to-use storage service for cloud users to store their data temporarily or permanently. Since the local copy usually will be deleted after being outsourced to the cloud server, it is paramount important to ensure the data are stored correctly in the clouds. In general, the security of data in cloud storage is captured by confidentiality, integrity, and reliability. For the data confidentiality, the users need to ensure that their data are really encrypted in the clouds. PoEs [6–8] are protocols to help users to ensure that the encryption process has been properly performed and the data is stored in an encrypted manner. The MLE [9–11] protocols are encryptions that enable secure deduplication, in which the storage space can be saved by detecting and removing redundant data, while the data confidentiality can be well protected. The integrity of cloud data can be attested through PoSs [12–14] and PoWs [15, 16, 18]. PoSs allow the cloud users to check integrity of data stored in the clouds. In addition, integrity checking is an effective strategy for the cloud server to obtain a PoW on a file during the client-side deduplication, which is what is known as "proofs of ownership". The reliability of data means the cloud data is continuously available over time, which can be guaranteed by placing multiple replicas of data in different cloud servers. Proofs of replications ensure the data are replicated multiple times in the clouds, and whether these replicas are stored exclusively at different disks can be tested through proofs of co-residence. In addition, since storing data in different countries may be subject to the laws of the jurisdiction where the data is stored, the cloud users will perform data geolocation to avoid legal issues.

14.4.1   Proofs of Encryption

For keeping client-side be lightweight, the cloud users may outsource encryption as well as the data being encrypted to the cloud. The cloud users, i.e., the data owner at this point, are trusted, while the cloud server is assumed to be *cheap-and-lazy*. To prevent the cloud server from fooling the cloud users that the encryption is performed while actually is not, the cloud users interact with the cloud server following PoEs [6–8].

Generally, the cloud server encrypts the outsourced data using encryptions from block-level and encapsulates each encrypted block through a time-consuming encoding algorithm. Due to computational limitation of the processor, as long as the algorithm is sufficiently expensive, it will be infeasible for the cloud server to store the original file and encryption key but instantly encrypt the original file to fool the cloud users that encryption was performed initially. The initial encryption process is shown in Figure 14.5a.

- The cloud user outsources the original file (f) and the encryption key (k) to the cloud server;
- The cloud server encrypts f with k to ciphertexts (C) through common encryption algorithms (e.g., AES-256);
- The cloud server seals C to an encapsulated format (H) through a time-consuming encapsulation algorithm (e.g., Butterfly transform in [6]);
- The cloud server computes the hash value (or a set of hash values) of H (or blocks in H), which is denoted by I, and sends I to the cloud user;
- The cloud user encrypts the entire file, or randomly selects several file blocks out of f, and encrypts them to ciphertext blocks (C_j) using k;
- The cloud user encapsulates the entire encrypted file, or randomly selected C_i into encapsulated block (H_i) using the same time-consuming encapsulation algorithm as what the cloud server should do;
- The cloud user computes the hash value of H_i and compares them to what received from the cloud server. When the two hash values of each selected file block are identical, the cloud user proceeds to the next step. Otherwise, the initial encryption is failed;
- The cloud user signs I with its signing private key, and the signed I will be sent to and stored by the cloud server (tag).
- The confidentiality of data then is ensured through checking integrity of the encapsulated data over time (as shown Figure 14.5b);
- The cloud user randomly picks c file blocks, i.e., $\{i_1, i_2,...,i_c\}$, for checking;
- The cloud server finds specific encapsulated file blocks according to $\{i_1, i_2,... ,i_c\}$, i.e., $\{H_i|1 \le i \le c\}$, and corresponding tag_i. The tuples (tag_i, Hi) are sent to the cloud user;
- The cloud user verifies whether the response is valid. Only when the cloud server can response correctly in time, the cloud server could be accepted as

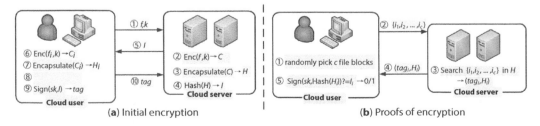

(a) Initial encryption   (b) Proofs of encryption

Figure 14.5 Wotrkflow of encryption checking.

Table 14.1 Performance comparison (*N* is exported data item).

		Butterfly [6]	**Hu *et al.* [7]**	**Jin *et al.* [8]**
Computation overhead	Sever-side	$O(NlogN)$	–	$O(N)C + O(Nm)$
	Client-side	$O(N)$	$O(N)C + O(Nm)$	$O(t)C + O(tm)$
Storage overhead	Server-side	$O(N)$	$O(N)$	$O(1)$
	Client-side	$O(N)$	$O(N)$	$O(1)$

an honest cloud server. The "correctly" here means the hash value of each returned encapsulated file blocks after decapsulation and decryption is identical to what is signed by the cloud user in the initial encryption phase.

The computational complexity of the three typical PoEs are listed in Table 14.1, in which *N* is the number of file blocks, *m* is the number of symbols in each file block, *C* is the time for generating a lookup table, which is used in encapsulation, and *t* is times of the encapsulation operation.

14.4.2   Secure Message-Locked Encryption

To protect the confidentiality of cloud data, the users may encrypt their data before outsourcing. However, encryption may create significant obstacle to deduplication, which is an effective and widely adopted technique in cloud storage to save storage by detecting and removing redundant data, resulting in a more economical and high-efficient cloud storage service. However, when two identical copies are encrypted into two different files using different encryption key, the deduplication cannot work. To deal with this conflict in deduplication-enabled cloud storage system, the user can encrypt their data using the MLE, in which the encryption key is derived from data itself. In this manner, as shown in Figure 14.6, if two encrypted files uploaded by different users are identical, then only one unique copy will be stored by the cloud server to avoid redundancy.

The naive MLE, i.e., the convergent encryption (CE) [23], has been proved to be vulnerable to the brute-force attack [24]. Fortunately, this attack has been mitigated in several secure MLE schemes at cost of requiring a trusted key server [10] or at least one valid data owner to stay online [11].

14.4.3   Proofs of Storage

The cloud data may be modified or corrupted due to careless management, various attacks, and unpredictable natural disasters, which is the most unacceptable issue for cloud users. PoSs [12–14] allow the client (i.e., the data owner) to ensure that the outsourced data is properly stored in cloud. Typical PoSs include the Provable Data Possession (PDP) [12] and the Proofs of Retrievability (PoRs) [13, 14].

PoSs are interactive protocols, and the main idea of them is to allow the data owner to embed secrets in the outsourced file, and then periodically checks existence of these secrets.

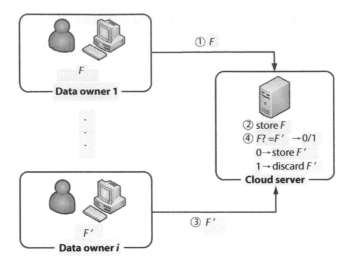

Figure 14.6 Sever-side deduplication.

Since the embedded secrets are distributed cross the entire file, and both content and distribution are unknown to the cloud server, it is infeasible for the untrusted cloud server to pass the integrity checking without possessing the entire file. Besides, considering performance, the data owner can perform spot checking, in which the data owner randomly selects several file blocks for integrity checking to efficiently detect corruption with a high probability rather than simply checks the entire file [12]. The integrity checking process includes the initial procession and PoSs is shown in Figure 14.7.

Before uploading the file to the cloud server, the cloud user pre-processes the outsourced file as follows (depicted by Figure 14.7a).

- The data owner splits the outsourced file (f) into several file blocks, i.e., $f = \{f_i | 1 \le i \le n\}$, and generates metadata for each f_i using its own secret (sk), which is denoted by tag_i.
- f and tag will be sent to and stored in the cloud server;
- Then, the cloud user can periodically check integrity of outsourced data by performing PoSs (as shown in Figure 14.7b);
- The data owner generates challenge (Q) and sends Q to the cloud server;

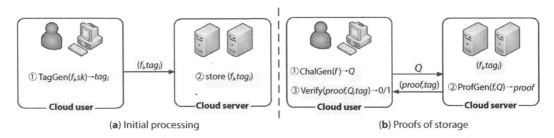

Figure 14.7 Workflow of integrity checking.

- The cloud server responses with integrity proofs (*proof*), which is supposed to be computed based on *f* and *Q*;
- Based on the received *proof, tag,* and locally stored *sk*, the data owner verifies the correctness of *proof.* If it is correct, then the data owner can be convinced that *f* is intact with a high confidence. Otherwise, *f* has been modified or corrupted.

14.4.4 Proofs of Ownership

The ownership of outsourced files is expected to be carefully managed in a secure cloud storage system. To correctly manage the ownership, the cloud server accepts a user as a valid data owner only after ensuring this user possesses the entire file. This assurance can be established by simply asking the user to upload the file, which, however, incurs significant bandwidth consumption. Fortunately, the communication overhead can be optimized by introducing PoWs, resulting in a more efficient cloud storage system supporting client-side deduplication (as shown in Figure 14.8). The process of PoW is similar to PoSs, but the roles of participants are inverse, that is, the cloud server is the verifier while the cloud users are the provers at this point.

Initially, the initial data owner who uploads the file for the first time is required to prepare PoW evidences as follows (depicted by "Initial upload" in Figure 14.8).

- The initial data owner asks the cloud server whether the file (*F*) has existed;
- The cloud server responses to the initial data owner that *F* has not existed;
- The initial data owner prepares metadata (M_F) of *F* to help the cloud server to do ownership checking;
- M_F and *F* will be uploaded to and stored by the cloud server.

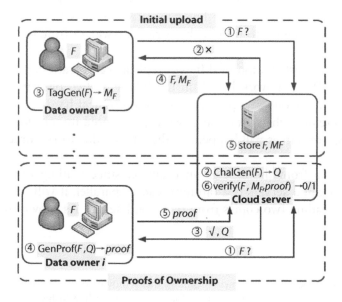

Figure 14.8 Client-side deduplication.

When another user comes and claims the ownership of F, which has existed in the cloud, the cloud server verifies the ownership of the cloud user as follows (depicted by "Proofs of Ownership" in Figure 14.8).

- The cloud server generates and sends ownership challenge (Q) to the prover, i.e., the cloud user;
- The prover computes ownership proof (*proof*) based on Q and F, which will be sent to the verifier, i.e., the cloud server;
- The cloud server checks the correctness of *proof* using M_F and Q. If the *proof* is correct, the cloud server adds the prover to the owner list of F.

14.4.5   Proofs of Reliability

Confidentiality and integrity checking ensure one data copy is stored properly in a protected format. However, storing data in the same cloud server is not secure enough for a cloud user. Once the cloud server is corrupted, confidentiality and integrity checking protocols do not provide capability for timely data recovery.

Proofs of reliability thus is designed to fill this gap. To enable data recovery from a potential corruption, the users may require the cloud server to store their outsourced data redundantly[2], e.g., through replication, and ensure the replication level through the proofs of replications [25]. In addition, these multiple data copies or shards need to be properly distributed to maintain the reliability level over time, which can be attested through proofs of co-residence [26, 27]. To avoid legal issues, the cloud users may determine whether their outsourced data is placed in a demanded place via data geolocation [17].

Similar to PoEs, in proofs of replications, the different replicas are generated in cloud through special encoding with different keys offered by the cloud users (as shown in Figure 14.9a). After that, for each replica, the cloud user challenges the cloud server with randomly selected file blocks. The computational complexity of encoding algorithms ensures that the cloud server has generated replicas honestly. Otherwise, the cloud server cannot respond to user with correct answer in time (as shown in Figure 14.9b).

Second, the proper distribution of different replicas can be attested through proofs of co-residence [26, 27]. They work based on the following two observations: 1) multiple instances running in a cloud server share the same physical hardware, including cache, bus, and disk. Therefore, when processing two copies stored in one cloud server, competition for hardware resources will happen; 2) the latency due to resources competition is distinguishable.

Take reading data from the disk as an example, since reading two different copies from two different cloud servers is a random read in parallel, it will be significant faster than sequentially reading two copies from one cloud server. As shown in Table 14.2, the

---

[2] Note that, different from deduplication in cloud storage that removing redundant data cross multiple users, reliability here means preparing multiple replicas for one user according to his/her security requirement, which usually is a paid service.

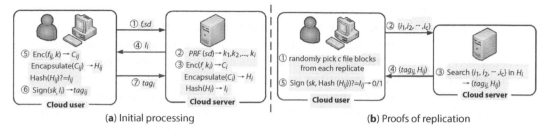

Figure 14.9 Workflow of replication checking.

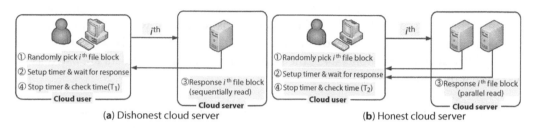

Figure 14.10 Workflow of proofs of co-residence.

Table 14.2 Benchmark of co-residence (two files) [26].

	15 MB	30 MB	50 MB	70 MB
Dishonest (two files stored in one disk)	8.87 ms	9.86 ms	11.25 ms	14.2 ms
Honest (two files stored in two disks)	6.41 ms	6.45 ms	7.97 ms	9.66 ms
Difference (%)	35.33	50.08	41.15	46.99

experimental results[3] show that it is easy for users to identify the dishonest cloud server (as shown in Figure 14.10a) and the honest (as shown in Figure 14.10b) one.

Note that, due to limitation of precision when measuring network based on response delay, geolocating cloud data cannot work well in proofs of co-residence, which requires ability to identify one cloud server from another. However, it is sufficient for cloud users to locate their data roughly to avoid legal issues from the region level.

Geolocating data in cloud implies two questions: 1) where the cloud server is, which stores the data; and 2) whether the data stored in located cloud server is intact. The first question usually turns to a network measurement problem, and the second question can be answered by proofs of integrity (as already introduced in Section 14.4.3).

---

[3] The experimental platform is a computer has an Intel Core i5 CPU 3.10 GHz and 4 GB RAM, over which running the Ubuntu 11.10 (32-bit). The two testing hard disks attached to the computer are Seagate ST3500418AS with 500 GB capability and 16 MB cache. The experiment was done on two files for 10 times.

The main idea of network measurement based on network delay is mapping the response latency to the physical distance. The network measurement methods can be broadly classified into two categorizations based on the topology of the network being measured. In a flatten network, e.g., networks in the United States and most European countries, where the network latency between two entities is strongly linear to the physical distance between them, the cloud user can build a mathematical model and geolocate the cloud server based on this model by taking the response time from the cloud server being tested as the input. The response time is recorded by the cloud user itself or multiple landmarks recruited by the cloud user. In a hierarchical network, e.g., network in the Mainland of China, the network latency between two entities is not strongly linear to the physical distance between them. In this case, the cloud user recruits multiple landmarks for testing, and approximates the location of the cloud server being tested to where the landmark is, which obtains the shortest response time. This rule is called "shortest-closest" principle. Combined with integrity checking introduced in Section 14.4.3, the steps of geolocating cloud data are listed as follows (shown in Figure 14.11).

- Suppose there are enough landmarks distributed evenly across the network. The cloud server recruits c landmarks and sends geolocation requests to them;
- Each landmark generates integrity challenge ($chal_i$, where $1 \le i \le c$), sends them to the cloud server, and starts a timer simultaneously;
- The cloud server computes and replies the integrity proof ($proof_i$) for each $chal_i$;
- Once receives $proof_i$, each landmark stops the timer, and the duration is recorded as T_i. The correctness of $proof_i$ will be verified at the same time;
- Each landmark sends T_i and integrity checking result to the cloud user;
- When detecting any corruption, the geolocation will terminate. Otherwise, the cloud user either geolocates the cloud server using the latency-distance

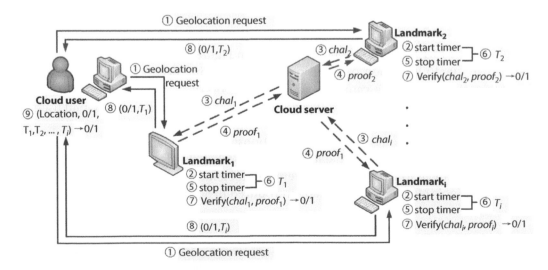

Figure 14.11 Geolocation of data in clouds.

model when testing a flatten network, or approximates the location of the cloud server to the landmark which obtains the shortest response time when testing a hierarchical network.

Note that, since the network is unstable and may be fluctuated due to the traffic jam, the poor connection, etc., the latency-distance model for a flatten network and location approximation in a hierarchical network could only provide a rough location of the cloud server being tested. Besides, the integrity checking is a probabilistic algorithm since it uses spot checking for performance. Therefore, geolocating data in cloud does not provide 100% correct geolocation result to the cloud user. But the confidence can be enhanced by performing geolocation repeatedly.

14.5   Protocols for Secure Cloud Systems

Besides the security of data in clouds, the security of the underlying cloud systems is significant as well. In general, the cloud system may be threatened by external and internal attackers. Access control can ensure that access to specific data is restricted to authenticated and authorized users and has been adopted by the cloud system to defend against various attacks.

From a high level, the access control mechanism usually includes three steps: identification, authentication, and authorization. The identification is to identify a user, e.g., with the help of the PKI. Authentication is an interactive process to verify a prover's claim about the identity, which can work based on what the prover knows, or what he/she has, or who he/she is. To achieve higher security levels, more advanced authentication techniques are expected, e.g., the two-factors authentications in which more than one authentication factor will be used together to validate a user. Existing authentication and authorization techniques can be directly used in the cloud computing systems for controlling access purpose.

Access control for the cloud users is not sufficient. Due to the out-of-place nature of clouds, virtual machines (VMs) belonging to different cloud users may be accessible to the cloud service manager as well, and the security of VMs is compromised. This problem is mitigated by using the hardware-driven Trusted Platform Module (TPM), resulting in a protocol enables secure VMs which are resistant to the cloud service manager [28]. The main idea of this protocol is to isolate a trusted execution environment using TPM, to establish trust between users and TPM, and to execute sensitive operations inside the TPM-enabled trusted execution environment. In this manner, the remote VM could run under full control of its owner, i.e., a cloud user, rather than the cloud service manager, and the security of VM can be strongly ensured at the hardware level.

14.6   Protocols for Cloud Security in the Future

Various advanced techniques are emerging in recent years, e.g., the artificial intelligence (AI), big data, the Internet of Thing (IoT), edge computing, quantum computing, and block-chain. As a critical network infrastructure, the cloud computing needs to be adapted to fulfill security requirements for those new applications.

In secure cloud computing, performance optimization is the first problem which needs to be resolved. For example, the homomorphic encryption enables data processions with privacy preserved at a great cost of performance. However, the computational power of peers in IoT network is always too limited to perform such expensive operations and lightweight cryptography is desired. In this case, the homomorphic encryption is not directly applicable to the IoT network. Second, input validation is not well addressed currently. As collaborations become increasingly common nowadays, accepting the input data from multiple parties to the same cloud computing unit without validation would be risky. The adversary may inject noises to disturb data processing, which is known as the "poisoning attack", causing problematic outputs even with the homomorphic encryption and the secure MPC in place. Therefore, how to efficiently validate input in the cloud setting deserves more attention.

For the SE in clouds, it has a trade-off among security, performance, and functionality. The efficient searchability comes at the cost of vulnerability to various attacks, in which the attackers can compromise the underlying databases and queries. Roughly speaking, these attackers can be classified into passive attackers and active attackers as defined in Section 14.2.2. The passive attackers passively exploit leakages which are allowed in SE and publicly available database, while the active attackers compromise the cloud server. Although several efforts [29] have been applied to mitigate these attacks by leveraging the hidden vector encryption (HVE) and bloom filter techniques, it still is an open question to design SEs that mitigate leakages as much as possible without significantly degrading performance and functionality.

Since most of existing security protocols for cloud data and cloud systems are based on computational security and fail to provide quantum security [30]. As the post-quantum era is coming, new security protocols for cloud computing which are quantum-resistant deserve further investigation.

In addition, a new decentralized cloud storage has been emerging in the past few years, in which each participant can be both the service provider and the consumer at the same time. The cloud users can store their data anywhere they want in the decentralized cloud storage network rather than in certain data centers controlled by a few CSPs. The consensus about storage transactions in such decentralized cloud storage network is accomplished via the block-chain. In this more complicate cloud architecture, establishing assurance on the confidentiality, integrity, reliability, and geolocation of the outsourced data, as well as the cloud system security would become more challenging in the decentralized cloud storage systems. Therefore, more protocols for securing the decentralized cloud storage are desired. The Protocol Lab has taken an initial step in implementing the decentralized cloud storage, called Filecoin [31], but a lot of security questions in this new architecture remain unknown and should be investigated in the near future.

14.7   Conclusion

Cloud computing has been increasingly used in real world. To address various security concerns arising due to the out-of-control nature of clouds, various secure protocols have been designed. To ensure secure cloud computing, protocols including the homomorphic encryption, the SE, the CP-ABE and the MPC can be used. To enable secure cloud storage, protocols including PoEs, PoSs, and proofs of reliability are proposed. To guarantee security of the underlying cloud systems, protocols including identity management, authentication, and launching VMs are designed. We also discuss possible research topics in the future, including efficient encryptions to secure cloud computing and cloud storage, as well as new protocols for decentralized cloud storage.

References

1. IDC Cooperation, Data age 2025: The digitization of the world, from edge to core, https://www.seagate.com/cn/zh/our-story/data-age-2025/, 2018.
2. Armknecht, F., Boyd, C., Carr, C., Gjsteen, K., Jaschke, A., Reuter, C.A., Strand, M., *A guide to fully homomorphic encryption*, vol. 2015, p. 1192, IACR Cryptol. ePrint Arch., 2015.
3. Curtmola, R., Garay, J., Kamara, S., Ostrovsky, R., Searchable symmetric encryption: improved definitions and efficient constructions. *J. Comput. Secur.*, 19, 5, 895–934, 2011.
4. Bethencourt, J., Sahai, A., Waters, B., Ciphertext-policy attribute-based encryption, in: *2007 IEEE Symposium on Security and Privacy (S&P 2007)*, 20-23, May 2007, IEEE Computer Society, Oakland, California, USA, pp. 321–334, 2007.
5. Yao, A.C., How to generate and exchange secrets (extended abstract), in: *27th Annual Symposium on Foundations of Computer Science*, 27-29 October 1986, IEEE Computer Society, Toronto, Canada, pp. 162–167, 1986.
6. Van Dijk, M., Juels, A., Oprea, A., Rivest, R.L., Stefanov, E., Triandopoulos, N., Hourglass schemes: how to prove that cloud files are encrypted, in: *Proceedings of the 2012 ACM conference on Computer and communications security*, Acm, pp. 265–280, 2012.
7. Hu, K. and Zhang, W., Efficient verification of data encryption on cloud servers, in: *2014 Twelfth Annual International Conference on Privacy, Security and Trust*, IEEE, pp. 314–321, 2014.
8. Fang, J., Liu, L., Lin, J., Practical Verification of Data Encryption for Cloud Storage Services, in: *16th International Conference on Services Computing*, Springer, pp. 16–31, 2019.
9. Bellare, M., Keelveedhi, S., Ristenpart, T., Message-locked encryption and secure deduplication, in: *Annual International Conference on the Theory and Applications of Cryptographic Techniques*, Springer, pp. 296–312, 2013.
10. Bellare, M., Keelveedhi, S., Ristenpart, T., DupLESS: Server-aided encryption for deduplicated storage, in: *USENIX Conference on Security*, Springer, pp. 179–194, 2013.
11. Liu, J., Asokan, N., Pinkas, B., Secure deduplication of encrypted data without additional independent servers, in: *Proceedings of the 22nd ACM SIGSAC Conference on Computer and Communications Security*, Springer, pp. 874–885, 2015.
12. Ateniese, G., Burns, R., Curtmola, R., Herring, J., Kissner, L., Peterson, Z., Song, D., Provable data possession at untrusted stores, in: *Proceedings of the 14th ACM conference on Computer and communications security*, Acm, pp. 598–609, 2007.
13. Juels, A. and Kaliski Jr., B.S., Pors: Proofs of retrievability for large files, in: *Proceedings of the 14th ACM conference on Computer and communications security*, Acm, pp. 584–597, 2007.
14. Shacham, H. and Waters, B., Compact proofs of retrievability, in: *International Conference on the Theory and Application of Cryptology and Information Security*, Springer, pp. 90–107, 2008.
15. Halevi, S., Harnik, D., Pinkas, B., Shulman-Peleg, A., Proofs of ownership in remote storage systems, in: *ACM Conference on Computer and Communications Security*, Acm, pp. 491–500, 2011.
16. You, W., Chen, B., Liu, L., Jing, J., Deduplication-friendly watermarking for multimedia data in public clouds, in: *Proceedings of the 25th European Symposium on Research in Computer Security*, Springer, pp. 67–87, 2020.

17. Jia, D., Liu, L., Jia, S., Lin, J., Votegeo: An iot-based voting approach to verify the geographic location of cloud hosts, in: *38th IEEE International Performance Computing and Communications Conference*, IEEE, pp. 1–9, 2019.
18. You, W. and Chen, B., Proofs of ownership on encrypted cloud data via intel sgx, in: *The First ACNS Workshop on Secure Cryptographic Implementation*, Springer, pp. 400–416, 2020.
19. Gentry, C. and Halevi, S., Implementing gentry's fully-homomorphic encryption scheme. *30th Annual International Conference on the Theory and Applications of Cryptographic Techniques*, Springer, pp. 129–148, 2011.
20. Cheon, J.H., Kim, A., Kim, M., Song, Y.S., Homomorphic encryption for arithmetic of approximate numbers. *23rd International Conference on the Theory and Applications of Cryptology and Information Security*, Springer, pp. 409–437, 2017.
21. Goyal, V., Pandey, O., Sahai, A., Waters, B., Attribute-based encryption for fine-grained access control of encrypted data, in: *Proceedings of the 13th ACM Conference on Computer and Communications Security*, Acm, pp. 89–98, 2006.
22. Rabin, M.O., How To Exchange Secrets with Oblivious Transfer[J]. IACR cryptology eprint archive, 2005.
23. Douceur, J.R., Adya, A., Bolosky, W.J., Dan, S., Theimer, M., Reclaiming space from duplicate files in a serverless distributed file system, in: *International Conference on Distributed Computing Systems*, Springer, pp. 617–624, 2002.
24. Gordon, D., *Discrete Logarithm Problem*, Springer US, Boston, MA, 2011.
25. Fisch, B., *Poreps: Proofs of space on useful data*, vol. 2018, p. 678, IACR Cryptol. ePrint Arch., 2018.
26. Wang, Z., Sun, K., Jajodia, S., Jing, J., Disk storage isolation and verification in cloud, in: *2012 IEEE Global Communications Conference, GLOBECOM 2012*, December 3-7, 2012, IEEE, Anaheim, CA, USA, pp. 771–776, 2012.
27. Atya, A.O.F., Qian, Z., Krishnamurthy, S.V., Porta, T.L., Marvel, L., Malicious co-residency on the cloud: Attacks and defense, in: *IEEE Conference on Computer Communications*, IEEE, 2017.
28. Khan, I., Anwar, Z., Bordbar, B., Ritter, E., Rehman, H., A protocol for preventing insider attacks in untrusted infrastructure-as-a-service clouds. *IEEE Trans. Cloud Comput.*, 6, 4, 942–954, 2018.
29. Lai, S., Patranabis, S., Sakzad, A., Liu, J.K., Mukhopadhyay, D., Steinfeld, R., Sun, S., Liu, D., Zuo, C., Result pattern hiding searchable encryption for conjunctive queries, in: *Proceedings of the 2018 ACM SIGSAC Conference on Computer and Communications Security*, Acm, pp. 745–762, 2018.
30. Mavroeidis, V., Vishi K., Zych, M.D., *et al.* The Impact of Quantum Computing on Present Cryptography[J]. *International Journal of Advanced Computer Science & Applications*, 9, 3, 2018.
31. Protocol Lab, Whitepaper of the Filecoin, https://filecoin.io, 2020.

Part IV

CASE STUDIES FOCUSED ON CLOUD SECURITY

15

A Study on Google Cloud Platform (GCP) and Its Security

Agniswar Roy[1]*, Abhik Banerjee[1] and Navneet Bhardwaj[2]

[1]Department of Computer Science and Engineering, Netaji Subhash Engineering College, West Bengal, India
[2]Department of Electronics and Communication Engineering, Netaji Subhash Engineering College, West Bengal, India

Abstract

This study on Google Cloud Platform (GCP) is solely based on different features of GCP like security (multi-layered security, from simple data level to hardware level), storage management (SSD for faster disk I/O higher performance, HDD for low-speed transfer with huge storage), computing (VMs, Google Kubernetes Engine, App Engine), networking (hot and cold potato), quality of service, cost and quality management, advantages of GCP over other existing public cloud providers. Google itself uses the cloud platform for its services of video streaming (YouTube), app/game management (Play Store), storage management (Google Drive), and Data Warehousing. A discussion of how the cloud platform functions to help Google seamlessly scale its services like Google Maps in case of unprecedented traffic has been made in this chapter.

In this COVID-19 scenario, a trend in many IT companies is toward shifting their office work, data, to the cloud as it offers near to zero downtime of services. This chapter is a case study on GCP and its security offerings with an insight into recent trends on usage of offerings on GCP.

Keywords: Serverless, stackdriver, IAM, Identity Aware Proxy, Security Command Center, logging, threat detection, secret manager

15.1   Introduction

Cloud is being used by IT companies due to work from home situations. There are a lot of public/private cloud providers in the market but the company needs to pick a cost-effective one and, most importantly, has strong security, especially the current news scenario where one news of selling user data in dark web comes in every week. This paper summarizes key security features of Google Cloud Platform (GCP), like how and where data is protected, and who can access user data if Google itself can access stored data so that the reader gets

---
**Corresponding Author*: agniswar999@gmail.com

Rajdeep Chakraborty, Anupam Ghosh and Jyotsna Kumar Mandal (eds.) *Machine Learning Techniques and Analytics for Cloud Security*, (315–338) © 2022 Scrivener Publishing LLC

a complete idea of how secure their data is. Alongside, we have also discussed some other key features of GCP so that readers get an idea of what sections to look further in case some features they find coinciding with their requirements.

GCP is the youngest among the current top three Cloud Service providers. The first cloud computer by Google, the "App Engine" was introduced by Google in April 2018 whose main purpose was to host websites/web applications on Google's data centers. It was publicly available by November 2011, compared to Microsoft Azure (February 2010) and Amazon Web Services (March 2006). Since then, Google has added a lot of cloud services.

Organization of the Chapter

The chapter is segregated as follows: Section 15.2 gives a brief overview of GCP's security, and then, Section 15.3 describes the architecture of GCP. Section 15.4 describes key security features in GCP which makes it more robust. Section 15.5 shows key application features which makes it more user friendly and helpful to developers and business. Sections 15.6, 15.7, 15.8, and 15.9 describe the four major pillars of GCP: compute, storage, network, and data, respectively. Section 15.10 describes the Machine Learning tools available to use very briefly, followed by the conclusion.

15.1.1 Google Cloud Platform Current Market Holding

This graph clearly describes the world is getting more dependent on cloud services. From Q3 2019 to Q3 2020, the spending has increased by 32.72%. Also to be noted that a lot of companies have started to build cloud platforms the top three leaders in the market are very clear. Google has also increased its market hold to 7% from 6% which is very small in front of Azure and Amazon Web Services, but it jumped from US$2.38bn to US$3.44bn which is a growth of 44.54% which is pretty significant, according to Alphabet [23].

To further discuss the growth of the GCP, we will take the Forrester Wave and Gartner Magic Quadrant. There exist a lot more security testing and market analysis but we are considering only these two as later we will discuss the security features in detail. Figure 15.1 summarize the statistics in a graph.

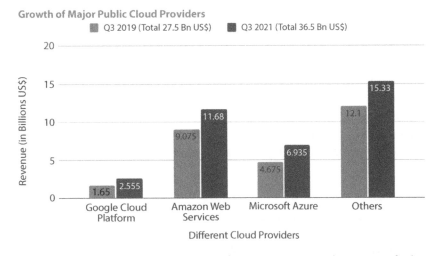

Figure 15.1 Current top 4 public cloud provider's growth over one year span. (Source: canalys.)

15.1.1.1   The Forrester Wave

Forrester Wave [22] is a review of the Infrastructure-as-a-Service (IaaS) native security report. It only validates top performers of the market on various parameters to evaluate its security. According to this, Google is one of the leaders with a strong market presence, great strategy, and services offered.

15.1.1.2   Gartner Magic Quadrant

The report published by Gartner [3] in September 2020 gives a comparative tally of cloud infrastructure and platform services, the top three of the market, as well as leaders in public cloud services. The report suggests that the open-source Kubernetes and TensorFlow, the Data Science tools like Dataproc and BigQuery developed by Google and available in the cloud, made them very popular. Currently, Google is developing Anthos which is a container-based middleware level that will help GCP to develop and deploy an application in a hybrid and multi-cloud environment.

15.1.2   Google Cloud Platform Work Distribution

Google pays a deep focus on the Security of the Cloud Platform. With constant security updates and patchworks, any flaw or loophole is very quickly removed. Apart from this, the security is separated into several sections each having their work. For the Cloud Engineer of the company, the most important thing is to know his limitations and power in the context of security.

The following Table 15.1 summarizes the responsibilities across cloud services.

Table 15.1 Responsibility division across SaaS, PaaS, and IaaS (source: BigCommerce).

Services	SaaS (Software-as-a-Service)	PaaS (Platform-as-a-Service)	IaaS (Infrastructure-as-a-Service)	On-Premise
Applications	Provider	User	User	User/Owner
Data	Provider	User	User	User/Owner
Runtime	Provider	Provider	User	User/Owner
Middleware	Provider	Provider	User	User/Owner
Operating System	Provider	Provider	User	User/Owner
Virtualization	Provider	Provider	Provider	User/Owner
Servers	Provider	Provider	Provider	User/Owner
Storage	Provider	Provider	Provider	User/Owner
Networking	Provider	Provider	Provider	User/Owner

This table clearly shows the work distribution. In the case of On-Premise User and Owner is the same as the old server concept before the cloud service era.

15.1.2.1   SaaS

SaaS or Software-as-a-Service [3] is the simplest form of a cloud service. Most of the work like security, maintenance, update, and programming are done by cloud providers and the user does not need to bother about the server, for example, the Cisco Webex meetings. A company can make purchases based on their need to add some features, but in the end, the company does not need to bother how Cisco is handling the video, which route it takes or they do not have to add any developer to set up the video platform, etc. With small monthly/annual plans, these services are cost-effective too.

15.1.2.2   PaaS

PaaS or Platform-as-a-Service [3] is a little more complicated than SaaS, where the company needs to hire a developer to do some work. In the basic platform, some code will be provided by the cloud provider so the developers do not need to work from scratch but the developers have to build the application/software themselves. PaaS is used to host software/applications. It runs on container/Virtual Machine (VM) technology. A very good example of PaaS is Heroku which is very commonly used to host websites at a small cost.

15.1.2.3   IaaS

IaaS [3] is the most complicated cloud service and the costliest one. When it is physically impossible to purchase and maintain a server (due to cost, maintenance, and place), IaaS comes to play. Here, the provider gives all other features of PaaS like basic code, some modules along heavy compute engines. Since the user does not need to bother about the physical maintenance cost of a server, it is quite cost-effective compared to maintaining personal servers, especially when your business is growing and you do not want to invest in a large server beforehand, as the cloud provider gives you the freedom to scale your server as your wish in runtime and the bill will come accordingly. Cloud Engineer, System Administrator, is needed to maintain this service.

15.1.2.4   On-Premise

A personal server [3] for companies, everything from security to physical maintenance costs, needs to be maintained by the company, pre-cloud service era.

15.2   Google Cloud Platform's Security Features Basic Overview

Google's data security can be broken down into several sections [4], from physical on-site security, data security to network security. Section 15.2.1 describes physical premises security, Section 15.2.2 describes hardware security, Section 15.2.3 describes inter-service security, Section 15.2.4 describes data security, Section 15.2.5 describes internet security, Section 15.2.6 is in-software security, Section 15.2.7 describes end-user security.

15.2.1   Physical Premises Security

Google stores data in their data center and, in some cases, other third-party centers [1]. In both cases, very few employees are allowed in the buildings, and each floor or section is locked by biometric, metal detection, CCTV, and laser alarming systems, entirely planned and monitored by Google. Those few employees are very closely monitored and their data access is always tracked. However, any change in the system always has to be approved by an engineer (other than the person making changes) and the owner so even if someone bypasses all monitoring and alarms, eventually he will have to get the owner's permission to do it.

15.2.2   Hardware Security

Google's computer's processors, NIC, and all other components are custom designed by Google to avoid any data leak or security breach [1]. In the context of this, we can mention the exploit in Intel 32 bit processors which were subject to a fatal data leak called Spectre, Identified by the team Meltdown and marked as a major issue in Common Vulnerabilities and Exposure [4].

The server boot devices, BIOS, kernel, grub (bootloader), and the OS image all are custom designed and stored in custom encrypted Google-designed chips so that they cannot be tampered with. Special updating programs are there to regularly update necessary software components, including removal of a machine from the system if any fatal flaw is detected. Each machine has its unique ID to make it trustworthy to the entire system.

15.2.3   Inter-Service Security

To make processes faster, Google does not use a firewall around each of the systems individually. Instead, it grants unique encrypted credentials to each of the services to make inter-service communications [1]. This procedure is called "Remote Procedure Calls" or RPCs. Figure 15.2 shows the core workflow of RPCs. This helps the machines to discard the security of the network path as encrypted data is transmitted, received, and decrypted (say, an HTTP packet re-encrypted). Recently, Google is deploying encryption accelerators so that in any case if Google's private WAN (we will discuss it later) gets compromised, all RPC traffic can be encrypted faster. The source code of system components (both old and new) is stored with a log. Any modification can be done by an author with credentials, but to put the change to affect, the system owner and at least one engineer other than the author need to approve it. As a result, even if someone manages to make changes in code, with the traceback in logging, then he/she can be tracked down.

To isolate one service from another, hardware + software virtualization, kernel + language-based sandboxes, user separation is done. High sensitive processes like Google Compute Engine and Google Kubernetes Engine are run in separate machines.

Then, his encrypted credentials are sent for authentication. In authentication, if it is found that the user can access Service 2, then it is sent to Service 2 where the credentials are

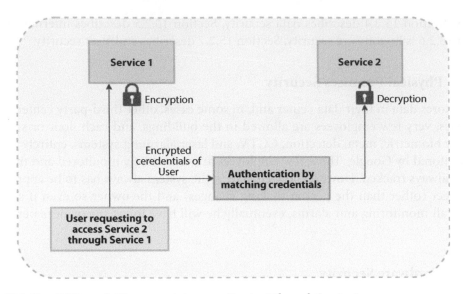

Figure 15.2 How RPCs work. User requests to access Service 2 through Service 1.

decrypted and used. During transmission of credentials, it is always encrypted so none can intercept communication between two services.

15.2.4 Data Security

Data is stored in physical disks in the encrypted form [1]. These encryption keys are generated, rotated, and maintained by a central Key Management Section (KMS). When a disk gets removed out of service for recycling/repair, it is wiped by a complex data wipe procedure and a two-step wipe verification process (data cannot be restored). If a disk fails to pass the verification, then it gets physically destroyed on-premise.

Data deletion is made as an application, not direct removal so that one can think to withdraw before data gets deleted. Also in case of any human or programmatic error, this scheduled deletion helps to recover lost data.

15.2.5 Internet Security

Google Front End (GFE) can stop harmful DoS (denial-of-service) attacks [1] ("Zombie Computer" or bots, constantly sending requests to servers, making the server crash or for large servers, makes the experience slower for other users) by monitoring the number of requests from a single IP. The load balancer observes the IP traffic and informs the central DoS service. When it detects that a DoS might happen, it throttles that IP's traffic. All data transmission over the network is secured with Transport Layer Security (TLS).

15.2.6 In-Software Security

Google has provided libraries for developers to patch up security vulnerabilities [4]. Also, a team of Google always looks for these leaks and constantly patches/create new libraries to fix them. Google also gives prizes to people who can find bugs/exploits their system. Hardware, network pipes have checkpoints. So, in case an uninformed large amount of data transfer is taking place, the checkpoint will alert the security personnel immediately who work round the clock 365 days.

15.2.7   End User Access Security

We have very commonly used Google our account to use many other sites, like YouTube, Calendar, Playstore, Contacts, and Drive. This is managed by cookies or tokens. When a user tries to enter service by logging in, the login credentials are sent to servers who verify it and return an "end-user permission ticket" which gets stored as a cookie. This cookie has an expiration time and within the time the user can do the communication without making any new request. The hardware and network details are also logged by Google so that we can use "Stay signed in for this device", and each time we try a new device, some verification is done [1].

15.3   Google Cloud Platform's Architecture

Here, it will be discussed how GCP works, from data storage to server location. Google has developed data centers all across the world [6]. All data centers are not the same; some have strong hardware support some do not. For example, a VM with a Tensor Processing Unit (TPU) (very useful for Graphics Card accelerated calculations during complicated Machine Learning model training) is not available at the Mumbai server but available in the central US server. But the basic working principle remains the same. In this section, we will discuss geographic zone in Section 15.3.1 and resource management in Section 15.3.2.

15.3.1   Geographic Zone

As mentioned before, Google developed multiple data centers over the world. To make sure that the data does not get lost or the service does not stop multiple data centers over the same or different locations can be used [6]. The type of thing that can be stored depends on the type of resource.

- Zonal Resources [6]: Stored within a single zone. These resources are mostly hardware dependent so the scope is limited. VMs and local persistent disks (PDs) are stored in a single zone [6].
- Regional Resources [6]: App Engine and Regional Cloud Storage Buckets are regional resources. (During bucket creation the option comes whether to use zonal or regional cloud buckets. Of course zonal has lower latency than regional and better for temporary uses, like crawling websites, training Neural Net models.)
- Multi-Regional Resources [6]: Data shared across regions. Nothing specific, based on the scale of business the user wants the data gets stored for faster access and security (less chance all regional servers break down together and data gets lost or the website comes down).

- Global Resources [6]: This is for large business organizations that want total data safety and have business all over the world. Google itself is a big example of it. Apart from it, the Speech to Text and Load Balancers are part of it.

15.3.2 Resource Management

A company can have many projects running simultaneously. It needs to be made sure that one project people cannot access another and the resources are kept isolated. That is why GCP has a project management system [2]. One project does not collide with another. Then comes who can access which project. The company email ID which is used to maintain the cloud account and has billing details attached can grant access to people as project managers who can further give access to people based on need [17]. The managers can permit two basic levels, Google account as developer and service account as an account to access an application from the user end. Developers can create VM and book a Cloud Bucket and all things needed. To make the developer access more detailed there are three IAM roles. Before getting to them, take a look at IAM.

15.3.2.1 IAM

Via Identity and Access Management (IAM) [2], one can grant access to people to work on projects. In a company, a lot of GCP projects might run simultaneously and one person cannot identify the requirements of all projects to allocate them. Hence, IAM creates a "policy" to identify roles for each person, or make a collection of roles and give the collection to the required people. Multiple policies can be created to give different types of access to different people/groups. Figure 15.3 shows the contents of an IAM Policy.

A policy consists of two key components. People granted the policy and what does the policy offer. The offerings are basically a combination of various roles.

Google account is a simple account. Google groups can be formed by combining a few email accounts. Taking the figure as an example, an "Admin" group can be used.

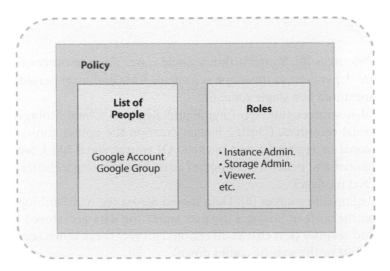

Figure 15.3 Structure of an IAM policy.

15.3.2.2 Roles

The access granting method done by IAM in GCP is done by giving roles [2] to people. These roles have a few types based on their access limitations.

15.3.2.2.1 Basic Roles

Viewer, Editor, and Owner: These are predefined roles [2]. Unless there is no option (i.e., the manager does not even know who needs what type of permission), basic roles should never be used. At least predefined roles should be used and the best practice is to use custom roles.

The following Table 15.2 shows the basic roles available.

15.3.2.2.2 Predefined Roles

IAM roles are more fine-tuning than basic roles [2]. For example, permission only to start VM instances or stop them but not allowing to create instances.

15.3.2.2.3 Custom Roles

This is the best practice and should be followed [2]. For example, owners can add resources to a project. Now the old problem comes that one person cannot know the needs of each project and hence some other people, say project manager is added as owner. The project manager grants permission of an "owner" to a developer. The developer can create random instances (VMs) and forget about them or use them for personal gain, but at the month-end, the company will get a big amount to pay. Instead, the project manager will allocate VM and the developer needs to start VM, stop VM, check logs, modify the machine type of existing instances but do not need to add or remove it; so that multiple resources cannot be purchased. These sets of roles can be granted to the developer policy group, whereas the project manager will get another policy to get roles to allocate resources.

15.3.2.3 Billing

Resources come with bills. To pay the bill, the organization account must be linked with a verified payment method. Billing [2] of cloud services is done by a cloud billing account, which only handles the billing of cloud resources. It is linked with Google payment profile which is used to store payment details (card details) to be used in all Google services (Playstore, AdSense). Now, there is a feature called sub-account. Usually, they are for resellers, like someone gives a sub-account to a person. That person can use as many resources as he/she wishes. At the month-end, the bill will be generated with his/her name and come to the reseller. Then, the reseller collects the money from him. But it is mostly

Table 15.2 Basic permission levels.

Role	Permissions
Viewer	Only see or read-only actions, no modifications allowed.
Editor	All viewer's permissions plus ability to modify existing resources state.
Owner	All editor roles plus the ability to grant roles to others, create/purchase cloud resources, and manage billing for projects.

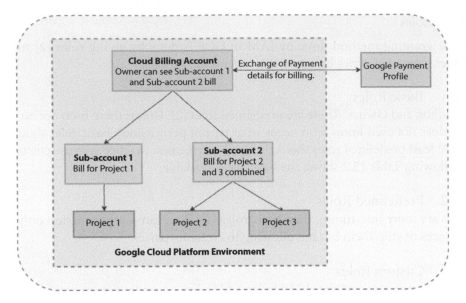

Figure 15.4 Sub-account billing method.

used in a single organization to run individual projects on individual sub-account so that the owner can see which project is costing how much.

Figure 15.4 show bill is generated for sub accounts, multiple projects. Here, a company can run three projects via two sub-accounts. At the end of the month, the bill for projects will generate for the sub-account, like sub-account 1 will have the bill of project 1 and sub-account 2 will have the bill of project 2. The owner can see each bill individually.

15.4 Key Security Features

We have got a brief overview of how GCP's security works. But there are some key security facilities in GCP apart from the aforementioned and these play key roles in reinforcing the security. Here, we will discuss Identity Aware Proxy (IAP) in Section 15.4.1, compliance in Section 15.4.2, policy analyzer in Section 15.4.3, Security Command Center (SCC) in Section 15.4.4, Data Loss Protection (DLP) in Section 15.4.5, key management in Section 15.4.6, secret manager in Section 15.4.7, and finally monitoring in Section 15.4.8.

15.4.1 IAP

IAP [8] is used to design a central authorization layer that gives control over the application layer instead of securing the network with firewalls. One can design one IAP policy and use it in all applications or create separate policies for individual applications.

IAP checks the user's request to access cloud resources. In case a user not signed in IAP responds with sign in, if the browser has no site settings, it requests a cookie to make the browser suitable for work. After the sign-in, browser details get confirmed, the user credentials get validated against IAM policy to check its access. Once it is cleared, the user can finally access the cloud resource.

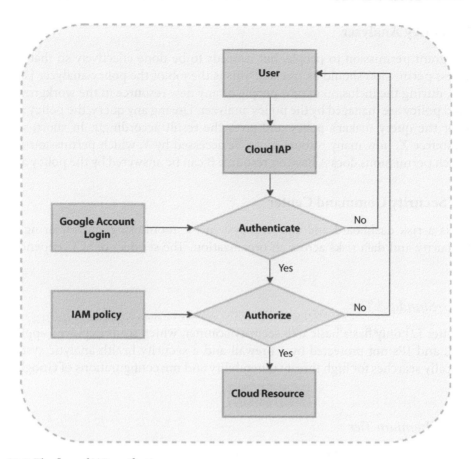

Figure 15.5 The flow of IAP verification.

Figure 15.5 shows the procedure of IAP verification. When a user tries to access a resource, first, he is checked with IAP. Then, his Google account is checked for authentication. Then, his account credentials are matched with IAM policies. Then, he gets authorized to access the resource based on his roles.

15.4.2   Compliance

GCP is a certified ISO/IEC 27001 company, meaning with best security practices and rules to follow to keep the information secure [6]. It has SOC 1 certification, which assures that the financial statements (Bills) made by Google are up to standard. The FedRAMP, Federal Risk and Authorization Management Program, is a US Federal government-run certification program for cloud services to provide a standardized security assessment, continuous monitoring, and authorization. The Health Insurance Portability and Accountability Act (HIPAA) is a federal law that shows data privacy and security requirements for organizations that are charged with safeguarding people's protected health information (PHI). Customers that are subject to HIPAA and want to utilize any Google Cloud products must review and accept Google's Business Associate Agreement (BAA). Google ensures that the Google products covered under the BAA meet the requirements under HIPAA.

15.4.3   Policy Analyzer

IAM can grant permission to people, but it needs to be done effectively so that who got what access permission should be tracked. This is the job of the policy analyzer [7]. Apart from this, during the inclusion of new people or any new resource in the workgroup, their access and policy are managed by the policy analyzer. During any query, the policy analyzer checks for the query maker's policy and gives the result accordingly. In short, who can access resource X, how many resources can be accessed by Y, which permission/access Z have, which permissions does A have on resource B can be answered by the policy analyzer.

15.4.4   Security Command Center

SCC [2] is a risk dashboard and analytics system for monitoring and repairing Google Cloud security and data risks across an organization. The services of SCC depend on the paid tier.

15.4.4.1   Standard Tier

Standard tier [2] only has a basic web security scanner, which scans deployed applications with URL and IPs not protected by a firewall and a security health analytic system that automatically searches for high threat vulnerability and misconfigurations of Google Cloud assets.

15.4.4.2   Premium Tier

Premium tier has some additional security features [2].

15.4.4.2.1   Event Threat Detection

Event threat detection [2] works by analyzing event logs. These near real-time logs contain various event information which is monitored by threat detection logic and threat intelligence to find a threat. If a threat is found, then it returns the finding to the SCC and Cloud Logging. From Cloud Logging, the findings can be exported to another system and can be analyzed with cloud functions. Some of the events that are marked as a threat are as follows:

- Exporting any data outside the project or organization.
- Trying to access a known malware-infected domain.
- Trying to connect to a known mining IP address.
- Outgoing Denial-of-Service (DoS) attacks.

Apart from pre-defined threats (some mentioned above), the owner can define custom events by using the Cloud Logging data that they want to be marked as a threat. Check Figure 15.6 to see how a threat is detected and managed.

15.4.4.2.2   Cloud Logging

Event threat detection cannot work without logging [2]. That is why logging is also a key part of security. By default, logging is off. To use event threat detection, it has to be turned on.

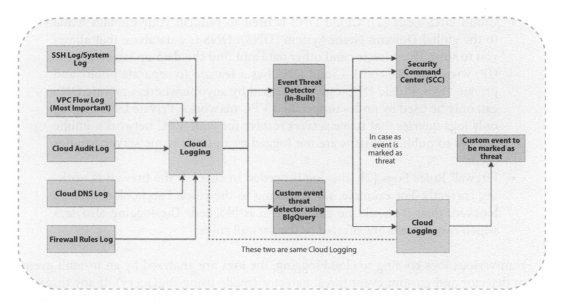

Figure 15.6 How event threat detection works.

Users can decide what sections of projects are needed to be logged. However, apart from event threat detection, a lot of applications can be monitored by using logging.

Currently, event threat detection uses only the following types of logging.

- SSH log/system log.
- VPC flow logs [2]: Virtual Private Cloud (VPC) flow logs records network traffic done by a VM instance. This can help to network surveillance, cost optimization, and most of the tasks done by the event threat detector. The event threat detector works best when this log is active.
- Cloud Audit Logs [2]: Cloud audit log saves four types of logs for each cloud project, folder, and organization.

  o Admin activity audit log: This log observes the administrative activities, like allocating new resources (creating a VM) and changing IAM policy. This log is free and it cannot be stopped or configured.
  o Data access audit log: This log checks any CRUD operation on user-provided resource data that is not publicly available, as these logs can be very big (each API call to access data will be an entry) and take resources to write. That is why this log is by default turned off (apart from BigQuery). This logging might cost additional charges. This logging can be configured.
  o System event audit logs: These look for events that are done by Google itself on a system (updating any resource, patch fix). It is free and cannot be stopped or configured.
  o Policy denied audit logs: When the system rejects someone's access request due to some security policy violation. This is generated automatically and charged with the cloud project but it can be stopped.

- Cloud DNS Logs [2]: Cloud DNS is used to publish your domain name to the global Domain Name System (DNS). DNS is a database that allows you to store IP addresses and other data and find the data up later by name (IP: www.example.com). Cloud DNS has a feature to separate public and private DNS. Public DNS can be accessed by anyone whereas private DNS can only be used by nodes in specified VPC networks. Private DNS logging only logs queries that name servers resolve for your VPC networks. Public queries to public domains are not logged as a public name server handles them.
- Firewall Rules Logs [2]: This log is needed to check if the firewall is working correctly. For example, say according to the rules, Facebook should be blocked, then it should be checked if it is blocked. The logging also says which connections are affected by the firewall rules.

From various logs coming to cloud logging, the logs are analyzed by an in-built event threat detector and custom event threat detector (made using BigQuery). If any threat is noticed, it is sent to SCC and Cloud Logging for further steps, otherwise, the analysis is discarded. Apart from these, there are user logs, i.e., multi-cloud and hybrid-cloud logs.

15.4.4.2.3   Container Threat Detection

This service's job is to monitor container images, evaluation of changes in images, and remote access attempts in near real time [2]. When it is enabled, event information and container identifier information is passed to the threat detector. Once it finds a threat, it informs SCC and Cloud Logging (optionally), otherwise, data is discarded. Incidents that are marked by this detection are as follows:

- A binary code that is not part of the original container image or modified version of the image is being executed.
- A library that is not part of the original container image or modified version of the image is loaded.
- Reverse Shell: a process started with the stream directly to a remotely connected socket. By this, an attacker can execute his desired commands.

15.4.4.2.4   Security Health Analytics

This tool finds and reports several vulnerabilities to the system [2]. Some are listed below:

- API Key: if an API key has too many users, unrestricted usage (untrusted apps can use the key), the key has not changed since a limit of days then these events are reported.
- Compute Image: Compute engine publicly accessible.
- Compute Instance: no OS login, the instance has a public IP address, load balancer targeting HTTP proxy instead of HTTPS, Secure Boot disabled (prevents rootkits and boot kits attacks), and many other vulnerability checks fall under this section.
- Dataset: dataset open to public access.

- Firewall: firewall logging disabled, firewall open to public access, firewall has opened ports for generic access.
- IAM: service account with administrative roles, using basic roles (owner, editor, viewer), service account key not changing over a certain time.
- Logging: storage bucket with no logging, resource with no proper log sink.
- Storage: storage bucket is publicly available.
- Monitoring: vulnerabilities of this section checks if all the resources are monitored properly. Usually, various log metrics and alerts are not monitored properly (changes in IAM permission, firewall rules, and audit configuration).

15.4.4.2.5 Web Security Scanner

This scanner [2] finds vulnerabilities in Google Kubernetes Engine (GKE), App Engine, and Compute Engine web applications. Starting from the initial URL, the scanner crawls all links (only public URLs, not protected by a firewall) within the scope of the initial URL and tries to take as many inputs and event handlers as possible. The scans run automatically once a week and the findings are reported to SCC. Some of the exploits that can be found are as follows:

- GIT repository exposed publicly.
- Password transmission without encryption.
- Library(es) used in the application has known vulnerabilities.

15.4.5 Data Loss Protection

To migrate data to a project for use, DLP [9] is needed. DLP does a lot of things other than simply taking the data. It can take the data (it can handle both structured and unstructured data), classify it, and store the data in their needed storage space, and the best thing is that this does not need any human monitoring. Since a lot of data might contain sensitive information (credit/debit card details, account number), DLP can de-identify data too. The de-identification can be done both one way and two way. One way encryption or hashing is used when it is sure the data would not be needed in the future. Two-way encryption is more popular as most of the time the data is needed further. Here, a Data Encryption Key (DEK) is used to encrypt and decrypt the data. The DEK must be given to a very small group of people.

15.4.6 Key Management

Previously in this paper, it was mentioned (Data Security, Section 15.2.4) that the data is written to disk in encrypted form all the time free of cost. The data is encrypted using the AES-256 method. Since this encryption is both ways, an encryption key is needed which should be stored for future use. This key management [10] is done by cloud KMS (Key Management Service). The encryption-decryption operation can be done by using cloud

KMS directly or cloud external key manager or Customer-Managed Encryption Keys (CMEK) integrations within other Google services.

15.4.7   Secret Manager

The secret manager [2] is used to store secrets of projects like API keys, passwords, and other critical data. Secret data is immutable and each access to the secret data is logged if Cloud Audit logging is enabled and the data can be used to track any unauthorized access. Like other cloud services, one must be granted permission through IAM to access the secrets but the project owner has access to the secrets.

15.4.8   Monitoring

Cloud monitor [5] collects metadata, metrics, and event data from applications and systems, processes it, and gives necessary feedback via dashboard, alerts, and charts. What data to be collected, custom alerts for user-defined cases based on log data, custom dashboard so that frequently used components come first, and globally observing online available VMs and APIs are all part of monitoring.

15.5   Key Application Features

We would not go into details about any specific applications available in the cloud, but some functions are there which is beneficial to everyone who uses GCP [15]. In this section, we will discuss the stackdriver in Section 15.5.1, network in Section 15.5.2, Virtual Machine Specifications in Section 15.5.3, and finally Preemptible VM in Section 15.5.4.

15.5.1   Stackdriver (Currently Operations)

It is the centralized method to collect logs, metrics, to quickly identify if anything is going wrong with your GCP resources [11]. It has six sections. Monitoring (see Section 15.4.8), logging (see Section 15.4.4.2.2), error reporting (see Section 15.4.4.2.1, event threat detection), profiler, debugger, and trace. Since monitoring, logging, and event reports fall under security, they are discussed before. Rest are briefed here.

15.5.1.1   Profiler

Profiler [12] gathers CPU and memory allocation information to inform you about which section of the application source code is taking the most resources, so the code can be further optimized.

15.5.1.2   Cloud Debugger

This is used for real-time running application debugging [13]. There is no need to stop or pause the application. The debug log comes with ~10-ms delay which is not noticeable.

During any moment, one can take a snapshot to note down call stack and variables or enter a log message which will be treated as if it is part of the actual code.

15.5.1.3   Trace

Trace [14] collects latency information of a running application from server to user end and generates reports where the performance drop is occurring (overtime by comparing two reports or any instant bottleneck) and why and it is automatic and near real-time. Some services like gaming, live streaming, and remote operations need minimal latency possible. That is why Trace is very useful.

15.5.2   Network

The default network tier one gets when using GCP is the premium tier [5]. It is for a reason. Most data centers of other cloud providers (Amazon Web Services, Microsoft Azure) are public, i.e., when you request data from America sitting in India, your data will hop from various data centers across the world, which is time-consuming. But, Google has made their own data centers across the world, and in the premium tier, the data travels from Google to Google data center before sending the data to local ISP, which makes it very fast compared to others. This method is called cold potato, and the other method is called hot potato. Also one can choose the standard edition which is a mix of public and private data centers for cost optimization and similar in performance to other cloud providers.

Figure 15.7 shows the hot potato network. Here, the data comes over the world by hopping shared public cloud data centers which makes the data transfer slow and more vulnerable.

Figure 15.8 shows the cold potato network. The data comes in Google's own network from and to Google's own data centers till it reaches the nearest data center then to the public web which makes the data transfer very fast and less vulnerable.

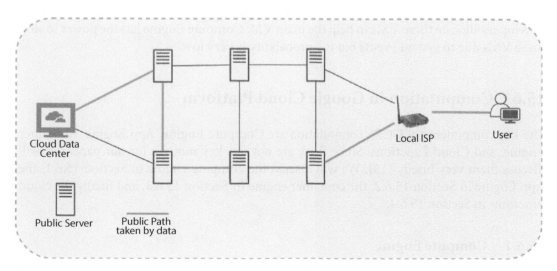

Figure 15.7 Hot potato, used by other cloud providers like AWS and Azure.

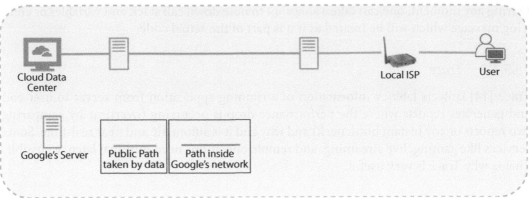

Figure 15.8 Cold potato, available in the premium network tier of GCP.

15.5.3   Virtual Machine Specifications

GCP has a unique feature to manually select the specifications of your VM. The no of core count in CPU and the amount of RAM can be done by user input, whereas other providers have a long list of almost all possible combinations you might need but they would not give you the freedom to customize a machine. Now, along with this Google's monitoring comes. If it can find out that the VM allotted for the specific task is too powerful, then it will suggest a lower-end version. For example, you allotted an 8 GB memory and 4 core processor. But after a week the monitor finds that your RAM usage never exceeded 5 GB and CPU usage was <40%. It will automatically suggest to scale down the VM, say, a 2 core 6 GB machine, which is helpful to minimize the cost.

15.5.4   Preemptible VMs

Preemptible VMs are 24-hour short-lived (unless the timer is reset) low-cost instances (up to 80% cheaper) which give additional power to the existing VM. Before heavy workload, like launching a game when massive downloads will come, sales in e-commerce sites the developers allocate these VMs to help the main VM. Compute Engine has the power to stop these VMs due to system events but the probability is very low.

15.6   Computation in Google Cloud Platform

The key components of GCP's computation are Compute Engine, App Engine, Container Engine, and Cloud Functions. Since these are not our key motives for our paper, we will discuss them very briefly [15]. We will discuss the compute engine in Section 15.6.1, the App Engine in Section 15.6.2, the container engine in Section 15.6.3, and finally the cloud functions in Section 15.6.4.

15.6.1   Compute Engine

Compute engines [2] are like real-life servers which have storage, processor, memory, SSD, etc. It allows users to create VM instances in Google cloud infrastructure. When you want a kernel-level modification, you want to run an app/package that cannot be containerized or have a custom image and complete control then you will need a compute engine. Machine learning model training or similar heavyweight applications run in compute engines [20].

15.6.2   App Engine

App Engine [2] is useful to host any website or web applications. The developer does not need to think about the host computer or any prior server handling, kernel module knowledge. Because of its simplicity, the App Engine is very popular [18, 20].

15.6.3   Container Engine

Google's container engine [2] is known as the Kubernetes engine. Say the App Engine handles server-side error but that does not remove the possibility of user-side error. So, in case a section of the code crashes, the entire application will come down. Here comes the Kubernetes engine. When the user does not want to mess with the kernel or touch server, he/she can shift the application to containers then use the container engine. The Kubernetes engine works on "Serverless" technology, i.e., no single server will be there. Each container will work separately and together they will be called clusters. If one container fails, then the rest will be up and running [20].

15.6.4   Cloud Functions

Cloud Function [2] is a simple function as a service. These functions are made available worldwide in all regions. Autoscale, no server management, run code from a phone, Google assistant, cloud anywhere, and many other features make this a very useful component. Some examples are a virtual assistant and conversion experiences (using Cloud Speech API, give voice and text-based conversation a more natural touch, like Google Assistant), and Sentiment analysis using Cloud Natural Language API.

15.7   Storage in Google Cloud Platform

Depending on the data type, various types of storage methods are used.

- Cloud Storage [2]: This is just a robust object storage space, huge in amount. The cost of this storage depends on the scale the data will be accessed. Based on the scale, it can be classified into four types:

    o Coldline Storage: Here, only redundant data is stored that is not used/very rarely used anymore. Source file backup, disaster recovery data is stored here. It is the cheapest.
    o Nearline Storage: More frequent and a bit costlier than Coldline. Usually, data backups, long time unused docs are stored here.
    o Regional Storage: Coding, computing machines, and data analytics are stored on a regional scale. Small-scale organizations use this type of storage.

- o Multi-Regional Storage: Here, very frequently data access is done. Hence, it is costliest. E-commerce and video stream/upload sites use kind of storage.

- Cloud SQL [2]: Here, relational databases can be stored via MySQL, PostgreSQL, and SQL server. It scales on the go and can be exported or imported from and to CSV files.
- Datastore: It is used to store NoSQL databases. It is also scalable. Currently, it is known as Firestore (with a lot of upgrades) and old datastore data can be migrated by users to Firestore or they will be automatically migrated in the future.
- BigTable: BigTable is also a high-performance scalable NoSQL database. The key difference between Datastore/Firestore and BigTable is that Datastore is easy to use but BigTable gives better performance.

15.8   Network in Google Cloud Platform

Components of GCP's network are DNS (see Section 15.4.4.2.2) and the rest are as follows:

- VPC [2]: It provides network functionality to VMs, App Engines, containers, etc.
- Load balancing [2]: It puts all cloud resources behind a single IP address. The scaling of the server (upscale or downscale) depends on the number of queries the load balancer is getting.
- Cloud Content Delivery Network (CDN) [19]: This is much like a processor cache. When the GFE gets a request, it searches inside CDN. If the answer is found it is sent to the user. If not found, the actual data is accessed. If the data is cacheable, then it is moved to CDN. Finding the data in CDN is called "cache hit" and not finding is called "cache miss" [17].
- Cloud Interconnect [2]: This service extends an on-premise network to a low latency connection in Google's network. It can be achieved by using a dedicated on-premise network to Google network by a physical medium or via a service provider who bridges the Google network and the on-premise network.

15.9   Data in Google Cloud Platform

Data can be accessed, analyzed, and visualized in GCP by various tools provided there.

- BigQuery [2]: Scalable, high performance, multi-cloud data warehouse. It is a very important component in Machine Learning (as it can analyze data) and security.
- DataFlow [2]: Fast, serverless batch data processing service based on Apache Beam SDK.
- Datalab: Used to explore, visualize, analyze, and transport data in Python, SQL, and other languages.

- Pub/Sub [2]: It is an asynchronous messaging service used for event ingestion and delivery for streaming analytics pipelines. It offers good message storage, real-time message delivery, and consistent performance at scale. Pub/Sub servers run in all GCP cloud regions over the world [16].

15.10   Machine Learning in Google Cloud Platform

There are various strong machine learning tools built-in GCP. Some of them are Cloud Vision API, Cloud Speech API, Cloud Natural Language API, AutoML, and Cloud Video intelligence. These pre-built codes are ready to use in other models or part of any larger projects. AutoML is a good classifier but you do not need to write a single line to use it. Combined with huge amounts of data and strong models, better training machines, machine learning in GCP has become a pretty simple thing. Most of the cloud providers are currently including these machine learning tools as prebuilt code for developers which makes a cloud engineer more valuable than machine learning developers unless the project entirely revolves around machine learning or deep learning methods. Google's data science tools, data analysis tools, and data management tools along with TensorFlow makes the GCP heaven for Machine Learning/Deep Learning/Data Science enthusiasts.

The following Table 15.3 summarizes all major components of the GCP.

Apart from these major six components, there are third party components too. Google's TensorFlow makes Google a stronger challenger to others in the Machine Learning field. This additional Table 15.4 [21] gives a chart of common terminology among public cloud providers.

Apart from these, a lot of cloud functionalities are there and they are continuously increasing.

15.11   Conclusion

We discussed here mainly the security of the GCP: how the data is stored at rest and at transit, who can access, and not only software but also physical security. We mentioned that

Table 15.3 The core of Google Cloud Platform.

Management	Compute	Storage	Networking	Data	Machine learning
Identity and Access Management (IAM) + Stackdriver (Currently Operations)	Compute Engine + Preemptive VM + App Engine + Container Engine (Kubernetes) + Cloud Functions	Cloud Storage + Cloud SQL + Cloud Datastore (Currently Firestore) + BigTable	Virtual Network + Content Delivery Network (CDN) + DNS + Interconnect	BigQuery + DataFlow + Datalab + Pub/Sub	AutoML + Speech API + Vision API + Translate API and many others

Table 15.4 Common terminology between Amazon Web Services, Microsoft Azure, and GCP.

Functionality	GCP	AWS	Azure
Compute Services	Compute Engine	Elastic Compute Cloud (EC2)	Virtual Machines
App Hosting	Google App Engine	Amazon Elastic Beanstalk	Azure Cloud Services
Serverless Computing	Google Cloud Functions	AWS Lambda	Azure Functions
Container Support	Container Engine (Kubernetes)	EC2 Container Service	Azure Container Service
Scaling options	Autoscaler	Autoscaling	Azure Autoscale
Object Storage	Cloud Storage	Amazon Simple Storage (S3)	Azure Blob Storage
Block Storage	Persistent Disks	Amazon Elastic Block Storage	Azure Managed Storage
Content Delivery Network (CDN)	Cloud CDN	Amazon CloudFront	Azure CDN
SQL Database	Cloud SQL	Amazon RDS	Azure SQL Database
NoSQL Database	Cloud Datastore	AWS DynamoDB	Azure DocumentDB
Virtual Network	Cloud Virtual Network	Amazon VPC	Azure Virtual Network
Private Connectivity	Cloud Interconnect	Private Connectivity	Azure Express Route
DNS Services	Cloud DNS	Amazon Route 53	Azure Traffic Manager
Log Monitoring	Cloud Logging	Amazon CloudTrail	Azure Operational Insights
Performance Monitoring	Stackdriver Monitoring	Amazon CloudWatch	Azure Application Insights
Administration and Security	Identity and Access Management (IAM)	AWS Identity and Access Management (IAM)	Azure Active Directory
Compliance	Google Cloud Platform Security	AWS CloudHSM	Azure Trust Center
Analytics	Cloud DataFlow	Amazon Kinesis	Azure Stream Analytics
Load Balancing	Cloud Load Balancing	Elastic Load Balancing	Load Balancing for Azure
Hybrid Cloud	Anthos	AWS Outposts	Azure Arc

Google prizes people who find bugs in their system and can exploit it. It is not only from the software end but also from the physical end too. The security drills at a Google data center consist of hiring people to break through the center not only externally but also internally, like a Google employee shaking hands with the thief. The security certifications earned by GCP can be found by visiting reference [6], which consists of 40 top global certificates for security standards. We mentioned some GCP exclusive features like best cost optimization by giving suggestions to the user if any resource is underused, 24x7 customer support, using personal data centers to transmit data instead of shared public data centers and, above all, great guides to train IT, people, and best security practices. With the preemptible VMs supporting main compute engines, a very stable serverless Kubernetes engine, and the zero-knowledge base friendly App Engine, Google has a solution for every need. GCP has claimed a lot of the market in a short term, a little below the leader Amazon Web Services because of their 7-year head start but they are covering the ground and continuously improvising, by adding new features and APIs to make the developer work easier, giving day zero security patches and updates, and designing custom firmware and hardware for less third party intervention. So, we think you will find it easier to decide to pick which cloud provider to get after going through the paper.

References

1. https://cloud.google.com/security/infrastructure/design
2. Google Cloud Whitepaper. Google Cloud security foundations guide, August 2020. Published and maintained by Google.
3. https://www.gartner.com/en/documents/3989743/magic-quadrant-for-cloud-infrastructure-and-platform-ser
4. https://cve.mitre.org/cgi-bin/cvename.cgi?name=CVE-2017-5754.
5. https://cloud.google.com/security/overview/whitepaper
6. https://cloud.google.com/security/compliance.
7. Gupta, D., Bhatt, S., Gupta, M., Kayode, O., Tosun, A.S., Access Control Model for Google Cloud IoT. *2020 IEEE 6th Intl Conference on Big Data Security on Cloud (BigDataSecurity), IEEE Intl Conference on High Performance and Smart Computing, (HPSC) and IEEE Intl Conference on Intelligent Data and Security (IDS)*, Baltimore, MD, USA, pp. 198–208, 2020.
8. https://cloud.google.com/iap/docs/concepts-overview.
9. Zhang, Q., Zhu, L., Bian, H., Peng, X., Cloud Storage-oriented Secure Information Gateway. *2012 International Conference on Cloud and Service Computing*, Shanghai, pp. 119–123, 2012.
10. https://cloud.google.com/kms/docs#docs.
11. https://versprite.com/blog/security-operations/google-stackdriver/#:~:text=Stackdriver%20provides%20a%20centralized%20method,BigQuery%2C%20CloudStorage%2C%20and%20more.
12. https://cloud.google.com/profiler/docs.
13. https://cloud.google.com/debugger.
14. https://cloud.google.com/trace.
15. Arif, H., Hajjdiab, H., Harbi, F.A., Ghazal, M., A Comparison between Google Cloud Service and iCloud. *2019 IEEE 4th International Conference on Computer and Communication Systems (ICCCS)*, Singapore, pp. 337–340, 2019.

16. Reza, M., Framework on large public sector implementation of cloud computing. *2012 International Conference on Cloud Computing and Social Networking (ICCCSN)*, Bandung, West Java, pp. 1–4, 2012.

17. Boza-Quispe, G., Montalvan-Figueroa, J., Rosales-Huamaní, J., Puente-Mansilla, F., A friendly speech user interface based on Google cloud platform to access a tourism semantic website. *2017 CHILEAN Conference on Electrical, Electronics Engineering, Information and Communication Technologies (CHILECON)*, Pucon, pp. 1–4, 2017.

18. Gupta, A., Goswami, P., Chaudhary, N., Bansal, R., Deploying an Application using Google Cloud Platform. *2020 2nd International Conference on Innovative Mechanisms for Industry Applications (ICIMIA)*, Bangalore, India, pp. 236–239, 2020.

19. https://cloud.google.com/cdn/docs/overview.

20. Posey, B. *et al.*, On-Demand Urgent High Performance Computing Utilizing the Google Cloud Platform. *2019 IEEE/ACM HPC for Urgent Decision Making (UrgentHPC)*, Denver, CO, USA, pp. 13–23, 2019.

21. Muhammed, A.S. and Ucuz, D., Comparison of the IoT Platform Vendors, Microsoft Azure, Amazon Web Services, and Google Cloud, from Users' Perspectives. *2020 8th International Symposium on Digital Forensics and Security (ISDFS)*, Beirut, Lebanon, pp. 1–4, 2020.

22. Cser, A., The Forrester Wave: Infrastructure-As-AService Platform Native Security, Q4 2020. The Seven Providers That Matter Most And How They Stack Up, December 7, 2020.

23. https://www.crn.com/news/cloud/alphabet-earnings-google-cloud-revenue-jumps-45-percent.

16

Case Study of Azure and Azure Security Practices

Navneet Bhardwaj[1]*, Abhik Banerjee[2] and Agniswar Roy[2]

[1]Department of Electronics and Communication Engineering, Netaji Subhash Engineering College, West Bengal, India
[2]Department of Computer Science & Engineering, Netaji Subhash Engineering College, West Bengal, India

Abstract

This study is meant for all potential customers who want to satisfy their business requirements using Azure. The main intention is to make them aware of the various security features offered by Azure. It provides a detailed description of the various security practices that will help the customers to take their data security to another level. With Microsoft Azure, we can define our Information Security Management System (ISMS) and build an entire set of security policies and define data safety. The paper also provides an overview of various security aspects ranging from identification, categorization, to access management using Azure. It also deals with various suggestions that can help the customer in securing the overall cloud infrastructure.

Azure plays a vital role in enabling companies in managing various workloads. These workloads can be from any domain. Microsoft Azure provides a plethora of services that are capable enough to manage any workload ranging from data computation, data security, to data encryption. Azure provides the organization of scaling up or scaling down according to the traffic. This helps the organization to maintain equal data flow distribution. This helps the organization to prevent any chances of data loss. Lack of this facility would make it practically impossible to ensure that there is no data wastage. A security breach can cause huge loss to the organization. The paper is meant for all those people who have an idea of the current business requirements and are well aware of the various basics that are used very frequently. These basics range from networking, OS, to the various security protocols which are a must while ensuring that there is no security breach.

Keywords: Azure API gateway, Azure functions, security center, key vault, Azure Virtual Network, Azure SQL Database, Azure sentinel, Azure active directory

16.1 Introduction

Microsoft Azure [4] is one of the leading cloud platforms currently available. The main ideology behind Microsoft Azure is satisfying the business requirements by making the best utilization of the available resources. Azure keeps an eye on the available resources and

---

*Corresponding author: navneetbhardwaj935@gmail.com

Rajdeep Chakraborty, Anupam Ghosh and Jyotsna Kumar Mandal (eds.) *Machine Learning Techniques and Analytics for Cloud Security*, (339–356) © 2022 Scrivener Publishing LLC

makes sure that all the things work properly to ensure the proper functioning of the business. It strives hard to come up with in time deployment of the services ensuring minimum downtime. There are four pillars on which the entire Cloud Platform [8] is dependent. They are availability, scalability, elasticity, and security. Azure is very much conscious when it comes to providing security to its users.

This whitepaper is meant to provide an overview of how Azure deals with security in brief. The main intention of this whitepaper is to throw light on the various services that Azure provides to maintain top-notch security to its end users.

Chapter Organization
The chapter is divided into multiple sections. Section 16.2 talks about the Azure security infrastructure. Section 16.3 deals with data encryption which is one of the best features offered by Azure. Security 16.4 gives a brief description about Azure cloud security architecture. Section 16.5 explores the Azure's architecture. Section 16.6 deals with the general features of Azure, whereas Section 16.7 deals with the security specific features of Azure.

16.1.1   Azure Current Market Holding

The Canalys graph describes the dependency of the world on the various cloud platform. According to Canalys, the expenditure grew 31% which amounts to US $34.6 billion. Azure reached a market share of 20% despite the current market crisis. This can be attributed to its strong end in the fiscal year. Azure holds a market share of US$6.92 billion which is a significant share.

The growth of Azure can be further discussed by considering the Forrester Wave and Gartner Magic Quadrant.

16.1.2   The Forrester Wave

Forester Curve is an overview of the Infrastructure-as-a-Service native security report. It evaluates the security of the top market performers on various parameters. It evaluates them based on their strategy and current offering. Azure Sentinel emerged as strategy leader in Forrester Wave in 2020.

16.1.3   Gartner Magic Quadrant

Azure emerged as a leader in the Gartner Magic Quadrant for full life cycle API Management 2020. Azure API management enables organizations of all scales to design, scale, secure, and monitor APIs across clouds and on premises which makes them discoverable and usable. These APIs can now be used by internal, partner, and public developers.

16.2   Microsoft Azure—The Security Infrastructure

Azure security infrastructure [1] is one of the best infrastructures available. It keeps an eye on the entire infrastructure to ensure that there is no chance of any security breach. It makes sure that it caters to the needs by providing the most flexible and agile cloud environment available. Microsoft Azure runs in data centers managed and operated by Microsoft. These data centers are distributed globally over multiple regions. Data center distribution certifies that there is no data loss in case of any failure. These data centers are in accordance with various industry key quality bars such as ISO/IEC 27001:2013 and NIST SP 800-53. This helps its users to be assured of the fact that their data is in safe hands. The data centers are managed by the skilled workforce of Microsoft.

With regular penetration testing, Azure ensures that there is not any possibility of having a security breach. It has an adequate level of automation to ensure thorough protection and monitoring of the underlying infrastructure.

These factors make Azure a business-friendly Cloud platform.

It is well known that "Security is a shared responsibility". There are some responsibilities that are on the user's side while some are on Azure's side.

Features such as compute power, storage, and database and networking services are managed by Azure, whereas service configuration and data is managed by the user.

16.2.1   Azure Security Features and Tools

Azure supports a list of security features and tools. These steps comprises design, code development monitoring operations, threat intelligence, and response. Azure is well aware of the fact that cloud demands a deep commitment to security technology and processes that few individual organizations can provide. The security specific features when coupled with services provides an easy pathway covering many security issues in one go. Figure 16.1 describes the flow of data encryption at rest. These security-specific products and tools feature configuration management, network security, and data access.

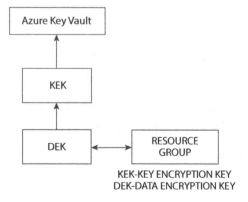

Figure 16.1 Data encryption at rest.

16.2.2   Network Security

Network security [2] has been one of the main concerns for Azure. It has made huge investments in security. Users can use virtual networks and the various security features and services to design, configure, and manage the various cloud applications deployed on Azure.

There are various features that Azure has got to offer to its security concerned customers.

Azure comes up with a variety of features to offer for Network Security. Some of the notable services are Network Access Control (NAC), Azure Firewall, Architecture Azure DDOS Protection Azure Front Door Traffic Manager, Monitoring, and Threat Detection.

These features ensure that there is no compromise with the Network Security. They make sure that any sort of malicious attack to the network gets prevented.

16.3   Data Encryption

Data encryption is one of the most important aspects of cloud security. It ensures that the data does not get into wrong hands.

There are generally two kinds of encryption widely used in Azure which are as follows:

- Data Encryption at Rest
- Data Encryption at Transit

16.3.1   Data Encryption at Rest

Data Encryption at rest deals with information that is stored on physical media irrespective of its digital format. The media can include all those data that is currently residing on any magnetic or optical media, archived data and data backups. It is available for services irrespective of the cloud service model. Azure is capable of managing the data encryption at rest if demanded by the user. It uses symmetric encryption which allows Azure to encrypt and decrypt large chunks of data in a small amount of time. Data encryption at rest is closely associated with the presence of a secret encryption key. It is mandatory to provide secure key creation, storage, access control, and management of access keys to get the secret encryption key.

16.3.2   Data Encryption at Transit

Data encryption at transit deals with such data that has to flow from one location to another. Figure 16.2 talks about the flow of data encryption at transit. It adds another level of security by encrypting data in transit using HTTPS.

Azure allows its users to enjoy various types of encryption models.

The following are some of the encryption models:

1. Client Side Encryption
2. Server Side Encryption
3. Disk Encryption
4. Azure Storage Service Encryption
5. Cell level Encryption

Table 16.1 talks about various types of encryption keys.

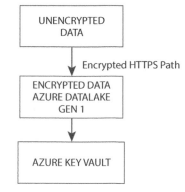

Figure 16.2 Data encryption at transit.

Table 16.1 Types of encryption keys.

Key	Associated with	Storage location	Type
Master Encryption	A DataLake Storage	Key Vault	Asymmetric
Key (MEK)	Gen 1 Account		
Data Encryption	A DataLake Storage	Persistent Storage	Symmetric
Key (DEK)	Gen 1 Account	Managed by a	
		DataLake Storage Gen	
		1 Account	
Block Encryption	Data block	None	Symmetric
Key (BEK)			

16.3.3   Asset and Inventory Management

Azure considers security to be one of its top priorities. It has always several measures to protect its users from any kind of potential security threat. The main aim of asset and inventory management [5] is to prevent unauthorized access. It focuses on all the issues that are linked with active management (inventory, track, and correction) of Azure resources. This is to make sure that only authorized users can access the resources. It helps in identification of unauthorized users and unmanaged resources and removes them. As a result, the speed increases exponentially. It makes resource management a lot simpler.

16.3.4   Azure Marketplace

Azure Marketplace is a one stop for organizations who want to integrate Azure in their business models. Figure 16.3 describes implementation of encryption keys in azure. It makes the work a lot easier for the user. It is a commercial marketplace with a catalog of solutions from the Independent Service Partners (ISV) of Microsoft. It contains services that

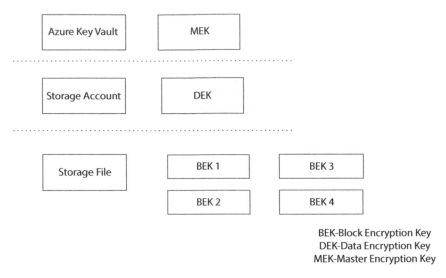

Figure 16.3 Implementation of encryption keys in Azure.

are identical or almost similar to currently used services while keeping an eye on the on-premise environment. Azure Marketplace also serves as an ideal location for all the security services. It keeps on consolidating with premium security partners to take its security to another height.

16.4   Azure Cloud Security Architecture

16.4.1   Working

Information security is always a critical thing for the organizations. It evolves in accordance with the creative ideas and implementations of the attackers and security researchers. Security is among the major aspects of any architecture. It brings many things on to the table such as confidentiality, integrity, and availability assurance. The security pillar revolves around the overview of design principles, best practices, and recommendation.

16.4.2   Design Principles

Security design principles [6] are the gateway that helps in building a secure infrastructure. Application of these principles drastically increases the likelihood of security architecture maintaining confidentiality, integrity and availability.

The following are the various design principles that help in developing a secure environment.

16.4.2.1   Alignment of Security Policies

Security resources are very limited in general. It requires prioritization of efforts by aligning it with the security strategy of the business using data classification. Security resources should be first used for the assets with intrinsic business values and administrative privileges.

16.4.2.2   Building a Comprehensive Strategy

A security strategy should be very comprehensive. It must include considerable investments in culture, processes, and security control across all systems. This strategy should include all those issues ranging from software supply chain to hardware.

16.4.2.3   Simplicity Driven

Complex systems often create confusion and errors. A simple and minimalist design helps in reducing the errors and ensures that there is no confusion. Simple systems make the system user friendly. It also helps in reducing the human efforts.

16.4.2.4   Leveraging Native Controls

Leveraging the native controls over the third party controls is always a good option. The native controls are maintained and supported by service providers. It becomes very easy to have regular updates while leveraging native controls.

16.4.2.5   Identification-Based Authentication

Identification-based authentication is the most common way of authentication for access control. The account control strategy should rely heavily on identity systems for access control rather than depending on direct usage of cryptographic keys.

16.4.2.6   Accountability

It is always considered good to clarify the ownership of assets and responsibilities to prevent future consequences. For a safe and secure design, it is always recommended to grant the entities in the least privileges needed.

16.4.2.7   Embracing Automation

Embracing automation is one of the first things that an organization should look at for ensuring no security breach happens in future. Automation when coupled with skilled humans governing the automation process makes the architecture safe from all potential security threats.

16.4.2.8   Stress on Information Protection

Information is one of the most precious things that an organization owns. By laying stress on information protection, the organization can ensure that data is safe in the constructed architecture.

16.4.2.9   Continuous Evaluation

Continuous evaluation proves to be a masterstroke in protecting an architecture. Regular evaluation of systems and controls help in protection against attackers who keep themselves updating with time.

Irregularity in evaluation might cause a potential threat to the entire organization.

16.4.2.10   Skilled Workforce

The whole system depends on the people who are managing it. Hence, it becomes very important to educate them and make them aware of the various advancements happening.

This helps in ensuring that the workforce is skilled and is capable of handling any potential security attack.

16.5   Azure Architecture

This section describes Azure architecture where Section 16.5.1 talks about components and Section 16.5.2 gives services.

16.5.1   Components

This section deals with Azure API gateway and Azure Functions which are described in Section 16.5.1.1 and Section 16.5.1.2, respectively.

16.5.1.1   Azure Api Gateway

Azure API management is a very strong tool for create modern day API calls for existing backend services. It helps organizations in publishing APIs. To developers, API management ensures a successful API program through developer engagement, business insights, and security. API gateway is an endpoint that accepts calls and routes them to the backend. It is responsible for verifying the API calls, certificates, and other credentials. It enforces rate limits and quotas. It is also responsible for logging call metadata for analytical purposes.

The diagram below explains API Management pictorially.

16.5.1.2   Azure Functions

Azure Functions is a "Compute On Demand" service by Azure. It can serve a list of requirements ranging from building a web API, processing IoT streams to responding to Database changes.

The most common use of Azure Functions is while building a web API. It helps in implementing an endpoint of the web application using a HTTP trigger. Figure 16.4 talks about working of Azure API. It is also a good option for code automation and function troubleshooting.

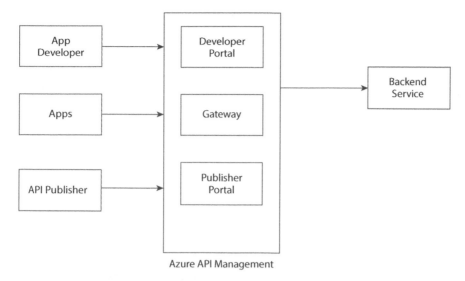

Figure 16.4 Working of Azure API.

16.5.2 Services

This section deals with Virtual Machines (VMs), Blob Storage, Azure Virtual Network, Content Delivery Network (CDN), and Azure SQL Database which are described in Section 16.5.2.1, Section 16.5.2.2, Section 16.5.2.3, Section 16.5.2.4, and Section 16.5.2.5, respectively.

16.5.2.1 Azure Virtual Machine

Azure VM is an on-demand scalable computing resource offered by Azure. Figure 16.5 denotes the graphical representation of Azure Virtual Machine. It is used in scenarios when we want more control over the computing environment. It is basically a computer created using Virtualization. It can be used in various ways. These ways include development and testing, running applications, and many more. VMs give us the freedom of deciding the operating system as well as the region where we want to place the VM.

16.5.2.2 Blob Storage

Azure Blob Storage is Microsoft's object storage solution. Figure 16.6 describes working of Azure Blob Storage. It is highly optimized for storing massive amounts of unstructured data.

Virtual Machine

Figure 16.5 Virtual Machine.

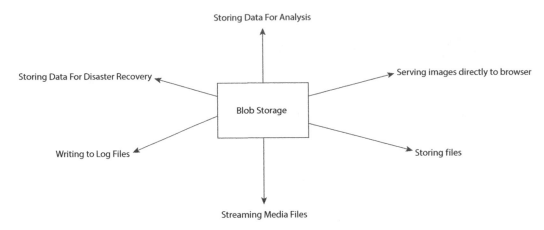

Figure 16.6 Working of Blob Storage.

The following diagram shows the various functions of Blob Storage.
Users can easily access the data stored in Blob via HTTP/HTTPS from any part of the world.

16.5.2.3 *Azure Virtual Network*

It is a fundamental block of building a private network in Azure. It is similar to the traditional network but it comes with Azure's special features which includes Scale, Availability, and Isolation.

All the virtual networks are separated from each other. This ensures that the network is safe from any potential security threat.

16.5.2.4 *Content Delivery Network*

CDN refers to a distribution of servers that ensure content delivery to the users. It accumulates cached content material on servers in Point of Presence (POP) places to make sure minimal latency.

It provides the developers with the ease to swiftly supply excessive bandwidth content material to customers with the aid of using caching content material at bodily nodes placed around the world. It can also handle dynamic content by leveraging network optimization using POPs.

Figure 16.7 explains the working of CDN pictorially.

- User 1 requests a file with a special domain name which can be either a custom domain or an endpoint host name. The DNS routes this request to the best suited POP.
- In case of file unavailability in the edge server available in the assigned POP, then the POP demands the report from the original server which can be any publically accessible web server
- The origin then returns the file to the POP which is then cached to an edge server in the POP. This file is now returned to User 1. Figure 16.8 describes the key features of CDN.

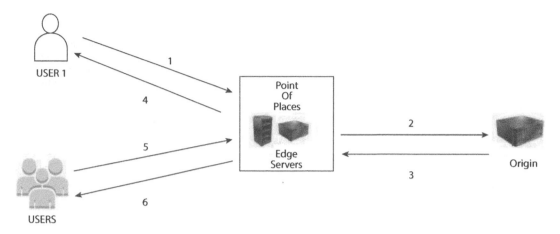

Figure 16.7 Working of CDN.

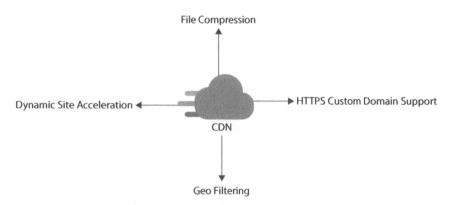

Figure 16.8 Key features of CDN.

- The file stays accumulated in the edge server till the TTL specified by the HTTPS servers does not expire.
- Other users can also access the file using the URL that was earlier used by User 1.

16.5.2.5   Azure SQL Database

It is a relational database model provided by Microsoft. It is a very handy tool which helps in data protection. It works on a security strategy that follows the layered defense in depth approach.

Figure 16.9 shows the layered defense in depth approach.

Azure SQL Database provides a relational database for cloud and enterprise applications. It identifies any potential threat in real time and diagnoses it before it causes any harm. It comes along with proactive vulnerability assessment alerts to make the system highly secure. It also comes along with a Always Encrypted Technology which makes sure that the encryption keys are never revealed to the database engine.

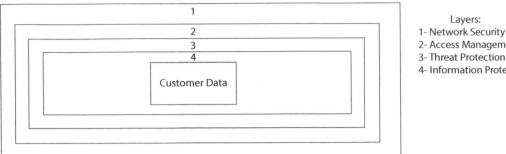

Figure 16.9 Defense in depth.

16.6   Features of Azure

Azure is among the most friendly cloud providers at the enterprise level. There are many enterprise level features that makes Azure a friendly platform.

16.6.1   Key Features

This section deals with Data Resiliency, Data Security, BCDR integration, Storage Management, and Single Pane view which are described in Section 16.6.1.1, Section 16.6.1.2, Section 16.6.1.3, Section 16.6.1.4, and Section 16.6.1.5, respectively.

16.6.1.1   Data Resiliency

Azure stores data in Microsoft's managed Data centers [9]. The default resiliency is called Locally Redundant Zone (LRS). In case of any software or hardware issue, if one copy is not available, then the data keeps on flowing in the system via the other two copies. Zone Redundant Zone (ZRS) and RA-GRS (Read only Geo Redundant Zone) create three copies each in two different zones, thus making six copies in total.

16.6.1.2   Data Security

Azure provides security in a tier architecture format. The DDOS (Data Denial of Service) is the outermost level which eradicates the threat once it reaches a threshold limit. Azure provides various mechanisms of security through Data Encryption at Rest. Azure Storage services by default are enabled for SSE (Storage Side Encryption).

16.6.1.3   BCDR Integration

Azure storage is directly merged with Business Continuity and Disaster Recovery strategy which guarantees that data does not get lost in case of any physical or software failure. Azure provides Azure Backup which deals with backup copies on premises, files and folders, and applications hosted in Hyper V.

16.6.1.4   Storage Management

Azure comes up with automated data tiering service. Automated Data Tiering Service helps place data in SSD, HDD, or cloud storage according to the usage pattern. It also comes along with a unique function called Deduplication. Deduplication makes sure that there is not duplicate data stored which helps in managing storage.

16.6.1.5   Single Pane View

Single Pane View ensures that there is transparency and helps gain visibility and insights about the things happening in infrastructure irrespective of the place where it is hosted.

Microsoft Operation Management Suite (OMS) is a Management As A Service (MAAS) which deals with a single pane view of a hybrid environment.

OMS additionally comes up with automation and security solutions to satisfy the new necessities of hybrid infrastructures. OMS can even be paired with BCDR for higher system potency.

16.7   Common Azure Security Features

This section deals with security center, key vault, and Azure Active Directory which are described in Section 16.7.1, Section 16.7.2, and Section 16.7.3, respectively.

16.7.1   Security Center

Azure Security Center [3] is a unified infrastructure security system that aims at strengthening the safety of the data center and provides advanced threat protection across the hybrid workload within the cloud regardless of the place where is it stored—be it cloud or on premises [7]. It is always said "Security is a shared responsibility". It is a collaborative effort between Azure and the customer. The Security Center provides all the necessary tools for ensuring top notch security posture. Azure Security Center deals with all the most urgent security challenges ranging from rapidly changing workloads to killing security threats in short supply. All the PaaS services in Azure are protected by security center without involving any deployment. Along with it, Security Center takes care of the non-Azure servers and the VMs for each windows and Linux servers by putting in a Log Analytics agent on them. Azure VMs are auto provisioned in Security Center. Security Center keeps analyzing the workloads that are being deployed dynamically. It makes sure that the workloads being deployed are according to the best security practices. It is also integrable with Microsoft Defender for Endpoint. This ensures that the windows and Linux machines are totally integrated with Security Center's recommendations and assessments. Security Center also enables the user automate application control over server environment.

16.7.2   Key Vault

Azure Key Vault is one of the best security features offered by Microsoft. It acts as a locker storing secrets, keys, and certificates in a secure cloud repository. It eradicates the need of storing credentials in the application. It lets the user tighten the security policies and make the system highly secure. Key vault comes up with a unique feature of RBAC (Role Back Access Control). RBAC is a set of instructions that decides the level of Access. The level of access is based on the role assigned.

The various roles are owner, contributor, and reader. These roles play a crucial role when it comes to who can access the data. These roles are a way to attach the extent of access for a particular scope.

This feature comes very handy when the data has to be shared with multiple people. RBAC ensures that there is no data manipulation done by any unauthorized person.

16.7.3   Azure Active Directory

Azure AD [10] is an identity management service provided by Microsoft. Azure AD allows users and organizations to sign in and access in internal as well as external resources.

Azure AD is generally meant for IT administrators when they want to limit the access of the app and its resources based on the business requirements.

Azure AD allows a list of features to work under it some of which are described below.

16.7.3.1   Application Management

Azure AD plays a vital role in application management using application proxy and SSO.

Azure AD is a Identity and Access Management (IAM) system. It acts as a centralized repository for storing information about digital identities. This reduces the burden of managing the credentials and information of applications separately.

Applications ranging from custom developed applications to on-premise applications can be easily integrated with Azure AD.

Application management also helps in recognizing potential security threats. It does daily analysis of the applications and helps in providing high level of security even at the granular level.

16.7.3.2   Conditional Access

Conditional access [11] is a frequently used feature in the modern scenario. Its main role is to integrate signals together, take decisions, and administer organizational policies. It can be called as the core of the new identity driven control plane. These policies can be as simple as IF-ELSE statements.

There are many things that conditional access takes into consideration while enforcing any policy. There are many simple policies such as requirement of MFA that are covered under conditional access.

Figure 16.10 explains the working of conditional access.

16.7.3.3   Device Identity Management

Azure AD reduces the burden of IT administrators by managing the device management. Identity Management can be called as the layout of the device-based conditional access. There are multiple features such as Azure AD joined and Azure AD registered.

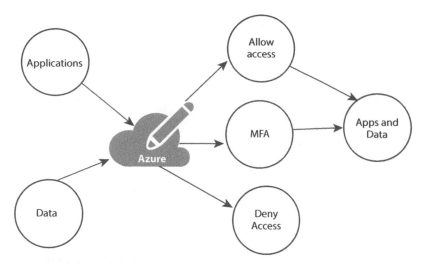

Figure 16.10 Working of conditional access.

Azure AD joined deals with devices that are owned by an organization and are signed with the organization's Azure AD account, whereas Azure AD registered deals with those devices that are personal devices that are signed in using a Microsoft account. These features add an additional layer of security thus saving the organization's precious data.

16.7.3.4   Identity Protection

Identity Protection is one of the most important aspects for an organization. Its main task is to automate the risk detection and provide solutions to it. It uses all the prerequisite knowledge acquired by Microsoft from its sources such as Microsoft Account to protect its user. Identity Protection comes with three role divisions such as Global Administrator, Security Administrator, and Security Operator. Global Administrator is the highest role who has full access to Identity Protection, whereas Security Operator is the lowest role who can only view all the Identity Protection Reports and Overview Reports.

16.7.3.5   Azure Sentinel

Azure Sentinel [12] is a cloud native SIEM and SORE solution that focuses on smart security analytics and threat intelligence, thus working as a one stop solution for alert detection, threat visibility, and threat response. It acts as a single solution covering alert detection, threat visibility, and threat response and much more.

It collects data at cloud scale across all users, devices, and applications. It detects previously undetected threats and also investigates threats with artificial intelligence.

Figure 16.11 describes about the functions of Sentinel pictorially.

One of the most amazing features that sentinel offers is the security automation. It automates all the tasks and simplifies it so that it can be used with services integrated with Azure. It provides a highly scalable architecture to enable scalable automation which is in accordance with development of new technologies and new threats. Sentinel helps us understand the

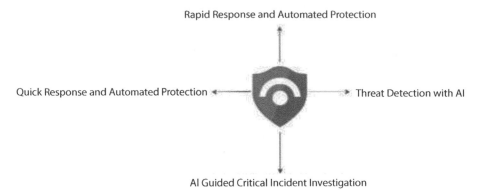

Figure 16.11 Functions of Azure Sentinel.

threat and also lets us know the root cause of the potential threat. This helps in data protection against those attacks which might have caused huge damage in near future.

16.7.3.6   Privileged Identity Management

Privileged Identity Management (PIM) is a handy tool from Azure that helps users to manage, protect, and monitor access to confidential data in the organization. It helps the organizations to limit the number of users who can access confidential data. PIM provides time and approval-based role activation to minimize the risk of any security breach.

There are generally two ways to authenticate using Azure AD for the administrators which are described below.

16.7.3.7   Multifactor Authentication

Multifactor authentication, in general, is a two-way verification. This adds another level of security.

During Multifactor authentication, once the user after entering the password is requested to add another identification which be the OTP shared over cell phone or fingerprint.

Using only passwords can be risky especially in cases where data is highly confidential. Hence, it is a good practice to add MFA to ensure the security of the data.

16.7.3.8   Single Sign On

Single Sign On (SSO) is generally used by App Developers. This allows the user to access the application using its pre-existing credentials. SSO is generally referred to as "Modern Day Authentication". SSO requires the creation of Azure AD in the on-prem which is done by Azure AD during setup. As the user visits the Azure AD sign in page, a Kerberos Ticket is raised which contains the credentials which is then forwarded to Azure AD. Upon verification, the user gets signed in without the need of any user id or password.

16.8   Conclusion

This whitepaper deals with the various security practices in Azure. It describes the various security practices that are generally used in industry. This ensures a top notch security at all levels. It ensures that security is maintained at both the levels be it hardware or software. It is one of the leading cloud service providers that caters to the need of the current business requirements. The various options explained in this white paper have laid stress on how users have safely connected their workloads with Azure. It simplifies the task in selecting the services needed. It helps the individual in understanding the core security concepts regarding the services offered by Azure. This whitepaper would help the individual in dividing which security feature is good for him and his organizations based on their requirements.

References

1. https://docs.microsoft.com/en-us/azure/security/fundamentals/infrastructure.
2. https://docs.microsoft.com/en-us/azure/security/fundamentals/network-overview.
3. Copeland, M., Getting Started with Azure Security Center, in: *Cyber Security onAzure*, Apress, Berkeley, CA, https://doi.org/10.1007/978-1-4842-2740-4_3, 2017.
4. Soh, J., Copeland, M., Puca, A., Harris, M., Microsoft Azure and Cloud Computing, in: *Microsoft Azure*, Apress, Berkeley, CA, https://doi.org/10.1007/978-1-4842-5958-0_1, 2020.
5. https://docs.microsoft.com/en-us/azure/security/benchmarks/security-control-inventory-asset-management.
6. https://docs.microsoft.com/en-us/azure/.
7. De Tender, P., Rendon, D., Erskine, S., Azure Security Center, in: *Pro Azure Governance and Security*, Apress, Berkeley, CA, https://doi.org/10.1007/978-1-4842-4910-9_5, 2019.
8. Copeland, M., Soh, J., Puca, A., Manning, M., Gollob, D., Microsoft Azure and Cloud Computing, in: *Microsoft Azure*, Apress, Berkeley, CA, https://doi.org/10.1007/978-1-4842-1043-7_1, 2015.
9. Chilberto, J., Zaal, S., Aroraa, G., Price, E., Building Solutions in the Azure Cloud, in: *Cloud Debugging and Profiling in Microsoft Azure*, Apress, Berkeley, CA, https://doi.org/10.1007/978-1-4842-5437-0_1, 2020.
10. https://docs.microsoft.com/en-us/azure/active-directory/fundamentals/active-directory-whatis.
11. https://docs.microsoft.com/en-us/azure/active-directory/conditional-access/overview.
12. Copeland, M. and Jacobs, M., Azure Security Center and Azure Sentinel, in: *Cyber Security on Azure*, Apress, Berkeley, CA, https://doi.org/10.1007/978-1-4842-6531-4_5, 2021.

17

Nutanix Hybrid Cloud From Security Perspective

Abhik Banerjee[1]*, Agniswar Roy[1], Amar Kalvikatte[2] and Navneet Bhardwaj[3]

[1]*Department of Computer Science and Engineering, Netaji Subhash Engineering College, Kolkata, India*
[2]*Field CTO/CSA - EMEA, UK, Scotland, Nutanix*
[3]*Department of Electronics and Communication Engineering, Netaji Subhash Engineering College, Kolkata, India*

Abstract

Cloud has become one of the most promising technologies in the industry. It is also one of the highest paying ones. This trend can be stated to have started with the US mandate on Federal Cloud Computing Strategy which led to many countries and companies following suit. But Cloud Computing has its fair share of risks, particularly because it operates on a shared responsibility model. The importance of Disaster Management and Recovery along with Zero-Day Patch Fixes has risen due to this massive cloud adoption. While a few companies have chosen to utilize Public Clouds like AWS, Azure, Google Cloud, Oracle, and more, others have chosen to use Hybrid Cloud. Nutanix is considered to be one of the best platforms for Hybrid Cloud Computing—a paradigm where a public cloud offering is combined with a private data center for the purpose of compliance and security. This chapter focuses on introducing the concepts of Control and Data Planes in Cloud Computing and then introduces key features of Nutanix Hybrid Cloud and the options for Disaster Management and Recovery. It covers the guide for Security Technical Implementation Guide (STIG) from Nutanix and discusses the various methods for hardening security and policy management.

Keywords: Hybrid cloud management, hyperconverged infrastructure, Nutanix hybrid cloud, prism, acropolis, disaster management and recovery, security technical implementation guide, Nutanix revenue growth

17.1 Introduction

Hybrid cloud is a paradigm which acts as a mid-way between public cloud and private cloud with the "best of both worlds". Unlike a pure public or private cloud solution, Hybrid Cloud solutions leverage the usage of a public cloud vendor (like AWS, Microsoft Azure, and Google Cloud) with a privately owned data center of an organization. This may be primarily due to two reasons: compliance-related issues and backup and disaster recovery strategy. Some compliance standards like the GDPR state that data of European Union Citizens must be kept within the EU. Germany also imposes such conditions of business. In such cases, an

---
**Corresponding author*: abhik.banerjee.1999@gmail.com

Rajdeep Chakraborty, Anupam Ghosh and Jyotsna Kumar Mandal (eds.) *Machine Learning Techniques and Analytics for Cloud Security*, (357–378) © 2022 Scrivener Publishing LLC

organization may choose to provision private cloud infrastructure or use infra provided by public cloud vendors specifically for this purpose (Microsoft Azure had provided such an arrangement for Germany). In other cases, the private part of the solution is used to backup data and configurations. Other organizations might choose a hybrid approach due to its flexibility and control.

Hybrid Cloud Management and Hyperconverged Infrastructure (HCI) have seen widespread adoption due to these reasons. At the time of writing, advisory giant Gartner has forecasted that the total market for public cloud service will grow from an estimated $227 billion (US) in 2019 to $354 billion in 2022. While Mordor Intelligence estimates that Hybrid Cloud Infrastructure Market will reach upward of $128 billion by 2025. This accelerated cloud adoption is brought on by the advantages of cost optimization, scalability, and better resource utilization.

In this chapter, we review the market leader of hybrid cloud infrastructure and hyperconverged infrastructure at the time writing—Nutanix. The chapter introduces Nutanix Hybrid Cloud and key terms and services related to it before assessing its security offerings and disaster management and recovery services. It closely follows the renowned Nutanix Bible and Security Technical Implementation Guide (STIG) while offering our views on it. We also surveyed the growth of Nutanix over the years in terms of market value, stocks, and services. Thus, this chapter acts as a primer for Nutanix Hybrid Cloud and its HCI from a security point of view.

17.2   Growth of Nutanix

Since its origin, Nutanix has seen rapid growth and has since become a recognized leader in the HCI market as well as a strong performer in the Hybrid Cloud Management market. It is worth noting that Nutanix has been the recipient of the NorthFace ScoreBoard Award from Customer Relationship Management Institute for seven times in a row. This award is given to the best performers in terms of Customer Experience. This section outlines the assessments of key advisory and research firms like Forrester and Gartner.

17.2.1   Gartner Magic Quadrant

Nutanix has enjoyed a steady place as a leader in the HCI market in the Magic Quadrant of Gartner [1]. Its position as a market leader is observed from 2017 to 2019 and in the recent report of 2020 which was released at the time of writing. The criteria for assessment in this report are the aggregation of compute and storage resources (true HCI). The 2019 report which names Nutanix as clear leader for its ability and ease of execution and vision also estimates that, by 2023, 70% organization would be utilizing HCI in one form or another. The report also underlines the growth of Nutanix's service offerings over the same time period along with its flexibility for third-party services. Nutanix has also won the Peer Insights Customer Choice award from Gartner for the year 2020.

17.2.2   The Forrester Wave

The Forrester Wave assesses vendors over four quarters in a year. It can be observed that Nutanix has been a market leader for HCI at the time of writing. The Forrester Wave evaluates HCI vendors based on broad categories of strategy and vision, strength, and number of current offerings and their presence in the market. Nutanix's position as a clear market leader is apparent on their graph from the Q3 Reports which were released in 2020 and 2018 [4, 5]. The 2018 report also goes on to state that the reduced operational expenditures (OpEx) might be one of the key reasons behind HCI adoption as mentioned by the customers interviewed.

A different pattern can be observed in The Forrester Wave for Hybrid Cloud Management in quarter four of 2020 however. This report states VMWare as the clear leader in terms of market presence, services and strategy. It notes that Nutanix is a new entrant to this market and has been gaining rapid attention courtesy of its position in the HCI market space. Nutanix has been underlined as a strong performer but has also been to have a lower market presence compared to Flexera in terms of offering strength. It is, however, a leader in its band of strong performers in terms of strategy. Please note that since the Forrester Wave Graph indicating Nutanix as leader in HCI could be quoted due to citation policy, we are limited to discussion of the reports released by them. Readers are encouraged to refer to the original reports for a complete market overview.

17.2.3   Consumer Acquisition

Nutanix has shown a steady consumer acquisition over its financial years as is evident from Figure 17.1. This also points to a statistic that has been seemingly unaffected by the COVID-19 pandemic. The Quarter 3 stats of consumer acquisition has seen a slight decline which is expected to recover in the fourth quarter at the time of writing. This points to an increasingly growing market share of Nutanix and consumer faith in its products.

17.2.4   Revenue

Nutanix is listed on NASDAQ (National Association of Securities Dealers Automated Quotations) as NTNX and has been trading since it is IPO on 30th September, 2016. In

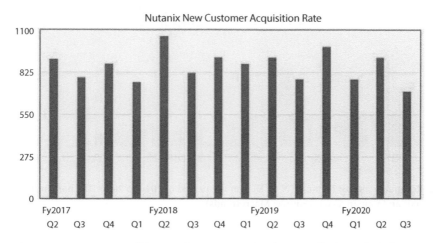

Figure 17.1 Consumer acquisition of Nutanix from 2017 to 2020 (Source: Blocks and Files).

this subsection, we present a brief visualization of Nutanix's Revenue and Gross Profit as a measure of its growth in the market.

As can be observed from Figure 17.2, Nutanix has reported steady growth in revenue and profits across its years of operations. These visualizations are reported upto 10th of December, 2020. As of writing, the quarter ending figures of revenue and gross profit on 31st of October, 2020 of Nutanix stood at an estimated $0.31 billion and $0.245 billion while the annual revenue and gross profit recorded at the time of writing was at $1.3 billion and $1.021 billion respectively. The quarterly growth from the figures is comparatively lower. This may be attributed to the COVID-19 pandemic.

The figures of revenue and gross profit indicate a steady growth of Nutanix in the market which is a mark of confidence and a result of its services offered to its customers—HCI and Hybrid Cloud Management being the core of it. A strong growth can point toward better customer faith in Nutanix Hybrid Cloud which as seen in the later section is warranted due to its services. This marks the end of the overview of technical and financial growth of Nutanix.

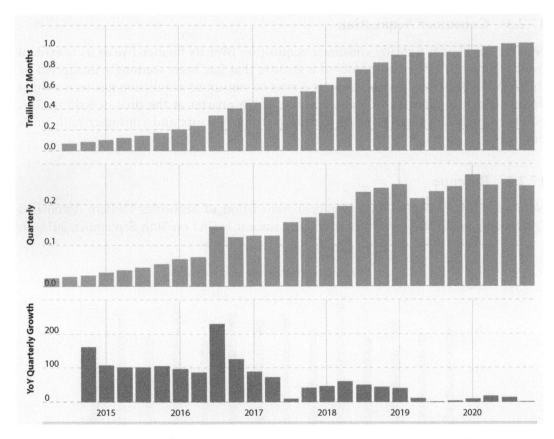

Figure 17.2 Revenue trends of Nutanix (NTNX) over the period of 2014 to 2020. The bars indicate $ (in billions) in y-axis and time in x-axis (Source: Macrotrends).

17.3 Introductory Concepts

This section introduces some key concepts relating to cloud computing and software defined data center in general along with two major concepts of STIG and SCMA before Nutanix Hybrid Cloud Platform is introduced in the next section.

17.3.1 Plane Concepts

The concept of plane arises out of the need to segregate the functioning of a solution for better understanding. This concept is observed in network segmentation as well as in container orchestration tool Kubernetes. In layman's terms, In case of networking, the control plane is termed as the part where the "path" the data is going to take, and the "rules" of travel are defined. While in the data plane the travel actually takes planes. Planes, in this context, are a part of Software-Defined Datacenter (SDDC). There is a subtle difference between the two concepts as discussed in the next part.

17.3.1.1 Control Plane

Control plane is the part of the solution where all the administrative operations take place. It is in the control plane that resource allocation like creating a VM, expanding or upgrading a cluster, is initiated. There are many control planes when it comes to cloud computing. It is not uncommon for different platforms to define planes in a service-specific way. For instance, you might have a "storage control plane" where you get to manage block and object storage services while the "compute" and "networking" control planes attend to their own set of services. However, there is always a "master control plane" which initiates the workflow.

17.3.1.2 Data Plane

Data plane is controlled by the control plane instructions. The control plane does not need to be up for every API hit and resource balancing. It is the data plane that is responsible for these. If we were to take an example, then one could start to provision a VM using the Control Plane but to interact with the virtual machine one needs to use the data plane. It is the part of the whole architecture where protocols like SSH and RDP would be utilized.

It is to be noted that the concept of planes is an abstraction and the boundary between the two is not a fixed line but a hazy one. There are other core concepts in a design that should be practiced for a near-perfect solution.

Security is another important point that one needs to remember. A Control Plane must not be vulnerable. At the time of writing, one of the most recent incidents of a vulnerable control plane was the cryptojacking of automotive giant Tesla's resources on AWS Cloud.

17.3.2   Security Technical Implementation Guides

STIGs are powerful automation and self-healing security models help to maintain continuous security in enterprise cloud environments with efficiency and ease. A complete set of Red Hat Enterprise Linux 7 STIG rules is configured on Nutanix Controller VM (CVM). Nutanix maintains additional STIGs for Acropolis Hypervisor. Nutanix publishes and tests their own custom security baseline documents, based on STIGs that prescribe steps to secure deployment in the field.

17.3.3   SaltStack and SCMA

Security Configuration Management Automation (SCMA) checks periodically for any unknown/unauthorized changes over 800 security entities in the Nutanix STIGs that cover both storage and built-in virtualization. If any component is found with bad configuration, then the component is set back to the supported security settings without any intervention. SaltStack Enterprise, built on Salt open source platform, provides system management software for the software-defined data center with the delivery of event-driven automation for natively integrated configuration management, infrastructure security and compliance, and any cloud or container control.

17.4   Nutanix Hybrid Cloud

Nutanix Hybrid Cloud builds on the concept of HCI. Generally speaking, any cloud platform has three main parts:

- Compute
- Storage
- Networking

In HCI, any two of these parts are merged together. The intention here is to reduce overhead arising out of these parts. For instance, data from the compute functionality may need to be stored. But this can incur costs if the storage medium and the compute medium are not together. In this case, the data needs to be sent through the network to the storage device. Bandwidth is regarded as the costliest resource in the network. The costs incurred due to this transfer can be avoided if the compute and storage are merged together. This is the idea behind Nutanix's Hyperconverged Infrastructure. As shown in Figure 17.3.

The two planes in Nutanix—Prism and Acropolis—are designed with this in mind. A brief description of the services in the Nutanix Hybrid Cloud environment has been presented in Table 17.1. As may be observed, there are a few services which Nutanix adopts from the open-source software world.

17.4.1   Prism

Prism is the control plane for the Nutanix Cloud. It is a User Interface built using HTML. Prism consists of two components—Prism Central and Prism Element. These show the

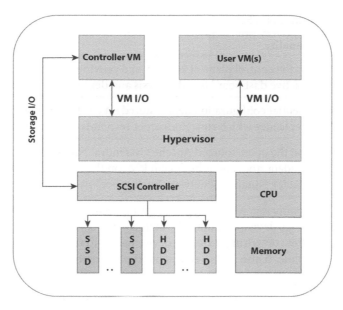

Figure 17.3 Nutanix Hybrid Cloud's Hyperconverged Infrastructure (HCI).

overall cloud status and run on the clusters for minute examinations respectively. Prism features a simplistic and intuitive User Interface. Unlike popular cloud platforms, the users are not overwhelmed by the choices of service available to them. In that respect, Prism helps the user gain control over the deployed Nutanix Solution without needing to manage everything manually. As mentioned before, Nutanix Hybrid Cloud prides on having a solution which focuses on Software Defined Intelligence and self-healing capability by automation. Prism is pivotal to that ideology. In the following sections, we shall explain the two components of Prism.

Since Nutanix is of SDDC and Network Paradigm, Prism—the control plane is used for the addition of new VMs to the cluster, the up-gradation of Hypervisor or any software and network segmentation. These details are hardware agnostic and can be dealt with ease from Prism. For any manner of upgradation, the strategy of "Rolling Update" is followed to ensure no downtime of operations.

17.4.1.1   Prism Element

It is a distributed application that runs on the Nutanix cluster and is responsible for managing the cluster. Every cluster in Nutanix has a Prism Element which is local to it. This Prism Element running on the cluster supervises the operations of the cluster and is crucial for generating the localized reports of cluster nodes' functioning. A Prism Element running in one cluster does not communicate with any other cluster. In the control and management hierarchy, it falls under a Prism Central instance running on a controller VM.

Prism Element features a User Interface which displays interactive dashboards based on the generated logs from the VMs in the cluster. Any localized health check management, container storage management and alert generation take place from Prism Element

Table 17.1 Nutanix Hybrid Cloud Services.

Service name	Functionality
Prism	Prism is the control plane of Nutanix and provides a User Interface for interactive dashboard based analysis and deployment of Nutanix's Services.
Zookeeper	Any essential configuration data is stored on cluster leveraging Zookeeper. The cluster leader which runs Zookeeper responds to all the requests.
Cassandra	Based on the open-sourced Apache Cassandra, Nutanix Cassandra is used as a metadata store and is by default kept on the first SSD of the cluster. It is crucial for Nutanix's "Software Intelligence" paradigm of Hybrid Cloud.
Stargate	Self-Monitoring, Analysis and Reporting Technology, or SMART test is run on a storage device monitored by Stargate in a cluster which fails to respond. At the time of writing, a storage device failing to respond three times is marked as offline. It also plays a role in backup operations.
Genesis	It runs on Nutanix nodes and manages the interactions between services. The services can be checked from the Controller VM from its CLI using the Genesis Command Line Utility.
Cerebro	(Discussed in Disaster Management and Recovery section) Cerebro work in tandem with Stargate for Disaster Recovery and Replication and the functionality also leverages Distributed Storage Fabric's replication and cloning capabilities.
Curator	A part of the HDD storage of the cluster is used for Curator Storage. The main functionality of this service is task scheduling and distribution as well as acting on disk failure. Curator scans on regular intervals for failures. It also functions as the DSF tier balancing agent for storage.
Pithos	Built on Cassandra, Pithos is a service which manages the configuration data of vDisks (discussed in section "Distributed Storage Fabric").
Chronos	It follows the Curator Scans on every node and then allots the required tasks. For instance allocation of extent groups for the writing of data or managing compression tasks to increase disk efficiency.

which is communicated to the Prism Central. Thus, each Prism Element is responsible for a single Acropolis Cluster (refer to later section for Acropolis). As explained in the Disaster Management and Recovery section, Nutanix has what is termed as a "Protection Domain". An Acropolis cluster under a Protection Domain is managed by Prism Element itself.

17.4.1.2 Prism Central

Prism Central shown in Figure 17.4 is the master Control Plane for Nutanix. It manages multiple clusters of VMs and receives statistics from the Prism Element running on Individual Clusters. Unlike Prism elements where the dashboards present interactive visualizations

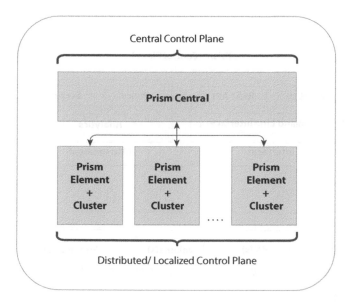

Figure 17.4 Prism control plane segments.

of the cluster data, Prism Central dashboards can be used to view a complete environment-wide statistic. Any detailed performance of multiple clusters can be viewed at this level. Alerts at this level are generated for environment-wide concerns.

17.4.2   Acropolis

Acropolis forms the data plane of the Nutanix Hybrid Cloud. Acropolis is in fact a reinforced Operating System designed by Nutanix to run seamlessly on its hardware and hypervisor. It is composed of three major components which are crucial to Nutanix's "Software-Defined" and "Software Intelligence" paradigms. These are also important for these to provide the features of high availability, scalability, and data redundancy across the environment for seamless functioning.

In this section, we will be focusing on Storage Fabric of Acropolis, while the next section discusses the Nutanix specific hypervisor which integrates with Acropolis. The third component of Acropolis which is App Mobility Fabric majorly deals with migration purposes. Since that is out of the scope at this time, it has not been discussed here. Figure 17.5 shows Acropolis and how it connects with other elements.

17.4.2.1   Distributed Storage Fabric

As mentioned earlier, Nutanix Hybrid Cloud Platform emphasizes on being Software-defined and focuses on Hyperconverged Infrastructure. Distributed Storage Fabric or DSF is a part of Acropolis' storage featuring containers or VMs in a cluster based on Nutanix's Distributed File System built to provide the best performance by localized handling of I/O. The Hypervisor and the Distributed Storage Fabric communicate using protocols such as iSCSI or SMBv3. Courtesy of Nutanix BlockStore, any filesystem kernel driver invocation can be avoided along with context switching.

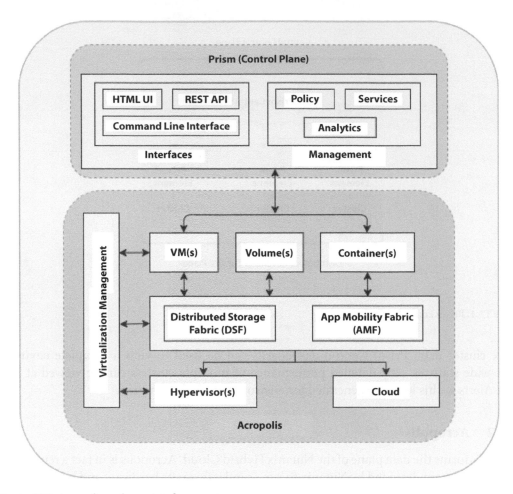

Figure 17.5 Acropolis and associated segments.

Distributed Storage Fabric consists of the following terminological abstractions:

- Containers: Virtual Machines running on the nodes in the cluster are termed as containers in the context of Nutanix DSF. This is different from the container which is run on the hypervisor and shares a kernel with the computer without a need for an OS like VM.
- vDisk: The term vDisk is used as a collective to identify files stored on the VM. This includes VM disks among others. At the time of writing, the minimum size has been set as 512 KB while it is stated that it may as well be close to 9 Exabytes as well in upper limit. A 1-GB space of vDisk is often referred to as an "episode".
- vBlock: vBlock is a higher unit of vDisk where 1 MB of vDisk address space is considered to be 1 vBlock.

Storage Pool - In a cluster of nodes in a Nutanix Cluster, Storage Pool consists of the storage media of HDD and SSD of the nodes. This storage pool is localized to a cluster and as the cluster expands or scales down, so does it is storage pool.

- Extent: A contiguous data allocation size 1 MB logically makes up 1 extent. Storing data in a contiguous manner has been observed to have allocated a consecutive address space which makes reference easier. This contiguous allocation is OS-dependent.
- Extent Group: While an extent forms a logical allocation, extent group forms physical allocation on the storage devices. A replication factor of 3 is often practised in DSF for data redundancy (in case of disaster incident). Depending on this, the size of an Extent Group on a storage medium can vary between 1 and 4 MB.

17.4.2.2 AHV

AHV is Nutanix's Hypervisor for Acropolis OS for Hybrid Cloud. It is offered by Nutanix in a license-free manner and is based on the CentOS KVM. AHV or Acropolis Hypervisor has been touted by Nutanix to be "Hyperconverged Infrastructure Centric". Nutanix provides freedom of choice when it comes to hypervisors. This implies Microsoft's Hyper-V or ESXi might be used or a VMWare hypervisor can be utilized. While it is not mandatory for a customer at this time to use AHV when building a Nutanix Solution, Nutanix's AHV is designed to deliver high performance natively with integrated support for management and security.

It utilizes Open vSwitch for networking and a native Acropolis IP Address Management for providing IP addresses to provisioned VMs and handle DHCP-based connections. AHV has a master-slave pattern where the master runs on a CVM and is implicit in monitoring the cluster state. In case of master failure, a new AHV master or leader is elected. AHV supports hot-addition of Memory and vCPU on the fly.

The Acropolis Distributed Scheduler is responsible for bringing up and managing VMs on a node based on the resource utilization of the node and the need of the VM. Instead of just focusing on the CPU memory, the scheduling also takes into account the disk throughput and latency of a node before allotting a VM to a node. This is done by the ADS Engine which uses machine learning based strategy for such allocations. It is to be noted that the advantages of AHV courtesy of the software-defined paradigm, the throughput and the built-in NUMA support is what made it the very first to be certified by SAP Lab for running SAP HANA workloads.

17.5   Reinforcing AHV and Controller VM

AHV can be reinforced by enforcing a minimum length and character-based requirement for a password. Apart from this, it features the usage of permission banners. These were designed with the United States Department of Defense in mind and as such offer varying levels of assessment based on the rank of the officer auditing the platform.

Nutanix also uses Advanced Intrusion Detection Environment (AIDE), a Linux-based utility that is utilized by Nutanix Hybrid Cloud for detection and acting against threats in real-time. It accomplishes this by using a list of files saved in its database. This is configured by the user from the CLI itself. The files in the database are treated as "trusted". Essentially what the AIDE does is takes a note of the configuration of the system and hashes it. This hash represents the "ideal" state of the solution. AIDE then creates a hash of the system configurations in a later time as dictated by the users. If the hashes do not match up, then this means that there has been a deviation from the planned architecture or configuration. This event is reported to the user.

17.6   Disaster Management and Recovery

Disaster Management and Recovery has always been an important part of any well-architected solution. With the rise of Cloud, it has assumed greater importance because companies which migrate or adopt cloud intend to run and store mission-critical data on their provisioned resources. There have been numerous incidents where an outage of a service being offered on a public cloud platform has been reported due to negligence on part of Clients or End Users' handling of Control Plane. Given that cloud is based on a shared responsibility model, Disaster Management and Recovery is one of the many fields where the clients need to have a clear understanding of DR capabilities and offerings of the cloud provider (in this case, Nutanix).

When it comes to DR, there are two terms which need to be understood for a proper design of disaster strategy and incident response. They are as follows:

1. RTO: RTO stands for Recovery Time Objective. This is the interval of time after an incident which is needed to bring back up service. This does not just refer to the service but also the application state. RTO needs to be drafted with the essential services having a lower RTO and higher priority.
2. RPO: RPO or Recovery Point Objective is crucial for determining the backup periods for data in the environment. It is the maximum permissible time interval where a business can afford a data loss. For instance, if the RPO is 12 hours, then it implies that in case of an incident, the business can afford a maximum downtime of 12 hours before it becomes seriously detrimental.

Nutanix provides multiple ways of Disaster Prevention and Management to its users. In this section, we discuss the Data Redundancy in Acropolis' DSF, Protection Domains and related concepts, Snapshots, Backups, Replications, and Cerebro which manages these facets.

17.6.1   Protection Domains and Consistent Groups

The Nutanix Backup and Disaster Recovery Strategy features (refer to Figure 17.6) terms which relate to the platform's abilities to withstand incidents in a production-grade environment. These are as follows:

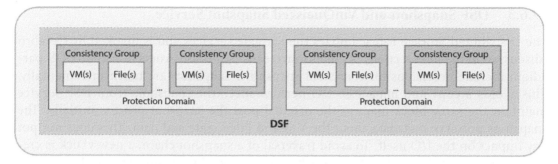

Figure 17.6 Nutanix DR constructs' hierarchy in distributed storage fabric.

- Snapshot Schedule: Snapshot Schedule defines the plan for replication of VMs in a node. As mentioned in the Protection Domain, snapshot schedules can be set for a group of VMs together. The snapshot is done incrementally and Nutanix recommends that this schedule should be within the RPO.
- Consistent Groups: These are groups of VMs which are always maintained at a consistent state. This is particularly important for mission-critical data. While stateless compute has been a rising trend at this time, the storage needs to be able to withstand failure. Database state needs to be maintained. Consistency Groups are used to mark VMs and files which need to come back up after a crash in a consistent state.
- Protection Domain: A protection domain concerns a bigger group of VMs and Files. These are replicated together courtesy of the snapshot schedule.
- Retention Policy: It may become challenging from a storage perspective to maintain multiple snapshots of your VMs and files. For this reason, Nutanix also offers Retention Policy where the point of time in future where the snapshot needs to be discarded may be set.
- Remote Site: The site where the backup and snapshots need to be stored. This is different from the site of the data center. This site is meant to be a secure location which might remain unaffected in case the data center might come under an incident or act of God.

17.6.2   Nutanix DSF Replication of OpLog

OpLog, as the name might suggest, is a log of the operations which is stored on the NVMe devices on at most 12 nodes in the environment in a write persistent manner. The Replication Factor or resiliency factor (synonymous when it comes to Nutanix Hybrid Cloud Solution) determines the number of other CVMs the local OpLog will be written to. Prism is used for fixing the RF in this case. The OpLog replication ensures fault tolerance. Stargate in this case performs checksum validation at regular intervals to ensure top notch performance and detection of any failures resulting from any supposed disk failures on node and other incidents.

17.6.3   DSF Snapshots and VmQueisced Snapshot Service

The Distributed Storage Fabric utilizes the Stargate services and is invoked by Cerebro (discussed in the next section). As mentioned earlier, the constructs in Nutanix DR paradigm include provisions for consistent snapshots. Snapshots are taken incrementally. This avoids a copy and impact on I/O performance. The snapshots from DSF service maintain the same block maps as the original post the snapshot process initially. The snapshots preserve metadata about the VM and Files' state and data. This does not put any impact on the I/O itself. To avoid traversal of a snapshot chain, a new vDisk is created per new snapshot and each of these have their own block maps as the VM continues to function after snapshot creation. The vDisk or the vDisk belonging to the previous state are locked in their moment in time and there are no R/W operations performed on them there on.

The term "Queisce" means "to pause" in middle of "operation". As the term might imply, VMQueisced Snapshot Service temporarily pauses the OS and file system of the VM in the middle of operation. This "stun" of the VM continues till the snapshot has been completed. The service ensures that the application is brought back up in the consistent state post incident.

17.6.4   Nutanix Cerebro

At the time of writing, after the 4.6 update of Acropolis Operating System, the CVM directly communicates with the VM whose snapshot is due to be taken. This has been changed as the "hypervisor-level" snapshot and communication is skipped which was the case before. It is Cerebro which initiates and completes the cycle of snapshot once it has received the instructions from the Control Virtual Machine. This instruction can be sent from Prism following the Protection Domain options.

The CVM relays the signal to Cerebro Leader running in CVM which then communicates to the Nutanix Guest Tool (NGT) instance running on the CVM. NGT is a framework which provides VM management functionality. These include VirtIO drivers for Acropolis Hypervisor and Self-Service Restore. The NGT on the CVM then communicates to the NGT on the VM due for snapshot. The NGT on the VM relays this instruction to the VSS which utilizes the Nutanix Provider to signal the Cerebro on CVM through the NGT on CVM after quiescing the VM. Cerebro then takes the snapshot of the VM. This completes the first cycle.

Cerebro then initiates the resume post the snapshot process by communicating to the Nutanix Provider through NGT on CVM. The Nutanix provider relays this to the VSS which resumes the VM operations from the last state in a consistent manner. This completes the snapshot cycle. It is to be noted that Stargate is involved in snaphoting the VM and storing the snapshot by the instructions provided from Cerebro.

As shown in Figure 17.7, Cerebro functions in a "Leader-Worker" fashion. Cerebro runs on every CVM on the nodes and only one of those Cerebro instances is a "Leader" at a given time. This leader is tasked with deciding what VM data to snapshot and maintaining coordination among the Cerebro Workers on other CVM. Naturally, in case of the failure of the Leader Cerebro instance, another from the fleet of Cerebro workers is elected.

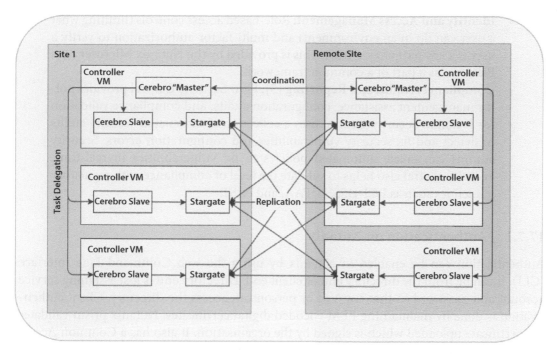

Figure 17.7 Nutanix Cerebro Service functioning.

The snapshot storage and backup can be done based on the topology adopted by the organization. Nutanix considers it a best practice to follow the Mesh topology in this case as the data from one site is backed up in another in the network and this topology ensures that all sites are interconnected. However, it also does support partial Mesh or any modified hybrid topology.

17.7   Security and Policy Management on Nutanix Hybrid Cloud

In practice, it is considered that the no network, application, storage, computational machine, or user is secured. This approach is known as "Zero Trust" Security Practice for obvious reasons. The security protocols are built around this assumption. This can be achieved through some steps. We will discuss each of the steps in brief in this section.

- **Secure Development Life Cycle:** Security starts from the software development process. The software should be continuously audited and tested for known vulnerabilities and secure design so that it can be patched/ upgraded.
- **Platform Hardening/Automation:** Security maintenance in the data center is done automatically to avoid human error. This also adds the feature of scalability and stability without compromising security.
- **Network Micro-Segmentation:** Using policies to restrict access to components and preventing the spread of malware and ransomware.

- **Identity and Access Management:** Role-based access controls (limiting what a user can do in an environment) and multi-factor authorization to verify a user is a key part of zero trust. This is provided by the Nutanix Microservices Platform as a part of a common framework.
- **Compliance, Audit, and Reporting [5]:** Flow Security Central provides policy management assistance, configuration audits, and compliance validation for Nutanix. Security Central uses a collection of automated security audits to detect and fix security vulnerabilities and configuration errors. Security admins can create automated policies to fix vulnerabilities in real-time. Security central also helps to validate the level of compliance with regulatory guidelines such as PCI-DSS, HIPAA, and NIST.

17.7.1   Authentication on Nutanix

Authentication can be enabled in Nutanix by using the web Command Line Interface (CLI). It can be from the directory end or client end. Directory end is just assigning service account and password so that any VM or person can access the directory. Client authentication is done by maintaining PEM encoded digital certificates. Nutanix prism validates the certificate uploaded which is signed by the organisation. It also has a Common Access Card (CAC) authentication which is useful for organizational employees. The card has a physical form and the data can be read by a CAC reader, which verifies the organization's digital signature and can fetch employee data and validate the employee's access limitation in the Active Directory (AD).

When a user is authenticated for a directory, initially he/she has no permission. These permissions are given to specify what a user has access in elements of AD. Permissions, called "Roles" can be given based on individual user, groups, or organizational units (OU). For example, cluster-admin, cluster viewer, and user admin are some roles that can be assigned.

17.7.2   Nutanix Data Encryption

Encryption is an important facet of data storage and transfer. There are two paradigms in this:

- Encryption at Rest: This concerns encrypting the data which is stored in a block or object storage service. This is to prevent unauthorised or unwanted access to data in case of vulnerable control planes.
- Encryption at Transit: This concerns encrypting the data while it is being sent over the network. A compromised network is always the presumption in a well-architected design. In-transit data encryption protects the data from prying eyes.

Nutanix AOS uses AES-256 to encrypt data at rest natively. Both Local and External KMS are supported by Nutanix. This is stronger than SEDs and included in the Ultimate license. In the case of AHV, data is encrypted on the cluster level. For ESXi and Hyper-V, encryption can be cluster or container level. In the case of container level, encryption for new containers must be enabled individually. It has all data protection features like SEDs like encrypted data so no chance of data leak, automatic rotation of encryption keys over time. This encryption is also the KMIP protocol standard.

Key Management Service (KMS): Data encryption can be done in two ways. One way, the encrypted data cannot be brought back to the original form (e.g., Hashing: Passwords are always stored in a server in hashed form so that they cannot be mishandled in case the password gets leaked or server admin wants to access), and the other way is two way, the data can both be encrypted and decrypted using Keys. These keys are crucial as without them the data will be lost forever, so a management service is used for them. Nutanix has a Local Key Manager but it can only be used if the cluster has more than or equal to three nodes. So, in the case of one node cluster, External Key Manager is used. One can also go for SEDs (discussed below) in case of single-node clusters. Two types of keys are managed.

- Data Encryption Key (DEK): Used to encrypt + decrypt the data, symmetric keys like AES-256.
- Key Encryption Key (KEK): A 32-bit long key used to encrypt DEK.

Self Encrypting Drives (SED): SEDs are drives where data is stored at rest in encrypted from. In this case, stolen drives cannot be used. The encryption key rotates automatically, giving further data protection. Nutanix uses open standard (TCG [1] and KMIP [2] protocols) and FIPS [3] validated SED for interoperability and strong security. Read/write is open in SEDs but to use the data, DEK is needed which is known to drive controllers. For authentication purposes, this DEK is encrypted/decrypted using a KEK.

It is considered best practice to have multiple KMS services. This redundancy is for preventing system failure in a real-time, production environment. In short, if CVM cannot get correct Keys from KMS, then it cannot access drive data. If a drive is stolen, the encrypted data cannot be used without the key which is located at KMS. If a node is stolen, then KMS can revoke the node certificates so that the node cannot access the data or drive anymore.

17.7.3   Security Policy Management

Nutanix Flow includes a policy-driven security framework that inspects traffic within the data center. The following are the objective for conducting the inspections:

- Security policies inspect traffic originating and terminating in a data center and eliminate the need of additional firewalls inside the data center.
- These policies are applied in categories (logical group of VMs) instead of individual VMs. So, a category of VM is always secured without administrator intervention irrespective of how many VMs are active.
- Prism central gives a visualized based approach to configuring policies and monitoring traffic to which a given policy applies.

Some of the policies are as follows:

Application Security Policy: Securing an application by specifying traffic sources and destinations. This policy is applied on groups of VM, instead of VM directly.

Isolation Environment Policy: When all types of traffic needs to be stopped between two VM groups then this policy is implemented. VMs of the same group can communicate.

Quarantine Policy: When a VM is suspected of infection and sent for testing, this policy is imposed to separate the VM from the system.

However, all security policies act on the whitelist method (only mentioned sources and destinations are allowed, since the number of allowed is much smaller than restricted and easier to monitor) by default, but the user can activate allow all in all cases. For quarantine policy, an allow none option is also there.

17.7.3.1   Enforcing a Policy

All policies can be enforced in two modes.

Apply mode: applying policies and allowing traffic based on whitelist.

Monitor mode: allowing all traffic (both whitelist and non-whitelist) to observe traffic and fine tune the policy before applying it.

17.7.3.2   Priority of a Policy

Two same types of policies have the same priority, as it only lists inbound and outbound rules and the list has no limit. But two different policies have different priorities, so that they never conflict. Quarantine policy has highest priority, followed by isolation policy and finally application policy.

17.7.3.3   Automated Enforcement

Connectivity between Prism Central and a registered AHV cluster is required while creating and modifying policies, changing the mode of operation. Policies are applied to the VMs in a cluster automatically even if the cluster temporarily loses network connection with the Prism Central instance with which it is registered. New policies and changes are applied to the cluster when connectivity is restored.

17.8   Network Security and Log Management

Nutanix achieves network security by separating management traffic with backplane traffic by creating separate virtual networks. The CVMs have virtual Network Interface Cards (vNIC) to communicate over the virtual networks. The backplane network can be further secured by splitting CVM and host VM in separate virtual networks. Some Nutanix platforms have Remote Direct Memory Access (RDMA) for Stargate to Stargate service communication. This network can be separated too using vNIC.

Traffic type in segmented network can be of broadly two types:

- **Backplane traffic:** It is intra-cluster traffic that comprises traffic between CVMs, CVM to host, and storage.
- **Management traffic:** Traffic associated with Prism and SSH connections, remote logging, SNMP, and user VM with CVM.

17.8.1   Segmented and Unsegmented Network

By default, the unsegment network in Nutanix cluster, the CVM has two virtual network interfaces, eth0 and eth1. eth1 is useful for CVM - hypervisor interaction and eth0 is connected with a built-in external switch which connects the external network via NIC team or bonds. Here, backplane and management traffic both used eth0. Figure 17.8 shows the differences between a default unsegmented network and segmented network.

In segmented network, management traffic uses eth0 interface and backplane traffic uses eth2 interface. During AOS upgrade, if AOS supports network segmentation, then an unsegmented network CVM also gets upgraded with a eth2 interface, even though the network stays unsegmented.

Apart from this, Nutanix also maintains log integrity by forwarding all logs to a central logging system. System and audit logs do not support local log retention period as it increases the chance of Distributed Denial-of-Service (DDoS) attacks. The central log acts as a support for other logs in case of system compromisation. The logs are an important part of the anomaly detection service from Nutanix which first establishes a baseline from observation of the logs generated over a fixed period of time before starting to report any deviation from these baselines during operations. Not to mention, the analysis dashboards of Prism leverage these logs for displaying environment stats to the user.

This completes the case study involving Nutanix Hybrid Cloud from a security point of view with regards to its Disaster Management and Recovery capabilities along with an overview of the beliefs on which the whole platform has been built on, namely, HCI, "Software Intelligence", and Automation-based "one-click" solutions.

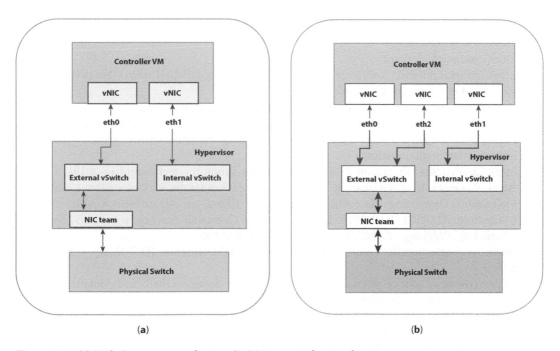

(a)   (b)

Figure 17.8 (a) Default unsegmented network. (b) Segmented network.

17.9   Conclusion

This concludes our case study on Nutanix Hybrid Cloud. In this chapter, we present Nutanix Hybrid Cloud from a security perspective and offer insights into its growth statistics. As is apparent, Nutanix is a clear leader in the HCI market due to its offerings which enable flexible, highly compliant and automated solutions for organizations wishing to adopt Hybrid Cloud. Not only does Nutanix present its own set of infrastructure and services but also extends support to third-party offerings. At the time of writing, the acquisition of Mainframe2 Inc, Calm, Minjar, and Netsil have enabled it to expand its arsenal of offerings and innovate in the HCI and Hybrid Cloud sphere and maintain its position as a clear market leader.

References

1. https://www.gartner.com/en/documents/3994054/magic-quadrant-for-hyperconverged-infrastructure-softwar

2. https://www.gartner.com/en/documents/3894101/magic-quadrant-for-hyperconverged-infrastructure

3. https://www.mordorintelligence.com/industry-reports/hybrid-cloud-market.

4. https://www.forrester.com/report/The+Forrester+Wave+Hybrid+Cloud+Management+Q4+2020/-/E-RES157479

5. https://www.forrester.com/report/The+Forrester+Wave+Hyperconverged+Infrastructure+Q3+2020/-/E-RES157285

6. https://www.forrester.com/report/The+Forrester+Wave+Hyperconverged+Infrastructure+Q3+2018/-/E-RES142274

7. https://www.macrotrends.net/stocks/charts/NTNX/nutanix/revenue.

8. https://blocksandfiles.com/2020/05/28/nutanix-new-customer-growth-and-subscription-push-rebuffs-pandemic.

9. https://nutanixbible.com/.

10. https://portal.nutanix.com/page/documents/details?targetId=Nutanix-Security-Guide-v5_10:Nutanix-Security-Guide-v5_10.

11. https://www.oasis-open.org/committees/tc_home.php?wg_abbrev=kmip

12. https://www.nist.gov/itl/publications-0/federal-information-processing-standards-fips.

13. https://www.virtualramblings.com/describe-and-manage-nutanixs-custom-security-technical-implementation-guides-stigs/.

14. https://analyticsindiamag.com/8-cloud-outages-that-shook-the-tech-world-in-2019/.

15. Aiyar, S., Gupta, K., Rajaraman, R., Shen, B., Sun, Z., Sundaram, R., Colocation, Colocation, Colocation: Optimizing Placement in the Hybrid Cloud, in: *Algorithmic Aspects of Cloud Computing*. ALGOCLOUD 2018. Lecture Notes in Computer Science, vol. 11409, Springer, Cham, https://doi.org/10.1007/978-3-030-19759-9_3, 2019.

16. https://www.ciosummits.com/media/solution_spotlight/Nutanix_IDC_Study_-_Summary.pdf

17. https://cdw-prod.adobecqms.net/content/dam/cdw/on-domain-cdw/brands/nutanix/o-reilly-ebook-designing-and-building-a-hybrid-cloud.pdf.

18. Maiti, A., Singh, R., Chandra, R., Shukla, H., QUEST: Search-Driven Management of Cloud-Scale Data Centers. *2017 IEEE International Conference on Cloud Engineering (IC2E)*, Vancouver, BC, pp. 175–182, 2017.

19. Shen, B. *et al.*, High Availability for VM Placement and a Stochastic Model for Multiple Knapsack. *2017 26th International Conference on Computer Communication and Networks (ICCCN)*, Vancouver, BC, pp. 1–9, 2017.
20. Divate, R., Sah, S., Singh, M., High Performance Computing and Big Data, in: *Guide to Big Data Applications. Studies in Big Data*, vol. 26, S. Srinivasan (Ed.), Springer, Cham, https://doi.org/10.1007/978-3-319-53817-4_6, 2018.
21. Nambiar, R., Ghandeharizadeh, S., Little, G., Boden, C., Dholakia, A., Industry Panel on Defining Industry Standards for Benchmarking Artificial Intelligence, in: *Performance Evaluation and Benchmarking for the Era of Artificial Intelligence*. TPCTC 2018. Lecture Notes in Computer Science, vol. 11135, R. Nambiar and M. Poess (Eds.), Springer, Cham, https://doi.org/10.1007/978-3-030-11404-6_1, 2019.
22. Li, D., Gong, Y., Shen, N., Qin, T., Design and Security Strategy Analysis for SaaS and Private Cloud-Based OA Platform, in: *Technology for Education and Learning. Advances in Intelligent Systems and Computing*, vol. 136, H. Tan (Ed.), Springer, Berlin, Heidelberg, https://doi.org/10.1007/978-3-642-27711-5_34, 2012.
23. Manakattu, S.S., Murugesh, S., Hirekurabar, R.N., Security Landscape for Private Cloud, in: *Inventive Computation Technologies. ICICIT 2019. Lecture Notes in Networks and Systems*, vol. 98, S. Smys, R. Bestak, Á. Rocha (Eds.), Springer, Cham, https://doi.org/10.1007/978-3-030-33846-6_8, 2020.
24. Olowu, M., Yinka-Banjo, C., Misra, S., Florez, H., A Secured Private-Cloud Computing System, in: *Applied Informatics*. ICAI 2019. Communications in Computer and Information Science, vol. 1051, H. Florez, M. Leon, J. Diaz-Nafria, S. Belli (Eds.), Springer, Cham, https://doi.org/10.1007/978-3-030-32475-9_27, 2019.

Part V
POLICY ASPECTS

A Data Science Approach Based on User Interactions to Generate Access Control Policies for Large Collections of Documents

Jedidiah Yanez-Sierra[1]*, Arturo Diaz-Perez[2] and Victor Sosa-Sosa[1]

[1]CINVESTAV-Tamaulipas, Cd. Victoria, Mexico
[2]CINVESTAV-Guadalajara, Guadalajara, Mexico

Abstract

A major concern of cloud storage users is the loss of control over the security and privacy of their information. The use of reliable and efficient access control schemes has proved to be mandatory for organizations whose operation involves sharing digital resources that must be kept private. However, defining access control policies (ACPs) is a non-trivial and critical process that is commonly delegated to expert humans. In this chapter, we propose a methodology based on data science composed of two main phases to comprehensively address the problem of generating APCs for attribute-based encryption schemes. Generated policies can be used to secure interactions with a large set of documents in cloud scenarios. The first phase is related to the detection of relevant users to spread information; the second phase focuses on the generation of policies based on propagation processes. In addition, we propose a strategy to analyze and evaluate the generated policies. The main contribution of this chapter is a method to spread ACPs through a graph of user interactions. We have tested our approach from real data obtained from the Instagram social network. The results obtained showed that the proposed strategies can effectively generate the ACPs to every user in an interaction graph from a small set of relevant users. Our proposal reduced in 96% the manual effort required to assign an ACP to each user in the tested dataset. Results also showed that generated ACPs are 92% effective when measuring the accuracy of the policies.

Keywords: Complex networks, access control policies, CP-ABE, security

18.1 Introduction

Information within organizations has shown an average growth of more than 25% per year [23]. A few examples of this trend are the large volume of content generated by scientific centers, hospitals, and news, space, and government agencies, for example. This massive generation of information has led to a growing demand for computing and storage resources. Cloud computing has proved to be one of the most efficient technologies to

---

*Corresponding author: jedidiah.yanez@cinvestav.mx

Rajdeep Chakraborty, Anupam Ghosh and Jyotsna Kumar Mandal (eds.) *Machine Learning Techniques and Analytics for Cloud Security*, (381–416) © 2022 Scrivener Publishing LLC

handle the problems of storing, processing, and sharing large sets of information. However, the main issue in cloud scenarios is to secure the data access and storage to preserve its confidentiality while facilitating its availability.

Privacy and more recent access control (at the cryptographic level) have been partially addressed by end-to-end encryption schemes based on ABE (attribute-based encryption) cryptography. But all proposals have one thing in common: they need a key to secure each piece of information [10]. Furthermore, they require an access control policy (ACP) for every object in the collection. When organizations need to share a large set of documents with a great number of users, individual policy generation becomes unfeasible. That is primarily because the definition of ACPs is a non-trivial and extremely critical process that is usually delegated to expert humans [13]. Recent works have studied the problem of mining ACPs form system logs [12, 25]. To the best of our knowledge, no proposal in the literature has addressed the problem of generating ACPs from the knowledge gathered through data science approaches.

Let us consider a scenario where there is a large number of users who need to securely share a large collection of documents through a cloud storage infrastructure. Users can be modeled as a network based on their interactions with the document collection, allowing for the discovery of knowledge. By employing data science techniques, users' relations can be processed to extract information such as communities, sub-communities, most relevant users, user hierarchies, correlated topics, among others. Our problem resides in assigning ACPs to users based on the knowledge extracted from the collection itself. Our results are the set of ACPs with the permissions to be fulfilled to access the collection. The ACPs can be used by an end-to-end tool to secure the entire collection of documents so that they can be safely stored and shared on a cloud storage infrastructure, preserving the privacy and sharing capabilities provided by ABE.

In this chapter, we present 1) a novel methodology based on network science and social network analysis to comprehensively address the problem of generating APCs for ABE schemes that can be used to secure the interactions with the large set of documents, and 2) a strategy to evaluate the complexity and effectiveness of the ACPs generated for each user.

Our method is based on the use of complex networks to take advantage of the underlying information discovered when modeling the interactions between the documents and the users as a network. The network is analyzed, and its underlying topology is used to discover a subset of relevant users which will spread APCs from an initial set using the network topology. The methodology to generate ACPs is composed of two main phases: relevant spreader detection and policy spreading and generation. In addition, an evaluation strategy allows us to measure two main characteristics of the generated ACPs: complexity and effectiveness.

The main contributions of this chapter are summarized as follows. First, we propose a new method to spread ACPs through the graph of user-user interactions, leveraging the topology, the inferred partitioning, and the identified relevant users. Second, while policy spreading is taking place, we develop a method to merge policies being aware of the hierarchy of users induced by the graph. Third, the adaptation of a metric for the evaluation of the structural complexity of the policies. Fourth, we describe a novel strategy for measuring policy effectiveness that considers the inclusion of rejected interactions, not explicitly present in the original data. By effectiveness, we refer to the evaluation of accuracy, sensitivity, precision, and F1 score of the generated ACPs, metrics commonly used in classification. We have tested our approach from real data obtained from an Instagram social network.

The results obtained showed that the strategies proposed in our methodology allow us to use the distinct users' interactions modeled as a network to generate the APCs to each user interaction. Results showed that our proposal reduces by 96% the manual effort required to assign an ACP to each user in the tested dataset. Experimentation also showed that generated ACPs have a 92% effectiveness when measuring the accuracy of the generated policies.

In the following, we first review in Section 18.2 some works related to the problem of APC generation for attributed-based encryption schemes. Section 18.3 describes the theoretical foundations of graph theory and network science relevant to this work. Section 18.4 describes the proposed methodology to generate policies from a network of interactions. Section 18.5 describes the experimental evaluation and the achieved results. Finally, we review some remarks in the conclusions and future work in Section 18.6.

18.2   Related Work

In the literature, there are few works related to the automatic or semi-automatic generation of APCs. Le *et al.* [13] propose a semiautomatic approach to infer APCs from Web-based applications. Their proposal infers APCs even when the web sites have not been prepared for it. They use role-based access control (RBAC) as a reference model to build access spaces for a set of known users and roles. Then, they apply machine learning techniques to infer access rules. These rules are presented to human experts for validating and detecting access control issues.

In [17], a multi-objective evolutionary algorithm is proposed to infer APCs in systems for data management. The approach is multi-objective because it aims to learn a policy that, at the same time, is consistent with the input requests, exhibits low complexity, and does not use those attributes which uniquely represent user and resource identities.

In [25], authors presented one of the first policy mining algorithms for attribute-based access control (ABAC). In their proposal, tuples of user-permission from existent access control lists are processed. From the set of identified tuples, authors select a relevant subset and use it as a seed to build access control rules that, through an iterative process, are generalized to cover as many tuples as possible. More recently, a learning-based approach for mining ABAC policies was proposed by Karimi and Joshi [12]. The authors process the system access logs to learn ABAC policy rules to assist the access control administration. Their proposal is based on a learning algorithm that is trained on the tuples of access rights, trying to detect patterns in those tuples. Patterns are used to infer rules, and then, the ABAC policies.

Although the works mentioned above address the problem of inferring APCs, there are three main issues with these algorithms. First, these entrust the security of the information solely to access control systems. Second, they are specific to their data model and policy frameworks. Third and most relevant, these proposals [12, 17, 25] work well with APCs whose rules and entities have few attributes but are inefficient when dealing with a high number of attributes and rules, which makes them unsuitable for most realistic scenarios.

From a data science approach, the policy generation problem can be divided into four core sub-components, 1) data modeling, 2) network characterizing, 3) relevant vertex selection, and 4) spreading and merge of ACPs. These components can be addressed through data science-based approaches, particularly through network science and social network analysis.

In network science literature, various models have been proposed to represent datasets as networks. Documents and users can be depicted as vertices, and the relations between them can be mapped as edges [4]. The modeled graph is bipartite, having documents and users as vertices [18].

Using projection, it is possible to transform a bipartite document-user graph into an only-users graph, i.e., an interaction network [4]. The resulting graph, in many cases, can exhibit those features often found in complex networks. Among others, the graph of user interactions can be used for three purposes: 1) to identify through community detection algorithms groups of users sharing common topological characteristics, 2) to identify users with overriding characteristics, and 3) to perform graph mining tasks to spread focalized information to the entire network.

A crucial problem in network science and social network analysis is related to how to identify influential spreaders in social networks. Spreaders detection is a crucial task for controlling diseases spreading, increasing product exposure, accelerating information diffusion, among other interesting problems [19]. Many works have shown the feasibility of extracting information from networks, such as roles, structures, leaders, or relevant nodes. Moreover, several works have shown the benefit of using partition algorithms (such as community detection schemes) as the foundation for vertex discrimination [3, 14]. Chen and Li [3] propose a structure that allows dividing the entities (members) of a network into different levels according to a belonging coefficient. The belonging factor reflects the strength of the relation between a member and its community. However, the proposed method relies on an earlier seed detection that is not described in their work. Lee *et al.* [14] propose a method to use the content-based behavioral features extracted from user-generated content and behavior patterns. This method allowed them to identify users' roles and to explore role change patterns in social networks. But their approach is not able to analyze large scale social networks.

In [24], an approach for the detection of leaders is proposed based on the analysis of various user interaction metrics. V.Marinescu *et al.* [24] present an approach to identify leaders in a social environment based on the chronological distribution of artifacts (emails). The leadership value is the number of relevant artifacts generated as a result of a temporal causality analysis. The proposed method also determines the behavior patterns that govern a socio-technical context. Authors observed in an email scenario that the speed of an individual's response to their average response time suggests a relative leadership weight between the sender and receiver. The person whose email triggered a series of responses is recognized as a leader and not necessarily the creator of the email.

In the network science field, many centrality metrics have been proposed to address the problem of identifying relevant nodes in a network, including degree, closeness, betweenness, neighborhood, among others. Ma *et al.* [16] proposed a gravity centrality metric to identify influential spreaders in complex networks. Authors use the idea of the gravity formula to determine the relevance of nodes.

18.3   Network Science Theory

In this section, we will summarize some of the key concepts of network science. We will cover the characteristics of the graphs used as part of our proposal, as well as the main

Table 18.1 Description of the neighborhood notation used in this work.

Symb	Description
δ_v	Neighbors of vertex v
δ_v^r	Neighbors of vertex v at distance r. $\delta_v = \delta_v^{r=1}$
δ_v^{IN}	Incoming neighbors of vertex v
δ_v^{OUT}	Outgoing neighbors of vertex v
δ_v^p	Neighbors of vertex v that have the same p policy
Δ_v^{IN}	Incoming neighbors of vertex v sourced from lower k-cores.

attributes and metrics required to characterize them. In general, an edge-weighted graph is defined as follows.

Definition 18.1 (Weighted Graph). *A weighted graph is represented with the tuple $G(V, E, w)$, where V is a set of vertices (or nodes), E is a set of edges (or ties) connecting some vertex pairs that are in V, and $w: E \to \mathbb{N}$, maps each edge $(u, v) \in E$ to a non-negative integer "weight" (or "length", or "cost"): $w(u,v) \in \mathbb{N}$. Numbers of vertices and edges of a network are $|V| = n$, and $|E| = m$, respectively.*

High-level graph metrics have been proposed to characterize them. Some examples are finding its average degree $\langle k \rangle$: $\dfrac{1}{n}\sum_{v \in V} k_v$; finding the connectivity between its neighbors (clustering coefficient) $\langle CC \rangle$: $\dfrac{2|E_u|}{k_u(k_u - 1)}$; finding the shortest path between two nodes d_{uv}; diameter: *diam*: $\max\{d(u, v)|u, v \in V\}$; closeness: $\left(\sum_{j \in V} d_{ij}\right)^{-1}$. Some common notation of the neighborhood is shown in Table 18.1.

Unlike random graphs[1] and graphs arising in scientific applications, like 3D meshes, complex networks show properties that only emerge when modeling real phenomena, commonly massive phenomena, and in some human-made systems such as the internet network. Although various proposals can be found in the literature, for the purpose of this chapter, we will apply the following definition of complex network.

Definition 18.2 (Complex Network). *A complex network is a graph $G = (V, E)$, with a vertex set V and edge set E with: (1) $n = |V|$, $m = |E|$, (2) low average degree $\langle k \rangle \ll n$, (3) low density density $\ll 1$, (4) scale-free distribution $P(k) = \sim k^{-\alpha}$, (5) low average path length $\langle L \rangle \ll n$, and (6) high average cluster coefficient $1/n \ll \langle CC \rangle < 1$.*

Complex networks have been studied due to the particular characteristics they present in comparison to other types of networks. Below are described some features that appear to be common to different types of networks.

---

[1] A random graph is a graph where the occurrence of edges depends on a given probability distribution.

The Small-World Effect. This feature is present in most complex networks and refers to the fact that the distance between any pair of vertices is astonishingly small. Watts and Strogatz found that the majority of the vertex pairs in complex networks are only a few steps away, despite their elevated number of vertices. This property can be mathematically characterized by the average shortest path, $\langle L \rangle$, and the graph diameter [1].

Clustering. Clustering quantifies the level of interconnection of a vertex with its neighbors. For a vertex, the max clustering coefficient value is obtained when the vertex and its neighbors form a clique, while the minimum value when the vertex is disconnected. A definition of the clustering coefficient given by Watts and Strogatz was shown above ($\langle CC \rangle$) [1].

Degree distribution (power law). This characteristic implies that a network has only a few vertices with a very high degree, called hubs (vertices with many neighbors), but that majority of vertices have a low degree (vertices with very few neighbors). Barabasi and Albert found that the degree distribution $P(k)$ of many real-world networks obeys a power law, in which the number of vertices of degree k is proportional to $k^{-\alpha}$ with $\alpha \in [2,3]$ [9]. Networks with a power-law distribution are also known as scale-free networks.

Community structure. A community is generally defined as a group of vertices that have a high density of edges between them and a lower density with other groups [8]. Many real networks present this connecting structure, and it is widely known that most social networks have a community topology since this structure reflects part of human behavior. In every social culture, people tend to organize in groups, either by common interests, work, age, religion, or any other purpose. In this regard, in network science, there are algorithms such as multilevel, modularity, edge betweenness, and label propagation that allows identifying communities in complex networks [20].

Networks characterization. Main efforts in network science have been focused on the statistical characterization of real-world graphs in terms of complex network metrics [1, 9]. Within the network analysis, it is possible to identify different metrics capable of providing information about the network. In general, metrics can be classified according to their scope or type. By their scope can be classified into local and global, and by their type into degree, clustering, distance, and centrality.

Local metrics give information about single elements of a graph, for example, the importance of a vertex in terms of its degree, neighborhood or its distance to other nodes. While *global* metrics can give information about the whole graph, for example, the average shortest path length, the network's diameter, or how much the degree distribution follows a scale-free form.

In a similar way, *Degree* metrics are directly derived from 1) the degree of the vertices, 2) the degree distribution, 3) the clustering around vertices, and 4) the vertex degree correlations. *Clustering* metrics quantify how well connected are the neighbors of a node. *Distance* metrics quantify how far or near are two nodes in terms of hops, weight, shortest paths, etc. Finally, *centrality* metrics quantify how relevant is a node for a defined phenomenon, i.e., for spreading information, relevant paths, and critical places. For more information about the most used metrics in network science, refer to [9].

k-*shell metric.* The k-core decomposition identifies internal cores and decomposes the networks layer by layer, revealing the structure of the different k-shells. A k-core of a graph is defined as the largest subgraph whose vertices have a degree of at least kc [6]. Let $G = (V, E)$

be the graph created from the set of vertices V and the set of edges E. The subgraph $H_{kc} = (W, E|W)$ induced by the set W is a k-shell or kernel of order kc if and only if $\forall\ v \in W$: $k_v \geq kc$ and H_{kc} is the maximum subgraph with this property [15]. The k_v term can be the in-degree, out-degree, or the sum of both for the vertex v, determining different types of cores.

Gravity k-shell metric. Based on the gravity formula proposed by Isaac Newton, the gravity k-shell metric weights the interactions between a node and its neighborhood. It is defined as follows:

$$G_{ks_v} \leftarrow \sum_{w \in \delta_v^r} \frac{ks(v)ks(w)}{d_{vw}^2} \qquad (18.1)$$

where d_{vw} is the shortest path between v and w, $ks(v)$ is the shell of node v, and δ_v^r is the neighborhood of v at r distance. Here, r is used to control the neighborhood of v [16].

18.4   Approach to Spread Policies Using Networks Science

We describe here the proposed methodology based on network science to generate APCs for a large set of documents based on the interaction of the users who use them. The methodology is composed of three main stages, (1) spreaders detection, (2) policy spreading and merging, and (3) policy refinement. The stages and processes required to perform the proposed methodology are shown in detail in Figure 18.1.

From a set of interactions between a large set of users and an equally large set of documents, complex network techniques and strategies can be applied to model a network of interactions, where vertices depict users (more specifically, owners, and consumers), and edges depict the explicit permissions between owners and consumers to interact with their content. It is possible to represent any dataset as a complex network as long as an adequate mapping model is used. Access logs in a cloud sharing environment, as well as social networks with content-sharing, are good examples of massive data sources that increasingly require attention for the confidentiality of their users' information. By applying complex network analysis techniques, it is possible to identify groups of users, their organization in hierarchical levels, and the interaction weights. Such information and a small set of initial policies can be used to generate and spread APCs through the network.

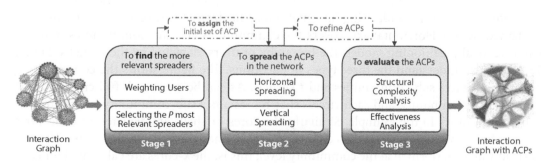

Figure 18.1 Main methodology to generate APCs from an interaction network.

The proposed methodology is based on a $G(V_G, E_G)$ graph that models a set of users and their interactions, which has also been processed through complex network techniques to generate, based on the underlying information, its partitioning from two axes, horizontal and vertical. The horizontal axis covers the communities and sub-communities of users, while vertical partitioning models the hierarchy of users, depicted by the k-shells.

As shown in Figure 18.1, in the *first stage* of the proposed methodology, the graph partitions are used as a reference to define the number of relevant vertices that can be used to properly represent the graph's topology, i.e., the minimum number of relevant vertices that can be used to describe the topology of the entire graph.

The process of assigning, generating, and spreading policies is defined in the *second stage*; this process begins with the assignment of a unique APC defined by an expert to the small subset of relevant vertices; policies are defined based on the context (communities and sub-communities) of users as well as groups of user closest to the spreaders. After the initial ACPs assignment, the process of spreading APCs to the remaining users is carried out. The spreading process consists of two parts: (1) a horizontal spreading on the same hierarchical level as the spreaders and (2) a vertical spreading toward the vertices of greater hierarchy. It is in this second part that new APCs are generated based on the hierarchical interactions of the users.

A proposal for the quality and complexity analysis is presented in the *third stage*. In the first subsection, a strategy to measure the complexity of the policies generated from the methodology described in the previous stage is analyzed, while the second subsection presents a strategy to measure the quality of the policies generated.

All the steps and processes of the methodology based on user interactions are described in detail in the following sections.

18.4.1   Finding the Most Relevant Spreaders

Identifying relevant vertices on a network has become a challenging field in network science. The modeled phenomenon, dataset, semantic information, and gathered information from network characterization play a crucial role when classifying the vertices of a graph. Once a vertex has been weighted, a ranking method and a selection process are needed.

In our proposal, the selection of relevant nodes is performed based only on topological information of the graph and the underlying data extracted during the processing. Our approach to identify and select a subset of relevant vertices from the G graph consists of four main steps: 1) hierarchy identification, 2) vertex ranking, 3) filtering, and 4) tagging relevant nodes.

The proposed methodology is based on a $G(V_G, E_G)$ graph that models a set of users and their interactions, which has also been processed through complex network techniques to generate, based on the underlying information, its horizontal and vertical partitioning, as explained before. Horizontal axis covers the communities and sub-communities of users, while vertical partitioning models the hierarchy of users, depicted by the k-shells. Figure 18.2 helps to understand the three types of partitions. The figure shows the community c_i partitioned into s sub-communities and t kernels. As can be seen, each full circular chart represents a community, and each circle's slice represents a sub-community; there are four sub-communities in the example. Similarly, the cores or shells are depicted as concentric rings, where lower cores are at the center, and higher ones are far from the center. Vertical partitioning is performed at the community level; this is, the k-cores are calculated for each community. This way allows deeply describing the community structure.

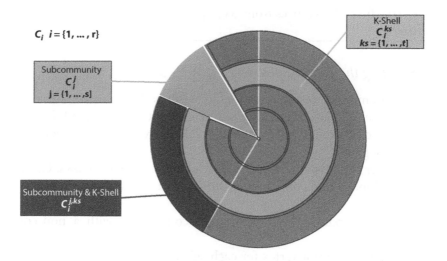

Figure 18.2 Example of a community partitioned into subcommunities and k-shells.

18.4.1.1   Weighting Users

When performing the partitioning by k-shells, the main objective is to identify the users whose information is the most used. On the other hand, the *ranking process* is focused on finding the users that consume the most information, more specifically, the vertices with higher weight in their output edges. In fact, given the structure of k-cores shown in Figure 18.2, it can be assumed that vertices with the highest out-interaction are in the most internal cores.

The output interaction (oi) for a given node v is calculated with Equation (18.2).

$$oi(v) = \sum_{w \in \delta_v^{OUT}} weight(v, w) \tag{18.2}$$

where δ_v^{OUT} are the outgoing neighbors of v and weight($\cdot, \cdot$) is the value of the edge going from v to w.

The weighting of users is performed for each sub-community of the graph, i.e., an induced sub-graph is built for each graph's sub-community. Then, for each node of the induced graph, the weight of its outgoing interactions is computed using Equation (18.2).

The outgoing interaction weight is kept as a vertex's attribute, being available for the process of ranking and selection of relevant vertices.

Algorithm 18.1 Function to select and assign the $\mathcal{P}$ spreaders defined for a sub-community.

Data: $GI_{sc_i^j}$: Graph induced by sub-community j from community i from user graph G

$\mathcal{P}_{sc_i^j}$: The number of vertices to select in the sub-community j of the community i.

Result: $vs = \{v : v \text{ are the vertices tagged as relevant}\}$

1   $V_{ks_0} \leftarrow$ get vertices from K-shell 0 of the induced graph $GI_{sc_i^j}$
2   $SV_{ks_0} \leftarrow$ sort the nodes in V_{ks_0} in descending order by their outgoing interaction weight

3 $vs \leftarrow \{$the first $\mathcal{P}_{sc_i^j}$ vertices from $SV_{ks_0}\}$

4 return vs

18.4.1.2   Selecting the Top $\mathcal{P}$ Spreaders

In this step, the number of relevant vertices to select is determined. The selection could be made at any level (global, community, sub-community, and k-shell). But regardless of where they are selected from, it is desirable that selected vertices can adequately represent the topology of the graph.

The total number of relevant vertices $\mathcal{P}$ to select is defined as follows. Given a graph G that has been partitioned into communities, sub-communities, and k-shells.

- Consider one relevant vertex for each community with a non-complex topology.
- Consider one relevant vertex for each sub-community with a non-complex topology.
- Consider one relevant vertex for each populated k-shell in the sub-community and community that has a complex topology.

A community is considered with a complex topology if (1) it has been partitioned into two or more sub-communities *and* k-shells, (2) it has been partitioned into two or more sub-communities *or* k-shells and its size fulfill $|c_i| \geq |V_{G_{UU}}|/|C|$, where $|c_i|$ is the community size, $|V_{G_{UU}}|$ is the number of vertices in the graph G_{UU}, and $|C|$ is the number of communities in the graph.

In similar way, a sub-community is considered with a complex topology if its size regard the upper level fulfill $|sc_i^j| \geq |c_i|/|sc_i|$, where $|sc_i^j|$ is the number of nodes in the sub-community j of the community c_i, $|c_i|$ is the number of vertices in the community i, and $|sc_i|$ is the number of sub-communities of the community i.

As can be seen, this process defines the number of spreaders to select for each i community $\mathcal{P}_{c_i}$ and for each sub-community, j of community i, $\mathcal{P}_{sc_i^j}$ when applicable. Once vertices are weighted and the mechanism to know the minimum number $\mathcal{P}$ of relevant nodes is defined, the next step is to rank, select and tag these $\mathcal{P}$ nodes in the graph.

As can be seen in Algorithm 18.1, given a sub-community sc_i^j with a complex topology, the induced graph $GI_{sc_i^j}$ is obtained and the $\mathcal{P}_{sc_i^j}$ vertices with the highest outgoing interaction weight [Equation (18.2)] from the first k-core are selected, that is, the vertices with only information consumption. Selected nodes are marked as relevant nodes using the appropriate attribute.

18.4.2   Assign and Spread the Access Control Policies

The spreading process of ACPs from the G graph is performed in two strategies. The *first* one performs a **horizontally spread** of policies among the users of the first k-shell, also called consumer users. This spread aims to group consumers who share common characteristics. Correspondingly, the *second* strategy performs a **vertical spreading** (bottom-up), in which the diffusion is carried out toward the producer users (highest k-core), assigning and merging new policies in the process. Producing users are those that mostly share information; as a result, they are in the upper k-shells since they have the largest amounts of input edges.

Figure 18.2 shows this process. In the first stage, policies would be distributed among all the vertices from the inner core, and in the second stage, ACPs are spread from inside-out (bottom-up strategy).

The initial policies assigned to the spreaders are specified by experts. The manually defined and assigned policies to the relevant nodes should suitably represent the interactions carried out by relevant users. Based on the weight of their incoming interactions, vertices of intermediate levels could take the ACP of the users in the lower cores with a strong relation or build a new one by merging the distinct incoming policies during the bottom-up strategy.

18.4.2.1   Access Control Policies

A standard form to specify ACPs is by using the disjunctive normal form (DNF). That is to say, an ACP should be composed of (1) *groups of attributes* tied by conjunctive operators; (2) each group, also called clause[2], is shaped by a *set of attributes* tied by disjunctive operators; (3) each attribute, in turn, is composed of *literals* of the form *variable = value*.

We call a DNF a permissive policy since the validation of any clause in the formula is sufficient to validate the entire formula, as each clause means an alternative to satisfy the policy. When the number of clauses increases, so does the capacity to satisfy the policy. In the following example, the elements in blue highlight attributes, the elements in red delimit clauses, and the elements in gray are ACP joins.

$$(v_{11} = x_{11} \text{ AND}\ldots\text{AND } v_{1m} = x_{1m}) \text{ OR}\ldots\text{OR } (v_{p1} = x_{p1} \text{ AND}\ldots\text{AND } v_{po} = x_{po})$$

Limiting the ACP specification allows us to combine two or more ACPs in a more controlled way. Further, the policy resulting from a merge of ACPs will maintain the same normal form as the original ACPs, so that the merge could be performed in 1) an incrementally way (one policy at a time), or 2) a complete fashion (with the full set of clauses of the final ACP).

In the topological structure induced by the graph of user interactions, users in the higher hierarchies are those with greater privileges. The vertical process spreads the policies into higher hierarchies by merging policies in permissive mode.

18.4.2.2   Horizontal Spreading

So-called consuming nodes are those vertices that only have out-edges, so their input degree is zero. The incoming degree is used to perform the vertical partitioning (k-shell); as a result, nodes that only consume information are always in the first core.

Since consuming nodes are in the first core, almost all remaining vertices of the community or sub-community may be reached from this core. Furthermore, it could be possible to group the outgoing edges from the first core based on the target vertices.

---

[2] Although in the mathematical literature, clauses refer to a disjunction of literals, it is usual in CP-ABE to name a set of attributes as clauses. In CP-ABE, sets of attributes are linked by conjunctions or disjunctions.

For this reason, the main problem for the horizontal spreading of ACPs is to define a similarity function that allows grouping vertices of the first core based on their outgoing edges. In addition, since the relevant nodes are part of the consuming nodes, they should be taken into account when forming the groups.

The relevant nodes become the group centroids, and the similarity regarding them is calculated to other nodes in the group. With this strategy, the problem of how many groups to form is solved. It also helps to reduce the number of similarity calculations.

Given any pair of vertices v, w, we define the Equation (18.3) to measure the similarity between them, which is calculated considering a scaled weight between v and w vertices and their respective neighborhoods. The scaled weight between any pair of vertices is inversely proportional to the difference of the k-core in which they are located so that the closest neighbors have a greater influence than the distant ones. Equation (18.3) shows the function to calculate the similarity [$sim(v, w)$] between pair of vertices while Equation (18.4) shows the function to calculate the scaled weights.

$$sim(v,w) = \frac{\sum_{i \in \delta_v \cap \delta_w} \varpi(v,i) + \sum_{i \in \delta_v \cap \delta_w} \varpi(w,i)}{\sqrt{\sum_{i \in \delta_v} \varpi(v,i) \cdot \sum_{i \in \delta_w} \varpi(w,i)}} \quad (18.3)$$

$$\varpi(v,i) = \frac{weight(v,i)}{abs(ks(i) - ks(v)) + 1} \quad (18.4)$$

where δ_v is the set of neighbors of v; $\varpi(v,i)$ is the scaled weight of the edge (v, i), v and w are in distant k-shells, lowering the scale of the edge weight; and $ks(v)$ is the k-core of the vertex v.

The horizontal diffusion process is performed for each community or sub-community, depending on the principles defined in Section 18.4.1.2. The process to perform the horizontal distribution is as follows:

1. For each community or sub-community, the induced graph is achieved.
2. Given the set of nodes and the list of spreaders tagged to the community/sub-community, perform the following: For each non-spreader vertex, update its policy using the spreader with the highest similarity.

This process is performed until all sub-communities and communities have been processed. It is necessary to realize that, for small communities having only one relevant node, all the vertices in the community will share the same ACP. Two considerations should be emphasized: 1) The manually assigned policy must consider that all users in the community will share the ACP. 2) The process of spreading the ACP is reduced to a direct assignment for each node in the community.

18.4.2.3   Vertical Spreading (Bottom-Up)

In the vertical spreading, policies are distributed from the inner k-shell to the outermost k-shells considering only the outgoing connections of vertices. In this way, as the process progresses toward the upper cores, policies are merged based on the connections that the vertices receive from the previous levels.

First, vertices in the lower k-shell are grouped by policy, and the vertices of the next core are processed; then, each core is individually processed until the upper core is reached. If a vertex receives edges of 2 or more groups (2 or more different policies), then the affinity to each group is evaluated.

The affinity of a node v regarding a policy p is given by the scaled weight for all the incoming neighbors of v in previous k-cores having the policy p. Equation (18.5) shows the function to calculate the affinity [$affinity(v, p)$] between any node v and any policy p.

$$affinity(v,p) = \sum_{w \in \delta_v^p} \varpi(w,v) \tag{18.5}$$

where $\varpi(v,w)$ is the scaled weight defined in Equation (18.4); $\delta_v^p = \{w \in \delta_v \mid p_w = p, ks(w) < ks(v)\}$, δ_v is the set of neighbors of v, p_w is the policy tagged to w, and $ks(w)$ is the k-core of vertex w, i.e., δ_v^p is the set of incoming neighbors v having p policy.

Based on the defined affinity between a node and a policy, it is possible to build a new policy by merging some of its neighbors' policies.

We define in Equation (18.6) a threshold that must be fulfilled by each distinct policy to decide when a policy should be combined or not. Figure 18.3 shows the three possible scenarios when combining a policy. In each case, the three vertices in the lower part are in a lower core, and they have outgoing edges to the vertex in a higher core. The weight in the edges corresponds to the sum of weights of all the neighbors that are inside each group, showing only one edge and weight for each distinct policy.

As can be seen in Figure 18.3, the threshold is the ratio between the sum of all weights of the incoming edges of v and the number of distinct policies ρ of the neighbors of v.

$$threshold(v) = \frac{\sum_{w \in \Delta_v^{IN}} \varpi(w,v)}{|\rho|} \tag{18.6}$$

where $\varpi(w,v)$ is the scaled weight of the edge between w and v [defined in Equation (18.4)]; $\Delta_v^{IN} = \{w \in \delta_v \mid ks(w) < ks(v)\}$, i.e., is the set of the incoming neighbors of v in lower cores; and ρ is the set of distinct policies in δ_v.

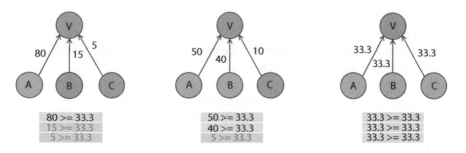

Figure 18.3 Bottom-up merger strategy. Keep one, keep the ones above the threshold, and keep all.

The equations to calculate the merging threshold [Equation (18.6)], the affinity [Equation (18.5)] of a vertex, and a policy, are the foundation for the vertical spreading process of ACPs.

The complete vertical policy spreading process for a given community or sub-community is shown in Algorithm 18.2. The algorithm shows the process for labeling ACPs to vertices in the core k from the vertices and policies of previous cores, symbolized as $k - 1$. To achieve this, Algorithm 18.2 receives two lists of vertices, the set of vertices to be processed V_k, and the set of vertices from the previous cores V_{k-1}. As a result, a new set of vertices $V_{k'}$ tagged with the new assigned policies is returned.

Algorithm 18.2 ends when all the vertices of the set V_k' have been processed, regardless of whether or not all of them have been labeled with an ACP. The set V_k' is returned, and the next core is evaluated, updating the input sets with $V_k = V_{k+1}$ and $V_{k-1} = V_k'$. The process described in Algorithm 18.2 must be executed for each k-cores of a community or sub-community.

Algorithm 18.2 Algorithm to spread ACPs vertically from lower to upper cores.

Data: V_k: List of vertices

V_{k-1}: List of vertices with a tagged ACP in lower cores $(k - 1)$

Result: V_k' : New list of vertices with tagged ACPs

1   $V_k' \leftarrow V_k$
2   **for each** vertex $v \in V_k'$ without policy **do**
3       $\delta_v \leftarrow$ incoming neighbors of v whose k-shell is lower than k
4   **if** $|\delta_v| > 0$ **then**
5           $\rho_v \leftarrow$ list of distinct policies assigned to δ_v
6   compute the policies *threshold* for v by using Equation (18.6)
7           $policy_v \leftarrow \{\varnothing\}$
8   **for each** policy $p \in \rho_v$ **do**
9   compute the *affinity* between v and p by using Equation (18.5)
10   **if** *affinity* > *threshold* **then**
11                  $policy_v \leftarrow policy_v \cup p$
12   **end**
13   **end**
14          $p_v \leftarrow buildNewPolicy(policy_v)$
15   update in V_k' the policy of v with p_v
16   **else**
17   *group* neighbors δ_v by policy
18   **for each** policy $p \in \rho_v$ **do**
19   compute and aggregate the *similarity* between v and all the neighbors with policy p by using Equation (18.3)
20   **end**
21   **if** there is at least one policy p with *similarity* > 0 **then**
22   update in V_k' the policy of v with the policy having the higher similarity value.
23   **else**
24   skip and continue...

25   end
26   **end**
27 end
28 return V_k'

18.4.2.4   Policies Refinement

In the DNF merging two policies means joining the set of clauses that conform them. However, before being assigned to the node, an improvement process is performed to refine the set of merged policies. For a clause to be satisfiable in DNF, all its attributes must be fulfilled. In this sense, if clause A is valid, and the attributes of A are a superset of attributes of B, then B must also be valid. Moreover, if the size of the clause is considered at the validation (if the smallest clauses are checked first), clause B would have precedence over A, thus, A can be removed.

Figure 18.4 shows an example of the process described above. The figure shows two ACPs (ACP_A y ACP_B) and the resulting ACP from the merging and refinement process. It can be observed that the clause $v4 = a4\_3$ $v5 = a5\_1$ $v6 = a6\_3$ 3 of 3 (in red) belonging to the ACP_B is a superset of the clause $v5 = a5\_1$ 1 of 1 (in blue) which belongs to the ACP_A. To fulfill the red clause, it is necessary that the attribute $v5 = a5\_1$ (highlighted in each of the clauses) be met. As a result, the clause marked in red can be eliminated from the final ACP, since fulfilling the attribute $v5 = a5\_1$, all the ACP is validated. The final resulting ACP is shown in Figure 18.4 as ACP_C.

18.4.3   Structural Complexity Analysis of CP-ABE Policies

In cloud scenarios where there is a large set of users sharing an equally large set of resources, generating and maintaining policies that control access is a complex task. In a naive scenario, given n users and m permissions, directly assigning permissions to users requires on the order of $O(m \times n)$ relationships to be maintained. However, in improved schemes, such as those based on functions, roles, or attributes, the number of relationships that must be maintained can be reduced to the order of $O(m + n)$. Furthermore, less complex policies have been shown in the literature to be easier to maintain [25].

The notion of weighted structural complexity (WSC) was first introduced by Molloy *et al.* This metric sums up the number of relationships with possibly different weights [17]. WSC is a generalization of policy size that was first introduced to evaluate policies generated from mining schemes [17]. WSC measures how concise the policies are. Informally, for a given policy, its WSC value will be given by the weighted sum of the number of its distinct elements.

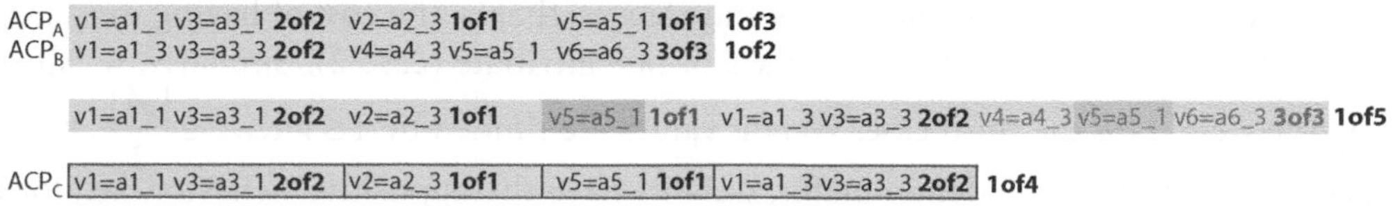

ACP_A v1=a1_1 v3=a3_1 **2of2**   v2=a2_3 **1of1**   v5=a5_1 **1of1** **1of3**
ACP_B v1=a1_3 v3=a3_3 **2of2**   v4=a4_3 v5=a5_1 v6=a6_3 **3of3** **1of2**

v1=a1_1 v3=a3_1 **2of2**   v2=a2_3 **1of1**   v5=a5_1 **1of1** v1=a1_3 v3=a3_3 **2of2** v4=a4_3 v5=a5_1 v6=a6_3 **3of3** **1of5**

ACP_C v1=a1_1 v3=a3_1 **2of2** | v2=a2_3 **1of1** | v5=a5_1 **1of1** | v1=a1_3 v3=a3_3 **2of2** | **1of4**

Figure 18.4 Merge and simplification of two ACPs in DNF model.

18.4.3.1   Assessing the WSC for ABE Policies

The notion of WSC has been adapted and extended for schemes such as RBAC and ABAC, where the policy complexity is given by the weighted sum of its different types of attributes. That is, weights are assigned for the rule types (resources, users, permissions, hierarchies, user-permission, operations, restrictions, etc.) [12, 25]. However, in those works, the weights for weighting the attribute types were equal to 1, but that leaves the WSC simply as the sum of attributes in the ACP, which is not enough to measure the complexity of ABE policies. Consequently, a distinction is made here considering the number of clauses, the number of attributes, and how these are distributed.

The policies for the ABE schemes have no limitations on the type, scope, or class of attributes. For this reason, the attributes are not linked to a user, resource, or location. But the number of clauses and attributes provide enough information to evaluate the cost of a policy.

To deal with ABE policies defined in DNF form, we propose the following extension of the WSC metric. Let R be the set of ABE policies for a dataset and let $\rho \in R$ be a policy assigned to a data. The WSC value for R is given by

$$WSC(R) = \sum_{\rho \in R} WSC(\rho) \tag{18.7}$$

$$WSC(\rho) = \frac{w_1 \cdot |\mathcal{A}_\rho|^2}{w_2 \cdot (|\mathcal{C}_\rho|^2 - b|\mathcal{C}_\rho| + c)} \tag{18.8}$$

where ρ is an ACP, $|\mathcal{C}_\rho|$ and $|\mathcal{A}_\rho|$ are respectively the number of clauses and attributes in policy ρ, w_1 and w_2 are the weights settle to balance the weight of the attributes regarding the number of clauses. Last, b and c can be achieved with a second-degree polynomial fit.

Given a set $\mathcal{A}$ of attributes in an ABE policy, the following cases can be identified: (1) a policy with $|\mathcal{A}|$ attributes in a single clause, (2) one attribute in at most $|\mathcal{A}|$ clauses, and (3) a combination of the above, i.e., variable sub-sets of attributes distributed among a number c of clauses, where $1 \leq c \leq |\mathcal{A}|$. The first two cases could be considered with similar complexity, but we believe that the first case has lower complexity since, on the DNF model, it is easier to evaluate if a single clause is fulfilled than to evaluate many independent clauses. In either case, the most expensive case is the third, in which there are several clauses, each with a variable number of attributes.

Based on the above observations, to determine the coefficients b and c, we propose to use the second-degree polynomial fit shown in Equation (18.9).

$$b,c = \text{polynomial}^2 - \text{fit}\left((1, w_3), \left(\frac{|\mathcal{A}_\rho|}{2}, w_4\right), (|\mathcal{A}_\rho|, w_5)\right) \tag{18.9}$$

where $|\mathcal{A}_\rho|$ is the number of attributes in policy ρ, w_3 and w_5 are the values that allow balancing the complexity between attributes and clauses, that is, the cost of having one clause and $|\mathcal{A}|$ attributes (case 1) or $|\mathcal{A}|$ clauses of one attribute (case 2). Similarly, w_4 allows setting the weight for the third case. Weight values are limited by $1 \leq w_3, w_4 \leq \frac{|\mathcal{A}|}{2}$, but, as the polynomial fit is in the denominator, weights have the oppositive behavior, i.e., lower weights will result in higher costs, and inversely.

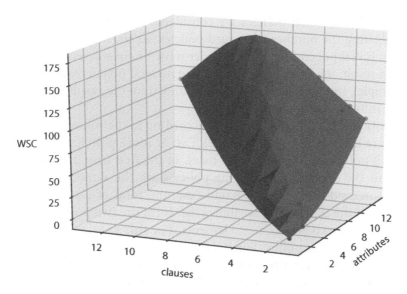

Figure 18.5 Overview of WSC landscape for ACPs from 1 to 13 clauses and attributes, showing the behavior due to the polynomial fitting.

Given the values $|\mathcal{A}| = 13, w_1 = w_2 = 1, w_3 = 2$ and $w_4 = 1.5$, Figure 18.5 shows the landscape of WSC values based on the Equations (18.7), (18.8), and (18.9). Based on the values of w_3 and w_4, the impact when all the attributes are in a single clause is 50% less than in the opposite case, i.e., when the number of clauses is the same as the attributes and each clause has one attribute. The figure shows the behavior of the complexity metric based on the growth trend of clauses and attributes.

For the clauses, Figure 18.5 shows that for the minimum case, the WSC value assigned is 1, increasing with a quadratic trend in terms of the number of clauses. The attributes, in turn, have similar behavior, assigning the lowest value of WSC for clauses with an attribute and having quadratic growth regarding the number of attributes. The figure also shows the impact of the polynomial adjustment. The highest costs are given in the middle-area based on the number of clauses, depicting a vertebral column in the middle points. For the maximum case of attributes (13 for the example), the lowest cost is found when the attributes are in one clause. To scatter the 13 attributes in a similar number of clauses leads to simple clauses (one attribute per clause), which reduces their complexity, hence its low WSC value, but greater than the last case. As described, the highest complexity value is found when are considered 50% of the clauses (7 for the example). In this case, there would be a considerable number of clauses with a high number of attributes, which increases the complexity of manual analysis, just as the metric models.

18.4.3.2   Assessing the Policies Generated in the Spreading Process

The complexity of the policies generated by the mechanism to merge ACPs can be evaluated at two levels. (1) Considering only the complexity due to the policy merging, that is, considering the initial policies as a unit. (2) Taking into account the initial policies defined for each spreader.

In the first level, the initial policies are considered as units. Then, the complexity is reduced to evaluating the number of merged policies. At the second level, the number of attributes in the initial policies for each spreader must be considered to perform the WSC evaluation. As a result, the WSC complexity of the merged policies will be lower-bounded by the least complex initial policy and upper-bounded by the resulting complexity when merging all the initial policies.

The complexity of the policies is analyzed according to the following three base cases: 1) No policies are merged (minimal case); 2) Two or more policies are merged (general case); and 3) All policies are merged (full case). In the first case, the number of clauses and attributes in the source and resulting policies are the same, so the complexity is given by the source policies. In the second case, the total of clauses and attributes is given by the sum of the clauses and attributes that form the two policies that are merged, validating that do not exist redundant elements. For this case, the complexity is given by the resulting size of the policy. Finally, the third one is an extreme case where the final number of clauses and attributes is given by the clauses resulting from the merging and refinement of all the source policies, and the complexity is given by the size of the resulting policy.

18.4.4   Effectiveness Analysis

One of the most important questions that arises after having the model for spreading ACPs is how to validate the quality/correctness of the generated policies. In our proposal, this validation is called effectiveness. Obtaining an evaluation of the ACPs is a relevant task to measure the quality of the entire process for defining policies.

An APC usability study presented by Beckerle and Martucci [2] proposes six main goals (from the perspective of information owners) to create usable sets of access control rules. The first two goals are as follows.

G_1. *Allow no more than the owner wants to be allowed.* This objective defines that a resource should only be accessed by users that are explicitly granted to have access. Therefore, access to resources not explicitly indicated by the owner is the result of non-restrictive or non-existent policies.

G_2. *Allow access to everything the owner wants to be accessed.* This goal settles that a resource must be accessible by the people that have explicitly received access by the owner. This goal complements G_1. Denying access to resources to which access has been explicitly granted is the result of too restrictive access policies, which are often the result of overfitted policies.

Two critical types of failures related to access control decisions are accesses that should be denied but are not; or accesses that should be allowed but are not. Naturally, the consequences of these failures have different impacts on the security and privacy of the information. For example, in a cloud-based sharing scenario, granting access to confidential/critical information for an organization or a public figure carries higher costs than granting access to public domain information. Similarly, denying access to necessary or critical information for authorized individuals carries more far-reaching consequences than denying access to leisure information to an ordinary user. Therefore, in cloud storage scenarios, it is essential to identify and reduce possible failures related to low restrictive or highly over-adjusted policies.

18.4.4.1   Evaluation Metrics

In binary classification, data is divided into two different classes, positives (P) and negatives (N). The binary model then classifies the input instances as positive or negative. Given the inputs, the model outputs (classification), and the actual (reference) outputs, four groups of results are identified; 2 types of correct classification (true), true positive (TP) and true negative (TN); and two types of incorrect classification, false positive (FP) and false negative (FN) [5].

A 2×2 table formulated with these four outcomes is called a confusion matrix, which is used to describe the performance of a classification model in a dataset for which both true values and resulting values from the model are known [21]. Figure 18.6 shows a typical confusion matrix. Cells in green represent correct model predictions, while red ones represent incorrect predictions.

When we need to evaluate the effectiveness of a classification model, we can use the metrics of precision, recall, F1 score, and accuracy, which are based on the confusion matrix.

Precision. It is the ratio of correctly predicted positive observations of the total predicted positive observations. High precision relates to a low FP rate, which in our scenario are unauthorized access. It is defined as follows:

$$precision = \frac{true\ positive}{actual\ results} = \frac{TP}{TP + FP} \tag{18.10}$$

Recall (Sensitivity). It is the ratio of correctly predicted positive observations to all observations in the actual class. High values of recall are related to low rates of FNs, which in our scenario are denials of authorized access. It is defined as follows:

$$recall = \frac{true\ positive}{predicted\ results} = \frac{TP}{TP + FN} \tag{18.11}$$

F1 Score. It is the harmonic mean (average) of the precision and recall. Therefore, this score takes both FPs and FNs into account. The F1 score gives higher weight to FNs and FPs while not letting large numbers of TNs influence the score. It is defined as follows:

$$F1\ score = 2 \times \frac{precision * recall}{precision + recall} \tag{18.12}$$

Accuracy. The accuracy metric can be defined as the ratio of the correctly classified inputs to the whole dataset. Accuracy metric is a great measure when dealing with datasets in which the costs of FPs and FNs are similar. Formally, it is defined as follows:

		Predicted/Classified Class	
		Negative	Positive
Actual	Negative	True Negative (TN)	False Positive (FP)
	Positive	False Negative (FN)	True Positive (TP)

Figure 18.6 An illustrative example of the confusion matrix for a binary model.

$$accuracy = \frac{correct\ predictions}{total\ predictions} = \frac{TP+TN}{TP+TN+FP+FN} \tag{18.13}$$

The accuracy metric allows assessing the ratio of accesses correctly represented by the policies, both TP and TN (synthetic). On the other hand, if the cost of FP and FN is similar, the F1 score metric allows to have a fair value of the model efficiency, it would be necessary to analyze the precision or recall for FP and FN, respectively.

18.4.4.2   Adjusting the Interaction Graph to Assess Policy Effectiveness

An interaction graph $G(V_G, E_G)$ models the real accesses of a set of users regarding the content owned by another set of users. The policies assigned to these interactions must preserve the accesses; however, given the nature of the information and the assignment of the policies, there is a possibility that policies do not fulfill the original authorizations of the owners. The policies assigned to that interaction can: (a) preserve or (b) break the accesses.

Based on goal G_2, it is possible to know that owners expect their information to be inaccessible when there is no explicit interaction. Furthermore, it is expected that assigned policies replicate the authorizations of the owners, i.e., the policies must prohibit access to information where there is no prior explicit interaction, and grant access when it exists.

From the previous analysis, it is possible to map the access control problem to a classification problem. Given the inputs (real access based on the interactions) and the assigned policies, it is possible to validate whether the explicit desire of the owner (i.e., there is an interaction and the assigned policy allows access) is being met, or conversely, there is an interaction, but the policy does not allow access. However, in an interaction-based graph, only explicit access permissions are reflected. Therefore, it is necessary to define a mechanism that allows enhancing the information, not only to evaluate whether the explicit permissions continue to be preserved (TP and FN) but also if the implicit permissions (TN and FP) are kept.

18.4.4.3   Method to Complement the User Interactions (Synthetic Edges Generation)

Due to the lack of real datasets having all the necessary cases described before, in the next two sections, a process to synthesize a large set of possible complementary interactions followed by a strategy to sample a representative set of them is described.

As a result of evaluating the APCs on the interactions, there are only two possible outputs, the policy allows or denies access. When the input is positive (there is access), and the result is also positive (the policy preserves the access), there is a TP. On the other hand, when the output is negative, i.e., the policy denies access, there is a FN.

In order to have the two remaining cases, TN and FP, it would be necessary to evaluate the set ES_G of all the possible combinations of edges not explicitly present in the set E_G, where $ES_G \rightarrow \{\{v, w\} \notin E_G, |v, w \in V_G\}$.

Since the interaction graph behaves like a complex network, it is sparse. Only those complementary edges (also called synthetic) in the scope of users and having meaningful characteristics need to be included. In addition, the set of possible missing interactions is large. Therefore, only a small subset below the actual number of interactions should be incorporated into the analysis of effectiveness. Otherwise, the actual interactions would be hidden.

Construction Based on Graph Partitioning

Partitions in the graph are used to generate synthetic edges that imitate the behavior of the original ones. As described in Section 18.4.2, consumers are in the lower k-shells while the producers are in the upper k-shells. It would be unlikely the existence of synthetic edges whose source is a vertex in an upper k-shell toward nodes in lower k-shells.

To complement the set of edges with synthetic edges that imitate the behavior of the original ones, it is proposed to use the existing partitions in the graph. That is, 1) consider only vertices within the same community or sub-community, and 2) preserve the hierarchy. In this way, only edges from lower shells to upper ones would be considered, as well as only vertices in the same partition.

Filtering Based on Similarity

The selection of possible synthetic edges to be added to the set ES_G can be further refined by applying strategies used in the link identification problem [11]. This problem is both of theoretical interest and practical significance in network science. The link prediction problem aims to identify possible/potential/missing links that might be added/exist to a network.

The most common approach taken has been focused on the so-called structural equivalence. Two vertices are considered structurally equivalent if they share many of the same network neighbors [22].

The Resource Allocation Index (RAI) is defined as the number of resources a node w receives from a node v through indirect neighbors. It was proposed to explain the nonlinear correlation between transportation capacity and connectivity, which can be mapped to the distribution of ACPs.

Let δ_i be the neighborhood of vertex i in a network, i.e., the nodes adjacent to vertex i, the RAI is defined as follows:

$$SI_{RA}(v,w) = \sum_{z \in \delta_v \cap \delta_w} \frac{1}{k(z)}, \qquad (18.14)$$

where $k(i) = |\delta_i|$, i.e., denotes the degree of i [26]. To preserve the topology of the interactions (from the lower k-shell to the upper ones), for the neighborhoods of vertices v and w, only vertices belonging to $z \in \delta_v^{out} \cap \delta_w^{in}$ are considered. The RAI with the above modification is used to compute the similarity between pairs of nodes, and a similarity value is associated with the possible synthetic links formed between a pair of vertices.

A high similarity value between two vertices means that an edge between them is highly likely to exist. That edge will have the same meaning as the current edges, but our goal is to add edges with the opposite meaning. In this regard, instead of the edges with a high similarity value, those with a low one, i.e., those edges with a low probability to exist, are used. However, values in the lower range of a similarity metric can have a bias, also called flattening, associated with the neighborhood wideness used in the similarity metric. As the analyzed neighborhood between two nodes becomes narrower, the proportional number of pairs of vertices with zero similarity becomes higher. That would bias the lower similarity values, an effect that will be called flattening low-range similarity.

Using a global approach to get the similarity may seem the best option to mitigate the effect of flattening the low-range similarity. But, performance is one of the main drawbacks of global similarity metrics, especially when analyzing complex graphs. Furthermore, since users are grouped into communities and sub-communities, neighborhoods cannot extend beyond these.

Sampling Based on a Probability Distribution

Using only vertex similarity to filter possible edges may not reduce the ES_G set enough. To overcome this, an edge-sampling procedure based on a probability distribution function F_X is being used to select a random subset, E'_G, of ES_G.

In summary, a set E'_G of synthetic edges to evaluate implicit permissions in the ACPs is built by A) considering edges only in the same partition, B) filtering edges based on vertex similarity, and C) random sampling based on a probability distribution function. Synthetic edges in E'_G will model denied access. Given the policies, it can be possible to validate, if the permissions are maintained, TNs; or on the contrary, if there is a problem with the policy and there are FP.

Algorithm 18.3 describes the complete process to generate the edges for the set E'_G that will complement the edges of the graph. The algorithm receives as input the interaction graph $G(V_G, E_G)$, a function associated with a probability distribution F_X and a probability of selection $P_{E'}$. The function F_X and the probability $P_{E'}$ are used in the sampling process to control the number of edges that will be added to E'_G. As output, Algorithm 18.3 returns the augmented graph $G^+(V_G, E_G \cup E'_G)$, which includes the synthetic edges; those will be considered the TN and FP cases.

Algorithm 18.3 Process to generate the synthetic edges.

> **Data:** $G(V_G, E_G)$: Graph of interactions
> F_X: Probability Distribution Function
> $P_{E'}$: Selection Probability
> **Result:** G^+: Graph complemented with the synthetic edges

1   $E'_G \leftarrow \{\varnothing\}$
2   $C \leftarrow getCommunities(G)$
3   **for each** $c \in C$ **do**
4     $G_C \leftarrow subgraph(G, c)$
5     $SC \leftarrow getCommunities(G_C)$
6   **for each** $sc \in SC$ **do**
7       $G_{SC} \leftarrow subgraph(G_C, sc)$
8       $KS \leftarrow getOrderedKS(G_{SC})$
9   **for each** $k \in KS$ **do**
10         $V_{ks} \leftarrow v \in V_{G_{SC}} \mid ks(v) == k$
11   **for each** $v \in V_{ks}$ **do**
12           $W_{ks} \leftarrow w \in V_{G_{SC}} \mid ks(w) > k \cup \{v, w\} \notin E_G$
13   **for each** $w \in W_{ks}$ **do**
14             $s \leftarrow Similarity(v, w)$
15             $p \leftarrow P(v, w, s, F_X)$
16   **if** $p \leq P_{E'}$ **then**

17 $E'_G \leftarrow E'_G \cup \{v, e\}$
18   **end**
19   **end**
20   **end**
21   **end**
22   **end**
23 end
24 return $G^+(V_G, E_G \cup E')$

Node traversal is performed considering the graph partitioning. For every vertex v in the k-shell ks (current), the similarity is calculated for the vertices w from the upper k-shells. Based on a probability distribution function and the similarity value for the edge $\{v, w\}$, its probability of being selected is computed. Then, if the probability is lower than or equal to the probability $P_{E'}$, the synthetic edge is added to the graph. Finally, a new network that includes the set of generated synthetic edges is returned.

18.4.5   Measuring Policy Effectiveness in the User Interaction Graph

It is possible to follow a node-based approach to assess the effectiveness of the APCs generated by the vertical and horizontal spreading processes. In this approach, for each vertex, the type of edge (real or synthetic) and the result of the ACP (access or deny) are evaluated. The proportions of TP, TN, FP, and FN for each node is calculated. This approach uses simple counters for each node according to the type of edge and the type of result after applying the ACP. However, instead of just counting edges, the metrics can be refined by considering their weights. The edge weights can be used to calculate the proportions of the confusion matrix.

18.4.5.1   Simple Node-Based Strategy

The node-based evaluation process is simple and straightforward. The evaluation process is carried out by doing a graph traversal. For each vertex v, its output neighborhood δ_v^{out} is evaluated. For each neighbor $w \in \delta_v^{out}$, the result of the ACP is evaluated, obtaining from the real edges, the proportion of edges that are TP and FN, and from the synthetic edges the proportion of δ_v^{out} that are TN and FP. Based on the edge type (real or synthetic) and the result of validating the v policy against the one of w, the edge is counted in one of the four possible cases: 1) real edges and positive access into TP, 2) real edges and denied access into FN, 3) synthetic edges and positive access into FP, and 4) synthetic edge and denied access into TN.

Algorithm 18.4 Function to perform a node-based evaluation of access control policies.

Data: $G(V_G, E_G \cup E'_G)$: Graph of interactions
Result: *precision, recall, f1score, accuracy*: Values of the evaluation metrics for the ACPs assigned to the network

1 $TP, TN, FP, FN \leftarrow 0$
2   **for each** $v \in V_G$ **do**
3   **for each** $w \in \delta_v^{out}$ **do**

4   **if** $\{v, w\} \in E_G$ **then**
5   **if** ACP_v **satisfies** ACP_w **then**
6           $TP \leftarrow TP + (1/|\delta_v^{out}|)$
7   **else**
8           $FN \leftarrow FN + (1/|\delta_v^{out}|)$
9   **end**
10   **else if** $\{v, w\} \in E'_G$ **then**
11   **if** ACP_v **satisfies** ACP_w **then**
12          $FP \leftarrow FP + (1/|\delta_v^{out}|)$
13   **else**
14          $TN \leftarrow TN + (1/|\delta_v^{out}|)$
15   **end**
16   **end**
17   **end**
18 **end**
19 *precision, recall, f1score, accuracy = metrics_evaluation(TP, TN, FP, FN)*
20 **return** *precision, recall, f1score, accuracy*

Algorithm 18.4 shows the complete process to compute the node-based evaluation for the ACPs assigned to the interaction graph. The algorithm receives as an input parameter the interaction graph, composed of the set of vertices V_G, the set of real edges E_G, and the set of synthetic edges E'_G. As a result, it returns the metrics values for the analyzed policies.

18.4.5.2   *Weighted Node-Based Strategy*

Each real edge in the interaction graph has an associated weight (interaction weight). The greater the relationship between a pair of users, the greater the weight of such interaction. The interaction weight can be used to weight the positive (access is maintained, TP) or negative (access is denied, TN) cost due to ACP. Then, the impact of each relationship will be linked to its weight, thus having weighted TP (wTP) and weighted FN (wFN).

Edge weight may have different meanings, such as quality, importance, strength, security level, etc., by using edge weights can help to enhance the meaning of the evaluation metric values. However, it is necessary to introduce weights to the synthetic edges for the FP or TN type of interactions.

Assigning Weights to Synthetic Edges. To compute the weights for the synthetic edges, two strategies are proposed. Let $z \leftarrow SI_{v,w}$ be the set of edges' weights linking the nodes that are in the intersection of v and w neighborhoods. If z is not empty, the weight is obtained by a random number with normal distribution with parameters μ_z and σ_z, the mean and the standard deviation of the weights associated with the edges in z, respectively. If z is empty, the weight is obtained using the mean and standard deviation from the weights associated to the set in the intersection of outgoing edges of v and incoming edges of w.

Using the Edge Weights. The node-based approach can be reformulated to consider weights. In the node-based weighted approach, lines 6, 8, 12, and 14 of Algorithm 18.4 are replaced by using Equation (18.15), where X stands for one of the four cases wTP, wFN, wTN, or wFP. Equation (18.16) shows the function to calculate the total weight of the outgoing neighborhood of node v, value that is needed to calculate the proportion of weight for each interaction. Once the total weight is calculated, the values of wTP, wFN, wFP, and wTN would be calculated as defined in Equation (18.15)

$$X \leftarrow X + weight(v, w) / W_{tot}^v \qquad (18.15)$$

$$W_{tot}^v \leftarrow \sum_{w \in \delta_v^{out}} weight(v, w) \qquad (18.16)$$

where v is a node, δ_v^{out} is the set of outgoing neighbors of v, X may be one of the confusion matrix values, and $weight(v, w)$ is the weight of the edge from v to w.

18.5   Evaluation

We use a dataset of real users and their interactions to test our proposal. The dataset was modeled as a complex network, which was analyzed using complex network techniques to deliver a graph with the partitioning this methodology requires. To perform the evaluation, first, the subset of relevant vertices is selected, and a set of initial ACPs is assigned. The initial set of ACPs is used to perform the spreading process. When the process finishes, all the vertices in the graph have an ACP assigned. These are the policies that are evaluated.

We build a prototype that performs all tasks presented in Section 18.4. The prototype was built using the *python programming language* and the *python-igraph*[3] library. The achieved results are shown in the following sections.

18.5.1   Dataset Description

In this section, we describe the results of the experimentation performed on a dataset of 17K Instagram users having more than 173K interactions. The methods to assess the complexity and effectiveness proposed in the Section 18.4.5 are used to evaluate the policies generated by our proposal.

The dataset used as a source was crawled through the Instagram API from January 20 to February 17, 2014, by Ferrara *et al.* It contains anonymized public media and user information from the social media Instagram.com, specifically, from the Instagram weekend hashtag project (WHP) promoted by Instagram's official blog [7]. The dataset was provided by the authors.

Table 18.2 shows a set of basic network science metrics that were calculated from the source Instagram users graph. As can be seen in Table 18.2, the graph fulfills the properties of a complex network despite the relatively low cluster coefficient. How the dataset was crawled and built is one of the main reasons for having a low clustering coefficient. The 17K vertices of the graph were grouped into 96 communities; these communities are partitioned into 312 sub-communities and 237 k-shells. From the 96 generated communities, only 22 communities were partitioned into 2 or more sub-communities, i.e., about 23%. The rate

---

[3] http://igraph.org/python/

Table 18.2 Main information obtained from the user-user graph partitioning. The full graph has 173K edges, avg., path length: 3.44, cluster coefficient: 0.11, diameter: 12, and assortativity index: 0.101.

Attribute	Full graph	Attribute	Full graph
Vertices	17,842	max ks/community	20
#Connected components	43	#Communities with sub-communities	22
#Communities	96	#Vertices in KS_0	16,114
#Sub-communities	312	#Vertices in $max(KS)$	674
#k-shells	237	#Vertices in-between KS	1,054
max sub-communities/community	28	#Spreaders	625

of partitioned communities might seem low; however, as can be seen in Table 18.2, the graph is already partitioned into 43 connected components. Therefore, if a community is considered for each sub-graph, there are only 53 real communities left; i.e., 54% of the real communities are broken into sub-communities. The number of sub-communities in which the communities were partitioned goes from 2 to 28, with an average distribution of 10.81 sub-communities per community.

As can be expected, the size of the communities does not follow a uniform distribution; on the contrary, there are few large communities (thousands of nodes), while the remaining are small-size communities with dozens of nodes. There are only six communities with a size greater than 1K nodes, 14 communities with a size between 11 and 1K vertices, and 76 communities with 10 or fewer nodes. All these values are usual in complex networks.

The maximum number of k-cores generated in the whole interaction graph is 237 for a single community, the maximum number of cores is 20. Partitioning by k-cores distributes the nodes based on their incoming degree, establishing a hierarchy between users, producers, and consumers. The number of vertices in each core depends exclusively on the degree and connectivity of vertices.

As shown in Table 18.2, the first core has the highest number of vertices (consumers), up to 2 orders of magnitude compared to the rest of cores; most of the remaining cores are in the highest k-cores (producers), and only few hundred are in the intermediate cores.

18.5.2   Results of the Complexity Evaluation

To measure the complexity of the control policies assigned to the interaction graph, the proposed WSC metric was used both in the initial ACPs and in the resulting ACPs after performing the process of vertical and horizontal distribution of policies, as well as the simplification process.

The interaction graph has 625 spreaders to which initial policies were generated with the process described in the next section.

Random ACPs. The number of clauses for each ACP was randomly selected based on the *gamma* distribution with shape $k = 2$ and a scale $\theta = 0.4$, this is, 1 to 5 clauses on average by

Table 18.3 Main results obtained for three sets of random ACPs generated for the spreaders of the interaction graph. § is the initial set; † is the merged set; ‡ is the refined set.

Set of ACPs	$|§|$	$|†|$	$|‡|$	Avg. WSC §	Max WSC §	Desv. Est. WSC §	Avg. WSC ‡	Max WSC ‡	Desv. Est. WSC ‡
S2	625	1,023	998	15.37	159.06	15.15	55.3	604.40	83.19
S16	625	1,013	993	15.90	115.62	17.64	49.82	738.18	71.33
S40	625	1,024	1,009	15.81	121.32	15.56	59.83	609.13	86.02

ACP. The number of attributes for each clause was defined randomly based on the *gamma* distribution with shape $k = 2$ and a scale $\theta = 0.6$, to get 1 to 8 attributes per clause on average. Values computed by the gamma functions were rounded to their nearest integer value. For the values of the tuples: *variable = value*, the normal distribution was used to select between 6 distinct variables and 4 different values for each variable. The values for shape and scale were selected so the number of clauses, and the number of attributes, were between the values [1 – 5] and [1 – 5], respectively.

Three different sets of random policies were generated using the above parameters for the 625 spreaders, S2, S16, and S40. For each set, the vertical and horizontal spreading process was carried out, as well as the simplification process according to the methodology presented in Section 18.4.2. The most relevant results for each set are shown in Table 18.3. It shows in the second column the source policies assigned to the spreaders, and in the third column, it can be seen that due to the merging of two or more source policies performed in the vertical distribution process, new policies are created. Likewise, in the fourth column, it can be seen that the simplification process was able to reduce some of these policies.

Columns 5–7 of Table 18.3 show the WSC costs for the simplified policy set, that is, the set of policies resulting from the simplification process. The minimum cost for the WSC metric is 1 as inferred from Equation (18.8). Likewise, the sixth column shows that the maximum cost grows up to 738 for the analyzed policy sets. However, as shown in the table, the mean and standard deviation is only 59.83 and 86.02 at most. This indicates that, on average, the policies used tend to have a relatively low complexity (based on the WSC value).

From the 1K policies generated on average for the three sets of test policies, it was observed that the average complexity is at least an order of magnitude less than the maximum complexity, and the standard deviation is at most double the average cost, which is consistent with the parameters used to generate the sets of policies.

18.5.3   Effectiveness Results From the Real Edges

Let G be a graph that models the interactions of a group of users, in which 1) its vertices have been partitioned horizontally in communities and sub-communities, and vertically in k-shells; 2) a group $\mathcal{P}_G \ll V_G$ of spreaders has been identified; 3) an APC (ACP) has been assigned to each spreader; 4) the process of horizontal and vertical spreading of ACPs has been performed; and 5) it has been performed the process to simplify the ACPs.

As stated in Section 18.4.5, if the effectiveness metrics are evaluated on the G graph, then only TP and FN values can be obtained. TP when the ACPs correctly preserve the accesses

Table 18.4 Relevant results of the accuracy metric calculation in the graph G, which has only real edges, so just TP and FN can be calculated, i.e., the TP rate.

Result without weights				Result with weights			
Nodes	TP	FN	Accuracy	Weight	wTP	wFN	wAccuracy
17842	16433.48	1408.52	92.11	17842	16642.58	1199.42	93.28

between users, and FN for the ones that despite the existence of explicit access, it is denied. For this scenario, although the information seems to be incomplete, it can be used as a basis for the subsequent cases in which is evaluated the graph $G^+(V_G, E_G \cup E'_G)$ that include the synthetic edges.

The most relevant results when evaluating the accuracy metric in the G graph are shown in Table 18.4. Columns 1 to 4 show the results for the simple vertex-based schema, while the last four show the results for the weighted-based one. In Table 18.4, it can be seen that the weighted-based scheme shows a slight increment of 1.17% in accuracy than the simple vertex-based approach. This difference can be associated with the use of edge weights. When all interactions are of the same weight, Table 18.4 also shows that the vertex-based approach obtains a 92.11% accuracy. Using the weighted-based scheme, accuracy increases up to 93.28%.

18.5.4 Effectiveness Results Using Real and Synthetic Edges

The set of real and synthetic interactions compose the graph $G^+(V_G, E_G \cup E'_G)$. Since the information in E'_G is synthetically generated, it is convenient that $|E'_G| \leq |E_G|$, to keep a balance between the amount of real data and the amount of synthetic one. To keep this relationship, for the aim of this work, the acceptable range for $|E'_G|$ is limited to $0 \leq |E'_G| \leq |E_G|$. In addition, the three considerations made in Section 18.4.4.3 about synthetic edges are taken into account.

To better describe and analyze the behavior of the method to complement the interaction graph by generating synthetic edges, the results obtained in Community 23, which is one of the largest and most representative of the interaction graph, will be used. The Community 23 has 3,150 vertex 23K edges, an average path length of 2.83, a cluster coefficient of 0.183, and a diameter of 6. If these values are compared with those obtained in the entire network (Table 18.2), then it is possible to see that the community can adequately represent the behavior of the full network. Actually, the effectiveness experiments conducted in Community 23 showed similar results to the full graph. For the sake of space, such results are not discussed here.

Results of the Filtering Based on Similarity
Figure 18.7 shows the histogram with the similarity distribution for the set of synthetic edges generated for Community 23. The normalized similarity values are shown on the horizontal axis. Each image shows a different range, the left image shows the range [0,0.01), the upper figure the range [0.01,0.03), and the lower one [0.03,1). On the vertical axis, it is shown the number of edges for each bucket.

After applying the method to generate synthetic edges based on the first filtering strategy, 78,904 synthetic edges were generated, of which 56,013 are in the range [0.01,0.03). In the

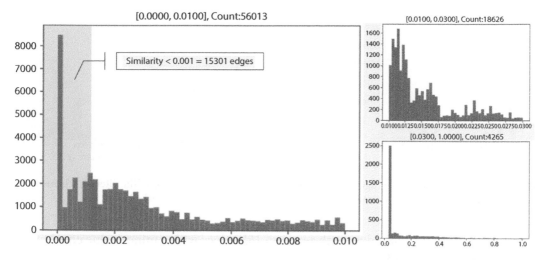

Figure 18.7 Distribution of the similarity values between pairs of nodes assigned to the 56K synthetic edges that conform the set E_G' for Community 23.

second range are 18,626 edges and the remaining 4,265 edges are in the last rank. It can be seen that there are few edges with large similarity values, since the third range, even though it is the widest, only has 5% of the edges, while the first range, the smallest, has more than 70%.

In the graph on the left of Figure 18.7, it can be observed the flattening effect for the lowest similarity values due to the metric used. Also, it can be seen that in the lowest range, there are more than 8K vertices and that in the range [0,0.001), there are 15,301 vertices, which is just over twice the real interactions in that community. Therefore, according to the second consideration in generating synthetic edges, for Community 23, only the edges in the range [0,0.001) were selected. This range varies according to community sizes.

Results of the Sampling Based on a Probability Distribution

As already stated, the third consideration about synthetic edges is to use a probability distribution to randomly select a subset of the synthetic edges.

Three different probability distribution functions were tested: *normal, chi* (χ), and *chi-square* (χ^2). The uniform distribution was selected as the base case since its density function is constant for all elements in the range, i.e., all the synthetic edges would have the same probability of being selected. On the other hand, chi (χ) and chi-square (χ^2) distributions were selected due to the shape of their density function, which generally have a decreasing behavior, which would assign a higher probability to edges with a lower similarity value, i.e., edges with an opposite meaning (see Figure 18.8). The three different probability functions illustrate three different ways of edge-sampling, and here they are used to show the accuracy behavior as more edges are added to E_G'.

The input parameters to shape the probability distributions are selected in such a way that it extended in the selected similarity range ([0.0,0.001] for Community 23). For the uniform distribution, the range of similarity is equivalent to the range defined for the distribution, i.e., [0.0,0.001). For the chi (χ) and chi-square distributions (χ^2) were used the values, $k = 1$ and scale of 2×10^{-3}, and $k = 3$ and a scale 1×10^{-3}, respectively.

For each probability distribution, Figure 18.8 shows the histogram with the average number of sampled edges. As mentioned above, many edges have a similarity value of zero

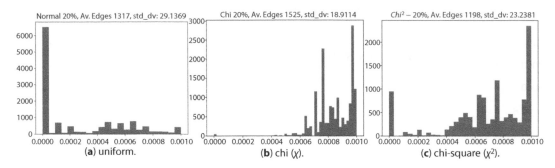

Figure 18.8 Histogram of the average number of selected edges for 31 executions of the filtering scheme in Community 23 of the interaction network, using a proportion of 20% regard to real edges.

or around it, more than 8K edges with zero and 15K edges with a minor value equal to 1×10^{-3}, as shown in Figure 18.7.

By using a uniform distribution, all synthetic edges have the same probability of being selected. This is corroborated by comparing the same range in Figures 18.7 and 18.8a. By using a chi distribution, the range selected is skewed toward the upper range of similarity (Figure 18.8b). In the case of chi-squared distribution, the range is also skewed to the upper range, but there is a higher selection of edges in the lowest range (Figure 18.8c).

Although chi and chi-square distributions assign a higher probability to the lower similarity range, due to the selection condition (Algorithm 18.3, line 16), they show a distinct behavior, since only edges with a probability p lower than $P_{E'}$ are selected.

18.5.4.1   Results of the Effectiveness Metrics for the Enhanced G^+ Graph

Let $G^+(V_G, E_G \cup E'_G)$ be a graph composed of a set of users V, E, and E', a set of (real) interactions denoting explicit accesses between users and a set of synthetic edges that depict the implicit accesses between users, respectively. When the accuracy metric is calculated using only the real edges, a base value is obtained. However, by including synthetic edges in the equation, different accuracy values can be calculated, which are directly related to the proportion of synthetic edges used. Furthermore, based on the probability distribution, sets of synthetic edges with different similarity characteristics are obtained, which also have an impact on the calculation of the accuracy.

Figure 18.9 shows the results when evaluating accuracy for different proportions (in the range $0 \leq |E'_G| \leq |E_G|$) of synthetic edges. The figure shows a graph for the two evaluation schemes described in Section 18.4.5. For each graph, the proportion of edges added to the set E'_G is shown on the horizontal axis. A vertical line indicates a suitable value for the proportion of synthetic edges.

The left end (0) means no synthetic edges added, and the right end (1.0), an inclusion of synthetic edges equivalent to the number of real edges. Similarly, the vertical axis shows the accuracy value for each proportion of synthetic edges used. Each point in the graphs shows the average accuracy values obtained for 32 runs for each proportion test of synthetic edges added. Figure 18.9a shows the results of the simple vertex-based evaluation, while Figure 18.9b shows the weight vertex-based evaluation.

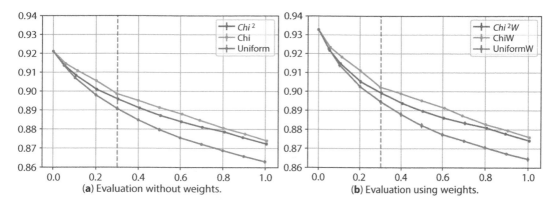

Figure 18.9 Results of the accuracy metric using the two evaluation approaches and the three random filtering schemes for the complete interaction graph G^+.

All the results in Figure 18.9 start in the base case, i.e., when no synthetic edges have been added, and from there, a reduction is observed as more synthetic edges are added. A slow loss in accuracy value is observed, which is more pronounced at the beginning (synthetic edges proportions <50%) and slightly smoother at the end (proportions >50%). The difference between including or not the weights in the vertex-based evaluation has a positive impact of 1.17% in the base value, and only 0.18% when considering a proportion of 100% and the chi-square distribution.

It can be observed that accuracy values differ based on the type of evaluation as well as on the probability distribution, but the loss trend is more or less the same in any case. Adding a number of synthetic edges greater than 100% of original edges would introduce too much noise to the information since synthetic data cannot fully replicate real data, especially if it tries to replicate non-existent behaviors; therefore, as more synthetic data is used, less relevant the data could be. In statistical analysis, it is difficult to define a threshold between the amount of synthetic data and the quality of the resulting information since it is difficult to generate synthetic data that is completely faithful to the original data. This is compounded in the scenario of the present work, where synthetic data must depict opposite behaviors to the real data.

To preserve an adequate balance between the source set and the synthetic data, a reasonable proportion of synthetic edges would be less than 30%. This range will allow the evaluation of the implicit accesses of the owners (unauthorized access) without reducing the quality of the information. This threshold is marked in all the graphs in Figure 18.9. Taking 30% of synthetic edges as a reference, using a node-based assessment and a uniform probability distribution, accuracy is 89.07% and 89.45%, for non-weighted and weighted approaches, respectively. If the chi probability distribution is used, then accuracy is 89.86% and 90.23%, for non-weighted and weighted approaches, respectively. That is, when using a uniform distribution, there is a difference of 0.89 when considering the weight of the edges, and a difference of 0.78 when selecting the chi distribution. Similarly, when using a chi distribution, there is a difference in the accuracy of 2.25% and 3.05% regarding the base case for the non-weight and weight evaluation scheme, respectively.

Figure 18.10 shows the behavior when evaluating the precision, recall, and F1 score metrics defined in Section 18.4.4.1, for different proportions (in the range $0 \leq |E'_G| \leq |E_G|$) of

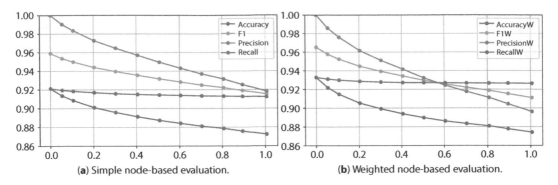

Figure 18.10 Average behavior of the *precision, recall, F1 score,* and *accuracy* metrics results when evaluating the network G^+ using chi sampling function.

synthetic edges. Figure 18.10a shows the behavior of the metrics when using the simple node-based evaluation, while Figure 18.10b shows the behavior when considering weights. In both figures, chi distribution was used for sampling. The proportion of edges added to the E'_G set is shown on the horizontal axis, while the metrics values are shown on the vertical axis. Each point in the figure shows the average accuracy values obtained for 32 runs for each proportion test of synthetic edges added.

As can be observed, the accuracy and recall metrics have the same value when no synthetic edges have been added. For the same proportion, the accuracy metric shows 100%, since all the TP have been correctly labeled and there are no FNs. Comparatively, the metric F1 score, which balances the precision and recall values, obtains an intermediate value. In the figures, it is possible to observe that using or not the weights changes the behavior of the metrics, mainly of the precision metric. This behavior is due to the weight of the FP interactions, making it evident that the growth rate of the FP weight is higher than the one obtained in the simple evaluation, producing a more pronounced fall in the precision values, and therefore in the F1 score.

The precision metric allows the evaluation of the FP ratio, which are the accesses allowed by the policies but not authorized by the owners. In Figure 18.10, it can be seen that even when considering a proportion of 100% of synthetic edges, the accuracy does not fall more than 8% for the simple method and 11% for the weighted node-based method.

Unlike other scenarios observed in works of the classification area, in our scenario, all the metrics described in Section 18.4.4.1 achieve a higher value than that obtained by the accuracy metric. This places the accuracy as a lower bound metric of our scheme since it also considers all the confusion matrix values.

Based on the results, it can be concluded that the quality of the policies generated according to the proposed methodology has a 93.28% accuracy when the policies and weights of the interactions for each vertex are considered. Whereas when only interactions are considered, there is a 92.11% accuracy. When the dataset is complemented with at most 30% of synthetic edges (compared to the total number of edges) showing an opposite behavior to real edges, our methodology has an accuracy value of 89.86% and 90.23% for each strategy, non-weighted and weighted. Also, it can be concluded that the synthetic edges adequately generate both FN and FP cases.

18.6   Conclusions

In this chapter, we presented an approach based on data science to generate APCs for a collection of users based on their interactions. In cloud-based applications, the interactions can represent information access like reading/writing, or access relationships in social networks such as follow, comment, and is-friend-of. This information can be processed using network science techniques and social network analysis to generate APCs for the collection.

The methodology was presented in two stages. In the first stage, taking advantage of the knowledge extracted from the network topology, a method to select and scatter a set of relevant users is presented. In the second stage, the network's topology (and its partitioning) is used as a basis for the spreading of the APCs. Our methodology receives as input a properly partitioned interaction network and provides as output the APCs based on CP-ABE attributes.

In addition, a study was also presented describing the evaluation of the structural complexity of the policies generated, as well as their effectiveness. The complexity metric assigns a ranking value based on a process that replicates a manual evaluation. The effectiveness, on the other hand, evaluates whether the policy preserves or not the user interactions (access). To overcome the lack of real datasets explicitly indicating true denial access, we also proposed a method to include synthetic interactions modeling explicit denials of access. Based on the proposed method, we developed a prototype to perform an experimental evaluation. We use a dataset of 17K users with 173K real interactions.

When there are no synthetic edges to validate the FP and FN, the results showed that the APCs assigned to the vertices have an accuracy value of 93.28% with a node-based weighted evaluation and 92.11% with the simple evaluation.

When a proportion of 30% synthetic edges is added, and a chi probability distribution is used to sample missing edges with negative behavior not present in original data, the reduction from accuracy base cases is only 2.25% for the unweighted vertex-based assessment and 3.05% when weights are considered. For the same proportion, the precision metric has 96.99% and 95.78% for the simple and weighted evaluations, respectively, while F1 score has 94.23% and 94.27% for the same evaluations.

In conclusion, our proposal reduces the complexity of assigning APCs compared to a manual assignment, and the generated policies show a high level of accuracy, even when adding noisy synthetic edges.

The use of complex network techniques makes our proposal suitable to analyze a large collection of information from other areas such as cloud storage schemes, medical files, government, or any other organization that requires the confidentiality of their information. Up to our knowledge, no other data-oriented approach to spread ACPs to a large set of users has been proposed.

Our evaluation demonstrates the viability of this approach and shows promising results for further exploration in the generation of policies to enforce privacy and provide access control to information. As a future work, we plan to explore strategies to modify the ACP spreading process to reduce FPs and FNs. Also, we are exploring the integration of the APCs generation into an end-to-end tool that allows us to propose strategies to make efficient use of the local resources while securing the collection. Finally, we consider that additional work is also required to simplify the APCs generated to optimize their complexity and facilitate their management.

References

1. Barabási, A.-L., Graph Theory, in: *Netw. Sci.*, p. 474, Cambridge University Press, University Printing House, Cambridge, United Kingdom, 2016.

2. Beckerle, M. and Martucci, L.A., Formal definitions for usable access control rule sets from goals to metrics. *SOUPS 2013 - Proc. 9th Symp. Usable Priv. Secur.*, 2013.

3. Chen, F. and Li, K., Detecting hierarchical structure of community members in social networks. *Knowl.-Based Syst.*, 87, 3–15, 2015.

4. Comin, C.H., Peron, T., Silva, F.N. *et al.*, Complex systems: Features, similarity and connectivity. *Phys. Rep.*, 861, 1–41, 2020.

5. Derczynski, L., Complementarity, F-score, and NLP evaluation. *Proceedings of the 10th International LRE Conference, LREC 2016*, pp. 261–266, 2016.

6. Dorogovtsev, S.N., Goltsev, A.V., Mendes, J.F.F., K-Core Organization of Complex Networks. *Phys. Rev. Lett.*, 96, 4, 1–5, Feb. 2006.

7. Ferrara, E., Interdonato, R., Tagarelli, A., Online popularity and topical interests through the lens of instagram, in: *Proc. 25th ACM Conf. Hypertext Soc. media - HT '14*, vol. i, ACM Press, New York, New York, USA, pp. 24–34, 2014.

8. Fortunato, S., Community detection in graphs. *Phys. Rep.*, 486, 3–5, 75–174, 2010.

9. Garcia-Robledo, A., Diaz-Perez, A., Morales-Luna, G., Characterization and Coarsening of Autonomous System Networks: Measuring and Simplifying the Internet. In *Advanced Methods for Complex Network Analysis*, Meghanathan, Natarajan (ed.), pp. 148–179. IGI Global, Hershey, PA, 2016. http://doi:10.4018/978-1-4666-9964-9.ch006

10. Gonzalez-Compean, J.L., Sosa-Sosa, V., Diaz-Perez, A., Carretero, J., Yanez-Sierra, J., Sacbe: A building block approach for constructing efficient and flexible end-to-end cloud storage. *J. Syst. Software*, 135, 143–156, 2018.

11. Hou, L. and Liu, K., Common neighbour structure and similarity intensity in complex networks. *Phys. Lett. Sect. A: General, Atomic Solid State Physics*, 381, 39, 3377–3383, 2017.

12. Karimi, L. and Joshi, J., An Unsupervised Learning Based Approach for Mining Attribute Based Access Control Policies. *Proc. - 2018 IEEE Int. Conf. Big Data, Big Data 2018*, pp. 1427–1436, 2019.

13. Le, H.T., Nguyen, C.D., Briand, L., Hourte, B., Automated Inference of Access Control Policies for Web Applications, in: *Proc. 20th ACM Symp. Access Control Model. Technol. - SACMAT '15*, pp. 27–37, 2015.

14. Lee, A.J.T., Yang, F.C., Tsai, H.C., Lai, Y.Y., Discovering content-based behavioral roles in social networks. *Decis. Support Syst.*, 59, 1, 250–261, 2014.

15. Liu, Y., Tang, M., Zhou, T., Younghae, D., Core-like groups result in invalidation of identifying super-spreader by k-shell decomposition. *Sci. Rep.*, 5, 1–21, 2015.

16. Ma, L.L., Ma, C., Zhang, H.F., Wang, B.H., Identifying influential spreaders in complex networks based on gravity formula. *Physica A Stat. Mech. Appl.*, 451, 205–212, 2016.

17. Medvet, E., Bartoli, A., Carminati, B., Ferrari, E., Evolutionary Inference of Attribute-Based Access Control Policies, in *Lecture Notes in Computer Science (including subseries Lecture Notes in Artificial Intelligence and Lecture Notes in Bioinformatics)*, vol. 9018, pp. 351–365, Springer, Cham, Switzerland, 2015.

18. Opsahl, T., Triadic closure in two-mode networks: Redefining the global and local clustering coefficients. *Soc. Networks*, 35, 2, 159–167, 2013.

19. Rahman, Q.M., Fariha, A., Mandal, A. *et al.*, A Sliding Window-Based Algorithm for Detecting Leaders from Social Network Action Streams. *2015 IEEE/WIC/ACM Int. Conf. Web Intell. Intell. Agent Technol.*, pp. 133–136, 2015.

20. Ruan, Y., Fuhry, D., Liang, J., Wang, Y., Parthasarathy, S., Community Discovery: Simple and Scalable Approaches. In *User Community Discovery. Human–Computer Interaction Series*, Paliouras, G., Papadopoulos, S., Vogiatzis, D., Kompatsiaris, Y. (eds), Springer, Cham, Switzerland, 2015. https://doi.org/10.1007/978-3-319-23835-7_2

21. Saito, T. and Rehmsmeier, M., The precision-recall plot is more informative than the ROC plot when evaluating binary classifiers on imbalanced datasets. *PLoS One*, 10, 3, 1–21, 2015.

22. Srilatha, P. and Manjula, R., Similarity Index based Link Prediction Algorithms in Social Networks: A Survey. *J. Telecommun. Inf. Technol.*, 2, 2, 87–94, 2016.

23. Turner, V., Gantz, J., Reinsel, D., Minton, S., *The Digital Universe of Opportunities: Rich Data and Increasing Value of the Internet of Things*, Framingham, MA, 2014.

24. M.-C. V. Marinescu, V. T. Rajan, and M. N. Wegman, "System and Method for detecting Leadership," US20120244500A1, 2012. https://patents.google.com/patent/US20120244500

25. Xu, Z. and Stoller, S.D., Mining Attribute-Based Access Control Policies. *IEEE Trans. Dependable Secure Comput.*, 12, 5, 533–545, 2015.

26. Zhou, T., Lü, L., Zhang, Y.C., Predicting missing links via local information. *Eur. Phys. J. B*, 71, 4, 623–630, 2009.

AI, ML, & Robotics in *iSchools*: An Academic Analysis for an Intelligent Societal Systems

P. K. Paul

Department of CIS, & Information Scientist (Offg.), Raiganj University, Raiganj, India

Abstract

The modern world is become more advanced and smart, sophisticated, and intelligent; and in this context, various tools, technologies, and systems are playing leading role in the development of the modern world toward more scientific, modern, and technologically equipped with, and it is also called as Machine Intelligence, it is dedicated in developing intelligence powered by machines, and it is referred as intelligent agents. The term Artificial Intelligence (AI) is often also used to describe machines and dedicated in learning and problem solving. It is also related with the computational statistics for giving prediction by the use of computers. Here, mathematical optimization plays a leading role with suitable methods, theory and applications of the sub field Machine Learning. Robotics is another allied area involves with the intelligent systems and robots designing, construction, operation, etc. Within the field of Information Technology apart from the basic technologies emerging technologies, *viz*,. AI, Big Data, and Robotics, are emerging. Academic institutions have started educational programs and degrees on AI and Robotics in the academic units of Computing Sciences and Mathematical Sciences. *iSchools* are the kind of consortium that develops with the collections of information and technology related schools and academic units, and in last decade, there is a significant growth in the development of such academic bodies. In recent past, a large amount of *iSchools* have started academic program on AI, Robotics, and on allied areas, and this work is devoted in exploring such programs with schools, nature, nomenclature, and curriculum facets with reference to the case study of *iSchools* in American region.

Keywords: *iSchools*, artificial intelligence, machine learning, robotics, intelligent systems, emerging degrees

19.1 Introduction

Technologies are changing rapidly with rapid speed and numerous developments, and as far as Information Technology is concerned, huge development is noticeable. Information Technology is consist with the technologies which help in information activities and processing, *viz.*, Database Systems and Technology, Multimedia Systems and Technology, Network Systems and Technology, and Software Systems and Technology, and among such

Email: pkpaul.infotech@gmail.com

Rajdeep Chakraborty, Anupam Ghosh and Jyotsna Kumar Mandal (eds.) Machine Learning Techniques and Analytics for Cloud Security, (417–438) © 2022 Scrivener Publishing LLC

broad field, Artificial Intelligence (AI), Machine Learning (ML), and Robotics are also important to note [1, 8]. AI comes with the benefits of AI system development in the tools, systems, products, and in services. Modern machines become more intelligent and here AI playing a leading role to perform healthier and better way [23, 27]. Furthermore in today's context, many machines are more intelligent, advanced, and having understanding of the human speech, inbuilt strategic systems, intelligent routing, and operating cars. As far AI is concerned, the major goals are include knowledge reasoning including planning and schedule, ML, computer vision, and Natural Language Processing (NLP). As far as approaches are concerned, important are mentioned in Figure 19.1.

AI is also connected with the Data Mining which is focused on exploratory data analysis by the unsupervised learning, and here, predictive analytics are also used. The field is gaining rapidly and inter connected with each other [24, 33, 37].

Robotics is an another branch and emerging technology and involving with the aspects like designing, construction, use of the robots in different systems, and products and services apart from in general or only Robotics uses [5, 12]. With the help of robotics and its allied systems intelligent machines, their day-to-day lives become easy. However, safety is the major concern in robotics and it has strong connections with major areas, *viz.*,

- Mechanical Engineering
- Electric Engineering
- Computer Engineering
- Information Technology, and so on [38, 39, 51].

Robotics is responsible in development of the machines which are able in substitute for humans and replicate human activities in many contexts [2, 13]. Robots are useful in many

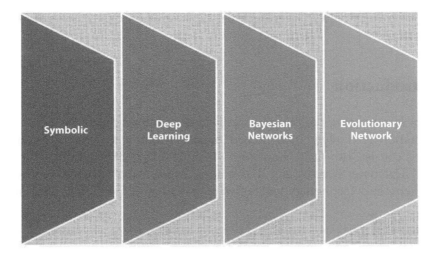

Figure 19.1 Basic approaches in Artificial Intelligence.

situations and many are in true reasons, *viz.*, dangerous environments and manufacturing processes where involvement of the human becomes difficult in many context. The areas like space, underwater, in high heat, and clean up, materials, and radiation robots are very useful. In replicating of walking, lifting, other human activity performance also robotics are very much useful. It is worthy to note that many of robots are inspired by nature and toward sustainability [32, 34, 52].

Initially, the concept of *iSchool* emerged in 1998 by three educationalist, *viz.*, Toni Carbo from the School of Information Science established by the University of Pittsburgh; Donald Marchan, who was from School of Information Studies under the Syracuse University; and also by Richard Lytle who belongs to the College of Information Science and Technology, Drexel University. However, the concerned established was known as *iSchool* Caucus [6, 16]. In the year 2001, total of five member institutes joined from "three" and though in the year 2003 several other Information related units academic bodies have joined and creates a wider arena regarding information system practice, research and development. University of North Carolina (UNC), North Carolina; USA Florida State University, Florida; USA, Indiana University, Bloomington; USA, University of Illinois, Champaign; USA, etc., are also joined in the group and makes it to the team of ten. Later, name of the school and units renamed as *iSchool* Caucus to simply *iSchools Organizations* with more interdisciplinary and sophisticated agenda in Information fields and also technological fields, *viz.*, Computing, IT, and Telecommunication and started to work as beyond traditional information field also [10, 35, 41]. Apart from the traditional nomenclature, various other emerging nomenclatures have also been started, *viz.*, Information Science and Technology (IST) Information Systems (IS) or Information Systems and Management, IT Management, Computer and Information Science, and also other emerging and interdisciplinary flavor/approaches and concentration.

In these schools, different educational programs related to the information, technologies related to the information are offered. Emerging technologies like AI, Data Analytics and Big Data, Cloud Computing and Virtualization, Robotics, and HCI have also been started as a program of studies and other interdisciplinary programs also offered. AI programs been started as specialization and also as a degree in many international *iSchools*. The details of such are depicted in next section [16, 26].

19.2   Objective

The present work entitled "AI, ML, & Robotics in *iSchools*: An Academic Analysis for an Intelligent Societal Systems" is associated with the following aim and objectives:

- To know about the basic features, functions, and role of the AI and ML.
- To know about the fundamental features, role, and importances in the Robotics.
- To get the knowledge of *iSchools* including fundation and root, features, and distribution of such schools worldwide.
- To learn about the basic programs and degrees on *iSchools* with emerging programs on the AI, ML, and Robotics of such schools.

- To get and analyzed about the nature and curricula of the AI, ML, and Robotics at the *iSchools*.
- To know about the nomenclatures and distribution of the AI, ML, and Robotics related programs in the American region as a special case study.

19.3   Methodology

The paper entitled "AI, ML, & Robotics in *iSchools*: An Academic Analysis for an Intelligent Societal Systems" is a kind of policy work and also interdisciplinary in nature. The work since technological and educational in nature therefore methods related to the educational and management science in nature. The paper is on AI, ML and Robotics related aspects; therefore, both primary sources and secondary sources are used such as journals and books to depict the basics on the subjects. Moreover, as the work is a kind of case study, therefore the *iSchools* official website has been mapped and analyzed in American region during April to June, 2020 to get the current picture of the *iSchools* and to report and present the work here with potentiality on offering AI, ML and Robotics programs, and as a method, the subjects, *viz.*, Data Science, Analytics, and Big Data, have been avoided in this work.

19.3.1   *iSchools*, Technologies, and Artificial Intelligence, ML, and Robotics

Technologies are rising rapidly in different sectors and areas and different Information Technological components are playing leading role in the development. The growing technological and management components are also changing the entire world toward a modern and digital society [3, 14, 22]. The educational institutes and universities are adopting latest strategies in respect of newer educational programs and degrees, and in this regard, the role of IT and Computing-oriented departments and units is noticeable. As far as *iSchools* are concerned, these are purely interdisciplinary and applied in nature; therefore in making of new age programs and toward digital society, *iSchools* are important [36, 42, 43].

It is worthy to note that *iSchools* are offering emerging, interdisciplinary, and skill-based nomenclature in the field of Information Sciences and Technologies with many domain centric Information Sciences, *viz.*, Bio Informatics, Health Informatics, and Ecological Informatics. The nomenclature of Information Science and Technology is considered as one of the popular in *iSchools* and was first used by the ASIST, i.e., American Society of Information Science and Technology as a new nomenclature title *from American Society of Information Science*. Here, at *iSchools*, major focus is on interaction of "Information-Technology-People" and more clearly for the Information and Technology solution [11, 15, 28]. Therefore, *iSchools* Organization are established with solving of such with skilled and educated manpower in the field in the traditional areas, *viz.*, Information Science/Information Studies/Communication Studies/Information Systems/Computing and Information Technology or in other fields directly or indirectly related to Information and technologies. Allied technologies and emerging are also important, *viz.*, Cloud Computing, Big Data, IoT, Cyber Security, Analytics, Data Science, AI, Robotics, and so on. Here, Table 19.1 depicted the *iSchools* with diverse nomenclature and locations.

Table 19.1 List of iSchools registered internationally under the iSchools Organization, United States.

Sl. no.	University and academic unit (iSchools)	Country
American Region		
1	College of Emergency Preparedness, Homeland Security and Cybersecurity established by University at Albany,	USA
2	School of Information under the University of Arizona	USA
3	School of Information (iSchools) under University of California, Berkley	USA
4	The School of Information, located at University of British Colombia	Canada
5	Heinz College of Information Systems and Public Policy under the Carnegie Mellon University (CMU)	USA
6	School of Information Technology under the University of Cincinnati	USA
7	Department of Information Science established by the University of Colorado	USA
8	Faculty of Computing and Information Science under the wing of Cornell University	USA
9	School of Information Studies (SIS) under Dominican University	USA
10	College Computing and Informatics (CCI) under Drexel University	USA
11	College of Communication and Information under Florida State University (FSU)	USA
12	College of Computing under the Georgia Institute of Technology	USA
13	School of Information Sciences under the University of Illinois at Urbana Champaign	USA
14	School of Informatics and Computing established by the Indiana University at IUPUI	USA
15	School of Informatics, Computing and Engineering (SICE) of diana University, Bloomington	USA
16	Donald Bren School of Information and Computer Science (DBSICS), University of California, Irvine	USA
17	School of Information established by the Kent State University (KSU)	USA
18	College of Communications and Information under the University of Kentucky	USA
19	Palmer School of Library and Information Science established by the Long island University	USA

(Continued)

Table 19.1 List of iSchools registered internationally under the iSchools Organization, United States. (*Continued*)

Sl. no.	University and academic unit (iSchools)	Country
20	School of Library and Information Science under Louisiana State University (LSU)	USA
21	Department of Information Systems established by University of Maryland, Baltimore County (UMBC)	USA
22	College of Information Studies (CIS) under University of Maryland	USA
23	School of Information Studies under the McGill University, Montreal	Canada
24	Department of Media and Information established by Michigan State University (MSU)	USA
25	School of Information (iSchools) established by University of Michigan	USA
26	School of Information Science and Learning Technologies (*iSchools*) University of Missouri	USA
27	School of Library and Information Science established by the University of Montréal	Canada
28	School of Information and Library Science under the University of North Carolina (UNC), Chapel Hill	USA
29	College of Information (CI) under the wing of University of North Texas (UNT)	USA
30	School of Library and Information Studies established by University of Oklahoma	USA
31	College of Information Science and Technology (CIST) established by The Pennsylvania State University (PSU)	USA
32	School of Computing and Information (SCI) under the University of Pittsburg	USA
33	Department of Information Science (DIS) Pontifical Xavierian University	Colombia
34	School of Information of Pratt Institute	USA
35	School of Communication and Information under the The State University of New Jersey, Rutgers,	USA
36	School of Information (SI) under the San Jose State University	USA
37	School of Communication and Arts (ECA), University of São Paulo	Brazil
38	School of Library and Information Science, under Simmons University, Boston	USA

(*Continued*)

Table 19.1 List of iSchools registered internationally under the iSchools Organization, United States. (*Continued*)

Sl. no.	University and academic unit (iSchools)	Country
39	School of Library and Information Science under the University of South Carolina (USC)	USA
40	School of Information (SI) under University of South Florida (USF)	USA
41	Department of Information Science under the State University of New York, Buffalo	USA
42	School of Information Studies (SIS), Syracuse University	USA
43	School of Information Sciences (SIS) of The University of Tennessee	USA
44	Department of Electrical Engineering and Computer Science established by the Texas A&M University – Kingsville	USA
45	School of Information (SI) at University of Texas at Austin (UTA)	USA
46	Faculty of Information under the University of Toronto (UT)	USA
47	Graduate School of Education and Information Studies at University of California at Los Angles (UCLA)	USA
48	The Information School of University of Washington (WU)	USA
49	School of Information Sciences at the Wayne State University (WSU)	USA
50	The Information School located at University of Wisconsin, Madison	USA
51	School of Information Studies located at University of Wisconsin, Milwaukee (UWM)	USA
European iSchools Directory		
52	Department of Communication and Psychology under Aalborg University, Denmark	Denmark
53	Graduate School of Humanities, Archives and Information Studies University of Amsterdam	Netherlands
54	Department of Information Science under the Bar-Ilan University	Israel
55	The Swedish School of Library and Information Science Established by University of Borås	Sweden
56	Department of Library and Documentation located within the University Carlos III of Madrid	Spain
57	Faculty of Computer Science, Multimedia and Telecommunications of The Open University of Catalonia	Spain

(*Continued*)

Table 19.1 List of iSchools registered internationally under the iSchools Organization, United States. (*Continued*)

Sl. no.	University and academic unit (iSchools)	Country
58	Institute of Information Studies and Librarianship (IISL) located at the Charles University in Prague	Czech Republic
59	Department of Information Studies established by the University of Copenhagen	Denmark
60	School of Information and Communication Studies located at University College Dublin (UCD)	Ireland
61	Humanities Advanced Technology and Information Institute established by the University of Glasgow, Glasgow	UK
62	Department of Information Management located at the Hacettepe University, Turkey	Turkey
63	Berlin School of Library and Information Science at The Humboldt University of Berlin	Germany
64	Department of Logic Uses, Social Sciences and Information at the IMT Atlantique (A Technological University)	France
65	Information Institute (iInstitute) located at the Linnaeus University	Sweden
66	Department of Information Studies located at University College London	United Kingdom
67	The College of Computing and Information Sciences established by Makerere University	Uganda
68	Department of Computing and Information Sciences (iSchools) at Northumbria University	United Kingdom
69	Information Management School at Nova University Lisabon	Portugal
70	Information and Communications at the Manchester Metropolitan University	United Kingdom
71	ALGORITMI Center School of Engineering at the The University of Minho	Portugal
72	Department of Archivistics, Library and Information Science, Established by the Oslo Metropolitan University	Norway
73	The Oxford Digital Information Group of the University of Oxford, Oxford	Oxford
74	School of Informatics established by the Polytechnic University of Valencia	Spain

(*Continued*)

Table 19.1 List of iSchools registered internationally under the iSchools Organization, United States. (*Continued*)

Sl. no.	University and academic unit (iSchools)	Country
75	Faculty of Engineering in cooperation with the Faculty of Arts of University of Porto	Portugal
76	Institute for Information and Media, Language and Culture Located at University of Regensburg	Germany
77	Department of Information Management, Aberdeen Business School, Robert Gordon University	United Kingdom
78	Information School established by the University of Sheffield	United Kingdom
79	School of Media and Information (iSchool), University of Siegen	Germany
80	Computer and Information Sciences established by the University of Strathclyde	United Kingdom
81	Department of Information Sciences of Josip Juray Strossmayer University of Osijek, Croatia	Croatia
82	Faculty of IT and Communication Sciences of the Tampere University	Finland
Asia Pacific iSchools Directory		
83	School of Information Management at Central China Normal University	China
84	School of Information Studies under the Charles Sturt University	Australia
85	Department of Library, Information and Archives Management located at The University of the Chinese Academy of Sciences	China
86	Human Communication, Development, and Information Sciences (CDIS) at The University of Hong Kong	China
87	School of Management at the Jilin University	China
88	Department of Information Science established by the Khon Kaen University (KKU)	Thailand
89	Department of Library and Information Science located at the Kyungpook National University (KNU)	Korea
90	Department of Library Science, Graduate School of Integrated Frontier Sciences established by the Kyushu University	Japan
91	Graduate Institute of Library Information and Archival Studies under the National Chengchi University	Taiwan

(Continued)

Table 19.1 List of iSchools registered internationally under the iSchools Organization, United States. (*Continued*)

Sl. no.	University and academic unit (iSchools)	Country
92	School of Economics and Management located at the Nanjing University of Science and Technology	China
93	School of Information Management located at the Nanjing University	China
94	Faculty of Information Technology located at the Monash University	Australia
95	Department of Computing and Information Systems established by the University of Melbourne	Australia
96	Department and Graduate Institute of Library and Information Science located at the National Taiwan University	Taiwan
97	Graduate Institute of Library and Information Studies located at the National Taiwan Normal University	Taiwan
98	School of Information Resource Management located at the Renmin University of China	China
99	Department of Library, Information and Archives located Shanghai University	China
100	Department of archives and e-government located Soochow University	China
101	School of Information Technology and Mathematical Sciences located at The University of South Australia	Australia
102	Department and Graduate Institute of Library and Information Science (LIS) established by the National Taiwan University	Taiwan
103	Department of Information Management at the Peking University	China
104	School of Library and Information Studies located at the University of the Philippines	Philippines
105	School of Information Management located at the Sun Yat-Sen University	China
106	Library and Information Science at The Sungkyunkwan University	South Korea
107	Faculty of Information Management located University of Technology, Malaysia (MARA)	Malaysia
108	Graduate School of Library, Information, and Media Studies Established at University of Tsukuba	Japan
109	School of Computing and Mathematical Sciences Located at the Waikato University	New Zealand

(Continued)

Table 19.1 List of iSchools registered internationally under the iSchools Organization, United States. (*Continued*)

Sl. no.	University and academic unit (iSchools)	Country
110	School of Information Management (SIM) located at the Wuhan University	China
111	Department of Library and Information Science (DLIS) located at Yonsei University	South Korea

19.4 Artificial Intelligence, ML, and Robotics: An Overview

AI as the tool and systems with developing intelligence in the products, services, and systems; these are the machines though it is act like a human and perform, mimic their action. AI is thus required in the activities of learning and also in problem-solving. AI has the ability regarding rationalize best goal, or simply, it is able in taking actions that is having best chance for achieving a specific or definite goal. AI is required in various areas, various sectors, and industries. AI is useful in effective utilizations in healthcare domains and in many others, *viz.*, governance, business and commerce, politics and administration, transport and tourism, and education and teaching. Automated machines, intelligent devices and products, and self-driving cars are the prime example of AI [4, 14, 19]. Financial industry, banking, and finance are increased with higher capacity of AI systems. The *iSchools* are rising with AI Programs due to its features and functions, *viz.*,

- AI is dedicated in the activities of simulation and acting like humans or simply the human intelligence in the devices and machines.
- Learning, reasoning, and perception are the core of AI systems.
- As AI is having two major types, i.e., weak AI and strong AI to do the tasks which are more complex and human-like.

Further AI is two types; and these are simply weak AI and strong AI. As far as weak AI is concerned, it is required in designing of the system that can do a particular job. Strong AI is more advanced and able in act like human [7, 17, 30]. Such systems are useful in more complex as well as in complicated system designing and development. Here, systems are able in performing the given task kike human. These tend to be more complex as well as complicated systems. Therefore, AI is required to solve the problem without having a person. ML in short called as ML and a subset of AI and considered within the emerging Computer Science. Here, various statistical techniques are able in computation, decision making assistance with proper data management [40, 44, 45]. In 1959, Arthur Samuel was coined the term first with deep involvement in exploring the study and construction of algorithms [9, 18, 20]. There are various approaches in ML, *viz.*,

- DTL, i.e., Decision Tree Learning
- ATL, i.e., Association Tree Learning
- ANM, i.e., Artificial Neural Networks
- Deep Learning or DL

- ILP or Inductive Logic Programming
- Clustering or Cluster.

Deep Learning, in short is called as DL, is another emerging area of the ML and closest with the AI. There are various architectures exists in DL or deep learning; and among these, important are recurrent neural networks (RNNs), deep neural networks (DNNs), deep belief networks (DBNs), etc. and these are applied in wide areas of computer vision, NLP, and audio recognition [10, 21, 29]. Though major emerging areas of Deep Learning are as under:

- Speech recognition with automatic systems
- Image recognition (i.e., Optical Character Recognition)
- Customer and HR relationship management
- Bioinformatics and pharma informatics
- Visual art processing or Software-based Visual Art Mechanism
- Drug discovery including its toxicology
- Digital and Mobile advertising
- Image restoration [23, 48, 49].

Therefore the applications of the AI, Robotics, ML etc. are well increasing in all the sectors and in this context introduction of such programs become important and valuable in the many academic institutions and *iSchools* are not exception of this trend [20, 46, 47].

19.5   Artificial Intelligence, ML, and Robotics as an Academic Program: A Case on iSchools—North American Region

The Information Science programs basically varies from country to country and it includes the foundational subjects, *viz.*, Information Science, Informatics, Information Systems, Computing, Data Science, to latest and emerging Technologies [35, 50] as depicted in Figure 19.2. However, such programs may be offered with different levels, *viz.*, Certificate, Advanced Certificate, Diploma, Minors, Bachelors, Masters, and Doctoral Degrees as far as AI, Robotics and allied areas are concerned, many programs are offered by the *iSchools* and with different levels. Internationally, many *iSchools* have started academic, training programs on AI, Robotics, ML, etc., and as far as American region is concerned, few important are Carnegie Mellon University, Drexel University, Indiana University, Bloomington, and The Pennsylvania State University [6, 22, 25].

The programs are available with the following:

- Certificate
- Bachelors
- Masters, etc.

As far as major disciplines are concerned, some of the important are Computer Science, Information Systems and Management, Intelligent System Engineering, etc. Further, as far as specializations are concerned, important nomenclatures are as follows:

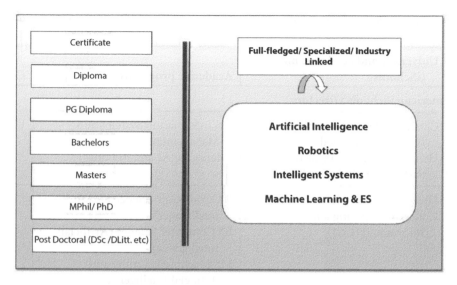

Figure 19.2 Possible programs on AI, ML, and Robotics at iSchools.

- Managing AI and Robotics
- AI
- ML and AI
- Intelligent Systems, etc.

However, here, in this study, the areas and nomenclature of Data Science, Data Analytics, and Big Data are not considered; though anything merged with AI, ML and Robotics considered. At the doctoral level, the subject is offered or area available as a full-fledged degree and also as a specialization in the allied subjects.

As most of the universities are located in United States (as depicted in Table 19.2), therefore M.Phil. Program is not noted according to this study. But some are offered PhD degree with such area of specialization as depicted in Table 19.3. Though the number of programs is depicted in Figure 19.3.

All these programs are academic in nature and there is no provision for the Professional Doctorate in these areas. All these programs are consisting with huge amount of courses and papers to enhance the skill sets. Such courses are from the core of the field, i.e., Computing/Information Technology, and also specialization papers from the field of study. As far as basic subjects are concerned, majority are from the Computer Architecture, Programming and Software Engineering, Mathematical Foundation of Computing, Operating Systems, Database Systems, and so on [17, 28, 31]. Whereas some of the basic AI, Robotics, and ML core are as follows:

- Basics of AI
- Robot Laboratory (RL)/Robotics Practical
- Advanced and Modern AI
- Game AI (GAI)
- Knowledge-based Agents and Systems
- ML and DL, etc.

Table 19.2 List of *iSchools* of American regions offering AI, ML, and Robotics programs at UG and PG.

Sl. no.	University and academic unit (iSchools)	Academic programs	Country
North American iSchools Directory			
1	Carnegie Mellon University (CMU), established Heinz College of Information Systems and Public Policy	MS Information Systems and Management (Managing AI and Robotics)	USA
2	Drexel University (DU) founded College Computing and Informatics (CCI)	BA Computer Science (Artificial Intelligence) BS Computer Science (Artificial Intelligence) MS Machine Learning and Artificial Intelligence Certificate (Post Bachelor)—AI and ML	USA
3	Indiana University (IUB), Bloomington by its founded School of Informatics, Computing and Engineering	BS Computer Science (Artificial Intelligence) BA Computer Science (Artificial Intelligence) BS Intelligent System Engineering	USA
4	Georgia Institute of Technology (GIT) established College of Computing	BS Computer Science (Intelligence Systems)	USA

Table 19.3 List of *iSchools* of American regions offering AI, ML, and Robotics programs at PhD.

Sl. no.	University and academic unit (iSchools)	Academic programs	Country
American iSchools offering degrees on the subject			
1	Drexel University's CCI, i.e., College Computing and Informatics	PhD Computer Science (Intelligent Systems)	USA
2	The Pennsylvania State University (PSU) College of Information Science and Technology (CIST)	PhD Informatics (AI and Big Data)	USA
3	Georgia Institute of Technology (GIT) established College of Computing	PhD Robotics PhD Machine Learning	USA

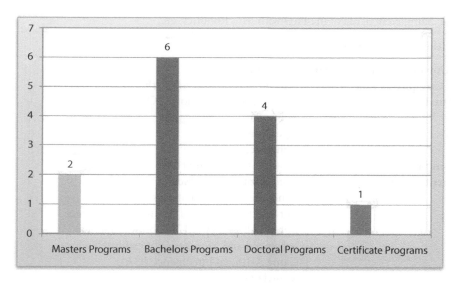

Figure 19.3 Number of programs on AI, ML, and Robotics.

However, the details of the paper are depicted in Table 19.4 herewith with description of all types of courses of the PhD programs. The specialization program is suitable in the sense that the educated on this subject can go with the two different areas, *viz.*, in IT and Computing; and other hand, in the areas of AI, ML, and Robotics. The Bachelors program is available with Arts and Science both the degrees, *viz.*, BA/BSc in some of the universities mentioned above. However, basic courses are different in each of these two programs. As far as specializations courses are concerned, that is also different in the context that if the programs is fully concentrated on AI, ML, and Robotics, then the nature is more computing centric whereas the courses as part of the specialization of the Information Science/System, etc., hold little different. Here, Table 19.5 depicted sample of the courses at Bachelors, Masters level. Further, it is worthy to note that Heinz College of Information Systems and Public Policy, under the Carnegie Mellon University basically offers MS Information Systems and Management (Managing AI and Robotics) program is little management centric; therefore, here, some of the programs are also offered in allied areas, *viz.*, Economic Analysis, Financial Accounting, and Principles of Finance.

19.6   Suggestions

iSchools are gaining popularity internationally and there are many reasons to introduce such interdisciplinary academic venture in modern educational systems and among them few important are depicted here. Since this topic of the work is interdisciplinary in nature, therefore some of the constructive suggestions include the following:

- According to this study, it is noted that majority of the programs are offered at Bachelors Degree only; therefore, it is important to offer the subjects at Masters level as well.

Table 19.4 Sample curricula of the PhD with ML, Robotics, etc.

Universities and programs	Papers/Courses
Drexel University (DU) founded College Computing and Informatics (CCI) **PhD Computer Science (Intelligent Systems)**	**Core Courses** Data Structures and Algorithms I Theory of Computation (TOC) Programming Languages Operating Systems Computer Graphics Developing User Interfaces **Specialization Courses** Fundamentals of Databases Introduction/Basics of Artificial Intelligence Robot Laboratory (RL)/Robotics Practical Advanced and Modern Artificial Intelligence Game Artificial Intelligence (GAI) Knowledge-based Agents and Systems Machine Learning and DL etc. Deep Learning Data Analysis at Scale Responsible Data Analysis
Georgia Institute of Technology (GIT) established College of Computing **PhD Robotics**	**Intro to Robotics Research (3 Credits)** A new course CS/AE/ECE/ME 7785, Introduction to Robotics Research. **Foundation Courses (9 Credits)** Three foundation courses, each selected from distinct core areas: Mechanics, Controls, Perception, Artificial Intelligence, Autonomy and Human-Robot Interaction (HRI). **Elective Courses (9 Credits)** Three targeted elective courses, each selected from the same three core areas used for the foundation courses. **Multidisciplinary Robotics Research (6 Credits)** Two new courses CS/AE/ECE/ME 8750 and CS/AE/ECE/ME 8751, Multidisciplinary Robotics Research I and II. **Outside Major Courses (9 Credits)** Three courses outside the major area to provide a coherent minor in accordance with Institute policies.

- Most of the specialization programs in AI and ML are offered in Computer Science track; however, such subjects may offered in wide areas of Information Sciences ranging from Informatics, Information Science, Computing, Information Systems, etc.
- Since Information Schools (*iSchools*) are different than traditoonal Computing School; therefore, it is better to include AI, ML, Robotics and allied programs more interdiscplinary with inclusion ofinformation and societal fundamentals.

Table 19.5 Sample courses of AI, ML, and Robotics programs at Master and Bachelors at the *iSchools*.

Universities and programs	Papers/Courses
Drexel University (DU) founded College Computing and Informatics (CCI) **BA/BS Computer Science (Artificial Intelligence)**	**Core Courses** Introduction to Computer Science Computer Programming I or Advanced Computer Programming I Computer Programming II Advanced Computer Programming II Data Structures Advanced Programming Tools and Techniques Mathematical Foundations of Computer Science Algorithms and Analysis Systems Architecture Systems Programming Programming Language Concepts Introduction to Software Engineering and Development Software Architecture I **Specialization Courses** Artificial Intelligence Machine Learning Evolutionary Computing Game AI Development Advanced Artificial Intelligence
Indiana University (IUB), Bloomington by its founded School of Informatics, Computing and Engineering	**Core Courses** Introduction to Software Systems Calculus II Discrete Structures for Computer Science Programming Languages Data Structures Fundamentals of Computing Theory Introduction to Algorithm Design and Analysis Database Concepts Principles of Machine Learning **Specialization Courses** Introduction to Software Systems Discrete Structures for Computer Science Data Structures Introduction to Statistical Inference Introduction to Artificial Intelligence Introduction to Data Analysis and Mining Principles of Machine Learning Fundamentals of Computing Theory Autonomous Robotics

(*Continued*)

Table 19.5 Sample courses of AI, ML, and Robotics programs at Master and Bachelors at the *iSchools*. (*Continued*)

Universities and programs	Papers/Courses
Carnegie Mellon University (CMU), established **Heinz College of Information Systems and Public Policy** **MS Information Systems and Management** **(Managing AI and Robotics)**	**Core Courses** Distributed Systems for ISM Database Management Managing Disruptive Technologies Object-Oriented Programming in Java Design Core Digital Transformation Organizational Design and Implementation Economic Analysis Financial Accounting Principles of Finance Decision Making Under Uncertainty Statistics for IT Managers Writing for ISM Professional Speaking Information Systems Capstone Project **Specializations Courses** Intro to Artificial Intelligence Robotic Process Automation Deep Learning for Information Systems Management AI, Society, and Humanity E-commerce Tech, Machine Learning, Analytics, and Bots
MS Machine Learning and Artificial Intelligence **Drexel University (DU) founded College Computing and Informatics (CCI)**	This interdisciplinary, 45-credit, 15-course program includes: **Five required core courses**; **Three elective courses**, one within each of the following focal areas: Data Science and Analytics, Foundations of Computation and Algorithms, or Applications of Artificial Intelligence and Machine Learning; **Seven free elective courses** may be selected from the above focal areas or Computer Science Department-approved courses; **A capstone course:** students work in teams to pursue an in-depth, multi-term capstone project applying computing and informatics knowledge in an artificial intelligence project, spanning two quarters (6 credits).

- According to the study, it is noted that Doctoral Degrees are highest level of degrees but Post Doctoral/Higher Doctoral Degree on the areas, *viz.*, AI, ML, and Robotics with D.Sc. degrees may be offered in the *iSchools*.
- Professional Doctorateal degrees like *Engg.D (Doctor of Engineering)* in the areas of AI, ML, and Robtics, *DBA (Doctor of Business Administration)* in the areas of Intelligent Systems and Management may be offered.

- Post Graduade Diploma is also considered as important qualification; therefore, AI, ML, and Robotics or allied areas may be offered in the *iSchools*.
- Post Graduate Certificate Program can also be started in respect of ML and AI perfectly.
- As many universities have started Post Doctoral Program leading to the Post Doctoral Certifiate therefore in the areas of AI, ML, and Robotics may be started.
- The AI, ML, and Robotics related programs should be offered with the fundamentals of Information Sciences, *viz.*, Information Management, Information Studies, and Knowledge Organization.
- Indistry Integrated Programs at different level (both higher and short term) may be offered at *iSchools* with the specilization in AI, ML, and Robotics.
- Initially *iSchools* may offer the specilization and later fullfledged AI, ML, and Robotics programs at the *iSchools*.
- The basic Information Science progams, *viz.*, BS and MS, can be offered with the specilizations of AI, ML, and Robotics programs.

Therefore, different strategies and policies are possible to enhance the subjects like AI, ML, and Robotics programs. Concerned institutions, collaborative efforts, industry integration, and inclusion of the societal aspects are important in developing healthy *iSchools* not only in American region but also in different regions and territories of the *iSchools*.

19.7   Motivation and Future Works

iSchools are emerging as an academic, training, and research program delivery institute, and therefore, it holds combination of different subjects concentrated on information and allied fields; and therefore, the work can be further possible to extend at individual levels, *viz.*, Bachelors, Masters, and Doctoral. Apart from the AI, ML, and Robotics programs, further study may be possible in some of the allied programs.

19.8   Conclusion

Internationally, many universities, educational institutes, and training centers have started programs on AI, ML, and Robotics (and few allied programs) and as *iSchools* are dealing with different strategies of integration of the society-technology-information approaches; therefore, such emerging programs may hold such features accordingly. *iSchools* are very innovative and emerging regarding the programs, subjects, and diversity in human resources (including faculty, staffs, and students); hence, AI, ML, and Robotics programs may also offer in diverse areas such as Healthcare, Education, Transport and Tourism, and Governance. Moreover, the countries and territories of *iSchools* may also join in the official of *iSchools* Organization (the association) for the better development of advanced and intelligent society with support of the healthy infrastructure, planning, and budget for the development of a healthy knowledge society. Moreover, as this work is specifically designed and considered for the area of iSchools located in around the world, therefore for the complete development of the AI, ML, and Robotics in the iSchools, complete support from all the organizations is highly solicited by the educational institutions, universities, research centers, Non-Government Organizations (NGOs), scientific society and associations, etc. In the research level, basic components of Computer Science must be integrated with the proposed degrees in the field of AI, ML, and Robotics.

References

1. Aasheim, C.L., Williams, S., Rutner, P., Gardiner, A., Data analytics vs. data science: A study of similarities and differences in undergraduate programs based on course descriptions. *J. Inf. Syst. Educ.*, 26, 103, 2015.
2. Brown, A.H., Simulated classrooms and artificial students: The potential effects of new technologies on teacher education. *J. Res. Comput. Educ.*, 32, 307, 1999.
3. Cao, L., Data science: a comprehensive overview. *ACM Comput. Surv. (CSUR)*, 50, 1, 2017.
4. Carrasquilla, J. and Melko, R.G., Machine learning phases of matter. *Nat. Phys.*, 13, 431, 2017.
5. Chiang, R.H., Goes, P., Stohr, E.A., Business intelligence and analytics education, and program development: A unique opportunity for the information systems discipline. *ACM Trans. Manage. Inf. Syst. (TMIS)*, 3, 3, 1, 2012.
6. Chowdhury, G. and Koya, K., Information practices for sustainability: Role of iSchools in achieving the UN sustainable development goals (SDGs). *J. Assoc. Inf. Sci. Technol.*, 68, 2128, 2017.
7. Chu, H., iSchools and non-iSchools in the USA: An examination of their master's programs. *Educ. Inf.*, 29, 1, 2012.
8. Cox, R.J. and Larsen, R.L., iSchools and archival studies. *Archival Sci.*, 8, 307, 2008.
9. Daniel, B.K., Big Data and data science: A critical review of issues for educational research. *Br. J. Educ. Technol.*, 50, 101, 2019.
10. Dillon, A., What it means to be an iSchool. *J. Educ. Libr. Inf. Sci.*, 53, 267, 2012.
11. Martin, S.B., Information technology, employment, and the information sector: Trends in information employment 1970–1995. *J. Am. Soc. Inf. Sci.*, 49, 1053, 1998.
12. Fahimirad, M. and Kotamjani, S.S., A Review on Application of Artificial Intelligence in Teaching and Learning in Educational Contexts. *Int. J. Learn. Dev.*, 8, 4, 106, 2018.
13. Foronda, V.R., Integrating information and communication technology into education: a study of the iSchools project in Camarines Sur, Philippines. *J. Dev. Sustain. Agric.*, 6, 101, 2011.
14. Goldstein, I. and Papert, S., Artificial intelligence, language, and the study of knowledge. *Cognit. Sci.*, 1, 84, 1997.
15. Golub, K., Hansson, J., Selden, L., Overview of the iSchool movement: an interview with Ronald L. Larsen, iCaucus Chair. *Bull. Assoc. Inf. Sci. Technol.*, 42, 12, 2016.
16. Ghahramani, Z., Probabilistic machine learning and artificial intelligence. *Nature*, 521, 7553, 452, 2015.
17. Holmberg, K., The Conceptual Landscape of iSchools: Examining Current Research Interests of Faculty Members. *Inf. Res.: An Int. Electronic J.*, 18, 33, 2013.
18. Huang, M.H. and Rust, R.T., Artificial intelligence in service. *J. Serv. Res.*, 21, 155–172, 2018.
19. ITS, A., *The Educational Intelligent Economy: Big Data, Artificial Intelligence, Machine Learning and the Internet of Things in Education*, vol. 5, p. 226, governance, Bigley, UK, 2019.
20. Ifenthaler, D., Are higher education institutions prepared for learning analytics? *TechTrends*, 61, 366, 2017.
21. Jordan, M., II and Mitchell, T.M., Machine learning: Trends, perspectives, and prospects. *Science*, 349, 255, 2015.

22. Kim, K., An Artificial Intelligence Education Program Development and Application for Elementary Teachers. *J. Korean Assoc. Inf. Educ.*, 23, 629, 2019.

23. Kotsiantis, S.B., Use of machine learning techniques for educational proposes: a decision support system for forecasting students' grades. *Artif. Intell. Rev.*, 37, 331, 2012.

24. Koya, K. and Chowdhury, G., Cultural heritage information practices and ischools education for achieving sustainable development. *J. Assoc. Inf. Sci. Technol.*, 71, 696, 2020.

25. Lopatovska, I. *et al.*, iSchools and l-schools: Converging or diverging communities? *Proc. Am. Soc. Inform. Sci. Tech.*, 49, 1, 2012.

26. Nalumaga, R., iSchools and Africa: Trends and developments. *Bull. Assoc. Inf. Sci. Technol.*, 42, 17, 2016.

27. Nilsson, N.J., Human-level artificial intelligence? Be serious! *AI Mag.*, 26, 68, 2005.

28. Lee, S., Analyzing the effects of artificial intelligence (AI) education program based on design thinking process. *J. Korean Assoc. Comput. Educ.*, 23, 49–59, 2020.

29. Lopatovska, I., Pattuelli, M.C., Bates, M.J., Buckland, M., Dalbello, M., Hastings, S., Giannini, T., iSchools and l-schools: Converging or diverging communities? *Proc. Am. Soc. Inf. Sci. Technol.*, 49, 1, 2012.

30. Lu, H., Li, Y., Chen, M., Kim, H., Serikawa, S., Brain intelligence: go beyond artificial intelligence. *Mob. Netw. Appl.*, 23, 368, 2018.

31. Obermeyer, Z. and Emanuel, E.J., Predicting the future—big data, machine learning, and clinical medicine. *New Engl. J. Med.*, 375, 1216, 2016.

32. Oh, S., The Asia-Pacific iSchools. *Bull. Assoc. Inf. Sci. Technol.*, 42, 22, 2016.

33. Ortiz-Repiso, V., Greenberg, J., Calzada-Prado, J., A cross-institutional analysis of data-related curricula in information science programmes: A focused look at the iSchools. *J. Inf. Sci.*, 44, 768, 2018.

34. Paul, P.K. and Sridevi., K.V., I Schools: An overview emphasizing need of versatile I-Programme in India: A Study. *Int. J. Embedded Syst. Comput. Eng.*, 4, 133, 2012.

35. Paul, P.K., Business Informatics: Emerging Domain of Interdisciplinary Information Science with Possibilities in I-Schools. *Int. J. Mark. Theory*, 3, 113, 2013.

36. Paul, P.K., Chatterjee, D., Bhuimali, A., Ghose, M., Rajesh, R., Karn, B., Data Science and increasing Carrier Opportunities: A Case of Masters programs in United Kingdom—*The Future of Intelligent Industries and Corporate. Int. J. Bus. Econ. Manage.*, 4, 4, 2016.

37. Paul, P.K. and Ghose, M.K., Why Green Computing and Green Information Sciences have potentialities in academics and iSchools: Practice and Educational Perspectives, in: *Advances in Smart Grid and Renewable, Energy* Lecture Note on Electric Engineering, vol. 435, K.S. Sherpa, A.K. Bhoi, A. Kalam, M.K. Mishra, (Eds.), pp. 103–112, Springer, Singapore, 2017.

38. Paul, P.K. and Chatterjee, D., iSchools promoting Information Science & Technology (IST) domain: towards Community, Business & Society with contemporary worldwide trend and emerging potentialities, in: *Encyclopaedia of Information science and Technology*, vol. 4, Khosrow-Pour (Ed.), pp. 4423–4735, IGI Global, Pennsylvenia, 2018.

39. Paul, P.K., Bhuimali, A., Aithal, P.S., Chatterjee, D., iSchools and It's Need for Promoting Information-Technology-Social Interaction: Overview and Need in Indian Educational Context. *Sci. Rev.*, 4, 1, 2018.

40. Paul, P.K. and Kumar, A., Big Data and Data Science in Engineering Platform: A Techno-educational Research Study in Indian Context, in: *Advances in Communication, Devices and Networking*, p. 837, 2018.

41. Paul, P., Saavedra M, R., Aithal, P.S., Aremu, P.S.B., Baby, P., Environmental Informatics: Potentialities in iSchools and Information Science & Technology Programs—An Analysis. *Int. J. Manage. Technol. Soc. Sci.*, 5, 238, 2020.

42. Ryu, M. and Han, S., AI Education Programs for Deep-Learning Concepts. *J. Korean Assoc. Inf. Educ.*, 23, 583, 2019.

43. Seadle, M., The European iSchools. *Bull. Assoc. Inf. Sci. Technol.*, 42, 26, 2016.

44. Subramaniam, M.M. and Jaeger, P.T., Weaving diversity into LIS: An examination of diversity course offerings in iSchool programs. *Educ. Inf.*, 28, 1, 2011.

45. Tilak, J.B., Transition from higher education as a public good to higher education as a private good: The saga of Indian experience. *J. Asian Public Policy*, 1, 220, 2018.

46. Topol, E.J., High-performance medicine: the convergence of human and artificial intelligence. *Nat. Med.*, 25, 44, 2019.

47. Wiggins, A. and Sawyer, S., Intellectual diversity and the faculty composition of iSchools. *J. Am. Soc. Inf. Sci. Technol.*, 63, 1, 8, 2012.

48. Williamson, B., Digital education governance: data visualization, predictive analytics, and 'real-time'policy instruments. *J. Educ. Policy*, 31, 123, 2016.

49. Wong, T.Y. and Bressler, N.M., Artificial intelligence with deep learning technology looks into diabetic retinopathy screening. *Jama*, 316, 2366, 2016.

50. Wu, D., He, D., Jiang, J., Dong, W., Vo, K.T., The state of iSchools: an analysis of academic research and graduate education. *J. Inf. Sci.*, 38, 15, 2012.

51. Yu, W.J., Jang, J.H., Ahn, J.M., Park, D.R., Yoo, I.H., Bae, Y.K., Kim, W.Y., Design of Artificial Intelligence Education Program based on Design-based Research. *Int. J. Adv. Smart Convergence*, 8, 113, 2019.

52. Zuo, Z., Zhao, K., Eichmann, D., The state and evolution of US iSchools: From talent acquisitions to research outcome. *J. Assoc. Inf. Sci. Technol.*, 68, 1266, 2017.

Index

Printed and bound by CPI Group (UK) Ltd, Croydon, CR0 4YY

27/10/2024

14580137-0002